EXPLORING
Earth Science

Anthea Maton
Former NSTA National Coordinator
Project Scope, Sequence, Coordination
Washington, DC

Jean Hopkins
Science Instructor and Department Chairperson
John H. Wood Middle School
San Antonio, Texas

Susan Johnson
Professor of Biology
Ball State University
Muncie, Indiana

David LaHart
Senior Instructor
Florida Solar Energy Center
Cape Canaveral, Florida

Maryanna Quon Warner
Science Instructor
Del Dios Middle School
Escondido, California

Jill D. Wright
Professor of Science Education
Director of International Field Programs
University of Pittsburgh
Pittsburgh, Pennsylvania

 Prentice Hall
Englewood Cliffs, New Jersey
Needham, Massachusetts

PRENTICE HALL EXPLORING Earth Science

Student Text and Teacher's Edition
Teaching Resources
Teacher's Desk Reference
Classroom Manager
Laboratory Manual and
   Annotated Teacher's Edition
Integrated Science Activity Book
Product Testing Activities

Transparency Box
Computer Test Bank with
   DIAL-A-TEST™ Service
Videos/Videodiscs
Level I Videodiscs
Level III Interactive Videodiscs
Level III Interactive Videodiscs/CD-ROM
Media Guide

The illustration on the cover, rendered by Raymond E. Smith, depicts a scene from the Age of Dinosaurs—a split-second glimpse into the long and dynamic history of Planet Earth.

Credits begin on page 832.

ISBN 0-13-807595-6

   6 7 8 9 10   98 97 96

Prentice Hall
Englewood Cliffs, New Jersey 07632

STAFF CREDITS

Editorial: Harry Bakalian, Pamela E. Hirschfeld, Julia A. Fellows, Lorraine Smith-Phelan, Lois B. Arnold, Maureen Grassi, Ann L. Collins, Robert P. Letendre, Natania Mlawer, Elisa Mui Eiger, Christine A. Caputo, Joseph Berman, Rekha Sheorey

Design: AnnMarie Roselli, Carmela Pereira, Laura Bird, Susan Walrath, Leslie Osher, Art Soares

Production: Suse F. Bell, Christina Burghard, Marianne Peters

Visual Research: Libby Forsyth, Emily Rose, Martha Conway

Publishing Technology: Andrew G. Black, Deborah J. Jones, Monduane Harris, Kathryn A. Foot, Louis A. Gorrell, Gregory Myers, Cleasta Wilburn

Marketing: Andrew Socha, Arthur C. Germano, Victoria Willows, Joel Gendler

Pre-Press Production: Laura Sanderson, Paula Massenaro, Denise Herckenrath

Manufacturing: Rhett Conklin

National Science Consultants: Kathy French, Jeannie Dennard, Janelle Conarton, Brenda Underwood

CONTENTS

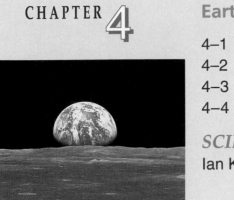

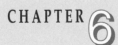

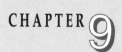

SCIENCE GAZETTE

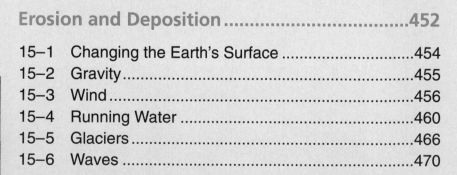

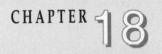

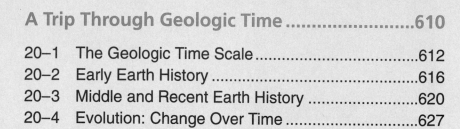

Calculating

Thinking

Writing

Reading

Laboratory Investigations

Activity Bank

Features

Careers

Connections

CONCEPT MAPPING

Throughout your study of science, you will learn a variety of terms, facts, figures, and concepts. Each new topic you encounter will provide its own collection of words and ideas—which, at times, you may think seem endless. But each of the ideas within a particular topic is related in some way to the others. No concept in science is isolated. Thus it will help you to understand the topic if you see the whole picture; that is, the interconnectedness of all the individual terms and ideas. This is a much more effective and satisfying way of learning than memorizing separate facts.

Actually, this should be a rather familiar process for you. Although you may not think about it in this way, you analyze many of the elements in your daily life by looking for relationships or connections. For example, when you look at a collection of flowers, you may divide them into groups: roses, carnations, and daisies. You may then associate colors with these flowers: red, pink, and white. The general topic is flowers. The subtopic is types of flowers. And the colors are specific terms that describe flowers. A topic makes more sense and is more easily understood if you understand how it is broken down into individual ideas and how these ideas are related to one another and to the entire topic.

It is often helpful to organize information visually so that you can see how it all fits together. One technique for describing related ideas is called a **concept map**. In a concept map, an idea is represented by a word or phrase enclosed in a box. There are several ideas in any concept map. A connection between two ideas is made with a line. A word or two that describes the connection is written on or near the line. The general topic is located at the top of the map. That topic is then broken down into subtopics, or more specific ideas, by branching lines. The most specific topics are located at the bottom of the map.

To construct a concept map, first identify the important ideas or key terms in the chapter or section. Do not try to include too much information. Use your judgment as to what is really important. Write the general topic at the top of your map. Let's use an example to help illustrate this process. Suppose you decide that the key terms in a section you are reading are School, Living Things, Language Arts, Subtraction, Grammar, Mathematics, Experiments, Papers, Science, Addition, Novels. The general topic is School. Write and enclose this word in a box at the top of your map.

SCHOOL

Now choose the subtopics—Language Arts, Science, Mathematics. Figure out how they are related to the topic. Add these words to your map. Continue this procedure until you have included all the important ideas and terms. Then use lines to make the appropriate connections between ideas and terms. Don't forget to write a word or two on or near the connecting line to describe the nature of the connection.

Do not be concerned if you have to redraw your map (perhaps several times!) before you show all the important connections clearly. If, for example, you write papers for Science as well as for Language Arts, you may want to place these two subjects next to each other so that the lines do not overlap.

One more thing you should know about concept mapping: Concepts can be correctly mapped in many different ways. In fact, it is unlikely that any two people will draw identical concept maps for a complex topic. Thus there is no one correct concept map for any topic! Even

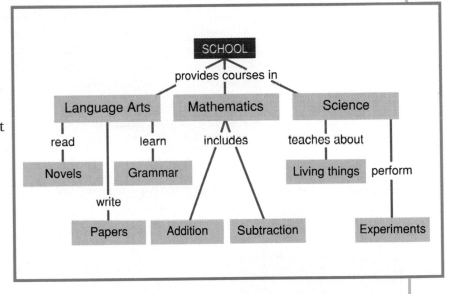

though your concept map may not match those of your classmates, it will be correct as long as it shows the most important concepts and the clear relationships among them. Your concept map will also be correct if it has meaning to you and if it helps you understand the material you are reading. A concept map should be so clear that if some of the terms are erased, the missing terms could easily be filled in by following the logic of the concept map.

UNIT ONE
Exploring the Universe

The Trifid Nebula is a huge mass of glowing gas and stars. It contains many young stars that generate a great deal of heat and light. The red portions of the nebula are mainly glowing hydrogen gas. The blue regions contain mostly dust particles that reflect light from the stars in the nebula. ▶

A nearly full moon was photographed by the Apollo 13 astronauts. ▼

Set aglow by fiery stars deep within its core, the gases of the Trifid Nebula sweep out into the blackness of space. The wispy red and blue cloud balloons out to a size that is almost unimaginable. It could gobble up thousands and thousands of solar systems! But it is so far away from the Earth that people can enjoy its beauty without fearing it will engulf them.

Although this dazzling cloud of gas is about 5000 light-years, or 50,000 trillion kilometers, from the Earth, it is one of the Earth's neighbors in space. The mysterious object astronomers call the Trifid Nebula is part of the Earth's starry neighborhood, the Milky Way Galaxy. Equally mysterious, but closer to home, are the objects with which the Earth and its moon share the solar system: the sun, the

planets and their moons, meteors, asteroids, and comets. In the pages that follow, you will explore these and other objects in space and perhaps begin to unravel some of their mysteries.

The rings of Saturn and six of its many moons can be seen in this composite photograph.

Discovery *Activity*

Colors of the Rainbow

Is white light really white? Find out for yourself.

1. Hold a prism in front of a sheet of white paper.

2. Shine a beam of white light through the prism onto the paper. What happens to the white light as it passes through the prism? How is this similar to a rainbow?

   ■ What do you think causes the colors of a rainbow?

   ■ What do you think would happen if you were to pass the beam of light through a second prism? Try it.

Exploring Earth Science

Guide for Reading

After you read the following sections, you will be able to

1–1 Science—Not Just for Scientists
- Describe the process of science and the branches of earth science.

1–2 The Scientific Method—A Way of Problem Solving
- Identify the steps in the scientific method.
- Compare an experimental setup and a control setup.

1–3 The Metric System
- Identify the metric units used in scientific measurements.

1–4 Tools of Earth and Space Scientists
- Identify some of the tools used by earth scientists.

1–5 Safety in the Science Laboratory
- Explain the importance of safety rules in the laboratory.

In the desert of northwestern New Mexico lies an interesting riddle. Two mysterious spirals are carved on a cliff wall behind three slanting stones. At noon on the first day of summer, a single ray of sunlight passes between two of the stones and strikes the larger of the two spirals through its center. At noon on the first day of spring and the first day of autumn, two rays of sunlight pass between the three stones and strike both spirals. At noon on the first day of winter, two rays of sunlight pass between the three stones and strike the large spiral on both sides. What do these spirals mean—and who carved them?

The mysterious spirals and slanting rocks are believed to be part of an astronomical observatory—a place where events in the sky were studied. Scientists think that the people who built the observatory were the Anasazi people, who lived in the area long before Columbus discovered America.

Modern astronomers have built far more complex observatories. But although the tools of today are more advanced, the basic ways in which scientists try to solve the mysteries of nature may not be very different from those used by the Anasazi people. In this chapter you will learn about some of the tools used to explore the world of earth science.

Journal *Activity*

You and Your World What would it be like to live in the Southwest before the time of Columbus? Imagine you are a member of the Anasazi Indian tribe. In your journal, describe a typical day in your life.

First winter sunlight at Fajada Butte, New Mexico.

1–1 Science—Not Just for Scientists

Why is the sky blue? Why do the planets revolve around the sun? What causes the daily tides? If you have ever asked questions such as these, then you were on the road to becoming a scientist. Does that surprise you? If it does, it is probably because you do not understand exactly what a scientist does. Whenever you observe the world about you and ask questions, you are acting like a scientist. Does that statement give you a clue to the nature of science and scientists?

Scientists also observe the world around them. For that reason, whenever you make an observation you are acting like a scientist. Of course, scientists do more than just observe. The word science comes from the Latin *scire,* which means "to know." So scientists go beyond just observing. They question what they see. They wonder what makes things the way they are. And they attempt to find answers to their questions.

You also wonder about and question what you see—at least some of the time. After reading this chapter, you will be better prepared to find answers to some of your questions. That is, you will be better able to approach the world as a scientist does.

Figure 1–1 *Would you describe yourself as a scientist? Probably not. Yet whenever you observe and ask questions about natural phenomena, such as a hurricane or a tornado, you are acting as a scientist does. What questions come to mind as you look at these photographs?*

The Nature of Science

If you think about it, you will quickly realize that there are many things you might question and seek answers to. Put another way, the universe is really a collection of countless mysteries. It is the job of scientists to solve those mysteries. **The goal of science is to understand the world around us.**

How do scientists achieve their goal? How do they go about solving the mysteries of nature? Like any good detective, scientists use special methods to determine truths about nature. Such truths are called facts. Here is an example of a fact: The Earth takes about 365 days to travel once around the sun. But science is more than a simple list of facts—just as studying science is more than memorizing facts. Jules Henri Poincaré, a famous nineteenth-century French scientist and mathematician who charted the motion of the planets, put it this way: "Science is built up with facts, as a house is with stones. But a collection of facts is no more a science than a heap of stones is a house."

As you might guess, scientists go far beyond making up a list of facts. Scientists use these facts to solve larger mysteries of nature. In a way, you can think of facts as clues to scientific mysteries. Facts are not the answers to mysteries, they are merely guideposts helping us find our way toward those answers. An example of a larger mystery is why the planets orbit around the sun rather than sailing off into the depths of space. (You will find out in Chapter 3.)

Having gathered as many relevant facts as they can, scientists often propose explanations for the events they observe. Whenever possible, they then perform experiments to test their explanations. In the next section of this chapter, you will learn more about how scientists go about performing experiments and solving some of the many mysteries of the universe.

Once a scientist has made observations, recorded facts, and performed experiments, the scientist may develop a **theory.** A theory is the most logical explanation for events that occur in nature. Keep in mind that scientists do not use the word theory as you do. For example, you may have a theory about why your local softball team is not winning. Your theory may or

Figure 1–2 *The goal of science is to understand events that occur in the world around us, such as how these beautiful barite (top) and wulfenite (bottom) crystals formed deep within the Earth.*

A Rocky Observation

To be useful, one person's observations must give meaningful information to another person.

1. Obtain four rocks of about equal size.

2. Place a small piece of masking tape on each rock and number the rocks 1 through 4.

3. On a sheet of paper, write down as many observations as you can about each rock next to its number.

4. Rewrite your observations without numbers on another sheet of paper. Give this sheet of paper and the rocks to a classmate.

5. Ask your classmate to match the observations to the rocks.

■ Did your classmate make correct matches? Why or why not?

may not make sense. But it is not a scientific theory. A scientific theory is not just a guess or a hunch. It is a powerful, time-tested concept that makes useful and dependable predictions about the natural world.

When a scientist proposes a theory, that theory must then be tested over and over again. If it survives the tests, the theory may be accepted by the scientific community. However, theories can be wrong and may be discarded or modified after additional tests and/or observations. In some cases, scientists may be able to express experimental results as a **law.** A law summarizes observed experimental facts—it does not explain the facts. The explanation resides in the appropriate theory. Laws, like theories, may change as new information is provided or new experiments are performed.

Branches of Earth Science

As you study science, you will discover that one of the skills you will master is the ability to organize things in a logical, orderly way—that is, to classify things. Classification systems are an important part of science. Earth scientists, for example, classify stars by their size and brightness.

Even the study of science can be classified into groups, or branches, of science. There can be many branches of science, each determined by the subject

Figure 1–3 *Scientists do not always agree about a particular event in nature. At this time, there are several alternative theories to explain the extinction of the dinosaurs some 65 million years ago. Why do you think these extinction theories are difficult to prove or disprove?*

matter being studied. However, the three main branches of science are life science, earth science, and physical science. Because this is an earth science book, let's now consider some of the main branches of earth science.

Earth science deals with the study of the Earth, its history, its changes, and its place in the universe. One branch of earth science is **geology** (jee-AHL-uh-jee). Geology is the study of the Earth's origin, history, and structure. Another branch of earth science is **meteorology** (mee-tee-uh-RAHL-uh-jee). Meteorology is the study of the Earth's atmosphere, weather, and climate. A third branch of earth science is **oceanography** (oh-shuh-NAHG-ruh-fee). Oceanography is the study of the Earth's oceans, including their physical features, life forms, and natural resources. Another branch of earth science is **astronomy** (uh-STRAHN-uh-mee). Astronomy is the study of the position, composition, size, and other characteristics of the planets, stars, and other objects in space.

As with any branch of science, earth science has many special terms that may be unfamiliar to you. The chart in Figure 1–6 gives the meanings of many common science prefixes and suffixes. Learning the meanings of these prefixes and suffixes will make learning new science terms easier. And knowing the meaning of science terms will increase your understanding of earth science. Suppose, for example, you see the term *isotherm* on a weather map. From the

ACTIVITY DOING

Branches of Earth Science

Read carefully the description of the various branches of earth science. Then look around and list some of the objects and events in the world around you. Decide which branch of earth science would study each of the objects and events you selected. Summarize your conclusions in a chart.

Figure 1–5 *Each of these photos—lightning striking, a volcano erupting, waves crashing—represents one branch of earth science. Can you match the photo with the branch of earth science it depicts?*

chart, you know that the prefix *iso-* means equal and the suffix *-therm* means heat. So you can quickly determine that isotherms are lines that connect areas of equal heat, or equal temperature.

It is important for you to remember that the branches of science are a handy way to classify the subject matter scientists study. But it would be a mistake to think that any branch works independently of the others. To the contrary, the branches of science actually interweave and overlap most of the time. Science does not happen in a vacuum, and the great discoveries of science do not usually occur unless scientists from many branches work together.

Prefix	Meaning	Prefix	Meaning	Suffix	Meaning
anti	reverse	in-	inside	-cline	incline
astro-	of a star	inter-	between	-graphy	description of
atmo-	vapor	iso-	equal	-logy	science of
bathy-	depth	litho-	stone	-meter	having to do with measuring
chromo-	color	meteor-	things in the air	-nomy	systemized knowledge of
chrono-	time	micro-	small	-oid	resembling
con-	together	petro-	rock	-scope	instrument for seeing
de-	undo	proto-	primitive	-sphere	round
dia-	away from	seismo-	earthquake	-therm	heat
epi-	over	strato-	covering	-verge	turn
ex-	out	sub-	under		
geo-	Earth	tele-	to a distance		
hemi-	half	trans-	across		
hydro-	water				

Figure 1–6 *Learning the meanings of prefixes and suffixes, such as those shown in this chart, will make it easier for you to learn new science terms. According to this chart, what does the word chronometer mean?*

1–1 Section Review

1. What is the goal of science?
2. Describe three branches of earth science. Give an example of a question that might be asked by scientists in each branch.
3. What is a theory? When does a scientific theory become a law?
4. You might use the word theory to mean a guess. How is this different from the way a scientist uses the word theory?

Critical Thinking—*Relating Concepts*

5. Sometimes an important scientific discovery must await new advances in technology. Explain why this is so.

ACTIVITY
THINKING

Prefixes and Suffixes

Use the prefixes and suffixes given in Figure 1–6 to form words that match the following definitions. Use at least one prefix and one suffix to form each word or phrase.

instrument for seeing small objects
instrument for seeing distant objects
one-half of a planet
study of water
study of Earth
method of measuring distant events

1–2 The Scientific Method— A Way of Problem Solving

Scientists investigate problems every day. Sometimes problems are quickly solved. Sometimes they take many years to solve. And sometimes a problem remains unsolved. When scientists try to solve a problem, they usually search for an answer in an orderly and systematic way. This systematic approach to problem solving is called the **scientific method. The basic steps in the scientific method are**

Stating the problem
Gathering information on the problem
Forming a hypothesis
Performing experiments to test the hypothesis
Recording and analyzing data
Stating a conclusion
Repeating the work

The following example shows how an earth scientist might use the scientific method to solve a problem.

Stating the Problem

Perhaps you have stepped into a lake or ocean during the winter. If so, you probably noticed that the temperature of the water was lower than it was during the summer. You may have even questioned why this was so. If you have wondered about such things, you have taken the first small step toward recognizing a scientific problem.

Before investigating any problem, scientists must develop a clear statement defining the problem. In this example, the earth scientist might state the problem the following way: What factor causes the temperature of the water to be lower during the winter than during the summer?

Figure 1–7 *As the sun slowly sinks in the west, would you be more likely to take a late afternoon swim in the middle of August or in the middle of December? Why is the water cooler in winter than in summer? You can use the scientific method to help you solve this problem.*

Gathering Information on the Problem

The earth scientist might begin to solve the problem by gathering information. The scientist would first find out how conditions during the winter when the water is cooler differ from conditions during the summer when the water is warmer. The information might include the position of the sun during the winter and the summer.

Forming a Hypothesis

After gathering information, the earth scientist would then suggest a possible solution to the problem. A proposed solution to a scientific problem is called a **hypothesis** (high-PAHTH-uh-sihs). A hypothesis almost always follows the gathering of information about a problem. But sometimes a hypothesis is a sudden idea that springs from a new and original way of looking at a problem.

One hypothesis the earth scientist might consider as a solution to the problem is the following: The water is cooler during the winter than during the summer because the sun, the Earth's source of heat, is farther from the Earth during the winter. But the scientist would soon discover that the sun is actually closer to the Earth during the winter.

Now the earth scientist would consider the situation again and arrive at a new hypothesis: The water is cooler during the winter than during the summer because the position of the sun is different during the two seasons. Position, in this case, means more than distance from the Earth. It also involves the angle at which the sun's rays strike the Earth.

Experimenting

Scientists must find evidence that either supports a hypothesis or does not support it. That is, they must test a hypothesis to show whether or not it is correct. Such testing is usually done by performing one or more experiments.

Figure 1–8 *Yosemite National Park in California appears blanketed in white, frozen in the icy grip of winter. On the same date, south of the equator, the Amazon Basin in Ecuador basks in the warmth of a summer day.*

ACTIVITY

DISCOVERING

Graphing Temperatures

1. Over a ten-day period, read the weather section of a newspaper.

2. Each day, record in a chart the day's date and the high and low temperatures for the town nearest where you live.

3. After ten days, plot your data in a graph. Use the vertical axis for temperature and the horizontal axis for day. Use red pencil for daily high temperatures and blue pencil for daily low temperatures.

4. Draw lines connecting the points for both the daily highs and lows.

■ Based on your graph, write a short essay describing the temperature patterns you observed.

Scientists perform experiments according to specific rules. By following these rules, they can be confident that the evidence they uncover will clearly support or not support a hypothesis. To test the hypothesis that the angle of the sun's rays affects the temperature of the water, the earth scientist would have to design an appropriate experiment. Let's see how this might actually be done.

First the earth scientist would place a measured amount of water into a container. The scientist would then place a thermometer into the water, just below the surface. Then the scientist would place a heat source above the container. Because the heat source requires an electric current, the scientist would take care to make sure that none of the electric wires comes in contact with the water. The heat source takes the place of the sun in the experiment. Since the scientist is testing the effect of the angle of the sun's rays during the winter, the heat source would be angled exactly as the sun is in relation to the Earth during the winter. In this experimental setup, then, the angle of the heat source is the **variable.** A variable in any experiment is the one factor that is being tested.

In any experiment, scientists ideally test only one variable at a time. In this way, they can be fairly certain that the results of the experiment are caused by one and only one factor. To avoid the possibility of hidden, unknown variables, scientists run a **control** experiment. The control experiment setup is exactly like the experimental setup except that the control experiment does not contain the variable.

Figure 1–9 *What is the variable in this experiment?*

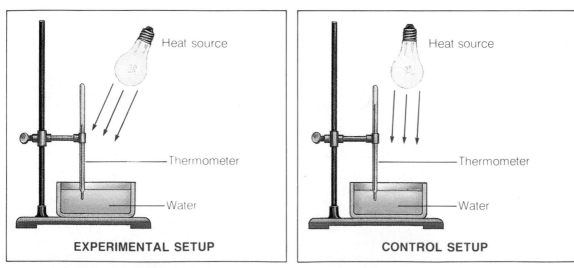

EXPERIMENTAL SETUP · CONTROL SETUP

In the control experiment for this example, the earth scientist would make sure that the setup is exactly the same as the experimental setup except for the angle of the heat source's rays. A container would be filled with the same amount of water. A thermometer would again be placed just below the surface of the water. The heat source would be placed at the exact same height above the container. But this time, the heat source would not be angled. It would be placed directly over the container. In this way, the earth scientist could be sure that the results of the experimental setup were due to the variable, the angle of the heat source's rays, and not to a hidden factor.

Recording and Analyzing Data

In any experiment, scientists must observe the experiment and write down important information. Recorded observations and measurements are called **data.**

In the earth science experiment, the data would include the time intervals at which the containers were observed and the temperature of the water in both containers at each interval. The earth scientist would record these observations for both the experimental setup and the control setup. The scientist might record the data for both setups in tables such as the following.

Figure 1–10 *Scientists often record their observations in data tables. What are the time intervals in these data tables?*

Heat Source at an Angle (*experimental setup*)

Time (min)	0	15	30	45	60	75	90	105	120	135	150
Temperature (°C)	20.0	20.5	21.0	21.5	22.0	23.0	23.5	24.0	25.0	26.5	27.5

Heat Source Directly Above (*control setup*)

Time (min)	0	15	30	45	60	75	90	105	120	135	150
Temperature (°C)	20.0	21.0	22.0	23.0	24.0	26.0	27.0	28.5	30.0	30.5	31.0

To visually compare the data, the scientist would construct a graph on which to plot the data. Since the data tables contain two types of measurements, the graph would have two axes. See Figure 1–11.

The horizontal axis of the graph would stand for the time measurements in the data tables. Time measurements were made every 15 minutes. So the horizontal axis would be marked with intervals of 15 minutes. The space between equal intervals would have to be equal. For example, the space between 15 minutes and 30 minutes would be the same as between 30 minutes and 45 minutes.

The vertical axis of the graph would stand for the temperature measurements in the data tables. The lowest temperature reached in the experiment was 20°C and the highest was 31°C. So the vertical axis would begin at 20°C and end at 31°C. Each interval of temperature would have to be equal to every other interval.

Figure 1–11 *The information in a data table can be placed on a graph. What conclusion can you draw from this graph about the rate of temperature change?*

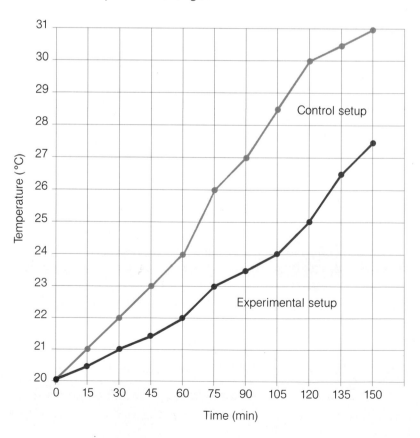

After the axes of the graph were set up, the earth scientist would first graph the data from the experimental setup. Each pair of data points from the data table would be plotted. At 0 minutes, the temperature was 20°C. So the scientist would place a dot where 0 minutes and 20°C intersected—in the lower left corner of the graph. The next pair of data points was 15 minutes and 20.5°C. So the scientist would lightly draw a vertical line from the 15-minute interval of the horizontal axis and then a horizontal line from the 20.5°C interval of the vertical axis. The scientist would then place a dot at the place where the two lines intersected. This dot would represent the data points 15 minutes and 20.5°C. The scientist would plot the rest of the data pairs from the data table in this manner.

When all the data pairs were plotted, the scientist would draw a line through all the dots. This line would represent the graph of the experimental setup data. Then the scientist would graph all the data pairs from the control setup. Figure 1–11 shows what the two lines would look like. After analyzing the lines on the graph, the scientist would quickly determine that the temperature of the water rose more slowly in the experimental setup than it did in the control setup.

Stating a Conclusion

After running the experiment and recording and analyzing the data, an earth scientist would likely conclude that the angle of the heat source's rays does indeed affect the temperature of the water. The scientist would further conclude that the temperature of the water rises higher when the sun's rays strike the water at a direct angle than when they strike the water at an indirect angle.

Why does this happen, you may ask? This question sounds very much like the beginning of a new puzzle. It often happens in science that the solution of one problem leads to yet another problem. Thus the cycle of discovery goes on and on.

Repeating the Work

Although the scientist conducting the experiment you just read about might be completely satisfied with

ACTIVITY READING

Dangerous Depths

Do you love an action-packed adventure story? If so, you will want to read *Twenty Thousand Leagues Under the Sea,* by Jules Verne.

the conclusion, he or she would repeat the experiment many more times to make sure the data were accurate. Moreover, before the conclusion would be accepted by the scientific community, other scientists would repeat the experiment and check the results. So when a scientist writes a report on his or her experiment, that report must be detailed enough so that scientists throughout the world can repeat the experiment for themselves. In most cases, it is only when an experiment has been repeated by scientists worldwide that it is considered to be accurate and worthy of being included in new scientific research.

The Scientific Method—Not Always So Orderly

It may seem to you that science is a fairly straightforward way of studying the world. After all, you state a problem, gather information, form a hypothesis, run an experiment, and end up with a conclusion. It certainly sounds very neat and tidy. Well, sometimes it is—and sometimes it isn't.

In reality, scientists do not always follow all the steps in the scientific method as they have been described to you. Nor do the steps always follow the same order. During an experiment, for example, a scientist might observe something totally unexpected. That unexpected event might cause the scientist to forget about the original hypothesis and suggest an entirely new one. In this example, the new hypothesis followed the experiment. In other situations, a scientist might not even start out with a particular problem to be studied. Let's go back to those unexpected results. Those results might cause the scientist to look at the world in a new and different way. They might suggest new problems that need to be considered. In this case, the problem followed the experiment.

Here's another way science does not always follow clean and simple rules. You read that each experiment should have only one variable. Sometimes, however, it is not possible to eliminate all but one variable. Naturally, the data in such experiments are much more difficult to analyze. For example, suppose a scientist wants to determine why the continents on the Earth's crust are moving away from one another. It is not likely that the scientist could eliminate all variables when studying the continents. So although a single variable is a good rule—and one that you will follow in almost all of the experiments you design or perform—it is not always practical in the real world.

The Scientific Method in Your World

"Why are we studying science? What does science have to do with my world?" You have probably heard these questions before—perhaps you have asked them yourself. Well the answer is—plenty! Oh you may not live near a body of water or care about the effect of the angle of the sun's rays on water temperature. But the same effect occurs when the sun's rays strike the Earth's soil. So if you live on a farm or plant a small garden, you will certainly be interested in the effect of the angle of the sun's rays. Or maybe you live in an area where electricity is very expensive. Surely if your family were putting a solar collector on your roof, you would want to know how to place it to maximize the heating effect of the sun—especially on those cold winter nights. How many other examples can you think of in which this principle of the effects of the angle of the sun's rays might impact your life?

It is important for you to keep in mind whenever you study science that the principles and concepts you study *do* have an effect on your life. Whenever possible, we will point out the relevance of earth science topics to your world. But that may not always be practical. So it's up to you to remember that science is not just for laboratory workers in white coats. Science affects all of us—each and every day of our lives.

Figure 1–12 *Why would it be virtually impossible for a scientist studying the effects of climate on plant life in this Peruvian rain forest to eliminate all but one variable?*

1–2 Section Review

1. List and describe the steps in the scientific method.
2. Why is it necessary to run both a control setup and an experimental setup?

Connection—*You and Your World*
3. It's your first big party and the guests are just about to arrive when you discover that your stereo no longer works. How might you apply the steps of the scientific method to determine the cause of the problem?

Create a Measurement System

Using objects found in your classroom as standards, create your own measurement system for length, mass, and volume. For each type of measurement, try to include units of several different sizes. Keep in mind that your "standards" must be things that will remain constant over time. Also keep in mind that you should be able to convert easily from one unit to another.

Once your measurement system is established, create a display of your standard objects and the units they represent. Then challenge members of your class to use your system to make measurements of various objects and distances.

1-3 The Metric System

Magnum est ut inter sese colloqui possint periti in scientiae rebus.

Having trouble reading the sentence written above? Don't worry, it's not a string of new vocabulary words you have to memorize. Actually, it is a very clear and concise sentence. It just happens to be written in a language you probably don't understand. And it's been included to make a simple but important point. Science is a worldwide topic, and scientists come from every country on Earth. If they are to work together and know what each other is doing, scientists must be able to communicate—in a sense, to speak the same language. In case you're wondering, the sentence above is in Latin. Its translation is:

> *It is important that scientists can communicate with each other.*

Metrics—The Universal Language of Measurement

Earlier, you learned that experiments are an important part of the scientific method. You also learned that most experiments require data in the form of measurements. It is important that measurements be accurate and easily communicated to other people. So a universal system of measurement having standard units must be used. You can imagine the confusion that would result if measurements were made without standard units. For example, suppose you ask a friend how far it is to his house, and his response is five. You do not know if he means five blocks, five kilometers, or that it takes about five minutes to get there. Obviously, such a response would be of little help to you—and you probably would not accept that answer.

Scientists are ordinary people just like you. In order to make sure there is little confusion about their work, all scientists use the same standard system of measurement. The scientific system of measurement is called the **metric system**. One form of the metric system is called the International System

COMMON METRIC UNITS

Length		Mass	
1 meter (m) = 100 centimeters (cm)		1 kilogram (kg) = 1000 grams (g)	
1 meter = 1000 millimeters (mm)		1 gram = 1000 milligrams (mg)	
1 meter = 1,000,000 micrometers (μm)		1000 kilograms = 1 metric ton (t)	
1 meter = 1,000,000,000 nanometers (nm)			
1 meter = 10,000,000,000 angstroms (Å)			
1000 meters = 1 kilometer (km)			

Volume		Temperature	
1 liter (L) = 1000 milliliters (mL) or 1000 cubic centimeters (cm³)		0°C = freezing point of water 100°C = boiling point of water	
kilo- = one thousand centi- = one hundredth milli- = one thousandth		micro- = one millionth nano- = one billionth	

of Units, or SI. Using the metric system, scientists all over the world can compare and analyze their data.

The metric system is a simple system to use. Like our money system, the metric system is a decimal system; that is, it is based on the number ten and multiples of ten. (There are ten pennies in a dime, ten dimes in a dollar, and so on.) In much the same way, each unit in the metric system is ten times larger or ten times smaller than the next smaller or larger unit. So calculations with metric units are relatively easy.

Scientists use metric units to measure length, volume, mass, weight, density, and temperature. Some frequently used metric units and their abbreviations are listed in Figure 1–13.

Length

The basic unit of length in the metric system is the **meter** (m). A meter is equal to 39.4 inches, or a little more than a yard. Your height would be measured in meters. Most students your age are between 1.5 and 2 meters tall.

To measure the length of an object smaller than a meter, scientists use the metric unit called the **centimeter** (cm). The prefix *centi-* means one-hundredth. As you might guess, there are 100 centimeters in a meter. The height of this book is about 27 centimeters.

Figure 1–13 *The metric system is easy to use because it is based on units of ten. How many centimeters are there in 10 meters?*

ACTIVITY

CALCULATING

Earthquake Waves

Earthquake waves, or seismic waves, travel at a speed 24 times the speed of sound. The speed of sound is 1250 km/hr. How fast do seismic waves travel?

Figure 1–14 *Which metric unit of length would be most appropriate when measuring the height of the Matterhorn in Switzerland or giraffes in Kenya?*

To measure even smaller objects, the metric unit called the **millimeter** (mm) is used. The prefix *milli-* means one-thousandth. So there are 1000 millimeters in a meter. In bright light, the diameter of the pupil of your eye is about 1 millimeter. How many millimeters are there in a centimeter?

Even millimeters are too large to use when describing the sizes of microscopic organisms such as bacteria. Bacteria are measured in micrometers, or millionths of a meter, and nanometers, or billionths of a meter. That may seem small enough for any measurement, but it's not. To describe the size of

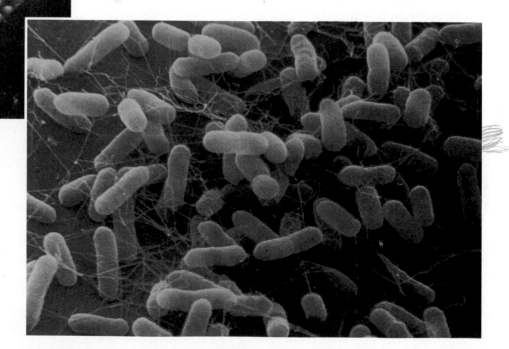

Figure 1–15 *The length of bacteria (right) are measured in micrometers or nanometers. What unit of length is used when measuring atoms such as these silicon atoms (left)?*

Figure 1–16 *To measure the length of long rivers, scientists would choose the unit of length called the kilometer.*

atoms, the building blocks of matter, scientists use the metric unit called the angstrom. An angstrom is equal to one ten-billionth of a meter!

Sometimes scientists need to measure large distances, such as the length of the Nile River in Africa. Such lengths can be measured in meters, centimeters, or even millimeters. But when measuring large distances with small units, the numbers become very difficult to work with. For example, the length of the Nile River is about 6,649,000,000 millimeters—not an easy number to use! To avoid such large numbers, scientists use the metric unit called the **kilometer** (km). The prefix *kilo-* means one thousand. So there are 1000 meters in a kilometer. The length of the Nile River is about 6649 kilometers. How many meters is this?

On Earth, meters and kilometers are very useful units of measurement. But in space, distances are often too great to be measured in kilometers. (Again, the numbers start getting very large.) To measure long distances in space, astronomers use a unit of distance called the **light-year.** A light-year is the distance light travels in one year. As you probably know, light travels mighty fast—about 300,000 kilometers per second. A light-year, then, is about 9.5 trillion kilometers. No, we won't ask you how many millimeters are in a light-year, but you might have fun figuring it out on your own. You can think of a light-year as a ruler made of light. But keep in mind that a light-year measures distance, not time.

A light-year may seem like an enormous distance, but in space, it is not very far at all. The closest star system to the Earth is over 4 light-years away. It takes the light from that star system over four years to reach the Earth. Yet even that distance seems quite short when compared to the distance of the farthest known star system, which is about 13 billion light-years away. The light from these most distant stars may take more than 13 billion years to reach Earth. Unbelieveable as it may seem, the light began its long journey toward Earth before the Earth had even formed.

Figure 1–17 *What unit of length is used to measure distant objects in space, such as this nebula?*

Volume

Volume is the amount of space an object takes up. In the metric system, the basic unit of volume is the **liter** (L). A liter is slightly larger than a quart. To measure volumes smaller than a liter, scientists use the **milliliter** (mL). Recall that the prefix *milli-* means one-thousandth. So there are 1000 milliliters in a liter. An ordinary drinking glass holds about 200 milliliters of liquid. How many milliliters are there in 10 liters?

Liters and milliliters are used to measure the volume of liquids. Of course, both you and scientists may need to measure the volume of solids as well. The metric unit used to measure the volume of solids is called the **cubic centimeter** (cm^3 or cc). A cubic centimeter is equal to the volume of a cube that measures 1 centimeter by 1 centimeter by 1 centimeter. It just so happens that a cubic centimeter is exactly equal in volume to a milliliter. (We told you the metric system is easy to use.) In fact, cubic centimeters can be used to measure the volume of liquids as well as solids. How many cubic centimeters are there in a liter?

Figure 1–18 *A cubic centimeter (cm^3 or cc) is the volume of a cube that measures 1 cm by 1 cm by 1 cm. How many milliliters are in a cubic centimeter?*

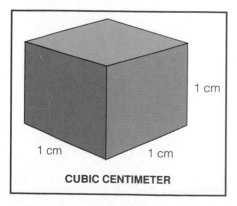

CUBIC CENTIMETER

Figure 1–19 *To measure the volume of water rushing over Iguassu Falls in Brazil, scientists would use the unit of volume called the liter. What unit of volume would they use to measure the amount of water in a pet's water dish?*

Mass

Mass is a measure of the amount of matter in an object. For example, there is more matter in a dumptruck than in a mid-sized car. So a dumptruck has more mass than a mid-sized car. Which has more mass, a mid-sized car or a bicycle?

Keep in mind that mass is different from volume. Volume is the amount of space an object takes up, whereas mass is the amount of matter in the object. The basic unit of mass in the metric system is the **kilogram** (kg).

The kilogram is a useful unit when measuring the mass of large objects. To measure the mass of small objects, such as a nickel, the **gram** (g) is used. If you remember what the prefix *kilo-* means, then you know that a kilogram contains 1000 grams. A nickel has a mass of about 5 grams. How many grams are in 20 kilograms?

Figure 1–20 *The buffalo is one of the largest land animals on Earth. Harvest field mice are the smallest mice on Earth. Which metric unit would be best for measuring the mass of the buffalo? Of field mice?*

As you might expect, scientists often need to measure the mass of objects much smaller than a nickel. To do so, they use the metric unit called the **milligram** (mg). Again, recall that the prefix *milli-* means one-thousandth. So there are 1000 milligrams in a gram. How many milligrams are there in a kilogram?

Weight

Weight is a measure of the attraction between two objects due to gravity. Gravity is a force of attraction. The strength of the gravitational force between objects depends in part on the distance between these objects. As the distance between objects becomes greater, the gravitational force between the objects decreases. On Earth, your weight is a measure of the Earth's force of gravity on you.

The basic unit of weight in the metric system is the **newton** (N), named after Isaac Newton who discovered the force of gravity. The newton is used because it is a measure of force, and weight is the amount of force the Earth's gravity exerts on an object. An object with a mass of 1 kilogram is pulled toward the Earth with a force of 9.8 newtons. So the weight of the object is 9.8 N. An object with a mass of 50 kilograms is pulled toward the Earth with a force of 50 × 9.8, or 490 N. That object's weight is 490 N. What is your weight on Earth?

Because the force of gravity changes with distance, your weight can change depending on your location. For example, you are farther from the center of the Earth when standing atop a tall mountain than when standing at sea level. And although the change may be small, you actually weigh less at the top of the mountain than you do at sea level. How might your weight change if you went into orbit above the Earth?

We often describe astronauts orbiting above the Earth as being weightless. You now know that this description is not correct. The distance between the astronauts and the center of the Earth is so great that the Earth's gravitational force is less strong. The astronauts appear to be weightless, but they actually are not. They still have weight because they

Figure 1–21 *Although we speak of astronauts as being "weightless," they are not. However, on Earth this astronaut would never have been able to lift this heavy communications satellite. But he was able to lift it with ease while floating above the Earth. Can you explain why?*

Figure 1–22 *The mass of planet Neptune is much greater than that of Earth, while the moon's mass is only about one sixth that of Earth. How would your weight on Neptune compare with your weight on Earth? On the moon? Is the same true of your mass?*

are still being pulled toward the Earth by the force of gravity.

As you just read, the strength of the gravitational force changes with distance. But it also changes depending on mass. An object with a large mass, such as the Earth, exerts a strong gravitational force on other objects. (Which is why you remain rooted to the ground and don't float off into space.) But any object with mass exerts a gravitational force—and that includes you! There is actually a gravitational force of attraction between you and this textbook. But don't worry, the book will not come flying at you as a result of gravity. Why? Your mass is much too small.

We tend to think of the Earth as being extremely large. But as objects in space go, the Earth is not so big. The mass of the planet Jupiter is more than two and one-half times that of Earth. If you could stand on Jupiter, you would find that your weight would be two and one-half times greater than your weight on Earth. The mass of the moon is about one sixth that of the Earth. How would your weight on the moon compare with your weight on Earth?

It should be clear to you by now that mass remains a constant, but weight can change. The amount of matter in an object does not change regardless of where the object is located. But the weight of an object can change due to its location.

Density

Sometimes scientists need to compare substances based on their mass and volume. The relationship between mass and volume is called **density.**

Density is defined as the mass per unit volume of a substance. That may sound complicated, but it really isn't. Perhaps the following formula, which shows the relationship between density, mass, and volume, will help:

$$\text{Density} = \frac{\text{Mass}}{\text{Volume}}$$

Suppose a substance has a mass of 10 grams and a volume of 10 milliliters. If you divide the mass of

10 grams by the volume of 10 milliliters, you obtain the density of the substance:

$$\frac{10 \text{ g}}{10 \text{ mL}} = \frac{1 \text{ g}}{\text{mL}}$$

As it turns out, this substance is water. The density of water is 1 g/mL. Objects with a density less than that of water will float on water. Objects with a density greater than that of water will sink. Does iron have a density less than or greater than 1 g/mL?

Temperature

In the metric system, temperature is measured on the **Celsius** scale. On this temperature scale, water freezes at 0°C and boils at 100°C. This is not an accident. The metric system of temperature was set up in such a way that there are exactly 100 degrees between the freezing point and boiling point of water. (Remember the metric system is based on units of 10.) Normal body temperature is 37°C. Comfortable room temperature is about 21°C.

Dimensional Analysis

You now know the basic units of measurement in the metric system. But there is still one more thing you must learn—how to go from one unit to another. The skill of converting one unit to another is called **dimensional analysis.** Dimensional analysis involves determining in what units a problem is

Figure 1–23 *To increase her density so that she can sink to the depths of the sea bottom, this scuba diver wears a belt of lead weights.*

Figure 1–24 *You can see by the way this lizard walks lightly across the hot desert sands that temperature has an effect on almost all living things. Scientists measure temperature in degrees Celsius.*

given, in what units the answer should be, and the factor to be used to make the conversion from one unit to another. Keep in mind that you can only convert units that measure the same thing. That is, no matter how hard you try, you cannot convert length in kilometers to temperature in degrees Celsius.

To perform dimensional analysis, you must use a **conversion factor.** A conversion factor is a fraction that *always* equals 1. For example, 1 kilometer equals 1000 meters. So the fraction 1 kilometer/ 1000 meters equals 1. You can flip the conversion factor and it still equals 1: 1000 meters/1 kilometer equals 1.

In any fraction, the top number is called the numerator. The bottom number is called the denominator. So in a conversion factor the numerator always equals the denominator and the fraction always equals 1.

This is probably beginning to sound a lot more complicated than it actually is. Let's see how it all works by using an example. Suppose you are told to convert 7500 grams to kilograms. This means that grams are your given unit and you are to convert grams to kilograms. (Your answer must be expressed in kilograms.) The conversion factor you choose must contain the relationship between grams and kilograms that has a value of 1. You have two possible choices:

$$\frac{1000 \text{ grams}}{1 \text{ kilogram}} = 1 \quad \text{or} \quad \frac{1 \text{ kilogram}}{1000 \text{ grams}} = 1$$

To convert one metric unit to another, you must multiply the given quantity times the conversion factor. Remember that multiplying a number by 1 does not change the value of the number. So multiplying by a conversion factor does not change the value of the quantity, only its units.

Now, which conversion factor should you use to change 7500 grams to kilograms? Since you want the given unit to cancel out during multiplication, you should use the conversion whose denominator has the same units as the units you wish to convert. Because you are converting grams into kilograms, the denominator of the conversion factor you use must be in grams and the numerator in kilograms.

The first step in dimensional analysis, then, is to write out the given quantity, the correct conversion factor, and a multiplication symbol between them:

$$7500 \text{ grams} \times \frac{1 \text{ kilogram}}{1000 \text{ grams}}$$

The next step is to cancel out the same units:

$$7500 \text{ \sout{grams}} \times \frac{1 \text{ kilogram}}{1000 \text{ \sout{grams}}}$$

The last step is to multiply:

$$7500 \times \frac{1 \text{ kilogram}}{1000} = \frac{7500 \text{ kilograms}}{1000}$$

$$\frac{7500 \text{ kilograms}}{1000} = 7.5 \text{ kilograms}$$

1–3 Section Review

1. What are the basic units of length, volume, mass, weight, and temperature in the metric system?
2. Compare mass and weight.
3. On what scale is temperature measured in the metric system? What are the fixed points on this scale?
4. What metric unit of length would be appropriate for measuring the distance from the Earth to the sun? Why?

Critical Thinking—*Applying Concepts*
5. Without placing an object in water, how can you determine if it will float?

1–4 Tools of Earth and Space Scientists

Earth scientists use many special tools to learn about the Earth and space. For example, meteorologists use a tool called an anemometer to measure wind speed. They also use a very complicated tool called a weather satellite, which orbits the Earth and takes photos that are used to predict weather conditions. Geologists use rock hammers and microscopes, which magnify objects that are too small to be seen by the human eye alone. The use of a microscope helps geologists study the tiny particles that make up rocks.

Sometimes great discoveries are not made until new tools are invented. For example, the moons of Jupiter did not become visible until the telescope was invented. The telescope is an instrument used to view and magnify distant objects in space. **Scientists use a variety of telescopes to study the universe: optical telescopes, radio telescopes, infrared telescopes, ultraviolet telescopes, and X-ray telescopes.** You will now read about these different types of telescopes and discover what kinds of information they provide.

Figure 1–25 *The invention of the telescope opened the door to the incredible vastness of outer space and showed that our sun is but one tiny drop in an ocean of stars.*

Optical Telescopes

The first telescopes used by early astronomers were optical telescopes.(Remember that the term optical refers to light.) An optical telescope collects and focuses visible light from distant objects such as stars and galaxies. Using a series of mirrors, lenses, or a combination of the two, the telescope magnifies the image formed by the light. The two types of optical telescopes are refracting telescopes and reflecting telescopes.

REFRACTING TELESCOPES In a **refracting telescope**, a series of lenses is used to focus light. (As you may know, an optical microscope uses a series of lenses to magnify microscopic objects.) In general, the larger the lens, the greater the light-gathering power of a telescope. The size of a telescope is given as the diameter of its largest lens. The world's largest refracting telescope is the "40-inch" telescope at Yerkes Observatory in Wisconsin. This telescope has a light-gathering power about 40,000 times greater than the human eye!

REFLECTING TELESCOPES In a **reflecting telescope,** a series of mirrors is used to collect and focus light from distant objects. For technical reasons, the mirrors in a reflecting telescope can be built much larger than the lenses in a refracting telescope. One of the world's largest reflecting telescopes is the "200-inch" Hale telescope on Mount Palomar in California. Telescopes like the Hale telescope can observe objects billions of light-years from Earth. They literally open the door to the very edge of the universe.

Figure 1–26 *The Hale Telescope on Mount Palomar in California uses one large mirror. What type of telescope is it?*

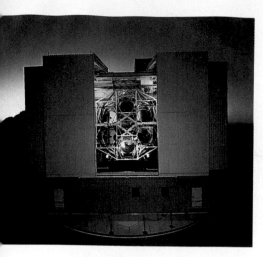

Figure 1-27 *The Multiple Mirror Telescope atop Mount Hopkins in Arizona uses six mirrors.*

MULTIPLE MIRROR TELESCOPES Large reflecting telescopes are extremely difficult and expensive to build. The mirrors in such telescopes must be perfectly constructed and flawless. For many years scientists believed that a 5-meter mirror (approximately 200 inches) was about the largest mirror they could construct. To get around that problem, the Multiple Mirror Telescope was constructed. Sitting high atop Mount Hopkins in Arizona, the Multiple Mirror Telescope contains six "72-inch" mirrors. The six mirrors work together to collect light from distant stars and provide even greater power than the single large mirror in the Hale telescope.

NEW ADVANCES IN OPTICAL TELESCOPES Many new types of optical telescopes are being designed and tested throughout the world. How many will go from the drawing board to actual construction remains to be seen. Each of these new types of telescopes uses a different design to enlarge the size of the mirror it houses. One of the most recently developed telescopes is the Keck telescope in Mauna Kea, Hawaii. The Keck telescope has a "400-inch" mirror. How have scientists solved the problem of building such a large mirror? In a sense, they haven't. For the Keck telescope actually contains 36 individual mirror segments joined together in what looks like a beehive. The 36 mirror segments make the Keck telescope the most powerful optical telescope on Earth—at least until an even newer and larger telescope is built.

Figure 1-28 *The Keck telescope in Hawaii houses a "400-inch" mirror made up of 36 segments (inset).*

CONNECTIONS

Messages From Outer Space?

Have we been receiving radio messages from outer space? In 1933, people believed we were. They were wrong, but their mistake is an interesting example of how luck, or serendipity, plays a role in science and, in this case, can shake up society for a little while.

Here's how it all happened. In 1931, Bell Telephone scientists wanted to find out what was causing static on some radio telephone lines. The scientists suspected (hypothesized) that the static might be caused by thunderstorms. They asked a young scientist named Karl Jansky to see if he could find out whether this was true. Jansky built a special antenna to try to solve the problem. He mounted his antenna on some wheels from an old car so that he could aim the antenna at any part of the sky. Because it could be turned around, Jansky's invention was nicknamed "the merry-go-round."

Jansky found that almost all of the static was indeed caused by radio waves from thunderstorms. But his an-

tenna had also picked up a faint hissing sound that he could not explain. Jansky could have shrugged his shoulders and ignored this hissing sound, but his curiosity got the best of him. So he decided to investigate. He would try to track down the hissing sounds.

Jansky carried on observations for two years. Eventually, he found that the hiss moved across the sky, as did the stars. In 1933, Jansky announced that the radio waves producing the hissing sound were actually coming to Earth from outer space! Jansky's discovery that radio waves were coming from space became an overnight sensation. Newspaper headlines throughout the world reported the finding. But after only a few weeks, most people seemed to forget Jansky's discovery.

Then, in 1937, an amateur radio operator named Grote Reber had a hunch that Jansky's discovery was important. So Reber built a 10-meter dish antenna in his backyard to capture the radio waves from space. This instrument became the world's first radio telescope. Jansky's unexpected discovery and Reber's hunch gave astronomers a new way of exploring the sky. The science of *radio astronomy,* which would produce many exciting discoveries of its own, had been born.

Radio Telescopes

No doubt when you think of stars you think of visible light. After all, that's what you see when you look up at the night sky. Visible light, however, is only one part of the **electromagnetic spectrum.** In addition to visible light, the electromagnetic spectrum includes forms of "light" we cannot detect with our eyes. These forms of invisible light include X-rays, ultraviolet rays and infrared rays, and radio waves. And as it turns out, many stars give off both visible and invisible light. Is there a way to view distant stars using invisible light? Yes, but obviously not with an optical telescope.

You just learned about the discovery of radio astronomy by Karl Jansky and Grote Reber. At that time we said that radio telescopes opened up a new view of the universe—and oh what a view! Because many stars give off mainly radio waves (not visible light), the invention of the radio telescope provided scientists with an opportunity to study the universe in a new and exciting way. It was almost as if a huge part of the universe had been hidden from us, waiting for the discovery of the radio telescope to reveal itself.

An optical telescope can be thought of as a bucket for collecting light waves from space. A **radio telescope** can be thought of as a bucket for collecting radio waves from space. In most radio telescopes, a curved metal dish gathers and focuses radio waves onto an antenna. The signal picked up

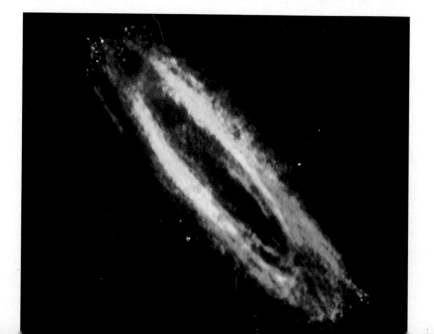

Figure 1–29 Radio telescopes have produced this image of the Andromeda galaxy, one of our nearest neighbors in space.

by the antenna is fed into computers, which then produce an image of the object giving off the radio waves. Radio telescopes are usually mounted on movable supports so they can be directed toward any point in the sky. These telescopes have been able to collect radio waves from objects as far away as 14 billion light-years!

In the desert of New Mexico stands a group of 27 radio telescopes known as the Very Large Array, or VLA. The VLA is extremely useful because it combines the radio-wave detecting power of 27 individual radio telescopes. With the VLA, scientists can get a clearer picture of many objects in space than they can with a single radio telescope.

Figure 1–30 *The Very Large Array in New Mexico is made up of 27 radio telescopes.*

Infrared and Ultraviolet Telescopes

In general, stars are the only objects in space that give off visible light. And some stars are so dim they do not give off enough visible light to be easily observed. But all objects, even dark, cold objects such as planets, give off infrared rays. Recall that infrared is part of the electromagnetic spectrum. Another term for infrared is heat energy. Unfortunately, infrared rays from distant objects in space are not easily detected once they enter Earth's atmosphere. So telescopes that operate using infrared rays are carried out of the atmosphere.

In January, 1983, the Infrared Astronomy Satellite, or *IRAS*, was launched. *IRAS*, the first **infrared telescope** in space, soon provided scientists with new and exciting information. For example, *IRAS* detected heat waves from newborn stars in clouds of gas and dust 155,000 light-years from Earth. *IRAS* also collected information that suggests that the distant star Vega is surrounded by a giant cloud of matter. This cloud may be an early stage in the development of planets. If so, *IRAS* has given us the first view of planets beyond our solar system.

Like infrared, ultraviolet light is an invisible form of light in the electromagnetic spectrum. In order to detect ultraviolet light given off by objects, scientists have constructed **ultraviolet telescopes.** Ultraviolet rays from space do not pass easily through Earth's atmosphere. So ultraviolet telescopes, like infrared telescopes, are usually carried out of the Earth's

ACTIVITY

WRITING

A New Comet

One of the first achievements of *IRAS* was finding a new comet in our solar system. Using library and other reference sources, find out the name of that comet—and the mystery of its triple name. Report your findings in a brief essay.

atmosphere. Some of the most dramatic photographs taken with ultraviolet telescopes are of our own sun, which gives off huge amounts of ultraviolet light daily. One of the primary tasks of the *Hubble Space Telescope,* which you will read about shortly, is to detect ultraviolet rays from space using an on-board ultraviolet telescope.

X-ray Telescopes

X-rays are another form of electromagnetic radiation given off by stars. In fact, almost all stars give off X-rays. By now you should not be surprised to learn that **X-ray telescopes** have been constructed to detect the invisible X-rays from space. Of all the forms of light in the electromagnetic spectrum, X-rays are the least able to pass through Earth's atmosphere. (A good thing because if they did, no life as we know it could survive on Earth.) So X-rays from space can only be detected by X-ray telescopes sent into orbit above the Earth.

In 1970, the first X-ray telescope, called *Uhuru,* was launched. *Uhuru* gave scientists their first clear view of X-ray sources in the sky. *Uhuru* and other orbiting X-ray telescopes have provided a wealth of information about the life cycle of stars, particularly what happens to very massive stars as they begin to age and die.

Space Telescope

You have no doubt read about a flaw in the 2.4-meter mirror of the *Hubble Space Telescope.* What you may not know is that the *Hubble Space Telescope* also houses several other kinds of telescopes. So you

Figure 1–31 *Compare the infrared image of the Dorados nebula (left) with the ultraviolet image of a spiral galaxy (right).*

Figure 1–32 *This X-ray image shows the remains of a star that exploded in what is called a supernova.*

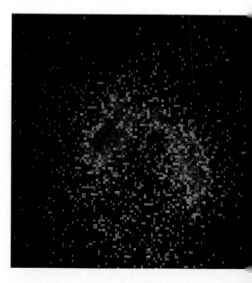

can think of the *Hubble Space Telescope* as a combination of telescopes—each of which provides a different picture of the universe. In fact, one of the first important discoveries of the *Hubble Space Telescope* was made by its ultraviolet telescope. In 1991, the ultraviolet telescope revealed what could be the beginning of a new solar system forming around a star called Beta Pictoris.

Scientists have nicknamed the *Hubble Space Telescope* the "eye in the sky." With it, they can obtain a detailed view of many objects long hidden from earthbound telescopes. The primary mirror, aided by a package of corrective optical equipment installed in 1993, enables the *Hubble Space Telescope* to provide excellent photographs of many distant objects. Combined with the other telescopes on board, the *Hubble Space Telescope* promises to expand our knowledge of the universe in as dramatic a fashion as van Leeuwenhoek's microscope opened up the microscopic world.

Figure 1–33 *Astronaut Story Musgrave, anchored to the end of the shuttle's robot arm, approaches the* Hubble Space Telescope *as it sits in the cargo bay of* Endeavour *during the eleven-day repair mission (left). Here astronaut Kathryn Thornton performs repair work on the telescope (right).*

1–4 Section Review

1. Compare refracting and reflecting telescopes.
2. Name and describe three types of telescopes that detect invisible light.

Connection—*You and Your World*
3. Doctors use X-rays to take pictures of broken bones and other internal body parts. Why can the doctor's X-rays pass through the atmosphere but X-rays from space cannot?

1–5 Safety in the Science Laboratory

To better understand the concepts you will read about in science, it is likely you will work in the laboratory. If you follow instructions and are as careful as a scientist would be, the laboratory will turn out to be an exciting experience for you.

Scientists know that when working in the laboratory, it is very important to follow safety procedures. **The most important safety rule is to always follow your teacher's directions or the directions in your textbook exactly as stated.** You should never try anything on your own without asking your teacher first. And when you are not sure what you should do, ask.

As you read the laboratory investigations in your textbook, you will see safety alert symbols. These symbols indicate that special safety precautions must be taken. Look at Figure 1–35 to learn the meaning of these safety symbols and the important safety procedures.

In addition to the safety procedures listed in Figure 1–35, there is a more detailed list of safety procedures in Appendix C at the back of this textbook. Before you enter the laboratory for the first time, make sure you have read each rule carefully. Then read all the rules over again, making sure you understand each rule. If you do not understand a rule, ask your teacher to explain it. You may even want to suggest further rules that apply to your classroom.

Figure 1–34 *These photographs illustrate some important laboratory safety rules. Never directly inhale the fumes from a beaker (top). Pour acids and bases over a sink (bottom).*

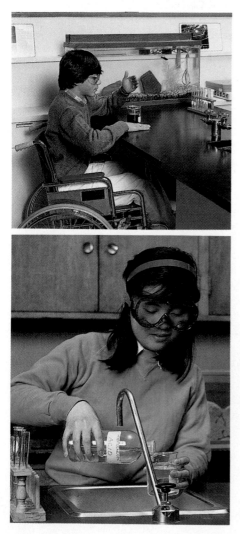

1–5 Section Review

1. What is the most important general rule to follow when working in the laboratory?
2. Suppose your teacher asks you to boil some water in a test tube. What precautions should you take to make sure this is done safely?

Connection—*You and Your World*
3. How can you apply the safety rules in Figure 1–35 to rules that should be followed when working in a kitchen? In a machine shop?

Glassware Safety

1. Whenever you see this symbol, you will know that you are working with glassware that can easily be broken. Take particular care to handle such glassware safely. And never use broken or chipped glassware.
2. Never heat glassware that is not thoroughly dry. Never pick up any glassware unless you are sure it is not hot. If it is hot, use heat-resistant gloves.
3. Always clean glassware thoroughly before putting it away.

Fire Safety

1. Whenever you see this symbol, you will know that you are working with fire. Never use any source of fire without wearing safety goggles.
2. Never heat anything—particularly chemicals—unless instructed to do so.
3. Never heat anything in a closed container.
4. Never reach across a flame.
5. Always use a clamp, tongs, or heat-resistant gloves to handle hot objects.
6. Always maintain a clean work area, particularly when using a flame.

Heat Safety

Whenever you see this symbol, you will know that you should put on heat-resistant gloves to avoid burning your hands.

Chemical Safety

1. Whenever you see this symbol, you will know that you are working with chemicals that could be hazardous.
2. Never smell any chemical directly from its container. Always use your hand to waft some of the odors from the top of the container toward your nose—and only when instructed to do so.
3. Never mix chemicals unless instructed to do so.
4. Never touch or taste any chemical unless instructed to do so.
5. Keep all lids closed when chemicals are not in use. Dispose of all chemicals as instructed by your teacher.

6. Immediately rinse with water any chemicals, particularly acids, that get on your skin and clothes. Then notify your teacher.

Eye and Face Safety

1. Whenever you see this symbol, you will know that you are performing an experiment in which you must take precautions to protect your eyes and face by wearing safety goggles.
2. When you are heating a test tube or bottle, always point it away from you and others. Chemicals can splash or boil out of a heated test tube.

Sharp Instrument Safety

1. Whenever you see this symbol, you will know that you are working with a sharp instrument.
2. Always use single-edged razors; double-edged razors are too dangerous.
3. Handle any sharp instrument with extreme care. Never cut any material toward you; always cut away from you.
4. Immediately notify your teacher if your skin is cut.

Electrical Safety

1. Whenever you see this symbol, you will know that you are using electricity in the laboratory.
2. Never use long extension cords to plug in any electrical device. Do not plug too many appliances into one socket or you may overload the socket and cause a fire.
3. Never touch an electrical appliance or outlet with wet hands.

Animal Safety

1. Whenever you see this symbol, you will know that you are working with live animals.
2. Do not cause pain, discomfort, or injury to an animal.
3. Follow your teacher's directions when handling animals. Wash your hands thoroughly after handling animals or their cages.

Figure 1–35 *You should become familiar with these safety symbols because you will see them in the laboratory investigations in this textbook.*

Laboratory Investigation

Constructing a Telescope

Problem

How does a refracting telescope work?

Materials *(per group)*

> meterstick
> 2 lens holders
> 2 convex lenses or magnifying glasses of different sizes
> unlined index card (to be used as a screen)
> card holder

Procedure 🧪

1. Put the two lenses in the lens holders and place them on the meterstick. Put the index card in its holder and place it between the two lenses.

2. Aim one end of the meterstick at a window or an electric light about 3 to 10 meters away. Light given off or reflected by an object will pass through the lens and form an image of the object on the screen (index card). Carefully slide the lens nearer to the light source back and forth until a clear, sharp image of the light source forms on the screen.

3. The distance between the center of the lens and the sharp image is called the focal length of the lens. Measure this distance to obtain the focal length of that lens. Record your measurement.

4. Turn the other end of the meterstick toward the light source. Without disturbing the screen or the first lens, determine the focal length of the second lens.

5. Point the end of the meterstick that has the lens with the longer focal length toward a distant object. Without changing the positions of the lenses, take the

screen out of its holder and look at the distant object through both lenses. You may have to adjust the lenses slightly to focus the image. You have now constructed a refracting telescope.

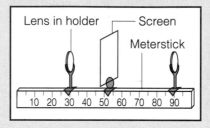

Observations

1. What was the focal length of the first lens? The second lens?

2. How does the image seen through the lens with the shorter focal length differ from the image seen through the lens with the longer focal length?

3. How does the image of an object seen through the lens with the longer focal length appear different from the object itself?

Analysis and Conclusions

1. In a telescope, the lens with the shorter focal length is called the eyepiece. The lens with the longer focal length is called the objective. You can calculate the magnifying power of your telescope by using the following formula:

$$\text{Magnifying power} = \frac{\text{Focal length of objective}}{\text{Focal length of eyepiece}}$$

Using the formula, calculate the magnifying power of your telescope.

2. **On Your Own**   What is the relationship between the telescope's magnifying power and the ratio between the focal lengths of the lenses?

Study Guide

Summarizing Key Concepts

1–1 Science—Not Just for Scientists

▲ The goal of science is to understand the world around us.

▲ Scientists use facts as clues to the large mysteries of nature.

▲ A theory is the most logical explanation for events that occur in nature.

1–2 The Scientific Method—A Way of Problem Solving

▲ The scientific method is a process scientists use to solve problems about nature.

▲ The basic steps of the scientific method are stating the problem, gathering information, forming a hypothesis, experimenting, observing and recording information, and stating a conclusion.

1–3 The Metric System

▲ Experimental measurements must not only be reliable and accurate but also be easily communicated to others.

▲ Mass is a measure of the amount of matter in an object. Weight is a measure of the force of attraction between objects caused by gravity.

▲ Density is the measurement of how much mass is contained in a given volume of an object.

1–4 Tools of Earth and Space Scientists

▲ The types of telescopes used by astronomers are refracting, reflecting, infrared, X-ray, and radio telescopes.

1–5 Safety in the Science Laboratory

▲ Whenever working in the laboratory, you should take all necessary safety precautions and use safety equipment when applicable.

Reviewing Key Terms

Define each term in a complete sentence.

1–1 Science—Not Just for Scientists
theory
law
geology
meteorology
oceanography
astronomy

1–2 The Scientific Method— A Way of Problem Solving
scientific method
hypothesis
variable
control
data

1–3 The Metric System
metric system
meter
centimeter
millimeter
kilometer
light-year
liter
milliliter
cubic centimeter
kilogram
gram
milligram
weight
newton
density
Celsius
dimensional analysis
conversion factor

1–4 Tools of Earth and Space Scientists
refracting telescope
reflecting telescope
electromagnetic
  spectrum
radio telescope
infrared telescope
ultraviolet telescope
X-ray telescope

Chapter Review

Content Review

Multiple Choice

Choose the letter of the answer that best completes each statement.

1. An orderly, systematic approach to a problem is called the
   a. investigation.
   b. scientific method.
   c. experiment.
   d. conclusion.

2. A proposed solution to a scientific problem is called a
   a. conclusion.
   b. control.
   c. hypothesis.
   d. theory.

3. In any experiment, the one factor being tested is called the
   a. control.
   b. data.
   c. variable.
   d. hypothesis.

4. The branch of earth science that deals with the Earth's history and structure is called
   a. geology.
   b. oceanography.
   c. astronomy.
   d. meteorology.

5. The meter is the basic unit of
   a. volume.
   b. temperature.
   c. density.
   d. length.

6. Very long distances in space are measured in
   a. kilograms.
   b. liters.
   c. centimeters.
   d. light-years.

7. The basic unit of mass is called the
   a. meter.
   b. kilogram.
   c. centimeter.
   d. gram.

8. The basic unit of volume is called the
   a. gram.
   b. kilogram.
   c. liter.
   d. degree Celsius.

9. Optical telescopes detect
   a. X-rays.
   b. infrared rays.
   c. visible light.
   d. radio waves.

10. The symbol of a hand next to a laboratory procedure means
    a. do not touch broken glassware.
    b. cover eyes with your hand.
    c. use heat-resistant gloves.
    d. wear safety goggles.

True or False

If the statement is true, write "true." If it is false, change the underlined word or words to make the statement true.

1. Any experiment must have <u>two variables</u> to be accurate.
2. The <u>control</u> experiment does not include a variable.
3. The prefix *kilo-* means <u>one hundred</u>.
4. Meters are used to measure <u>volume</u>.
5. The unit of density is <u>g/cm³</u>.
6. The degree <u>Fahrenheit</u> is the basic unit of temperature in the metric system.
7. Astronomers study the skies with different kinds of <u>microscopes</u>.
8. A series of <u>mirrors</u> is used in reflecting telescopes.
9. The symbol of a <u>flask</u> means you will be working with a sharp instrument.

Concept Mapping

Complete the following concept map for Section 1–3. Then construct a concept map for the entire chapter.

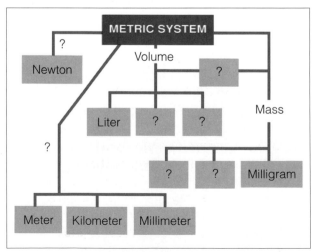

44

Concept Mastery

Discuss each of the following in a brief paragraph.

1. Describe the steps in the scientific method.
2. To investigate a problem why might you go to a library? To a laboratory?
3. Compare refracting and reflecting telescopes.
4. Why must an experiment contain only one variable?
5. Explain why mass is a constant, but weight can change.

Critical Thinking and Problem Solving

Use the skills you have developed in this chapter to answer each of the following.

1. **Making charts** Construct a chart that shows the different types of telescopes and the kinds of energy each type can detect.
2. **Expressing an opinion** A great deal of money is spent each year on space exploration. Many people feel that this money could be better spent improving conditions on Earth. Other people feel that knowledge gained from space exploration will ultimately bring great benefits to human society. Still others suggest that scientific knowledge is valuable for its own sake and should not be thought of in terms of dollars and cents. What is your opinion? Explain your answer.
3. **Designing an experiment** Ocean water, unlike fresh water, contains salt. The amount of salt in ocean water is called salinity. Design an experiment to determine if the salinity of ocean water changes as the depth of the ocean changes.
4. **Drawing conclusions** At the beginning of this chapter we stated that the way the Anasazi people tried to solve the mysteries of nature may not be very different from those used by modern scientists. Now that you have completed the chapter, explain whether you agree or disagree with that statement.
5. **Using the writing process** If telescopes could talk, what stories would they tell? Write a telescope story. *Hint:* First decide what type of telescope you are.
6. **Using the writing process** Write a short story that begins, "It was a dark and stormy night. As the lost hikers knocked on the door of the scientist's laboratory, they suddenly realized. . ."

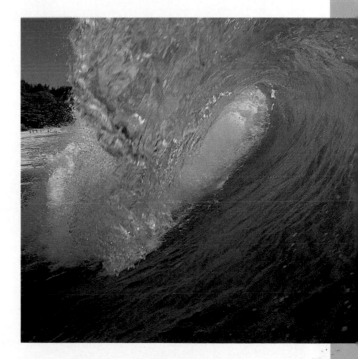

Stars and Galaxies

Guide for Reading

After you read the following sections, you will be able to

2–1 A Trip Through the Universe
- Describe the groups into which stars are classified.
- Describe the Milky Way galaxy.

2–2 Formation of the Universe
- Describe the big-bang theory and relate it to the formation of the universe.
- Explain how red shift is used to determine the movements of galaxies.

2–3 Characteristics of Stars
- Classify stars by size, mass, color, temperature, and brightness.

2–4 A Special Star: Our Sun
- Describe the four main layers of the sun.

2–5 The Evolution of Stars
- Describe the life cycles of stars.

Where does the sun fit into the universe? In 1914, American astronomer Harlow Shapley asked himself this question. Until then most astronomers believed that the sun was the center of the entire universe. Shapley, however, was not so sure.

Shapley began studying large groups, or clusters, of stars. He made a model showing where these clusters were located. Using his model, Shapley found that the clusters were grouped together in a gigantic sphere whose center was thousands of light-years from the sun. Shapley believed the center of this gigantic sphere was the real center of the universe. If so, our sun and nearby stars were actually near the edge of the universe!

Most of the stars that were known in Shapley's time were in a part of the sky called the Milky Way. The Greek name for the Milky Way is *galaxias kylos*, which means milky circle. So Shapley's universe came to be called the galaxy. Shapley believed that all the matter in the universe was located in this single galaxy. Outside the galaxy there was empty space.

But was Shapley right? Had he found the center of the universe? To shed some light on the answer, read on.

Journal *Activity*

You and Your World   What would it be like to experience the wonders of outer space? In your journal, write a letter to NASA describing why you should be selected for the first trip to a distant star.

 Notice the bright stars shining amidst the glowing gas and dust of the Orion nebula.

Guide for Reading

Focus on these questions as you read.

▶ What are galaxies? What are the three main types of galaxies?

▶ What is the size and shape of the Milky Way galaxy?

2–1 A Trip Through the Universe

Look up at the stars on a clear moonless night. Hundreds, perhaps thousands, of stars fill the sky. Each of these twinkling lights is actually a sun—a huge sphere of hot, glowing gas. Many of these suns are much larger and brighter than our own sun. But even a person with extremely good eyesight can see only a tiny fraction of the stars in the entire universe. Telescopes, of course, reveal many more stars. Most of the stars are so far away, however, that they cannot be seen individually, even with the most powerful telescope. Fortunately, although astronomers are unable to locate most individual stars, they can detect huge groups of stars.

To better understand what astronomers have learned about the stars, you can begin with a quick journey through the known universe. Most scientists believe that nothing can travel faster than the speed of light, which is about 300,000 kilometers per second. That's fast, but not fast enough for your trip. For even at the speed of light a journey through the universe would take billions of years. So in the spaceship of your mind you will have to travel much faster, stopping only occasionally to view some of the wonders of space.

Figure 2–1 *Only a small portion of the billions upon billions of stars in the universe are shown in this photograph.*

ACTIVITY

DISCOVERING

Using Star Charts

1. Turn to the star chart appendices at the back of this textbook.

2. Take the star chart outside on a starry night. Make sure you hold the star chart in the proper position for the time and date you are observing.

3. Make a drawing of what you see.

4. Repeat this activity in about one month.

How many constellations can you find in your first drawing? In your second drawing?

■ Are there any other changes in your drawing? If so, how can you explain them?

Multiple-Star Systems

You begin your trip by heading directly toward the star closest to the sun, Alpha Centauri. Although it is "close" by space standards, Alpha Centauri is still about 4.3 light-years from Earth.

Because our sun is a single-star system, astronomers believed for many years that most stars form individual star systems. For example, Alpha Centauri, when viewed from Earth, appears as a single speck in the sky. As you approach Alpha Centauri, however, you quickly discover that early astronomers were wrong. Alpha Centauri is not a single star at all, but three stars that make up a triple-star system! So Alpha Centauri is a multiple-star system. In fact, only one of the stars, called Proximi Centauri, is actually the closest to Earth.

As you continue your journey, you begin to realize that Alpha Centauri is not unusual. You discover that about half the stars in the sky have at least one companion star. Most of these stars are double-star systems in which two stars revolve around each other. Double-star systems are called **binary stars** (the prefix *bi-* means two). See Figure 2–2.

Thousands of years ago Arab shepherds discovered that about every three days a certain bright star suddenly became dim and disappeared, only to brighten again. In fear of this strange star, they

Figure 2–2 *This photograph shows Sirius, the Dog Star, and its small binary companion star. What are binary stars?*

Figure 2–3 *Algol is a binary star system. Each time the large dark star passes between the bright star and Earth, the bright star seems to dim and disappear. When does it reappear?*

Algol

Dim companion star

named it Algol, the "ghoul." Since your journey steers you by Algol, you will be able to discover the reason for Algol's winking on and off. Algol is a binary-star system. One of Algol's stars is a small, bright-blue star. It is visible from Earth. The other star is a large, dim, yellow star. It is not visible from Earth, so the Arabs could not have known of its existence. About every three days the large star passes between the smaller star and Earth, blocking off some of the smaller star's light. So every three days the smaller star seems to disappear. Can you explain why it reappears again?

Constellations: Star Groups That Form Patterns

From Algol you can continue your journey in any direction. One path may take you past the Dog Star—Sirius—which is more than 8 light-years from Earth. Another path may take you to the North Star—Polaris—more than 700 light-years from Earth. Polaris has long been an important star to navigators. at sea because they knew if they steered toward Polaris they were heading north.

Figure 2–4 *These are some of the constellations you can see in the night sky. What do the pointer stars point to?*

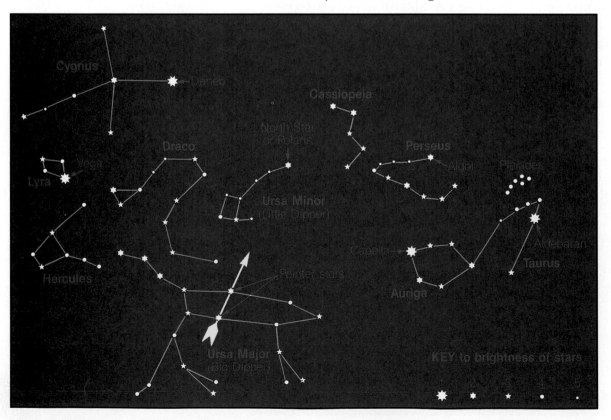

Polaris is at the end of the handle of a group of stars called the Little Dipper. The Little Dipper, in turn, makes up the **constellation** of stars called Ursa Minor, or the Little Bear. Constellations are groups of stars in which people at one time thought they saw imaginary figures of animals or people. See Figure 2–4.

One of the best-known constellations is the Big Bear, or Ursa Major. The seven stars in the back end and tail of the Big Bear form the Big Dipper, which can be easily seen in the northern sky. Two bright stars in the cup of the Big Dipper are known as the pointer stars because they point toward Polaris.

On clear winter nights, you can see the large constellation Orion, the Hunter. There are two bright stars in this constellation: Betelgeuse (BEET-uhl-jooz) and Rigel (RIGH-juhl). Nearby are other constellations: Gemini, Canis Major, or the Big Dog, and Canis Minor, or the Little Dog. Some of the summer constellations that are easy to recognize are Scorpius, Leo, and Virgo. What constellations do you know?

Novas

No time to dally with the constellations, as there is much more to see. The Little Dipper fades into the distance as you steer your ship toward a web of glowing stars. Then, without any warning, a tiny star seems to explode in a burst of light. You are fortunate indeed. For you have witnessed a rare event in space—you have seen a **nova.**

A nova is a star that suddenly increases in brightness up to 100 times in just a few hours or days. Soon after it brightens, the nova slowly begins to grow dim again. Astronomers believe that almost all novas are members of binary-star systems. Gases from the companion star in the system occasionally strike the surface of the nova star. When this happens, a nuclear explosion results, and heat, light, and gases burst into space. See Figure 2–5.

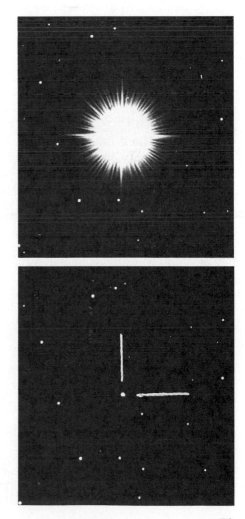

Figure 2–5 In 1935, a star in the constellation Hercules erupted in a rare nova. A month later the same star, shown by the arrows, had returned to normal.

Figure 2–6 *The Pleiades is an open cluster of stars (right). The Hercules cluster of stars is globular (left).*

Star Clusters

When the light from the nova finally fades, you are able again to pay close attention to the mass of stars you are approaching. When you do, you notice that although there are stars almost everywhere you can see, a great many stars seem to be grouped in huge clusters.

There are two types of star clusters. See Figure 2–6. Open clusters such as the Pleiades are not well organized and contain hundreds of stars. Globular clusters, which are more common, are arranged in a spherical, or round, shape. Globular clusters, such as the cluster in the constellation Hercules, contain more than 100,000 stars.

Star clusters appear to the unaided eye on Earth as one star or as a faint, white cloud. Why do you think that you cannot see the individual stars in a cluster?

Nebulae

Once you have passed what seems like a thousand or more globular clusters, you begin to notice that the number of stars is thinning. You are rapidly approaching an area of space that seems empty. But before you get there, it is time to put on a special pair of glasses. Up until now you have seen with your eyes alone, so you have been limited to seeing only the visible light rays your eyes can detect. The special glasses will allow you to see all the different kinds of rays stars can give off.

Figure 2–7 *Most stars are born in the gas and dust that make up a nebula. The photographs show the Red Nebula (right) and the Tarantula Nebula (left).*

You are completely unprepared for the spectacle that awaits you when you put on your glasses. To your left you notice a mass of brilliant stars that shine mainly with X-rays. Ahead you see stars beaming ultraviolet light at you. Strangely enough, almost all the stars seem to be giving off some radio waves as well. You wonder briefly why you have never heard the stars on your radio. Then you remember that astronomers do just that when they "listen" to the sky with radio telescopes.

Of all the views your glasses give you, there is one that seems most exciting. Now that you can see infrared rays—or heat rays—an entirely new universe is revealed. And nothing could be more spectacular than the huge clouds of dust and gas you see glowing between the stars. Each massive cloud, probably the birthplace of new stars, is called a **nebula.** See Figure 2–7.

Galaxies

You began this chapter by learning how astronomer Harlow Shapley believed the entire universe could be found in one huge **galaxy,** the Milky Way. In 1755, long before Shapley was born, the German philosopher-scientist Immanuel Kant suggested a different theory. Kant believed that the sun was part of a vast galaxy, but that there were other "island universes," or galaxies, scattered throughout space as well.

Your ship has finally reached the area of space that seemed empty before. You are about to leave the Milky Way galaxy. Was Shapley right—will there

A CTIVITY READING

Psychohistory

Interested in societies of the future when people have moved to distant planets? Want to know how science and history can be combined into a single subject that can be used to rule the universe? If so, then you are guaranteed to enjoy the *Foundation Series* by Isaac Asimov.

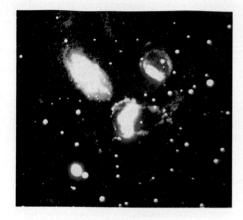

Figure 2–8 *Each galaxy in this cluster of galaxies might hold several trillion or more stars. Astronomers believe there may be over 100 billion galaxies in the universe.*

Figure 2–9 *Three different spiral galaxies are shown in these photographs. What is the major feature of a spiral galaxy?*

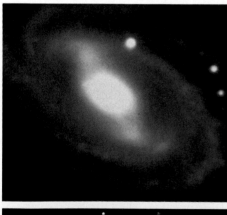

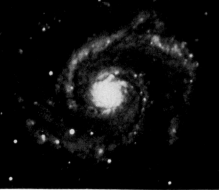

be nothing but empty space from here on? Or was Kant correct and will there be countless more worlds to visit? Seconds later the answer is clear. Before you, stretching out in every direction, thousands and thousands of galaxies shine in an awesome display of size and power. Even though the Milky Way is so large that it would take light more than 100,000 years to travel from one end to another, it is but one tiny galaxy in a sea of galaxies. **Galaxies, which contain various star groups, are the major features of the universe.** In fact, astronomers now believe there may be more than 100 billion major galaxies, each with billions of stars of its own! See Figure 2–8.

You cannot visit more than a handful of galaxies on your journey, but it really doesn't matter. For you quickly find that most galaxies fit one of three types. Many galaxies are **spiral galaxies.** See Figure 2–9. Spiral galaxies, such as Andromeda, which is 2 million light-years from Earth, are shaped like pin-wheels. They have huge spiral arms that seem to reach out into space, ready to grab passing visitors that stray too close. The Milky Way, in which planet Earth is located, is another example of a spiral galaxy.

Galaxies that vary in shape from nearly spherical to flat disks are called **elliptical galaxies.** These galaxies contain very little dust and gas. The stars in elliptical galaxies are generally older than those in

other types of galaxies. This should not be surprising, since you learned that stars are born in huge clouds of gas and dust (nebula), which are rare in elliptical galaxies.

The third type of galaxy does not have the orderly shape of either the elliptical or spiral galaxies. These galaxies are called irregular galaxies. Irregular galaxies have no definite shape. The Large and Small Magellanic Clouds are irregular galaxies. They are the closest galaxies to the Milky Way. Several hundred irregular galaxies have been observed by astronomers, but they are much less common than spiral or elliptical galaxies.

The Milky Way Galaxy

It is almost time for our journey to end. You have traveled in a huge circle. In the distance you see the familiar spiral shape of your own galaxy, the Milky Way. In your mind, at least, you are the first person to observe the Milky Way from outside the galaxy. From this distance you can see that the Milky Way is a huge pinwheel-shaped disk with a bulge in the center. See Figure 2–11.

Most of the older stars in the Milky Way are found near the nucleus, or center, of the galaxy. The stars there are crowded together thousands of times more densely than in the spiral arms. This nucleus,

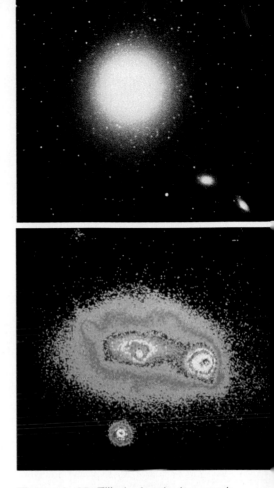

Figure 2–10 *Elliptical galaxies, such as the giant M87 galaxy, are oval-shaped and do not contain spiral arms (top). Irregular galaxies have no definite shape (bottom).*

Figure 2–11 *From the side, the Milky Way appears to be a narrow disk with a bulge in the center. Seen from the front, the galaxy reveals its spiral structure.*

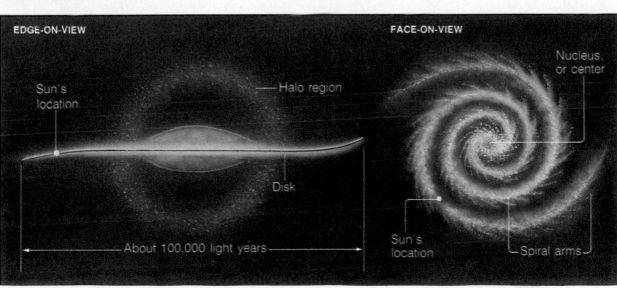

almost 20,000 light-years across, is hidden from our view on Earth by thick clouds of hot dust and gases.

Scientists estimate the Milky Way to be about 100,000 light-years in diameter and about 15,000 light-years thick. So even at the speed of light, it would take 100,000 years to travel across the Milky Way! If you could spot the light from Earth's sun, shining among the 100 billion stars in the Milky Way, you would notice that the sun is located in one of the pinwheel's spiral arms, almost 30,000 light-years from the central bulge. Earth's sun, along with many of the stars in the spiral arms, is among the younger stars in the Milky Way.

As you approach the Milky Way from above, you notice that all its many stars are rotating counter-clockwise about its center. In fact, scientists estimate that it takes our sun and its planets about 200 million years to rotate once about the center of the galaxy.

Well, your trip was an exciting one, but it is time to come back to Earth. You have traveled unimaginable distances in your mind and returned safely. Now it is time to look into how the extraordinarily beautiful and majestic universe formed. For the remainder of your study of stars and galaxies, you will have to travel through the pages of this textbook. But don't worry—it won't be any more dangerous than your trip through the universe.

Figure 2–12 *This edge-on-view of the Milky Way was made by plotting the locations of over 7000 known stars. Where is the sun located in the Milky Way?*

CONNECTIONS

Signs of the Zodiac

About 2000 years ago, astronomers wondered what the sky would look like if the stars could be seen during the day. Based on their observations of the night sky, some astronomers determined that during the daytime the sun would appear to move across the sky, entering a different constellation each month. These twelve constellations, one per month, came to be called the *zodiac*. Each constellation was called a sign of the zodiac. Many ancient people believed that the month a person was born in, and hence that person's sign, influenced the person's behavior, emotions, and even his or her fate. Even today, thousands of years later, some people still believe in the powers of the zodiac and read their horoscope daily. Most people read their horoscope for fun, however, not because they believe it to be true.

The illustration shows the original symbols for the twelve signs of the zodiac and the constellation each sign relates to. Many of these symbols may be familiar to you, as they are commonly used in jewelry. Under what sign were you born? Do you know how your emotions are supposed to be affected by your sign?

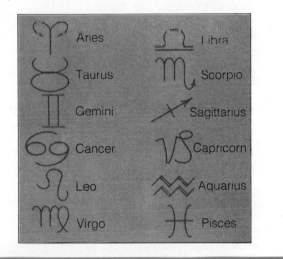

2–1 Section Review

1. Why are galaxies considered the major features of the universe?
2. Name and describe the three main types of galaxies.
3. Many binary stars are called eclipsing binaries. Explain why this term is appropriate. (*Hint:* Think about Algol when you answer this question.)

Connections—*Science and Technology*

4. How has our ability to detect "invisible" forms of light contributed to our knowledge of the universe?

2–2 Formation of the Universe

Astronomers use various telescopes to study stars. Optical telescopes detect visible light from stars. Radio telescopes detect radio waves emitted by stars. X-ray telescopes detect X-rays; ultraviolet telescopes detect ultraviolet rays. Finally, infrared telescopes examine infrared radiation from stars. Since stars give off some or all of these types of rays, telescopes are important tools for the astronomer.

Telescopes, however, are not the only tools of astronomers. An equally important tool is the **spectroscope.** Although visible light from stars appears white to your eyes, the light given off by stars usually contains a mixture of several different colors, all of which combine to make white light. A spectroscope can break up the light from a distant star into its characteristic colors. See Figure 2–14.

When light enters a spectroscope, the light is first focused into a beam by a lens. The beam of light then passes through a prism. A prism separates light into its different colors. (If you have a prism, you can prove this for yourself.) The band of colors formed when light passes through a prism is called

Figure 2–13 *Telescopes have been developed to detect the many types of light stars emit—both visible and invisible. The photograph of the Andromeda Galaxy was taken using an infrared telescope (right). The image of the galaxy called Centaurus A was taken with a radio telescope (top left). Parts of the constellation Sagittarius are seen in this X-ray photograph (bottom left).*

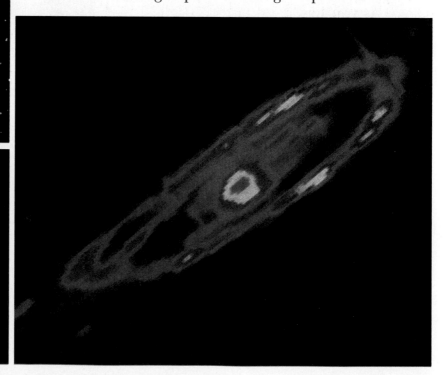

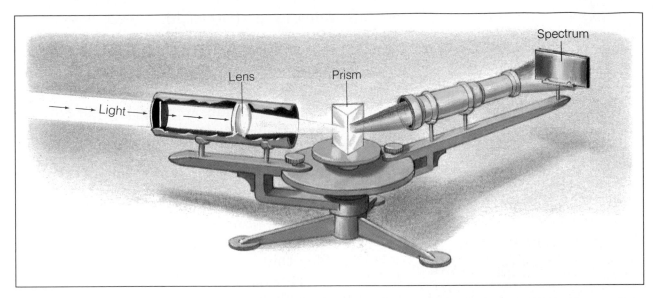

Figure 2–14 *In a spectroscope, light passes through a prism and is broken into a band of colors called a spectrum.*

a **spectrum.** The kind of spectrum produced by the light from a star tells astronomers a lot about that star.

Stars on the Move

Every single object in the universe is on the move. The moon, for example, moves around the Earth. The Earth, in turn, travels around the sun. The sun moves about the center of the Milky Way galaxy. As you have read, astronomers suggest there may be as many as 100 billion major galaxies. And like the other objects in space, each and every galaxy is on the move. By using a spectroscope, astronomers can determine whether a particular galaxy is moving toward the Earth or away from the Earth.

The Red Shift

Drop a stone into a pool of water and you will see water waves traveling away from the stone in all directions. The distance from the top of one wave (crest) to the top of the next wave is called the wavelength.

Light from stars travels to Earth as light waves. You have read that a spectroscope breaks up light into a spectrum. This happens because each color of light has a different wavelength. When light strikes the prism in a spectroscope, the prism bends the

Activity Bank

All the Colors of the Rainbow, p.749

Figure 2–15 *Despite the vastness of space, galaxies do collide on occasion, as demonstrated by this rare photograph of two galaxies colliding. Such collisions may last many millions of years.*

light according to the wavelength of each color. Some wavelengths are bent more than others by the prism. So the white light that enters the prism comes out as a band of colors. Each color has a different wavelength.

Suppose a star is rapidly approaching the Earth. The light waves from the star will be compressed, or pushed together. In fact, wavelengths from an approaching star often appear shorter than they really are. Shorter wavelengths of light are characteristic of blue and violet light. So the entire spectrum of an approaching star appears to be shifted slightly toward the blue end of the spectrum. This shifting is called the blue shift.

If a star is moving away from the Earth, the light waves will be slightly expanded as they approach the Earth. The wavelengths of the light will appear longer than they really are. Longer wavelengths of light are characteristic of the red end of the spectrum. So the spectrum of a star moving away from the Earth appears to be shifted slightly toward the red end. This is called the **red shift.** Astronomers know that the more the spectrum of light is shifted toward the blue or red end of the spectrum, the faster the star is moving toward or away from the Earth.

The apparent change in the wavelengths of light that occurs when an object is moving toward or away from the Earth is called the **Doppler effect.** You have probably "heard" another kind of Doppler effect right here on Earth. If you are in a car at a railroad crossing when a train is approaching, the first sound of the train's whistle will be high-pitched. The sound of the whistle will become low-pitched as the train passes by and moves away from you. In this example, the Doppler effect involves sound waves. But the same principle applies to light waves moving toward or away from Earth. See Figure 2–16.

When astronomers first used the spectroscope to study the light from stars in distant galaxies, they had a surprise. None of the light from distant galaxies showed a blue shift. That is, none of the galaxies was moving toward the Earth. Instead, the light from every distant galaxy showed a red shift. Every galaxy in the universe seemed to be moving away from the Earth.

ACTIVITY

THINKING

Red or Blue Shift?

The top spectrum represents a star not moving toward or away from Earth. The bottom two spectra show what would happen if the star were moving with respect to Earth.

1. Compare the bottom two spectra with the top spectrum.

2. Determine which spectrum is of a star moving toward Earth and which is of a star moving away.

Explain your answer in terms of red and blue shift.

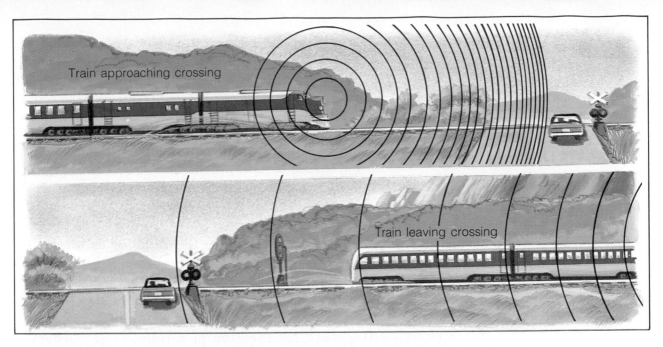

Figure 2–16 *As the train approaches the crossing (top), sound waves are crowded together and reach the listener's ears with a high pitch. As the train leaves the crossing (bottom), sound waves are farther apart and have a lower pitch. What term is used to describe this effect?*

After examining the red shifts of distant galaxies, astronomers concluded that the universe is expanding. Galaxies near the edge of the universe are racing away from the center of the universe at tremendous speeds. Galaxies closer to the center are also moving outward, but at slower speeds. What can account for an expanding universe?

The Big-Bang Theory

Astronomers believe that the expanding universe is the result of an enormous and powerful explosion called the big bang. The **big-bang theory** may explain how the universe formed. **The big-bang theory states that the universe began to expand with the explosion of concentrated matter and energy and has been expanding ever since.** According to the theory, all the matter and energy in the universe was once concentrated into a single place. This place, of course, was extremely hot and dense. Then some 15 to 20 billion years ago, an explosion—the big bang—shot the concentrated matter and energy in all directions. The fastest moving matter traveled farthest away. Energy, too, began moving away from the area of the big bang.

Figure 2–17 *What does this illustration tell you about galaxies?*

Swing Your Partner, p.750

ACTIVITY

An Expanding Universe

Use a balloon and small circles cut from sticky labels to make a model of an expanding universe. First, decide how to put your model together. What will represent the galaxies? How will the balloon enable you to show how the universe is expanding?

■ Do the galaxies get any larger as the universe expands?

■ What relationship exists between the speed of the galaxies moving apart and their initial distances from one another?

If the big-bang theory is correct, the energy left from the big bang will be evenly spread out throughout the universe. This energy is known as background radiation. And indeed, scientists have discovered that the background radiation is almost the same throughout the entire universe. This constant background radiation is one observation that supports the big-bang theory.

After the initial big bang, the force of **gravity** began to affect the matter racing outward in every direction. Gravity is a force of attraction between objects. All objects have a gravitational attraction for other objects. The more massive the object is, the stronger its gravitational attraction. This force of gravity began to pull matter into clumps.

At some time, the clumps formed huge clusters of matter. These clumps became the galaxies of the universe. But even as the galaxies were forming, the matter inside the galaxies continued to race away from the area where the big bang had occurred. And this is just what astronomers have discovered. All of the galaxies are speeding away from the center of the universe.

An Open Universe

Most astronomers feel that the big-bang theory leads to two possible futures for the universe. Perhaps the galaxies will continue racing outward. In this case, the universe will continue to expand. Such a universe is called an open, eternal universe. But eternal does not mean "forever" when it comes to the universe. In an open universe, the stars will eventually die off as the last of their energy is released. So the future of an open universe is one in which there will be nothing left. An open universe leads to total emptiness. But even if the universe is open, its end will not occur for many billions of years.

A Closed Universe

Most astronomers do not feel that the universe is an open universe. Instead, they suspect that the gravitational attraction between the galaxies will one day cause their movement away from each other to slow down. The expansion of the universe will finally

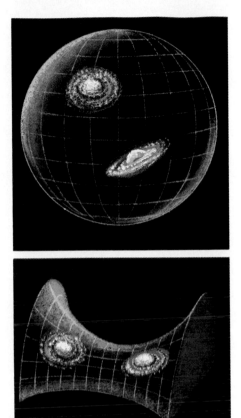

Figure 2–18 *A closed universe will eventually contract. Scientists picture a closed universe as similar to the surface of a ball (top). An open universe will expand until all of the stars die off. Scientists picture an open universe in the shape of a saddle (bottom).*

come to a halt. Then gravity will begin to pull the galaxies back toward the center of the universe. When this happens, every galaxy will begin to show a blue shift in its spectrum. Recall that a blue shift means that a galaxy is moving toward the Earth.

As the galaxies race back toward the center of the universe, the matter and energy will again come closer and closer to the central area. After many billions of years, all the matter and energy will once again be packed into a small area. This area may be no larger than the period at the end of this sentence. Then another big bang will occur. The formation of a universe will begin all over again. A universe that periodically expands and then contracts back on itself is called a closed universe. In a closed universe, a big bang may occur once every 80 to 100 billion years.

Quasars

If the universe is expanding, then objects near the edge of the universe are the oldest objects in the universe. Put another way, these objects took longer to reach their current position than objects closer to the center of the universe did. The most distant known objects in the universe are about 12 billion light-years from Earth. They are called **quasars** (KWAY-zahrz). The word quasar stands for quasi-stellar radio sources. The prefix *quasi-* means something like. The word *stellar* means star. So a quasar is a starlike object that gives off radio waves.

Quasars are among the most studied, and the most mysterious, objects in the universe. They give off mainly radio waves and X-rays. The mystery of quasars is the tremendous amount of energy they give off. Although they may seem too small to be galaxies, they give off more energy than 100 or more galaxies combined!

If the big-bang theory is correct, quasars at the edge of the universe were among the first objects formed after the big bang. In fact, scientists now believe that quasars may represent the earliest stages in

Figure 2–19 *This quasar, seen through an X-ray telescope, is some 12 billion light-years from Earth. How long does it take the quasar's light to reach Earth?*

the formation of a galaxy. So when scientists observe quasars, they are observing the very edge and the very beginning of the universe. Keep in mind that the light from a quasar 12 billion light-years from the Earth has traveled more than 12 billion years to reach the Earth. Astronomers observing quasars are, in a sense, looking back into time.

2–2 Section Review

1. How does a spectroscope enable astronomers to determine the characteristics of distant stars and galaxies?
2. Briefly describe the big bang. What two pieces of information provide evidence of the big bang?
3. What role did gravity play in the formation of galaxies?

Connection—*Social Studies*
4. The German philosopher Nietzsche went mad because he believed that he had already taken every action he took. How did the concept of a closed universe affect Nietzche's beliefs?

Guide for Reading

Focus on this question as you read.

▶ *How do the size, mass, color, temperature, and brightness of stars vary?*

2–3 Characteristics of Stars

Astronomers estimate that there may be more than 200 billion billion stars in the universe. **Stars differ in many features, including size, mass, color, temperature, and brightness.** It might seem an impossible task for astronomers to study so many different stars. While stars do vary in a great many ways, however, there are certain forces that govern all stars. By studying the stars that can be examined in detail and the forces that they must obey, astronomers gain knowledge about the vast numbers of stars they cannot closely observe.

How Large Are Stars?

Most stars are so far away that they appear as tiny points of light through even the most powerful

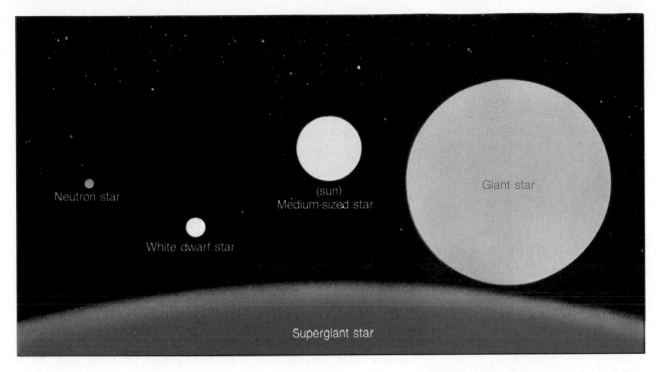

Neutron star

White dwarf star

(sun)
Medium-sized star

Giant star

Superglant star

telescopes. However, looks can be deceiving. For stars actually vary tremendously in size. Astronomers have divided stars into five main groups by size. See Figure 2–20.

Our sun has a diameter of about 1,392,000 kilometers, or about 109 times the diameter of Earth. That may seem enormous to you, but the sun is actually a medium-sized star. Medium-sized stars make up the majority of the stars you can see in the sky. They vary in size from about one-tenth the size of the sun to about ten times its size. Many of these stars are very bright. Sirius, for example, is about twice the diameter of the sun and is the brightest star in the night sky.

Stars with diameters about 10 to 100 times as large as the sun are called **giant stars.** For example, the diameter of the orange giant Aldebaran is 45 times the sun's diameter. Even the giant stars, however, seem tiny in comparison to the largest of all stars—the **supergiant stars.** Supergiants have diameters up to 1000 times the diameter of the sun. Some of the best-known supergiants are Rigel, Betelgeuse, and Antares. To get some idea of just how large these stars can be, suppose the red supergiant Antares were to replace the sun. It would burn Earth to cinders; in fact, it would extend well

Figure 2–20 *Stars come in a variety of sizes. What are the largest stars called? The smallest?*

beyond planet Mars. Supergiants, however, pay a price for their huge size. They die off quickly and are the shortest-lived stars in the universe.

Not all stars are larger than the sun. Some, such as **white dwarfs,** are even smaller than Earth. The smallest known white dwarf, Van Maanen's star, has a diameter that is less than the distance across the continent of Asia.

The smallest stars of all are called **neutron stars**. A typical neutron star has a diameter of only about 16 kilometers. That may be less than the total distance you travel to and from school.

Composition of Stars

Suppose you were given an unknown substance and asked to discover what it was made of. You might start by looking closely at the object from all sides. You might touch it to see how it feels and smell it to see if you could recognize its aroma. You would probably want to perform some other tests on it as well.

Astronomers cannot take a bit of a star and test it to see what it is made of. But they can determine the composition of stars, even stars many light-years from Earth. To determine the composition of a star, astronomers turn to the spectroscope.

How can a spectroscope show what a star is made of? Let's begin with the simple example of ordinary table salt. Table salt, or sodium chloride, is made of the elements sodium and chlorine. If table salt is placed in a flame, the flame will burn bright yellow.

Figure 2–21 *Scientists cannot take a bit of a star from the Large Magellanic Cloud in order to study the star's composition. How do astronomers know what elements make up the stars in the Large Magellanic Cloud?*

The yellow flame is caused by the sodium in salt. A yellow flame, then, is a characteristic of the element sodium.

Suppose the yellow light from the flame is passed through a spectroscope. No matter how many times this is done, two thin lines will always appear in the spectrum produced by the spectroscope. These two thin lines will always appear in exactly the same place in the spectrum. See Figure 2–22. In fact, no other element will produce the same two lines as sodium. In a way, these two lines are the "fingerprint" of the element sodium.

Other elements also produce a characteristic set of lines when they are heated and the light given off is passed through a spectroscope. So every known element has a fingerprint. By passing the light from a star through a spectroscope, astronomers can determine exactly what elements are in that star. How? They compare the spectral lines from the star to the spectral lines, or fingerprints, of the known elements.

By using the spectroscope, astronomers have found that almost all stars have the same general composition. The most common element in stars is hydrogen. Hydrogen is the lightest element. It makes up 60 to 80 percent of the total mass of a star. Helium is the second most common element in a typical star. It is the second lightest element. In fact, the combination of hydrogen and helium makes up about 96 to 99 percent of a star's mass. All other elements in a star total little more than 4 percent of the star's mass. These other elements often include oxygen, neon, carbon, and nitrogen.

Surface Temperature of Stars

Are you familiar with the heating coil on top of an electric stove? When the stove is off, the coil is dark. Then, when the stove is turned on, the coil begins to change color. Soon the coil is bright red, and you know that it is very hot. As you can see, the color a hot object gives off is a good indicator of its temperature.

The sun is a yellow star. But stars come in many other colors. By studying the color of a star, astronomers can determine its surface temperature.

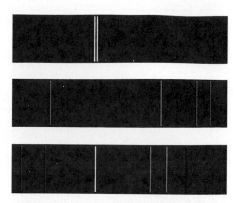

Figure 2–22 *With the spectrum produced by a spectroscope, scientists can identify the elements in distant stars. These spectra are of the elements sodium (top), hydrogen (center), and helium (bottom).*

STAR COLORS AND SURFACE TEMPERATURES		
Color	Average Surface Temperatures (°C)	Examples
Blue or blue-white	35,000	Zeta Eridani Spica Algol
White	10,000	Sirius Vega
Yellow	6000	Procyon Sun Alpha Centauri A
Red-orange	5000	Alpha Centauri B
Red	3000	Proxima Centauri Barnard's star

Figure 2–23 *How do scientists use color to determine the surface temperature of distant stars?*

Keep in mind that the surface temperature of a star is much lower than the temperature in the star's center, or core. For example, the sun has a surface temperature of about 6000°C. Yet the temperature of the sun's core can reach 15,000,000°C.

Using color as their guide, astronomers have determined that the surface temperature of the hottest stars is about 50,000°C. Such stars shine with a blue-white light. Red stars, which are among the coolest stars, have a surface temperature of about 3000°C. Most other stars have surface temperatures between these two extremes. See Figure 2–23.

Brightness of Stars

Suppose you were given a small flashlight and a large spotlight. You know, of course, that the spotlight is much bigger and brighter than the flashlight is. However, if a friend held the dim flashlight about a meter away from you and another friend held the spotlight a long distance away, the flashlight would appear brighter. So the brightness you saw would depend on the strength of the light, the size of the light source, and the distance the light source was from your eyes.

Figure 2–24 *The brightness of these stars in the Trifid Nebula, as seen from Earth, is called apparent magnitude. What term is used for the actual brightness of a particular star?*

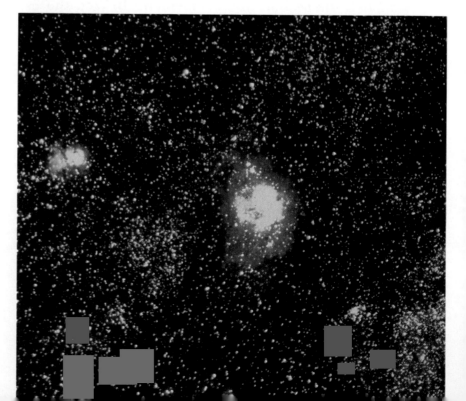

The brightness of a star depends on its size, its surface temperature, and its distance from Earth. When you look at the night sky, some stars appear brighter than others. As in the case of the flashlight and the spotlight, however, the star that appears brighter may not really be brighter at all. So astronomers call the brightness of a star as it appears from Earth its **apparent magnitude.**

If astronomers could take two stars and place them exactly the same distance from Earth, they could easily tell which star was really brighter. Astronomers cannot move stars, of course, but they can calculate a star's actual brightness. The amount of light a star actually gives off is called its **absolute magnitude.**

The brightness of most stars is constant. Some stars, however, vary in brightness and are called variable stars. One type of variable star changes size as well as brightness in regular cycles. Stars of this type are called pulsating variable stars. The North Star, Polaris, for example, changes from bright to dim and back again in a four-day cycle. Astronomers call these pulsating stars Cepheid (SEF-ee-id) variables because the first one was discovered in a group of stars called Cepheus.

The Hertzsprung-Russell Diagram

In the early 1900s, Danish astronomer Ejnar Hertzsprung and American astronomer Henry Norris Russell, working independently, found a relationship between the absolute magnitude and the temperature of stars. They discovered that as the absolute magnitude of stars increases, the temperature usually also increases. The relationship between the absolute magnitude and the surface temperature is shown in Figure 2–25 on page 70. You can see a definite pattern. This pattern forms the **Hertzsprung-Russell (H-R) diagram**. The Hertzsprung-Russell diagram is the single most important diagram astronomers use today.

On the Hertzsprung-Russell diagram, the surface temperature of stars is plotted along the horizontal axis. The absolute magnitude, or actual brightness, of stars is plotted along the vertical axis. If you study Figure 2–25, you will see that most stars fall in an

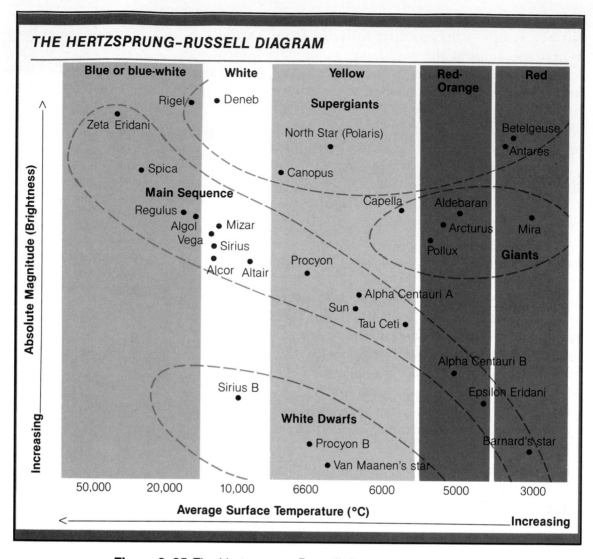

THE HERTZSPRUNG-RUSSELL DIAGRAM

Blue or blue-white | **White** | **Yellow** | **Red-Orange** | **Red**

Rigel • • Deneb

Zeta Eridani •

Supergiants

North Star (Polaris) •

Betelgeuse •

• Antares

• Spica • Canopus

Main Sequence

Capella • Aldebaran •

Regulus • • Arcturus • Mira •

Algol • • Mizar

Vega • • Sirius Pollux • **Giants**

• Alcor • Altair Procyon •

• Alpha Centauri A

Sun •

Tau Ceti •

Alpha Centauri B •

Sirius B • Epsilon Eridani •

White Dwarfs

• Procyon B Barnard's star •

• Van Maanen's star

Absolute Magnitude (Brightness) → Increasing

50,000   20,000   10,000   6600   6000   5000   3000

Average Surface Temperature (°C) → Increasing

Figure 2–25 *The Hertzsprung-Russell diagram shows that, for most stars, as the absolute magnitude increases, the surface temperature also increases.*

area from the upper left corner to the lower right corner. This area is called the main sequence. The stars within this area are called **main-sequence stars.**

Main-sequence stars make up more than 90 percent of the stars in the sky. The hottest main-sequence stars shine with a blue or blue-white light and are located in the upper left corner of the H-R diagram. Cool, dim main-sequence stars appear in the lower right corner.

The Hertzsprung-Russell diagram also identifies the other 10 percent of stars. These stars are no longer on the main sequence. They have changed to their present condition as they have aged. In the area above the main sequence are stars called red giants and supergiants. In the area below the main sequence are the white dwarfs. These white dwarfs are smaller and dimmer than main-sequence stars.

Measuring Star Distance

Since we cannot travel to stars and there certainly aren't any tape measures long enough to stretch anyway, how do astronomers determine the distance to different stars? Actually, it's a pretty complicated problem and sometimes some guesswork is involved.

One method of measuring the distance to stars is called **parallax** (PAR-uh-laks). Parallax refers to the apparent change in the position of a star in the sky. This apparent change in position is not due to the movement of the star. Instead, it is due to the change in the Earth's position as the Earth moves around the sun. So the star stays in the same place and the Earth moves.

In Figure 2–26, you can see how parallax is used to determine the distance to a star. First, the apparent position of the star in June and in December is noted. A line is then drawn between the Earth's position in these months and the center of the sun. This straight line will become the base of a triangle. The length of this base line is known to astronomers because it has already been carefully measured.

Next, a diagonal line is drawn from each end of the base line to the apparent position of the star in June and in December. These three lines form a triangle. The tip of the triangle is the true position of the star. Then a vertical line is drawn from the true position of the star to the base of the triangle. This line, labeled X, is the actual distance to the star. Since astronomers can determine the angles within the parallax triangle, they can calculate the length of line X. In this way, they can measure the true distance from the Earth to the star.

Parallax is a reliable method for measuring the distance to stars relatively close to Earth. The distance to stars more than 100 light-years away, however, cannot be found using parallax. Why? The angles within the parallax triangle are too small to be accurately measured.

To determine the distance to a star more than 100 light-years away, astronomers use the brightness

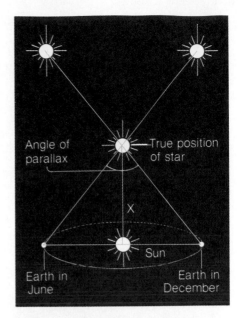

Figure 2–26 *Scientists can use an apparent change in position called parallax to measure star distance. By calculating the length of the line marked X, they can find the actual distance to the star.*

of the star. They plug the star's apparent magnitude and its absolute magnitude into a complicated formula. The formula provides a close approximation of the distance to that star.

Neither brightness nor parallax will work when a star is more than 7 million light-years from Earth—and most stars are at least that far away. To determine the distance to these stars, astronomers once again use the spectroscope. As you have read, light from a star moving away from Earth has a red shift in its spectrum. Astronomers measure the amount of red shift in a star's spectrum and use complex formulas to calculate how far from Earth a star is located. This method of calculating star distances is controversial, and not all scientists agree as to just how far away many stars are from Earth.

Why Stars Shine

You have learned how light from a star can be used to determine its composition, surface temperature, and distance. But what exactly causes a star to shine? To answer this question, you must look deep into the core of the star.

Within the core of a star, gravitational forces are extremely strong. In fact, gravity pulls together the

Figure 2–27 *Although we think of the sun as giving off only visible light, these photographs prove us wrong. The photograph on the right is a combination of an X-ray and ultraviolet light. The photograph on the left shows our sun as seen through a radio telescope.*

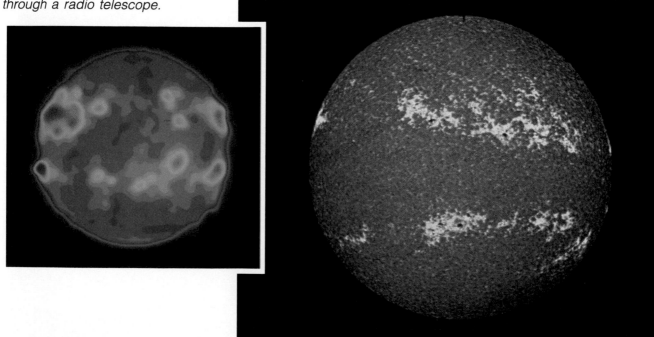

atoms of hydrogen gas in the core so tightly that they become fused together. This process is called **nuclear fusion.** During nuclear fusion, hydrogen atoms are fused to form helium atoms. Nuclear fusion, then, allows a star to produce a new element by combining other elements.

The sun changes about 600 billion kilograms of hydrogen into 595.8 billion kilograms of helium every second. As you can see from these numbers, during this fusion process 4.2 billion kilograms of the original mass of the hydrogen seem to be lost every second. Magic? Not really. The missing mass has been changed into energy. Most of the rest of the mass is changed into heat and light. And that is why a star shines. Of course, not all the light from nuclear fusion is visible light. Some of it may be infrared radiation, ultraviolet radiation, radio waves, and X-rays.

Back on Earth, nuclear fusion can be both constructive and destructive. The most destructive force known is the hydrogen bomb, in which hydrogen atoms are fused to form helium atoms, and huge amounts of energy are released. But one day nuclear fusion may become the most constructive force known. For controlled nuclear fusion in a nuclear-power plant would provide unlimited energy that is relatively pollution-free. Scientists hope that sometime in the next century nuclear-fusion power plants may solve much of Earth's energy needs.

Fusion Power

Our sun changes 600 billion kilograms of hydrogen into 595.8 billion kilograms of helium every second. The remaining 4.2 billion kilograms are changed into the energy that pours out from the sun.

Determine how many grams of hydrogen are converted into energy in one minute. In one hour.

2–3 Section Review

1. Describe how stars vary in size, composition, temperature, color, mass, and brightness.
2. How do astronomers determine the surface temperature of stars?
3. Compare absolute magnitude and apparent magnitude.

Critical Thinking—*Making Inferences*
4. Why does the parallax method of measuring star distances require observations of a star made six months apart?

PROBLEM Solving

A Question of Intensity

Light intensity can be simply defined as the amount of light that falls on a given area. The intensity of a star is of great interest to astronomers. But astronomers are not the only ones who need to know about light intensity. Anyone who uses a camera understands the importance of light intensity on the quality of his or her photographs and how it affects the type of film that must be used. But how does the intensity of light change as you move farther away from a light source?

Relating Cause and Effect

Using a light source, a light meter, and a one-meter cardboard square, determine how light intensity changes over distance. Explain the results of your experiment (*Hint:* The total amount of light does not change over distance.)

2–4 A Special Star: Our Sun

About 150 million kilometers from Earth there is a very important star—our sun. The sun is not unusual compared to other stars in the universe. It is a medium-sized, middle-aged yellow star about 4.6 billion years old. But without the sun, there would be no life on Earth.

Layers of the Sun

The sun is a ball-shaped object made of extremely hot gases. It is an average star in terms of size, temperature, and mass. It measures 1.35 million

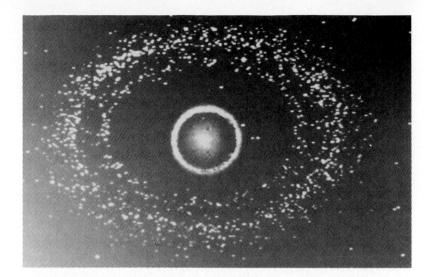

Figure 2–28 *This computer-enhanced photograph surprised astronomers when it revealed a giant ring of dust circling the sun. The ring is almost 1.5 million kilometers from the sun.*

kilometers in diameter. If the sun were hollow, more than 1 million planet Earths could fit inside it! Although the sun's volume is more than 1 million times greater than that of Earth, its density is only one quarter that of Earth. Why do you think the Earth is more dense than the sun?

Since the sun is made only of gases, there are no clear boundaries within it. But four main layers can be distinguished. **Three layers make up the sun's atmosphere, and one layer makes up its interior.** See Figure 2–29.

Figure 2–29 *The three main layers of the sun's atmosphere are the corona, the chromosphere, and the photosphere. What is the hottest part of the sun?*

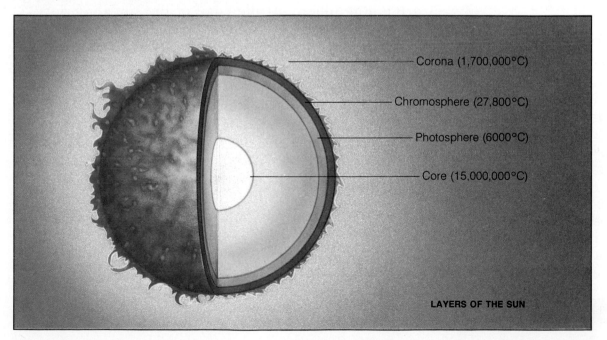

Corona (1,700,000°C)

Chromosphere (27,800°C)

Photosphere (6000°C)

Core (15,000,000°C)

LAYERS OF THE SUN

Figure 2–30 *The sun's corona becomes visible during a total solar eclipse. What object in space blocks out the rest of the sun during a solar eclipse?*

How Can You Observe the Sun Safely?, p.751

Word Search

Have you ever wondered about the origins of words? Very often, especially in science, you can figure out the meaning of a word if you understand its parts. The terms *photosphere* and *chromosphere* are good examples.

Using reference materials, look up the meanings of the parts *chromo-, photo-,* and *-sphere.* How do they relate to the terms scientists use for parts of the sun's atmosphere?

CORONA The outermost layer of the sun's atmosphere is called the **corona** (kuh-ROH-nuh). Gas particles in the corona can reach temperatures up to 1,700,000°C. But if a spacecraft could pass through the corona and be shielded from the rest of the sun's heat, the temperature of the spacecraft would barely rise! The reason for this is simple. The gas particles in the corona are spread so far apart that not enough particles would strike the spacecraft at any one time to cause a rise in temperature.

CHROMOSPHERE Beneath the corona is the middle layer of the sun's atmosphere, the **chromosphere** (KROH-muh-sfir). The chromosphere is several thousand kilometers thick. But sometimes gases in the chromosphere suddenly flare up and stream as far as 16,000 kilometers into space. Temperatures in the chromosphere average 27,800°C.

PHOTOSPHERE The innermost layer of the sun's atmosphere is called the **photosphere.** The photosphere is about 550 kilometers thick and is often referred to as the surface of the sun. Temperatures in the photosphere usually do not exceed 6000°C.

CORE You may have noticed that the temperature decreases greatly from the corona through the photosphere. But the temperature begins to rise again in the interior of the sun. The interior of the sun includes all of the sun except the three layers of the atmosphere. At the edge of the sun's interior, near the photosphere, temperatures may reach 1 million degrees Celsius. But in the center of the sun, called the **core,** temperatures may reach up to 15 million degrees Celsius. It is here in the sun's core that hydrogen and helium gases churn in constant motion, and hydrogen atoms are fused into helium atoms, releasing the sun's energy as heat and light.

The Active Sun

The sun is a relatively calm star compared to stars that expand and contract or erupt violently from time to time. But there is still a lot of activity going on in the sun.

PROMINENCES Many kinds of violent storms occur on the sun. One such solar storm is called

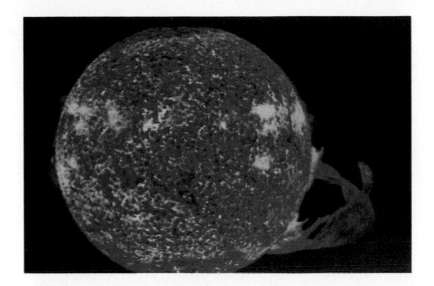

Figure 2–31 *A huge solar prominence rises out of the sun like a twisted sheet of gas. What is a solar prominence?*

a **prominence** (PRAHM-uh-nuhns). Prominences are seen from Earth as huge bright arches or loops of gas. These twisted loops of hot gas usually originate in the chromosphere. Prominences sometimes bend backward and shower the gases back onto the sun. Other prominences from the chromosphere erupt to heights of a million kilometers or more above the sun's surface. During a solar prominence, gases and energy are sent into space. One incredibly large prominence, photographed on June 4, 1946, grew to almost the size of the sun in one hour before it disappeared a few hours later. Figure 2–31 shows a solar prominence shooting into space.

SOLAR FLARES Another kind of storm on the sun shows up as bright bursts of light on the sun's surface. These bursts of light are called **solar flares.** A solar flare usually does not last more than an hour. But during that time, the temperature of the solar-flare region can be twice that of the rest of the sun's surface. Huge amounts of energy are released into space during a solar flare.

SOLAR WIND A continuous stream of high-energy particles is released into space in all directions from the sun's corona. This stream is the **solar wind.** Solar flares sometimes increase the speed and strength of the solar wind. This increase in the solar wind can interfere with radio signals and telephone communications on Earth.

SUNSPOTS When astronomers observe the sun, they sometimes see dark areas on the sun's surface.

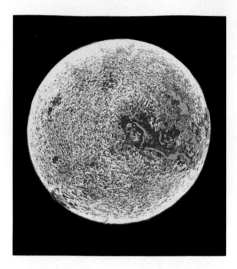

Figure 2–32 *The green dots on the surface of the sun are colorized images of sunspots. What are sunspots?*

These dark areas are called **sunspots.** Sunspots appear dark because they are cooler than the rest of the sun's surface.

Sunspots are storms in the lower atmosphere of the sun. They may be as small as 16 kilometers in diameter or as large as 160,000 kilometers in diameter. The number of sunspots that appear on the sun at any one time is always changing. But periods of very active sunspot activity seem to occur every ten to eleven years. This activity interferes with communication systems on Earth.

Astronomers have observed that sunspots move across the sun's surface. This movement indicates that the gases in the sun spin, or rotate. The sun rotates on its **axis.** The axis is an imaginary vertical line through the center of the sun. Gases around the middle of the sun appear to rotate on the axis once every 25 days. But not all parts of the sun rotate at the same speed. Some parts of the sun take longer to rotate than others. What do you think accounts for this?

2–4 Section Review

1. List and describe the four main layers of the sun.
2. Describe four types of storms on the sun.
3. How have astronomers determined that the sun rotates on its axis?

Connection—*Meteorology*
4. Explain the difference between the solar wind and winds on Earth.

Guide for Reading

Focus on these questions as you read.
▶ What is the life cycle of a star?
▶ How does the starting mass of a star relate to its evolution?

2–5 The Evolution of Stars

Does it surprise you that the title of this section is called The Evolution of Stars? If you are like most people, you may think of evolution as something that deals with changes in living things. The definition of evolution, however, can be thought of in simple terms as change over time. Using that definition, many things can be considered to evolve. Planet Earth, for example, has changed greatly since it

Figure 2–33 *These rock formations in Arches National Park, Utah, demonstrate that planet Earth evolves, or changes, over time. What forces carved out the unusual rock formations?*

formed some 4.5 billion years ago. Rivers have carved canyons out of solid rock; plants have produced oxygen and turned a poisonous atmosphere into one in which animals can survive; mountains have risen, eroded away, and been carried as sediments to the sea.

Astronomers agree that stars also evolve, or change over time. The stars you see, including the sun, did not always look the way they do today. These stars will continue to change. Changes may take place over a few million years, or perhaps several billion years. Astronomers refer to the evolution of a star as the life cycle of a star.

Some stars have existed almost since the origin of the universe. Other stars, such as the sun, have come from the matter created by the first stars. From their studies of stars, astronomers have charted the life cycle of a star from its "birth" to its "death." According to the present theory of star evolution, the many different kinds of stars in the sky represent the various stages in the life cycle of a star.

Protostars

You have read that galaxies contain huge clouds of dust and gases called nebulae. The most current theory of star formation states that new stars are born from the gases in a nebula. Over time, some of the hydrogen gas in a nebula is clumped together by gravity. The hydrogen atoms form a spinning cloud of gas within the nebula. Over millions of years more and more hydrogen gas is pulled into the spinning cloud. Collisions between hydrogen atoms become more frequent. These collisions cause the hydrogen gas to heat up.

Figure 2–34 *New stars and protostars are forming today in the dust and gas that make up the Orion Nebula. The sun formed in a similar nebula over 5 billion years ago.*

When the temperature within the spinning cloud reaches about 15,000,000°C, nuclear fusion begins. The great heat given off during nuclear fusion causes a new star, or **protostar,** to form. As a result of nuclear fusion, the protostar soon begins to shine and give off heat and light. At that point, a star is born.

Medium-Sized Stars

Once a protostar forms, its life cycle is fixed. Everything that will happen to that star has already been determined. **The main factor that shapes the evolution of a star is how much mass it began with.**

For the first few billion years, the new star continues to shine as its hydrogen is changed into helium by nuclear fusion in the star's core. But eventually most of the star's original supply of hydrogen is used up. By this time, most of the star's core has been changed from hydrogen to helium. Then the helium core begins to shrink. As it shrinks, the core heats up again. The outer shell of the star is still composed mainly of hydrogen. The energy released by the heating of the helium core causes the outer hydrogen shell to expand greatly. As the outer shell expands, it cools and its color reddens. At this point, the star is a red giant. It is red because cooler stars shine red. And it is a giant because the star's outer shell has expanded from its original size.

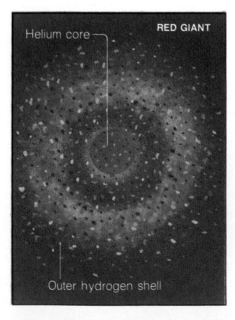

Helium core
Outer hydrogen shell
RED GIANT

Figure 2–35 *This illustration shows a red giant star. What does the red color of the outer shell indicate?*

As the red giant ages, it continues to "burn" the hydrogen gas in its shell. The temperature within the helium core continues to get hotter and hotter too. At about 200,000,000°C, the helium atoms in the core fuse together to form carbon atoms. Around this time, the last of the hydrogen gas surrounding the red giant begins to drift away. This drifting gas forms a ring around the central core of the star. This ring is called a planetary nebula—although it has nothing to do with planets. See Figure 2–36.

At some point in the red giant's life, the last of the helium atoms in its core are fused into carbon atoms. The star begins to die. Without nuclear fusion taking place in its core, the star slowly cools and fades. Finally gravity causes the last of the star's matter to collapse inward. The matter is squeezed so tightly that the star becomes a tiny white dwarf.

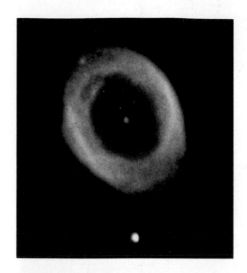

Figure 2–36 *This ring nebula, or planetary nebula, is all that is left of the gases that once surrounded a red giant star.*

White Dwarfs

The matter squeezed into a white dwarf is extremely dense. In fact, a single teaspoon of matter in a white dwarf may have a mass of several tons. But a white dwarf is not a dead star. It still shines with a hot white light.

At some point, the last of the white dwarf's energy is gone. It becomes a dead star. The length of time it takes a medium-sized star to become a white dwarf and die depends on the mass of the star when it first formed. It will take about 10 billion years for a medium-sized star such as the sun to evolve from formation to death. A smaller medium-sized star may take as long as 100 billion years. But a larger medium-sized star may die within only a few billion years. As you can see, the smaller the starting mass of a star, the longer it will live.

Massive Stars

The evolution of a massive star is quite different from that of a medium-sized star. At formation, massive stars usually have at least six times as much mass as our sun. Massive stars start off like medium-sized stars. They continue on the same life-cycle path until they become red giants, or even supergiants. Unlike

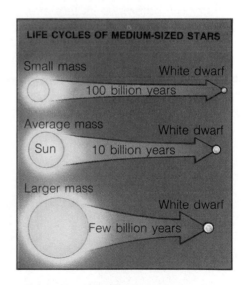

Figure 2–37 *Medium-sized stars all end up as white dwarfs. What is the relationship between mass and the time it takes a medium-sized star to become a white dwarf?*

Figure 2–38 *These photographs show a star before and after a supernova. What characteristic of the star will determine its fate after the supernova?*

medium-sized stars, however, massive stars do not follow the path from red giant to white dwarf. They take a completely different path.

Recall that a red giant becomes a white dwarf when all the helium in its core has turned to carbon. In a massive star, gravity continues to pull together the carbon atoms in the core. When the core is squeezed so tightly that the heat given off reaches about 600,000,000°C, the carbon atoms begin to fuse together to form new and heavier elements such as oxygen and nitrogen. The star has begun to become a factory for the production of heavy elements. The core of the massive star is so hot that fusion continues until the heavy element iron forms. But not even the tremendous heat of the massive star can cause iron atoms to fuse together.

Supernovas

By the time most of the nuclear fusion in a massive star stops, the central core is mainly iron. Although the process is not well understood, the iron atoms begin to absorb energy. Soon this energy is released, as the star breaks apart in a tremendous explosion called a **supernova.** A supernova can light the sky for weeks and appear as bright as a million suns. (Keep in mind that a supernova is very different from the nova you read about earlier. Only the names are similar.)

Figure 2–39 *Notice the ring of gas surrounding the red giant star that has undergone a supernova explosion.*

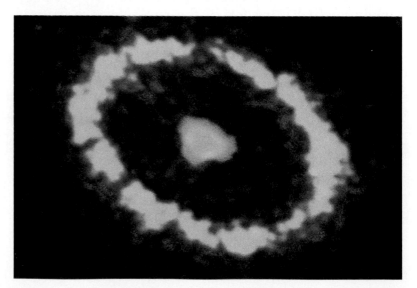

During a supernova explosion, the heat in a star can reach temperatures up to 1,000,000,000°C— that is, one billion degrees Celsius! At these extraordinarily high temperatures, iron atoms within the core fuse together to form new elements. These newly formed elements, along with most of the star's remaining gases, explode into space. The resulting cloud of dust and gases forms a new nebula. The gases in this new nebula contain many elements formed during the supernova. At some point new stars may form within the new nebula.

Most astronomers agree that the nebula from which our sun and its planets formed was the result of a gigantic supernova many billions of years ago. Why do you think astronomers feel the sun and its planets could not have formed in a nebula of only hydrogen and helium gases?

The most famous supernova ever recorded was observed by Chinese astronomers in 1054. The supernova lit the day sky for 23 days and could be seen at night for more than 600 days. Today the remains of this supernova can be seen in the sky as the Crab Nebula. One day, perhaps, new stars will form within the Crab Nebula, and the cycle will begin all over again.

Neutron Stars

What happens to the remains of the core of a star that has undergone a supernova? Again, the evolution of the star depends on its starting mass. A star that began 1.5 to 4 times as massive as the sun will end up as a neutron star after a supernova. A neutron star is about as massive as the sun but is often less than 16 kilometers in diameter. Such a star is extremely dense. A teaspoon of neutron matter would have a mass of about 100 million tons!

Neutron stars spin very rapidly. As a neutron star spins, it may give off energy in the form of radio waves. Usually the radio waves are given off as pulses of energy. Astronomers can detect these pulses of radio waves if the pulses are directed toward the Earth. Neutron stars that give off pulses of radio waves are called **pulsars.** Thus the end result of a supernova may be a pulsar. And in fact, astronomers have found a pulsar at the center of the Crab Nebula.

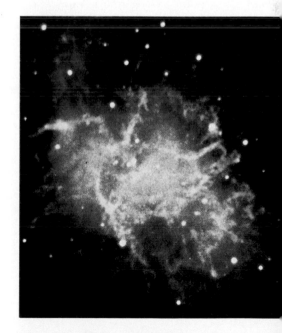

Figure 2–40 *The Crab Nebula formed from the supernova explosion of a dying star.*

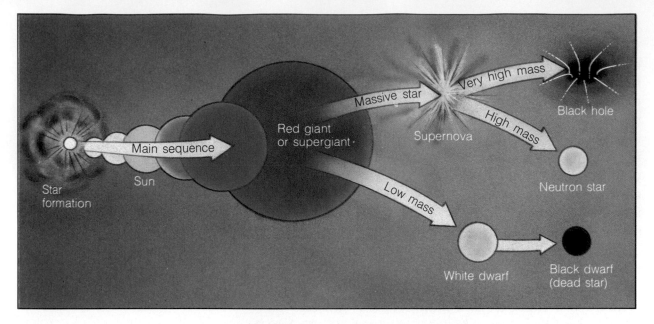

Figure 2–41 *The fate of a star depends on its mass when it first formed. The sun is a low-mass star that will one day become a white dwarf and finally a dead black dwarf.*

The neutron star in the Crab Nebula pulses at a rate of about 30 times a second. So you can see that a superdense neutron star spins very rapidly.

Black Holes

Stars with 10 or more times the mass of the sun will have even shorter life spans and a stranger fate than those that wind up as white dwarfs or neutron stars. After a supernova explosion, the core that remains is so massive that, without the energy created by nuclear fusion to support it, the core is swallowed up by its own gravity. The gravity of the core becomes so strong that not even light can escape. The core has become a **black hole.** A black hole swallows matter and energy as if it were a cosmic vacuum cleaner.

If black holes do not allow even light to escape, how can astronomers find them? Actually, it is difficult to detect black holes. But some black holes have a companion star. When the gases from the companion star are pulled into the black hole, the gases are heated. Before the gases are sucked into the black hole and lost forever, they may give off a burst of X-rays. So scientists can detect black holes by the X-rays given off when matter falls into the black hole. See Figure 2–42.

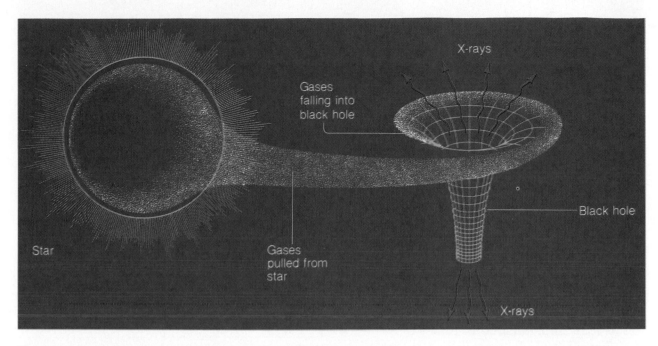

Figure 2–42 *Some black holes have a companion star. Gases from the companion star are pulled into the black hole. When this occurs, the black hole releases a huge burst of X-rays.*

What happens to matter when it falls into the black hole? Probably the matter is squeezed out of existence, just as a star that becomes a black hole is. But some scientists think strange things may go on inside a black hole. The laws of science may be different within a black hole. Some scientists theorize that black holes are passageways to other parts of the universe, to other universes, or even into time!

2–5 Section Review

1. How is the evolution of a star determined by its starting mass?
2. What is the next stage in the sun's evolution?
3. Why are supernovas considered factories for the production of heavy elements?

Critical Thinking—*Making Inferences*

4. A scientist observes a pulsar in the center of a large nebula. What can the scientist infer about the relationship of the nebula and the pulsar's life cycle?

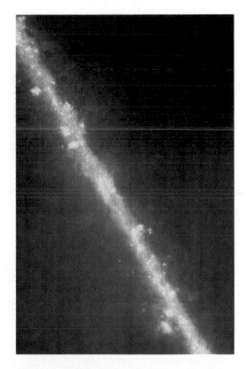

Figure 2–43 *This photograph of the center of the Milky Way Galaxy was taken with an infrared telescope. Many scientists now believe there is a black hole in the center of the Milky Way.*

Laboratory Investigation

Identifying Substances Using a Flame Test

Problem

How can substances be identified by using a flame test?

Materials *(per group)*

safety goggles
Bunsen burner
heat-resistant gloves
stainless steel teaspoon
1 unmarked bottle each of sodium chloride, potassium chloride, and lithium chloride

Procedure 🔥 👈 🧰 👁

1. Put on the safety goggles. Carefully light the Bunsen burner. **CAUTION:** *If you are not sure how to light a Bunsen burner safely, have your teacher show you the correct procedure.*

2. Put on the heat-resistant gloves.

3. Place the tip of the clean teaspoon in water. Then dip the tip of the spoon into one of the unmarked powders. Make sure that some of the powder sticks to the wet tip.

4. Hold the tip of the spoon in the flame of the Bunsen burner until most of the powder has burned. Observe and record the color of the flame.

5. Repeat steps 3 and 4 using the powder in the second and third unmarked bottles. Observe and record the color of the flame for each powder.

Observations

Flame Test	Color of Flame	Name of Substance
Powder 1		
Powder 2		
Powder 3		

Analysis and Conclusions

1. Sodium chloride burns with a yellow flame. Potassium chloride burns with a purple flame. And lithium chloride burns with a red flame. Using this information, determine the identity of each of the unmarked powders. Record the names of the substances.

2. Why is it important to make sure the spoon is thoroughly cleaned before each flame test? Try the investigation without cleaning the spoon to test your answer.

3. Relate this investigation to the way astronomers study a star's composition.

4. **On Your Own** Predict the color of the flame produced when various combinations of the three powders are used. With your teacher's permission, perform an investigation to test your prediction.

Study Guide

Summarizing Key Concepts

2–1 A Trip Through the Universe

▲ Nebulae are huge clouds of dust and gas from which new stars are born.

▲ The three types of galaxies are spiral, elliptical, and irregular. Our sun is in the spiral-shaped Milky Way galaxy.

▲ Many stars are found in multiple-star systems.

2–2 Formation of the Universe

▲ Every distant galaxy shows a red shift, indicating that the universe is expanding.

▲ Most astronomers agree that the universe began with the big bang.

2–3 Characteristics of Stars

▲ Stars range in size from huge supergiants to tiny neutron stars.

▲ The surface temperature of a star can be determined by its color.

▲ Most stars are made up primarily of hydrogen and helium gases.

▲ A star's brightness as observed from Earth is its apparent magnitude. A star's true brightness is its absolute magnitude.

▲ The Hertzsprung-Russell diagram shows the relationship between a star's absolute magnitude and its temperature.

2–4 A Special Star: Our Sun

▲ The layers of the sun are the corona, chromosphere, photosphere, and core.

2–5 The Evolution of Stars

▲ The main factor that affects the evolution of a star is its starting mass.

Reviewing Key Terms

Define each term in a complete sentence.

2–1 A Trip Through the Universe

binary star
constellation
nova
nebula
galaxy
spiral galaxy
elliptical galaxy

2–2 Formation of the Universe

spectroscope
spectrum
red shift
Doppler effect
big-bang theory
gravity
quasar

2–3 Characteristics of Stars

giant star
supergiant star
white dwarf
neutron star
apparent magnitude
absolute magnitude
Hertzsprung-Russell diagram
main-sequence star
parallax
nuclear fusion

2–4 A Special Star: Our Sun

corona
chromosphere
photosphere
core
prominence
solar flare
solar wind
sunspot
axis

2–5 The Evolution of Stars

protostar
supernova
pulsar
black hole

Chapter Review

Content Review

Multiple Choice

Choose the letter of the answer that best completes each statement.

1. Light can be broken up into its characteristic colors by a(an)
   a. optical telescope. c. spectroscope.
   b. flame test.   d. parallax.
2. The shape of galaxies such as the Milky Way is
   a. elliptical.   c. globular.
   b. irregular.   d. spiral.
3. The most common element in an average star is
   a. hydrogen.   c. helium.
   b. oxygen.   d. carbon.
4. During nuclear fusion, hydrogen atoms are fused into
   a. carbon atoms.   c. iron atoms.
   b. nitrogen atoms. d. helium atoms.
5. The main factor that shapes the evolution of a star is its
   a. mass.   c. composition.
   b. color.   d. absolute magnitude.

6. The color of a star is an indicator of its
   a. size.   c. surface temperature.
   b. mass.   d. inner temperature.
7. Supermassive stars end up as
   a. main-sequence stars. c. black holes.
   b. neutron stars.   d. white dwarfs.
8. The innermost layer of the sun's atmosphere is the
   a. corona.   c. chromosphere.
   b. photosphere.   d. core.
9. The most distant objects in the universe are
   a. pulsars.   c. quasars.
   b. neutron stars. d. binary stars.
10. A star's brightness as seen from Earth is its
    a. absolute magnitude.
    b. average magnitude.
    c. apparent magnitude.
    d. parallax.

True or False

If the statement is true, write "true." If it is false, change the underlined word or words to make the statement true.

1. Our sun is in the <u>Andromeda</u> galaxy.
2. Most stars are <u>main-sequence</u> stars.
3. A solar storm in the form of a huge, bright loop is called a <u>solar flare</u>.
4. Heavy elements are produced in a star during a <u>nova</u> explosion.
5. Most of the core of a red giant is made of <u>helium</u>.
6. In an <u>open universe</u>, all the galaxies will eventually move back to the center of the universe.
7. The <u>blue shift</u> indicates that the universe is expanding.

Concept Mapping

Complete the following concept map for Section 2–2. Then construct a concept map for the entire chapter.

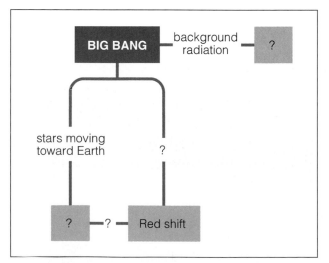

Concept Mastery

Discuss each of the following in a brief paragraph.

1. Compare the evolution of a medium-sized star and a massive star.
2. When you look at the light from distant stars, you are really looking back in time. Explain what this statement means.
3. Describe the Hertzsprung-Russell diagram and the information it provides.
4. What are the different ways astronomers use starlight to study stars?

Critical Thinking and Problem Solving

Use the skills you have developed in this chapter to answer each of the following.

1. **Making predictions** Predict how people in your town would react to a visit by living things from a distant star.
2. **Making comparisons** Compare a pulsar to a lighthouse.
3. **Interpreting diagrams** Examine the spectral lines, or fingerprints, of the elements hydrogen, helium, sodium, and calcium. Compare them with the spectral lines in the spectra labeled X, Y, and Z. Determine which elements produced spectral lines in spectra X, Y, and Z.
4. **Relating cause and effect** Once every three days a small but bright star seems to disappear, only to reappear within six hours. Based on this data, what is causing the small star to disappear?
5. **Using the writing process** You have been on board Earth's first spaceship to another star system for more than six months. Write a letter home to your friends describing your experiences and the wonders you have seen.

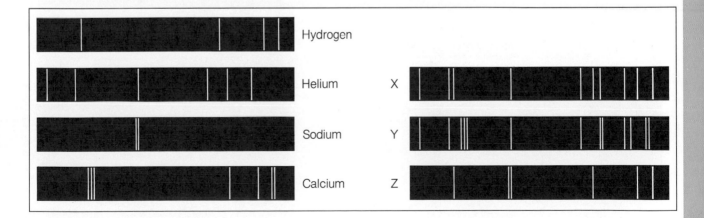

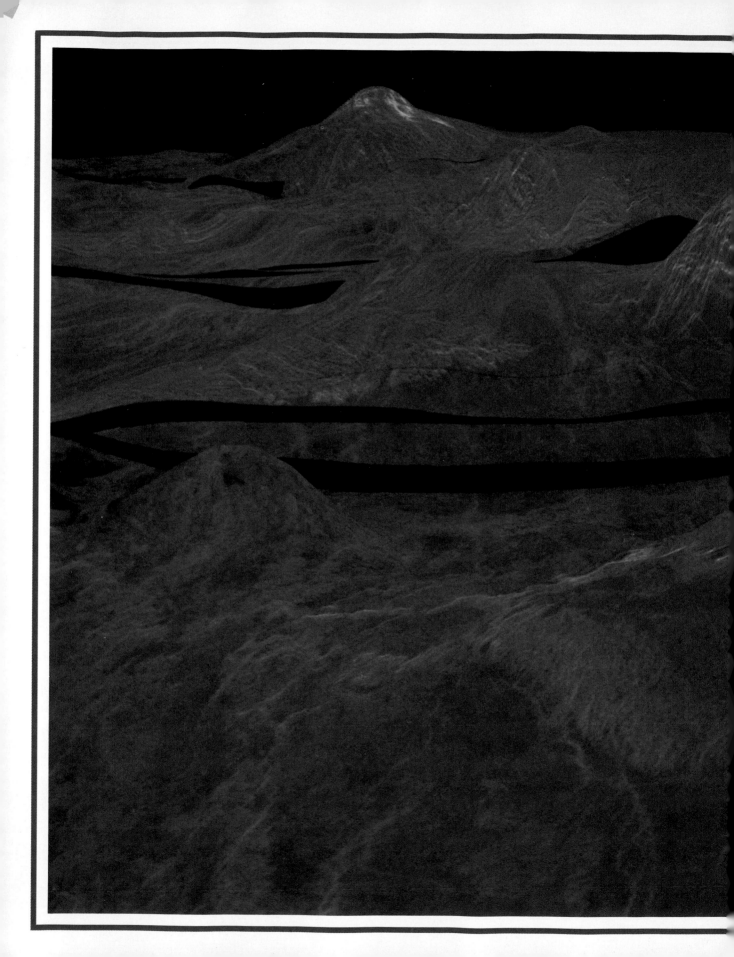

The Solar System

Guide for Reading

After you read the following sections, you will be able to

3–1 The Solar System Evolves

■ Describe the nebular theory and the formation of the solar system.

3–2 Motions of the Planets

■ Identify the shape of a planet's orbit and the factors that contribute to that shape.

3–3 A Trip Through the Solar System

■ Describe the major characteristics of the planets, moons, asteroids, comets, and meteoroids in the solar system.

3–4 Exploring the Solar System

■ Describe the principle behind how a reaction engine works.

Planet Venus, next to the sun and moon the brightest object in the night sky, has long been a subject of fascination for Earth-bound observers. One reason for the interest in Venus is that thick clouds blanket the planet, making it impossible to study the Venusian surface from Earth.

How can we study a planet hidden from view? The answer, it turns out, is radar. On August 10, 1991, the United States spacecraft *Magellan* went into orbit above Venus. *Magellan* is a radar-mapping spacecraft. Using complex computers, the craft can produce images of the planet's surface from radar data.

Although it will take many years to analyze the data sent back from *Magellan,* scientists were immediately astounded by some of its discoveries. Pancake-shaped domes that appear to be volcanic in origin are splattered across the surface of Venus. Evidence of lava flows millions of years old crisscross the planet and reveal a highly volcanic planet.

Venus is but one of nine planets in our solar system. One planet—Earth—you call home. In this chapter you will study the other eight planets—and perhaps discover how lucky you are to live on Earth.

Journal *Activity*

You and Your World Do you already have some idea about what the other planets are like? In your journal, draw and describe one of the planets in the solar system. Then, after you read the chapter, go back and see how close your ideas were to scientific data.

◀ *Scientists constructed this photograph of the Venusian surface using radar data transmitted to Earth from* Magellan.

3–1 The Solar System Evolves

In Chapter 2 you read about the evolution and life cycle of stars, one of which is our sun. You can also think of the formation of our solar system as a kind of evolution. For, like stars, the solar system changes over time. That is, evolution takes place on a planetary scale. To understand how the solar system formed and has changed, let's take a brief trip back about 5 billion years in time.

In the vast regions between the stars you find yourself in a huge cloud of gas and dust drifting through space. The cloud is cold, colder than anything you can imagine. There is no sun. There are no planets. Slowly moving gases are all that exist. Yet astronomers suggest that our **solar system** formed from this cloud. The solar system includes our sun, its planets, and all the other objects that revolve around the sun.

Many explanations have been proposed to account for the formation of the solar system. But

Figure 3–1 *The tiny speck of light in this photograph is the distant star Vega. Scientists believe planets may one day form from the ring of gas and dust surrounding the star.*

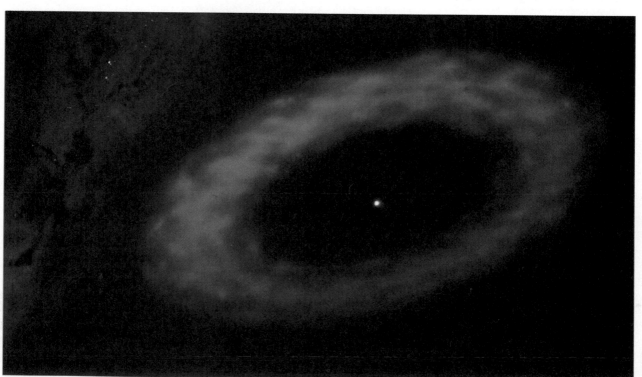

today virtually all astronomers believe in the **nebular theory** of formation. **The nebular theory states that the solar system began as a huge cloud of dust and gas called a nebula, which later condensed to form the sun and its nine planets.** The nebular theory has been revised many times as new data have been gathered. And it will likely be revised many more times. However, studying this theory can reveal much about the mighty forces at work in the formation of our solar system.

The Sun Forms First

The nebula from which our solar system evolved was composed primarily of hydrogen and helium gases. Yet Earth and the other planets are not made only of these gases. As a matter of fact, the planets contain a wide variety of elements. Where did the elements that make up rivers and mountains, trees and flowers, and even your own body come from? The incredible answer is—from a star!

About 5 billion years ago, according to the nebular theory, a star exploded in a huge supernova. In Chapter 1 you learned that the tremendous heat of a supernova can cause heavy elements to stream into space. These elements rained down on a nearby nebula, seeding it with the chemicals that would become

A *New Planetary System?*

Photographs taken by the *Hubble Space Telescope* have revealed a gaseous disk surrounding a distant star called Beta Pictoris. Astronomers believe the photographs may show that planets orbit Beta Pictoris.

Using reference books in the library, write a report detailing the information about Beta Pictoris that has been discovered by the *Hubble Space Telescope*. Have astronomers found a planet outside our solar system?

Figure 3–2 *According to the nebular theory, shock waves from a supernova disrupted a nearby nebula. The nebula began to rotate, and gravity pulled more and more matter into a central disk. That central disk became the sun. Clumps of gas and dust around the central disk formed the planets and other objects in the solar system.*

the sun and its planets. At the same time, the shock wave produced by the supernova ripped through the nebula, disrupting the stable gas cloud.

The nebula, which had been slowly spinning, began to collapse. Gravitational forces pulled matter in the nebula toward the center. As the nebula shrank, it spun faster and faster. Gradually, the spinning nebula flattened into a huge disk almost 10 billion kilometers across. At the center of the disk a growing protosun, or new sun, began to take shape.

As the gas cloud continued to collapse toward its center, the protosun grew more and more massive. It became denser as well. In time, perhaps after many millions of years, gravitational forces caused the atoms of hydrogen in the protosun to fuse and form helium. This nuclear fusion gave off energy in the form of heat and light. A star—our sun—was born.

The Planets Form

Gases and other matter surrounding the newly formed sun continued to spin around the sun. However, the particles of dust and gas were not spread out evenly. Instead, gravity caused them to gather into small clumps of matter. Over long periods of time, some of these clumps came together to form

Figure 3–3 *This illustration shows the relative sizes of the planets in the solar system. Which planet is the largest?*

larger clumps. The largest clumps became proto-planets, or the early stages of planets.

Protoplanets near the sun became so hot that most of their lightweight gases, such as hydrogen and helium, boiled away. So the inner, hotter proto-planets were left as collections of metals and rocky materials. Today these rocky inner planets are called Mercury, Venus, Earth, and Mars.

The protoplanets farther from the sun were less affected by the sun's heat. They retained their lightweight gases and grew to enormous sizes. Today these "gas giants" are known as Jupiter, Saturn, Uranus, and Neptune.

As the newly formed planets began to cool, smaller clumps of matter formed around them. These smaller clumps became satellites, or moons. Astronomers believe that one of the satellites near Neptune may have broken away from that planet. This satellite became the farthest known planet in the solar system: Pluto. This theory explains why Pluto is similar in composition to many of the icy moons surrounding the outer planets.

Objects other than moons were also forming in the solar system. Between Mars and Jupiter small clumps of matter formed asteroids. These rocklike objects are now found in a region of space between Mars and Jupiter called the asteroid belt. Farther out in space, near the edge of the solar system, other clumps of icy matter formed a huge cloud. Today astronomers believe that this cloud may be the home of comets.

3–1 Section Review

1. Briefly describe how the solar system formed according to the nebular theory.
2. What was the main factor that contributed to the differences between the inner and the outer planets?

Critical Thinking—*Applying Concepts*
3. Hold a rock in your hand and you are holding stardust. Explain what this statement really means.

Guide for Reading

Focus on these questions as you read.

▶ What two factors cause planets to move in elliptical orbits around the sun?

▶ What is a planet's period of revolution? Period of rotation?

ACTIVITY

DISCOVERING

Ellipses

The orbits of the planets are elliptical. Every ellipse has two fixed points called foci (singular: focus). In any planetary orbit, one of the foci is the sun.

1. Stick two thumbtacks into a sheet of stiff paper. The tacks should be about 10 centimeters apart. Wind a 30-centimeter string around the thumbtacks and tie the ends together. Place a sharp pencil inside the string and trace an ellipse. Keep the string tight at all times.

2. Repeat step 1, but this time place the thumbtacks 5 centimeters apart.

■ Compare the two ellipses you have drawn. Does the distance between two foci affect the ellipses' shape?

■ Predict what shape you will draw if you remove one of the thumbtacks (foci). Try it.

3–2 Motions of the Planets

Long before there were cities or even written language, people looked to the sky for answers to the nature of life and the universe. People used the stars to guide them in traveling and to tell them when to plant crops. Sky watchers knew that although the stars seemed to move across the sky each night, they stayed in the same position relative to one another. For example, a constellation kept the same shape from one night to the next.

In time, however, people who carefully observed the night sky discovered something strange. Some of the "stars" seemed to wander among the other stars. The Greeks called these objects planets, or wanderers. But how were the planets related to Earth and the sun? In what ways did the planets move?

Earth at the Center?

In the second century AD, the Greek scientist Ptolemy proposed a theory that placed Earth at the center of the universe. Ptolemy also thought that all objects in the sky traveled in **orbits** around an unmoving Earth. An orbit is the path one object takes when moving around another object in space.

In addition, Ptolemy believed that the universe was perfect, unchangeable, and divine. Because the circle was considered the most perfect of all forms, Ptolemy assumed that all objects in space moved in perfectly circular orbits around Earth. The first major challenge to Ptolemy's theory did not come for about 1400 years.

Sun at the Center?

Between 1500 and 1530 the Polish astronomer Nicolaus Copernicus developed a new theory about the solar system. Copernicus became convinced that Earth and the other planets actually revolved, or traveled in orbits, around the sun.

Based on his theory, Copernicus drew several conclusions regarding the motions of the planets. For one thing, he reasoned that all the planets revolved around the sun in the same direction.

Copernicus also suggested that each planet took a different amount of time to revolve around the sun.

Although Copernicus correctly described many of the movements of the planets, he was wrong about one important concept. Like Ptolemy before him, Copernicus believed that the orbits of the planets were perfect circles.

Elliptical Orbits

The sixteenth-century German mathematician and astronomer Johannes Kepler supported the theory of Copernicus that planets revolve around the sun. But he discovered something new. After a long and careful analysis of observations made by earlier astronomers, Kepler realized that the planets do not orbit in perfect circles. Instead, each planet moves around the sun in an ellipse, or oval orbit. An oval orbit is approximately egg-shaped.

Today astronomers know that Kepler was correct. Each planet travels in a counterclockwise elliptical

Figure 3–4 *All the planets revolve around the sun in elliptical orbits. Note that at some points, the orbit of Pluto falls inside that of Neptune. In fact, from 1979 to the year 2000 Neptune will be farther from the sun than Pluto.*

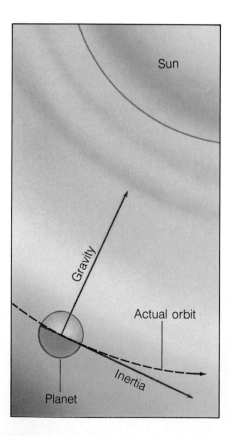

Figure 3–5 *Inertia makes a planet tend to travel in a straight line (blue arrow). But gravity pulls the planet toward the sun (red arrow). What is the effect of the combined action of inertia and gravity?*

orbit around the sun. Naturally, the planets closest to the sun travel the shortest distance. They complete one orbit around the sun in the shortest amount of time. The more-distant planets travel a longer distance and take a longer time to complete one orbit around the sun. Which planet takes the longest time to complete one orbit?

Inertia and Gravity

Although Kepler correctly explained the shape of the planets' orbits, he could not explain why the planets stayed in orbit around the sun instead of shooting off into space. In the seventeenth century, the English scientist Sir Isaac Newton provided the answer to that puzzling question.

Isaac Newton began his explanation using the law of inertia. This law states that an object's motion will not change unless that object is acted on by an outside force. According to the law of inertia, a moving object will not change speed or direction unless an outside force causes a change in its motion.

Newton hypothesized that planets, like all other objects, should move in a straight line unless some force causes them to change their motion. But if planets did move in a straight line, they would sail off into space, never to be seen again. Newton realized that some force must be acting on the planets, tugging them into elliptical orbits. That force, he reasoned, is the sun's gravitational pull.

According to Newton, a planet's motion around the sun is the result of two factors: inertia and gravity. Inertia causes the planet to move in a straight line. Gravity pulls the planet toward the sun. When these two factors combine, the planet moves in an elliptical orbit. See Figure 3–5.

Period of Revolution

Another way to say a planet orbits the sun is to say it revolves around the sun. The time it takes a planet to make one revolution around the sun is called its **period of revolution.** A planet's period of revolution is called a year on that planet. For example, Mercury—the planet closest to the sun—takes about 88 Earth-days to revolve once around the sun.

Figure 3–6 *Mars, like all planets, rotates on its axis while it revolves around the sun. The time it takes to rotate once is called its day. What is the time it takes to make one revolution called?*

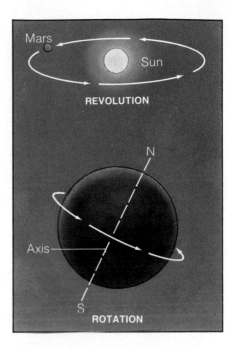

So a year on Mercury is about 88 Earth-days long. Pluto—normally the planet most distant from the sun—takes about 248 Earth-years to revolve around the sun. So a year on Pluto is about 248 Earth-years long.

Period of Rotation

Aside from revolving around the sun, planets have another kind of motion. All planets spin, or rotate, on their axes. The axis is an imaginary line drawn through the center of the planet. The time it takes a planet to make one rotation on its axis is called its **period of rotation.**

The Earth takes about 24 hours to rotate once on its axis. Does that number seem familiar to you? There are 24 hours in an Earth-day. So the time it takes a planet to go through one period of rotation is called a day on that planet.

Mercury takes almost 59 Earth-days to rotate once on its axis. A day on Mercury, then, is almost 59 Earth-days long. Pluto takes just over 6 Earth-days to rotate once on its axis. So a day on Pluto is a little more than 6 Earth-days long.

3–2 Section Review

1. What two factors cause planets to move in elliptical orbits?
2. Describe the two types of planetary motion.
3. Compare the contributions of Ptolemy, Copernicus, Kepler, and Newton to our understanding of planetary motion.

Connection—*You and Your World*
4. Many stock-car races are run on a track called a tri-oval. Describe or draw the shape of a tri-oval racetrack.

ACTIVITY DOING

Investigating Inertia

Inertia is the tendency of an unmoving object to remain in place, or of a moving object to continue in a straight line. Using a toy truck and a rubber band, observe inertia.

1. First, attach the rubber band to the front of the truck. Then fill the truck with small rocks or any heavy material.

2. Pull on the rubber band until the truck starts to move. Make a note of how much the rubber band must stretch to get the truck moving.

3. Continue pulling the truck with the rubber band. Does the rubber band stretch more or less once the truck is moving? Explain.

3–3 A Trip Through the Solar System

As you have read, people have wondered about the planets for many centuries. But it was not until recently that spacecraft were sent to examine the planets in detail. From spacecraft observations, one thing about the planets has become clear. **The nine planets of the solar system have a wide variety of surface and atmospheric features.** Figure 3–11 on pages 104–105 presents data about the planets gained from spacecraft and from observations from Earth.

To really appreciate the objects in our solar system, you would have to travel to each of them as spacecraft do. One day you may be able to do this, but for now you will have to use your imagination. So climb aboard your imaginary spaceship and buckle up your safety belt for a journey through the solar system.

Mercury—Faster Than a Speeding Bullet

Your first stop is a rocky world that has almost no atmosphere. A blazing sun that appears nine times as large as it does from Earth rises in the morning sky. The sun appears huge because Mercury is the closest planet to the sun. Mercury also moves more swiftly around the sun than does any other planet. This tiny world races around the sun at 48 kilometers a second, taking only 88 Earth-days to complete one revolution (one year). This fact explains why the planet was named after the speedy messenger of the Roman gods.

As you approach Mercury, your view is far better than is the view astronomers get from Earth. Mercury is so close to the blinding light of the sun that astronomers on Earth rarely get a good look at it. However, in 1975 the United States spacecraft *Mariner 10* flew past Mercury and provided scientists with their first close look at the planet.

Mariner 10 found a heavily crater-covered world. The craters were scooped out billions of years ago

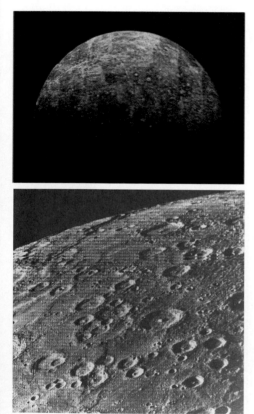

Figure 3–7 *These photographs of Mercury were taken by Mariner 10. The craters were scooped out of the surface billions of years ago. Why have they remained unchanged over all that time?*

by the impact of pieces of material striking the surface of the planet. Because Mercury has almost no atmosphere, it has no weather. Since there is no rain, snow, or wind to help wear down the craters and carry away the soil particles, the craters of Mercury appear the same as when they were created. As a result, Mercury has changed very little for the past few billion years.

Photographs from *Mariner 10* also revealed long, steep cliffs on Mercury. Some of the cliffs cut across the planet for hundreds of kilometers. There are also vast plains. These plains were probably formed by lava flowing from volcanoes that erupted billions of years ago. There is no evidence today of active volcanoes on Mercury.

As you read, Mercury rotates on its axis very slowly, taking about 59 Earth-days for one complete rotation. In fact, Mercury rotates three times about its axis for every two revolutions around the sun. The combined effect of these two motions produces a sunrise every 175 Earth-days. So the daytime side of the planet has lots of time to heat up, while the nighttime side has plenty of time to cool off. This long period of rotation causes temperatures on Mercury to range from a lead-melting 427°C during the day to −170°C at night. Mercury is, therefore, one of the hottest and one of the coldest planets in the solar system.

Figure 3–9 *This photograph of the Venusian surface was taken by a Soviet* Venera *spacecraft, a portion of which can be seen at the bottom of the photograph. Soon after taking this photograph, the spacecraft went silent—a harsh reminder of the extreme conditions on Venus.*

After taking off and leaving Mercury behind, you speed deeper into the solar system. Your next stop is the second planet from the sun.

Venus—Greenhouse in the Sky

Venus, the next stop on your imaginary journey, was named for the Roman goddess of beauty and love. Venus has about the same diameter, mass, and density as Earth does. For these reasons, astronomers once called Venus Earth's twin. People even imagined that Venus, like Earth, might be covered with vast oceans and tropical forests. For many years no one was sure whether this was true or not.

The uncertainty about Venus was due to its thick cloud cover, which has covered Venus for 400 to 800 million years. Clouds on Venus are more than five times as dense as are clouds on Earth. From Earth, astronomers can see only the yellowish Venusian clouds.

In recent years, however, data from spacecraft have slowly revealed the surface of Venus to astronomers. In 1975, two Soviet spacecraft (*Venera 9* and *Venera 10*) landed on Venus. The spacecraft were not able to withstand the harsh conditions and functioned for only a few hours. But before they failed, they were able to send back the first photographs of the Venusian surface. More recently, two United States spacecraft, *Pioneer Venus Orbiter* and *Magellan,* were placed in orbit around Venus. Radar instruments were able to penetrate the thick cloud cover and map much of the Venusian surface. The story that follows is based on information gathered from such probes.

As you approach Venus, your instruments detect winds of more than 350 kilometers per hour pushing the upper cloud layers around the planet. When you descend into the yellow clouds, you discover that they are not made of water vapor, as clouds on Earth are. These clouds consist of droplets of sulfuric acid and carbon dioxide. As you descend farther into this hostile atmosphere, the temperature and pressure rise rapidly. Sulfuric-acid rain falls through the cloud layers but evaporates in midair, never reaching the surface. Bolts of lightning flash near your ship.

Finally, you reach the surface. The atmosphere near the surface contains mainly carbon dioxide and is bathed in an eerie orange glow. Temperatures climb to 480°C, even hotter than on the surface of Mercury. No water has been found on Venus. The thick atmosphere bears down on you with a pressure 91 times greater than the atmospheric pressure at sea level on Earth.

As your craft skims over the surface of Venus, you discover deep canyons, craters, and vast plains. The remains of once-active volcanoes dot the surface, appearing like pancakes or upside-down cereal bowls. Venus also has a few continent-sized highland areas. In the distance you spot mountains as tall as any on Earth. Scientists feel these mountains were formed by ancient Venusian volcanoes. These volcanoes were likely the source of the thick atmosphere that covers Venus. You also notice a huge crack, or channel, in the surface. This channel runs for almost 7000 kilometers, longer than the Nile River and deeper than the Grand Canyon back on Earth.

From the surface, the cloud cover completely hides your view of the sun. But if you could see the sun, you would see something that would be a totally new experience. The sun would slowly rise in the west and later set in the east. The sun follows this pattern because, unlike Earth, Venus rotates from east to west. Astronomers call this reverse motion **retrograde rotation.** Another unusual aspect of Venus is that it rotates once on its axis every 243 Earth-days. However, Venus takes only 224 Earth-days to revolve once around the sun. A Venusian day, then, is actually longer than a Venusian year.

Figure 3–10 *As you can see in this photograph, Venus is a planet covered by thick clouds.*

THE SOLAR SYSTEM

Name	Average Distance From Sun (millions of km)	Diameter (km)	Period of Revolution in Earth-time Days	Years	Period of Rotation Days	Hours	Number of Moons
Mercury	58	4880	88	—	58	16	0
Venus	108	12,104	225	—	243 Retrograde	—	0
Earth	150	12,756	365	—	—	24	1
Mars	228	6794	—	1.88	—	24.5 (about)	2
Jupiter	778	142,700	—	11.86	—	10 (about)	16
Saturn	1427	120,000	—	29.46	—	10.5 (about)	23?
Uranus	2869	50,800	—	84.01	— Retrograde	16.8 (about)	15
Neptune	4486	48,600	—	164.8	—	16	8
Pluto	5890	2300	—	247.7	6	9.5	1

Figure 3–11 *This chart shows the most current information known about the planets. Which planets show retrograde rotation?*

Your stay on Venus is almost over. By now you have discovered that Venus is certainly not the twin of Earth. But why is Venus, the closest planet to Earth, so vastly different from our world? Why is it such a dry, hot world? Billions of years ago, when the solar system was still forming, the sun was much cooler than it is today. In those early days, Venus may have been covered with planet-wide oceans. In fact, the remains of coastlines and sea beds can still be detected today. Then, as the sun grew hotter, water began to evaporate into the atmosphere. This water vapor helped to create a heat-trapping process

Temperature Extremes (°C) High	Low	Orbital Velocity (km/sec)	Atmosphere	Main Characteristics
427	−170	47.8	Hydrogen, helium, sodium	Rocky, cratered surface; steep cliffs; extremely thin atmosphere
480	−33	35.0	Carbon dioxide	Thick cloud cover, greenhouse effect, vast plains, high mountains
58	−90	29.8	Nitrogen, oxygen	Liquid water, life
−31	−130	24.2	Carbon dioxide, nitrogen, argon, oxygen, water vapor	Polar icecaps, pink sky, rust-colored surface, dominant volcanoes, surface channels
29,700	−95	13.1	Hydrogen, helium, methane, ammonia	Great red spot, thin ring, huge magnetosphere, rocky core surrounded by liquid-hydrogen ocean
?	−180	9.7	Hydrogen, helium, methane, ammonia	Many rings and ringlets, Titan only moon with substantial atmosphere
?	−220	6.8	Hydrogen, helium, methane	Rotates on side, 9 dark mostly narrow rings of methane ice, worldwide ocean of superheated water
?	−220	5.4	Hydrogen, helium, methane	Unusual satellite rotation, 4 rings, great dark spot, rocky core surrounded by slush of water and frozen methane
?	−230	4.7	Methane	Smallest planet, possibly a double planet

called the **greenhouse effect.** The greenhouse effect occurs when heat becomes trapped beneath the clouds.

As the temperature rose further, the oceans evaporated completely. However, even after all the water was gone from Venus, the greenhouse effect continued. The atmosphere of Venus is mainly carbon dioxide. The carbon dioxide, like the water vapor before it, traps heat and produces a greenhouse effect. So today, even during the long nights on Venus, the dark side of the planet remains about as hot as the bright side.

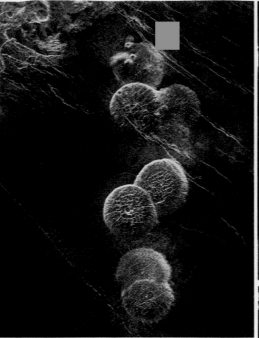

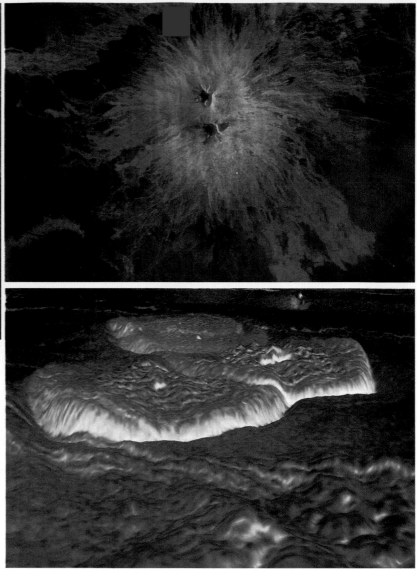

Figure 3–12 *These remarkable photographs of the Venusian surface were developed using radar data from the* Magellan *spacecraft. They show a planet dominated by volcanoes and deep valleys. The pancake-shaped structures are the domes of volcanoes.*

ACTIVITY

Build a Greenhouse

How did the greenhouse effect get its name? Fill two containers with potting soil. Place a thermometer on the surface of the soil in each container. Cover one container with a sheet of glass. Put both containers in a sunny window. Observe what happens to the temperature in each container.

If the term greenhouse effect seems familiar to you, it is probably because scientists warn of a similar problem on Earth. The Earth's atmosphere also acts as a greenhouse. Up until now, this has kept the Earth warm enough for life to evolve and survive. However, the burning of fossil fuels such as coal and oil adds carbon dioxide to the Earth's atmosphere. Scientists fear that this increased carbon dioxide may cause a runaway greenhouse effect, much like the one that left Venus dry, hot, and barren. What are some ways to prevent a runaway greenhouse effect from happening on Earth?

Even on an imaginary trip, the harsh conditions on Venus make you uncomfortable. So you decide to continue your journey. For now, however, you will skip the third planet, Earth.

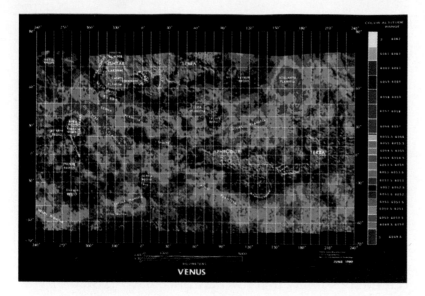

Figure 3–13 *This map of the Venusian surface was produced using radar data from a spacecraft orbiting Venus.*

Mars—The Rusty Planet

Your imaginary ship is now approaching Mars, the fourth planet from the sun. As you reach Mars, the first thing you notice is its reddish color. In ancient times, this color reminded people of blood, and they thought of Mars as a warrior planet. Today it still bears the name of the Roman god of war. Appropriately, the two tiny moons that circle Mars are called Phobos and Deimos, from the Greek words for fear and terror.

In late July 1976, a spacecraft landed successfully on Mars. This was not an easy task, for the surface of Mars is rocky and heavily cratered. The ship, named *Viking 1* after early explorers on Earth, was soon followed by a second ship, *Viking 2*. Both quickly began to send back detailed photographs of the Martian surface. Another giant step in the exploration of the solar system had been taken.

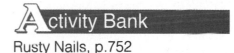

Activity Bank

Rusty Nails, p.752

Figure 3–14 *Notice the characteristic red color of the Martian soil in this photograph taken by a* Viking *spacecraft that landed on Mars. What causes the soil on Mars to appear red?*

Figure 3–15 *You can actually see the thin Martian atmosphere over the horizon in this photograph taken by* Viking 1.

One of the most imporant tasks of the *Viking* spacecraft was to analyze Martian soil. To do so, a robot arm scooped up some of the soil and placed it in the on-board laboratory. Tests revealed that Martian soil is similar to Earth's soil in many ways. But there are differences. For centuries Mars had been known as the red planet. Soil tests showed why this is so. Martian soil is coated with a reddish compound called iron oxide. Perhaps you know iron oxide by its more common name—rust!

The *Viking* spacecraft also tested the soil for signs of life. Although the tests did not reveal any signs of life or life processes, the data did not rule out the possibility that life may once have existed on Mars.

The *Viking* spacecraft as well as observations from the Earth aided in the discovery of many other features on Mars. Mars appears to be a planet that has had a very active past. For example, four huge volcanoes are located on Mars. These volcanoes are dormant, or inactive. But large plains covered with lava indicate that the volcanoes were once active. The largest volcano on Mars is *Olympus Mons*. *Olympus Mons* is wider than the island of Hawaii, and it is almost three times as tall as Mount Everest. In fact, *Olympus Mons* is the largest known volcano in the solar system.

Astronomers now believe that when the Martian volcanoes were active, they poured out both lava and steam. As the steam cooled, it fell as rain. Rushing rivers may have once crossed the Martian surface, gouging out channels that wander across Mars. Today there is no liquid water on Mars. But frozen water can be found in the northern icecap and may also be located under the soil.

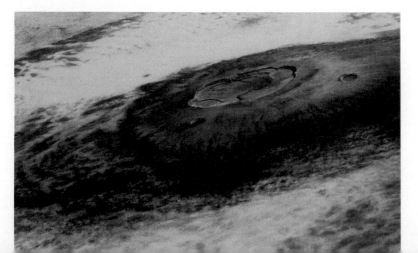

Figure 3–16 *The dead volcano* Olympus Mons *on Mars is the largest volcano ever discovered.*

The northern icecap of Mars is made mostly of frozen water, which never melts. But the southern icecap is mostly frozen carbon dioxide. Much of this icecap melts during the Martian summer. But do not be misled by the word summer. Since Mars has a very thin atmosphere made mostly of carbon dioxide, it does not retain much heat from the sun. So even during the summer, temperatures on Mars are well below 0°C. That, of course, is why water on Mars stays frozen all year round.

Another interesting feature of Mars is an enormous canyon called *Valles Marineris*. The canyon is 240 kilometers wide at one point and 6.5 kilometers deep. If this canyon were on the Earth, it would stretch from California to New York.

Although the atmosphere of Mars is very thin, winds are common. Windstorms sweep across the surface at speeds up to 200 kilometers per hour. These storms stir up so much dust that the sky may turn a dark pink.

As you have read, Mars has two moons called Phobos and Deimos. These rocky, crater-covered moons are much smaller than Earth's moon. The maximum diameter of Phobos is only 25 kilometers. The diameter of Deimos is only 15 kilometers.

Your stay on Mars is just about over—and just in time. Another dust storm has begun to develop.

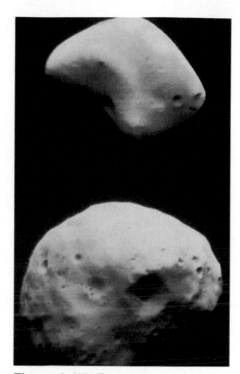

Figure 3–17 *Both moons of Mars, Phobos and Deimos, are shown in this composite NASA photograph.*

The Asteroid Belt

Your journey from Mars to Jupiter holds a new kind of danger. Thousands, perhaps hundreds of thousands, of rocks and "flying mountains" lie in your path. These objects are the "minor planets," which sweep around the sun between the orbits of Mars and Jupiter. You have entered the **asteroid belt.**

Asteroids may be made of rocks, metals, or a combination of the two. Most asteroids are small and irregularly shaped. A few, however, are huge. The largest asteroid, Ceres, has a diameter of almost 1000 kilometers. Earth's moon, by comparison, is about 3400 kilometers in diameter.

At one time, astronomers thought that the fragmented objects in the asteroid belt were the remains of a planet that broke apart long ago. However, it now appears that the asteroid belt is made up of clumps of matter that failed to join together to form a planet during the birth of the solar system. Why? Scientists suspect that Jupiter's strong gravitational pull kept the asteroids from coming together.

Not all asteroids are found in the asteroid belt. For example, some asteroids hurtle through space close to the Earth. Fortunately, these "flying mountains" are rarely on collision courses with Earth. However, collisions do occur from time to time. Many impact scars on Earth have been identified. At least seventy of these scars are thought to be the results of asteroids plowing into Earth's crust at tremendous speeds. Many of the craters on the moon and on other planets may also be due to the impact of asteroids.

One theory that has prompted a good deal of scientific debate states that the collision of a huge asteroid some 65 million years ago resulted in changes that led to the extinction of the dinosaurs and almost 90 percent of all other life on Earth at that time. It has been estimated that the force of the asteroid collision may have been some 10,000 times greater than the force that would result if all the nuclear weapons on Earth were exploded at one time!

Although you have had to steer your ship carefully, you have managed to pass safely through the asteroid belt. The giant planet Jupiter looms ahead.

Figure 3–18 *The asteroid belt is a region located between the orbits of Mars and Jupiter. What is the composition of most asteroids?*

Figure 3–19 *Many scientists believe that the extinction of the dinosaurs was caused by the collision of an asteroid some 65 million years ago. How might such a collision have caused this to happen?*

Jupiter—The Planet That Was Almost a Star

The first thing you notice as you approach Jupiter is its size. Our sun contains about 99.8 percent of all the matter in the solar system. Jupiter contains about 70 percent of what is left. A hundred Earths could be strung around Jupiter as if they were a necklace of pearls. Jupiter is so big and bright in the night sky that the Romans named this planet after their king of the gods.

In many ways Jupiter rivals the sun. Like the sun and other stars, Jupiter is made primarily of hydrogen and helium gases. The temperature is cold at the cloud tops but rises considerably beneath the upper cloud layers. At Jupiter's core, scientists believe temperatures may reach 30,000°C, almost five times the surface temperature of the sun. Scientists think that if Jupiter had grown larger during the formation of the solar system, gravitational forces might have caused nuclear fusion to occur and a star to form. So you can think of Jupiter as a planet that was almost a star.

From Earth, all that can be seen of Jupiter's atmosphere is its thick cloud cover. These clouds,

Comparing Diameters

Jupiter has a diameter of 142,800 kilometers. Mercury has a diameter of 4900 kilometers. How many times larger is Jupiter than Mercury?

which appear as bands of color, are made mostly of hydrogen and helium. Other gases, such as ammonia and methane are also found in Jupiter's atmosphere.

As your imaginary ship nears Jupiter, you notice that the clouds are very active. Huge storms swirl across the surface of the atmosphere. These storms can be observed because the colored bands of the clouds are twisted and turned by the strong winds. Perhaps the best-known feature of Jupiter's cloud cover is a giant red spot three times the size of Earth. This Great Red Spot, which is probably a hurricanelike storm, has been observed for more than 100 years. (Scientists estimate it may be well over 20,000 years old.) If it is a storm, it is the longest-lasting storm ever observed in the solar system.

Unlike the other planets you have read about, Jupiter probably has only a small solid core. The clouds become thicker and denser as they get closer to the center of the planet's core. As their density increases, the clouds may change into a giant ocean of liquid hydrogen.

Because of the thick cloud cover, the atmospheric pressure on Jupiter is enormous. In fact, the pressure near the center of the planet is so great that the liquid-hydrogen ocean probably changes into a form of liquid hydrogen that acts like a metal. This liquid metallic layer may surround a rocky core about the size of Earth. The liquid metallic layer is the cause of Jupiter's gigantic magnetic field. The magnetic field, called the magnetosphere,

Figure 3–20 *This photograph of Jupiter was taken by a* Voyager *spacecraft. The ring has been added by an artist. Can you find the Great Red Spot on Jupiter?*

Figure 3–21 *In this composite photograph, Jupiter and its four largest moons are shown. What are the four large inner moons called?*

stretches for millions of kilometers beyond the planet. Jupiter's magnetosphere is the largest single structure in the solar system. Jupiter is unusual in other ways. For example, it gives off more heat than it receives from the sun.

In 1979, two *Voyager* spacecraft (*Voyager 1* and *Voyager 2*) flew past Jupiter. These spacecraft took thousands of photographs of the gas giant. From these photographs, astronomers discovered a thin ring circling Jupiter. They also discovered gigantic bolts of lightning in the atmosphere and mysterious shimmering sheets of light in the sky.

In 1610, the scientist Galileo Galilei observed four moons orbiting Jupiter. Today these moons are known as the Galilean satellites. And although at least sixteen moons have now been found orbiting Jupiter, the four largest and most interesting are the moons discovered by Galileo more than 300 years ago.

Io The innermost of Jupiter's large moons is Io. Io is perhaps the most dramatic object in the solar system. The moon seems painted in brilliant orange, yellow, and red hues, which are due mainly to the high sulfur content of Io's surface. This mix of colors

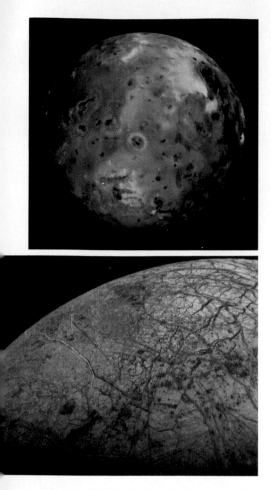

Figure 3–22 *Io, the innermost of Jupiter's moons, has a surface that is constantly changed by volcanic eruptions (top). Europa shows tan streaks that may be shallow valleys (bottom).*

prompted one scientist to compare the colorful moon to a pepperoni pizza. Scientists originally assumed Io's surface would be heavily cratered. They expected to see the scars of impacts with large objects that occurred over the past few billion years. Instead, the scientists found a young, active surface. The surface looked so young because it was constantly being covered by new material from Io's active volcanoes. Today scientists consider Io the most geologically active object in the solar system.

EUROPA Next out from Jupiter is Europa. Europa is an ice-covered world slightly smaller than Io. Europa has the brightest, whitest, and smoothest surface of any object astronomers have observed in the solar system. It has been described as a giant "billiard ball in the sky." Some of the photographs from the *Voyager* spacecraft indicate that Europa may have a volcano that spews out water and ammonia ice. Such a volcano would be far different from those on Earth, which spew out molten rock.

GANYMEDE Beyond Europa is Ganymede, Jupiter's largest moon. Ganymede, in fact, is the largest moon in the solar system. It is larger even than the planet Mercury. Ganymede is an icy world, about half rock and half water ice. It has some smooth regions, but it also has craters.

Some regions on Ganymede look as though they have been shaken by "earthquakes." Pieces of the moon's surface look as though they have cracked and slipped past one another. If that is what happened, Ganymede is the first object in the solar system besides Earth and its moon that is known to have earthquakes.

CALLISTO Your next stop is Callisto, the most heavily cratered object in the solar system. Although they are very small, Callisto's craters cover almost every part of this moon's surface. Scientists estimate that it would have taken several billion years of impacts to punch out all the craters of Callisto. Therefore, the surface of Callisto, which is mainly rock and ice, appears much as it did billions of years ago. This further suggests that Callisto is, and has been, a very quiet world. If volcanoes such as those on Io existed on Callisto, they would have filled in many of the craters.

There is much that can still be learned about the moons of Jupiter. Now, however, it is time to journey to the gas giant that is the second largest planet in the solar system.

Figure 3–23 *Ganymede is a moon that is half covered by ice and half covered by rock (left). The bright spots on the surface of Callisto are craters billions of years old (right).*

Saturn—A World of Many Rings

As you approach Saturn, you notice that it is surrounded by a series of magnificent rings. Saturn's rings were discovered by Galileo, and it was the first planet found to have rings. Many astronomers consider Saturn's rings to be the most beautiful sight in the solar system—so enjoy your view.

The rings of Saturn are made mainly of icy particles ranging in size from one thousandth of a millimeter to almost 100 kilometers in diameter. When observed through a telescope, Saturn appears to have three main rings. However, photographs taken by *Voyager* spacecraft showed that Saturn's ring system is far more complex than we could ever tell from Earth. *Voyager* revealed that Saturn has at least seven major rings, lettered from A to G. The outer edge of the most distant ring is almost 300,000 kilometers from Saturn. In addition, the main rings are made up of tens of thousands of ringlets that weave in and out of the main rings.

While Saturn's rings are its most spectacular feature, the planet is also interesting in other ways. Like Jupiter, Saturn spins rapidly on its axis and is made mainly of hydrogen and helium gases. Because

Orbital Velocities

Using the data in Figure 3–11, make a graph of the orbital velocities of the planets in our solar system. Plot orbital velocity on the vertical axis and the nine planets in order on the horizontal axis.

■ What conclusions can you draw from the curve on your graph?

Figure 3–24 *Saturn's ring system may well be the most beautiful sight in the solar system. What is the composition of Saturn's rings?*

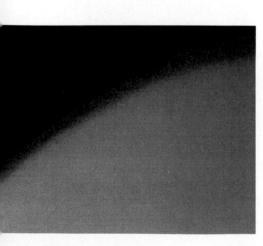

Saturn spins so fast, it is flattened at the poles, and it bulges at the equator. Near the equator, winds speed around Saturn at about 1800 kilometers per hour. This superfast jet stream is four times as quick as the fastest winds of Jupiter. Also like Jupiter, Saturn has violent storms. *Voyager 2* detected one enormous lightning storm that lasted more than ten months.

Saturn's clouds, like Jupiter's, form colored bands around the planet. Light-colored bands alternate with darker bands. There is even a reddish-orange oval feature in Saturn's southern hemisphere, a smaller version of Jupiter's Great Red Spot. Saturn is colder than Jupiter, yet it gives off almost three times as much energy as it gets from the sun. Saturn also has a huge magnetic field, second in size only to Jupiter's magnetosphere. Scientists suspect that the core of Saturn may also be similar to Jupiter's small, inner core.

Another unusual feature of Saturn is its very low density. In fact, Saturn is the least dense planet in the solar system. If all the planets could be placed in a giant ocean, Saturn would be the only planet to float on water.

As you fly by Saturn you must be careful not to collide with one of its moons. Saturn has more moons than any other planet. So far, twenty-one— and possibly two more—moons have been found orbiting Saturn. The largest of Saturn's moons is Titan. Only Ganymede is larger than Titan. However, size is not the only thing that makes Titan an unusual moon. Titan has a substantial atmosphere. The atmosphere is mainly nitrogen, but also contains methane, hydrogen cyanide, carbon monoxide, carbon dioxide, and other gases. The combination of these gases gives Titan a hazy orange glow. Many of these gases are deadly to life on Earth. But it is interesting to note that before life formed, the Earth had an atmosphere very similar to that on Titan. Some scientists have speculated that living things could evolve in the atmosphere of Titan, although no life has been detected.

Figure 3–25 *Notice the haze, indicating an atmosphere, surrounding Saturn's moon Titan. What is the composition of Titan's atmosphere?*

Figure 3–26 *In this composite photograph you can see Saturn surrounded by six of its moons. The large moon in front is Dione. The other moons (clockwise) are Enceladus, Rhea, Titan, Mimas, and Tethys.*

Uranus—A Planet on Its Side

You have now traveled almost 1.5 billion kilometers on your imaginary trip through the solar system. But you still have quite a distance to go before you reach the seventh planet, Uranus. Named for the father of Saturn in Roman mythology, Uranus was discovered in 1781 by the English astronomer Sir William Herschel. With Herschel's discovery, the size of the known solar system doubled, for Uranus is almost twice as far from the sun as is Saturn. See Figure 3–31 on pages 120–121 for the relative distances of the planets from the sun.

As you approach Uranus, you notice immediately that it is a gas giant, much like Jupiter and Saturn. Uranus is covered by a thick atmosphere made of hydrogen, helium, and methane. The clouds of Uranus do not have bands, but rather the entire

Figure 3–27 *This photograph of the gas giant Uranus was taken by a Voyager spacecraft as it passed the distant planet.*

Figure 3–28 *Notice the craters on Miranda, a moon of Uranus.*

Figure 3–29 *This composite photograph shows a portion of Uranus with Miranda, one of its moons, in the foreground.*

planet is tinged with a greenish-blue color. Temperatures at the top of the clouds may dip to as low as −220°C.

Data from *Voyager 2* provide strong evidence that Uranus is covered by an ocean of superheated water that may have formed from melted comets. Because of the extreme pressure from an atmosphere 11,000 kilometers thick, the superheated water does not boil. This worldwide ocean is about 8000 kilometers thick and encloses a rocky, molten core about the size of Earth.

The axis on which Uranus rotates is one of the most unusual features of this gas giant. The axis of Uranus is tilted at an angle of about 90°. So Uranus seems to be tipped completely on its side. Uranus has nine known rings. But unlike the rings of Saturn, these rings are dark and probably made of methane ice. Because of the tilt of the axis of Uranus, the rings appear to circle the planet from top to bottom.

The *Voyager 2* flyby confirmed the fact that Uranus has fifteen moons, ranging in diameter from 32 to 1625 kilometers. Some of the more interesting

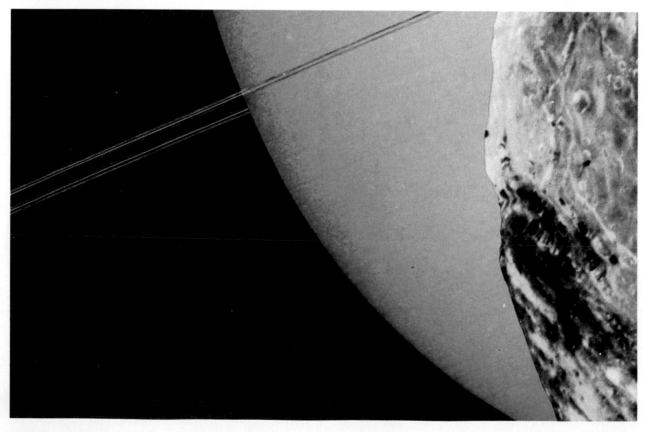

moons include Miranda and Ariel. Both Miranda and Ariel are geologically active, and their surfaces show many fault lines. (Faults are places where landmasses collide and are the cause of earthquakes on Earth.)

Neptune—The Mathematician's Planet

Soon after the discovery of Uranus, astronomers found that the blue-green planet was not behaving as expected. Uranus was not following exactly the orbital path that had been carefully calculated for it by taking into account the gravitational pull of the other planets. Astronomers decided that there must be another object beyond Uranus. The gravitational pull from this distant object in space, it was assumed, was affecting the orbit of Uranus.

In 1845, a young English astronomer John Couch Adams calculated where such an object should be. For the most part his results were ignored. Meanwhile, in France, Urbain Jean Joseph Leverrier also calculated the location of this new planet. Leverrier's calculations were also largely ignored. However, one scientist, Johann Galle at Germany's Berlin Observatory, took Leverrier seriously. Galle immediately began searching for the unknown object. Before his first night of observation was over, he had discovered a new planet. It was located exactly where both Adams and Leverrier had predicted the mysterious object would be. And it is that mysterious object you will visit next on your tour of the solar system.

The new planet, a giant bluish world, was named Neptune, for the Roman god of the sea. Neptune and Uranus are often called the twin giants. They are about the same size, mass, and temperature. Neptune also glows with a blue-green color.

Like Uranus, Neptune is covered by a thick cloud cover. Huge clouds of methane float in an atmosphere of hydrogen and helium. Temperatures at the cloud tops may dip to a chilly −220°C. Neptune's surface is probably an ocean of water and liquid methane, covering a rocky core.

Data from *Voyager 2* confirmed that Neptune has five rings. These rings are made of dust particles that may have formed when meteorites crashed into Neptune's moons millions of years ago.

ACTIVITY THINKING

Outer Planetary Weather

Saturn and Neptune are the windiest planets in the solar system, and Jupiter is the stormiest. Using information from the chapter, create a weather forecast for the planets Jupiter, Saturn, and Neptune. Assume you are a local weather forecaster providing a traveler's forecast for people on Earth who will be journeying to these distant planets.

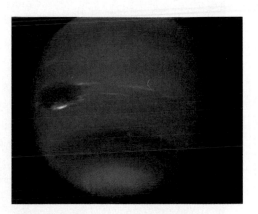

Figure 3–30 *After passing by Uranus,* Voyager *continued on to Neptune, where it took this photograph of the gas giant. Why are Uranus and Neptune called the twin giants?*

Neptune also has at least eight moons. The most interesting moon is Triton, the fourth largest moon in the solar system. Triton appears to be an icy world covered with frozen methane. Like Titan, Triton has an atmosphere. Triton is an unusual moon because it orbits Neptune in a backward, or retrograde, direction. This fact has led some astronomers to conclude that Triton is not an original moon of Neptune. Instead, it may be an object captured by Neptune's gravity.

Your journey through the solar system is not quite over. Now it is time to travel to the only planet that was not discovered until this century.

Figure 3–32 *Triton, Neptune's largest moon, is a world covered with frozen methane.*

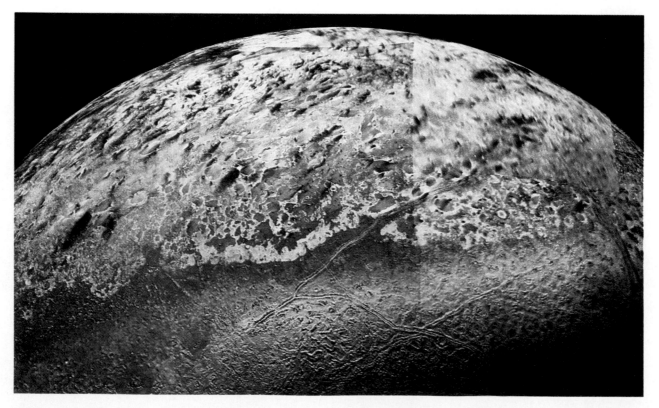

Pluto—A Double Planet

Neptune's discovery helped to explain some of the unexpected changes in the orbit of Uranus. But it did not account for all the changes. To complicate matters, the newly discovered Neptune did not orbit the sun as predicted either. In the early 1900s, astronomer Percival Lowell attempted to explain the mystery. He suggested that there was another planet whose gravity was pulling on both Neptune and Uranus.

In 1930, after an intense search, a young astronomy assistant named Clyde Tombaugh found the ninth planet near where Lowell had predicted it would be. The planet was named Pluto, for the Roman god of the underworld. However, the discovery of Pluto still did not solve the riddle of the strange orbits of Uranus and Neptune.

Lowell had calculated the position of a world that he thought was huge—a world massive enough to pull the two gas giants Uranus and Neptune out of their expected orbits. But, as it turns out, Pluto is much too small to have any real effect on either of these giant planets. In fact, Pluto is the smallest and least massive planet in the solar system.

Pluto is little more than a moon-sized object and may be an escaped moon of Neptune. It appears to be made mainly of various ices, primarily methane ice. Although the methane is frozen on the dark side of Pluto, it seems likely that some of the methane on the part of the planet facing the sun may have evaporated and formed a thin, pink atmosphere. If so, Pluto would be the only planet with an atmosphere on its sunny side and no atmosphere on its dark side.

As your imaginary ship approaches Pluto, you notice something that remained hidden to Earthbound astronomers for forty-eight years after

ACTIVITY DOING

Planetary Sizes

Examine the diameters of the planets in our solar system as shown in Figure 3–11. Using art materials and measuring tools, illustrate visually the relative sizes of the planets. Keep in mind that everything in your model must be done to the same scale.

Figure 3–33 *This NASA illustration shows Pluto and its moon Charon. Why do some people call Pluto a double planet?*

the discovery of Pluto. In 1978, astronomer James Christy was studying photographs of Pluto when he noticed some that appeared to be defective. In the "defective" photograph, Pluto seemed to have developed a bump. Looking more closely, Christy realized that the bump was not part of the planet. It was a moon. He named the moon Charon, after the mythological boatman who ferried the souls of the dead into the underworld. Charon is about half the size of Pluto. Because of this closeness in size, astronomers consider Pluto and Charon to be a double planet.

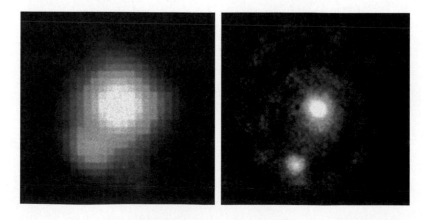

Figure 3–34 *The photograph on the left shows Pluto and its moon as seen from Earth. The photograph on the right was taken by the Hubble Space Telescope.*

Planet X—The Tenth Planet?

As you have just read, the orbits of Uranus and Neptune led to the discovery of Pluto. But the mass of Pluto is far too small, and therefore its gravitational pull too weak, to account for the unexpected orbits of Uranus and Neptune. Astronomers suspected that something else must be pulling on these planets, tugging them slightly from their expected orbits around the sun. Is this mysterious "something" a tenth planet? Astronomers have been looking for such a planet, nicknamed Planet X, which would be a giant planet some 8 billion kilometers beyond the orbit of Pluto.

What if no giant planet is found out there? Is there something else that might be tugging at Uranus and Neptune? Other possibilities exist. Many stars have a dark companion star. The sun may be part of such a binary-star system. Its dark companion could even be a brown dwarf, a massive object far larger than any planet but too small to have become a star. The brown dwarf would exert an enormous gravitational pull on the outer planets and might be found more than 80 billion kilometers from the sun.

Some astronomers have proposed an even more "far-out" explanation. They suggest that a black hole some 160 billion kilometers in space may be the source of the unexpected changes in the orbits of Uranus and Neptune. The black hole, at least ten times the mass of our sun, would exert a tremendous gravitational pull on these planets. Even from such a long distance it could reach into the solar system and disturb the orbits of Uranus and Neptune.

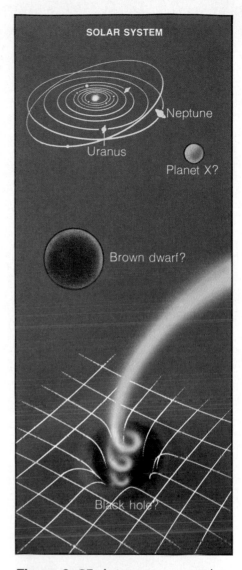

SOLAR SYSTEM

Neptune

Uranus

Planet X?

Brown dwarf?

Black hole?

Figure 3–35 *Astronomers wonder what unknown object may be tugging on the orbits of Uranus and Neptune. There are three possibilities: a tenth planet called Planet X, a brown dwarf, or a black hole.*

Comets

You have gone a long way on your tour of the solar system and are now far beyond the outermost reaches of Pluto's orbit. You are about to visit the Oort cloud, named for the Dutch astronomer Jan Oort.

The Oort cloud is a vast collection of ice, gas, and dust some 15 trillion kilometers from the sun. Every once in a while, the gravitational pull of a

Figure 3–36 *Why does the tail of a comet always point away from the sun?*

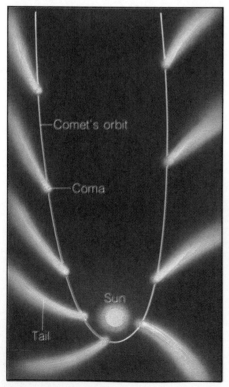

nearby star will tug a "dirty snowball" out of the Oort cloud and send it speeding toward the sun. For most of its trip toward the sun, this mountain-sized object, commonly called a **comet,** travels unnoticed. As it comes closer and closer to the sun, it grows warmer. Some of its ice, gas, and dust heat up enough to form a cloud around its core.

The core of a comet is called its nucleus. The cloud of dust and gas surrounding the nucleus is known as the coma. The nucleus and coma make up the head of the comet. During its approach to the sun, the head of the comet continues to grow warmer and to expand. In time, the head can expand to become as large as a few hundred thousand or even a million kilometers in diameter. Yet the head forms only a small part of the entire comet.

The sun produces a powerful solar wind made of high-energy particles. This solar wind blows the coma outward into a long tail that always streams away from the sun. The tail of an incoming comet streams out behind it. The tail of an outgoing comet streams in front of it. See Figure 3–36. In fact, the glowing tail was the basis for the term comet, which comes from the Greek word meaning long-haired. The tail of a comet often stretches out for millions of kilometers. A comet's tail is an astronomical wonder. It can sweep across a huge portion of the sky, yet it is so thin that distant stars can be seen shining through it.

Most of the 100,000 or so comets in the solar system orbit the sun over and over again. Many are long-period comets that have long, elliptical orbits, perhaps reaching out to the very edge of the solar system. Long-period comets may take thousands of years before they return to Earth's neighborhood again.

Short-period comets, however, return to the sun every few years. Perhaps the most famous short-period comet is Halley's comet, named for the English astronomer Edmund Halley. Halley's comet returns every 75 to 79 years. Although Halley did not discover the comet, he was the first to realize that the comets seen in 1456, 1531, 1607, and 1682 were really the same periodic comet. Halley predicted that the comet would return again in 1759, but he died without ever knowing whether his prediction

Figure 3–37 *This photograph of Halley's comet was taken in 1910. The colors were added later by a computer. Ancient Babylonians recorded a sighting of what is now called Halley's comet in 164 BC on this clay tablet.*

would actually come true. It did. The last time Halley's comet was seen was in 1986. It is due back again around 2062.

Meteoroids, Meteors, and Meteorites

Earth is often "invaded" by objects from space. Most of these invaders are **meteoroids** (MEE-tee-uh-roids), chunks of metal or stone that orbit the sun. Scientists think that most meteoroids come from the asteroid belt or from comets that have broken up. Each day millions of meteoroids plunge through Earth's atmosphere. When the meteoroid rubs against the gases in the atmosphere, friction causes it to burn. The streak of light produced by a burning meteoroid is called a **meteor.** Meteors are also known as shooting stars.

Most meteors burn up in the atmosphere. A few, however, survive to strike Earth's surface. A meteor that strikes Earth's surface is called a **meteorite.** Meteorites vary in composition, but most contain iron, nickel, and stone.

While most meteorites are small, a few are quite large. The largest meteorite ever found is the Hoba West meteorite in South West Africa. It has a mass of more than 18,000 kilograms.

When a large meteorite crashes to Earth, it produces a crater. Some of the world's largest meteorite craters are found in Canada. In the United States, the most famous crater is the enormous Barringer Meteorite Crater, between Flagstaff and Winslow in Arizona.

Figure 3–38 *This meteorite, discovered in Antarctica, is believed to have come from Mars.*

Figure 3–39 *The Barringer crater in Arizona is 1.2 kilometers wide. What caused this huge crater?*

A meteorite found recently in Antarctica appears to have come from the moon. It is made of materials very similar to those brought back from the moon by astronauts. Even more exciting is an Antarctic meteorite that may have come from Mars. It appears similar in composition to the Martian soil tested by *Viking 1.* If so, it is the first known visitor from Earth's red neighbor in space.

Life in the Solar System

In your mind, you have traveled across billions of kilometers as you explored the solar system. Yet nowhere in your travels have you come across living things. As far as scientists know, Earth is the only planet in our solar system that contains life. However, that does not mean that living things do not exist somewhere "out there."

For life as we know it to develop, certain conditions must be met. Two very important conditions are moderate temperatures and liquid water. And both must be present for billions of years for life to evolve. By chance, Earth has possessed these two conditions for most of its estimated 4.6-billion-year history. This is due partly to the fact that Earth happens to be in the very narrow "life zone" of its star, the sun.

If Earth had formed only 7.5 million kilometers closer to the sun, temperatures probably would have

Figure 3–40 *The center illustration shows Earth as it is today. The illustration on the top shows what Earth might be like if its orbit were slightly farther from the sun. On the bottom is a view of Earth if its orbit were slightly closer to the sun.*

been too hot to support life. A location just 1.5 million kilometers more distant from the sun would have produced an Earth covered with frozen water. Again, life would not have developed. Yet these are simply probabilities. Even on Earth, living things have been found in the most improbable places.

3–3 Section Review

1. Briefly describe the major characteristics of the planets and other objects in the solar system.
2. What gives Mars its red color?
3. Which planet is thought to have lost its oceans due to the greenhouse effect?
4. Why is Neptune called the mathematician's planet?
5. Compare a meteoroid, meteor, and meteorite.
6. Why does a comet's tail always stream away from the sun?

Connection—*Ecology*

7. During the process of photosynthesis, plants take in carbon dioxide from the atmosphere. Based on that information, why are scientists so concerned about the cutting down of huge patches of tropical rain forests on Earth?

3–4 Exploring the Solar System

Much of the information you have read in this chapter was provided by spacecraft sent to probe distant planets in our solar system. However, before a spacecraft can be sent to another planet, it has to be launched off the surface of the Earth. And to do

Guide for Reading

Focus on these questions as you read.

▶ What is the principle behind the reaction engine used in rockets?

▶ What were the contributions of the various spacecraft sent by the United States to probe the solar system?

that we need rockets. So we will begin our examination of the spacecraft we send to other planets by looking into the history of rocketry.

Rocketry

Blow up a balloon and pinch the nozzle so that no air can escape. Hold the balloon at arm's length; then let it go. What happens?

When the balloon nozzle is released, air shoots out of it. At the same time, the balloon moves in a direction opposite to the movement of the escaping air. The released balloon is behaving like a rocket.

This example illustrates the idea of a **reaction engine.** Its movement is based on Sir Isaac Newton's third law of motion, which states that every action produces an equal and opposite reaction. The escaping rush of air out of the balloon nozzle causes the balloon to shoot off in the opposite direction. A reaction engine works in much the same way. **In a reaction engine, such as a rocket, the rearward blast of exploding gases causes the rocket to shoot forward.** The force of this forward movement is called thrust.

Long before Newton's time, the ancient Chinese, Greeks, and Romans made use of reaction engines. The Greeks and the Romans used steam to move toys. One toy consisted of a kettle on wheels with a basket holding glowing embers beneath it. Heat from the embers caused water in the kettle to boil. As the water boiled, steam hissed out of a horizontal nozzle on the kettle. In reaction to the escape of steam in one direction, the wheeled kettle rolled off in the opposite direction.

The first useful reaction engines were rockets developed by the Chinese around the year 1000. Their first known use was as weapons of war. These early Chinese rockets were long cylinders, probably sections of hollow bamboo, filled with gunpowder. One end of the cylinder was sealed, usually by a metal cap. The other end was open and had a fuse running through it into the gunpowder. When the gunpowder was ignited, burning gases shot out the open end of the cylinder. In reaction to this movement of gases, the cylinder shot off in the opposite direction.

By the end of the nineteenth century, some scientists began dreaming of using rockets to explore

Activity Bank

Action, Reaction, p. 753

Figure 3–41 *The action of the rocket's thrusters causes an opposite reaction and the rocket goes forward (top). Similar types of thrusters in this manned maneuvering unit (MMU) allow an astronaut to move in any direction in space (bottom).*

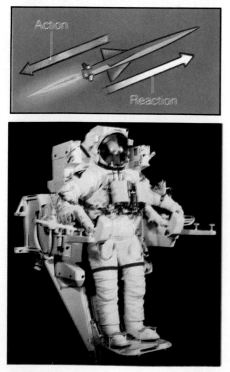

space. But would it be possible to build a rocket large enough and powerful enough to travel out of Earth's atmosphere? Late in the century a number of scientists studied this question. And at least one of them, a Russian named Konstantin E. Tsiolkovsky, considered it a definite possibility.

As a teenager, Tsiolkovsky had experimented with reaction engines. Using his lunch money to pay for materials, he had built a carriage powered by a reaction engine. But his experiment did not work. The engine could not develop enough thrust to move the carriage.

From his failure, Tsiolkovsky actually learned a lot about reaction engines. (Science is often like that.) He started to think about using such engines for space travel. Drawing on the work of Newton and other scientists and mathematicians, Tsiolkovsky worked out mathematical formulas for space flight. He even dreamed of creating human colonies in space. But before such colonies could be built, Tsiolkovsky knew that scientists would have to solve the enormous problems involved in building rockets powerful enough to escape the Earth's gravitational pull.

Escape Velocity

In order for a rocket to escape Earth's gravitational pull, the rocket must achieve the proper velocity. This **escape velocity** depends on the mass of the planet and the distance of the rocket from the planet's center. The escape velocity from Earth is 11.2 kilometers per second, or 40,320 kilometers per hour. From the moon, it is just 2.3 kilometers per second. From mighty Jupiter, the escape velocity is 63.4 kilometers per second. Can you relate these differences in escape velocity to the mass of each planet?

The first step into space involves escape from the Earth. Tsiolkovsky predicted that through the use of a huge reaction engine, a vehicle would someday leave Earth's gravitational pull. But he also concluded that a rocket powered by gunpowder or some other solid fuel would not be able to accomplish this feat. Why not?

Solid fuels burn rapidly and explosively. The pushing force that results is used up within seconds.

Figure 3–42 *This table shows the escape velocities for the nine planets in our solar system, the sun, and several other stars. Why is the escape velocity of Pluto so much lower than that of the other planets?*

ESCAPE VELOCITIES

Object	Escape Velocity (km/sec)
Mercury	4.2
Venus	10.3
Earth	11.2
Moon	2.3
Mars	5.0
Jupiter	63.4
Saturn	39.4
Uranus	21.5
Neptune	24.2
Pluto	0.3*
Sun	616
Sirius B	3400*
Neutron star	200,000*

* Estimated

Although the force provides an enormous early thrust, it cannot maintain that thrust. As the rocket soars upward, the pull of Earth's gravity would tend to slow its climb and eventually bring it back to Earth.

In order for a rocket to build up enough speed to overcome the Earth's downward pull, the rocket must have a fuel that continues to burn and provide thrust through the lower levels of the atmosphere. Although Tsiolkovsky proposed this idea, he never built such a rocket. But in the 1920s, the American scientist Dr. Robert H. Goddard did. In 1926, Goddard combined gasoline with liquid oxygen and burned this mixture, launching a small rocket. The rocket did not go very far or very fast, but it did prove the point that liquid fuels could be used to provide continuous thrust.

Goddard built bigger and bigger rockets. And he drew up plans for multistage rockets. As each stage in such a rocket used up its fuel, the empty fuel container would drop off. Then the next stage would ignite, and its empty fuel container would drop off. In this way, a vehicle could be pushed through the atmosphere and out of Earth's grip. Today's rockets work in much the same way as Goddard's early rocket did. Now, however, the fuel is liquid hydrogen and liquid oxygen. Using such rockets, scientists are able to send spacecraft from Earth to the other planets in our solar system.

Deep-Space Probes

The first spacecraft to travel beyond the solar system, in June 1983, was *Pioneer 10.* It was intended, along with *Pioneer 11,* to explore the outer planets of

Figure 3–43 *You can see how the last stage of this rocket—the nose cone—is released into space.*

the solar system. In February 1990, seventeen years after it was launched, *Pioneer 11,* too, flew beyond the solar system.

Pioneers, Vanguards, Explorers, Mariners, Rangers, Vikings, Surveyors, and Voyagers have been the workhorses of the effort of the United States to explore the solar system. And their record has been impressive. The first successful probe of Venus was made by *Mariner 2* in 1962. The spacecraft approached to within 35,000 kilometers of the cloud-wrapped planet. *Mariner 2* quickly discovered that Venus, unlike Earth, does not have a magnetic field. And, as you have read earlier, Venus continues to be studied by spacecraft such as the *Magellan* probe.

The first successful probe of Mars was made by *Mariner 4,* in 1965. Going to within 10,000 kilometers of the red planet, the spacecraft sent back twenty-one photographs and other data. Two later probes, *Mariner 7* in 1969 and *Mariner 9* in 1971, sent back thousands of photographs of the Martian surface and the first detailed pictures of Mars's two moons.

The achievements of *Mariners 7* and *9* paved the way for the successful landings of *Vikings 1* and *2* on Mars in 1975, the first time spacecraft ever landed on another planet.

Mariner 10 was the only spacecraft to fly by Mercury, innermost planet of the solar system. During three passes in 1974, *Mariner 10* mapped ancient volcanoes, valleys, mountains, and plains on the tiny planet.

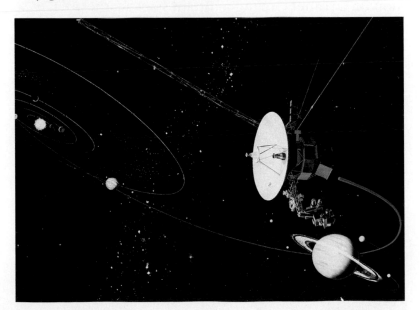

Figure 3–44 *Here you see an artist's idea of how* Voyager *appeared as it passed by Saturn and made its way toward the very edge of our solar system and beyond.*

A Different Viewpoint

We view the solar system from the center of our world, which is Earth. Imagine how the solar system might look to intelligent creatures on another planet. In particular, how might those creatures view Earth? Use your ideas to write several pages that would be included in an alien's textbook on the solar system. (Of course, the book might be called *Neptune Science*—not *Earth Science*.)

Outward-bound *Pioneer 10* took a look at the giant planet Jupiter in December 1973 and sent back more than three hundred photographs. It also provided data on Jupiter's stormy atmosphere and its many moons. These findings were confirmed by the photographs sent back by *Pioneer 11* a short time later.

Six years later, two larger spacecraft, *Voyager 2* and *Voyager 1*, flew by Jupiter and sent back data that revealed surprises about the giant planet. Faint rings of particles and many new moons were discovered. The *Pioneer* and *Voyager* spacecraft examined Saturn and its ring system. *Voyager* photographs showed that what were considered to be a few broad rings are actually thousands of thin ringlets.

The missions of the *Voyager* spacecraft were far from over with the exploration of Saturn. Continuing on in the late 1980s and early 1990s, the *Voyager* spacecraft passed by and photographed Uranus and then Neptune, the twin giants of the outer solar system. Data from both spacecraft provided evidence regarding the atmosphere, core, and moons of these distant planets. Many scientists consider the *Voyager* spacecraft to be the most successful effort in the entire United States space program.

Pioneer 10 and *Pioneer 11* are now beyond the solar system. By the end of this century, the *Voyagers* will follow into outer space. In case it should ever be found by people from another world, *Pioneer 10* contains a plaque with a message from the people of Earth. Who can say, but one day the most important discovery *Pioneer* may make is an advanced civilization on a planet circling a distant star!

3–4 Section Review

1. Identify at least one discovery made by each of the following spacecraft: *Mariner, Pioneer, Viking,* and *Voyager.*
2. How does the concept of action/reaction relate to rocketry?

Connection—*You and Your World*
3. Discuss some of the ways sending spacecraft to distant planets has improved the quality of life for people on Earth.

CONNECTIONS

The First Magellan Probe

You began this chapter by reading about the exploration of Venus by the *Magellan* probe. The *Magellan* probe did not get its name by accident. It was named for one of the greatest explorers in *history*—Ferdinand Magellan.

Born in Portugal in the late fifteenth century, Magellan became convinced that a ship could sail around the world. In those days some people still did not believe the Earth was round, and they were convinced that any ship that sailed far enough would sail right off the edge of the Earth.

Before his famous trip to circle the world, Magellan studied astronomy and navigation for several years. Then in 1519, he commanded a fleet that set sail from Spain. The fleet traveled across the stormy Atlantic and reached the coast of Brazil. It then sailed down the coast of South America and wintered near what is now called Argentina. A mutiny broke out among Magellan's crew and several crew members were executed.

In 1520, the fleet set sail again and soon discovered a passage beneath South America that led them to a vast ocean, which Magellan called the Pacific Ocean, meaning peaceful ocean. To this day, the passage is called the Strait of Magellan.

Sailing across the Pacific was a great hardship for Magellan and his crew. Many suffered from a disease called *scurvy* caused by a lack of Vitamin C. Finally, the fleet reached the island of Guam. It was on Guam that Magellan suffered a fatal wound and died in 1521.

Magellan's crew continued the trip and eventually circled the planet by ship. And although Magellan did not live to see his dream completed, he is the first European to provide evidence that the Earth is a sphere.

Many historians consider Magellan's trip the greatest navigational feat in history. So it is not surprising that a twentieth-century spacecraft would be named after this courageous and daring explorer.

Laboratory Investigation

Constructing a Balloon Rocket

Problem

How can a balloon rocket be used to illustrate Newton's third law of motion?

Materials *(per group)*

> drinking straw
> scissors
> 9-m length of string
> balloon
> masking tape
> meterstick

Procedure

1. Cut the drinking straw in half. Pull the string through one of the halves.
2. Blow up the balloon and hold the end so that the air does not escape.
3. Have someone tape the drinking straw with the string pulled through it to the side of the balloon as shown in the diagram. Do not let go of the balloon.
4. Have two students pull the string tight between them.
5. Move the balloon to one end of the string. Release the balloon and observe its flight toward the other end of the string.
6. Record the flight number and distance the balloon traveled in a data table.
7. Repeat the flight of the balloon four more times. Record each flight number and length in your data table.

Observations

1. What was the longest flight of your balloon rocket? The shortest flight?
2. What was the average distance reached by your balloon?

Analysis and Conclusions

1. Using Newton's third law of motion, explain what caused the movement of the balloon.
2. Compare your balloon rocket to the way a real rocket works.
3. Suppose your classmates obtained different results for the distances their balloons traveled. What variables may have caused the differences?
4. **On Your Own** As you have read, rockets require a certain thrust to escape Earth's gravitational pull. How might you increase the thrust of your balloon rocket? Try it and see if you are correct.

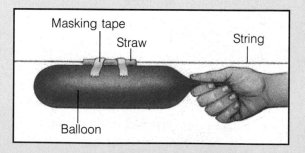

Masking tape · Straw · String · Balloon

Study Guide

Summarizing Key Concepts

3–1 The Solar System Evolves

▲ According to the nebular theory, the solar system formed from a huge cloud of gas and dust called a nebula.

3–2 Motions of the Planets

▲ A planet's period of revolution is the time it takes that planet to make one complete revolution around the sun, or a year on that planet.

▲ A planet's period of rotation is the time it takes that planet to make one complete rotation on its axis, or a day on that planet.

▲ The combined effects of inertia and gravity keep planets orbiting the sun in elliptical orbits.

3–3 A Trip Through the Solar System

▲ Mercury is a crater-covered world with high temperatures on its daylight side and low temperatures on its nighttime side.

▲ Venus is a cloud-covered world with high temperatures. The greenhouse effect is the main cause of its high temperatures.

▲ Mars is coated with iron oxide, or rust, which gives the planet its reddish color.

▲ The atmosphere of Jupiter is primarily hydrogen and helium.

▲ Jupiter's core is probably a rocky solid surrounded by a layer of liquid metallic hydrogen.

▲ Jupiter has sixteen moons.

▲ Saturn is similar in appearance and composition to Jupiter.

▲ Saturn's spectacular rings are made mostly of water ice.

▲ Uranus and Neptune are cloud-covered worlds. The atmosphere of both planets is primarily hydrogen, helium, and methane.

▲ The axis of Uranus is tilted at an angle of almost 90°. Uranus has at least fifteen moons and nine rings. Neptune has five known rings and eight known moons.

▲ Pluto is a moon-sized, ice-covered world with a large moon, Charon.

▲ The trail of hot gases from a burning meteoroid is called a meteor. If part of a meteoroid strikes the Earth, it is called a meteorite.

▲ As a comet approaches the sun, some of the ice, dust, and gas heat up and form a cloud around the nucleus.

3–4 Exploring the Solar System

▲ Much of the information about our solar system has been provided by spacecraft .

Reviewing Key Terms

Define each term in a complete sentence.

3–1 The Solar System Evolves
solar system
nebular theory

3–2 Motions of the Planets
orbit
period of revolution
period of rotation

3–3 A Trip Through the Solar System
retrograde rotation
greenhouse effect
asteroid belt
comet
meteoroid
meteor
meteorite

3–4 Exploring the Solar System
reaction engine
escape velocity

Chapter Review

Content Review

Multiple Choice

Choose the letter of the answer that best completes each statement.

1. The outer gas giants do not include
   a. Jupiter.
   b. Pluto.
   c. Neptune.
   d. Saturn.

2. The observation that planets move in elliptical orbits was first made by
   a. Copernicus.
   b. Ptolemy.
   c. Kepler.
   d. Newton.

3. The time it takes a planet to make one complete trip around the sun is called its
   a. period of rotation.
   b. day.
   c. period of revolution.
   d. axis.

4. A planet with retrograde rotation is
   a. Venus.
   b. Jupiter.
   c. Pluto.
   d. Earth.

5. The Oort cloud is the home of
   a. asteroids.
   b. comets.
   c. meteorites.
   d. Pluto.

6. Rocklike objects in the region of space between the orbits of Mars and Jupiter are called
   a. comets.
   b. protoplanets.
   c. asteroids.
   d. meteorites.

7. The reddish color of Mars is due to
   a. carbon dioxide.
   b. oxygen.
   c. iron oxide.
   d. methane.

8. The planet that appears to be tipped on its side is
   a. Saturn.
   b. Uranus.
   c. Neptune.
   d. Venus.

True or False

If the statement is true, write "true." If it is false, change the underlined word or words to make the statement true.

1. Due to the tremendous heat of the sun, the <u>outer</u> planets were unable to retain their lightweight gases.

2. The time it takes for a planet to travel once on its axis is called its <u>period of revolution</u>.

3. Newton recognized that planets do not sail off into space due to <u>gravity</u>.

4. The tail of a comet always streams <u>away</u> from the sun.

5. A <u>meteor</u> is a streak of light produced when a small object shoots through the atmosphere.

6. The <u>nebular theory</u> accounts for the formation of the solar system.

7. Newton's third law of motion states that for every action there is an <u>equal</u> and <u>opposite</u> reaction.

Concept Mapping

Complete the following concept map for Section 3–1. Then construct a concept map for the entire chapter.

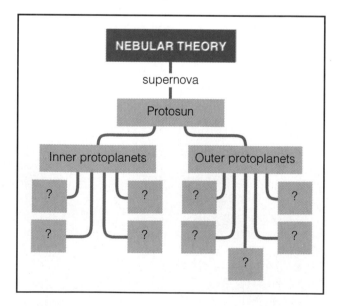

Concept Mastery

Discuss each of the following in a brief paragraph.

1. Why do astronomers consider Jupiter a planet that was almost a star?
2. Describe the two types of planetary motion.
3. What factors led to the great differences between the rocky inner planets and the gaseous outer planets?
4. Describe the evolution of the solar system according to the nebular theory.
5. How has our understanding of the solar system been increased through mathematics?
6. Discuss the greenhouse effect in relation to Venus.

Critical Thinking and Problem Solving

Use the skills you have developed in this chapter to discuss each of the following.

1. **Making comparisons** Compare the theories of Copernicus and Ptolemy.
2. **Relating cause and effect** Mercury is closer to the sun than Venus is. Yet temperatures on Venus are higher than those on Mercury. Explain why.

3. **Making predictions** Predict what the outer planets would be like if the sun were three times as large as it is.
4. **Making graphs** Using the chart on pages 104–105, draw a graph that plots the high and low temperatures on each planet. What conclusions can you draw from your graph?
5. **Making comparisons** Compare a meteoroid, meteor, and meteorite.
6. **Expressing an opinion** Sending spacecraft to probe the planets of our solar system costs many billions of dollars. Should the United States continue to spend money on space research, or could the money be better spent to improve conditions on Earth? What's your opinion?
7. **Using the writing process** Write a short story called "A Trip Around Planet Earth" in which you describe your home planet to an alien from another star system. Assume the alien has never been to Earth.

Earth and *Its Moon*

Guide for Reading

After you read the following sections, you will be able to

4–1 The Earth in Space
- Relate Earth's rotation and revolution to day and night and to the seasons.

4–2 The Earth's Moon
- Describe the characteristics of the moon.
- Discuss several theories for the origin of the moon.

4–3 The Earth, the Moon, and the Sun
- Identify the interactions among the Earth, the moon, and the sun.

4–4 The Space Age
- Describe the functions of various types of artificial satellites.
- Discuss some of the uses of space technology on Earth.

Hundreds of meters below the tiny spacecraft loomed a dusty plain strewn with boulders and craters—the strangest landscape humans had ever seen. But the two astronauts in the spidery craft had no time for sightseeing. Their job was to find a safe landing site—and fast, for they were running out of fuel. After traveling almost 400,000 kilometers from the Earth, they now had about 90 seconds to find a place to land on the moon.

"Down two and a half . . . forward, forward . . . good." Now they were just 12 meters above the plain called the Sea of Tranquility.

"Down two and a half . . . kicking up some dust." Nine meters to go!

"Four forward . . . drifting to the right a little." Finally, a red light flashed on the control panel.

"Contact light! Houston, Tranquility Base here. The *Eagle* has landed."

The date was July 20, 1969. For the first time in history, humans had left the Earth to explore its nearest neighbor in space, the moon. In the pages that follow, you will learn about the Earth's place in the solar system and about the relationship between the Earth and its moon.

Journal *Activity*

You and Your World   Go outdoors on a clear night and look at the moon. What features can you see? In your journal, describe the appearance of the moon and include a sketch of what you see.

Astronaut Edwin E. Aldrin, Jr., walks on the surface of the moon. Notice the reflection of the Lunar Module Eagle *in his faceplate.*

A Foucault Pendulum Model

In 1851, the French physicist Jean Foucault proved that the Earth rotates on its axis.

1. Tie a small weight such as an eraser to a piece of string. Tie the opposite end of the string to the arm of a ring stand.

2. Hang the pendulum over a turntable. The center of the turntable represents the North Pole. With a pen, make a reference mark on one side of the turntable.

3. Set the pendulum swinging and slowly turn the turntable. You will see that the direction of swing appears to change relative to the mark on the turntable.

If a Foucault pendulum is swinging above the North Pole, how long will it take for its direction of swing to appear to make one complete rotation? Explain.

4–1 The Earth in Space

Early observers saw the sun and the moon rise in the east and set in the west, just as we do today. Unlike modern observers, however, these people thought that the Earth stood still while the sun and the moon moved around it. Today we know that sunrise and sunset, as well as moonrise and moonset, are actually caused by the movements of the Earth in space.

Earth is the third planet from the sun in the solar system. Like all the other planets, Earth rotates on its axis as it travels around the sun. The Earth's axis is an imaginary line from the North Pole through the center of the Earth to the South Pole. And like the other planets, Earth revolves around the sun in an elliptical, or oval, orbit. **These two movements of the Earth—rotation and revolution—affect both day and night and the seasons on Earth.** Let's examine the effects of the Earth's rotation and revolution more closely.

Day and Night

At the equator, the Earth rotates at a speed of about 1600 kilometers per hour. (This is about 400 kilometers per hour faster than the speed of sound in air.) It takes the Earth about 24 hours to rotate once on its axis. The amount of time the Earth takes

Figure 4–1 *This dramatic photograph taken by the Apollo 11 astronauts shows the Earth rising above the moon's horizon.*

7:30 A.M.

10:30 A.M.

NOON

3:30 P.M.

7:30 P.M.

to complete one rotation is called a day. So a day on the Earth is about 24 hours long.

As the Earth rotates, part of it faces the sun and is bathed in sunlight. The rest of it faces away from the sun and is in darkness. As the Earth continues to rotate, the part that faced the sun soon turns away from the sun. And the part that was in darkness comes into sunlight. So the rotation of the Earth causes day and night once every 24 hours. Figure 4–2 shows a 12-hour sequence from sunrise to sunset.

If you could look down on the Earth from above the North Pole, you would see that the Earth rotates in a counterclockwise direction—that is, from west to east. The sun appears to come up, or rise, in the east, as the Earth turns toward it. The sun appears to go down, or set, in the west, as the Earth turns away from it. So a person standing on the rotating Earth sees the sun appear in the east at dawn, move across the sky, and disappear in the west at dusk.

You have probably noticed that throughout the year the length of day and night changes. This happens because the Earth's axis is not straight up and down. The Earth's axis is tilted at an angle of 23½°. If the Earth's axis were straight up and down, all parts of the Earth would have 12 hours of daylight and 12 hours of darkness every day of the year.

Because the Earth's axis is slightly tilted, when the North Pole is leaning toward the sun, the South Pole is leaning away from the sun. And when the South Pole is leaning toward the sun, the North Pole is leaning away from the sun. As a result, the •

Figure 4–2 *This five-photo sunrise-to-sunset sequence was taken by a satellite orbiting the Earth above South America. What causes day and night on Earth?*

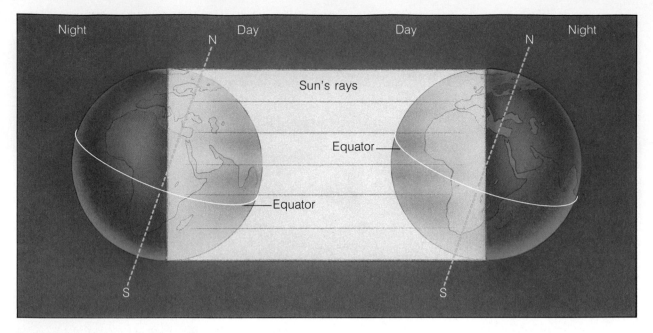

Night | Day | Day | Night

Sun's rays

Equator

Equator

N

N

S

S

Figure 4–3 *Because of the tilt of the Earth's axis, the length of day and night is not constant. At the beginning of summer in the Northern Hemisphere (left), the North Pole is always in daylight and the South Pole is always dark. What happens at the beginning of winter (right)?*

number of daylight hours in the Northern and Southern Hemispheres is not constant. (Recall that the Earth is divided into two halves, or hemispheres, by the equator.) The hemisphere that leans toward the sun has long days and short nights. The hemisphere that leans away from the sun has short days and long nights. Today, is the Northern Hemisphere leaning toward or away from the sun? How do you know?

A Year on Earth

At the same time that the Earth is rotating on its axis, it is also revolving in its orbit around the sun. The Earth takes about 365.26 days to complete one revolution, or one entire trip, around the sun. The time the Earth takes to complete one revolution around the sun is called a year. So there are 365.26 days in one Earth year. How many times does the Earth rotate in one year?

You do not have to look at a calendar to know that there are only 365 days in a calendar year. But the Earth rotates 365.26 times in the time it takes to make one complete revolution around the sun. So about one fourth (0.26) of a day is left off the calendar each year. To make up for this missing time, an extra day is added to the calendar every four years. This extra day is added to the month of February, which then has 29 days instead of its usual 28. What is a year with an extra day called?

Activity

DISCOVERING

Temperature, Daylight, and the Seasons

1. In your journal, keep a log of the high and low temperatures for each day in the school year.

2. Record the time at which the sun rises and sets each day.

3. Calculate the length of daylight, in hours and minutes, for each day.

■ What relationship do you see between the length of daylight and the temperature? Explain.

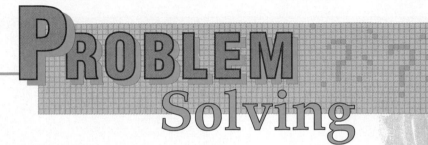

PROBLEM Solving

What Causes Summer?

When the Northern Hemisphere is tilted toward the sun, that part of the Earth receives more direct rays of sunlight than the Southern Hemisphere does. The Southern Hemisphere, which is tilted away from the sun, receives slanting rays of sunlight. As a result, it is summer in the Northern Hemisphere and winter in the Southern Hemisphere.

During the summer season, the Earth's land surface, oceans, and atmosphere receive the greatest amount of heat from the sun. Why is this so? Using a globe, a light source, and one or two thermometers, design an experiment to compare the amount of heat produced by direct rays of light and by slanting rays of light.

Finding cause and effect Think about a typical sunny day. Do the sun's rays feel hotter at noon when the sun is directly overhead, or in the late afternoon when the sun is low in the sky? Explain.

Seasons on Earth

Most people live in a part of the Earth that has four distinct seasons: winter, spring, summer, and autumn. If you could spend a year on each of the other eight planets in the solar system, you would find that five of them (Mars, Saturn, Uranus, Neptune, and possibly Pluto) share this characteristic with the Earth. The other three planets (Mercury, Venus, and Jupiter) either have no seasons at all or have seasons that vary so slightly they are not noticeable. Why do some planets have seasons and others do not?

If you study all the planets that have seasons, you will find that they all have one characteristic in common. They are all tilted on their axes. This is not true of the planets that do not have seasons. So you might conclude that the different seasons on Earth are caused by the tilt of the Earth's axis. And you would be correct.

ACTIVITY
READING

A Seasonal Journal

Read *Circle of the Seasons* by the American naturalist Edwin Way Teale (1899–1980).

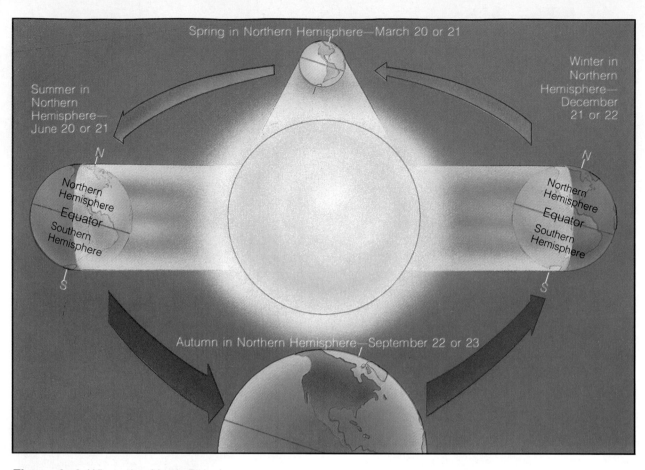

Spring in Northern Hemisphere—March 20 or 21

Summer in Northern Hemisphere— June 20 or 21

Winter in Northern Hemisphere— December 21 or 22

N

Northern Hemisphere

Equator

Southern Hemisphere

S

N

Northern Hemisphere

Equator

Southern Hemisphere

S

Autumn in Northern Hemisphere—September 22 or 23

Figure 4–4 *When the North Pole is tilted toward the sun, the Northern Hemisphere receives more sunlight. It is summer. When the North Pole is tilted away from the sun, the Northern Hemisphere receives less sunlight. It is winter. Is the same true for the South Pole and the Southern Hemisphere?*

Activity

CALCULATING

The Earth on the Move

The Earth moves at a speed of about 30 km/sec as it orbits the sun. What distance, in kilometers, does the Earth travel in a minute? An hour? A day? A year?

As the Earth revolves around the sun, the axis is tilted away from the sun for part of the year and toward the sun for part of the year. This is shown in Figure 4–4. When the Northern Hemisphere is tilted toward the sun, that half of the Earth has summer. At the same time, the Southern Hemisphere is tilted away from the sun and has winter. How is the Earth's axis tilted when the Southern Hemisphere has summer?

It is interesting to note that summer and winter are not affected by the Earth's distance from the sun. In fact, when the Northern Hemisphere is experiencing summer, the Earth is actually farthest away from the sun in its elliptical orbit. The same is true for summer in the Southern Hemisphere.

The hemisphere of the Earth that is tilted toward the sun receives more direct rays of sunlight and also has longer days than the hemisphere that is tilted away from the sun. The combination of more direct sunlight and longer days causes the Earth's surface and atmosphere to receive more heat from the sun. The result is the summer season.

Figure 4–5 *These photographs were taken on the same day in the Northern and Southern hemispheres. It is winter for the bison in Yellowstone National Park, Wyoming. But it is summer for the kangaroos in Australia. On this day, is the North Pole tilted toward or away from the sun?*

Summer begins in the Northern Hemisphere on June 20 or 21. This is the day when the North Pole is tilted a full 23½° toward the sun. The Northern Hemisphere has its longest day at this time, while the Southern Hemisphere has its shortest day. The longest day of the year is known as the **summer solstice** (SAHL-stihs). The word solstice comes from two Latin words meaning sun and stop. It refers to the time when the sun seems to stop moving higher in the sky each day. The sun reaches its highest point in the sky on the summer solstice.

After the summer solstice, the sun seems to move lower and lower in the sky until December 21 or 22, when the **winter solstice** occurs. At this time, the North Pole is tilted a full 23½° away from the sun. The shortest day of the year in the Northern Hemisphere and the longest day of the year in the Southern Hemisphere occur on the winter solstice.

Twice a year, in spring and in autumn, neither the North Pole nor the South Pole is tilted toward the sun. These times are known as equinoxes (EE-kwuh-naks-uhz). The word equinox comes from Latin and means equal night. At the equinoxes, day and night are of equal length all over the world. In the Northern Hemisphere, spring begins on the **vernal equinox,** March 20 or 21. Autumn begins on the **autumnal equinox,** September 22 or 23. What season begins in the Southern Hemisphere when spring begins in the Northern Hemisphere?

Figure 4–6 *Stonehenge, on Salisbury Plain in England, was built 4000 to 6000 years ago. Its massive stones were aligned to point to the rising or setting positions of the sun at the summer and winter solstices.*

A Magnet in Space

In Figure 4–7 you can see the pattern that forms when iron filings are sprinkled on a plate of glass covering a bar magnet. The pattern of iron filings reveals the invisible lines of force that connect the two poles, or ends, of the magnet. These invisible lines of force are called a magnetic field.

The Earth, much like a magnet, is surrounded by similar lines of force. In fact, you might think of the Earth as having a giant bar magnet passing through it from pole to pole. The Earth's magnetism forms a magnetic field around the Earth similar to the magnetic field around a bar magnet. Where does the Earth's magnetism come from? Although scientists are not sure, they think the Earth's magnetism is probably the result of the movement of materials in the Earth's inner core. The Earth's inner core is made mainly of the metals iron and nickel.

You can see in Figure 4–7 that the Earth's magnetic poles are not in the same place as the geographic North and South poles. The geographic poles are at the opposite ends of the Earth's tilted axis. But the magnetic poles, like the poles of a bar magnet, are at the ends of the lines of force that form the Earth's magnetic field.

The Earth's magnetic field is called the **magnetosphere.** The magnetosphere begins at an

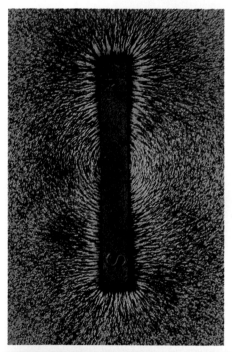

Figure 4–7 *The Earth is enveloped in a huge magnetic field called the magnetosphere (bottom), whose lines of force produce the same pattern as those of a small bar magnet (top). The solar wind from the sun blows the magnetosphere far into space in the shape of a long tail.*

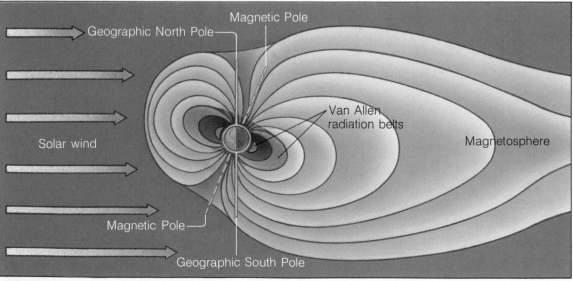

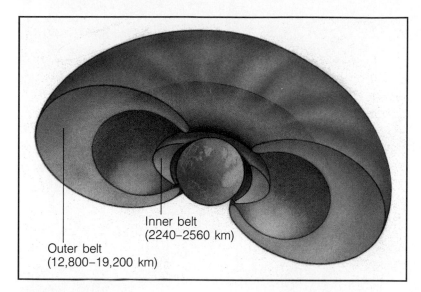

Figure 4–8 *Particles in the solar wind are trapped to form the doughnut-shaped Van Allen radiation belts. What is it that traps the particles from the solar wind?*

Inner belt
(2240–2560 km)

Outer belt
(12,800–19,200 km)

altitude of about 1000 kilometers. It extends to an altitude of 64,000 kilometers on the side of the Earth facing toward the sun. But on the side of the Earth facing away from the sun, the magnetosphere extends in a tail millions of kilometers long! This long tail is caused by a stream of charged particles, called the solar wind, blowing from the sun. The solar wind constantly reshapes the magnetosphere as the Earth rotates on its axis. The magnetosphere is shown in Figure 4–7.

Two doughnut-shaped regions of charged particles are formed as the magnetosphere traps some of the particles in the solar wind. These regions are called the **Van Allen radiation belts.** They were named after Dr. James Van Allen, the scientist who first identified them. The outer Van Allen belt contains mostly electrons, or negatively charged particles. The inner Van Allen belt contains mainly protons, or positively charged particles.

Charged particles trapped by the Van Allen radiation belts may travel along magnetic lines of force to the Earth's poles. Here they collide with particles in the Earth's upper atmosphere. These collisions cause the atmospheric particles to give off visible light, producing an **aurora** (aw-RAW-ruh). The aurora may appear as bands or curtains of shimmering colored

ACTIVITY

DISCOVERING

Lines of Force

1. Place a thin sheet of glass or plastic over a bar magnet.

2. Sprinkle iron filings onto the glass or plastic.

3. Gently shake the glass or plastic back and forth until a clear pattern of lines forms.

4. Draw the pattern of lines of force that you observe.

How do the lines of force you observed compare with those shown in Figure 4–7?

■ How would the lines of force change if you placed another magnet under the glass or plastic? Test your prediction.

Figure 4–9 *The eerie green glow of the aurora australis, or southern lights, was photographed from the Space Shuttle* Discovery.

lights. Near the North Pole, the aurora is called the aurora borealis, or northern lights. Near the South Pole, the aurora is called the aurora australis, or southern lights.

4–1 Section Review

1. What causes day and night on the Earth?
2. How does the tilt of the Earth's axis, combined with the Earth's revolution, cause the occurrence of the seasons?
3. What do the words solstice and equinox mean? How are they related to the position of the Earth's axis?
4. What is the magnetosphere? What are the Van Allen radiation belts?
5. What causes an aurora?

Connection—*You and Your World*
6. Describe the season you are experiencing today in terms of the Earth's position in space relative to the sun.

CONNECTIONS

Solar Wind Blows Out the Lights

Storms on the sun send forth huge bursts of charged particles. When these charged particles reach Earth, they can move the magnetic field that surrounds the Earth. When a magnetic field moves in relation to a conductor, an electric current results. In this case, the conductor is the Earth itself.

Usually, electric charges in the Earth equalize themselves by flowing back and forth through soil or rocks. Trouble results, however, when the electric current encounters dense igneous rocks. *Electricity* cannot flow easily through these rocks. As a result, the electric current seeks an easier path—and electric power lines provide the perfect alternative.

Because the equipment that manufactures electric power cannot handle the electric current produced by a solar storm, power systems can be seriously damaged or destroyed. This is what happened in March 1989 when a solar storm caused a power blackout in Quebec, Canada, and ruined two huge transformers at a nuclear power plant in southern New Jersey.

Due to the destructive potential of solar storms, several electric-power companies have suggested that a satellite "watchdog" be placed in orbit around the Earth. Such a satellite would be able to predict a solar storm in advance because charged particles in the solar wind travel much more slowly than electromagnetic radiation from the sun does. Sensors in the satellite would pick up signals from the electromagnetic radiation about an hour before the burst of charged particles actually took place. This advance warning would give power companies at least a chance to reduce power loads on certain transformers and possibly prevent sensitive equipment from being knocked out.

4–2 The Earth's Moon

"That's one small step for a man, one giant leap for mankind." With those words, astronaut Neil Armstrong became the first human to set foot on the moon. After landing, Armstrong and Edwin (Buzz) Aldrin left the Lunar Module *Eagle* to explore the moon. (The word lunar comes from the Latin word for moon.) While they walked on the surface, their fellow astronaut Michael Collins remained in orbit around the moon in the Apollo Command Module *Columbia*.

Guide for Reading

Focus on this question as you read.

▶ *What are the major characteristics of the moon?*

Figure 4–10 *Landing people on the moon was a complex mission. Here you see the Lunar Module approaching the moon (bottom). The Apollo Command Module (top), which remained in lunar orbit during the mission, was photographed from the Lunar Module shortly after it separated from the Command Module. After landing, the astronauts walked on the moon (right).*

ACTIVITY
READING

A Voyage to the Moon

For a fictional account of the first exploration of the moon, read *From the Earth to the Moon* by the French novelist Jules Verne (1828–1905).

Although Armstrong and Aldrin were the first astronauts to step onto the moon's dusty surface, they would not be the last. By the time the Apollo moon-landing project ended in 1972, twelve American astronauts had explored the moon. Scientists learned more about the moon from the Apollo missions than they had learned in the previous thousands of years. Here is some of what they now know about the moon.

The Moon's Characteristics

The moon measures 3476 kilometers in diameter, or about one fourth the diameter of the Earth. It is much less dense than the Earth. The gravity of the moon is also less than that of the Earth. The moon's gravity is only one sixth that of the Earth. So objects weigh less on the moon than they do on Earth. To find out how much you would weigh on the moon, divide your weight by six. What would your weight be on the moon?

Today scientists know that the average distance to the moon is 384,403 kilometers. How do they know this? Among the instruments left on the moon by the Apollo astronauts was a small mirror. Scientists bounced a beam of laser light from the Earth off the mirror. Then they measured the amount of time it took the beam to bounce back to the Earth. Using

the known speed of light, they could then calculate the distance to the moon accurately.

Astronauts also left instruments on the moon to measure moonquakes. These instruments have measured as many as 3000 moonquakes per year. From these data, scientists now know that the moon's outer layer, or crust, is about 60 kilometers thick. Below the crust, there appears to be another layer of denser rock that is about 800 kilometers thick. Beneath this layer is a central core that may be made of melted iron.

Apollo astronauts also brought back samples of moon rocks. The oldest moon rocks are about 4.6 billion years old, which is about the same age as the Earth. So it seems likely that the moon and the Earth formed at about the same time.

The moon rocks brought back to Earth by the astronauts show no traces of water. So scientists believe that there never was any water on the moon. And the moon has no atmosphere. Without an atmosphere, there is no weather on the moon.

The temperature range on the moon is extreme. Noonday temperatures may rise above 100°C. During the long lunar nights, and in the shadows cast by crater walls, surface temperatures may drop to –175°C. **In short, the moon is a dry, airless, and barren world.**

Features of the Moon

In 1609, Galileo Galilei became the first person to look at the moon through a telescope. He saw light areas and dark areas on the surface. The light areas he saw are mountain ranges soaring thousands of meters into the black sky. They are called **highlands.** Some of the highlands on the moon reach 8 kilometers above the surrounding plains. The broad, smooth lowland plains are the

Figure 4–12 *The chart lists some important facts about the moon. How much greater is the moon's circumference than its diameter?*

FACTS ABOUT THE MOON
Average distance from Earth 384,403 kilometers
Diameter About 3476 kilometers (about 1/4 Earth's diameter)
Circumference About 10,927 kilometers
Surface area About 37,943,000 square kilometers
Rotation period 27 days, 7 hours, 43 minutes
Revolution period around Earth 29 days, 12 hours, 44 minutes
Length of day and night About 14 Earth-days each
Surface gravity About 1/6 Earth's gravity
Mass 1/81 Earth's mass
Volume 1/50 Earth's volume

Figure 4–13 *Astronaut James Irwin explores the moon in a Lunar Rover. The surface of the moon has changed very little since Galileo studied it in 1609. What evidence of their presence did the Apollo astronauts leave on the moon?*

Figure 4–14 *Here you see a moon rock brought back to Earth by the Apollo astronauts. What have scientists learned about the moon by studying these rocks?*

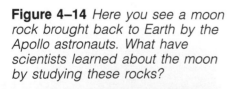

dark areas Galileo saw through his telescope. He called them **maria** (MAHR-ee-uh). *Maria* (singular, *mare*) is the Latin word for seas. Although the name maria seems to indicate that there is water on the moon, scientists now know that the moon has no surface water. Why do you think Galileo called the plains maria?

Among the most striking features of the moon are its many craters. Craters ranging in size from microscopic to hundreds of kilometers across cover the moon's surface. One of the largest craters on the moon is called Copernicus. (Many craters are named for famous scientists. Copernicus was a Polish astronomer who first stated the theory that Earth and the other planets revolve around the sun.) The crater Copernicus is approximately 91 kilometers in diameter. Imagine a crater about the same distance across as the distance between Houston, Texas, and Galveston, Texas. Most of the moon's craters are in the highlands. Few craters are located in the maria.

Scientists think that most craters were formed by the continuous bombardment of meteorites. These meteorites blasted out craters when they hit the moon. A few of the craters, however, seem to be the result of volcanic activity. In fact, the maria are filled with hardened rock that may have flowed into the plains as hot lava billions of years ago. And lava comes from active volcanoes.

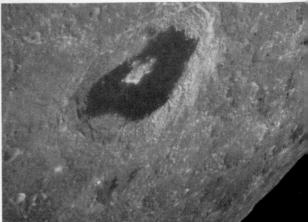

Figure 4–15 *Meteorites have been crashing into the moon for billions of years and have carved out many craters. Here you see the large crater Tsiolkovsky on the far side of the moon (right).*

Other evidence that the moon once had active volcanoes may be the long valleys, or **rilles,** that crisscross much of its surface. Hadley Rille is one such valley. It is about 113 kilometers long. Because there was no running water to carve the rilles, they might have been cut into the moon's surface by rivers of flowing lava. Another possible explanation is that the rilles may be cracks caused by moonquakes. Or the rilles may have opened up billions of years ago when the moon's hot surface cooled and shrank. Whatever caused the rilles, scientists agree that today's cold and inactive moon was once hot and active.

Movements of the Moon

As the Earth revolves around the sun, the moon revolves around the Earth in an elliptical orbit. At **perigee** (PEHR-uh-jee), the point of the moon's orbit closest to the Earth, it is about 350,000 kilometers from the Earth. At **apogee** (AP-uh-jee), the point of the moon's orbit farthest from the Earth, it is about 400,000 kilometers away.

Like the sun, the moon seems to move west across the sky. This apparent movement is caused by the Earth's rotation. When viewed against a background of stars, however, the actual movement of the moon eastward can be observed. You can

Figure 4–16 *This photograph of the far side of the moon clearly shows some of the thousands of craters scattered across the moon's surface.*

prove this by observing the moon when it is at the western edge of a cluster of stars. If you observe carefully for several hours, the moon's eastward movement can be seen as it passes in front of each star, one after the other.

Recall that it takes the Earth about 24 hours to rotate once on its axis. The moon takes much longer. The moon rotates once on its axis every 27.3 days. This is the same amount of time it takes the moon to revolve once around the Earth. Thus the moon's period of rotation is the same as its period of revolution. This means that a day on the moon is just as long as a year on the moon! As a result, the same side of the moon always faces toward the Earth. For many years, scientists could observe only the side of the moon that faces the Earth. Then the Lunar Orbiter space probe photographed the far side of the moon for the first time. The astronauts of the Apollo 8 mission, which circled the moon, were the first humans to see the far side directly. The entire surface of the moon has now been photographed. These photographs show a bleak, lifeless landscape of boulders, craters, plains, and valleys.

Origin of the Moon

One of the most interesting questions scientists have asked about the moon is: Where did the moon come from? There are several theories concerning the moon's origin. According to one theory, the moon may have been formed millions or billions of kilometers away from the Earth and later "captured" by the Earth's gravity. Most scientists, however, do not think that is what happened. Another theory is that the moon formed from the same swirling cloud of gas and dust from which the sun, Earth, and other planets were formed. Indeed, the composition of the moon is similar enough to the composition of the Earth to indicate that they could have formed from the same material.

Probably the most likely explanation for the origin of the moon is that the moon was "born" when a giant asteroid the size of the planet Mars struck the early Earth, tearing a chunk of material from the planet. According to this theory, the Pacific Ocean may be the hole left when the moon was torn from the Earth. This explanation, based on evidence from moon rocks, would explain why the moon is so similar to Earth and yet has no water. Any water in the material that was blasted off the Earth would have been vaporized (turned into a gas) when the material was blown into orbit. When the material came together again to form the moon, there would have been no water left.

Scientists are still not sure how the moon was formed. But clues gathered by astronauts and robot space probes are helping scientists to solve the mystery of the moon's origin.

4–2 Section Review

1. What are the main characteristics of the moon?
2. How might the moon's craters and rilles have formed?
3. Why is a day on the moon the same length as a year on the moon?
4. Describe three possible theories to explain the origin of the moon.

Critical Thinking—*Making Inferences*
5. Why is the distance between the Earth and the moon usually given as an average?

CAREERS

Aerospace Engineer

Engineers are people who make things work. The people who design spacecraft and satellites are **aerospace engineers.** They may plan and develop navigation and communications systems, scientific instruments, and safety devices. Aerospace engineers will design safe and comfortable space stations for the twenty-first century.

A career in aerospace engineering requires high school courses in physics, trigonometry, and geometry, as well as a college degree in engineering. To learn more about a career in aerospace engineering, write to the National Aeronautics and Space Administration, Johnson Space Center, Houston, TX 77058.

Guide for Reading

Focus on this question as you read.

▶ How are the motions of the Earth, the moon, and the sun related to the moon's phases and to eclipses?

4–3 The Earth, the Moon, and the Sun

We can think about the motions of the Earth and the motions of the moon separately. Usually, however, scientists consider the motions of the Earth–moon system as a whole. As the Earth moves in its yearly revolution around the sun, the moon moves in its monthly revolution around the Earth. At the same time, both the Earth and the moon rotate on their axes. Gravitational attraction keeps the moon in orbit around the Earth and the Earth in orbit around the sun. **The relative motions of the Earth, the moon, and the sun result in the changing appearance of the moon as seen from the Earth and the occasional blocking of the sun's light.**

Phases of the Moon

The moon revolves around the Earth. The revolution of the moon causes the moon to appear to change shape in the sky. The different shapes are called phases of the moon. The phases of the moon are shown in Figure 4–17. The moon goes through all its phases every 29.5 days.

Why does the moon go through phases? The moon does not shine by its own light. Rather, the moon reflects sunlight toward the Earth. The phase of the moon you see depends on where the moon is in relation to the sun and the Earth. Refer to Figure 4–17 as you read the description that follows.

When the moon comes between the sun and the Earth, the side of the moon facing the Earth is in darkness. The moon is not visible in the sky. This phase is called the new moon. Sometimes the new moon is faintly visible because it is bathed in earthshine. Earthshine is sunlight reflected off the Earth onto the moon.

As the moon continues to move in its orbit around the Earth, more of the lighted side of the moon becomes visible. First a slim, curved slice called a crescent appears. This is the waxing crescent phase. The moon is said to be waxing when the lighted area appears to grow larger. When the lighted area appears to grow smaller, the moon is said to be waning.

ACTIVITY DOING

Observing the Moon

The best time to observe the moon is on the second or third day after the first-quarter phase. At this time, the moon is in a good position in the evening sky. Many surface features are clearly visible because the moon is not reflecting full light toward the Earth. Details are easier to see.

1. Using binoculars or a small telescope and a labeled photograph of the moon, locate some of the most prominent surface features on the moon.

2. Draw a sketch of the moon and label the features you were able to identify.

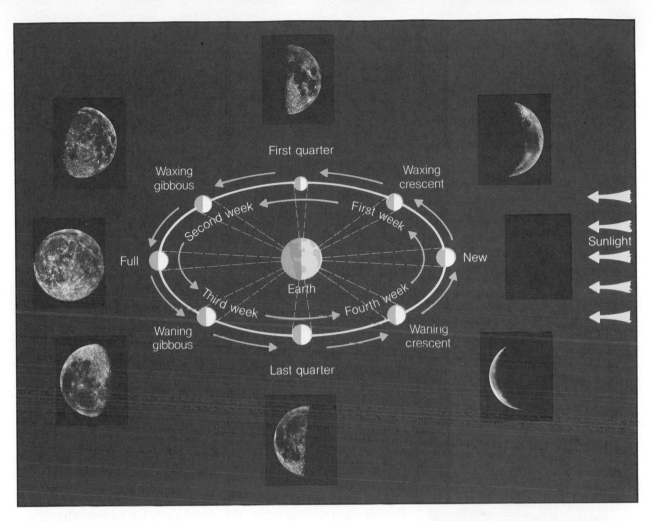

Figure 4–17 *The eight phases of the moon you see from Earth depend on where the moon is in relation to the sun and the Earth. How many days does it take for the moon to pass through all eight phases?*

About a week after the new moon, the moon has traveled a quarter of the way around the Earth. At this time, half the moon appears lighted. This phase is the first-quarter phase. As the days pass, more of the lighted area can be seen during the waxing gibbous phase.

About two weeks after the new moon, the entire lighted side of the moon is visible in the sky. This phase is called the full moon. The Earth is then between the moon and the sun. The moon takes another two weeks to pass through the waning-gibbous, last-quarter, and waning-crescent phases, and back to the new moon. The phases of the moon then start all over again. What phase of the moon was visible to you last night?

Eclipses

More than 2000 years ago, a great war was about to begin. The two armies faced each other across a vast plain. Suddenly, the sky turned dark. The sun seemed to be swallowed up. Both armies thought the sun's disappearance was a sign that they should not fight. Although the sun soon reappeared, the frightened soldiers went home without fighting. There was no battle that day. The soldiers never knew that what they had witnessed was not a sign but one of Earth's most dramatic natural events—an eclipse.

As the moon revolves around the Earth and the Earth and the moon together revolve around the sun, they occasionally block out some of the sun's light. The long, cone-shaped shadows that result extend thousands of kilometers into space. Sometimes the moon moves into the Earth's shadow. At other times the moon casts its shadow onto the Earth. Each event results in an eclipse.

There are two types of eclipses. The two types of eclipses are named depending on which body—the sun or the moon—is eclipsed, or blocked. A **solar eclipse** occurs when the new moon comes directly between the sun and the Earth. As the Earth moves into the moon's shadow, sunlight is blocked from reaching the Earth. Any shadow has two parts. The small, inner shadow is called the **umbra** (UHM-bruh). The larger, outer shadow is called the **penumbra** (pih-NUHM-bruh). Only people directly in the path of the umbra see a total solar eclipse, in which the sun is completely blocked out. People in the penumbra see a partial solar eclipse, in which only part of the sun is blocked out.

As you have read, a new moon occurs once a month. But as you probably know from experience, this is not true for a solar eclipse. Why is there not a solar eclipse once every month? The answer is that the orbit of the moon is slightly tilted in relation to the orbit of the Earth. A solar eclipse takes place only when the new moon is directly between the Earth and the sun, which happens only rarely.

To anyone who has ever seen a total solar eclipse, the experience is awe-inspiring. When the sky begins to darken, birds are fooled into thinking it is evening, and so they stop singing. Dogs begin to howl. The air temperature drops sharply. For a few minutes, day becomes night. If you are ever fortunate enough to view a solar eclipse, you must remember one very important rule. Never look directly at the sun. Your eyes may be burned by

Figure 4–18 *The magnificent pearly light of the sun's corona is visible during a total solar eclipse.*

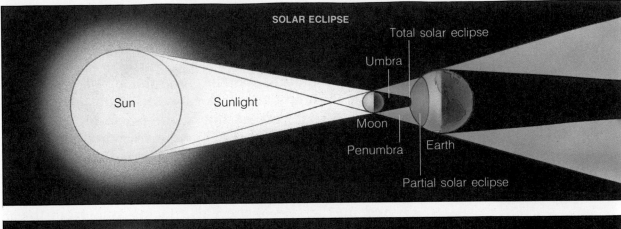

SOLAR ECLIPSE

Total solar eclipse
Umbra
Sun
Sunlight
Moon
Earth
Penumbra
Partial solar eclipse

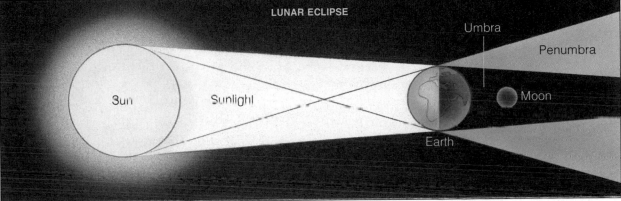

LUNAR ECLIPSE

Umbra
Penumbra
Sun
Sunlight
Earth
Moon

the sun's rays—even when they do not appear to be visible—and you may be blinded.

The second type of eclipse occurs when the Earth comes directly between the sun and the full moon. This event is called a **lunar eclipse.** A lunar eclipse takes place when the moon passes through the Earth's shadow. When the moon moves through the umbra, a total lunar eclipse occurs. When the moon moves through the penumbra, a partial lunar eclipse occurs. Earth's shadow falling on the full moon dims the moon's glow to a dark coppery color. This eerie reddish color results when sunlight reflected off the moon is bent as it passes through Earth's atmosphere.

Figure 4–19 *During a solar eclipse, the moon passes between the sun and the Earth. During a lunar eclipse, the Earth passes between the sun and the moon. When does a total eclipse of the moon occur?*

Tides

Because the moon is close to the Earth, there is a gravitational attraction between the Earth and the moon. As a result of the gravitational pull of the Earth on the moon, the side of the moon facing the Earth has a distinct bulge. But the moon also exerts a gravitational pull on the Earth. This pull results in the rise and fall of the oceans as the moon moves in its orbit around the Earth.

Activity Bank

What Causes High Tides?, p. 754

If you have ever spent a day at the beach, you probably noticed that the level of the ocean at the shoreline did not stay the same during the day. For about six hours, the ocean level rises on the beach. Then, for another six hours, the ocean level falls. The rise and fall of the oceans are called **tides.**

As the moon's gravity pulls on the Earth, it causes the oceans to bulge. The oceans bulge in two places: on the side of the Earth facing the moon and on the side of the Earth facing away from the moon. Each of these bulges causes a high tide.

At the same time that the high tides occur, low tides occur between the two bulges. The diagram in Figure 4–20 shows the positions of high tides and low tides on the Earth. Because the Earth rotates on its axis every 24 hours, the moon's gravity pulls on different parts of the Earth at different times of the day. So at a given place on the Earth, there are two high tides and two low tides every 24 hours. But because the moon rises about 50 minutes later each day, the high and the low tides are also 50 minutes later each day.

Some high tides are higher than other high tides. For example, during the full moon and the new moon phases, the high tides are higher than at other times. These higher tides are called **spring tides.** Spring tides occur because the sun and the moon are in a direct line with the Earth. The increased

Figure 4–20 *The pull of the moon's gravity causes tides. During a 12-hour period, Los Angeles moves from a high tide (left) to a low tide (center) to another high tide (right). At the same time, the moon moves in its orbit. As a result, the tides occur slightly later each day.*

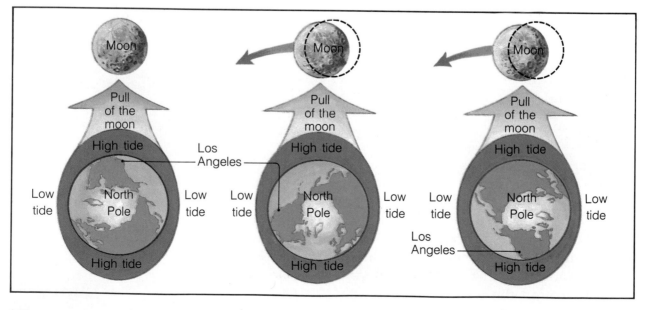

Figure 4–21 *At high tide, boats float serenely at their moorings in the Bay of Fundy in Nova Scotia (left). A few hours later, at low tide, the boats are left sitting in the mud (right).*

effect of the sun's gravity on the Earth causes the ocean bulges to be larger than usual.

When the moon is at the first and last quarter phases, its gravitational pull on the oceans is partially canceled by the sun's gravitational pull. This results in high tides that are lower than usual. These lower high tides are called **neap tides.** What is the position of the sun and the moon with respect to each other during neap tides?

The varying distance between the Earth and the moon as the moon moves in its orbit also affects the tides. The closer the moon is to the Earth, the greater the pull of the moon's gravity on the Earth. If the moon is at perigee during a new moon or a full moon, extremely high tides and low tides will occur.

4–3 Section Review

1. How is the relative motion of the Earth, the moon, and the sun related to the phases of the moon? To eclipses?
2. When would you be able to see a lunar eclipse? A solar eclipse?
3. How does the moon affect tides on the Earth?

Critical Thinking—*Relating Concepts*
4. Why does a lunar eclipse occur either two weeks before or two weeks after a total solar eclipse?

4–4 The Space Age

The first exciting step into space was taken on October 4, 1957. On that historic day, a Soviet rocket boosted *Sputnik 1,* the world's first artificial satellite, into Earth orbit. The Space Age had begun!

Since that day, thousands of artificial satellites have been placed in orbit around the Earth. Astronauts have gone to the moon and returned. People have lived and worked in Earth orbit for extended periods of time. Slowly, humans are taking their first tentative steps beyond the home planet and into the solar system. At the same time, we are learning more about our planet and finding ways to improve our lives.

Artificial Satellites

Artificial satellites are satellites built by people. Like the moon, which is Earth's natural satellite, artificial satellites travel just fast enough so that they neither escape the Earth's gravity nor fall back to the Earth's surface. There are several different types of satellites orbiting the Earth. **Communications satellites, weather satellites, navigation satellites, and scientific satellites are among the artificial satellites that orbit the Earth today.** Each of these types of satellites has a specific function.

Figure 4–22 *In spite of problems with its main mirror, astronomers hope the* Hubble Space Telescope *will reveal many secrets about the universe. This view is from inside the Space Shuttle as the telescope was being held by the robot arm before being released from the cargo bay.*

COMMUNICATIONS SATELLITES   Many of the satellites orbiting the Earth are communications satellites. Communications satellites beam television programs, radio messages, telephone conversations, and other kinds of information all over the world. You can think of a communications satellite as a relay station in space. The satellite receives a signal from a transmitting station on Earth. The satellite then beams the signal to a receiving station somewhere else on Earth. In this way, information is quickly transmitted from one place to another, even on the other side of the world.

Communications satellites are often placed in **geosynchronous** (jee-oh-SIHNG-kruh-nuhs) **orbit.** A geosynchronous orbit is one in which the satellite revolves around the Earth at a rate equal to the Earth's rotation rate. As a result, the satellite stays in one place above a certain point on the Earth's surface. Three such satellites placed equal distances apart at an altitude of about 35,000 kilometers above the Earth can relay signals to any place on Earth.

WEATHER SATELLITES   Artificial weather satellites have greatly improved our ability to track weather patterns and forecast weather conditions all over the world. By studying and charting weather patterns, scientists can predict the weather with greater accuracy than ever before. These predictions are particularly important in tracking dangerous storms such as hurricanes. Through the use of weather satellites, scientists today can better predict when and where a hurricane will strike. This information gives people in the path of a hurricane time to protect themselves and their property and often saves lives.

NAVIGATION SATELLITES   Navigation satellites are another type of artificial satellite. They send precise, continuous signals to ships and airplanes. Using information from navigation satellites, sailors and pilots can determine their exact locations within seconds. This information is especially useful during storms when other kinds of navigation equipment may not provide accurate information. Someday it may even be possible for cars and trucks to use navigation satellites to pinpoint their locations.

SCIENTIFIC SATELLITES   Many different types of scientific satellites now orbit the Earth. Long before

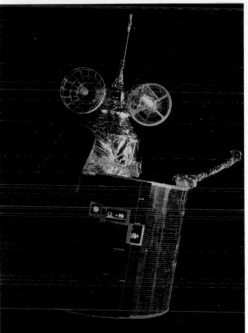

Figure 4–23 *A communications satellite floats above Africa after being released into orbit by the Space Shuttle* Columbia *(top). The GOES satellite makes it possible for meteorologists to track the paths of severe storms (bottom). What type of satellite is GOES?*

Figure 4–24 *Advance warning of a hurricane provided by weather satellites helps to prevent property damage and may even save lives. Manhattan is visible in the center of this satellite map of New York City and the surrounding area.*

Sputnik, scientists looked forward to the day when they could observe the Earth and the universe from orbiting satellites. They thought scientific satellites would help them to solve old mysteries and to make new discoveries about the universe. And they were correct!

In 1958, the first satellite launched by the United States, *Explorer 1,* discovered the Van Allen radiation belts around the Earth. Since that time, other scientific satellites have added greatly to our knowledge of the universe. One satellite in particular—the Infrared Astronomy Satellite, or *IRAS*—has solved many mysteries of the universe. *IRAS* has found evidence of planetary systems forming around distant stars, as well as evidence of massive black holes at the center of the Milky Way and other galaxies. (A black hole is a collapsed star that is so dense that nothing—not even light—can escape its grip.)

Other scientific satellites focus their attention on Earth. In 1991, the Upper Atmosphere Research Satellite was sent into orbit to study the Earth's protective ozone layer. This satellite was the first in a series of environmental science satellites launched as part of Mission to Planet Earth. Mission to Planet Earth is a long-term research program that will use scientific satellites to study the Earth's environment.

Laboratories in Space

In 1973, the United States launched Skylab into orbit. Skylab was a space station designed to allow astronauts to perform experiments in space. Astronauts could dock their spacecraft with Skylab and enter its laboratory. Later the astronauts could re-enter their spacecraft and return to Earth with their data. Visiting crews aboard Skylab made detailed studies of the sun, conducted several health-related experiments, and learned to work in space. Skylab was the United States' first laboratory in space.

Today Spacelab has taken the place of Skylab. Spacelab is a laboratory that is designed to be carried into orbit by the Space Shuttle. The laboratory can be fitted with different types of scientific equipment, depending on the types of experiments being performed.

In 1986, the Soviet Union launched a space station called *Mir*. (The Russian word *mir* means peace.) Space station *Mir* was designed as a series of modules that could be added to the original basic module. Today, *Mir* consists of four permanent modules. Eventually, two more modules may be added on. Cosmonauts, who often remain on the space station for months, perform a variety of scientific experiments aboard *Mir*.

Mir is now the largest and most complex space station ever to orbit the Earth. The United States, however, is planning to build its own space station, possibly as a joint venture with Russia, Japan, and several other nations. The space station will be built in orbit from parts carried into space by the Space Shuttle. Someday the space station may serve as a base for return trips to the moon and for the exploration of Mars.

Figure 4–25 *The* Mir *space station orbits 320 kilometers above the Earth (bottom right). Here you see an artist's idea of what a United States space station might look like (bottom left). Astronaut Mae Jemison performs experiments in the science module of Spacelab J inside the cargo bay of the Space Shuttle* Endeavour *(top).*

Figure 4–26 *Multilayer insulation was developed to protect experiments in the Space Shuttle's open cargo bay. It is now used to make cold weather clothing. The Newtsuit, an experimental diving suit made possible by space technology, will be used as a model for twenty-first century space suits. The bicyclist is wearing a miniature insulin pump first developed for NASA.*

Space Technology Spinoffs

Although most of the major discoveries of the space program have been made far from the Earth, many aspects of space technology have practical applications. Because these applications have been "spun off" the space program, they are called space technology spinoffs. They owe their existence to the exploration of space. Thousands of spinoffs—from heart pacemakers to lightweight tennis rackets—have resulted from applications of space technology.

In 1967, NASA scientists and engineers searched for a fabric to use in spacesuits. The fabric would have to be strong enough to withstand the extreme temperature variations in space and yet flexible enough to fashion into a spacesuit. It was not long before such a fabric was invented. Astronauts walking in space and on the moon found themselves dressed properly—and safely—for conditions in space. Soon after, the same fabric was used to make roofs for a department store in California, an entertainment center in Florida, and a football stadium in Michigan.

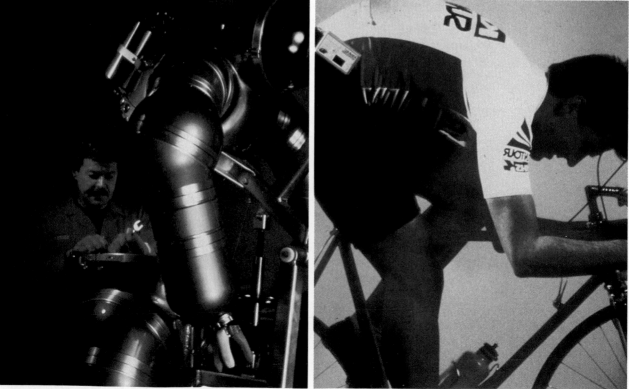

An astronaut exposed to direct sunlight in space runs the risk of overheating. To reduce the danger of overheating, space scientists developed various devices to be fitted into spacesuits. One of these devices was a gel packet that draws excess heat away from the body. These gel packets are now used by marathon runners to absorb excess heat from their foreheads, necks, and wrists.

One of the questions that puzzled scientists was how the human body would react to the new environment of space. To find the answers, scientists designed a series of automatic monitoring devices that would relay to Earth an astronaut's blood pressure, heart rate, and other vital statistics. Such devices are now used by paramedics when they answer emergency calls. These devices provide rapid and accurate information about a patient's condition. Such information can often mean the difference between life and death.

The message seems clear. Space technology—even if it is intended for use far beyond the frontiers of Earth—may have practical applications for billions of people who will never get farther from the Earth's surface than an energetic leap can take them.

ACTIVITY

WRITING

Space Technology Facilities

Space-technology facilities are located throughout the world. Some of those run by NASA in the United States are listed below. Choose one that sounds interesting to you and find out more about that facility. Write a brief report of your findings. Be sure to include where the facility is located, what technological development occurs there, and what the plans are for future research.

Goddard Space Flight Center
Jet Propulsion Laboratory
Kennedy Space Center
Langley Research Center
Lewis Research Center
Marshall Space Flight Center

4–4 Section Review

1. What are four kinds of artificial satellites? Describe the basic function of each.
2. How can space technology be beneficial to people? Why are applications of space technology called spinoffs?
3. Describe one practical application for each of the following: the fabric used in spacesuits; gel packets used to keep astronauts from overheating; automatic monitoring devices used to keep track of an astronaut's vital signs.

Critical Thinking—*Applying Concepts*

4. Explain what you think is meant by the following statement: "The space program is a down-to-Earth success."

Laboratory Investigation

Observing the Apparent Motion of the Sun

Problem

How can the sun's apparent motion in the sky be determined by observing changes in the length and direction of a shadow?

Materials *(per student)*

wooden stick and base
piece of cardboard, 25 cm x 25 cm
compass
wide-tip felt pen
metric ruler

Procedure

1. Place the stick attached to a base in the middle of a piece of cardboard. Trace the outline of the base on the cardboard so that you will be able to put it in the same position each time you make an observation of the sun.

2. Place the stick and the cardboard on flat ground in a sunny spot.

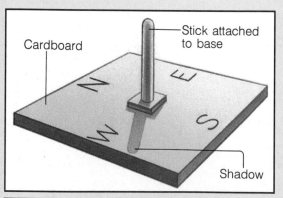

Cardboard
Stick attached to base
N E
S W
Shadow

3. Using the compass, locate north, south, east, and west. Write the appropriate directions near the edges of the cardboard.

4. With the felt pen, trace the shadow of the stick on the cardboard. Write the time of day along the line. Measure the length of the shadow. Determine in which direction the shadow is pointing. Determine the position of the sun in the sky. **CAUTION:** *Do not look directly at the sun!* Record your observations in a data table similar to the one shown here.

5. Repeat step 4 five more times throughout the day. Be sure to include morning, noon, and afternoon observations.

Observations

1. In which direction does the sun appear to move across the sky?

2. In which direction does the shadow move?

3. At what time of day is the shadow the longest? The shortest?

Analysis and Conclusions

1. Why does the length of the shadow change during the day?

2. What actually causes the sun's apparent motion across the sky?

3. **On Your Own** How is it possible to tell time using a sundial? Turn your shadow stick into a sundial by writing the correct time of day in the appropriate places on the cardboard.

Time of Day	Shadow Length	Direction of Shadow	Location of Sun

Study Guide

Summarizing Key Concepts

4–1 The Earth in Space

▲ The rotation and revolution of the Earth affect both day and night and the seasons on Earth.

▲ The apparent motions of the sun and the moon in the sky are caused by the rotation of the Earth.

▲ The tilt of the Earth's axis, combined with its revolution, causes the seasons.

▲ The Earth is surrounded by a magnetic field called the magnetosphere.

4–2 The Earth's Moon

▲ The moon has neither water nor an atmosphere.

▲ The main features of the moon are highlands, maria, craters, and rilles.

▲ The moon revolves around the Earth in an elliptical orbit.

▲ There are three possible theories to explain how the moon was formed.

4–3 The Earth, the Moon, and the Sun

▲ The relative motions of the Earth, the moon, and the sun result in the phases of the moon and in eclipses.

▲ As the moon revolves around the Earth, its shape appears to change; the moon goes through all its phases in 29.5 days.

▲ There are two types of eclipses: solar eclipses and lunar eclipses.

▲ The gravitational pull of the moon on the Earth causes the tides.

4–4 The Space Age

▲ Artificial satellites include communications satellites, weather satellites, navigation satellites, and scientific satellites.

▲ Space stations, such as Skylab, Spacelab, *Mir,* and *Freedom,* serve as laboratories in space.

▲ Space technology spinoffs have many practical applications on Earth.

Reviewing Key Terms

Define each term in a complete sentence.

4–1 The Earth in Space
summer solstice
winter solstice
vernal equinox
autumnal equinox
magnetosphere
Van Allen radiation
    belts
aurora

4–2 The Earth's Moon
highlands
maria
rille
perigee
apogee

4–3 The Earth, the Moon, and the Sun
solar eclipse
umbra
penumbra
lunar eclipse
tide
spring tide
neap tide

4–4 The Space Age
geosynchronous orbit

Chapter Review

Content Review

Multiple Choice

Choose the letter of the answer that best completes each statement.

1. Smooth lowland areas on the moon are
   a. maria.
   c. highlands.
   b. rilles.
   d. craters.
2. The phase of the moon that follows the waning-crescent phase is called the
   a. full moon.
   c. waxing crescent.
   b. new moon.
   d. last quarter.
3. The sun reaches its highest point in the sky on the
   a. summer solstice.
   c. vernal equinox.
   b. winter solstice.
   d. autumnal equinox.
4. Which of the following are examples of space technology spinoffs?
   a. heart pacemakers
   b. heat-absorbing gel packets
   c. blood-pressure monitors
   d. all of these
5. The magnetic field around the Earth is called the
   a. solar wind.
   c. magnetosphere.
   b. aurora australis.
   d. aurora borealis.

6. The Earth's axis is tilted at an angle of
   a. 90°.
   c. 23½°.
   b. 45°.
   d. 30°.
7. Of the following, the one that is a natural satellite of the Earth is
   a. the moon.
   b. a communications satellite.
   c. a scientific satellite.
   d. a weather satellite.
8. The first satellite launched by the United States was
   a. *IRAS.*
   c. *Explorer 1.*
   b. Skylab.
   d. *Sputnik.*
9. Every four years, an extra day is added to the month of
   a. January.
   c. March.
   b. February.
   d. December.
10. Another name for the aurora borealis is the
    a. magnetosphere.
    c. northern lights.
    b. Van Allen belts.
    d. southern lights.

True or False

If the statement is true, write "true." If it is false, change the underlined word or words to make the statement true.

1. The Earth rotates in a <u>clockwise</u> direction.
2. When the Northern Hemisphere is tilted toward the sun, it is <u>summer</u> in the Southern Hemisphere.
3. The Earth's magnetic poles <u>are</u> in the same place as the geographic poles.
4. The longest day of the year occurs on the <u>winter</u> solstice.
5. The moon goes through all its phases every <u>30</u> days.
6. The outer part of a shadow is called the <u>umbra</u>.
7. Exceptionally high tides that occur during a full-moon phase are called <u>neap</u> tides.

Concept Mapping

Complete the following concept map for Section 4–1. Then construct a concept map for the entire chapter.

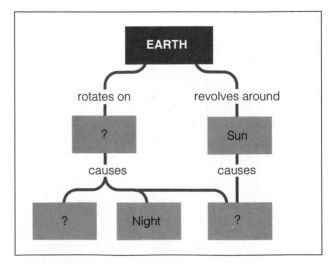

170

Concept Mastery

Discuss each of the following in a brief paragraph.

1. Explain why one side of the moon always faces toward the Earth while the other side always faces away from the Earth.
2. Describe the functions of the various kinds of artificial satellites.
3. How is the direction of the Earth's rotation related to the apparent motion of the sun across the sky?
4. What is the difference between a solstice and an equinox?
5. Explain why there are tides on the Earth.
6. Why should you never look directly at the sun?
7. Why is an Earth year (the time it takes the Earth to complete one revolution around the sun) different from a calendar year? What is done to make up for this difference?
8. What is the difference between a solar eclipse and a lunar eclipse? When can you see a total solar eclipse? A total lunar eclipse?

Critical Thinking and Problem Solving

Use the skills you have developed in this chapter to answer each of the following.

1. **Applying concepts** Lunar eclipses occur during a full moon. The moon goes through a full-moon phase every month. Yet lunar eclipses are fairly rare. Why is there not a lunar eclipse every month? *Hint:* You may want to use models to arrive at your answer.
2. **Making predictions** Describe how living conditions on the Earth might change if the Earth's axis were straight up and down instead of tilted.
3. **Interpreting diagrams** Identify each of the phases of the moon in the diagram.
4. **Identifying relationships** The moon seems to move westward across the sky. But when it is viewed against the background of stars, it appears to move eastward. Explain why this is so.
5. **Making comparisons** How is the Earth like a magnet?
6. **Using the writing process** Write a science-fiction story describing what you think life would be like on an orbiting space station or a moonbase in the twenty-first century.

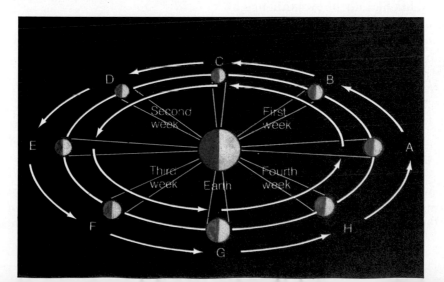

SCIENCE GAZETTE

IAN K. SHELTON DISCOVERS AN EXPLODING S*T*A*R

The time: 170,000 years ago. Much of North America is covered by huge sheets of ice. Herds of woolly mammoths and other unusual creatures roam the land. From time to time, the ancestors of modern humans gaze up at the stars twinkling in the night sky. Although these human ancestors have no way of knowing, in a galaxy 170,000 light years away a giant star is exploding.

The time: February 24, 1987. Ian K. Shelton, a young Canadian scientist, prepares to spend another long night at the Cerro Tololo Inter-American Observatory in Chile, South America. Shelton assumes it will be another quiet night. But little does he know that light produced when that giant star exploded more than 170,000 years ago will finally reach the Earth this night!

Shelton has been studying photographs of a small galaxy called the Large Magellanic Cloud. By early morning, he is ready to call it a night. "I had decided," he recalls, "that enough was enough. It was time to go to bed." Yet before going to sleep, Shelton decided to develop one last photograph.

As he studied the last photograph, Shelton realized there was something most unusual in the picture. A bright spot could be seen. Photographs taken of the same area on previous nights had not shown this bright spot. "I was sure there was some flaw on the photograph," he recalled. But then he did something astronomers rarely do. He went outside and looked up at the area of the sky he had just photographed. And without the telescope, or even a pair of binoculars, Shelton saw the same bright spot in the Large Magellanic Cloud. He knew right away that this was something new and unusual.

Shelton could hardly believe what he was seeing. "For more than three hours," he explained later, "I tried several logical explanations. It took me a long time to actually accept that what I had just seen was a supernova."

Supernovas are the last stage in the life of certain giant stars. As the star dies it begins to contract. Then, in its last moments of life, the star explodes and sends matter and energy blasting through the universe.

During a supernova, a star reaches temperatures of billions of degrees Celsius. At those temperatures, atoms in the star fuse and new elements are produced. The light

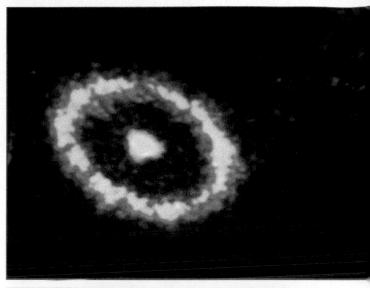

◀ ▲ **On February 24, 1987, Ian K. Shelton observed the supernova pictured top left. The bottom left photograph, taken three years before, shows the star that became Supernova 1987A. The photograph above shows a view of Supernova 1987A taken by the Hubble Space Telescope in 1990. The green ring is gas released before the star exploded and the pink blob is debris from the explosion.**

produced by a supernova is brighter than the light produced by a million normal stars. It was that bright light Shelton observed in 1987, after the light had traveled 170,000 years toward Earth.

Shelton immediately sent telegrams to astronomers all over the world. Observatories in other parts of the world soon confirmed Shelton's discovery. "It's like Christmas," remarked astronomer Stan Woosley from the University of California. This was the first supernova close to the Earth that modern astronomers had ever had a chance to study. A few weeks after the discovery, the new supernova was officially named Supernova 1987A.

Why, you might wonder, is the discovery of a new supernova so important? Many as-

tronomers believe that supernovas cause the birth of new stars. So, by studying supernovas, astronomers can learn a great deal about the life cycles of stars. Also, the elements a supernova produces shower nearby areas of space. In fact, most of the elements on the Earth probably formed some 6 billion years ago during a supernova. "The calcium in our bones, the iron in hemoglobin and the oxygen we all breathe came from explosions like this one," says astronomer Woosley.

For Ian K. Shelton, the discovery of an exploding star would change his life. Shelton knows he owes some of the credit for the discovery to modern technology. "We couldn't conduct modern astronomy without these wonderful instruments," he has said. "But without the romance, most of us would never have been attracted to this wonderful science in the first place. Just look at that beautiful supernova up there. Isn't that enough to make you glad you're alive?"

UNIT TWO
Exploring Planet Earth

As the *Voyager* spacecraft began its epic journey among the planets of the solar system, it sent back a portrait of the Earth and its moon. During its 13-year voyage, the sturdy spacecraft was to send back thousands of stunning images of the outer planets and their moons before disappearing into the depths of space. But of all the planets and moons on *Voyager*'s travels, Planet Earth is unique.

▲ *From the moon, Earth appears as a watery blue planet with swirls of white clouds.*

▲ *This photograph of clouds near the top of the Matterhorn in Switzerland illustrates two features of Earth—landmasses and an atmosphere.*

◄ *Of all the planets, only Earth contains liquid water.*

Of all the planets in our solar system, only Earth has oceans and rivers of liquid water on its surface. And only Earth is surrounded by a blanket of breathable air. In the pages that follow, you will learn about the Earth's oceans, its freshwater lakes and rivers, and the atmosphere that surrounds it. You will also learn about Earth's landmasses—its mountains, plains, and plateaus. And you will take a journey to the center of the Earth to study its interior.

Voyager has given us a valuable glimpse of the worlds that make up the sun's family. In this textbook, you will explore the world that interests us most—our home, Planet Earth.

Raging Iguassu Falls in Brazil demonstrates how Earth's surface is changed by moving water. ▶

Discovery *Activity*

Neighborhood Mapping

Use a large sheet of plain, white paper and colored pencils to draw a map of your neighborhood. Show the location of houses, schools, libraries, streets, and other local features, as well as any natural features such as bodies of water. Include a scale and a key to indicate direction on your neighborhood map.

■ Trade maps with a classmate. Can you find your way around using your classmate's map? Can your classmate use your map to find a specific location in your neighborhood?

■ What features make a map useful?

Earth's Atmosphere

People have walked on the surface of the moon. Machines have landed upon and scratched at the surface of Mars. Rockets have carried satellites on photographic missions into the darkness of space beyond the farthest reaches of our solar system. These voyages of exploration represent great leaps that took the minds—and sometimes even the bodies—of humans far from the comforts of their Earthly home.

Yet people forget that Earth too is a wondrous planet on a fantastic voyage. In just one year's time, Earth will make a complete trip around the sun—taking you, your family and friends, and the remainder of humanity on a fabulous journey. In many ways, Earth is like a giant spacecraft transporting a special cargo of life.

Why is Earth the only planet in our solar system uniquely able to support life? In this chapter you will learn about the Earth's atmosphere—the special envelope of air that surrounds our planet home as it journeys through space. The atmosphere is one reason there is life on Earth.

Journal *Activity*

You and Your World Have you ever thought about being an astronaut? What kind of training do you think you would need to become an astronaut? In what ways do you think life in space would be different from life on Earth? Draw a picture in your journal of what you think it would be like to float in space and describe some of the conditions you would expect to encounter.

Towering clouds are a familiar sight in the Earth's atmosphere.

Guide for Reading

Focus on this question as you read.

▶ *What are some features of planet Earth?*

5–1 A View of Planet Earth: Spheres Within a Sphere

Have you ever seen a carved doll like the one in Figure 5–1? This doll holds some surprises within its painted wooden shell. When it is opened you can see that what appeared to be a single doll is actually a series of dolls, snugly nesting one within the other. These sets of dolls are made in Russia and are part of the folk heritage of the Russian people.

In some ways, the Earth is similar to this set of dolls. What appears to be a simple structure is, upon close examination, found to have many hidden layers of complexity. And along with this complexity comes a kind of awe-inspiring beauty.

Size of the Earth

Exactly how large is planet Earth? Its size can be described by two measurements: its diameter and its circumference. The diameter of the Earth (or the distance from the North Pole to the South Pole through the center) is about 12,740 kilometers. When compared with Jupiter, the largest planet in the solar system with a diameter of 142,700 kilometers, the Earth may not seem to be very large at all. But the Earth is the largest of the inner planets—Mercury, Venus, Earth, and Mars—in the solar system. The diameter of Mars, for example, is only about one-half the diameter of the Earth.

The circumference of the Earth, or the distance around the Earth, is about 40,075 kilometers at the **equator.** The equator is an imaginary line around Earth that divides Earth into two **hemispheres.** These hemispheres are called the Northern Hemisphere and the Southern Hemisphere. In which hemisphere do you live?

Figure 5–1 *Dolls such as these are part of Russian folk heritage. In what way are these dolls similar to planet Earth?*

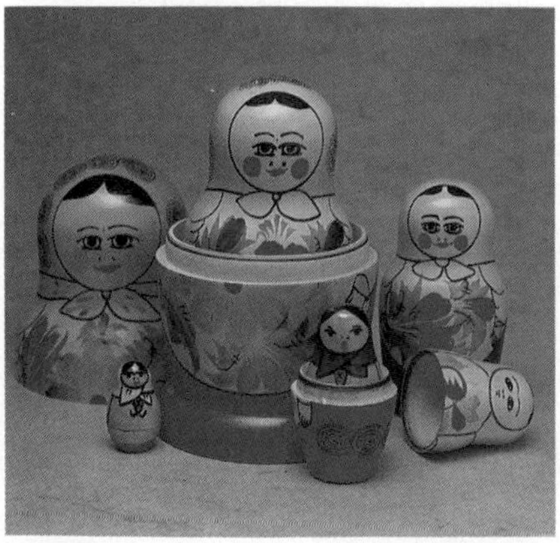

Features of the Earth: The Lithosphere, Hydrosphere, and Atmosphere

The word earth has many meanings. It can mean the ground you walk on or the soil in which plants grow. Most importantly, the word Earth can mean

Figure 5–2 *In this shot of Earth from space you can see the atmosphere, land areas, and oceans. How much greater is the Earth's circumference than its diameter?*

your planet home. Looking at the Earth from space—actually a relatively new way to view the planet—you can appreciate its extraordinary beauty. You can also observe the three main features that make up your "home."

Photographs from space show that the Earth is a beautiful planet indeed. From space the Earth's land areas can be seen easily. The outlines of continents, in the past seen only as two-dimensional drawings on a map, become real when photographed by satellite cameras. From space, the oceans and other bodies of water that cover much of the Earth can clearly be identified. In fact, about 70 percent of the Earth's surface is covered by water. From space, the Earth's atmosphere can be observed, if only indirectly. The clouds in the photograph in Figure 5–2, floating freely above land and water, are part of the normally invisible atmosphere that surrounds the Earth.

The three main features of the Earth are the land, the water, and the air. The land areas of the Earth are part of a solid layer of the Earth known as the crust. Land areas include the seven continents and all other landmasses. Such land areas are clearly visible as part of the Earth's surface. But there is also land that is not visible—land that exists beneath the oceans and beneath the continents. You will learn more about this solid layer of the Earth in Chapter 8. Scientists call all the land on Earth the **lithosphere,** a word that means "rock-sphere." Why do you think this is an appropriate name?

The water on Earth makes up the **hydrosphere.** (The prefix *hydro-* means water.) The hydrosphere includes the Earth's oceans, rivers and streams, ponds and lakes, seas and bays, and other bodies of water. Some of the hydrosphere is frozen in the polar ice caps at the North and South poles, as well as in icebergs and glaciers.

You might be surprised to learn that about 97 percent of the hydrosphere is composed of salt water. The most common salt in salt water is sodium chloride, which you are more familiar with as table salt. You might think that the remaining 3 percent

FACTS ABOUT THE EARTH

Average distance from sun
About 150,000,000 kilometers

Diameter through equator
12,756.32 kilometers

Circumference around equator
40,075.16 kilometers

Surface area
Land area, about 148,300,000 square kilometers, or about 30 percent of total surface area; water area, about 361,800,000 square kilometers, or about 70 percent of total surface area

Rotation period
23 hours, 56 minutes, 4.09 seconds

Revolution period around sun
365 days, 6 hours, 9 minutes, 9.54 seconds

Temperature
Highest, 58°C at Al Aziziyah, Libya; lowest, -90°C at Vostok in Antarctica; average surface temperature, 14°C

Highest and lowest land features
Highest, Mount Everest, 8848 meters above sea level; lowest, shore of Dead Sea, 396 meters below sea level

Ocean depths
Deepest, Mariana Trench in Pacific Ocean southwest of Guam, 11,033 meters below surface; average ocean depth, 3795 meters

Figure 5–3 *These unusual rock formations in Canyonlands National Park, Utah, are part of the Earth's crust.*

Figure 5–4 *Don't let this creek in California fool you. Most of the Earth's fresh water is locked up in the great polar ice caps. Here you see the southern polar cap in Antarctica. To which sphere does the Earth's fresh and salt water belong?*

of the hydrosphere is fresh water that can be used by humans for a variety of purposes. You would not be correct, however. Almost 85 percent of the fresh water on Earth exists as ice locked up in the great polar ice caps. That leaves about 15 percent of the 3 percent as liquid fresh water. And keep in mind that this liquid fresh water is not evenly distributed over the Earth. The deserts of the Earth have very little fresh water, whereas the tropical areas have a great

deal. Remember also that it is liquid water that makes life on this planet possible. Without water, no life would exist on Earth.

The oxygen that you breathe is found in the last great sphere that makes up planet Earth, the **atmosphere** (AT-muhs-feer). The atmosphere is the envelope of gases that surrounds the Earth. The atmosphere protects the Earth and also provides materials necessary to support all forms of life on the Earth. In the next three sections, you will learn more about Earth's atmosphere. In later chapters, you will learn about the other spheres of planet Earth.

5–1 Section Review

1. What are the three main features of the Earth?
2. What percentage of the hydrosphere is fresh water? What percentage of the hydrosphere is available for drinking?
3. What is the envelope of gases that surrounds the Earth called?

Connection—*Astronomy*
4. *Viking* was the name of the lander that explored the surface of Mars. One of its primary missions was to determine if life existed there. What one test do you think *Viking* performed in order to get an answer to this question?

5–2 Development of the Atmosphere

When astronauts walk in space, they must wear space suits. The space suits provide a protective covering. They enclose the astronauts in an artificial environment, providing them with comfortable temperatures as well as with moisture and oxygen. Space suits also protect the astronauts from harmful ultraviolet rays given off by the sun. In a similar way, the atmosphere of the Earth provides protection for you. And it also provides some of the materials necessary to support life on Earth.

Guide for Reading

Focus on these questions as you read.

▶ *How does the atmosphere on Earth today compare with the atmosphere long ago?*

▶ *What gases are present in the atmosphere?*

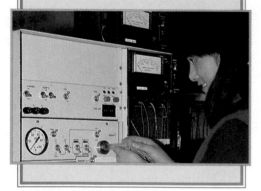
Cameras and other instruments aboard space satellites have provided much data about the structure and composition of the present atmosphere. From this information, and from other studies, scientists have developed a picture of what the Earth's atmosphere may have been like billions of years ago. Scientists are certain that the atmosphere of the Earth has changed greatly over time. And they believe that the present atmosphere is still changing! What are some of the conditions that may be responsible for changes in the atmosphere?

The Past Atmosphere

It is theorized that the Earth's atmosphere 4 billion years ago contained two deadly gases: methane and ammonia. Methane, which is made up of the elements carbon and hydrogen, is a poisonous compound. Ammonia, also poisonous, is composed of the elements nitrogen and hydrogen. There was also some water in the atmosphere 4 billion years ago.

As you well know, the air is no longer deadly. In fact, you could not live without it. How did this important change in the atmosphere occur?

To explain this change, it is necessary to picture the atmosphere 3.8 billion years ago. At that time, sunlight triggered chemical reactions among the methane, ammonia, and water in the air. As a result

Figure 5–5 *Scientists use a variety of tools to study the atmosphere, including weather balloons and satellites orbiting in space. Gases trapped in the ice caps thousands of years ago provide scientists with a glimpse of Earth's ancient atmosphere.*

Figure 5–6 *An artist's idea of what the Earth may have looked like billions of years ago. What two deadly gases were common in the ancient atmosphere?*

of many chemical reactions, new materials formed in the atmosphere. Among the new materials were nitrogen, hydrogen, and carbon dioxide. The methane and ammonia broke down, but the water still remained.

Hydrogen is a very lightweight gas, so lightweight in fact, that it escaped the pull of the Earth's gravity and disappeared into space. That left nitrogen in greatest abundance, as well as carbon dioxide and water vapor. In the upper parts of the ancient atmosphere, sunlight began to break down the water vapor into hydrogen and oxygen gases. The lightweight hydrogen gas again escaped into space. But, the atoms of oxygen gas began to combine with one another to form a gas known as **ozone.** Eventually a layer of ozone gas formed about 30 kilometers above the Earth's surface.

The ozone layer is sometimes referred to as an "umbrella" for life on Earth. This is because the ozone layer absorbs most of the harmful ultraviolet radiation from the sun. Without the protection of the ozone layer, few living things could survive on Earth.

Before the ozone layer formed, the only living things on Earth were microscopic organisms that lived far below the surface of the oceans. Here these

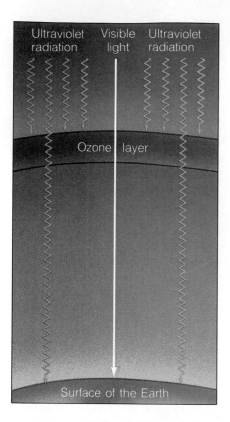

Ultraviolet radiation   Visible light   Ultraviolet radiation

Ozone layer

Surface of the Earth

Figure 5–7 *The ozone layer absorbs most of the sun's harmful ultraviolet radiation before it reaches the Earth's surface. Visible light is not absorbed by the ozone layer.*

organisms were protected from most of the ultraviolet radiation from the sun. After the formation of the ozone layer, certain types of microorganisms called blue-green bacteria started to appear on or near the water's surface. These bacteria used the energy in sunlight to combine carbon dioxide from the air with water to produce food.

A byproduct of this food-making process would change the planet forever. This byproduct was oxygen. Unlike ozone, which formed high in the atmosphere, oxygen remained near the surface of the Earth. It would be this oxygen that animals would later breathe.

In time, green plants began to grow on the land. And they, too, took in carbon dioxide and released oxygen during the food-making process. The oxygen content in the atmosphere increased greatly. Then, around 600 million years ago, the amounts of oxygen and carbon dioxide in the atmosphere began to level off. Since that time, the composition of the atmosphere has remained fairly constant.

Figure 5–8 *Billions of years ago, microscopic organisms such as blue-green bacteria helped to change the Earth's atmosphere by producing oxygen as a byproduct of their food-making process. This increase in the oxygen levels in the atmosphere permitted the evolution of green plants and eventually the animals that feed on green plants.*

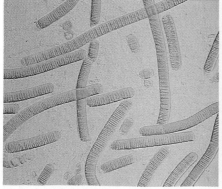

The Present Atmosphere

The atmosphere that surrounds the Earth today contains the gases necessary for the survival of living things. The air you breathe is among the Earth's most important natural resources. What is the air made of?

The atmosphere is a mixture of gases. **The atmospheric gases include nitrogen, oxygen, carbon dioxide, water vapor, argon, and trace gases.** Nitrogen gas makes up about 78 percent of the atmosphere. Another 21 percent of the atmosphere is oxygen. The remaining 1 percent is a combination of carbon dioxide, water vapor, argon, and trace gases. Among the trace gases, which are present in only very small amounts, are neon, helium, krypton, and xenon.

NITROGEN The most abundant gas in the atmosphere is nitrogen. Living things need nitrogen to make proteins. Proteins are complex compounds that contain nitrogen. These compounds are required for the growth and repair of body parts. The muscles of your body are made mostly of protein, as are parts of the skin and internal organs.

Figure 5–9 *This diagram shows the nitrogen cycle. How is nitrogen returned to the soil?*

Nitrogen compounds released

Volcano

Nitrogen compounds

Nitrogen in atmosphere

Nitrogen-fixing blue-green bacteria

Decaying leaves

Animal dies

Nitrogen-fixing bacteria in roots

Bacteria decompose wastes forming nitrogen compounds

Shallow-water sediments

Argon, carbon dioxide, water vapor, and other gases 1%

Oxygen 21%

Nitrogen 78%

Figure 5–10 *The atmosphere is a mixture of many gases. Which two gases make up most of the Earth's atmosphere?*

However, plants and animals are not able to use the nitrogen in the air directly to make proteins. Certain kinds of bacteria that live in the soil are able to combine the nitrogen from the atmosphere with other chemicals to make compounds called nitrates. These bacteria are called nitrogen-fixing bacteria. Plants are able to use the nitrates formed by the nitrogen-fixing bacteria to make plant proteins. In turn, animals get the proteins they need by eating plants.

Nitrogen is returned to the atmosphere when dead animals and plants decay. Decay is the breaking down of dead organisms, usually by bacteria, into simple chemical substances. Thus the organisms that bring about decay return the nitrogen to the atmosphere. The movement of nitrogen from the atmosphere to the soil then to living things and finally back to the atmosphere makes up the nitrogen cycle.

OXYGEN Oxygen is the second most abundant gas in the atmosphere. Oxygen is used directly from the atmosphere by most plants and animals. It is essential for respiration (rehs-puh-RAY-shuhn). During respiration, living things chemically combine oxygen with food. This breaks down the food and releases the energy needed by living things. Why do you think all living things need energy?

Oxygen is also necessary for the combustion, or burning, of fuels such as oil, coal, and wood. Combustion will not take place without oxygen. This is why many fire extinguishers contain special chemicals to fight fires. When sprayed on a fire, the chemicals prevent oxygen from reaching the burning material and supporting any further combustion. Without oxygen, the fire goes out.

CARBON DIOXIDE The amount of carbon dioxide in the atmosphere is very small. However, carbon dioxide is one of the important raw materials used by green plants to make food.

Carbon dioxide is removed from the atmosphere by plants during the food-making process. It is returned to the atmosphere by the respiration of

Figure 5–11 *Bacteria and other decay organisms play an important role, as they remove nitrogen and other substances from dead organisms and return these chemicals to the environment.*

Carbon dioxide used by plants

Carbon dioxide given off by animals

Carbon dioxide given off by decaying leaves

Oxygen given off by plants

Oxygen used by animals

Oxygen from food-making process available to animals

Carbon dioxide from respiration available to plants

plants and animals. The decay of dead plants and animals also returns carbon dioxide to the air.

Scientists believe that the amount of carbon dioxide used by plants equals the amount returned to the atmosphere by respiration, decay, and other natural processes. But the burning of fossil fuels such as oil and coal is adding even more carbon dioxide to the atmosphere. Scientists are concerned that the amount of carbon dioxide in the atmosphere is increasing to a level that may become dangerous. Studies have shown that the increased level of carbon dioxide traps more of the sun's heat energy in the Earth's atmosphere. Thus an increase in the level of carbon dioxide in the air could significantly increase the overall temperature of the Earth.

WATER VAPOR Water vapor in the atmosphere plays an important role in the Earth's weather. Clouds, fog, and dew are weather conditions caused by water vapor in the air. Rain and other forms of precipitation (snow, sleet, and hail) occur when water vapor forms droplets that are heavy enough to fall. Water vapor is also involved in the heating of the atmosphere. Water vapor absorbs heat energy given off by the sun. The amount of water vapor in

Figure 5–12 *Carbon dioxide and oxygen are continuously exchanged among plants and animals. How is oxygen returned to the atmosphere?*

Figure 5–13 *Where would you find more water vapor in the atmosphere—in a rain forest in Hawaii or the sand dunes of the Sahara?*

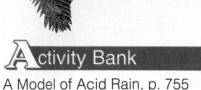

Activity Bank

A Model of Acid Rain, p. 755

ACTIVITY

DISCOVERING

Clean Air Anyone?

1. Spread a thin layer of petroleum jelly on each of three clean microscope slides. With your teacher's permission, place the slides in different locations in and around your school building. Leave the slides in place for several days.

2. Collect the slides and examine each one under a microscope. Count the particles you find. Draw what you observe.

Where was the slide with the fewest particles placed? Where was the slide with the most particles placed?

■ How can you account for the differences?

the atmosphere varies from place to place. In desert regions, the amount of water vapor in the air is usually very small, although most deserts have rainy seasons that last for short periods of time. In tropical regions, the amount of water vapor in the air may be as high as 4 percent. Where else on Earth would you expect to find a great deal of water vapor in the air?

SOLID PARTICLES Many tiny particles of solid material are mixed with the air's gases. These particles are so small that they can float on even the slightest movements of the air. You may have noticed these particles if you have observed a flashlight beam in a darkened room. These particles in the air are dust, smoke, dirt, and even tiny bits of salt. Where do these particles come from?

Every time a wave breaks, tiny particles of salt from ocean water enter the atmosphere and remain suspended in the air. Much of the dust in the air comes from the eruption of volcanoes. In 1883, the massive eruption of Krakatoa, a volcano in the East Indies, spewed huge amounts of volcanic dust and other materials into the air. As a result of this eruption, skies as far away as London became dark. The average temperature of the Earth fell 1.5°C as volcanic dust from this single eruption filled the air, preventing sunlight from warming the atmosphere. You will learn more about volcanoes in Chapter 11.

Dirt and smoke particles are also added to the air by

Figure 5–14 *Volcanoes and factories that burn fossil fuels add solid particles to the atmosphere. How are these bikers in Holland helping to keep the Earth's atmosphere a bit cleaner?*

the actions of people as they burn fuels, and as they drive cars and other vehicles. Factories and power plants that burn fossil fuels also add particles to the air. However, new kinds of smoke stacks reduce the amount of particles being added to the air by actually "scrubbing" the smoke before it is released into the air. Do you have any suggestions about what you and your family and friends can do to reduce the amounts of these particles that affect the quality of the air?

5–2 Section Review

1. What two gases were present in the greatest amounts in the atmosphere of Earth 4 billion years ago?
2. What four gases are present in the greatest amounts in the Earth's atmosphere today?
3. Describe the nitrogen cycle and the water cycle. Why is it important that certain substances in the atmosphere are used over and over again?
4. Why are scientists concerned that the level of carbon dioxide in the air is increasing?

Critical Thinking—*Relating Cause and Effect*
5. How have living organisms changed the composition of the atmosphere over time?

Figure 5–15 *Some pollutants found in the atmosphere include asbestos particles (top) and ash from burning coal (bottom).*

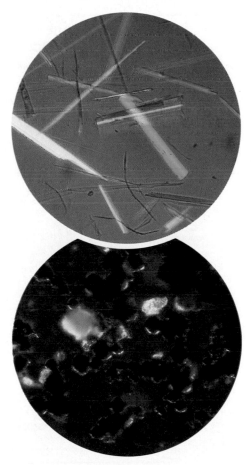

PROBLEM Solving

Protection From the Sun

All life on Earth depends upon the sun. But the sun also poses certain dangers. You learned that the ozone layer acts like a shield that protects organisms on Earth from some of the dangerous radiation given off by the sun. Newspaper and magazine articles, television and radio programs issue warnings—on an almost daily basis—of the dangers posed to the ozone layer by certain chemicals. This graph shows the effects of limiting the release of ozone-damaging chemicals into the atmosphere.

Interpreting Graphs

1. How has the amount of ozone-damaging chemicals changed from 1975 to 1985?

2. What amount of ozone-damaging chemicals is projected to be in the atmosphere in 1995?

3. How does this amount compare with the amount in the atmosphere today?

4. Two meetings proposed controls on the amount of ozone-damaging chemicals that could be released into the atmosphere. What would happen to the amounts of ozone-damaging chemicals released in the air in 2005 according to the London agreement? According to the Montreal agreement?

■ Which agreement offers some protection for the ozone layer?

5. On Your Own Find out what you can do to limit the amounts of ozone-damaging chemicals that are released into the air.

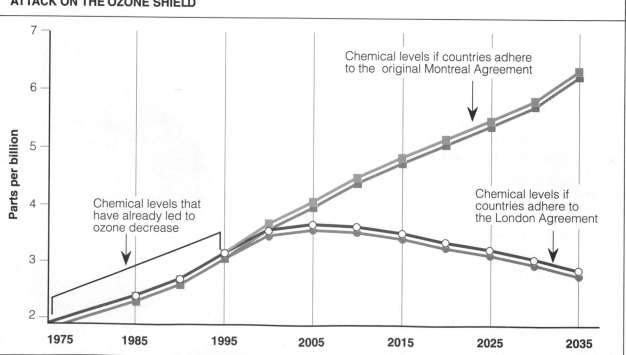

ATTACK ON THE OZONE SHIELD

Chemical levels if countries adhere to the original Montreal Agreement

Chemical levels that have already led to ozone decrease

Chemical levels if countries adhere to the London Agreement

Parts per billion

1975   1985   1995   2005   2015   2025   2035

5–3 Layers of the Atmosphere

If you were able to soar up from the surface of the Earth to the high edge of outer space, you would notice many changes in the atmosphere. The mixture of gases, the temperature, and the electrical and magnetic forces of the atmosphere change as the distance from the Earth's surface increases. For example, there is less oxygen in the upper atmosphere than in the lower atmosphere. You may have seen pictures of mountain climbers wearing oxygen masks when they were climbing very high mountains. They do this because there is only half as much oxygen available 5.5 kilometers above the Earth's surface as there is at the Earth's surface.

If you ever climb a high mountain yourself, you will notice that as you climb upward the air gets colder. At an altitude (height above sea level) of 3 kilometers, you will probably need a heavy jacket to keep warm! The temperature of the air decreases as the altitude increases because the air becomes less dense. That is, there are fewer and fewer particles of air in a given amount of space. The thin, less dense air cannot hold as much heat.

The atmosphere is divided into layers according to major changes in its temperature. The layers of air that surround the Earth are held close to it by the force of gravity. Gravity is a force of attraction by which objects are pulled toward each other. Because of gravity, the layers of air surrounding the Earth push down on the Earth's surface. This push is called air pressure.

The upper layers of air push down on the lower layers. So the air pressure near the surface of the Earth is greater than the air pressure further from the surface. If you have ever flown in an airplane, you may have felt your ears "pop." This popping was caused by a change in air pressure. Where else might you experience a change in air pressure?

It is interesting to note that 99 percent of the total mass of the atmosphere of the Earth is below an altitude of 32 kilometers. The remaining 1 percent of the atmosphere's mass is in the hundreds of kilometers above an altitude of 32 kilometers.

AIR PRESSURE AND ALTITUDE

Altitude (meters)	Air Pressure (g/cm^2)
Sea level	1034
3000	717
6000	450
9000	302
12,000	190
15,000	112

Figure 5–16 *Climbers need warm clothing and oxygen masks on a high mountain because the air is colder and thinner (less dense). How does air pressure change as altitude increases?*

191

Figure 5–17 *Convection currents in the atmosphere, caused by heat from the sun, contribute to the Earth's weather. In what layer of the atmosphere does most weather occur?*

ACTIVITY

DISCOVERING

The Temperature Plot

1. At three times during both the day and evening, use an outdoor thermometer to measure air temperature 1 centimeter above the ground and 1.25 meters above the ground. Record the time of day and the temperature for both locations.

2. On graph paper, plot time (X axis) versus temperature (Y axis) for each thermometer location. Label both graphs.

In which area did the temperature change most rapidly? In which area did the temperature change a greater amount over the entire time period?

■ Why do you think the temperatures changed as they did?

Now let's pretend that you are able to soar upward from the Earth's surface through the levels of the atmosphere. What will each layer look and feel like? Read on to find out.

The Troposphere

The layer of the atmosphere closest to Earth is the **troposphere** (TRO-po-sfeer). It is the layer in which you live. Almost all of the Earth's weather occurs in the troposphere.

The height of the troposphere varies from the equator to the poles. Around the equator, the height of the troposphere is about 17 kilometers. In areas north and south of the equator, the height is about 12 kilometers. At the poles, the troposphere extends upward between 6 and 8 kilometers.

As the heat energy from sunlight travels through the atmosphere, only a small amount of the heat energy is trapped by the atmosphere. Most of the heat energy is absorbed by the ground. The ground then warms the air above it. Warm air is less dense than cool air. The warm, less dense air rises and is replaced by cooler, denser air. Currents of air that carry heat up into the atmosphere are produced.

These air movements are called **convection** (kuhn-VEHK-shuhn) **currents.** You might be familiar with convection currents if you have observed a convection oven in use. This kind of oven contains a fan that continuously moves the hot oven air over the food. Food cooks more quickly and evenly in a convection oven than in a conventional oven.

Remember that temperature decreases with increasing altitude because the air becomes less dense. The temperature of the troposphere drops about 6.5°C for every kilometer above the Earth's surface. However, at an altitude of about 12 kilometers, the temperature seems to stop dropping. The zone of the troposphere where the temperature remains fairly constant is called the tropopause (TRO-po-pawz). The tropopause divides the troposphere from the next layer of the atmosphere.

The Stratosphere

The **stratosphere** (STRAT-uh-sfeer) extends from the tropopause to an altitude of about 50 kilometers. In the lower stratosphere, the temperature of the air remains constant and extremely cold—around −60°C. This temperature equals the coldest temperature ever recorded in a location other than Antarctica. It was recorded in Snag, in the Yukon Territory, Canada. The world's coldest recorded temperature, −90°C, occurred in Vostok, Antarctica.

The air in the lower stratosphere is not still. Here very strong eastward winds blow horizontally around the Earth. These winds, called the **jet stream,** reach speeds of more than 320 kilometers per hour. What effect do you think jet streams have on weather patterns in the United States?

A special form of oxygen called ozone is present in the stratosphere. Ozone has a clean sharp smell. You have probably smelled ozone after a thunderstorm or when you are near an electric motor that is running. In both cases ozone forms when electricity passes through the atmosphere. In the case of a thunderstorm, the electricity is in the form of lightning.

Most of the ozone in the atmosphere is found in the ozone layer located between 16 kilometers and

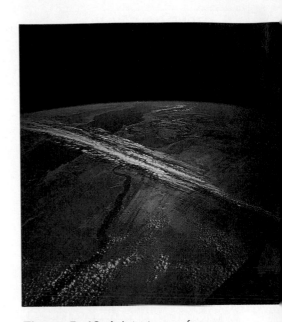

Figure 5–18 *A jet stream forms where cold air from the poles meets warmer air from the equator. This high-altitude jet stream is moving over the Nile Valley and the Red Sea.*

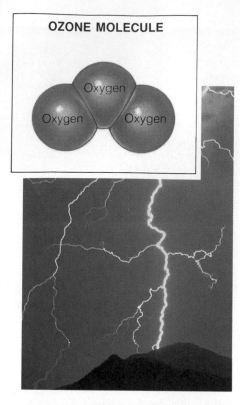

OZONE MOLECULE

Oxygen
Oxygen   Oxygen

Figure 5–19 *The ozone layer forms a protective umbrella in the stratosphere. Ozone, a molecule made up of three oxygen atoms, is formed when lightning passes through the atmosphere.*

ACTIVITY

CALCULATING

How Thick Are the Atmosphere's Layers?

Figure 5–20 shows the layers of the Earth's atmosphere and the altitudes at which they begin and end. Use the information in the diagram to calculate the average thickness of each layer.

60 kilometers above the surface of the Earth. Below and above these altitudes, there is little or no ozone. Although the total amount of ozone in the stratosphere is actually very small, ozone is extremely important to life on Earth. Ozone acts as a shield for the Earth's surface. As you learned in the previous section, ozone absorbs most of the ultraviolet radiation from the sun. Ultraviolet radiation is harmful to living things. Overexposure of the skin to ultraviolet radiation (often in the form of a bad sunburn) has been linked to skin cancer.

You may already know that you can get a bad sunburn on a cloudy day, even when it seems as if little sunlight is reaching the Earth. Ultraviolet rays are able to pass through cloud layers. In some ways, the ozone layer acts like a sunblock. Without it, more of the sun's harmful ultraviolet radiation would reach the Earth's surface, and you would always be in great danger of being badly burned by the sun's rays.

Ozone is also responsible for the increase in temperature that occurs in the upper stratosphere. Heat is given off as ozone reacts with ultraviolet radiation. This heat warms the upper stratosphere to temperatures around 18°C. The zone in which the temperature is at its highest is called the stratopause (STRAT-uh-pawz). The stratopause separates the stratosphere from the next layer of the atmosphere.

The Mesosphere

Above the stratopause, the temperature begins to decrease. This drop in temperature marks the beginning of the **mesosphere** (MEHS-oh-sfeer). The mesosphere extends from about 50 kilometers to about 80 kilometers above the Earth's surface. The temperature in the mesosphere drops to about −100°C. The upper region of the mesosphere is the coldest region of the atmosphere. If water vapor is present, thin clouds of ice form. You can see these feathery clouds if sunlight strikes them after sunset.

The mesosphere helps protect the Earth from large rocklike objects in space known as meteoroids (MEET-ee-uh-roidz). When meteoroids enter the atmosphere, they burn up in the mesosphere. The heat caused by the friction, or rubbing, between the meteoroid and the atmosphere causes this burning.

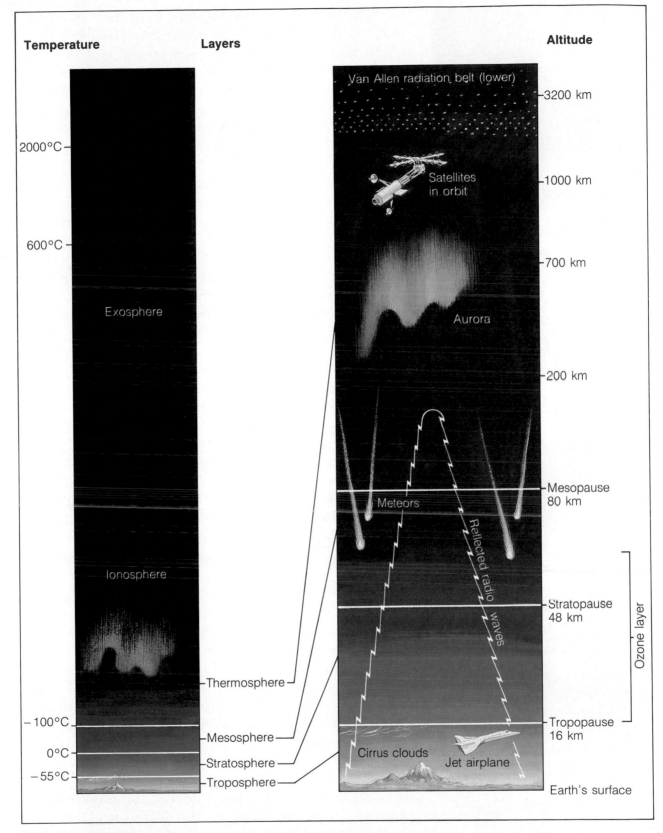

Figure 5–20 *The four main layers of the atmosphere and their characteristics are shown here. In which layer do you live? In which layer is the temperature the highest?*

Figure 5–21 *A meteorite crater in Arizona formed when a meteorite struck the Earth around 20,000 years ago.*

At night, you may see a streak of light, or "shooting star," in the sky. What you are actually seeing is a bright trail of hot, glowing gases known as a meteor.

Most meteoroids burn up completely as they pass through the Earth's atmosphere. But some are large enough to survive the passage and actually strike the Earth. These pieces are called meteorites (MEET-ee-er-rights). A few large meteorites have produced huge craters on the Earth. The most famous is the Barringer meteorite crater in Arizona. It is 1.2 kilometers wide. Scientists estimate that the meteorite that caused this crater fell to the Earth within the last 20,000 years.

When artificial satellites fall from orbit, they also burn up as they pass through the atmosphere. However, pieces of the United States's *Skylab* and the Soviet Union's *Cosmos* satellite have fallen out of orbit and reached the Earth's surface. Why do you think some meteoroids and satellites do not burn up completely as they pass through the layers of the atmosphere?

The Thermosphere

The **thermosphere** (THER-moh-sfeer) begins above the mesosphere at a height of about 80 kilometers. The thermosphere has no well-defined upper limit. The air in the thermosphere is very thin. The density of the atmosphere and the air pressure are only about one ten-millionth of what they are at the Earth's surface.

The word *thermosphere* means "heat sphere," or "warm layer." The temperature is very high in this layer of the atmosphere. In fact, the temperature of the thermosphere may reach 2000°C or more! To give you some idea of how hot this is, the temperature at the bottom of a furnace used to make steel reaches 1900°C. At this temperature, the steel mixture is a liquid! You may wonder why the temperature of the thermosphere is so high. (After all, for most of the atmosphere, temperature decreases as altitude increases.) The nitrogen and oxygen in the thermosphere absorb a great deal of the ultraviolet radiation from space and convert it into heat.

The temperature in the thermosphere is measured with special instruments, not with a thermometer.

Figure 5–22 *Temperatures in the thermosphere reach 2000°C, which is higher than the temperatures in a steel furnace.*

If a thermometer were placed in the thermosphere, it would register far below 0°C! This may seem strange since the thermosphere is so hot. How can this be explained? Temperature is a measurement of how fast particles in the air move. The faster the air particles move, the higher the temperature. And the particles present in the thermosphere are moving very fast. Therefore the particles themselves are very hot.

But these particles are very few and very far apart. There are not enough of them present to bombard a thermometer and warm it. So the thermometer would record a temperature far below 0°C.

THE IONOSPHERE The lower thermosphere is called the **ionosphere** (igh-AHN-uh-sfeer). The ionosphere extends from 80 kilometers to 550 kilometers above the Earth's surface. The size of the ionosphere varies with the amount of ultraviolet and X-ray radiation, two types of invisible energy given off by the sun.

Nitrogen oxides, oxygen, and other gas particles in the ionosphere absorb the ultraviolet radiation and X-rays given off by the sun. The particles of gas become electrically charged. Electrically charged particles are called **ions.** Hence the name ionosphere.

The ions in the ionosphere are important to radio communication. AM radio waves are bounced

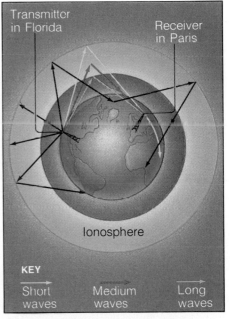

Figure 5–23 *Radio waves are bounced off the ionosphere to transmit radio messages overseas or across continents. There are three types of waves, and each travels to a different height in the ionosphere. Why do storms on the sun interfere with the transmission of radio waves in the ionosphere?*

Figure 5–24 *Weather satellites orbiting the Earth transmit information used by scientists to track weather patterns. What type of weather do you think the southeastern United States is having?*

off the ions in the ionosphere and back to the Earth's surface. As a result, AM radio messages can be sent over great distances.

Sometimes large disturbances on the sun's surface, known as solar flares, cause the number of ions in the ionosphere to increase. This increase in ions can interfere with the transmission of some radio waves.

THE EXOSPHERE The upper thermosphere is called the **exosphere** (EHKS-oh-sfeer). The exosphere extends from about 550 kilometers above the Earth's surface for thousands of kilometers. The air is so thin in the exosphere that one particle can travel great distances without hitting another particle.

It is in the exosphere that artificial satellites orbit the Earth. Satellites play an important role in television transmission and in telephone communication. Does it surprise you to learn how great a distance a long distance call actually travels if the signal bounces off a satellite in the exosphere before it returns to the Earth? Satellites are also used to keep a 24-hour watch on the world's weather. And because the very thin air in the exosphere makes seeing objects in space easier, telescopes are often carried aboard satellites.

5–3 Section Review

1. How are the layers of the atmosphere divided? What are the four main layers?
2. Identify one significant characteristic of each layer of the atmosphere. How is that characteristic important to you on Earth?
3. Why is ozone important to life on Earth?
4. Why is the temperature in the thermosphere not measured with a thermometer?

Connection—*Ecology*
5. Scientists are concerned that "holes" are being created in the ozone layer. In such a hole, the amount of ozone is reduced. Predict what would happen to life on Earth if the amount of ozone in the ozone layer were depleted.

CONNECTIONS

Sneezing and Wheezing— It's Allergy Time

It's spring again. The days get longer. The sun seems warmer and friendlier. Plants once again begin to grow. After the short, cold days of winter, most people look forward to spring as a promise of the season to come. But for many others, spring brings the misery of allergies. An allergy is a reaction caused by an increased sensitivity to a certain substance. With every breath they take, allergy sufferers are reminded of the many natural sources of air pollution.

Pollen grains are one kind of particle normally found in the air. Pollen grains are male plant reproductive cells. During certain times of the year, different kinds of pollen are released into the air. For example, maple and oak trees flower in the early spring, releasing millions upon millions of pollen grains into the air. These pollen grains are lightweight and float on air currents. If a person with an allergy to maple and oak tree pollen breathes in these pollen grains, certain cells in the respiratory system overreact, producing a chemical called histamine. This chemical causes the nose to run, the throat to tickle, and the eyes to water and itch.

You have probably heard of the condition called hay fever. Hay fever is neither a fever nor is it caused by hay. Hay fever is another example of an allergy. In this case, the culprit is ragweed pollen. Ragweed pollen also causes histamine to be produced.

There is no complete cure for allergies. If the particular pollen cannot be avoided, sufferers can take allergy-relief medicines prescribed by their physicians. As you can see, for some people, there are dangers hidden in the beauty of the natural world.

Ragweed pollen (left), ragweed plant (right)

Guide for Reading

*Focus on this question as
you read.*

▶ *What are some
characteristics of the
magnetic field of the Earth?*

5–4 The Magnetosphere

Recall from Chapter 4 that the area around the Earth that extends beyond the atmosphere is called the **magnetosphere** (mag-NEET-oh-sfeer). The Earth's magnetic force operates in the magnetosphere. The magnetosphere begins at an altitude of about 1000 kilometers. On the side of the Earth that faces the sun, the magnetosphere extends out into space about 4000 kilometers. It extends even farther into space on the other side of the Earth. See Figure 5–25. The difference in size of the magnetosphere is caused by the solar wind, which is a stream of fast-moving ions given off by the outermost layer of the sun's atmosphere. (Ions, recall, are electrically charged particles common to the ionosphere.) The solar wind pushes the magnetosphere farther into space on the side of the Earth away from the sun.

The magnetosphere is made up of positively charged protons and negatively charged electrons. Protons and electrons are two of the most important particles that make up atoms. An atom is considered the basic building block of matter, or the smallest unit from which all substances are made. Protons and electrons are given off by the sun and captured by the Earth's magnetic field. The charged particles

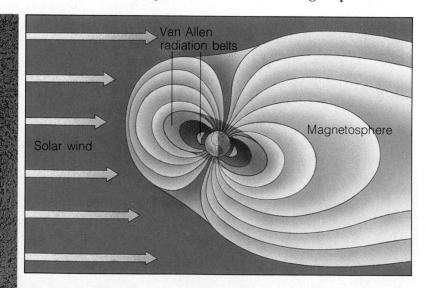

Figure 5–25 *The Earth acts like a giant bar magnet whose lines of force produce the same pattern as a small bar magnet. Why does the magnetosphere formed by the Earth extend farther on one side than on the other?*

Figure 5–26 *Electrically charged particles from the sun collide with particles in the upper atmosphere and produce the multicolored lights called an aurora. Here you see the aurora borealis, or northern lights.*

are concentrated into belts, or layers, of high radiation. These belts are called the **Van Allen radiation belts.** They were discovered by satellites in 1958 and named after James Van Allen, the scientist whose work led to their discovery.

The Van Allen radiation belts pose a problem for space travelers. Space flights have to be programmed to avoid the radiation or suitable protection must be provided for astronauts who travel through the belts. However, the Van Allen belts are important to life on the Earth. They provide protection by trapping other deadly radiation.

When there is a solar flare, the magnetosphere is bombarded by large quantities of electrically charged particles from the sun. These charged particles get trapped in the magnetosphere. Here they collide with other particles in the upper atmosphere. The collisions cause the atmospheric particles to give off light. The multicolored lights are called the aurora borealis, or northern lights, and the aurora australis, or southern lights.

After a heavy bombardment of solar particles, sometimes called a magnetic storm, the magnetic field of the Earth may change temporarily. A compass needle may not point north. Radio signals may be interrupted. Telephone and telegraph communications may also be affected.

5–4 Section Review

1. What is the magnetosphere made of?
2. Why are the Van Allen radiation belts important to life on Earth?
3. How can scientists predict when an aurora will be visible?

Critical Thinking—*Relating Concepts*
4. How did technology contribute to the discovery of the Van Allen radiation belts?

Laboratory Investigation

Radiant Energy and Surface Temperature

Problem

Does the type of surface affect the amount of heat absorbed both in and out of direct sunlight?

Materials *(per group)*

> 10 thermometers
> stopwatch or clock with sweep second hand
> 2 shallow containers of water

Procedure 🧪

1. Place a thermometer on the grass in the sun. Place a second thermometer on the grass in the shade.
2. Place the remaining thermometers—one in the sun and one in the shade—on bare soil, on concrete, on a blacktop surface, and in water.
3. After 2 minutes, record the temperature of each surface.
4. Continue recording the temperature of each surface every 2 minutes for a period of 10 minutes.
5. Record your results in a data table similar to the one shown here.

Observations

1. Which surface was the warmest? Which surface was the coolest?
2. By how many degrees did the temperature of each surface in direct sunlight change during the 10-minute time period?
3. By how many degrees did the temperature of each surface in the shade change during the 10-minute period?

Analysis and Conclusions

1. Why do you think the warmest surface was the warmest?
2. How do you explain the temperature change that occurred in water?
3. What conclusions can you reach about the amount of heat energy different surfaces absorb from the sun?
4. **On Your Own** How can you apply your observations to the kinds of clothing that should be worn in a warm climate? In a cold climate? In what other ways do the results of this investigation affect people's lives?

Surface	Temperature in the Sun					Temperature in the Shade				
	2 min	4 min	6 min	8 min	10 min	2 min	4 min	6 min	8 min	10 min
Grass										
Soil										
Concrete										
Blacktop										
Water										

Study Guide

Summarizing Key Concepts

5–1 A View of Planet Earth: Spheres Within a Sphere

▲ The solid parts of planet Earth make up the lithosphere.

▲ Parts of the Earth that are made up of water compose the hydrosphere.

▲ The envelope of gases that surrounds the Earth is the atmosphere.

5–2 Development of the Atmosphere

▲ About 3.8 billion years ago, chemical reactions triggered by sunlight produced new substances in the atmosphere.

▲ The ozone layer is sometimes referred to as an "umbrella" for life on Earth. The ozone layer absorbs much of the harmful radiation from the sun.

▲ The present atmosphere consists mainly of nitrogen, oxygen, carbon dioxide, water vapor, argon, and several other gases present in trace amounts.

5–3 Layers of the Atmosphere

▲ The four main layers of the atmosphere are the troposphere, stratosphere, mesosphere, and the thermosphere.

▲ Almost all of the Earth's weather occurs in the troposphere.

▲ Temperature decreases with increasing altitude in the troposphere. The zone of the troposphere where the temperature remains fairly constant is called the tropopause.

▲ Most of the ozone in the atmosphere is located in a layer of the stratosphere.

▲ The upper mesosphere is the coldest region of the atmosphere.

▲ The thermosphere is made up of the ionosphere and the exosphere.

5–4 The Magnetosphere

▲ The magnetosphere extends from an altitude of about 1000 kilometers far into space.

▲ The Van Allen radiation belts are layers of high radiation that form as a result of the concentration of charged particles.

Reviewing Key Terms

Define each term in a complete sentence.

5–1 A View of Planet Earth: Spheres Within a Sphere
equator
hemisphere
lithosphere
hydrosphere
atmosphere

5–2 Development of the Atmosphere
ozone

5–3 Layers of the Atmosphere
troposphere
convection current
stratosphere
jet stream
mesosphere
thermosphere
ionosphere
ion
exosphere

5–4 The Magnetosphere
magnetosphere
Van Allen radiation belt

Chapter Review

Content Review

Multiple Choice

Choose the letter of the answer that best completes each statement.

1. The envelope of gases that surrounds the Earth is called the
   a. lithosphere.
   b. atmosphere.
   c. hydrosphere.
   d. equator.

2. Oceans, lakes, and the polar ice caps are part of the Earth's
   a. crust.
   b. argons.
   c. fresh water.
   d. hydrosphere.

3. Four billion years ago the Earth's atmosphere contained the deadly gases
   a. nitrogen and oxygen.
   b. methane and ammonia.
   c. methane and oxygen.
   d. nitrogen and ozone.

4. The most abundant gas in the atmosphere is
   a. oxygen.
   b. carbon dioxide
   c. argon.
   d. nitrogen.

5. The layer of the atmosphere where the temperature may reach 2000°C is called the
   a. stratosphere.
   b. mesosphere.
   c. thermosphere.
   d. troposphere.

6. Ultraviolet radiation from the sun is absorbed by ozone in the
   a. troposphere.
   b. stratosphere.
   c. thermosphere.
   d. ionosphere.

7. Artificial satellites orbit the Earth in the part of the thermosphere called the
   a. ionosphere.
   b. mesosphere.
   c. exosphere.
   d. troposphere.

8. The lowest layer of the atmosphere is called the
   a. stratosphere.
   b. mesosphere.
   c. thermosphere.
   d. troposphere.

True or False

If the statement is true, write "true." If it is false, change the underlined word or words to make the statement true.

1. Almost <u>85 percent</u> of the fresh water on Earth is <u>trapped</u> in ice.

2. The envelope of gases that surrounds the Earth is called the <u>hydrosphere</u>.

3. Few living things could survive on Earth without the presence of <u>methane</u>, the gas that absorbs ultraviolet radiation.

4. The <u>magnetosphere</u> is the area that extends beyond the atmosphere.

5. Electrically charged particles are called <u>molecules</u>.

6. As altitude increases, the temperature of the air <u>increases</u>.

7. Because of the increased burning of fossil fuels, the level of <u>carbon dioxide</u> in the air is increasing.

Concept Mapping

Complete the following concept map for Section 5–1. Then construct a concept map for the entire chapter.

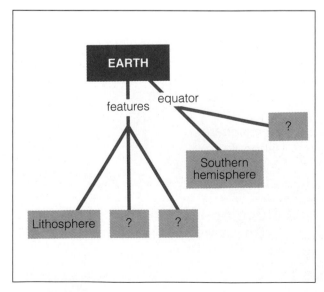

204

Concept Mastery

Discuss each of the following in a brief paragraph.

1. How did living organisms change the atmosphere of ancient Earth?
2. Tell how each of the following items would be useful for an astronaut on a trip to Mars: a supply of oxygen, a space suit, radiation protection.
3. What are the four most common gases in the troposphere? In what percentages do these gases occur?
4. Explain why air pressure decreases as altitude increases.
5. What is ultraviolet radiation? What effect does this type of radiation have on living things?
6. How have satellites contributed to our knowledge of the atmosphere?

Critical Thinking and Problem Solving

Use the skills you have developed in this chapter to answer each of the following.

1. **Applying concepts** Could animals have lived on ancient Earth before green plants? Explain your answer.
2. **Applying concepts** Traveling from New York to San Francisco, California takes about 5 hours and 30 minutes. The return trip from San Francisco to New York, however, takes about 5 hours. Use your knowledge of the jet stream to explain the difference in travel time.

3. **Relating cause and effect** Scientists are concerned that certain chemicals, when released into the atmosphere, cause the level of ozone to decrease. Predict what might happen to living things on Earth if the ozone layer continues to decrease.
4. **Sequencing events** Make a series of drawings or small dioramas to show how the atmosphere of Earth has changed over time.
5. **Making diagrams** The diagrams on pages 185 and 187 show the nitrogen and the oxygen-carbon dioxide cycles. Use these diagrams as a guide to draw pictures of each cycle as it occurs in your surroundings. Include plants and animals found in your area.
6. **Using the writing process** People have walked on the moon during your parents' or your teachers' lifetime. Conduct an interview with your parents or a teacher. Ask them if they saw the first step onto the moon. Have them describe their feelings at the time of the first moon walk. Organize the information from the interview into a short essay.

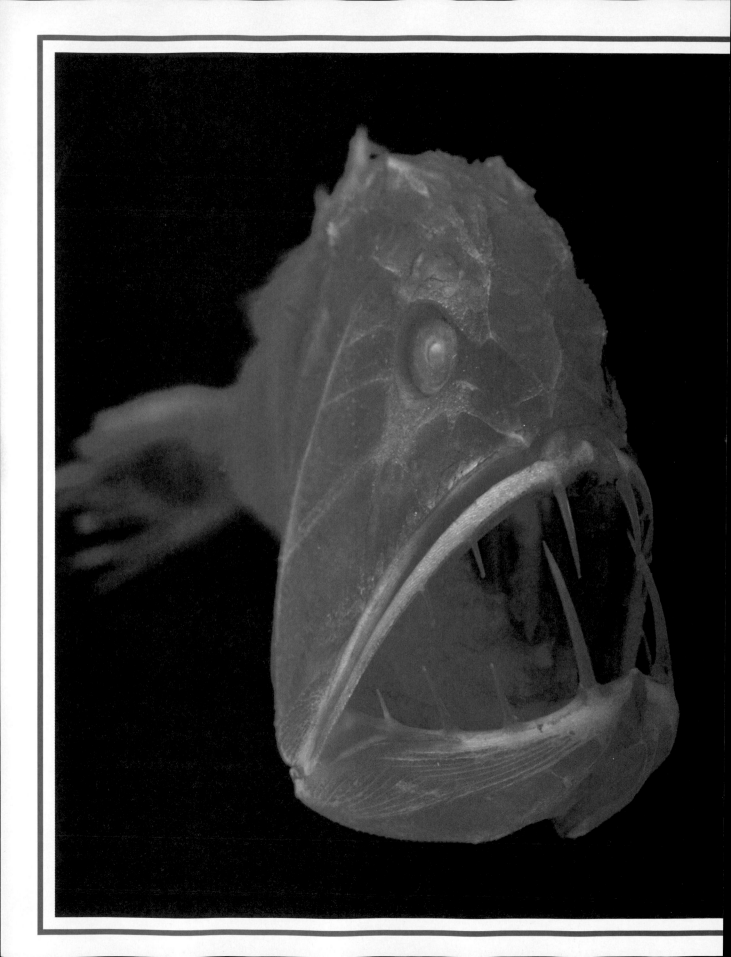

Earth's Oceans

Many bizarre living things make their home deep beneath the ocean waves. Indeed, some fish look as if they recently swam out of the pages of the strangest science fiction novel. The anoplogaster on the opposite page is but one example. With its needlelike teeth bared, the 15-centimeter fish stalks its prey. Food, however, is scarce in the 6000-meter-deep water this fish calls home.

At this profound depth, the water temperature is near freezing, the pressure tremendous. But in this blue-black ocean water where no sunlight penetrates, the anoplogaster is a fearsome predator.

The oceans are rich in many forms of life. Tiny single-celled plants share the salt waters of the Earth with mammoth whales. A wide variety of organisms obtain the gases and foods they need from ocean water. The ocean plays an important role in your survival, as well. It is a direct source of food and an indirect source of fresh water for all living things.

In this chapter, you will learn more about the oceans—their properties, motions, and the land beneath them. And you will become more familiar with the variety of living things that make the oceans their home.

Journal *Activity*

You and Your World In 1492, it took Christopher Columbus weeks to reach the New World by sailing across the Atlantic in ships powered by winds. Would you have liked to be a member of Columbus's crew? What do you think that long voyage was like? In your journal, keep a diary for a week in which you are a member of Columbus's crew.

Tiny but terrifying, an anoplogaster patrols the ocean depths in search of food.

6–1 The World's Oceans

Suppose a contest was held in which you were asked to rename the Earth. What would you call it? If you looked at the Earth's surface features from space, you might call it Oceanus. This would probably be a good name to choose because about 71 percent of the Earth's surface is covered by ocean water. In fact, the oceans contain most of the Earth's water—about 97 percent. And although each ocean and sea has a separate name, all of the oceans and seas are actually one continuous body of water.

The Atlantic, Indian, and Pacific oceans are the three major oceans. Smaller bodies of ocean water, such as the Mediterranean Sea, the Black Sea, and the Arctic Ocean, are considered part of the Atlantic Ocean. A sea is a part of an ocean that is nearly surrounded by land. Can you name any other seas?

The Pacific Ocean is the largest ocean on Earth. Its area and volume are greater than those of the Atlantic and Indian oceans combined. The Pacific Ocean is also the deepest ocean. Its average depth is 3940 meters. The Atlantic Ocean is the second largest ocean. The average depth of the Atlantic Ocean is 3350 meters. Although the Indian Ocean is much smaller than the Atlantic, its average depth is greater.

The ocean, which you may already know is made of salt water, plays an important role in the water cycle. During this cycle, the sun's rays heat the surface of the ocean. The heat causes the water to evaporate, or change from the liquid phase to the gas phase. The evaporating water—pure, fresh water—enters the atmosphere as water vapor. The salts remain in the ocean.

Winds carry much of the water vapor over land areas. Some of the water vapor in the atmosphere condenses to form clouds. Under the right conditions, the water in clouds falls as precipitation (rain, snow, sleet, and hail). Some of this water runs into

Figure 6–1 *Notice the sea stacks that have been carved by ocean waves off Big Sur in California. What percent of the Earth's surface is covered by water?*

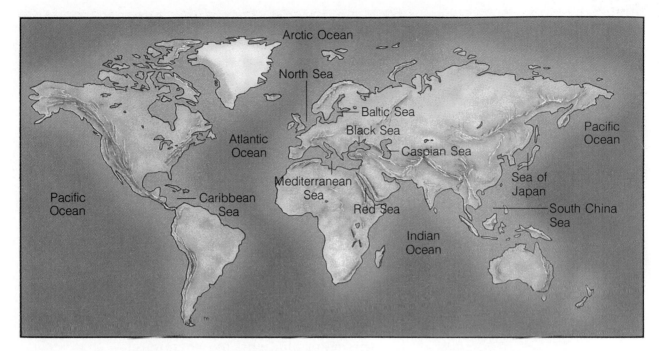

Figure 6–2 *The major oceans and seas of the world are actually part of one continuous body of water. What are the three major oceans?*

rivers and streams that flow directly back into the ocean. Some of it seeps deep into the soil and rocks of the Earth to become part of the groundwater beneath the Earth's surface. As you can see, the ocean is a source of fresh water for all living things.

6–1 Section Review

1. What are the three main oceans of the world?
2. What is a sea?
3. What part does the ocean play as a source of fresh water for all living things?

Critical Thinking—*Relating Cause and Effect*
4. The state of Washington lies on the Pacific Ocean. Certain parts of this state receive large amounts of rain throughout the year. Predict which parts receive the most rain. Explain why.

6–2 Properties of Ocean Water

Ocean water is a mixture of gases and solids dissolved in pure water. Scientists who study the ocean, or **oceanographers** (oh-shuh-NAHG-ruh-fuhrz), believe that ocean water contains all of the natural elements found on Earth. Ninety elements are known to exist in nature. So far, about 85 of these have been found in ocean water. Oceanographers are hopeful that with improved technology, they will find the remaining elements.

Ocean water is about 96 percent pure water, or H_2O. So the most abundant elements in ocean water are hydrogen (H) and oxygen (O). The other 4 percent consists of dissolved elements. Figure 6–3 lists the major elements in ocean water.

Salts in Ocean Water

Sodium chloride is the most abundant salt in ocean water. If you have ever accidentally swallowed a mouthful of ocean water, you have probably recognized the taste of sodium chloride. Sodium chloride is, in fact, common table salt. It is made of the elements sodium and chlorine.

Sodium chloride is only one of many salts dissolved in ocean water. Figure 6–4 shows the other salts. Oceanographers use the term **salinity** (suh-LIHN-uh-tee) to describe the amount of dissolved salts in ocean water. Salinity is the number of grams of dissolved salts in 1 kilogram of ocean water. When 1 kilogram of ocean water evaporates, 35 grams of salts remain. Of these 35 grams, 27.2 grams are sodium chloride. How many grams are magnesium chloride?

The salinity of ocean water is expressed in parts per thousand. It ranges between 33 and 37 parts per thousand. The average salinity of ocean water is 35 parts per thousand.

Salts and other materials dissolved in ocean water come from several different sources. One important source is volcanic activity in the ocean. When volcanoes erupt, rock materials and gases spew forth. These substances dissolve in ocean water. Chlorine

Figure 6–3 *Ocean water is composed of hydrogen, oxygen, and about 85 other elements. Of those other elements, which two are the most abundant?*

MAJOR ELEMENTS IN OCEAN WATER	
Element	**Percent of Total (%)**
Oxygen Hydrogen	96.5
Chlorine	1.9
Sodium	1.1
Magnesium Sulfur Calcium Potassium Bromine Carbon Strontium Silicon Fluorine Aluminum Phosphorus Iodine	0.5
	100

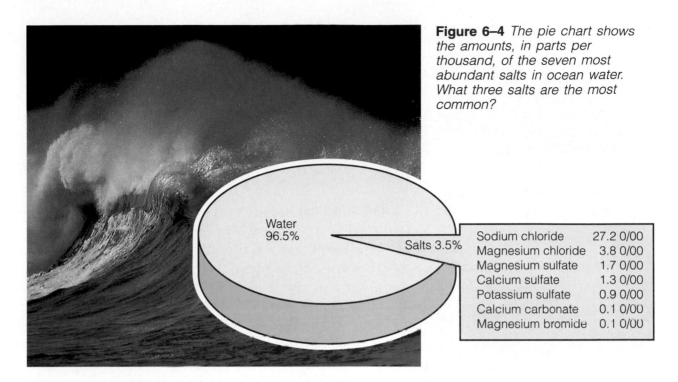

Figure 6–4 *The pie chart shows the amounts, in parts per thousand, of the seven most abundant salts in ocean water. What three salts are the most common?*

Water
96.5%

Salts 3.5%

Sodium chloride	27.2 0/00
Magnesium chloride	3.8 0/00
Magnesium sulfate	1.7 0/00
Calcium sulfate	1.3 0/00
Potassium sulfate	0.9 0/00
Calcium carbonate	0.1 0/00
Magnesium bromide	0.1 0/00

gas is one substance that is added to ocean water as a result of volcanic activity.

Another source of dissolved materials is the erosion of the land by rivers, streams, and glaciers. As rivers, streams, and glaciers move over rocks and soil, they dissolve salts in them. Sodium, magnesium, and potassium reach the ocean in this way.

The action of waves breaking along the shore is also a source of salts and other dissolved materials. As waves pound the shoreline, they dissolve the salts contained in the rocks along the coast.

In most areas of the ocean, the salinity is about the same. But in some areas, greater or lesser amounts of dissolved salts cause differences in the salinity. Several reasons explain these differences. The salinity is much lower in areas where freshwater rivers run into the ocean. This is especially true where major rivers such as the Mississippi, Amazon, and Congo flow into the ocean. Can you suggest a reason for the lower salinity? At these points, huge amounts of fresh water pour into the ocean, diluting the normal amount of salts in the ocean water.

In warm ocean areas where there is little rainfall and much evaporation, the amount of dissolved salts in the water is greater than average. Thus, the salinity is higher. The salinity is higher in the polar regions also. Here temperatures are cold enough for

ACTIVITY

Temperature and Salinity

1. Pour 100 mL of hot tap water into a glass.

2. Add salt, one teaspoonful at a time, to the water. Stir the water after each addition. Stop adding salt when no more can be dissolved. Record the number of teaspoons of salt added. Empty the contents of the glass. Wash the glass.

3. Now pour 100 mL of cold water into the same glass. Repeat steps 1 and 2.

In which glass did more salt dissolve?

What relationship have you illustrated by doing this investigation?

ocean water to freeze. When ocean water freezes, pure water is removed and the salts are left behind.

Scientists believe that the salinity of ocean water is also affected by animal life. Animals such as clams and oysters use calcium salts to build their shells. They remove these salts from ocean water, thus lowering the salinity of the water.

Gases in Ocean Water

The most abundant gases dissolved in ocean water are nitrogen, carbon dioxide, and oxygen. Two of these gases, carbon dioxide and oxygen, are vital to ocean life. Most plants take carbon dioxide from the water and use it to make food. In the presence of sunlight, the plants combine carbon dioxide with water to make sugars. During this process, oxygen is released into the water. Plants and animals use oxygen to break down food and provide energy for all life functions.

The amount of nitrogen, carbon dioxide, oxygen, and other gases in ocean water varies with depth. Nitrogen, carbon dioxide, and oxygen are more abundant at the ocean's surface. Here sunlight easily penetrates and plant growth abounds. The abundant plant growth ensures a large supply of oxygen—certainly a great deal more than is found in the depths of the oceans. Can you explain why?

The amount of dissolved gases is also affected by the temperature of ocean water. Warm water holds less dissolved gas than cold water. When ocean water cools, as in the polar regions, it sinks. (Cold water is

Figure 6–5 *One source of minerals in ocean water is the erosion of cliffs by ocean waves.*

Figure 6–6 *The salinity of the ocean is fairly constant. However, in areas where rivers dump sediment-laden fresh water into the ocean, the salinity is reduced. Ocean animals such as flame scallops also reduce salinity.*

denser, or heavier, than warm water.) It carries oxygen-rich water to the ocean depths. As a result, fish and other animals can live in deep parts of the ocean.

Temperature of Ocean Water

The sun is the major source of heat for the ocean. Because solar energy enters the ocean at the surface, the temperature of the water is highest there. Motions of the ocean, such as waves and currents, mix the surface water and transfer the heat downward. The zone where the water is mixed by waves and currents is called the **surface zone.** The surface zone extends to a depth of at least 100 meters. Sometimes it extends as deep as 400 meters.

The temperature of the water remains fairly constant within a surface zone. It does not change much with depth. But the temperature in a surface zone does change with location and with season. Water near the equator is warmer than water in regions farther north and south. Summer water temperatures are warmer than winter water temperatures. For example, the summer water temperature near the surface of the Caribbean Sea may be 26°C. Farther north, off the coast of England, the temperature near the surface may be 15°C. What do you think happens to the water temperature at these two places during the winter?

Below the surface zone the temperature of the water drops very rapidly. This zone of rapid temperature change is called the **thermocline** (THER-moh-klighn). The thermocline does not occur at a specific depth. The season and the flow of ocean currents alter the depth of the thermocline.

The thermocline exists because warm surface water does not easily mix with cold deep water. The difference in the densities of the warm water and the cold water keeps them from mixing. The less dense warm water floats on top of the denser cold water.

The thermocline forms a transition zone between the surface zone and the **deep zone.** The deep zone is an area of extremely cold water that extends from the bottom of the thermocline to depths of 4000 meters or more. Within the deep zone, the temperature decreases only slightly. At depths greater than

ACTIVITY

DISCOVERING

A Drink of Water

■ Use your knowledge of the properties of salt water to devise a procedure for obtaining fresh water from ocean water by freezing. Describe the steps to your teacher. With permission, try your procedure using the following: Dissolve 3 grams of table salt in 100 mL of water. Report your results to your class.

Figure 6–7 *There are three temperature zones in the ocean.*

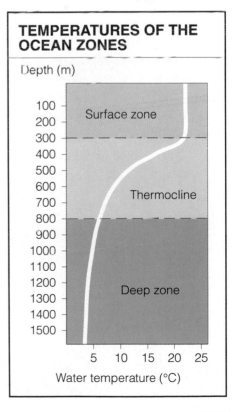

Figure 6–8 *Ocean temperatures vary from the Caribbean Sea to the White Cliffs of Dover to the polar regions. Notice the blue-green bacteria below the frozen surface of Lake Hoare in Antarctica.*

1500 meters, the temperature is about 4°C. So the temperature of most ocean water is just above freezing (0°C)!

The three ocean zones are not found in the polar regions. In the Arctic and Antarctic oceans, the surface waters are always very cold. The temperature changes only slightly as the depth increases.

Sink or Swim—Is It Easier to Float in Cold Water or Hot?, p. 756

6–2 Section Review

1. What does ocean water consist of?
2. What is salinity?
3. What three gases are most abundant in ocean water?
4. What are the three zones of the ocean? On what property of ocean water are these zones based?

Critical Thinking—*Applying Concepts*

5. Fish get the oxygen they need by removing it from water. Would you expect to find greater numbers of fish near the equator or in ocean areas farther north and south of the equator? Explain your answer. (*Hint:* Consider the effect of temperature on the amount of gases that can dissolve in water.)

6–3 The Ocean Floor

A description of the shape of the ocean floor—its characteristics and major features—is known as its topography. The topography of the ocean floor is different from the topography of the continents. The ocean floor has higher mountains, deeper canyons, and larger, flatter plains than the continents. The ocean floor also has more volcanoes than the continents. Earthquakes occur with greater frequency under the ocean than on the land. The rocks that form the ocean floor are very different from the rocks that form the crust of the continents. The crust of the Earth is much thinner under the ocean than under the continents.

Edges of the Continents

On a continent, there is a boundary where the land and the ocean meet. This boundary is called a **shoreline.** A shoreline marks the average position of sea level. It does not mark the end of the continent.

The edge of a continent extends into the ocean. The area where the underwater edge of a continent meets the ocean floor is called a **continental margin.** Although a continental margin forms part of the ocean floor, it is more a part of the land than it is a part of the ocean.

A continental margin generally consists of a continental shelf, a continental slope, and a continental rise. Sediments worn away from the land are deposited in these parts of a continental margin.

The relatively flat part of a continental margin that is covered by shallow ocean water is called a **continental shelf.** A continental shelf usually slopes very gently downward from the shoreline. In fact, it usually slopes less than 1.2 meters for every 100 meters from the shoreline.

The width of a continental shelf varies. Off the Atlantic coast, the continental shelf extends more than 200 kilometers into the ocean. Off the Arctic shore of Siberia, the continental shelf extends over 1200 kilometers into the ocean. Off the coast of southeastern Florida, there is almost no continental shelf.

Figure 6–9 *An offshore oil rig drills for oil trapped beneath the ocean floor in the continental shelf.*

The Great Whale

Moby Dick is one of the greatest stories ever written in the English language. This tale of the sea and the whalers who sailed it describes a time when people made a living by hunting the great whales. You might enjoy reading this book written by Herman Melville and reporting on it to your class.

The best fishing areas of the ocean are found in waters over a continental shelf. Large mineral deposits, as well as large deposits of oil and natural gas are also found on a continental shelf. Because of the presence of these precious resources, many countries have extended their natural boundaries to include the continental shelf that lies off their shores.

At the edge of a continental shelf, the ocean floor plunges steeply 4 to 5 kilometers. This part of the continental margin is called a **continental slope.** A continental slope marks the boundary between the crust of the continent and the crust of the ocean floor. Separating a continental slope from the ocean floor is a **continental rise.** You can see the parts of a continental margin and other features of the ocean floor in Figure 6–10.

A continental rise is made of large amounts of sediments. These sediments include small pieces of rocks and the remains of plants and animals washed down from the continent and the continental slope. Sometimes the sediments are carried down the slope in masses of flowing water called **turbidity** (ter-BIHD-uh-tee) **currents.** A turbidity current is a flow of water that carries large amounts of sediments. A turbidity current is like an underwater avalanche.

Figure 6–10 *In this illustration, you can see the major features of the ocean floor. What are some of these features?*

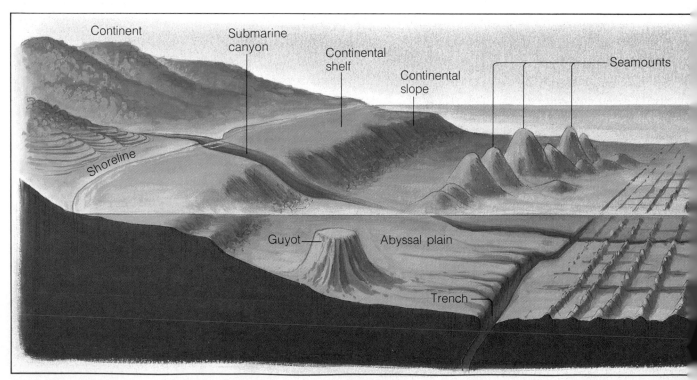

In many areas, **submarine canyons** cut through a continental shelf and slope. Submarine canyons are deep, V-shaped valleys that have been cut in rock. Some of the canyons are very deep indeed. For example, the Monterey Submarine Canyon off the coast of central California reaches depths of more than 2000 meters. It is actually deeper than the Grand Canyon!

Many scientists believe that submarine canyons are formed by powerful turbidity currents. Submarine canyons may also be caused by earthquakes or other movements that occur on a continental slope. Scientists still have much to learn about the origin and nature of submarine canyons.

Features of the Ocean Floor

Scientists have identified several major features of the ocean floor. (The ocean floor is also called the ocean basin.) Refer back to Figure 6–10 as you read about these features.

ABYSSAL PLAINS Large flat areas on the ocean floor are called **abyssal** (uh-BIHS-uhl) **plains.** The abyssal plains are larger in the Atlantic and Indian oceans than in the Pacific Ocean. Scientists believe

Figure 6–11 *These divers are exploring a submarine canyon in the continental shelf. How are submarine canyons formed?*

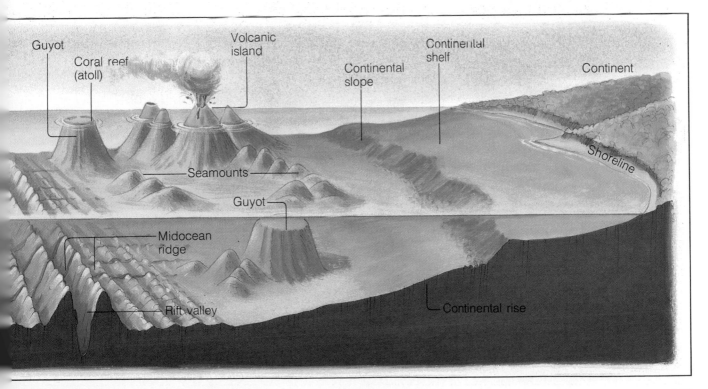

Figure 6–12 *The submersible* Alvin *searches for unusual organisms in the sediments covering the abyssal plains.*

that two reasons account for the difference in the size of these abyssal plains.

First, the world's greatest rivers flow directly or indirectly into the Atlantic and Indian oceans. These rivers include the Mississippi, Congo, Nile, and Amazon, which flow into the Atlantic Ocean, and the Ganges and Indus rivers which flow directly into the Indian Ocean. These major rivers, and many smaller ones, deposit large amounts of sediments on the abyssal plains.

Second, the floor of the Pacific Ocean contains a number of deep cracks along the edges of the continents. These long, narrow cracks trap sediments that are carried down a continental slope.

Deep-sea drilling operations and sound-wave detection equipment have shown that the sediments of the abyssal plains close to continents consist of thick layers of mud, sand, and silt. Farther out on the abyssal plains, some of the sediments contain the remains of tiny organisms. These organisms are so small they can be seen only with the aid of a microscope. They form a sediment called ooze. Where ocean life is not abundant, the floor of the ocean is covered with a sediment called red clay. Red clay is made of sediments carried to the oceans by rivers.

SEAMOUNTS AND GUYOTS Scattered along the floor of the ocean are thousands of underwater mountains called **seamounts.** Seamounts are volcanic mountains that rise more than 1000 meters above the surrounding ocean floor. Seamounts have steep sides that lead to a narrow summit (or top). To date, oceanographers have located more than 1000 seamounts. They expect to find thousands more in the future as more ocean areas are explored. Many more seamounts have been found in the Pacific Ocean than in either the Atlantic or the Indian Ocean.

Some seamounts reach above the surface of the ocean to form islands. The Azores and the Ascension Islands in the Atlantic Ocean are examples of volcanic islands. Perhaps the most dramatic and familiar volcanic islands are the Hawaiian Islands in the Pacific Ocean. The island of Hawaii is the top of a great volcano that rises more than 9600 meters from the ocean floor. It is the highest mountain on Earth when measured from its base on the ocean floor to its peak high above the surface of the ocean.

Activity

THINKING

Strolling Under the Seas

Imagine that all the water has been drained from all the oceans on Earth. Every feature once hidden under the waves is now seen easily. You and a friend decide to take a hike across the dry ocean floor. Choose a starting point and a destination. In a report, describe the features of the ocean floor you observe on your trip.

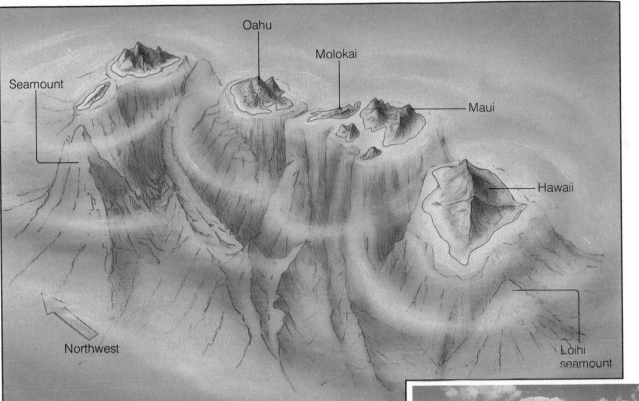

Oahu

Molokai

Seamount

Maui

Hawaii

Northwest

Loihi seamount

Figure 6–13 *The Hawaiian island of Kauai is the top of a seamount that extends above the ocean's surface (bottom). The age of the Hawaiian Islands increases as you travel toward the northwest. Loihi Seamount, off the coast of Hawaii, is slowly growing taller. Loihi will eventually become the newest Hawaiian island (top).*

During the mid-1940s, scientists discovered that many seamounts do not rise to a peak. Instead they have a flat top. These flat-topped seamounts are called **guyots** (gee-OHZ). Scientists believe that the flat tops are the result of wave erosion. Waves broke apart the tops of seamounts that once were at sea level. The flattened volcanic seamounts were later submerged.

TRENCHES The deepest parts of the ocean are not in the middle of the ocean floor. The greatest depths are found in **trenches** along the edges of the ocean floor. Trenches are long, narrow crevices (or cracks) that can be more than 11,000 meters deep.

The Pacific Ocean has more trenches than the other oceans. The Mariana Trench in the Pacific Ocean contains the deepest spot known on the Earth. This spot is called Challenger Deep. Challenger Deep is more than 11,000 meters deep. To

MAJOR OCEAN TRENCHES	
Trench	**Depth (meters)**
Pacific Ocean	
Aleutian	8100
Kurile	10,542
Japan	9810
Mariana (Challenger Deep)	11,034
Philippine	10,497
Tonga	10,882
Kermadec	10,800
Peru-Chile	8055
Mindanao	10,030
Atlantic Ocean	
Puerto Rico	8648
South Sandwich	8400

Figure 6–14 *Ocean trenches are the deepest parts of the ocean floor. Which ocean, the Atlantic or Pacific, has the most trenches?*

give you some idea of the depth of Challenger Deep, consider this: The Empire State Building in New York is about 430 meters tall. It would take a stack of 26 Empire State Buildings to break the ocean surface from the bottom of Challenger Deep!

MIDOCEAN RIDGES Some of the largest mountain ranges on Earth are located under the oceans. These mountain ranges are called **midocean ridges.** They form an almost continuous mountain belt that extends from the Arctic Ocean, down through the middle of the Atlantic Ocean, around Africa into the Indian Ocean, and then across the Pacific Ocean north to North America. In the Atlantic Ocean, the mountain belt is called the Mid-Atlantic Ridge. In the Pacific Ocean, the mountain belt is called the Pacific-Antarctic Ridge or East Pacific Rise or Ridge.

The midocean ridges are unlike any mountain ranges on land. Why? Mountain ranges on land are formed when the Earth's crust folds and is squeezed together. Midocean ridges are areas where molten (or hot liquid) material from deep within the Earth flows up to the surface. At the surface, the molten material cools and piles up to form new crust.

Figure 6–15 *This map shows the topography of the ocean floor.*

Figure 6–16 *This illustration shows a submarine above a rift valley surrounded by mountains that make up part of the oceanic ridge system. In the central part of the rift valley you can see molten rock that has cooled. This rock will eventually become new ocean floor (inset).*

Running along the middle of the midocean ridges between the rows of almost parallel mountains are deep crevices, or rift valleys. Rift valleys are about 25 to 50 kilometers wide and 1 to 2 kilometers below the bases of the surrounding midocean ridges. Rift valleys are regions of great earthquake and volcanic activity. In fact, rift valleys may mark the center of the areas where new crust is formed. Scientists have learned about changes in the Earth's crust by studying the rocks in and around the midocean ridges. Why do you think this is so?

REEFS Sometimes unusual-looking volcanic islands can be seen in tropical waters near a continental shelf. Surrounding these islands offshore are large masses and ridges of limestone rocks. The limestone structures contain the shells of animals and are called **coral reefs.** Because the reef-building organisms cannot survive in waters colder than 18°C, reefs are found only in tropical waters. Reefs are found in the warmer parts of the Pacific Ocean and in the Caribbean Sea. The organisms that build reefs also cannot live in deep water. They need sunlight to make their hard limestone skeletons. Not enough sunlight for these organisms to survive penetrates water deeper than 55 meters.

There are three types of coral reefs. One type is called **fringing reefs.** Fringing reefs are coral reefs that touch the shoreline of a volcanic island. Fringing reefs are generally less than 30 meters; however, some may be several hundred meters wide.

ACTIVITY
DOING

Ocean Floor Model

1. Use some papier-mâché, plaster of Paris, or modeling clay to construct a model of the ocean floor. Use Figures 6–10 and 6–15 to help you construct your model.

2. Label each feature in your model.

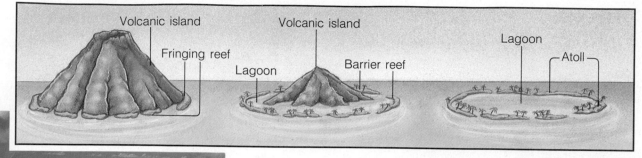

Barrier reefs are another type of coral reef. Barrier reefs are separated from the shore by an area of shallow water called a lagoon. Barrier reefs are generally larger than fringing reefs. And the islands that barrier reefs surround usually have sunk farther into the ocean than the islands that fringing reefs surround. The largest barrier reef on Earth is the Great Barrier Reef of Australia. It is about 2300 kilometers long and ranges from 40 to 320 kilometers wide. The Great Barrier Reef is rich in many kinds of animal and plant life.

The third type of coral reef can be found farther out in the ocean. It is a ring of coral reefs called an **atoll.** An atoll surrounds an island that has been worn away and has sunk beneath the surface of the ocean. Figure 6–17 shows the three types of coral reefs.

Figure 6–17 *The development of the three types of coral reefs is shown in the illustration. A barrier reef is separated from the shore by a lagoon (top photograph). An atoll surrounds only a lagoon because the island has been worn away and is no longer above the ocean surface (bottom photograph).*

6–3 Section Review

1. What is the continental margin? Describe the parts of a continental margin.
2. Identify five major features of the ocean floor.
3. What are three types of coral reefs?

Connection—*Literature*

4. A famous science fiction writer once said that "... good science fiction must also be good science." In a new science fiction movie, a giant sea monster lives in a coral reef off the coast of Maine near the Canadian border. During the day, the monster terrorizes the local population, devouring pets and people. At night it returns to the safety of its reef. Is this plot good science fiction? Explain your answer.

6–4 Ocean Life Zones

Guide for Reading

Focus on these questions as you read.

▶ *What are the three major groups of animals and plants in the ocean?*

▶ *What are the three major life zones in the ocean?*

A visit to a public aquarium will convince you that a great variety of life exists in the ocean. But even the most well-stocked aquarium is home to relatively few kinds of fishes and plants. People who visit a real coral reef, for example, swim away amazed at the colors, shapes, and variety of the fishes that inhabit the reef.

The animal and plant life found in the ocean is affected by several factors. One factor is the amount of sunlight that penetrates the ocean. Another factor is the temperature of the water. Because there is less sunlight deep in the ocean, the temperature is much lower. So more plants and animals are found in the upper layers of the ocean and near the shoreline than in the deeper layers. Another factor that affects ocean life is water pressure. Water pressure increases as depth increases. Do you know why? With increasing depth, the amount of water pushing down from above increases. This increases the pressure. Organisms that live deep in the ocean must be able to withstand great pressure.

The animals and plants in the ocean can be classified into three major groups according to their habits and the depth of the water in which they live. The largest group of animals and plants is called **plankton** (PLANGK-tuhn). Plankton float at or near the surface of the ocean where sunlight penetrates. Near the shore, they live at depths of about 1 meter. In the open ocean, they can be found at depths of up to 200 meters.

Most plankton are very small. In fact, many forms are microscopic. These organisms drift with the currents and tides of the ocean. Tiny shrimplike organisms and various forms of algae are all plankton. Plankton are the main food for many larger organisms, including the largest organisms on Earth—whales. Certain kinds of whales strain plankton from the water. It is interesting to note that the throat of some of the largest whales is so small that they cannot swallow food larger than a fifty-cent piece!

Forms of ocean life that swim are called **nekton** (NEHK-ton). Whales, seals, dolphins, squid, octopuses, barracudas, and other fishes are all nekton.

Figure 6–18 *Microscopic plankton (top) are the main source of food for many large sea creatures. The Southern right whale uses its strainerlike mouth to filter plankton from ocean water. Can you imagine how many plankton it must take to satisfy this whale's appetite?*

Figure 6–19 *Among the most-feared nekton, or forms of life that swim, are the sharks. Here you see the dangerous great white shark (left), the huge and harmless whale shark (top right), and the bottom-dwelling leopard shark (bottom right).*

Figure 6–20 *The sea anemone's "tentacles" carry stinging cells that enable it to capture unsuspecting fish. The clownfish swimming between the tentacles is immune to the anemone's poison. It helps attract other fish to the anemone. How does this unusual behavior help the clownfish survive?*

Because they can swim, nekton are able to actively search for food and avoid predators. Predators are organisms that eat other organisms. The organisms that get eaten are called prey. Some types of sharks are feared predators in the ocean; other fish are their prey.

Nekton can be found at all levels of the ocean. Some swim near the ocean surface, others along the bottom. Some are found in the deepest parts of the ocean. Because they can swim, nekton can move from one part of the ocean to another. But they remain in areas where conditions are most favorable.

Organisms that live on the ocean floor are called **benthos** (BEHN-thahs). Some benthos are plants that grow on the ocean floor in shallow waters. Plants are able to survive in water only where sunlight penetrates. Other benthos are animals such as barnacles, oysters, crabs, and starfish. Many benthos, such as sea anemones, attach themselves to the ocean floor. Others live in shore areas. A few kinds live on the ocean floor in the deepest parts of the ocean.

Intertidal Zone

As you just read, there are three major groups of ocean life. There are also three major environments, or life zones, in the ocean. **The classification of the ocean into life zones is based on the conditions in the ocean—conditions that vary widely.** There are

Figure 6–21 *The intertidal zone lies between the low- and high-tide lines. Organisms that live in the intertidal zone include starfish (inset), giant limpets (inset), clams (top right), barnacles (center), and sea anemones (bottom right).*

shallow beach areas that dry out twice a day and then become wet again. There are ocean depths where no ray of sunlight ever reaches and where the temperature stays a few degrees above freezing all year round. And in between these extremes is the open ocean with a range of environments at different depths. Scientists know a great deal about these areas, but much of the ocean still remains an unexplored frontier.

The region that lies between the low– and high–tide lines is the **intertidal zone.** This region is the most changeable zone in the ocean. Sometimes it is ocean. Sometimes it is dry land. These changes occur

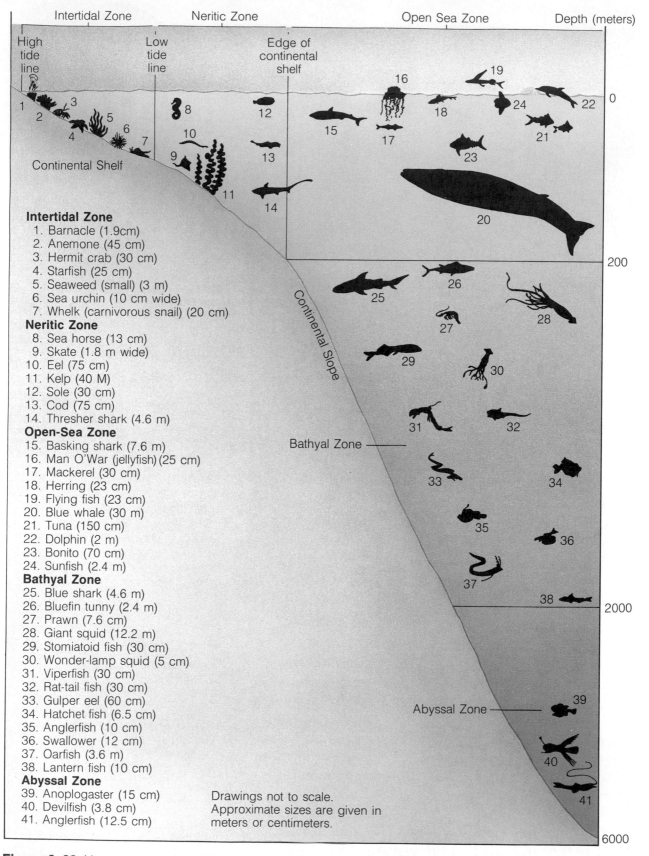

Intertidal Zone   Neritic Zone   Open Sea Zone   Depth (meters)

High tide line   Low tide line   Edge of continental shelf

Continental Shelf

Continental Slope

Bathyal Zone

Abyssal Zone

Intertidal Zone
1. Barnacle (1.9 cm)
2. Anemone (45 cm)
3. Hermit crab (30 cm)
4. Starfish (25 cm)
5. Seaweed (small) (3 m)
6. Sea urchin (10 cm wide)
7. Whelk (carnivorous snail) (20 cm)

Neritic Zone
8. Sea horse (13 cm)
9. Skate (1.8 m wide)
10. Eel (75 cm)
11. Kelp (40 M)
12. Sole (30 cm)
13. Cod (75 cm)
14. Thresher shark (4.6 m)

Open-Sea Zone
15. Basking shark (7.6 m)
16. Man O'War (jellyfish) (25 cm)
17. Mackerel (30 cm)
18. Herring (23 cm)
19. Flying fish (23 cm)
20. Blue whale (30 m)
21. Tuna (150 cm)
22. Dolphin (2 m)
23. Bonito (70 cm)
24. Sunfish (2.4 m)

Bathyal Zone
25. Blue shark (4.6 m)
26. Bluefin tunny (2.4 m)
27. Prawn (7.6 cm)
28. Giant squid (12.2 m)
29. Stomiatoid fish (30 cm)
30. Wonder-lamp squid (5 cm)
31. Viperfish (30 cm)
32. Rat-tail fish (30 cm)
33. Gulper eel (60 cm)
34. Hatchet fish (6.5 cm)
35. Anglerfish (10 cm)
36. Swallower (12 cm)
37. Oarfish (3.6 m)
38. Lantern fish (10 cm)

Abyssal Zone
39. Anoplogaster (15 cm)
40. Devilfish (3.8 cm)
41. Anglerfish (12.5 cm)

Drawings not to scale.
Approximate sizes are given in meters or centimeters.

0

200

2000

6000

Figure 6–22 *Here are the major life zones in the ocean, their depths, and some of the living things usually found in these zones. Above what depth is most ocean life found?*

Figure 6–23 *Mandarin, or psychedelic, fish (left) and the highly venomous lion fish (right) are but two of the many types of fishes that inhabit Earth's oceans.*

twice a day as the ocean surges up the shore at high tide and retreats at low tide. It is difficult for living things to survive in the intertidal zone. The tides and the waves breaking along the shore constantly move materials in this zone. Because the tide rises and falls, organisms must be able to live without water some of the time.

Some of the organisms that live in the intertidal zone are anemones, crabs, clams, mussels, and plants such as certain kinds of seaweeds. To keep from being washed out to sea, many of these organisms attach themselves to sand and rocks. Others, such as certain worms and some kinds of shellfish, burrow into the wet sand for protection.

Neritic Zone

The **neritic** (nee-RIHT-ihk) **zone** extends from the low-tide line to the edge of a continental shelf. This zone extends to a depth of about 200 meters.

The neritic zone receives plenty of sunlight. The water pressure is low and the temperature remains fairly constant. Here the ocean floor is covered with seaweed. Many different animals and plants live in this zone, including plankton, nekton, and benthos. In fact, the neritic zone is richer in life than any other ocean zone. Most of the world's great fishing areas are within this zone. Fish, clams, snails, some types of whales, and lobsters are but a few of the kinds of organisms that live in the neritic zone. This

Figure 6–24 *This California spiny lobster searching for food at night is among the many interesting creatures in the neritic zone.*

ACTIVITY DOING

Fish for the Table

Visit a supermarket or a fish market. List the different foods available that come from the ocean. Answer the following questions about the foods you listed:

1. Which foods are plankton? Nekton? Benthos?

2. From which ocean-life zone did each food come?

3. Where did the store obtain each food?

4. Which foods are sold fresh? Which are sold frozen?

5. Which foods have you eaten?

zone is the source of much of the seafood people eat. The neritic zone ends where there is too little sunlight for seaweed to grow.

Open-Ocean Zones

There are two open-ocean zones. The first is the **bathyal** (BAHTH-ee-uhl) **zone.** It begins at a continental slope and extends down about 2000 meters. Sunlight is not able to penetrate to the bottom of this zone. Many forms of nekton live in the bathyal zone, including squid, octopus, and large whales. Because there is little sunlight in the lower parts, plants do not grow near the bottom of this zone.

At a depth of about 2000 meters, the **abyssal zone** begins. This is the second open-ocean zone. The abyssal zone extends to an average depth of 6000 meters. This zone covers the large, flat plains of the ocean. No sunlight is able to penetrate to this zone. Thus little food is available. The water pressure is very great. What do you think the temperatures are like in the abyssal zone?

Even with extremely harsh conditions, life exists in the abyssal zone. Most of the animals that live here are small. Many are quite strange looking. Look again at the anoplogaster shown in the chapter opener. Some of the animals that live in this zone are able to make their own light.

Figure 6–25 *Organisms that live in the open-ocean zone include deep-sea anglerfish (top left), hatchet fish (bottom left), and krill (right).*

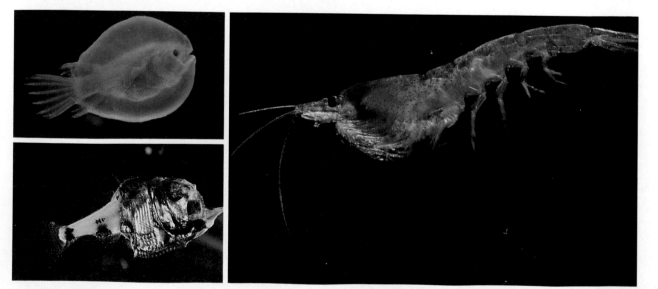

6–4 Section Review

1. What are the three major groups of ocean life?
2. What are some factors that affect ocean life?
3. Describe the three major ocean life zones.
4. Which zone contains the greatest variety of ocean life? Why?

Critical Thinking—*Applying Concepts*
5. Most commercial fishing occurs near the ocean surface. Why would fishing in extremely deep water prove to be unsuccessful?

6–5 Mapping the Ocean Floor

The oceans have been called the last great unexplored places on Earth. In fact, we probably know more about some of our neighbors in outer space than we do about the waters that make up almost 71 percent of our planet.

In 1872, the first expedition to explore the ocean began when the *Challenger* sailed from England. Equipped for ocean exploration, the *Challenger* remained at sea for $3\frac{1}{2}$ years. Scientists aboard the *Challenger* used wire to measure ocean depth. They used nets attached to heavy ropes to collect animals and plants from the ocean floor. Organisms that had

Guide for Reading

Focus on this question as you read.

▶ *How is the ocean floor mapped?*

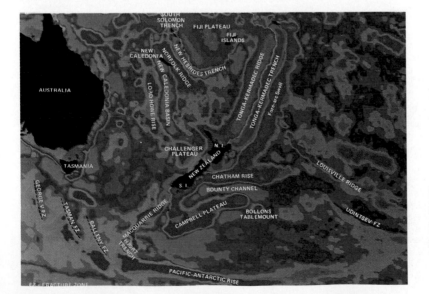

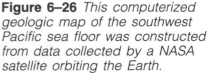

Figure 6–26 *This computerized geologic map of the southwest Pacific sea floor was constructed from data collected by a NASA satellite orbiting the Earth.*

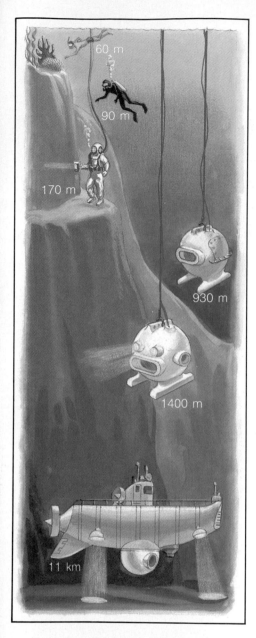

Figure 6–27 *Different instruments are used to explore the ocean. The type of instrument used is determined by the ocean depth. To what depth can a person descend without special breathing equipment?*

long remained undisturbed—free from the probing eyes of humans—were brought to the surface. Special thermometers enabled the scientists to record deep-ocean temperatures. And samples of ocean water were collected in special bottles.

Today oceanographers have many modern instruments to aid them in the exploration of the oceans. Underwater cameras provide pictures of the ocean floor. Devices called corers bring up samples of mud and sand from the ocean bottom. And a variety of vehicles, including bathyspheres, bathyscaphs, and other submersibles, are able to dive deep under the surface to explore the ocean depths.

One of the most important goals of oceanographers is to map the ocean floor. **Mapping the ocean floor can only be done by indirect methods, such as echo sounding, radar, sonar, and seismographic surveys.** All of these methods are based on the same principle: Energy waves, such as sound waves, sent down to the ocean surface are reflected from (bounce off) the ocean floor and return to the surface, where they are recorded. Knowing the speed of sound in water, which is about 1500 meters per second, and the time it takes sound waves to make a round trip, oceanographers can determine the ocean depth at any location along the ocean floor.

The most complete picture of the ocean floor has been pieced together from information gathered by *Seasat*, a scientific satellite launched in 1978. From the 8 billion readings radioed back by *Seasat*, scientists have created the most accurate map yet.

6–5 Section Review

1. Name three instruments used by oceanographers today to explore the ocean. How do these instruments compare with ones used in the earliest expeditions?
2. What two pieces of information are needed to map the ocean depth using sonar?

Connection—*You and Your World*
3. Even though the oceans are one of the grandest features of Planet Earth, we know relatively little about them. What are some reasons to explain this lack of knowledge?

6–6 Motions of the Ocean

Ocean water never stops moving. **There are three basic motions of ocean water: the up and down movement of waves, the steady movement of ocean currents, and the rise and fall of ocean water in tides.** In this section you will read more about each of these ocean movements.

Waves

Waves are pulses of energy that move through the ocean. Waves are set in motion by winds, earthquakes, and the gravitational pull of the moon. The most common source of energy for waves, however, is wind blowing across the surface of the ocean.

Have you ever observed ocean waves—first far out at sea and then closer to shore? If not, perhaps you have seen pictures of them. Ocean waves begin as wind-stirred ripples on the surface of the water. As more energy is transferred from wind to water, the waves formed look like great forward surges of rapidly moving water. But the water is not moving forward at all! Only energy moves forward through the water, producing one wave after another. The energy is passed from one particle of water to another. But the particles of water themselves remain in relatively the same positions.

Wave energy is not only passed forward from one water particle to another, it is also passed downward from particle to particle. With increasing depth, the motion of the particles decreases. At a certain depth, motion stops. In deep water, there are no waves except for those caused by tides and earthquakes.

The height of surface waves depends upon three different factors. Do you know what they are? These factors are the wind's speed, the length of time the wind blows, and the distance the wind blows over the water. As each of these factors increases, the height of a wave increases. And some waves can become really huge. The largest surface wave ever measured in the middle of any ocean occurred in the North Pacific on February 7, 1933. At that time, a wind storm was sweeping over a stretch of water thousands of kilometers long. A ship in the United States Navy, the *U.S.S. Ramapo,* was plowing through

Figure 6–28 *Waves are set in motion as energy is transferred from wind to water. The wave pulses of energy are passed forward from particle to particle, as well as downward from particle to particle. Notice that it is not the water that is moving forward, but the pulse of energy.*

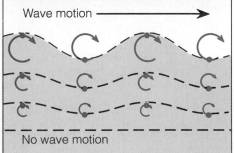

Wave motion ⟶

No wave motion

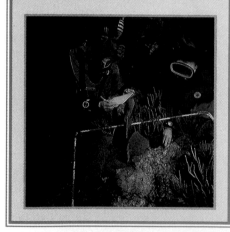
FACTORS THAT AFFECT THE HEIGHT OF SURFACE WAVES

Wind Speed (m/sec)	Length of Time Wind Blows (hr)	Distance Wind Blows Over Water (km)	Average Height of Wave (m)
5.1	2.4	18.5	0.27
10.2	10.0	140.0	1.5
15.3	23.0	520.0	4.1
20.4	42.0	1320.0	8.5
25.5	69.0	2570.0	14.8

Figure 6–29 *The factors that affect the height of surface waves are shown in this chart. What happens to the height of a wave as the wind speed increases?*

the sea when its officers spotted and measured a gigantic wave. It was at least 34 meters high! Such a wave would rise above a ten-story apartment house.

WAVE CHARACTERISTICS Ocean waves, like all other waves, have several characteristics. The highest point of a wave is called the **crest.** The lowest point of a wave is called the **trough** (TRAWF). The horizontal distance between two consecutive (one after the other) crests or two consecutive troughs is called the **wavelength.** The vertical distance between a crest and a trough is called the wave height. Waves have various wavelengths and wave heights. The basic characteristics of waves are shown in Figure 6–30.

Figure 6–30 *Characteristics of ocean waves are shown in this diagram. What is the distance between two consecutive crests called? What is the lowest point of a wave called?*

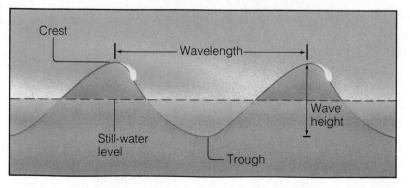

The amount of time it takes consecutive crests or troughs to pass a given point is called the wave period. The number of crests or troughs passing a given point in a certain wave period is called the wave frequency. What is the relationship between wavelength and wave frequency?

Out in the open ocean, waves stay about the same distance apart for thousands of kilometers. So wavelength is usually constant. These waves are called swells. Swells are long, wide waves that are not very high.

But waves change as they approach the shore. They slow down, and they get closer and closer together. Their wavelength decreases and their wave height increases. They finally crash forward as breakers and surge onto the shore. This surging water is called the surf.

The water then flows back toward the ocean. Bits of seaweed, sand, and pebbles are pulled back by the retreating water. This retreating water is called an undertow. Undertows can be quite strong. Occasionally, they can be strong enough to pose danger to swimmers, pulling them farther out into the ocean and under the water. Undertows can also extend for several kilometers offshore.

TSUNAMIS Some ocean waves are caused by earthquakes. These waves are called **tsunamis** (tsoo-NAH-meez). Tsunami is a Japanese word meaning "large wave in a harbor." Tsunamis are the highest ocean waves.

Figure 6–31 *The pattern of a swell as it reaches a sloping beach is shown in this diagram. What happens to the wavelength and the wave height as the wave nears the beach?*

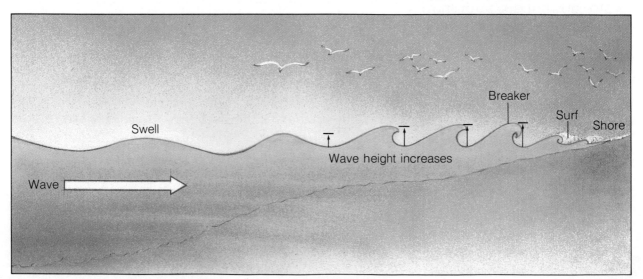

Swell

Breaker

Surf

Shore

Wave height increases

Wave

Figure 6–32 *The power of a tsunami left this boat high and dry on the dock.*

Tsunamis have very long wavelengths and are very deep. They carry a huge amount of energy. As tsunamis slow down in shallow water, they pile closer and closer together. Their wave heights increase. The energy that was once spread throughout a great depth of water is now concentrated in much less water. This energy produces the tsunamis, which can reach heights of 35 meters or more when they strike the shore. To give you some idea of the imposing height of a tsunami, consider this: The average height of a building story is between 3 and 4 meters. So a 35-meter wave is about the height of a ten-story building!

As you might suspect, tsunamis can cause great damage and loss of life along coastal areas. One of the most famous groups of tsunamis was caused by the volcanic eruption of Krakatoa between Java and Sumatra in 1883. Nine tsunamis that rose up to 40 meters high hit along the Java coast. Nothing was left of the coastal towns and about 36,000 people died.

Currents

You can easily see water moving on the surface of the ocean in the form of waves. But it is not only water on the surface that moves. Water below the surface also has motion. This water moves in streams called currents. Some currents are so large—up to several thousand kilometers long—that they are better described as "rivers" in the ocean. In fact, the mighty Mississippi River can be considered a mere brook when compared with the largest of the ocean currents. But long or short, all ocean currents are caused by the same two factors: wind patterns and differences in water density.

SURFACE CURRENTS Currents caused mainly by wind patterns are called **surface currents.** These currents usually have a depth of several hundred meters. Some surface currents are warm-water currents, others are cold-water currents. The temperature of a current depends upon where the current originates. A warm current begins in a warm area. A cold current begins in a cold area.

Surface currents that travel thousands of kilometers are called long-distance surface currents. The

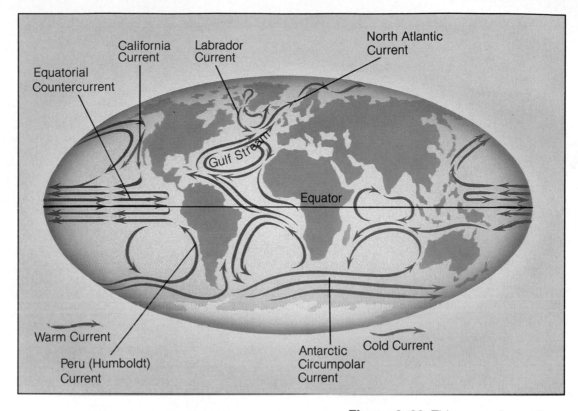

California Current
Labrador Current
North Atlantic Current
Equatorial Countercurrent
Gulf Stream
Equator
Warm Current
Peru (Humboldt) Current
Antarctic Circumpolar Current
Cold Current

Gulf Stream is a well-known long-distance surface current. It is about 150 kilometers wide and may reach a depth of about 1000 meters. It carries warm water from the southern tip of Florida north along the eastern coast of the United States. It moves along at speeds greater than 1.5 meters per second. And more than 150 million cubic meters of water may pass a given point each second!

Figure 6–33 shows the major warm and cold surface currents of the world and the general directions in which they flow. Because all the oceans are connected, these ocean currents form a continuous worldwide pattern of water circulation.

You will notice from Figure 6–33 that the water in each ocean moves in a large, almost circular pattern. In the Northern Hemisphere, the currents move clockwise, or the same way the hands of a clock move. In the Southern Hemisphere, the currents move counterclockwise, or in the opposite direction. These motions correspond to the direction of wind circulation in each hemisphere.

As you might expect, surface currents that move over short distances are called short-distance surface currents. These currents usually are found near a shoreline where waves hit at an angle. When the

Figure 6–33 *This map shows the directions of flow of the major long-distance surface currents. Is the Gulf Stream a warm or a cold current?*

Figure 6–34 *Two surface currents converge, or come together, in the Atlantic Ocean near Bermuda.*

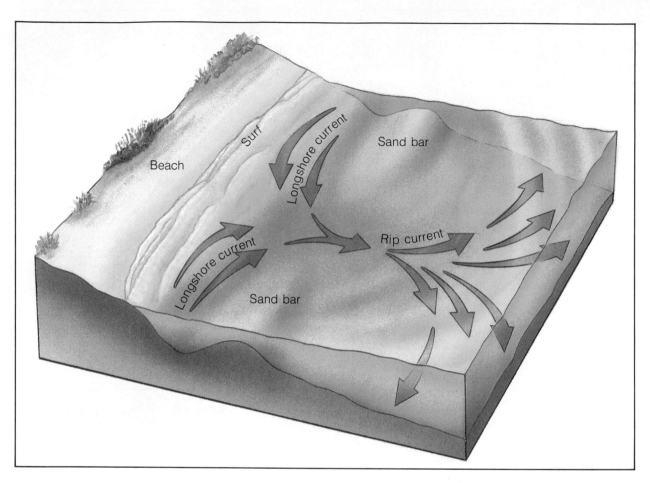

Figure 6–35 *When longshore currents cut through a sand bar, a rip current is formed.*

waves hit the shoreline, the water turns and produces currents that move parallel to the shoreline. These streams of water are called longshore currents.

As longshore currents move parallel to the shoreline, they pick up large quantities of material, such as sand from the beach. The sand is deposited in water close to the shoreline. A long, underwater pile of sand called a sand bar builds up.

Longshore currents can become trapped on the shoreline side of a sand bar. These currents may eventually cut an opening in the sandbar. The currents then return to the ocean in a powerful narrow flow called a rip current. A rip current is a type of undertow.

DEEP CURRENTS Some currents are caused mainly by differences in the density of water deep in the ocean. Such currents are called **deep currents.** The density, which you can think of as the heaviness of water, is affected by temperature and salinity. (Density is actually defined as mass per unit volume of a substance.) Cold water is more dense than warm water. And the saltier water is, the more dense it is. For example, cold dense water flowing from the polar regions moves downward under less dense warm water found in areas away from the poles.

Cameras lowered to the ocean floor have photographed evidence of powerful deep currents. The photograph in Figure 6–36 shows ripples carved into the sand of the ocean floor. In places on the floor, heavy clay has been piled into small dunes, as if shaped by winds. These "winds," scientists conclude, must be very strong ocean currents.

Most deep currents flow in the opposite direction from surface currents. For example, in the summer the Mediterranean Sea loses more water by evaporation than it gets back as rain. The salinity and density of the Mediterranean Sea increase. As a result, deep currents of dense water flow from the Mediterranean into the Atlantic Ocean. At the same time, the less salty and thus less dense water of the Atlantic Ocean flows into the Mediterranean at the water's surface.

The densest ocean water on Earth lies off the coast of Antarctica. This dense, cold Antarctic water sinks to the ocean floor and tends to flow north through the world's oceans. These deep Antarctic currents travel for thousands of kilometers. At the same time, warm surface currents near the equator tend to flow south toward Antarctica.

As the deep Antarctic currents come close to land, the ocean floor rises, forcing these cold currents upward. The rising of deep cold currents to the ocean surface is called **upwelling.** Upwelling is very important because the rising currents carry with them rich foodstuffs that have drifted down to the ocean floor. The foodstuffs are usually the remains of dead animals and plants. Wherever these deep currents rise, they turn the ocean into an area of plentiful ocean life. For example, deep currents move upward off the coasts of Peru and Chile. The nutrients they carry to the surface produce rich fishing grounds and important fishing industries in these areas.

Figure 6–36 *In this photograph you can see ripples carved into the ocean floor by a slow-moving deep current.*

Figure 6–37 *Areas of upwelling are important fishing areas because ocean life is plentiful. What factors cause upwelling?*

Figure 6–38 *The daily rise and fall of tides is magnificently evident at Mont-St.-Michel in France.*

Tides

As you learned in Chapter 4, tides are the regular rise and fall of ocean water caused by the gravitational attraction among the Earth, moon, and sun. The Earth's gravity pulls on the moon. But the moon's gravity also pulls on the Earth, producing a bulging of the ocean. The ocean bulges in two places: on the side of the Earth that faces the moon, and on the side of the Earth that faces away from the moon. Both bulges cause a high tide on nearby shorelines.

At the same time that the high tides occur, low tides occur between the two bulges. Observations show that at most places on Earth there are two high tides and two low tides every 24 hours.

Figure 6–39 *Spring tides occur when the sun and the moon are in line with the Earth. Neap tides occur when the sun and the moon are at right angles to the Earth.*

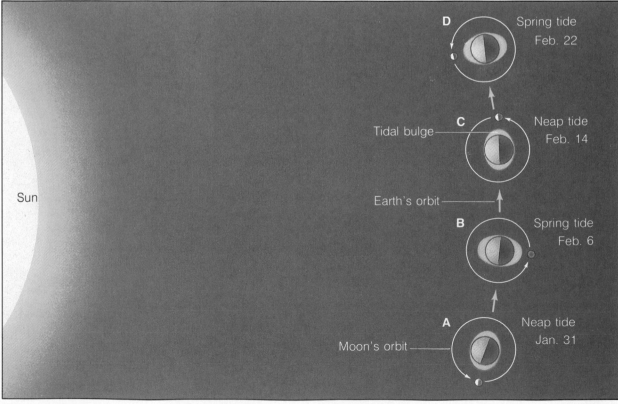

Recall from Chapter 4 that some high tides are higher than other high tides. These higher tides are called spring tides. Neap tides are the high tides that are lower than usual. Look at Figure 6–39. What is the position of the sun and moon with respect to each other during spring tides? During neap tides?

6–6 Section Review

1. What are the three basic motions of the ocean?
2. What are four characteristics of a wave?
3. What are currents? What is the difference between surface currents and deep currents?
4. What are tides? What causes them?

Critical Thinking—*Relating Cause and Effect*
5. For maximum excitement, a surfer wants to find the highest waves possible. In what ocean would the surfer have the best chance of finding enormous waves? Why?

ACTIVITY
DOING

The Moon's Attraction

Tide forecasts for each month are usually given in the newspaper on the first day of the month. You can also find tide forecasts in the *Farmer's Almanac.*

Use the information to plot a graph of daily high- and low-tide heights for the month. There are two high and two low tides given for each day. Plot only the heights that occur earlier in the day.

What is the relationship of the phases of the moon to the tide heights?

CONNECTIONS

The Sound of the Surf

Waves are beautiful to watch and thrilling to listen to. Even the smallest waves do not creep silently onto a beach. Instead they break with a gentle sigh. And when large waves break on shore, the crashing sounds are quite impressive. Did you ever wonder why waves make noise when they roll onto shore? The explanation may surprise you.

The answer to this question is as near as the bubble gum in your mouth. When you blow a bubble, you trap air in the gum. When the bubble breaks, it makes a popping sound. Breaking bubbles of trapped air also cause a sound when waves break. Ocean water picks up tiny bubbles of air, bubbles that become trapped within the water. When waves crash on the shore, the tiny air bubbles in the waves break. The characteristic sound of waves is produced. Keep this in mind, however. Even though there is a sound scientific reason that explains the *physics* of the noise, waves are still beautiful to look at and still wonderful to listen to.

Laboratory Investigation

The Effect of Water Depth on Sediments

Problem

To determine the effects that differences in water depth have on the settling of sediments.

Materials *(per group)*

plastic tubes of different lengths that contain sediment samples and salt water

Procedure

1. Obtain a plastic tube from your teacher.
2. Make sure that both ends of the tube are securely capped.

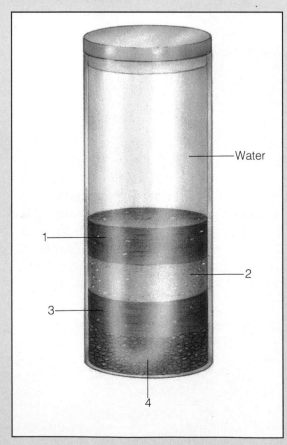

3. Hold the tube by both ends and gently tip it back and forth until the sediments in the tube are thoroughly mixed throughout the water.
4. Set the tube in an upright position in a place where it will not be disturbed.
5. Repeat steps 1 through 4 for each of the remaining tubes.
6. Carefully observe the sediments in each tube.

Observations

1. Make a detailed sketch to illustrate the heights of the different layers formed when the sediments in each tube settled.
2. What general statement can you make about the size of the sediment particles and the order in which each type of sediment settled in the tube?

Analysis and Conclusions

1. What effect does the length of the water column have on the number and types of sediment layers formed in each tube?
2. How are these tubes accurate models of what happens to sediments carried to the ocean?
3. What is the variable present in this investigation? What variables that may be present in the ocean are not tested in this investigation?
4. **On Your Own** Design an investigation to determine the effect of different amounts of salinity on the formation of sediment layers.

Study Guide

Summarizing Key Concepts

6–1 The World's Oceans

▲ The Atlantic, Pacific, and Indian oceans are the three major oceans.

6–2 Properties of Ocean Water

▲ Ocean water is a mixture of gases and solids dissolved in pure water.

▲ Ocean water is classified into three zones based on water temperature: surface zone, thermocline, and deep zone.

6–3 The Ocean Floor

▲ A continental margin consists of a continental shelf, a continental slope, and a continental rise.

▲ Major features of the ocean floor include, abyssal plains, seamounts, guyots, trenches, midocean ridges, rift valleys, and reefs.

6–4 Ocean Life Zones

▲ Ocean life forms are classified by habits and depth in which they live.

▲ The three major ocean life zones are the intertidal, neritic and open-ocean zones.

6–5 Mapping the Ocean Floor

▲ The ocean floor is mapped by echo sounding, radar, sonar, and seismographic surveys.

6–6 Motions of the Ocean

▲ Motions of the ocean include waves, currents, and tides.

▲ Waves have the following characteristics: crests, troughs, wavelength, wave height, wave period, and wave frequency.

▲ Surface currents are caused mainly by wind patterns; deep currents by differences in the density of ocean water.

▲ Tides are the regular rise and fall of ocean water caused by the gravitational attraction among the Earth, moon, and sun.

Reviewing Key Terms

Define each term in a complete sentence.

6–2 Properties of Ocean Water
oceanographer
salinity
surface zone
thermocline
deep zone

6–3 The Ocean Floor
shoreline
continental margin
continental shelf
continental slope
continental rise
turbidity current
submarine canyon
abyssal plain
seamounts
guyot
trench
midocean ridge
coral reef
fringing reef
barrier reef
atoll

6–4 Ocean Life Zones
plankton
nekton
benthos
intertidal zone
neritic zone
bathyal zone
abyssal zone

6–6 Motions of the Ocean
crest
trough
wavelength
tsunami
surface current
deep current
upwelling

Chapter Review

Content Review

Multiple Choice

Choose the letter of the answer that best completes each statement.

1. The three major oceans of the world are the Atlantic, Pacific, and
   a. Arctic.   c. Mediterranean.
   b. Indian.   d. Caribbean.

2. The amount of dissolved salts in ocean water is called
   a. salinity.   c. upwelling.
   b. turbidity.   d. current.

3. The zone in the ocean where the temperature changes rapidly is called the
   a. surface zone.   c. tide zone.
   b. benthos.   d. thermocline.

4. The amount of time it takes consecutive wave crests or troughs to pass a given point is called the
   a. wavelength.   c. wave height.
   b. tsunami.   d. wave period.

5. All ocean currents are caused by
   a. winds and earthquakes.
   b. volcanoes and tides.
   c. winds and water density.
   d. tides and water density.

6. The most common source of energy for surface waves is
   a. wind.   c. tides.
   b. earthquakes.   d. volcanoes.

7. The deepest parts of the ocean are found in long, narrow crevices called
   a. guyots.   c. reefs.
   b. seamounts.   d. trenches.

8. Organisms that live on the ocean floor are called
   a. nekton.   c. diatoms.
   b. plankton.   d. benthos.

9. The rising of deep cold currents to the ocean surface is called
   a. surfing.   c. mapping.
   b. upwelling.   d. reefing.

10. High tides that are higher than other high tides are called
    a. tsunamis.   c. spring tides.
    b. neap tides.   d. ebb tides.

True or False

If the statement is true, write "true." If it is false, change the underlined word or words to make the statement true.

1. The most abundant salt in the ocean is <u>magnesium bromide</u>.
2. The lowest point of a wave is called the <u>crest</u>.
3. The Gulf Stream is a <u>long-distance</u> surface current.
4. Tides are caused mainly by the gravitational attraction of <u>Jupiter</u>.
5. The relatively flat part of a continental margin covered by shallow water is called a <u>continental slope</u>.
6. <u>Spring tides</u> occur during the first- and last-quarter phases of the moon.

Concept Mapping

Complete the following concept map for Section 6–1. Then construct a concept map for the entire chapter.

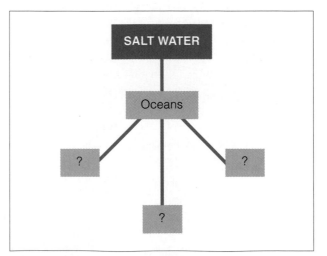

242

Concept Mastery

Discuss each of the following in a brief paragraph.

1. How do surface waves and deep waves differ?
2. How does the salinity of ocean water change with temperature?
3. Some of the largest animals in the oceans, (certain whales, for example) depend upon some of the smallest living organisms in the sea. Explain this statement.
4. List the three temperature zones of the ocean. Describe the physical conditions present in each zone.
5. Describe the topography of the ocean floor.
6. What are the three types of coral reefs? How are they alike? How are they different?

Critical Thinking and Problem Solving

Use the skills you have developed in this chapter to answer each of the following.

1. **Applying concepts** Many countries in the world extend their borders to a "two hundred mile limit" from shore. What are several reasons countries might impose this limit?
2. **Making inferences** Suppose conditions in the ocean changed and a major upwelling occurred off the coast of New York City. How would this change the life in the ocean in this area?
3. **Drawing conclusions** Suppose you were asked to design a special suit that would allow people to explore areas deep under the surface of the ocean. What are some important features the suit would need in order to help a diver survive?
4. **Applying concepts** Many legends tell of the appearance and disappearance of islands. Explain why such legends may be fact rather than fiction.
5. **Making calculations** Sound travels about 1500 meters per second in water. How deep would the ocean be if it took twenty seconds for a sound wave to return to the surface from the ocean bottom?
6. **Relating concepts** How do nekton organisms differ from benthos organisms?
7. **Identifying parts** The accompanying illustration shows a typical wave. Provide labels for the parts shown.
8. **Using the writing process** Suppose you and your family and friends lived in a huge glass bubble deep beneath the ocean waves. Write several pages in a diary to explain what life is like over a week's time.

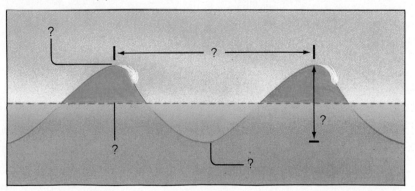

Earth's Fresh Water

Guide for Reading

After you read the following sections, you will be able to

7–1 Fresh Water on the Surface of the Earth

- Identify the sources of fresh water on the Earth's surface.
- Describe a watershed.

7–2 Fresh Water Beneath the Surface of the Earth

- Identify the sources of fresh water beneath the Earth's surface.
- Explain how fresh water forms caverns, stalactites, and stalagmites

7–3 Water as a Solvent

- Describe how the polarity of water makes it a good solvent.
- List ways in which supplies of fresh water can be protected.

The newspaper headlines said it all. Water, a substance most people take for granted, was creating problems all over the country. In some places there was too little water, in other places too much.

A severe drought in the West had left hundreds of square kilometers of forest dry. Forest fires raged in these areas, causing heavy damage. Firefighters battled in vain to stem the fire's destructive path.

Meanwhile, heavy rains in some southern states had flooded rivers, lakes, and streams. Dams could no longer hold the huge quantities of water building up behind them. In several places, dams collapsed. Water and thick streams of mud buried land and homes under a heavy sheet of wet, brown dirt.

Perhaps you have never thought of water as the cause of such problems. To you, water is a natural resource you use every day to stay alive. In fact, more than 500 billion liters of water are used every day in the United States alone. Within the next 20 years, this staggering volume will probably double! Where does our supply of fresh water come from? Will there always be enough? In this chapter you will learn about the Earth's supply of fresh water, as well as the answers to these questions.

Journal *Activity*

You and Your World The average American family uses 760 liters of water a day. In some parts of the world, however, the average family uses 7 to 10 liters of water a day! Suppose your family's supply of water were limited to 10 liters a day. In your journal, make a list of the things you would use this water for. Make a list of the things you couldn't do.

Fresh water is one of the Earth's most important natural resources.

Guide for Reading

*Focus on this question as
you read.*

▶ *What are the major
sources of fresh water on
the Earth's surface?*

7–1 Fresh Water on the Surface of the Earth

When you look at a photograph of Planet Earth taken from space, you can observe that water is one of the most abundant substances on Earth's surface. In fact, astronauts—whose views of Earth differ from those of most people—have described the Earth as the blue planet!

A casual glance at a world map might make you think that the Earth has an unending supply of fresh water—a supply that can meet the needs of living things forever. After all, the oceans cover more than 70 percent of the Earth's surface. Actually, about 97 percent of all the water on Earth is found in the oceans. But most of the ocean water cannot be used by living things because it contains salt. The salt would have to be removed before ocean water could be used.

Figure 7–1 *Most water on Earth is salt water found in the oceans. Only a small percent is fresh water, most of which is trapped as ice in the polar icecaps. That leaves only a small portion of fresh water available for use by living things.*

Fresh water makes up only about 3 percent of the Earth's water. However, most of this fresh water cannot be used because it is frozen, mainly in the icecaps near the North and South poles and in glaciers. In fact, only about 15 percent of the Earth's fresh water can be used by living things. This extremely small percent represents the Earth's total supply of fresh water. With such a limited supply, you might wonder why the Earth does not run out of fresh water. Fortunately, the Earth's supply of fresh water is continuously being renewed.

The Water Cycle

Most of the fresh water on the Earth's surface is found in moving water and in standing water. Rivers, streams, and springs are moving water. Ponds, lakes, and swampy wetlands are standing water.

Water moves among these sources of fresh water, the salty oceans, the air, and the land in a cycle. A cycle has no beginning and no end. It is a continuous chain of events. The **water cycle** is the movement of water from the oceans and freshwater sources to the air and land and finally back to the oceans. The water cycle, also called the hydrologic cycle, constantly renews the Earth's supply of fresh water.

Three main steps make up the water cycle. The first step involves the heat energy given off by the sun. This energy causes water on the surface of the Earth to change to water vapor, the gas phase of water. This process is called **evaporation** (ih-vap-uh-RAY-shuhn). Enormous amounts of water evaporate from the oceans. Water also evaporates from freshwater sources and from the soil. Animals and plants release water vapor into the air as well. You might be surprised to learn just how much water actually evaporates into the air from a single plant. (As you might suspect, a scientist has measured it!) In one day, a single large tree can move more than 1800 liters of water from the ground, through its stems and branches, to its leaves, and finally into the air! Other organisms do not move quite the same amount of water as this single large tree. But if you consider the vast number of plants, animals, and other living things that are part of the water cycle, you can see that the total amount of water given off by living things is very large indeed.

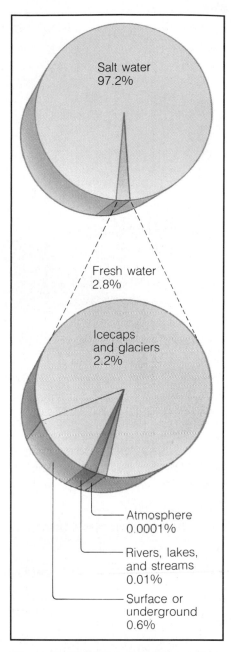

Figure 7–2 *This graph shows the distribution of Earth's water. What percent is fresh water? Is all this water available for use? Explain.*

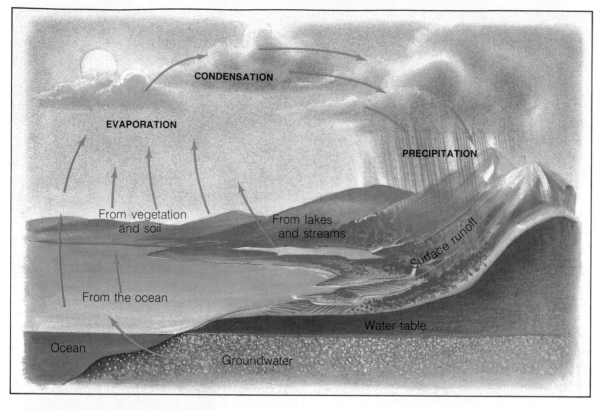

Figure 7–3 *The water cycle constantly renews the Earth's supply of fresh water. What three processes make up the water cycle?*

Figure 7–4 *A large tree can release up to 1800 liters of water a day into the atmosphere. By what process does liquid water in a tree become water vapor in the atmosphere?*

The second step of the water cycle involves a process called **condensation** (kahn-dehn-SAY-shuhn). Condensation is the process by which water vapor changes back into a liquid. For condensation to occur, the air containing the water vapor must be cooled. And this is exactly what happens as the warm air close to the Earth's surface rises. As it moves farther from the Earth's surface, the warm air cools. Cool air cannot hold as much water vapor as warm air. In the cooler air, most of the water vapor condenses into droplets of water that form clouds. But these clouds are not "salty" clouds. Do you know why? When water evaporates from the oceans, the salt is left behind. Water vapor is made of fresh water only.

During the third step of the cycle, water returns to the Earth in the form of rain, snow, sleet, or hail. This process is called **precipitation** (prih-sihp-uh-TAY-shuhn). Precipitation occurs when the water droplets that form in clouds become too numerous and too heavy to remain afloat in the air. The water that falls as rain, snow, sleet, or hail is fresh water. After the water falls, some of it returns to the

Figure 7–5 *The third step of the water cycle is precipitation, which may occur as rain, snow, sleet, or hail.*

atmosphere through evaporation. The cycle of water movement continues. The Earth's supply of fresh water is continuously renewed.

Some of the water that falls as precipitation may run off into ponds, lakes, streams, rivers, or oceans. Some may soak into the ground and become **groundwater.** Groundwater is the water that remains in the ground. At some point, the groundwater flows underground to the oceans. You will learn more about groundwater in the next section.

Frozen Water

If you make a snowball out of freshly fallen snow and hold it tightly in your hands for awhile, the warmth of your body will cause the snow to melt. Snow is actually a solid form of water. You may also notice that some of the snow pressed together by your hands forms ice. The same thing happens when new snow falls on top of old snow. The pressure of the piled-up snow causes some of the snow to change into ice. In time, a **glacier** forms. A glacier is a huge mass of moving ice and snow.

ACTIVITY

DISCOVERING

Making a Model of the Water Cycle

1. Stir salt into a small jar filled with water until no more will dissolve. Pour a 1-cm deep layer of the salt water into a large, wide-mouthed jar.

2. Place a paper cup half filled with sand in the center of the jar.

3. Loosely cover the jar's mouth with plastic wrap. Seal the wrap around the jar's sides with a rubber band.

4. Place a small rock or weight on the plastic wrap directly over the paper cup.

5. Place the jar in direct sunlight. After several hours, observe the setup. Carefully remove the plastic wrap and try to collect a few drops of the water that cling to the undersurface. Taste this water.

What is the purpose of sealing the jar? What did you notice about the taste of the water? What processes of the water cycle are in this model?

■ Develop another model to show the effect of temperature on the water cycle.

ACTIVITY

WRITING

The Water Cycle

Write a 250-word essay describing the water cycle. Use the following words in your essay:

    water cycle
    vapor
    evaporation
    condensation
    precipitation
    groundwater
    surface runoff
    watershed

Figure 7–6 *Valley glaciers are long, narrow glaciers that move downhill between mountain valleys. Here you see valley glaciers in the Alps (left) and in Alaska (right).*

Glaciers form in very cold areas, such as high in mountains and near the North and the South poles. Because of the extremely cold temperatures in these areas, the snow that falls does not melt completely. As more snow falls, it covers the older snow. As the snow builds up, the pressure on the older snow squeezes the snow crystals together. Eventually ice forms. When the layers of ice become very thick and heavy, the ice begins to move.

Glaciers contain about 2 percent of the available fresh water on the Earth. As sources of fresh water become more scarce, scientists are trying to develop ways to use this frozen supply of fresh water.

VALLEY GLACIERS Long, narrow glaciers that move downhill between the steep sides of mountain valleys are called **valley glaciers.** Usually, valley glaciers follow channels formed in the past by running water. As a valley glacier moves downhill, it bends and twists to fit the shape of the surrounding land. The valley walls and the weight of the ice itself keep the glacier from breaking apart. But on its surface, the ice cracks. Cracks on the surface of glaciers are called crevasses (krih-VAS-sehz).

As a valley glacier slides downward, it tears rock fragments from the mountainside. The rock fragments become frozen in the glacier. They cut deep grooves in the valley walls. Finer bits of rock smooth the surfaces of the valley walls in much the same way

Figure 7–7 *A crevasse, or crack in a glacier, can make mountain climbing a difficult sport indeed.*

as a carpenter's sandpaper smooths the surface of a piece of wooden furniture.

Mountains located anywhere from the equator to the poles can contain glaciers. Many glaciers are found in the United States. Mount Rainier in Washington State and Mount Washington in New Hampshire contain small glaciers. Glaciers can also be found in many mountains of Alaska.

As a valley glacier moves, some of the ice begins to melt, forming a stream of water. This water is called meltwater. Meltwater is usually nearly pure water. Some cities use meltwater as a source of their drinking water. Boulder, Colorado, uses meltwater from the nearby Arapaho Glacier. Meltwater is also used in some places to generate electricity in hydroelectric plants. But some problems arise in the use of meltwater in these ways. Building channels or pipelines to transport meltwater from glaciers to cities can be costly. And the construction of hydroelectric plants in the underdeveloped areas where glaciers are located could alter the surrounding environment.

CONTINENTAL GLACIERS   In the polar regions, snow and ice have built up to form thick sheets. These thick sheets of ice are called **continental glaciers,** or polar ice sheets. Continental glaciers cover millions of square kilometers of the Earth's surface and may be several thousand meters thick. Continental glaciers move slowly in all directions.

Figure 7–8 *Continental glaciers such as Mertz Glacier in Antarctica cover millions of square kilometers.*

Continental glaciers are found in Greenland and Antarctica. Nearly 85 percent of Greenland is covered by ice. More than 98 percent of Antarctica is covered by ice. These huge glaciers are more than 4800 meters thick at the center. In the future, continental glaciers could be another source of fresh water.

ICEBERGS At the edge of the sea, continental glaciers form overhanging cliffs. Large chunks of ice, called **icebergs,** often break off from these cliffs and drift into the sea. Some icebergs are as large as the state of Rhode Island! The continental glaciers of Greenland and Antarctica are the major sources of icebergs in ocean waters.

Icebergs can pose a major hazard to ships. In 1912, the ocean liner *Titanic* sank after smashing into an iceberg in the North Atlantic Ocean. Many lives were lost as this ship, thought to be unsinkable, plunged to the ocean bottom on her first voyage. Today, sea lanes are patrolled constantly by ships and planes on the lookout for icebergs.

Much fresh water is frozen in icebergs. Attempts have been made to develop ways of towing icebergs to areas that need supplies of fresh water, such as deserts. But transporting icebergs from Greenland and Antarctica poses several problems. First, the effects of an iceberg on local weather conditions must be evaluated. Second, the cost and time involved in moving the iceberg must be considered.

Figure 7–9 *Icebergs, which often have spectacular shapes, are large chunks of ice that break off glaciers and drift into the sea. Only a small part of an iceberg rises above the water's surface. Can you explain the meaning of the phrase "tip of the iceberg"?*

Third, scientists would have to find a way of preventing the iceberg from melting during the ocean journey. Can you think of ways to use icebergs?

Running Water

Rivers and streams are important sources of fresh water. Many cities and towns were built near rivers and streams. The water is used for irrigating crops, generating electricity, drinking, and other household uses. Rivers and streams are also used for recreational purposes, such as fishing, swimming, and boating. Industry and commerce depend on rivers for transporting supplies and equipment and for shipping finished products. River and stream water is also used to cool certain industrial processes. In the past, industries and towns used rivers and streams as natural sewers to carry away waste products. Today, although pollution is still a problem, strict controls regulate the kinds and amounts of wastes that can be dumped into rivers and streams.

Rain and melted snow that do not evaporate or soak into the soil flow into rivers and streams. The water that enters a river or stream after a heavy rain or during a spring thaw of snow or ice is called **surface runoff.**

The amount of surface runoff is affected by several factors. One factor is the type of soil the precipitation falls on. Some soils soak up more water

ACTIVITY
CALCULATING

I Am Thirsty

An average person needs about 2.5 L of water a day to live.

Use this amount to calculate how much water an average person needs in a year. How much water is needed by your class to live in a day? In a year?

Figure 7–10 *Running water from rivers and streams is an important resource used for crop irrigation and for generating electricity in hydroelectric plants.*

Figure 7–11 *Over the course of millions of years, the Colorado River has carved the Grand Canyon out of the Earth's rocky crust.*

than others. These soils have more spaces between their particles. The space between particles of soil is called **pore space.** The more pore space a soil has, the more water it will hold. The condition of the soil also affects the amount of runoff. If the soil is dry, it will soak up a great deal of water and reduce the surface runoff. If the soil is wet, it will not soak up much water. Surface runoff will increase.

The number of plants growing in an area also affects the amount of surface runoff. Plant roots absorb water from the soil. In areas where there are many plants, large amounts of water are absorbed. There is less surface runoff. The season of the year is another factor that affects the amount of surface runoff. There will be more runoff during rainy seasons and during the spring in areas where large amounts of snow are melting.

A land area in which surface runoff drains into a river or a system of rivers and streams is called a **watershed.** Watersheds vary in size. Especially large watersheds can cover millions of acres and drain their water into the oceans. Watersheds prevent floods and water shortages by controlling the amount of water that flows into streams and rivers. Watersheds also help to provide a steady flow of fresh water into the oceans. How do you think the construction of roads in a watershed area might affect nearby rivers and streams?

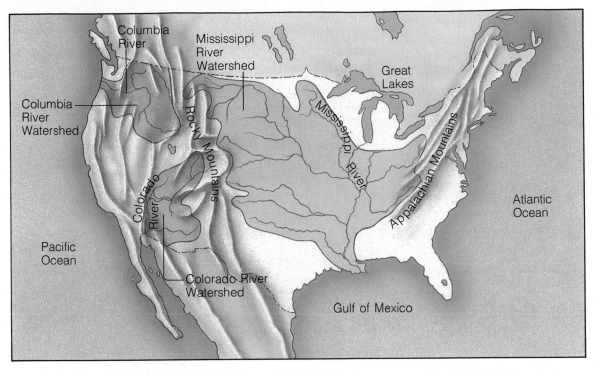

Many rivers are sources of fresh water. The amount of water in a river and the speed at which the water flows affect the usefulness of a river as a source of fresh water. Rivers that move quickly carry a lot of water. But because the water is moving rapidly, fast-moving rivers also carry a large amount of soil, pebbles, and other sediments. The water in these rivers often looks cloudy. Slow-moving rivers do not churn up as much sediment. Their water is clearer. These rivers are better sources of fresh water.

In recent years, pollution has had an effect on the usefulness of rivers and streams as sources of fresh water. If a river or stream has many factories along its banks that discharge wastes into the water, the water becomes polluted. Water in a polluted river or stream must be cleaned before it can be used. Some rivers are so heavily polluted that they cannot be used as a source of fresh water. You will learn more about pollution in Chapter 23.

Standing Water

Within a watershed, some of the surface runoff gets caught in low places. Standing bodies of fresh water are formed there. Depending on their size, these bodies of water are called lakes or ponds.

Figure 7–12 *The major watersheds of the United States are shown in this map. Which watershed is the largest?*

Figure 7–13 *Our supply of fresh water is reduced every year by dangerous wastes released into the water. In what ways can you personally reduce water pollution?*

Activity Bank

How Does a Fish Move?, p. 757

Like rivers and streams, lakes and ponds receive their water from the land. Surface runoff keeps lakes and ponds from drying up. In many areas, these standing bodies of water are important sources of fresh water. Moosehead Lake, in Maine, is a natural source of fresh water. It is 56 kilometers long and varies from 3 to 16 kilometers wide. The pine-forested shores of the lake hold huge amounts of water from rains and melting snow. The water is released slowly to the lake, so flooding is not likely. During times of drought (long periods with little rainfall), the lake holds water in reserve.

LAKES AND PONDS Lakes are usually large, deep depressions in the Earth's crust that have filled with fresh water. Rain, melting snow, water from springs and rivers, and surface runoffs fill these depressions. A lake is sometimes formed when there is a natural obstruction, or blockage, of a river or stream. Lakes can be found in many places on the Earth. They are found most frequently at relatively high altitudes and in areas where glaciers were once present.

Ponds are shallow depressions in the Earth's crust that have filled with fresh water. They are usually smaller and not as deep as lakes. Because the water is shallow, sunlight can penetrate to the bottom of a pond. Plants need light to make food, so plants can be found throughout a pond. Lakes, however, often have very deep parts where sunlight cannot reach. Will you find plants at the bottom of a deep lake?

Figure 7–14 *Standing water is found in lakes and ponds throughout the world. What is the difference between a lake and a pond?*

RESERVOIRS The most frequently used sources of fresh water are artificial lakes known as **reservoirs** (REHZ-uhr-vwahrz). A reservoir is built by damming a stream or river that runs through a low-lying area. When the stream or river is dammed, water backs up behind the dam, forming a reservoir. Reservoirs have been built near cities and towns and in mountainous regions throughout the country.

Reservoirs serve several purposes. They help to prevent flooding by controlling water during periods of heavy rain and runoff. Reservoirs store water. During periods when rainfall and runoff are scarce, reservoirs serve as sources of drinking water for nearby towns and cities. In certain areas, reservoirs provide irrigation water for farms. The water held in reservoirs can also be used to generate electricity. Hydroelectric generators are built in the walls of a dam. The water stored in the reservoir can generate electricity when it moves through turbines, which are connected to the dams. Hydroelectric plants convert the energy of moving water into electrical power.

A reservoir, however, cannot be used for all purposes at the same time. Why is this so? Suppose a reservoir is used to store water. To use the water to generate electricity, the water would have to be drawn from the reservoir. The reservoir would no longer be storing water.

Figure 7–15 *The effects of a drought in California in 1991 can be seen in the low water level in the San Luis Reservoir.*

7–1 Section Review

1. What are the major sources of fresh water on the Earth's surface?
2. How much of the Earth's supply of fresh water is available for use? Where is the bulk of fresh water on Earth found?
3. Briefly outline the water cycle.

Critical Thinking—*Applying Concepts*

4. A builder wants to level all the trees in a watershed area to construct homes. What would be some effects of the builder's actions on the watershed and on nearby rivers and streams?

ACTIVITY

CALCULATING

Hydroelectric Power

The total potential hydroelectric power of the world is 2.25 billion kilowatts. Only 363 million kilowatts of this is actually being utilized, however. The United States uses one sixth of the world's hydroelectric power. Calculate the percent of the world's hydroelectric power that is actually being used. What percent of the world's hydroelectric power is used in the United States?

CONNECTIONS

Water, Water Everywhere— And Everyone Wants to Use It

There is nothing more soothing than the sound of raindrops hitting a windowpane. Most outdoor activities are postponed during a heavy rain. But you can be sure that the rain will eventually stop, and the sun will shine once again. You might not be happy when it rains, but you should be thankful. For rain replenishes the Earth's supply of fresh water.

Water is needed by all forms of life on Earth. Without water, Earth would be a dry and lifeless planet. Visit a desert after a heavy rain and you will see plants appear in the once dry, blowing sands. These plants take advantage of the rain to flower and make seeds before the soil again becomes too dry to support life.

People make great demands on the Earth's supply of fresh water. The average American family uses 760 liters of water a day—and not just to satisfy their thirsts. About half of that total is used to flush away wastes and for showers and baths. Seventy-five liters or more is used each time a dishwasher or a clothes washer cleans up after us.

The *technology* to manufacture the many products that contribute to our way of life takes water—often a great deal of water. For example, about 3.8 million liters of water are used to produce a ton of copper—the metal used to make electric wires and the pennies jingling in your pocket. Almost 1.1 million liters of water are used to make a ton of aluminum—a metal used to make cooking utensils and food containers. It even takes about 3.7 liters of water to make a single page in this textbook. We hope you feel that this was water well used!

7–2 Fresh Water Beneath the Surface of the Earth

Not all of the water that falls to the Earth as rain, snow, sleet, or hail runs off into lakes, ponds, rivers, and streams. Some of the water soaks into the ground. Water contained in the ground is one of the Earth's most important natural resources. There is more fresh water below the surface of the land than in all the lakes and reservoirs on the Earth's surface.

Groundwater

If you live in a rural, or country, area, you probably do not get your water from a reservoir or river. More likely, your water is pumped from a well in the ground. As you learned in the previous section, the water stored in the ground is known as groundwater. In many areas, groundwater provides a continuous supply of fresh water.

Groundwater is present because the various forms of precipitation—rain, snow, sleet, and hail—do not stop traveling when they hit the ground. Instead, the precipitation continues to move slowly downward through pores, or spaces, in the rocks and soil. If the rocks and soil have many pores between their particles, they can hold large quantities of groundwater. Sand and gravel are two types of soil that contain many pores.

As the water seeps down, it passes through layers of rocks and soil that allow it to move quickly. Material through which water can move quickly is described as **permeable** (PER-mee-uh-buhl). Sandstone is a rock that is very permeable. But clay, which has small pores between its particles, is not as permeable. Clay is sometimes described as **impermeable.**

UNDERGROUND ZONES Groundwater continues to move downward through permeable rock and soil until it reaches an impermeable layer of rock. When it reaches an impermeable layer, it can go no farther. So the groundwater begins to fill up all the pores above the impermeable layer. This underground region in which all the pores are

Figure 7–16 *Some of the water that falls to Earth as rain, snow, sleet, or hail soaks into the ground. In some places this water is very close to the Earth's surface. So a well such as this can be used to obtain water.*

filled with water is called the **zone of saturation** (sach-uh-RAY-shuhn).

An example from the kitchen may help you to understand what happens when spaces in the ground become filled with water. You may never have looked closely at the sponge on a kitchen sink. When a sponge is barely moist, only some of the spaces in the sponge are filled with water. Most of the spaces hold air. When you place the sponge in water, it swells. Eventually, all the spaces are filled and the sponge cannot take up any more water. The ground acts in much the same way as the sponge. Once the spaces in the ground are filled, the ground is saturated. It cannot hold any more water.

Above the water-filled zone, the ground is not as wet. Pores in the soil and rocks are filled mostly with air. This drier region in which the pores are filled mostly with air is called the **zone of aeration.**

The surface between the zone of saturation and the zone of aeration is an important boundary. It

Figure 7–17 *A cross section of the zones of underground water is shown here. What separates the zone of aeration from the zone of saturation?*

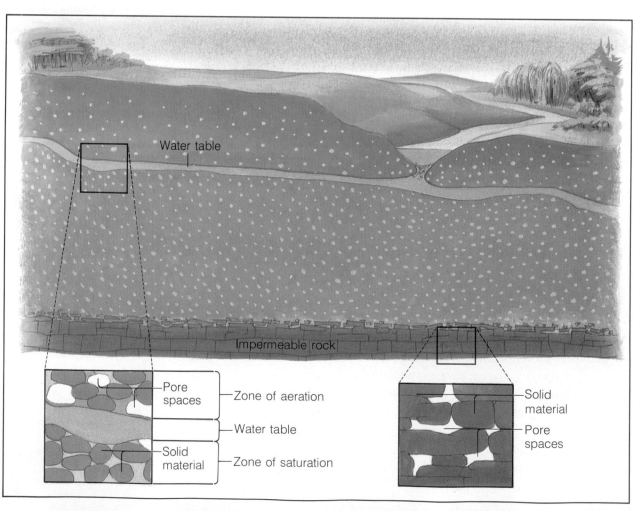

Water table

Impermeable rock

Pore spaces
Solid material

Zone of aeration
Water table
Zone of saturation

Solid material
Pore spaces

Figure 7–18 *What factors influence the levels of the water table in this marsh (left) and at this Saharan oasis (right)?*

marks the level below which the ground is saturated, or soaked, with water. This level is called the **water table.** See Figure 7–17.

At the seashore, the water table is easy to find. After you dig down 10 or 20 centimeters, you may notice that the hole you are digging fills with water. At this point, you have located the water table. In general, the water table is not very deep near a large body of water.

In areas near hills or mountains, the water table may be deep within the ground. In low-lying areas such as valleys with swamps and marshes, the water table may be close to or at the surface. The depth of the water table also varies with the climate of an area. It may be deep in very dry areas, such as deserts. It may be close to the surface in wet, low-lying forest areas. In very moist climate regions, the water table may come right to the surface and form a swamp, lake, or spring. Why do you think low-lying areas have a water table that is close to the surface?

Even in the same area, the depth of the water table may change. Heavy rains and melting snows will make the water table rise. If there is a long, dry period, the water table will fall. The depth of the water table will also change if wells are overused or if many wells are located in a small area. Wells are

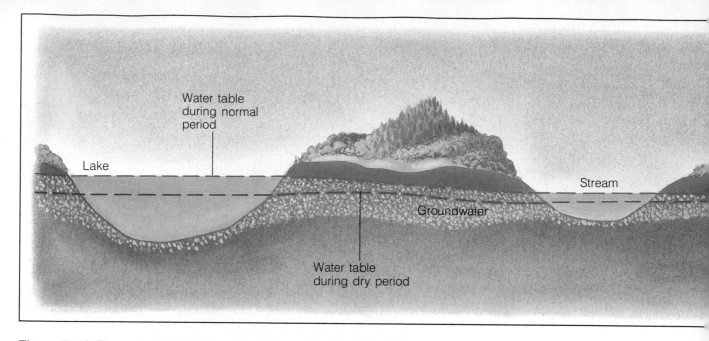

Figure 7–19 *The water table follows the shape of the land. Springs, swamps, and ponds sometimes form where the water table meets the land's surface. What happens to the water table during a dry period?*

holes drilled or dug to the water table to bring water to the surface. The use of several wells in an area may draw so much water from the water table that only very deep wells are able to pump water to the surface. Figure 7–19 shows some characteristics of the water table.

The depth of the water table may have other effects. In order to provide a proper foundation for a tall building, a builder must dig a deep hole. In some places in New York City, the water table is very high, and water rapidly fills the foundation hole. This water must be pumped out in order for construction to proceed. This extra work adds to the cost of a building. In certain areas, wells are dug to provide a source of household water. It is relatively inexpensive to dig a well in areas where the water table is high. In areas where the water table is deep, however, it can be very expensive to dig a well. Remember—a water table is always present, no matter where you live. And you will always reach it if you dig deep enough!

AQUIFERS As groundwater moves through a permeable rock layer, it often reaches an impermeable rock layer or the water table. At this point, the groundwater may move sideways through a layer of rock or sediment that allows it to pass freely. Such a layer is called an **aquifer** (AK-wuh-fer). Aquifers are

Spring

Stream

Swamp

Sea

usually layers of sandstone, gravel, sand, or cracked limestone.

Because rocks form in layers, a layer of permeable rock may become trapped between two layers of impermeable rock. Sandstone (permeable rock) trapped between two layers of shale (impermeable rock) is an example. If the layer of sandstone contains water, an aquifer forms. An aquifer may also form when soil saturated with groundwater is located above an impermeable rock layer.

An aquifer is a source of groundwater. To reach this water, a well is often dug or drilled into the aquifer. Groundwater moves into the well hole and forms a pool. Each time water is pumped from the well, more water moves through the aquifer into the well hole. Nassau and Suffolk counties in New York State pump much of the water used by their inhabitants from huge aquifers.

Because water often moves great distances through aquifers, these underground water sources are extremely vulnerable to pollution. Any pollutants added to an aquifer may spread through the aquifer, endangering water sources far from the pollutants' point of origin.

In some places where the underground rock layers slope, an aquifer carries water from a higher altitude to a lower altitude. If the aquifer is trapped between two layers of impermeable rock, pressure may build up at the lower altitude. A well

ACTIVITY

DISCOVERING

Drought and the Water Table

1. Fill a deep clear-glass baking dish about halfway with sand. Make sure that the sand covers the bottom.

2. Slowly add enough water so that 1 cm of water is visible above the surface of the sand.

3. Add more sand above the water in only one half of the baking dish.

4. Observe the water level during the next few days.

What changes do you notice in the water level?

■ What different conditions of the water table does your model represent?

■ Design an experiment to show the effect of drought on the water table in an area with a clay soil.

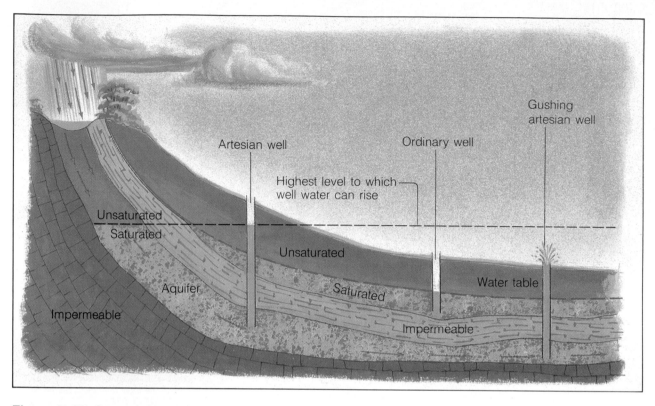

Figure 7–20 Groundwater can be obtained from an aquifer by means of an ordinary well or an artesian well. The amount of water pressure in an artesian well depends on how close the well is to the water table.

drilled into the aquifer at this point will provide water without pumping. A well from which water flows on its own without pumping is called an artesian (ahr-TEE-zhuhn) well. See Figure 7–20.

Groundwater Formations

In some areas, the underlying rock is limestone. Because limestone is affected by groundwater in a particular way, underground **caverns** (KAV-ernz) often form in these areas. As water moves down through the soil, it combines with carbon dioxide to form a weak acid that can dissolve limestone. This acid, called carbonic acid, is the weak acid found in seltzer water and other carbonated beverages. You are probably familiar with this weak acid as the "fizz" in a carbonated beverage.

When groundwater enters cracks in limestone, the carbonic acid it contains causes the cracks to become wider. If this process continues long enough, underground passages large enough to walk through may be formed.

Sometimes large underground caverns with many passages are formed. If you walk through these caverns, you will see what looks like long stone icicles

Figure 7–21 This giant sinkhole in Winter Park, Florida, was caused when groundwater dissolved the limestone base on which part of the town was constructed.

hanging from the ceilings. These icicles are called stalactites (stuh-LAK-tights). Stalagmites (stuh-LAG-mights) look like stone icicles built up from the floors of the caverns. Stalactites and stalagmites are formed when dissolved substances in groundwater are deposited. You will learn more about the dissolving properties of water in the next section.

Figure 7–22 *In many caverns, underground lakes are formed as groundwater moves through limestone. This lake is found in Hams Caves, Spain. What are the cavern formations hanging from the ceiling and rising from the ground called?*

7–2 Section Review

1. How does groundwater form?
2. What are the three underground zones through which groundwater moves?
3. What causes differences in the depth of the water table?
4. Describe the formation of the following: aquifer, artesian well, cavern.

Connection—*Ecology*
5. Because it is too expensive to truck dangerous pollutants away from the plant, the factory manager proposes that a hole be dug deep in the ground on the side of the factory building and that wastes be dumped into this hole. Predict the effects of this action on the water pumped from wells a short distance from this factory.

265

7–3 Water as a Solvent

Water is the most common substance on Earth. It exists as a solid, a liquid, or a gas. Water moves in a cycle among the oceans, the air, and the land. Water changes form as it moves through this cycle. In this section, you will take a look at the chemical makeup of water and some of its important properties.

Composition of Water

A water molecule (MAHL-uh-kyool) is the smallest particle of water that has all the properties of water. A water molecule forms when two atoms of hydrogen and one atom of oxygen combine. (Atoms are the basic building blocks of all materials on Earth.) The chemical formula for water is H_2O. As you can see, this formula describes the number of atoms of hydrogen (2) and oxygen (1) that combine to form a water molecule.

In a water molecule, the atom of oxygen has a slight negative charge (−). Each atom of hydrogen has a slight positive charge (+). So a molecule of water has oppositely charged ends. See Figure 7–23. These charged ends give a water molecule the property known as **polarity** (poh-LAR-uh-tee). You might be familiar with the property of polarity as it applies to a magnet. A magnet has two poles—a positive pole and a negative pole. Each pole attracts the oppositely charged pole of another magnet.

It is the polarity of water molecules that makes water a **solvent** (SAHL-vuhnt). A solvent is a substance in which another substance dissolves. The dissolving process produces a **solution.** A solution contains two or more substances mixed on the molecular level.

For example, if you pour a small quantity of salt into a container of water, the salt will dissolve in the water. Although you will not be able to see the dissolved salt, you will know that it is there if you taste the water. The water molecules, having oppositely charged ends, attract the charged particles that make up the salt. It is as if the water molecules "pull" the charged particles out of the solid salt, dissolving the salt.

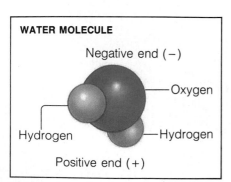

WATER MOLECULE

Negative end (−)

Oxygen

Hydrogen

Hydrogen

Positive end (+)

Figure 7–23 *A molecule of water exhibits the property of polarity. Why is this property important?*

Because of its polarity, water is able to dissolve many different substances. Water can dissolve so many different substances, in fact, that it is called the universal solvent. You probably use water as a solvent every day without realizing it. For example, flavoring and carbon dioxide gas are dissolved in water to make soft drinks. In fact, all the beverages you drink contain substances dissolved in water. What other products can you name that are made with water?

Farmers use water to dissolve fertilizers for crops. Many medicines use water to dissolve the medication. Certain minerals and chemicals are dissolved in water in water-treatment plants to remove harmful minerals, chemicals, and wastes. For example, chlorine, a chemical that kills bacteria, is added to drinking water. In some cities and towns, fluorides are also added to water. The dissolved fluorides help to prevent tooth decay.

Figure 7–24 *In this sewage-treatment plant in California, water hyacinths are used to help purify "dirty" water.*

PROBLEM Solving

How Sweet It Is

Several factors affect the rate at which a substance dissolves in water.

Making inferences Use the photographs to determine these factors.

Figure 7–25 *As water evaporates from the hot springs, piles of salts are left behind. Is the water most likely hard or soft? Why?*

Hardness of Water

The taste, odor, and appearance of water vary from area to area. The differences depend on the amounts and types of materials dissolved in the water.

The water that you drink may come from a surface source or from a groundwater source. This water may be "hard" or "soft." The hardness or softness of water depends on the source of the water and the types of rocks and soils the water comes in contact with. **Hard water** contains large amounts of dissolved minerals, especially calcium and magnesium. Soap will not lather easily in hard water. Also, hard water causes deposits of minerals to build up in water heaters and plumbing systems. **Soft water** does not contain these minerals. Soap lathers easily in soft water, and mineral deposits do not build up when soft water is used.

Some water is softened naturally as it passes through and reacts with rock formations that contain certain minerals. These minerals remove the calcium and magnesium from the water, making it soft. Many homes with hard water have water softeners that remove the minerals that make the water hard. Do you know what type of water you have in your home? How could you experiment to find out?

Quality of Water

Water is necessary to all life on Earth. So it is important to maintain the quality of our water.

Unfortunately, many of Earth's freshwater sources are becoming polluted. In nature, water is usually filtered as it passes through soil and sand. This filtering removes impurities. But the careless dumping of sewage, silt, industrial wastes, and pesticides into water has produced many serious problems. Because so many different substances can be dissolved in water, water is becoming more and more polluted.

Water pollution limits the amount and kinds of wildlife that can live in water. Water pollution also affects supplies of drinking water and destroys recreational areas. Among the chemicals that cause water pollution are nitrates and phosphates. These chemicals are used on farms to improve the growth of plants or to kill harmful insects. Nitrates and phosphates have entered the groundwater in many areas and must be removed before water can be used for drinking or swimming.

Federal laws have been passed to prevent industries from dumping certain chemical wastes into the Earth's waters. Waste-water treatment systems are being built to remove pollution from water before it enters rivers and lakes. Although Earth is called the water planet (and the supply of water seems unending), the truth is that we have a limited supply of fresh water. This water must be protected from sources of pollution. Can you think of some other steps that might be taken to do just this?

Figure 7–26 *One of the most serious problems facing society is the pollution of its water supply. Here you see an oil spill in Galveston Bay, Texas.*

What Is the Effect of Phosphates on Plant Growth?, p. 758

7–3 Section Review

1. Describe the structure of a molecule of water. How is this structure related to its ability to act as a solvent?
2. What is hard water? Soft water?
3. What are three sources of water pollution? Why must the water supply be protected from pollutants?

Critical Thinking—*Designing an Experiment*
4. Design an experiment to compare the hardness of two sources of water using only common, everyday substances. You can use tap water from your home, bottled water, or water from your school or the home of a friend or relative.

Laboratory Investigation

Porosity of Various Soils

Problem

How can the water-holding capability, or porosity, of various soils be determined?

Materials *(per group)*

250 mL sand
250 mL clay
250 mL gravel
4 small paper cups
2 L water
500-mL graduated cylinder

Procedure 🧪

1. Fill the first paper cup about three-fourths full of sand. Fill the second paper cup about three-fourths full of clay. Fill the third paper cup about three-fourths full of gravel. Fill the fourth paper cup about three-fourths full of a mixture of sand, clay, and gravel.

2. Fill the graduated cylinder with water to the 500 mL mark. Slowly pour water into the first cup. Let the water seep through the sand. Slowly add more water until a small pool of water is visible on the surface of the sand. At this point, the sand can hold no more water.

3. Determine the amount of water you added to the sand by subtracting the amount of water left in the graduated cylinder from 500 mL. Record this figure in the appropriate place in a data table similar to the one shown here.

4. Repeat steps 2 and 3 for the cups of clay, gravel, and the mixture of sand, clay, and gravel.

Observations

1. Which soil sample holds the most water?
2. Which soil sample holds the least water?

Soil	Amount of Water Added to Soil
Sand	
Clay	
Gravel	
Sand, clay, gravel	

Analysis and Conclusions

1. Why can some soil samples hold more water than others?

2. What can you conclude about the porosity of the soil samples you used?

3. If you wished to test the porosity of the soil found on your school grounds, what procedure would you follow? Which tested soil sample do you think the soil of the grounds at your school would most resemble?

4. **On Your Own**   What effects, if any, do the roots of plants have on the porosity of soil? Design an experiment to test your hypothesis.

Study Guide

Summarizing Key Concepts

7–1 Fresh Water on the Surface of the Earth

▲ Fresh water—one of the Earth's most precious resources—is found in lakes, ponds, rivers, streams, springs, and glaciers.

▲ The water cycle is the continuous movement of water from the oceans and sources of fresh water to the air and land and then back to the oceans.

▲ The three steps in the water cycle are evaporation, condensation, and precipitation.

▲ A land area in which surface runoff drains into a river or system of streams and rivers is called a watershed.

7–2 Fresh Water Beneath the Surface of the Earth

▲ Fresh water beneath the ground's surface is called groundwater.

▲ The water table is the underground level below which all the pore spaces are filled with water. The water table separates the zone of aeration from the zone of saturation.

▲ The depth of the water table depends on the location of groundwater, the climate of the area, the amount of rainfall, the type of soil, and the number of wells drawing water.

▲ Groundwater formations include caverns, stalactites, and stalagmites.

7–3 Water as a Solvent

▲ A molecule of water is made up of two atoms of hydrogen combined with one atom of oxygen.

▲ Because of the polarity of water molecules, water is a good solvent. It can dissolve many substances.

▲ Water may be hard or soft depending on the kinds and amounts of minerals in it.

▲ People must protect and conserve their sources of fresh water.

Reviewing Key Terms

Define each term in a complete sentence.

7–1 Fresh Water on the Surface of the Earth
water cycle
evaporation
condensation
precipitation
groundwater
glacier
valley glacier
continental glacier
iceberg
surface runoff
pore space
watershed
reservoir

7–2 Fresh Water Beneath the Surface of the Earth
permeable
impermeable
zone of saturation
zone of aeration
water table
aquifer
cavern

7–3 Water as a Solvent
polarity
solvent
solution
hard water
soft water

Chapter Review

Content Review

Multiple Choice

Choose the letter of the answer that best completes each statement.

1. The continuous movement of water from the oceans and freshwater sources to the air and land and back to the oceans is called the
   a. nitrogen cycle.   c. runoff.
   b. water cycle.   d. oxygen cycle.
2. The process in which water vapor changes to a liquid is called
   a. precipitation.   c. condensation.
   b. evaporation.   d. runoff.
3. Very thick sheets of ice found mainly in polar regions are called
   a. aquifers.
   b. crevasses.
   c. valley glaciers.
   d. continental glaciers.
4. The space between soil particles is called
   a. pore space.
   b. zone of aeration.
   c. surface runoff.
   d. polarity.

5. The underground region where all the pores are filled with water is called the
   a. zone of saturation.
   b. aquifer.
   c. watershed.
   d. zone of aeration.
6. The level below which all of the pore spaces in the soil are filled with water is called the
   a. water table.   c. meltwater.
   b. groundwater.   d. watershed.
7. The property of water that enables it to dissolve many substances easily is called
   a. hardness.   c. softness.
   b. polarity.   d. permeability.
8. A substance in which another substance dissolves is called a
   a. solution.
   b. saturated substance.
   c. solvent.
   d. molecule.

True or False

If the statement is true, write "true." If it is false, change the underlined word or words to make the statement true.

1. The process by which water changes to a gas is <u>condensation</u>.
2. Rain, snow, sleet, and hail are all forms of <u>precipitation</u>.
3. Water that enters a river or a stream after a heavy rain or during thawing of snow or ice is called <u>groundwater</u>.
4. In dry desert areas, the water table is usually very <u>shallow</u>.
5. Materials through which water can move quickly are described as <u>saturated</u>.

Concept Mapping

Complete the following concept map for Section 7–1. Then construct a concept map for the entire chapter.

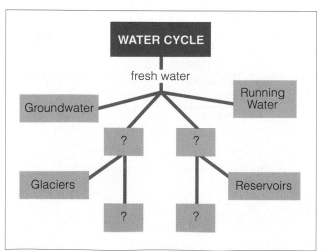

Concept Mastery

Discuss each of the following in a brief paragraph.

1. What is the water cycle? How does this cycle renew the Earth's supply of fresh water?
2. Describe the structure of a molecule of water. How does this structure affect its ability to dissolve substances?
3. What is a watershed? Why are watersheds important?
4. Why is it important to keep from polluting underground sources of water?
5. What is the difference between a lake and a reservoir? How could both bodies of water be used to supply a city with water?
6. Why is it important to protect our sources of fresh water? Why is it important to develop new sources?
7. What is hard water? How does hard water differ from soft water?
8. What is an aquifer? How can aquifers be used as a source of fresh water?

Critical Thinking and Problem Solving

Use the skills you have developed in this chapter to answer each of the following.

1. **Making diagrams** Two different areas of the United States receive the same amount of rainfall during a day. Area A has soil that contains many large pores and rocks made of sandstone. The soil in Area B is mainly heavy clay. Area A is a desert. Area B is a swamp. For each area draw two diagrams: one that shows the level of the water table before a day of rain and one that shows the level after a day of rain.
2. **Designing an experiment** Clouds are not salty. The salt from the oceans is left behind when the water evaporates. Devise an experiment to illustrate this fact. Describe the problem, materials, procedure, expected observations, and your conclusions.

3. **Applying concepts** Water molecules have polarity. Explain how water molecules can attract each other. Illustrate your explanation.
4. **Applying concepts** Pure water evaporates continuously from the oceans while salts are left behind. Explain why the salinity of ocean water does not increase over time.
5. **Relating concepts** A factory dumps harmful chemical wastes into a huge hole dug in the ground behind the building. Explain why and how these chemicals might affect a well located in a town several kilometers away from the factory site.
6. **Designing an experiment** Soap does not lather easily in hard water. It does so, however, in soft water. Devise a simple test to determine if water from a tap in your school is hard or soft.
7. **Using the writing process** Develop an advertising campaign to warn people about the dangers of polluting rivers and streams. You might want to design a poster campaign and/or write a letter to your neighbors to enlist their help.

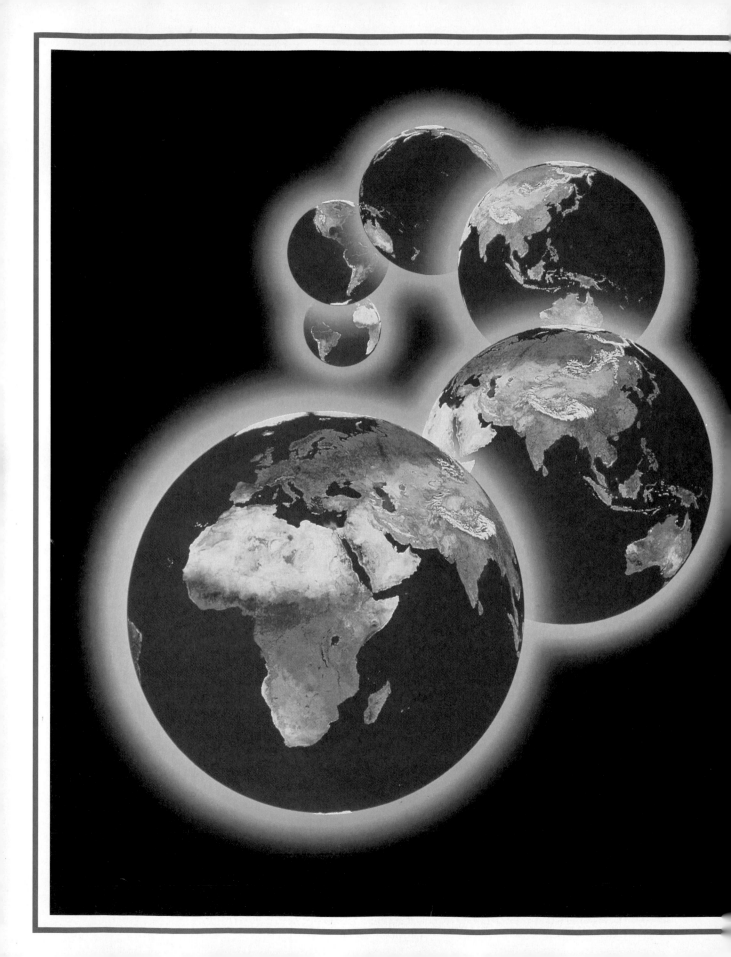

Earth's Landmasses

Guide for Reading

After you read the following sections, you will be able to

8–1 The Continents
■ Identify the continents.
■ Explain the relationship of continents to the Earth's landmasses.

8–2 Topography
■ List the characteristics of mountains, plains, and plateaus.

8–3 Mapping the Earth's Surface
■ Recognize the importance of longitude and latitude in mapping the Earth.
■ Identify the time zones and time differences in the United States.

8–4 Topographic Maps
■ Identify ways in which the Earth's features are shown on topographic maps.

Just imagine how hard it would be to visit a strange place for the first time without a map to guide you. Although someone might be able to give you accurate directions to this unfamiliar location, it is certainly easier and more helpful if you look at a map and visualize the trip before you begin.

The same idea holds true for the pilots of an airplane. Without maps, it would be very difficult for an airplane leaving Illinois to arrive in Germany. With accurate maps, however, you can enjoy a frankfurter at a baseball game in Chicago, and the next day eat a knockwurst at a soccer game in Berlin.

Throughout history, as people explored Planet Earth, maps became more and more accurate. By the middle of the eighteenth century, maps showed the Earth's land areas in the same shapes and sizes you see on maps today. Today, map-making is aided by photographs taken by high-flying satellites.

In this chapter, you will learn about different land features. You will also learn how these land features are represented on maps, and you will gain a better understanding of maps in general.

Journal *Activity*

You and Your World If you live in a city or town, make a map of your neighborhood. If you live in a rural area, make a map of the road you live along. Include places of interest and landmarks that would make it easy for a relative or friend to find your home if they wanted to visit you.

◀ In centuries past, maps of Earth were drawn by the skilled hands of artists. Today a new type of Earth map—made from thousands of images relayed by satellite—shows just how remarkably beautiful Earth is.

8–1 The Continents

All the land on Earth is surrounded by oceans. There are many **islands**, or small landmasses completely surrounded by water, scattered throughout the oceans. But there are only four major landmasses on Earth. Each major landmass consists of one or more **continents**. A continent is a landmass that measures millions of square kilometers and rises a considerable distance above sea level. Each continent has at least one large area of very old rock exposed at its surface. This area is called a shield. Shields form the cores of the continents. The shield of North America is located in Canada.

There are seven continents on the Earth: Asia, Africa, Europe, Australia, North America, South America, and Antarctica. Some of the continents are joined to form a single landmass. See Figure 8–2. For example, Asia and Europe are joined together as one landmass, called Eurasia. And Africa is connected to Asia by a small piece of land. These three continents—Asia, Africa, and Europe—make up one giant landmass, the largest landmass on Earth.

The second largest landmass consists of the continents of North America and South America. Central America is located just to the south of North America. Central America is part of the North American continent. At the point where Central America connects to South America, the continents of North America and South America are joined.

The third largest landmass is the continent of Antarctica. Antarctica is about twice the size of the United States. Antarctica has only recently been explored. In fact, the first known exploration of Antarctica occurred in 1901.

Antarctica is very different from the other continents. It is almost completely covered by a thick icecap. In fact, the Antarctic icecap is the largest in

Figure 8–1 *Mount Everest is considered to be the highest point on Earth. The lowest point on Earth is the Dead Sea. The difference in altitude between these two points is 9200 meters!*

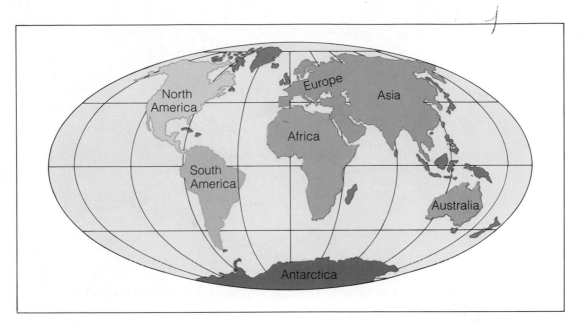

Figure 8–2 *This map shows the major islands and the seven continents of the world. Which continents make up the Earth's largest landmass?*

the world and covers an area of 34 million square kilometers! The Antarctic icecap is so large that it extends into the surrounding ocean. It contains almost 90 percent of the ice on the Earth's surface.

Antarctica is certainly the coldest area on Earth. In July 1983, the temperature in Vostok, Antarctica, dropped to nearly −89.2°C, the lowest temperature ever recorded on Earth. Many scientific stations have been built on Antarctica. Some scientific teams study life on the continent. Others study the land beneath the ice. Still others study conditions in the atmosphere over Antarctica. Today, one of the major areas of study is the depletion of the ozone layer over Antarctica. In the past several years, "holes" in the ozone layer have been observed there. Scientists study these areas in an attempt to determine the long-term effects of ozone depletion. Because of the extreme cold, however, the scientists who live and work in Antarctica are only temporary visitors to this continent.

Australia is the smallest landmass still considered a continent. It is the only continent that is a single country. Sometimes, Australia is referred to as the island continent. Why do you think this term is used to describe Australia?

Figure 8–3 *Australia is a continent country completely surrounded by water. These steep cliffs border on the Indian Ocean.*

8–1 Section Review

1. Identify the seven continents.
2. What is a landmass? A continent? An island?
3. What makes the continent of Antarctica unusual? What makes Australia unusual?

Critical Thinking—*Applying Concepts*
4. Predict what would happen if the average temperature of Antarctica rose to 5°C.

8–2 Topography

Over billions of years, the surface of the Earth has changed many times. These changes are produced by several factors. Weather conditions such as wind and heat change the surface. Running water reshapes the land. Earthquakes and volcanoes cause major changes in the Earth's surface. Earthquakes can build up or level mountains, and volcanoes can produce new islands. Surtsey, an island off the coast of Iceland, was produced in 1963 by volcanic eruptions on the seabed. Even people alter the Earth's appearance. For example, they use huge earth-moving machinery to smooth the Earth's surface in order to construct the buildings that make up a large city. What other human activities can you think of that might change the shape of the land?

Scientists refer to the shape of the Earth's surface as its **topography** (tuh-PAHG-ruh-fee). The Earth's topography is made up of different kinds of **landscapes**. A landscape is the physical features of the Earth's surface found in an area. Figure 8–5 shows landscape regions of the United States. In which landscape region do you live?

There are three main types of landscape regions: mountains, plains, and plateaus. Each type has different characteristics. One characteristic of a landscape region is **elevation**, or height above sea level. Some landscape regions have high elevations; others have low elevations. Within a landscape region, the elevation can vary from place to place. The difference in a region's elevations is called its **relief**. If a landscape region has high relief, there are large differences in the elevations of different areas within the landscape region. What do you think is true of a landscape region with low relief?

Figure 8–4 *Earth's landmasses are constantly undergoing changes. The island of Surtsey appeared in 1963 as a result of volcanic eruptions on the ocean floor.*

Figure 8–5 *This map shows the major landscape regions of the continental United States. What type of landscape region covers most of the land shown? In what type of landscape region do you live?*

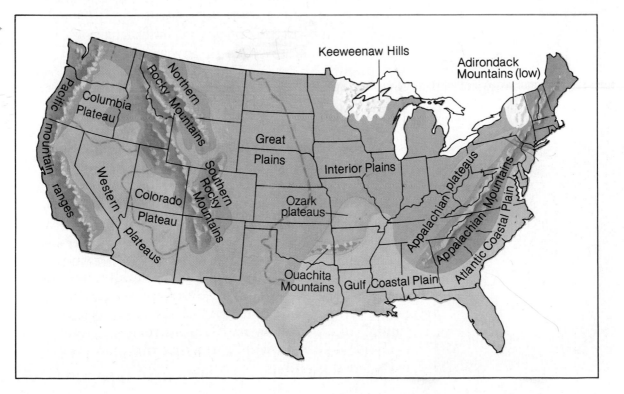

CALCULATING

Mountain Landscapes

Mountain landscapes cover about one fifth of the Earth's surface. The total land area of the Earth's surface is about 148,300,000 km². How much of the surface of the Earth has a mountain landscape?

Figure 8–6 *Mountains may form when the Earth's crust breaks into great blocks that are then tilted or lifted (top). Folded mountains form when layers of the Earth's crust wrinkle into wavelike folds (bottom).*

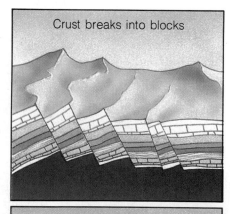

Crust breaks into blocks

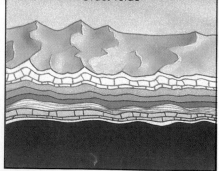

Crust folds

Mountains

Mountains make up one type of landscape region. Mountains are natural landforms that reach high elevations. Mountains have narrow summits, or tops, and steep slopes, or sides. Mountain landscapes have very high relief.

What do you think is the difference between a hill and a mountain? Most geologists agree that a mountainous area rises at least 600 meters above the surrounding land. But the actual height of a mountain is given as its height above sea level. For example, Pike's Peak in Colorado rises about 2700 meters above the surrounding land. But its actual height above sea level is 4301 meters.

The highest mountain in the world is Mount Everest. Mount Everest is part of the Himalayas, a great chain of mountains in Asia that extends from Tibet to Pakistan. The peak of Mount Everest soars more than 8 kilometers! The highest mountain in the United States is Mount McKinley in the state of Alaska. It is more than 6 kilometers high. What mountains are closest to your home?

All mountains did not form at the same time. Some mountains are old; others are relatively young. Mountains are built very slowly. It is thought that the Rocky Mountains began to form about 65 million years ago. It took about 10 million years for these mountains to reach their maximum height. You might be surprised to learn that geologists consider the Rocky Mountains to be "young" mountains. In this case, "young" and "old" are relative terms compared to the age of the Earth.

Mountains can be formed in several ways. Some mountains result from the folding and breaking of the Earth's surface. Other mountains are created when hot magma (liquid rock) from the Earth's interior breaks through the Earth's surface. (You will learn more about the Earth's interior in Chapter 9.)

Streams and rivers in mountain areas move very quickly. The higher and steeper the mountain slopes, the faster the water flows. Mountain streams and rivers carry rocks of all sizes. When there is heavy rainfall or when snow melts, the streams and rivers become so swollen with water that they can even carry small boulders.

Figure 8–7 *Some of the world's mountains are described below. In what state is the highest mountain in North America located?*

SOME OF THE WORLD'S MOST FAMOUS MOUNTAINS

Name	Height Above Sea Level (meters)	Location	Interesting Facts
Aconcagua	6959	Andes in Argentina	Highest mountain in the Western Hemisphere
Cotopaxi	5897	Andes in Ecuador	Highest active volcano in the world
Elbert	4399	Colorado	Highest mountain of Rockies
Everest	8848	Himalayas on Nepal-Tibet border	Highest mountain in the world
K2	8611	Kashmir	Second highest mountain in the world
Kanchenjunga	8598	Himalayas on Nepal-India border	Third highest mountain in the world
Kilimanjaro	5895	Tanzania	Highest mountain in Africa
Logan	5950	Yukon	Highest mountain in Canada
Mauna Kea	4205	On volcanic island in Hawaii	Highest island mountain in the world
Mauna Loa	4169	On volcanic island in Hawaii	Famous volcanic mountain
McKinley	6194	Alaska	Highest mountain in North America
Mitchell	2037	North Carolina	Highest mountain in the Appalachians
Mont Blanc	4807	France	Highest mountain in the Alps
Mount St. Helens	2549	Cascades in Washington	Recent active volcano in the United States
Pikes Peak	4301	Colorado	Most famous of the Rocky Mountains
Rainier	4392	Cascades in Washington	Highest mountain in Washington
Vesuvius	1277	Italy	Only active volcano on the mainland of Europe
Whitney	4418	Sierra Nevadas in California	Highest mountain in California

Figure 8–8 *The Rocky Mountains are considered "young" mountains because they formed a mere 65 million years ago (left). Mountains in the Appalachian Range are "old" mountains, having formed more than 300 million years ago (top right). Mount Kilimanjaro in Africa is an example of a mountain formed by volcanic activity (bottom right).*

Figure 8–9 *This stream, swollen with water from mountain snows, flows quickly.*

Streams and rivers often carve valleys in mountains. Valleys in older mountains are usually wide. Valleys in younger mountains are usually narrow. Why do you think this is so?

Individual mountains, which are mountains that are not part of a group, can be found in all parts of the world. These mountains are usually the products of volcanic activity during which magma broke through the Earth's surface. Examples of volcanic mountains are Fujiyama in Japan, Vesuvius in Italy, and Kilimanjaro in Tanzania.

Most mountains, however, are part of a group of mountains called a **mountain range**. A mountain range is a roughly parallel series of mountains that have the same general shape and structure. A group of mountain ranges in one area is called a **mountain system**. The Great Smoky, Blue Ridge, Cumberland, and Green mountain ranges are all in the Appalachian mountain system in the eastern United States.

Most mountain ranges and mountain systems are part of an even larger group of mountains called a **mountain belt.** The pattern of mountain belts on the Earth is shown in Figure 8–10.

There are two major mountain belts in the world. The Circum-Pacific belt rings the Pacific Ocean. The Eurasian-Melanesian belt runs across northern

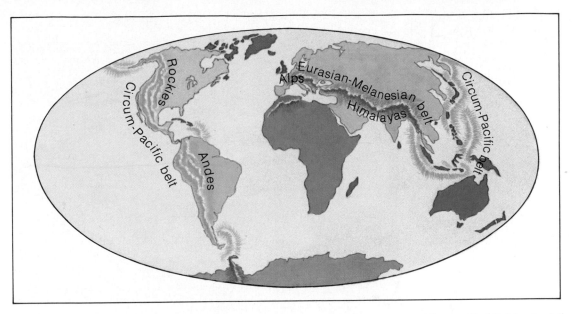

Figure 8–10 *Most of the Earth's mountains are located within the two major mountain belts shown on this map: the Circum-Pacific belt and the Eurasian-Melanesian belt. Which major belt runs through the United States?*

Africa, southern Europe, and Asia. The Eurasian-Melanesian belt and the Circum-Pacific belt meet in Indonesia, just north of Australia. These mountain belts may have been formed by movements of the Earth's crust.

Plains

Another type of landscape region is made up of **plains**. Plains are flat land areas that do not rise far above sea level. Plains, then, have very small differences in elevation. They are areas of low relief. The difference between the highest and lowest elevations in a plain may be less than 100 meters. Plains areas are characterized by broad rivers and streams. Most of the plants that grow well here are grasses, related to the grass plants that are grown in a lawn or on a baseball field. Some plains are located at the edges of a continent. Others are located in the continent's interior.

COASTAL PLAINS A coast is a place where the land meets the ocean. Low, flat areas along the coasts are called **coastal plains.** The Atlantic and Gulf coastal plains of the United States are typical coastal plains. The change in elevation of the land from the Gulf of Mexico to southern Illinois is very small. Over a distance of more than 1000 kilometers, the land rises only about 150 meters above sea level.

The coastal plains of the United States were formed when soil and silt were deposited on the edge of the continent. In the past, shallow oceans

283

Figure 8–11 *This area in Jacksonville Beach, Florida, is located within the Atlantic coastal plain. What characteristic of plains regions is visible in this photograph?*

ctivity Bank

Making Soil, p. 760

Figure 8–12 *The land in interior plains regions has fertile soil. In the past, these lands supported huge herds of grazing animals, such as buffaloes. Today crops are grown in these areas.*

covered these areas. As these oceans disappeared, large deposits of sand and silt were left behind. More sediments have been deposited onto coastal plains by rivers and streams. The soil in these areas has been enriched by these deposits.

Because of the abundance of fertile soil, farming is a major activity of great economic importance on coastal plains. In the United States, cotton, tobacco, vegetables, and citrus crops are grown in these areas.

INTERIOR PLAINS Some low flat areas are also found inland on a continent. These areas are called **interior plains**. Interior plains are somewhat higher above sea level than coastal plains. For example, the interior plains of the United States have an elevation of about 450 meters above sea level. This is considerably higher than the elevation of the Atlantic and Gulf coastal plains. But within an interior plain itself, the differences in elevation are small. So interior plains also have low relief.

The Great Plains of the United States are large interior plains. They were formed as mountains and hills that were later worn down by wind, streams, and glaciers. Large interior plains are found in the Soviet Union, central and eastern Europe, and parts of Africa and Australia.

Interior plains have good soil. The sediments deposited by rivers and streams make the soil suitable for farming. In the United States, grasses and grains such as wheat, barley, and oats are grown in the interior plains. Cattle and sheep are raised in these areas, too.

Plateaus

A third type of landscape region consists of **plateaus**. Plateaus are broad, flat areas of land that rise more than 600 meters above sea level. Some plateaus reach elevations of more than 1500 meters. Plateaus are not considered mountains because their surfaces are fairly flat. Like plains, plateaus have low relief. But unlike plains, plateaus rise much higher above sea level.

Most plateaus are located inland. But a few plateaus are near oceans. The plateaus near oceans often end in a cliff at the edge of a coastal plain. If a plateau is directly next to an ocean, it ends in a cliff at the coast.

Plateaus often have the same landscape for thousands of kilometers. Some plateaus have been deeply cut by streams and rivers that form canyons. The Colorado River cuts through the Colorado Plateau to form the Grand Canyon in Arizona. The river flows 1.5 kilometers lower than the surface of the surrounding plateau. Have you ever visited the Grand Canyon or seen pictures of it?

Many plateaus of the world are dry, nearly desert areas. They are often used for grazing cattle, sheep, and goats. Plateaus in the western United States are rich in coal and mineral deposits such as copper and lead.

ACTIVITY
WRITING

A Dream Vacation

Imagine that you are taking a trip around the United States. You will see many different landscape features. Write a 200-word essay about what you see on your trip. Include the following vocabulary words in your essay: coastal plain, interior plain, mountain, mountain range, plateau, elevation. Be sure to mention specific locations such as the Gulf Coastal Plain and the Colorado Plateau.

Figure 8–13 *Plateaus are broad, flat areas of land with low relief. Some plateaus have been cut by streams and rivers that form canyons. Cut by the relentless action of the Colorado River, the Grand Canyon is among the most impressive on Earth.*

285

CONNECTIONS

Frozen Foods—An Idea From Frigid Lands

Near the North Pole—in climates almost as severe as those found in Antarctica—native peoples have lived for many thousands of years. They survive primarily by fishing and hunting. And a long time ago, they discovered that the extreme cold in which they live can have significant value—it can preserve food.

Clarence Birdseye was a businessman and inventor, who at his death owned more than 300 patents on his inventions. Early in his career, Birdseye traded in furs. In 1912 and 1916 he visited Labrador, a part of Canada. While there, he observed the people freezing food for use in the winter because it was difficult for them to get a fresh supply during the very cold months. Birdseye spent years experimenting on ways to freeze food commercially. In 1929 he achieved success and began selling his quick-frozen foods. As a result of this technology, Birdseye became quite wealthy and famous. Today, his name is practically synonymous with frozen foods.

The idea seems a simple one. Extremely cold temperatures can protect foods from spoiling almost indefinitely. (Some Russian scientists claim that they have eaten the meat of a mammoth frozen 20,000 years ago and have found it edible!) But keep in mind that the original idea came from native peoples whose primary motive was to survive in a cold, hostile environment.

8–2 Section Review

1. What is a landscape? What are the three main landscape types found in the United States?
2. What do scientists mean by the Earth's topography?
3. Describe the following: mountain, mountain range, mountain system, mountain belt.
4. What is a coastal plain? An interior plain?

Connection—*Ecology*

5. Why are plains and plateaus good areas to grow crops, whereas the sides of mountains usually are not?

8–3 Mapping the Earth's Surface

Guide for Reading

Focus on this question as you read.

▶ *What are some features of the Earth shown on maps and globes?*

A **map** is a drawing of the Earth, or a part of the Earth, on a flat surface. There are many ways to show the Earth's surface features on maps. Some maps show only a small area of the Earth. Others show the Earth's entire surface. Maps are often grouped together in a book called an atlas. Have you ever thumbed through an atlas and visited, if only in your imagination, distant and foreign places?

The most accurate representation of the entire surface of the Earth is a **globe**. A globe is a spherical, or round, model of the Earth. It shows the shapes, sizes, and locations of all the Earth's landmasses and bodies of water.

Both maps and globes are drawn to **scale**. A scale compares distances on a map or globe to actual distances on the Earth's surface. For example, 1 centimeter on a map might equal 10 kilometers on the Earth's surface. Different maps may have different scales. However, all maps and globes should have the scale used to represent the distances shown on that particular map or globe. Why is including a scale important?

Meridians

When you look at a globe or a map, you see many straight lines on it. Some of the lines run between the points that represent the geographic North and South poles of the Earth. These lines are called **meridians** (muh-RIHD-ee-uhnz).

Each meridian is half of an imaginary circle around the Earth. Geographers have named the meridian that runs through Greenwich, England, the **prime meridian**. Because meridians run north and south, they measure distance east and west. The

Figure 8–14 *Satellites that orbit the Earth provide information used to make maps. In the center of the photograph of Washington, DC, you can make out the mall that runs from the United States Capitol to the Washington Monument. Satellite images can also show evidence of living organisms. The yellow areas in the photograph represent great numbers of microscopic life in the oceans along the coasts of continents.*

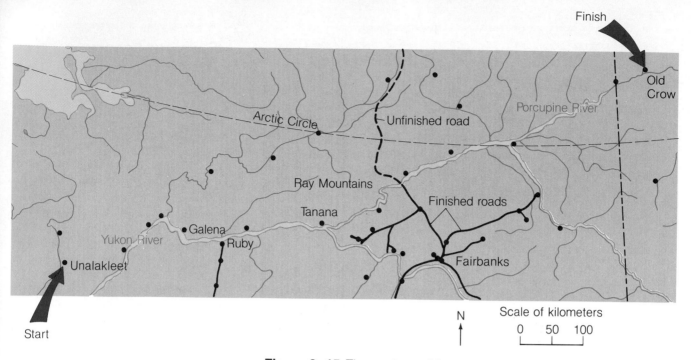

Figure 8–15 *The scale on this map is useful in finding the distance between two cities. If you took a plane ride from Unalakleet to Old Crow, how many kilometers would you fly?*

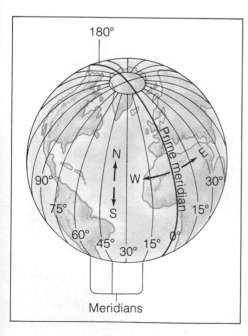

Meridians

Figure 8–16 *Meridians are lines running north to south on a map or globe. What are meridians used to measure?*

measure of distance east and west of the prime meridian is called **longitude**. Meridians are used to measure longitude.

The distance around any circle, including the Earth, is measured in degrees. The symbol for degree is a small circle written at the upper right of a number. All circles contain 360°. Each meridian marks 1° of longitude around the Earth. But not all meridians are drawn on most globes or maps. (Just think how crowded a map would look if all 360 meridians were drawn.)

The prime meridian is labeled 0° longitude. Meridians to the east of the prime meridian are called east longitudes. Meridians to the west of the prime meridian are called west longitudes. Meridians of east longitude measure distances halfway around the Earth from the prime meridian. Meridians of west longitude measure distances around the other half of the Earth from the prime meridian. Because half the distance around a circle is 180°, meridians of east and west longitude go from 0° to 180°.

Time Zones

On Earth, a day is 24 hours long. During these 24 hours, the Earth makes one complete rotation. You can think of this in another way. In one day, the Earth rotates 360°. If you divide 360° by the number of hours in a day (24), you will find that the Earth rotates 15° every hour. Thus the Earth has been divided into 24 zones of 15° of longitude each. These zones are called **time zones**. A time zone is a longitudinal belt of the Earth in which all areas have the same local time.

Suppose it is 6:00 AM in Miami, Florida. It is also 6:00 AM in Washington, DC, because Miami and Washington are in the same time zone. But it is not 6:00 AM in Dallas, Texas. Dallas is one time zone away from Miami and Washington. How can you tell whether it is earlier or later in Texas?

ACTIVITY WRITING

Technology and Mapmaking

In the past, mapmakers drew maps of landmasses based on personal experience. Today, technology has made mapmaking a more accurate science. Using reference materials in the library, find out how the space program resulted in the production of more accurate maps of the Earth.

Figure 8–17 *The Earth has been divided into 24 time zones. All areas within a single time zone have the same local time.*

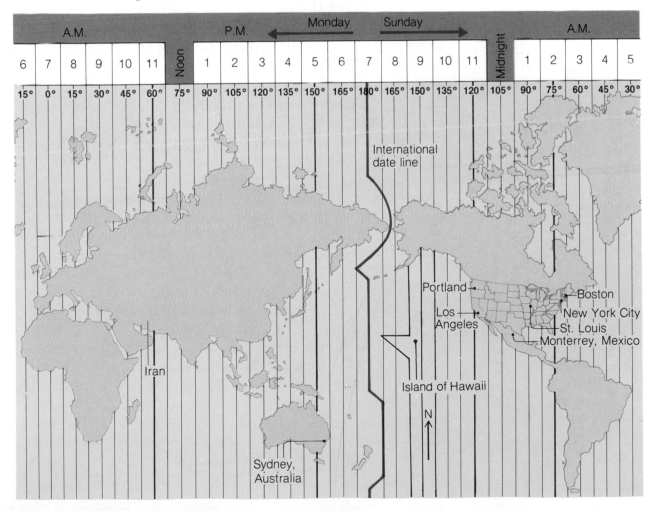

ACTIVITY DOING

Mapping Your Neighborhood

1. Draw a detailed map of your neighborhood. Be sure to draw the map to scale.

2. Use different colors for buildings, industrial areas, crop fields, and bodies of water.

3. Make a legend that includes the symbols in the map and their meanings.

The Earth rotates on its axis from west to east. This direction of rotation makes the sun appear to rise in the east and travel toward the west. So the sun comes into view first in the east. Suppose the sun rises in New York City at 6:00 AM. After the Earth rotates 15°, the sun rises in Dallas. It is 6:00 AM in Dallas. But it is now 7:00 AM in New York City. Dallas is one time zone west of New York City.

After the Earth rotates another 15°, the sun rises in Denver. It is 6:00 AM in Denver. But by now it is 7:00 AM in Dallas and 8:00 AM in New York City. Denver is one time zone west of Dallas and two time zones west of New York City.

If it were not for time zones, the sun would rise in New York City at 6:00 AM, in Dallas at 7:00 AM, in Denver at 8:00 AM, and in Los Angeles at 9:00 AM. And the sun would not rise in Hawaii until 11:00 AM! Because of time zones, the sun rises at 6:00 AM in each city. Is this an advantage? Why?

There are four time zones in the contiguous United States. From east to west they are: the Eastern, Central, Mountain, and Pacific time zones. The states of Alaska and Hawaii are further west than the Pacific time zone. Use a globe to find these two states. What is the time in Alaska and Hawaii if it is 9:00 AM in Los Angeles?

When you cross from one time zone to another, the local time changes by one hour. If you are traveling east, you add one hour for each time zone you cross. If you are traveling west, you subtract one hour for each time zone you cross.

Now suppose you are taking a 24-hour trip around the world. You travel west, leaving Miami, Florida, at 1:00 PM Sunday. Because you are traveling west, you subtract one hour for each time zone you cross. One day later, you arrive back in Miami. It is now 1:00 PM Monday. But because you have subtracted a total of 24 hours as you traveled, you think that it is still 1:00 PM Sunday!

This situation is quite confusing. But geographers have established the **international date line** to simplify matters. The international date line is located

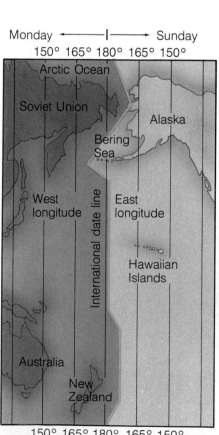

Figure 8–18 *Travelers going west across the international date line gain a day. Those going east across it lose a day. Why does the international date line zigzag?*

along the 180th meridian. When you cross this line going east, you subtract one day. When you cross this line going west, you add one day. So in your trip around the world, you should have added one day, or gone from Sunday to Monday, as you crossed the international date line traveling west. You would then have arrived back in Miami, as expected, at 1:00 PM Monday afternoon.

Parallels

There are also lines from east to west across a map or globe. These lines are called **parallels**. Parallels cross meridians at right angles. The parallel located halfway between the North and South poles is the **equator**. Because parallels run east and west, they measure distance north and south. So in relation to the equator, locations of other parallels are either north or south. The measure of distance north and south of the equator is called **latitude**. Parallels are used to measure latitude.

The equator is labeled 0° latitude. Parallels to the north of the equator are north latitudes. Parallels to the south of the equator are south latitudes. The distance from the equator to either the North or South pole is one quarter of the distance around the Earth.

ACTIVITY DOING

Latitude and Longitude

1. Select ten specific places on the Earth. Use a map or globe and determine the approximate latitude and longitude of each place. For example, if you select New Orleans, Louisiana, your answer will be 30°N, 90°W. If you select Tokyo, Japan, your answer will be 35°N, 140°E.

2. Write down ten random combinations of latitude and longitude. Refer to a map or globe to find the corresponding locations. For example, if you write down 50°S, 70°W, the corresponding location will be southern Argentina.

Why are latitude and longitude important?

Figure 8–19 *Parallels are lines running from east to west on a map or globe. Parallels and meridians form a grid used to determine exact locations. On what continent is 40° north latitude and 90° west longitude located?*

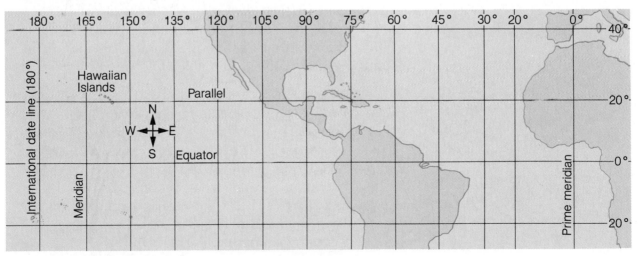

Because one quarter of the distance around a circle is 90°, north and south parallels are labeled from 0° to 90°. The North Pole is at 90° north latitude, or 90°N. The South Pole is at 90° south latitude, or 90°S. Just as there is a meridian for every degree of longitude, there is a parallel for every degree of latitude. But not all parallels are drawn on most globes or maps.

Meridians and parallels form a grid, or network of crossing lines, on a globe or map. They can be used to determine the exact locations east and west of the prime meridian and north and south of the equator. For example, if a ship reported its position as 30° south latitude and 165° east longitude, it would be off the coast of Australia. Why is this system of locating points helpful in shipping?

Types of Maps

Maps of the Earth are very useful. **Maps show locations and distances on the Earth's surface. They also show many different local features. Some maps show the soil types in an area. Some show currents in the ocean. Some maps show small, detailed areas of the Earth. Maps of cities may show every street in those cities.**

However, maps have one serious drawback. Because they are flat, maps cannot represent a round surface accurately. Like a photograph of a person, a map is only a **projection**, or a representation of a three-dimensional object on a flat surface. When the round surface of the Earth is represented on the flat surface of a map, changes occur in the shapes and sizes of landmasses and oceans. These changes are called distortion. Despite distortion, maps are still useful.

MERCATOR PROJECTIONS There are many different ways to project the Earth's image onto a map. One type of map projection is a **Mercator projection**. Mercator projections are used for navigation. They show the correct shape of the coastlines. But the sizes of land and water areas become distorted in latitudes far from the equator. For example, on the Mercator projection in Figure 8–20, Greenland appears much larger than it really is.

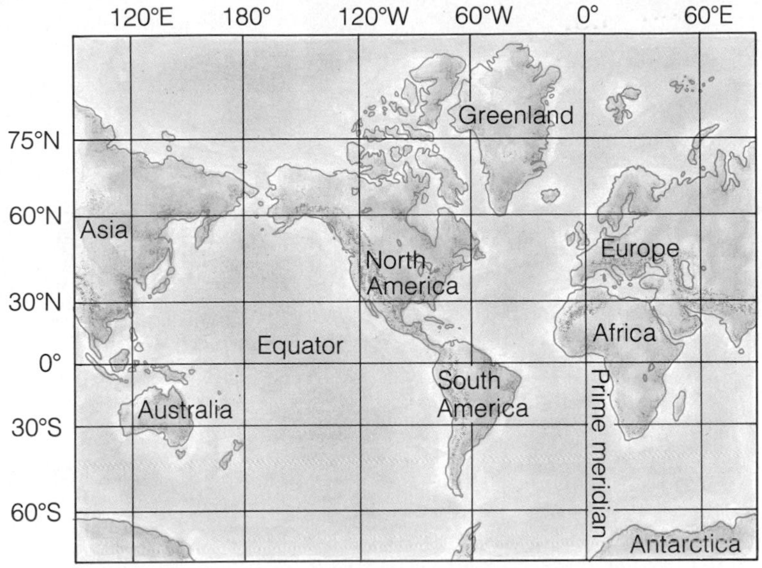

Figure 8–20 *This type of map is called a Mercator projection. What feature of this map is distorted?*

EQUAL-AREA PROJECTIONS   Another type of map projection is called an **equal-area projection**. Equal-area projections show area correctly. The meridians and parallels are placed on the map in such a way that every part of the Earth is the same size on the map as it is on a globe. But the shapes of the areas are distorted on an equal-area projection. What areas in Figure 8–21 look distorted to you?

Figure 8–21 *The correct areas of the Earth's landmasses are shown on this map. But the correct shapes are not. What type of map is this?*

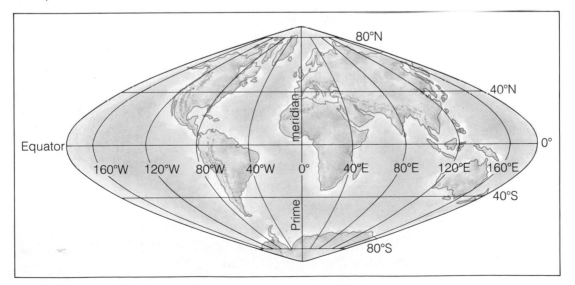

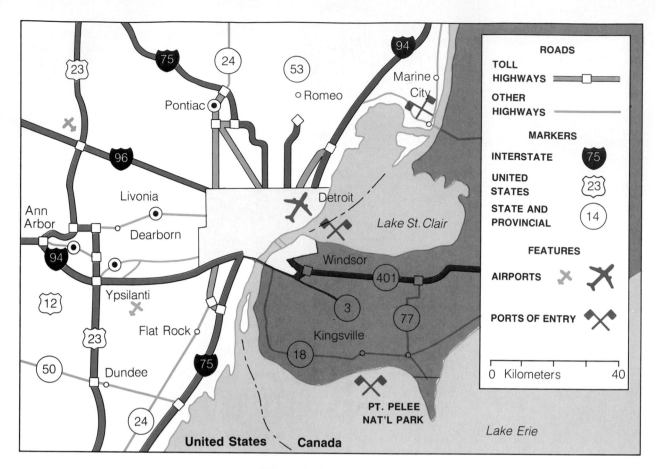

Figure 8–22 *One of the most familiar types of maps is a road map. What kinds of information are provided by the legend of this map?*

8–3 Section Review

1. In what ways are maps useful?
2. Under what circumstances would a globe be more useful than a map?
3. What is a scale? Why is it important?
4. What is longitude? Latitude?
5. What is the international date line? How is this meridian used?
6. What is a time zone? Explain why the Earth has been divided into 24 time zones.
7. What is a projection? What are the two kinds?

Critical Thinking—*Applying Concepts*
8. Why was it important for people to agree on the location of the prime meridian?

PROBLEM Solving

Famous People—Famous Places

Famous people often make places famous. Use the following clues to locate the places on Earth being described. You will need a world atlas to discover the locations.

Interpreting Maps

1. The French artist Gauguin fled Paris to this tropical paradise, whose location is 17°S, 149°W.

2. Marie Curie discovered radium while working in a country whose capital is located at 48.5°N, 2°E.

3. Napoleon spent the last years of his life at 16°S, 5°W.

4. Ponce de Leon found the fountain of youth at 29.5°N, 81°W. The waters, alas, were not all that effective, for he died in 1521.

5. Cecil B. DeMille directed many epic films that were supposed to take place in foreign locations, but which were filmed for the most part at 34°N, 118°W.

6. Betsy Ross was supposed to have sewn the first American flag in this city, located at 40°N, 75°W.

■ Add to this list of famous places by identifying and locating some other important sites. Here are a few examples: where you live; where you were born; where your favorite sports team plays; where you would like to spend a vacation.

8–4 Topographic Maps

You have learned that the Earth has a varied topography. Perhaps you have even noticed some of the Earth's varied features if you have ever flown in an airplane across the United States. High above the ground, you can easily see mountains, plains, valleys, rivers, lakes, and other features. At ground level, some of these features are more difficult to observe. However, certain types of maps that show even small details of the topography of an area have been drawn. A map that shows the different shapes and sizes of a land surface is called a **topographic map**. This type of map may also show cities, roads, parks, and railroads.

Topographic maps show the relief of the land. Most topographic maps use contour lines to show relief. A **contour line** is a line that passes through all points on a map that have the same elevation. Some topographic maps show relief by using different colors for different elevations.

The difference in elevation from one contour line to the next is called the contour interval. For example, in a map with a contour interval of 5 meters, contour lines are drawn only at elevations of 0 meters, 5 meters, 10 meters, 15 meters, and so on. Look at the contour lines in Figure 8–23. What contour interval is being used here? What is the highest elevation on the hill?

Like other maps, topographic maps use symbols to represent features. Symbols for buildings and roads are usually black. Symbols for bodies of water such as rivers, lakes, and streams are blue. Green represents woods and swamps. And contour lines are brown or red. All symbols on a map are placed in a legend. The legend explains what each symbol represents. See the legend in Figure 8–24 for some common map symbols and their meanings. (Appendix F on page 800 of this textbook contains a more extensive list of map symbols.)

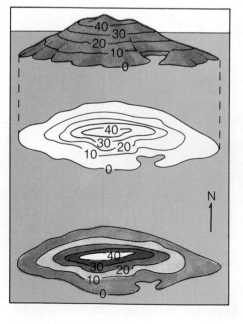

Figure 8–23 *Some topographic maps use colors to indicate different elevations. Others use contour lines to show different elevations.*

TOPOGRAPHIC MAP SYMBOLS

Symbol	Meaning	Symbol	Meaning	Symbol	Meaning
■	House	⊁═⊀	Bridge	⣿⣿⣿	Gravel beach
▐🚩	School	╪╪╪	Railroad	~	Contour line
▬▬▬	Primary highway	～	Perennial stream	⬭	Depression
＝＝＝＝	Unimproved road	⣿	Dry lake	⩣⩣⩣	Swamp

Figure 8–24 *The symbols in this legend are commonly found on topographic maps. What is the symbol for a school? A railroad?*

The first time you look at a topographic map, you may be somewhat confused. All those lines and symbols can seem awesome. But once you become familiar with contour maps and gain experience in interpreting them, a great deal of confusion will be cleared up. The information in a topographic map is quite useful, especially for people who like to hike or who enjoy camping. The following simple rules will make it easier for you to read this type of map:

- A contour line of one elevation never crosses, or intersects, a contour line of another elevation. Each contour line represents only one elevation. Contour lines can never cross because one point cannot have two different elevations.

- Closely spaced contour lines represent a steep slope. The lines are close together because the elevation of a steep slope changes greatly over a short distance. Contour lines spaced far apart represent a gentle slope. The lines are far apart because the elevation of a gentle slope changes only slightly over a short distance.

- Contour lines that cross a valley are V shaped. If a stream flows through the valley, the V will point upstream, or in the direction opposite to the flow of the stream.

ACTIVITY

WRITING

The History of Mapmaking

Using reference materials in the library, write a short essay on the history of mapmaking from the time of the Babylonians to the present. Include information on the following:
Gerhardus Mercator
Christopher Columbus
Claudius Ptolemy
Amerigo Vespucci
Satellite mapping
Include drawings and illustrations with your essay.

■ Contour lines form closed loops around hilltops or depressions. Elevation numbers on the contour lines indicate whether a feature is a hilltop or a depression. If the numbers increase toward the center of the closed loop, the feature is a hilltop. If the numbers decrease, the feature is a depression. Sometimes elevation numbers are not given. Instead short dashes called hachures (HASH-oorz) are used to indicate a depression. Hachures are drawn perpendicular to the contour line that loops around a depression. The hachures point to the inside of the loop.

Now look at Figure 8–25. You should be able to understand all of the information on the map. What is the location of the depression? Which mountain has the steepest slope? In what direction does the Campbell River flow? Now look at Figure 8–26, Figure 8–27 on page 300 and Figure 8–28 on page 301. Use the legend in Figure 8–24 and the rules you have just learned to identify other topographic features.

Figure 8–25 *Once you learn the meanings of map symbols, topographic maps such as this one are easy to read. What does the symbol in green at the bottom of this map represent?*

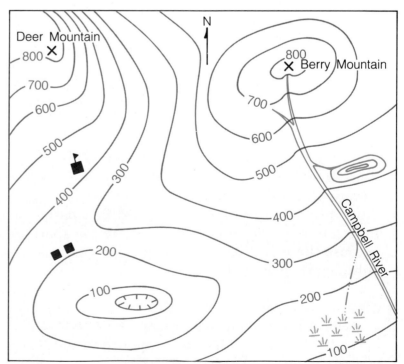

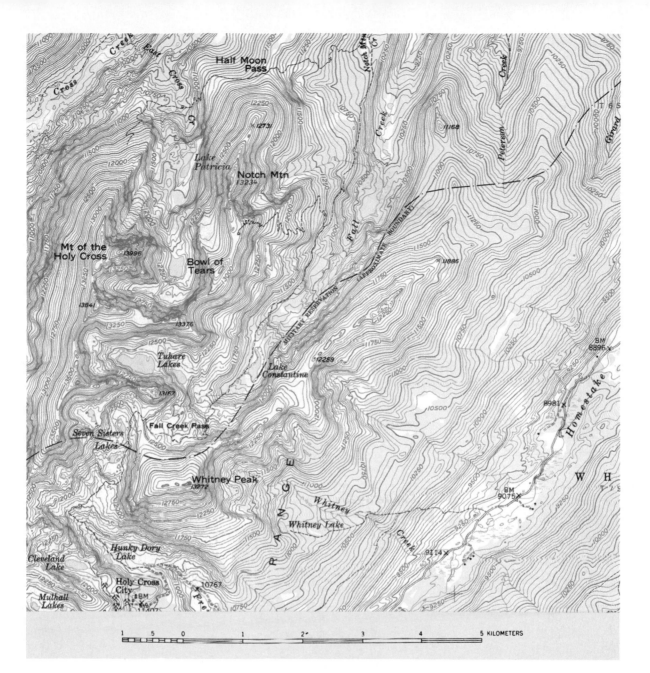

Figure 8–26 *This is a topographic map of Holy Cross Quadrangle, Colorado. What type of landscape region do you think this area is part of? How are changes in elevation shown? What is the highest point shown on this map?*

8–4 Section Review

1. How do topographic maps represent features of the Earth's surface?
2. What is a contour line? A contour interval?
3. Why is a map's legend important?

Critical Thinking—*Relating Concepts*

4. Why would it be difficult to show a vertical cliff on a topographic map?

Figure 8–27 *This topographic map shows part of a county in New York State. What landscape features can you identify?*

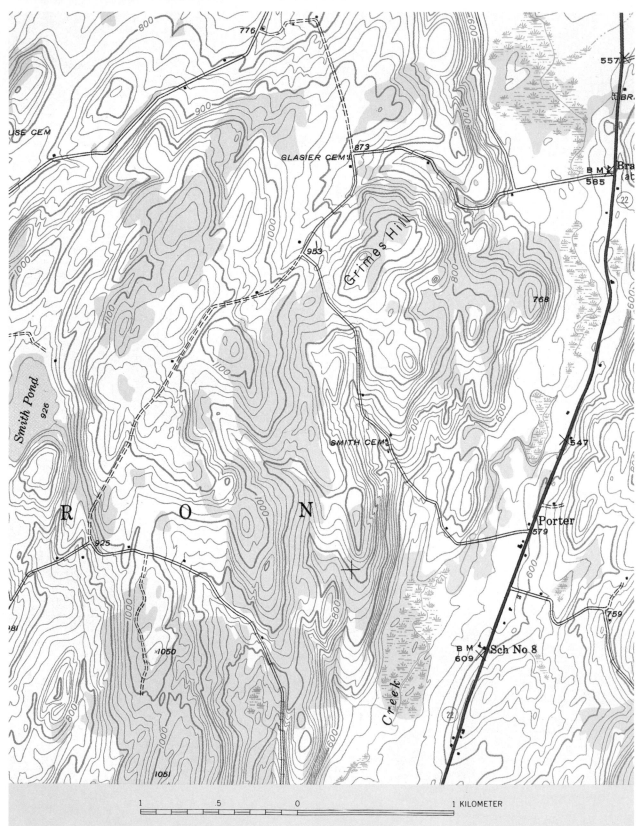

USE CEM

800

776

800

900

GLASIER CEM

873

953

Grimes Hill

768

Smith Pond

926

R   O   N

925

1100

1100

1100

1000

1000

1000

1000

1050

1051

081

×1050

800

800

600

600

800

600

557

BR.

B M
585

22

Br
(at

Porter
579

×547

B M
609   Sch No 8

759

600

600

22

Creek

1   .5   0   1 KILOMETER

Figure 8–28 *This topographic map shows part of the shoreline of California. What type of landscape region is this area part of?*

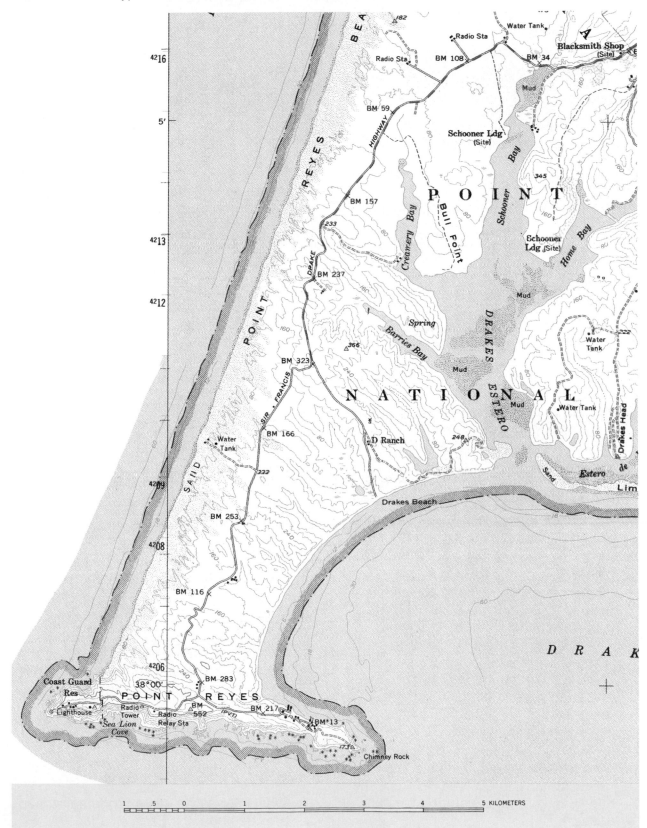

Laboratory Investigation

Making a Topographic Map

Problem

What information can a topographic map provide about the surface features of the Earth?

Materials *(per group)*

modeling clay	glass-marking pencil
metric ruler	1 L water
rigid cardboard	pencil
pane of clear glass	sheet of unlined,
aquarium tank or	white paper
deep-sided pan	

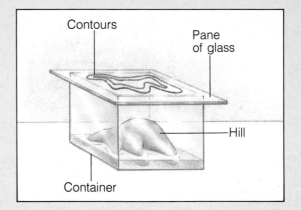

Contours
Pane of glass
Hill
Container

Procedure

1. Cut the cardboard to fit the bottom of the tank or pan.

2. On top of the cardboard, shape the clay into a model of a hill. Include on the model some gullies, a steep slope, and a gentle slope.

3. When the model is dry and hard, place the model and cardboard into the tank or pan. Pour water into the container to a depth of 1 cm. This will represent sea level.

4. Place the pane of glass over the container. Looking straight down into the container, use the glass-marking pencil to trace the outline of the container on the glass. Also trace on the glass the contour, or outline, of the water around the edges of the model. Carefully remove the pane of glass from the container.

5. Add another centimeter of water to the container. The depth of the water should now be 2 cm. Place the glass in exactly the same position as before. Trace the new contour of the water on the pane of glass.

6. Repeat step 5, adding 1 cm to the depth of the water each time. Stop when the next addition of water would completely cover the model.

7. Remove the pane of glass. With a pencil, trace the contours on the glass onto a sheet of paper. This will be your topographic map.

8. Assume that every centimeter of water you added to the first centimeter (sea level) equals 100 m of elevation on the map. Label the elevation of each contour line on your topographic map.

Observations

1. What is the approximate elevation of the top of the hill?

2. How can you determine if the hill has a steep slope by looking at the contour lines?

3. How can you determine if the hill has a gentle slope by looking at the contour lines?

4. How do contour lines look when they show gullies on the model?

Analysis and Conclusions

What information can a topographic map provide about the Earth's surface?

Summarizing Key Concepts

8–1 The Continents

▲ There are seven continents on Earth: Africa, Antarctica, Asia, Australia, Europe, North America, and South America.

8–2 Topography

▲ The shape of the Earth's surface is called its topography.

▲ The different physical features of an area are called its landscape.

▲ The three main types of landscape regions are mountains, plains, and plateaus.

▲ One characteristic of a landscape region is elevation. The difference in a region's elevations is called its relief.

▲ Mountains have high elevations, and are areas of high relief.

▲ Mountains are usually part of larger groups called mountain ranges, mountain systems, and mountain belts.

▲ Plains are flat land areas that are not far above sea level. They are areas of low relief.

▲ Low, flat areas along the coast are called coastal plains. Low, flat areas found inland are called interior plains.

▲ Plateaus are broad, flat areas that rise more than 600 meters above sea level.

8–3 Mapping the Earth's Surface

▲ A map is a drawing of the Earth, or part of the Earth, on a flat surface. The most accurate representation of the Earth is a globe.

▲ The Earth is divided by lines that run from north to south, called meridians, and by lines that run from east to west, called parallels.

▲ Meridians are used to measure longitude. Parallels are used to measure latitude.

▲ The Earth is divided into 24 time zones.

8–4 Topographic Maps

▲ Topographic maps show the different shapes and sizes of land surfaces.

▲ Topographic maps use contour lines to show relief.

Reviewing Key Terms

Define each term in a complete sentence.

8–1 The Continents
island
continent

8–2 Topography
topography
landscape
elevation
relief
mountain
mountain range
mountain system
mountain belt

plain
coastal plain
interior plain
plateau

8–3 Mapping the Earth's Surface
map
globe
scale
meridian
prime meridian
longitude

time zone
international date line
parallel
equator
latitude
projection
Mercator projection
equal-area projection

8–4 Topographic Maps
topographic map
contour line

Chapter Review

Content Review

Multiple Choice

Choose the letter of the answer that best completes each statement.

1. The smallest landmass that is still considered a continent is
   a. North America.   c. Africa.
   b. Australia.   d. Greenland.
2. Large areas of very old, exposed rock that form the core of a continent are called
   a. icecaps.   c. shields.
   b. mountains.   d. meridians.
3. Tops of mountains are called
   a. gorges.   c. summits.
   b. elevations.   d. projections.
4. Individual mountains are usually
   a. volcanic mountains.
   b. mountain systems.
   c. plateaus.
   d. none of these.
5. The landscape region with the lowest overall elevation is a(an)
   a. mountain belt.   c. plateau.
   b. coastal plain.   d. interior plain.

6. Broad, flat areas of land more than 600 meters above sea level are called
   a. plains.   c. farmland.
   b. plateaus.   d. mountains.
7. The measure of distance east or west of the prime meridian is called
   a. latitude.   c. projection.
   b. parallel.   d. longitude.
8. A map projection that shows the correct shape of coastlines but distorts the sizes of regions far from the equator is called a(an)
   a. Mercator projection.
   b. topographic map.
   c. equal-area projection.
   d. contour projection.
9. Lines on a map that pass through points with the same elevation are called
   a. meridians.   c. parallels.
   b. contour lines.   d. lines of relief.

True or False

If the statement is true, write ''true.'' If it is false, change the underlined word or words to make the statement true.

1. Central America is part of the continent of South America.
2. The three main types of landscape regions are mountains, plains, and continents.
3. Plains are flat areas of land that rise more than 600 meters above sea level.
4. The distance around the world is measured in degrees.
5. The prime meridian divides the parallels of north latitude from those of south latitude.
6. The time in a city one time zone west of another city will be one hour earlier.

Concept Mapping

Complete the following concept map for Section 8–1. Then construct a concept map for the entire chapter.

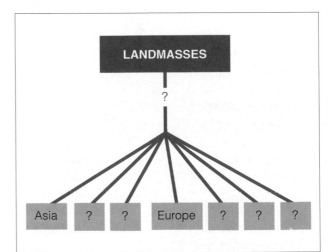

Concept Mastery

Discuss each of the following in a brief paragraph.

1. List the continents. Which continent is also a country? Which continent is almost completely covered by a thick icecap? Which continents are joined to form larger landmasses?
2. How is the topography of an area changed by moving water?
3. Define relief as it relates to Earth's topography. What landscape feature would have high relief? Low relief?
4. What are the similarities and differences between interior plains and coastal plains?
5. Why is the international date line important to travelers?
6. In what ways are maps and globes useful?
7. Why is a map's legend important? What kinds of information can you find in a map's legend?

Critical Thinking and Problem Solving

Use the skills you have developed in this chapter to answer each of the following.

1. **Applying concepts** Explain why the distance measured by degrees of latitude always stays the same, while the distance measured by degrees of longitude varies.
2. **Making predictions** Most of the Earth's ice is found on or around Antarctica. Suppose the temperature of the area around the South Pole climbs above freezing and all of Antarctica's ice melts. Which landscape regions in the rest of the world would be most affected? Why?
3. **Interpreting maps** In Figure 8–27, what contour interval is used? At what elevation is School Number 8? If you wanted to take an easy climb up Grimes Hill, which slope would you choose to climb? Why? Why would you not want to hike in the area located just west of the major highway? Locate the unpaved road west of Grimes Hill. How many kilometers would you walk if you walked from one end of the road to the other? Does the stream flow in or out of Smith Pond? How can you tell?
4. **Relating concepts** Suppose you are the captain of a large ocean liner sailing across the Pacific Ocean from Asia to North America. You notice that the maps in your cabin have the same projection as the map shown in Figure 8–21 on page 293. Are you in trouble? Why?
5. **Applying concepts** You want to go camping with some friends in a national park. You plan to hike into the park on a highway, then leave the road to make your own trails in the forest. How would a road map help you? How would a topographic map of the area help you?
6. **Making maps** Draw topographic maps of three imaginary areas. The first area has a mountain landscape; the second has a plains landscape; the third has several plateaus separated by rivers.
7. **Using the writing process** You are lost in the deep woods with only a scrap of paper, a pencil, a small amount of supplies, and your faithful homing pigeon, Homer. You plan to send Homer for help. Write a note to tie to Homer's leg. Include a map of your location.

Earth's Interior

Guide for Reading

In 1864, Jules Verne wrote *Journey to the Center of the Earth.* In this exciting and imaginative tale, Verne describes his idea of what lies hidden beneath the surface of planet Earth.

Verne was not the only person to be fascinated by this unknown world. For many years, scientists have explored the interior of the Earth. But they have not been able to use mechanical probes such as those that explore outer space. The tremendous heat and pressure in the Earth's interior make this region far more difficult to explore than it is to explore planets millions of kilometers away.

In this chapter you will learn about the structure and composition of each layer of the Earth. Afterward, you may want to read *Journey to the Center of the Earth*—and compare Jules Verne's description with the scientific model of the Earth's interior.

Journal *Activity*

You and Your World Have you ever visited a cave or a cavern? If so, in your journal write about your feelings upon first entering the cave's depths. If you have never visited a cave, use your imagination to describe what you think it might be like to walk beneath the surface of the Earth.

 Dangling by what appears to be a slender thread, a group of scientists descend into the Earth.

9–1 The Earth's Core

Scientists use telescopes and space probes to gather information about the planets and the stars. They use microscopes to examine unseen worlds of life on Earth. They use computers and other instruments to gather information about atoms, the building blocks of all matter. Most of the information scientists have gathered about the Earth's interior has come not only from complex instruments but also from earthquakes.

Earthquakes and Seismic Waves

As you will learn in Chapter 11, earthquakes are produced when a part of the Earth's uppermost layer moves suddenly. During an earthquake, the ground shakes and trembles. Sometimes the movement is so violent that buildings crash to the ground and roads and highways are destroyed. Earthquakes produce shock waves that travel through the Earth. These shock waves, which are actually waves of energy, are called seismic (SIGHZ-mihk) waves. You can make a simple model to show how shock waves move. Fill a sink or basin half full with water and then drop a small pebble onto the center of the water's surface. You will observe waves that move outward from the pebble's point of impact in circles of ever-increasing size.

All earthquakes produce at least two types of seismic waves at the same time: P waves and S waves. These waves are detected and recorded by a special

Figure 9–1 *An earthquake in San Francisco twisted and cracked this highway (left). An earthquake in Armenia reduced buildings to rubble (right).*

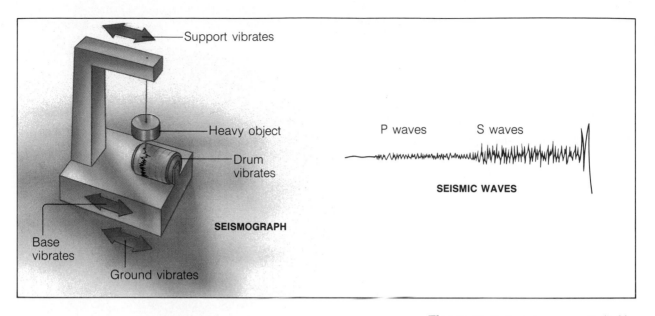

Support vibrates

Heavy object

Drum vibrates

Base vibrates

Ground vibrates

SEISMOGRAPH

P waves   S waves

SEISMIC WAVES

instrument called a seismograph (SIGHZ-muh-graf). You will learn more about how a seismograph works and about seismic waves in Chapter 11. What you need to know now is that seismic waves penetrate the depths of the Earth and return to the surface. During this passage, the speed and direction of the waves change. The changes that occur in the movement of seismic waves are caused by differences in the structure and makeup of the Earth's interior.

Exactly how have P waves and S waves helped scientists develop a model of the Earth's inner structure? At a depth of 2900 kilometers below Earth's surface, P waves passing through the Earth slow down rapidly. S waves disappear. Scientists know that P waves do not move well through liquids and that S waves are stopped completely. So the changes in the movement of the two seismic waves at a depth of 2900 kilometers indicate something significant. Do you know what it is? You are right if you say that 2900 kilometers is the beginning of a liquid layer of the Earth. At a depth of 5150 kilometers, P waves increase their speed. This increase indicates that P waves are no longer traveling through a liquid layer. Instead, P waves are passing through a solid layer of the Earth.

After observing the speeds of P waves and S waves, scientists have concluded that the Earth's center, or core, is actually made up of two layers with different characteristics.

Figure 9–2 *A seismograph (left) detects and records earthquake waves, or seismic waves. A typical pattern of seismic waves is shown (right). What are two types of seismic waves?*

ACTIVITY

What Is the Cause of Earthquakes?

1. Obtain four carpet samples of different colors.

2. Stack the samples on top of one another.

3. Place one hand on each side of the carpet pile and gently press toward the center. Describe what happens.

If the layers of carpet were actually layers of rock, what would happen?

Figure 9–3 *The paths of seismic waves change as they travel through the Earth. P waves slow down as they pass through the liquid outer core. As they leave the outer core and pass through the inner core, P waves speed up. This change in speed bends the waves. S waves disappear as they enter the outer core. Why? Notice that a wave-free shadow zone extends all the way around the Earth. The shadow zone is produced by the bending of seismic waves.*

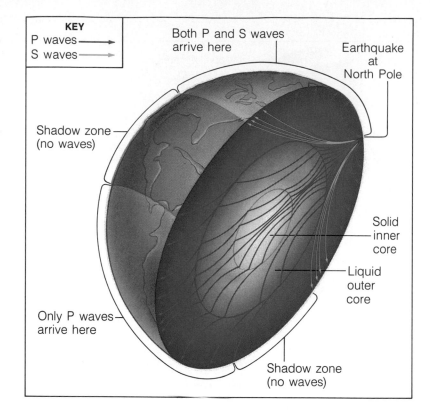

KEY
P waves ——→
S waves ——→

Both P and S waves arrive here

Earthquake at North Pole

Shadow zone (no waves)

Solid inner core

Liquid outer core

Only P waves arrive here

Shadow zone (no waves)

The Earth's Core

Both layers of the Earth's core are made of the elements iron and nickel. The solid, innermost layer is called the **inner core.** Here iron and nickel are under a great deal of pressure. The temperature of the inner core reaches 5000°C. Iron and nickel usually melt at this temperature. The enormous pressure at this depth, however, pushes the particles of iron and nickel so tightly together that the elements remain solid.

The radius, or distance from the center to the edge, of the inner core is about 1300 kilometers. The inner core begins at a depth of about 5150 kilometers below the Earth's surface. The presence of solid iron in the inner core may explain the existence of the magnetic fields around the Earth. Scientists think the iron produces an effect similar to the effect around a magnet—that is, a magnetic field. Have you ever experimented with iron filings and a bar magnet? If so, were you able to observe the pattern of the filings around the magnet? This pattern identifies the magnetic field. Perhaps your teacher can help you do this activity so that you can see a magnetic field for yourself.

ACTIVITY
WRITING

Shake and Quake

Write a 250-word horror story describing the disaster that would occur in the aftermath of a fictitious earthquake that levels a major American city. Make your story as descriptive as you can.

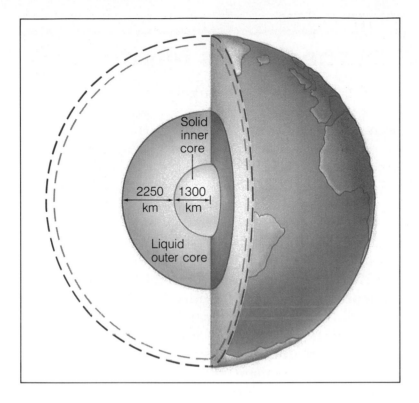

Labels in figure: Solid inner core; 2250 km; 1300 km; Liquid outer core

Surrounding the inner core is the second layer of the Earth, called the **outer core.** The outer core begins about 2900 kilometers below the Earth's surface and is about 2250 kilometers thick. The outer core is also made of iron and nickel. In this layer, the temperature ranges from about 2200°C in the upper part to almost 5000°C near the inner core. The heat makes the iron and nickel in the outer core molten, or changed into a hot liquid.

9–1 Section Review

1. What evidence has caused scientists to conclude that the Earth's core is made of two different layers?
2. Name two types of seismic waves. How are these waves the same? How are they different?
3. How are the inner and the outer cores of the Earth alike? How do they differ?

Critical Thinking—*Making Predictions*
4. Predict what would happen to P waves and S waves if the Earth's outer core were solid and its inner core were liquid.

ACTIVITY

CALCULATING

The Speed of Seismic Waves

Some kinds of seismic waves travel at 24 times the speed of sound. The speed of sound is 1250 km/hr. How fast do such seismic waves travel?

311

9–2 The Earth's Mantle

The layer of the Earth directly above the outer core is the **mantle.** The mantle extends to a depth of about 2900 kilometers below the surface. About 80 percent of the volume of the Earth and about 68 percent of the planet's mass are in the mantle.

In 1909, the Yugoslav scientist Andrija Mohorovičić (moh-hoh-ROH-vuh-chihch) observed a change in the speed of seismic waves as they moved through the Earth. When the waves reached a depth of 32 to 64 kilometers below the Earth's surface, their speed increased. The change in the speed of the waves at this depth indicated a difference in either the density (how tightly together the particles of material are packed) or the composition of the rock. Mohorovičić discovered a boundary between the Earth's outermost layer and the mantle. In his honor, this boundary is now called the **Moho.**

Scientists have made many attempts to determine the composition of the mantle. They have studied rocks from volcanoes because these rocks were formed deep within the Earth. They have also studied rocks from the ocean floor. **After studying rock samples, scientists have determined that the**

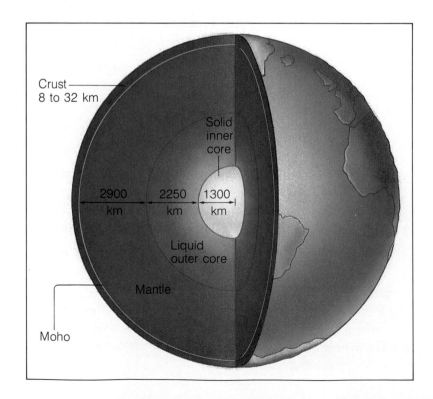

Figure 9–5 *The mantle is the Earth's layer that lies above the outer core. The crust is only a very thin layer of the Earth. Most of the crust is covered with soil, rock, and water. What is the name of the boundary between the mantle and the crust?*

Crust 8 to 32 km

Solid inner core

2900 km　2250 km　1300 km

Liquid outer core

Mantle

Moho

mantle is made mostly of the elements silicon, oxygen, iron, and magnesium. The lower mantle has a greater percentage of iron than the upper mantle has.

The density of the mantle increases with depth. This increase in density is perhaps due to the greater percentage of iron in the lower mantle. The temperature and the pressure within the mantle also increase with depth. The temperature ranges from 870°C in the upper mantle to about 2200°C in the lower mantle.

Studies of seismic waves suggest that the rock in the mantle can flow like a thick liquid. The high temperature and pressure in the mantle allow the solid rock to flow slowly, thus changing shape. When a solid has the ability to flow, it has the property of **plasticity** (plas-TIHS-uh-tee).

Figure 9–6 *Kilauea is an active volcano in Hawaii. Here you can see lava being thrown into the air as the volcano erupts (right). Lava, either from a volcano or from a rift valley in the ocean floor, forms these "pillow" shapes when it is rapidly cooled by ocean water (left).*

9–2 Section Review

1. What elements make up most of the mantle?
2. Where is the mantle located? How far does it extend below the Earth's surface?
3. What is the Moho?
4. What is plasticity?

Connection—*You and Your World*

5. In areas where earthquakes are common, the foundations of buildings are constructed so that they can move slightly on special slippery pads. Architects believe that these buildings will not be damaged during an earthquake. How would this type of construction make a building safer during an earthquake?

ACTIVITY

DOING

A Model of the Earth's Interior

1. Obtain a Styrofoam ball 15 cm or more in diameter.

2. Carefully cut out a wedge from the ball so that the ball is similar to the one in Figure 9–5.

3. Draw lines on the inside of the ball and on the inside of the wedge to represent the four layers of the Earth.

4. Label and color each layer on the ball and wedge.

Figure 9–7 *Natural rock formations, such as these in Big Bend National Park, Texas, often take beautiful, and sometimes surprising, forms. The elements that make up the Earth's crust are listed in this chart. What two elements are the most abundant?*

ELEMENTS IN THE EARTH'S CRUST

Element	Percentage in Crust
Oxygen	46.60
Silicon	27.72
Aluminum	8.13
Iron	5.00
Calcium	3.63
Sodium	2.83
Potassium	2.59
Magnesium	2.09
Titanium	0.40
Hydrogen	0.14
Total	99.13

9–3 The Earth's Crust

The Earth's crust is its thin outermost layer. The **crust** is much thinner than the mantle and the outer and inner cores. You can think of the crust as being similar to the peel on an apple. All life on Earth exists on or within a few hundred meters above the crust. Most of the crust cannot be seen. Do you know why? It is covered with soil, rock, and water. There is one place, however, where the crust can be seen. Where do you think that might be?

The crust is made of three types of solid rocks: igneous rocks, sedimentary rocks, and metamorphic rocks. Igneous rocks form when hot liquid rock from deep within the Earth cools and hardens as it reaches the surface. The word igneous means "born of fire," a term that explains with accuracy how these rocks are formed. Sedimentary rocks form when sediments—small pieces of rocks, sand, and other materials—are pressed and cemented together by the weight of layers that build up over long periods of time. Metamorphic rock forms when igneous and sedimentary rocks are changed by heat, pressure, or the action of chemicals.

The thickness of the Earth's crust varies. Crust beneath the oceans, called oceanic crust, is less than 10 kilometers thick. Its average thickness is only about 8 kilometers. Oceanic crust is made mostly of silicon, oxygen, iron, and magnesium.

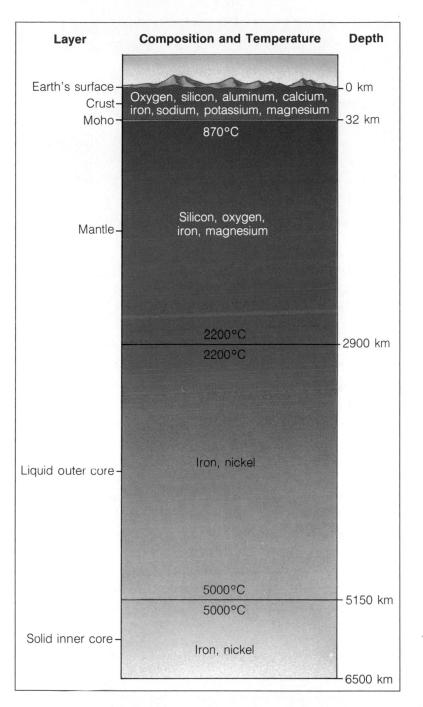

Layer	Composition and Temperature	Depth
Earth's surface	Oxygen, silicon, aluminum, calcium, iron, sodium, potassium, magnesium	0 km
Crust		
Moho		32 km
	870°C	
Mantle	Silicon, oxygen, iron, magnesium	
	2200°C	2900 km
	2200°C	
Liquid outer core	Iron, nickel	
	5000°C	5150 km
	5000°C	
Solid inner core	Iron, nickel	
		6500 km

Figure 9–8 *This diagram summarizes the major characteristics of the Earth's layers. Which layers are solid? Which layer is liquid?*

Activity Bank

How Hard Is That Rock?, p. 761

Crust beneath the continents, called continental crust, has an average thickness of about 32 kilometers. Beneath mountains, continental crust is much thicker. Under some mountains, the crust's thickness is greater than 70 kilometers. Continental crust is made mostly of silicon, oxygen, aluminum, calcium, sodium, and potassium.

The Earth's crust forms the upper part of the **lithosphere** (LIHTH-uh-sfeer). The lithosphere is the

ACTIVITY

CALCULATING

How Many Earths?

The distance from the center of the Earth to the surface is about 6450 kilometers. The distance from the Earth to the sun is 150 million kilometers. How many Earths lined up in a row are needed to reach the sun?

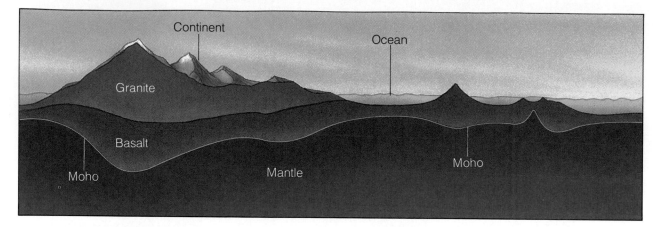

Figure 9–9 *The Earth's crust consists of two layers. The top layer is made of granite and is found only under the continents. The bottom layer is made of basalt and is found under both the continents and the oceans.*

solid topmost part of the Earth. It is between 50 and 100 kilometers thick and is broken up into large sections called lithospheric plates. There are at least seven major plates.

The layer directly beneath the lithosphere is called the **asthenosphere** (az-THEEN-oh-sfeer). The asthenosphere, which is 130 to 160 kilometers thick, is actually considered to be the upper edge of the mantle. The asthenosphere is made of hot, molten material. This material has the property of plasticity and thus can flow easily. The lithospheric plates move on the hot molten material that forms the asthenosphere. You can get a better idea of this concept by making your own model of the lithosphere and the asthenosphere. Try the following: Use a slice of bread to represent a lithospheric plate and a layer of jelly spread on a piece of cardboard to represent the asthenosphere. Place the bread on top of the jelly. Move the slice of bread back and forth slightly. What do you observe?

9–3 Section Review

1. What is the Earth's crust?
2. Compare oceanic crust with continental crust.
3. What are the characteristics of the asthenosphere? What floats on this layer?

Critical Thinking—*Relating Concepts*

4. Explain why metamorphic rock could not form before igneous or sedimentary rock.

Beauty From Beneath the Earth's Surface

The Smithsonian Institution in Washington, D.C., has often been called the nation's attic. But you should not think of a dusty attic filled with unwanted and unused objects. For the Smithsonian Institution is a treasure-filled attic: a storehouse of items of great artistic merit made by talented women and men, as well as of treasures from the Earth itself. Here you will find diamonds, rubies, sapphires, and other gems valuable beyond price—all handcrafted by the forces of nature in a "laboratory" you know as the Earth.

For example, scientists believe that diamonds form within the upper part of the Earth's mantle. Here the pressure is tremendous—about 65,000 times the pressure at the Earth's surface—and the temperature is close to 1500°C! Under these extreme conditions of pressure and temperature, carbon can be transformed into diamonds. Diamond-laden molten rock is forced to the surface of the Earth by volcanic explosions. Mines cut into the crust expose the diamonds formed long ago in the Earth's mantle. These rough diamonds vary in quality. Those that are gem quality are cut and shaped into precious stones used in jewelry. Those that are not fine enough to be made into jewelry are used to make drills and saws. Such *industrial-grade diamonds* are so strong that they cut through many materials, including steel. Small bits of diamond are often used in the dental drills that remove decayed parts of teeth and in the needles that follow the grooves in a record to produce the sounds of music.

If you are able to visit the Smithsonian Institution at some future time, keep this in mind: Not all the great treasures preserved and protected within the walls of this great museum were made by the hands of people; many were shaped by forces at work deep within the Earth.

Gemstones, like this green beryl, are quite beautiful. Diamonds, highly valued for their beauty, also have important uses in industry. Small diamond particles are often imbedded in drills (left) and in saws (right).

Laboratory Investigation

Simulating Plasticity

Problem

How can the plasticity of the Earth's mantle be simulated?

Materials *(per group)*

15 g cornstarch
2 small beakers
10 mL cold water
medicine dropper
metal stirring rod or spoon

Procedure 🧪

1. Put 15 g of cornstarch in one of the beakers. Into the other beaker, pour 10 mL of cold water.

2. Use the medicine dropper to gradually add one dropperful of water to the cornstarch. Stir the mixture.

3. Continue to add the water, one dropperful at a time. Stir the mixture after each addition. Stop adding the water when the mixture becomes difficult to stir.

4. Try to pour the mixture into your hand. Try to roll the mixture into a ball and press it.

Observations

1. Before the addition of water, is the cornstarch a solid, liquid, or gas? Is the water a solid, liquid, or gas?

2. When you try to pour the mixture into your hand, does the mixture behave like a solid, liquid, or gas?

3. When you try to roll the mixture into a ball and apply pressure, does the mixture act like a solid, liquid, or gas?

Analysis and Conclusions

1. How is the mixture of cornstarch and water similar to the Earth's mantle? Different from the Earth's mantle?

2. How might the plasticity of the mantle influence the movement of the Earth's lithospheric plates?

3. **On Your Own** Make a model of a lithospheric plate. Devise a way to show how the plasticity of the mantle allows the Earth's lithospheric plates to move.

Study Guide

Summarizing Key Concepts

9–1 The Earth's Core

▲ An earthquake is a sudden movement of the Earth's outermost layer.

▲ Shock waves produced by an earthquake are called seismic waves.

▲ Seismic waves are detected and recorded by an instrument called a seismograph.

▲ Seismic waves called P waves and S waves are used to study the structure and composition of the Earth's interior.

▲ The core of the Earth is made of a liquid outer core and a solid inner core. Both core layers are composed of iron and nickel.

▲ Although the temperature is high enough to melt iron and nickel, the inner core is solid because of the enormous pressure.

▲ The dense iron and nickel in the inner core may be the cause of the Earth's magnetic field.

▲ The temperature range of the Earth's outer core is from about 2200°C to almost 5000°C.

▲ P waves do not move very well through liquids. S waves do not move through liquids at all. This information has helped scientists determine that the outer core is liquid and the inner core is solid.

9–2 The Earth's Mantle

▲ The mantle is the layer of the Earth that lies above the outer core.

▲ The mantle makes up about 80 percent of the Earth's volume and 68 percent of the Earth's mass.

▲ The boundary between the Earth's outermost layer and the mantle is called the Moho.

▲ The mantle is made mostly of silicon, oxygen, iron, and magnesium.

▲ Pressure and temperature increase with depth in the mantle.

▲ Because of the tremendous heat and pressure in the mantle, rocks in the mantle exhibit the property of plasticity.

9–3 The Earth's Crust

▲ The crust is the thin outermost layer of the Earth.

▲ The crust is made of igneous, sedimentary, and metamorphic rocks.

▲ The most abundant elements in the crust are oxygen, silicon, aluminum, iron, calcium, sodium, potassium, and magnesium.

▲ Oceanic crust is about 8 kilometers thick. Continental crust is about 32 kilometers thick.

▲ The crust forms the upper part of the lithosphere. The lithosphere contains large sections called lithospheric plates.

▲ Lithospheric plates move about on the asthenosphere, the outermost edge of the mantle. The asthenosphere exhibits the property of plasticity.

Reviewing Key Terms

Define each term in a complete sentence.

9–1 The Earth's Core
inner core
outer core

9–2 The Earth's Mantle
mantle
Moho
plasticity

9–3 The Earth's Crust
crust
lithosphere
asthenosphere

Chapter Review

Content Review

Multiple Choice

Choose the letter of the answer that best completes each statement.

1. The shock waves produced by an earthquake are measured with a
   a. radiograph.
   b. seismograph.
   c. sonograph.
   d. laser.
2. The Earth's inner core is made of
   a. oxygen and silicon.
   b. iron and nickel.
   c. iron and silicon.
   d. copper and nickel.
3. The boundary between the mantle and the outermost layer of the Earth is called the
   a. Moho.
   b. outer core.
   c. lithosphere.
   d. bedrock.
4. The crust of the Earth is made mostly of
   a. oxygen and silicon.
   b. iron and silicon.
   c. iron and nickel.
   d. copper and nickel.
5. When P waves and S waves reach the Earth's outer core,
   a. both keep moving at the same speed.
   b. both stop completely.
   c. P waves stop and S waves slow down.
   d. S waves stop and P waves slow down.
6. The layer that makes up most of the Earth's mass and volume is the
   a. mantle.
   b. magma.
   c. crust.
   d. core.
7. The ability of a solid to flow is called
   a. ductility.
   b. plasticity.
   c. seismology.
   d. porosity.
8. The thin outermost layer of the Earth is called the
   a. mantle.
   b. Moho.
   c. crust.
   d. core.

True or False

If the statement is true, write "true." If it is false, change the underlined word or words to make the statement true.

1. The <u>atmosphere</u> is the outermost layer of the mantle on which the plates move.
2. The innermost layer of the Earth is called the <u>inner</u> core.
3. The <u>outer</u> core is <u>molten</u>.
4. <u>S waves</u> slow down as they pass through liquids.
5. The outermost layer of the Earth is called the <u>crust</u>.
6. The topmost solid part of the Earth is broken up into <u>lithospheric plates</u>.
7. The presence of <u>copper</u> in the inner core may explain the <u>magnetic field</u> that exists around the Earth.

Concept Mapping

Complete the following concept map for Section 9–1. Then construct a concept map for the entire chapter.

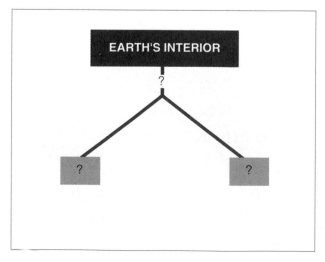

Concept Mastery

Discuss each of the following in a brief paragraph.

1. How have scientists learned about the composition of the Earth's interior?
2. How does oceanic crust differ from continental crust?
3. How do temperature and pressure change as you move from the Earth's crust to the inner core? How do temperature and pressure affect the properties of materials found in the Earth?
4. Briefly describe the work of Andrija Mohorovičić. What did this scientist discover?
5. What is igneous rock? Sedimentary rock? Metamorphic rock?
6. How does the property of plasticity shown by the asthenosphere account for the movement of lithospheric plates?

Critical Thinking and Problem Solving

Use the skills you have developed in this chapter to answer each of the following.

1. **Analyzing data** The temperature of the inner core reaches about 5000°C. The temperature of the outer core begins at 2200°C. Explain why the outer core is liquid and the inner core is solid.
2. **Relating concepts** It has been said that "Every cloud has a silver lining." What could be the "silver lining" in an earthquake?
3. **Analyzing illustrations** This illustration shows the layers of the Earth. Something is wrong with this artist's ideas, however. Identify the errors and describe what you would do to correct them.

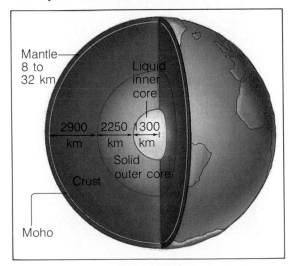

4. **Making models** Use the information in this chapter to make a model of the four layers of the Earth's interior. You may use clay of different colors, papier-mâché, or other materials to make your model. Keep the depth and thickness of each layer of your model in scale with the actual depth and thickness of the Earth's layers. Include a key to the scale you use to construct your model. For example, 1 centimeter in your model might equal 1000 kilometers in the Earth.
5. **Interpreting diagrams** Look at Figure 9–3 on page 310. You will notice an area of the Earth labeled the shadow zone. Use this diagram and your knowledge of seismic waves and the structure of the Earth's interior to explain what the shadow zone is.
6. **Using the writing process** Write a short story about an imaginary trip taken in a machine that is able to drill through the Earth. Make your destination an exotic country on the side of the Earth opposite the city or town in which you live. Use a globe to help. You might like to illustrate this story with appropriate pictures.

Vast canyons and craggy mountains make the ocean floor as mysterious as the surface of a far-off planet. It may be centuries before the bottom of the world's seas are fully explored. Yet using information from space satellites, geologist William Haxby has created startling maps of the undersea landscape. The remarkable maps are almost as detailed as if the water had been drained from the seas to reveal the features of the ocean floor.

William Haxby works at the Lamont Doherty Earth Observatory in Palisades, New York. Using data from space satellites and a computer, Haxby produces three-dimensional maps in vivid colors. These maps provide a view of the ocean floor never before seen. Cracks in the sea bottom, underwater volcanoes, and other features of the ocean floor are easily observed on Haxby's maps. The existence of such features provides new evidence about some of the most important earth science theories.

One theory, called plate tectonics, states that the Earth's crust is made up of a number of very large plates. Heat and motion deep within the Earth cause the plates to move slowly but constantly. The movement of plates triggers earthquakes, thrusts up mountain ranges, and cuts deep ridges.

Haxby's maps show many signs of plate movement along the ocean floor. One deep crack under the Indian Ocean may have been made when India drifted away from Antarctica and moved toward Asia millions of years ago. Geologists believe a twisting ridge on the ocean floor off the southern tip of Africa was also formed millions of years ago, when Africa, South America, and Antarctica separated. The ridge, concealed under layers of sediment, was detected by Haxby's computer imaging.

William Haxby Maps a Strange World

BENEATH

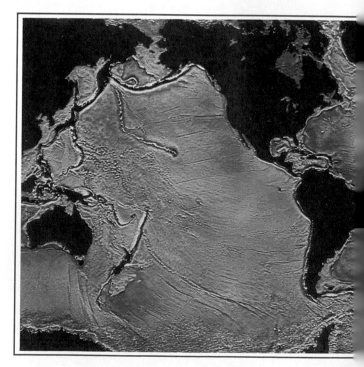

Haxby started his mapping project, which took 18 months, in 1981. His work was based on data from the space satellite *Seasat*. *Seasat's* measurements showed that there were height differences on the ocean's surface. Haxby discovered that the height of the ocean's surface varies by dozens of meters from one place to another. And as he points out, these differences are not due to waves or wind. The surface of the ocean is simply not flat.

The reason for the variations in the ocean's surface is the gravitational pull of structures on the ocean bottom. Structures with large mass, such as underwater mountains, pull on the water with more force than structures with less mass, such as canyons. The stronger the pull of the underwater structure, the greater the amount of water that is attracted to a place above it. "As a result," says Haxby, "water piles up and there is a bump in the ocean over a big object." So the ocean surface imitates the ocean bottom.

Launched in 1978 for a five-year orbit, *Seasat* became silent after three months due to a short circuit in its electrical system. But the eight billion readings it had radioed back to tracking stations on the Earth were enough for Haxby to begin working on his maps. And today, data collected by another space satellite, *Geosat*, allow Haxby to continue.

Haxby has been interested in geology since his boyhood, when he was a "rockhound." At the University of Minnesota, he became interested in continental drift and plate tectonics. He eventually did graduate work in geophysics, leading to a doctoral degree from Cornell University. When he first began computer analysis of the satellite information, he did not intend to map the entire ocean bottom. All he wanted to do was chart some small areas by matching ocean surface heights with the gravitational forces that created them. His first maps were so detailed, however, that he decided to go further.

The detail—Haxby can pinpoint objects as small as 30 kilometers across—and colors reveal structures that are not on other large maps of the ocean bottom. In fact, the images produced by Haxby's computer look so real that people looking at them feel as if they are standing on the bottom of the ocean. And around the world, scientists use Haxby's maps to help them learn more about the ever-changing Earth.

THE SEA

◀ **This is an example of the type of map that William Haxby draws with the help of a computer that analyzes measurements taken by an orbiting satellite.**

UNIT THREE

Dynamic Earth

It is midnight on the island of Hawaii. The stars shine brightly in a coal-black sky; they look close enough to touch. But in one part of the sky above a distant mountain ridge, something strange is happening.

Red and purple clouds swirl rapidly and restlessly, rumbling with thunder. Just below them, there is an eerie reddish glow. Orange and yellow flames flicker along the ridge, forming a shimmering curtain of fire.

Through your binoculars, you can see that this is no ordinary fire. Fountains of molten rock the colors of flame leap from cracks in the Earth and fall back to the ground in showers of black cinders. Scarlet streams of molten rock ooze from the cracks and flow away, creating twisted formations of black rock as they cool.

▲ *Waterfalls and streams slowly wear away the rock of the island's interior.*

Lava spews forth from the top of Mauna Loa and flows in orange rivers down its slopes. ▶

CHAPTERS

Even as the island is being built up in one place, it is being broken down in another. Waves pound against the island's shore, grinding the rocks of the coast into sand and carrying the sand away. Farther inland, rocks are broken down into soil by wind, rain, and plants. Like the rest of the dynamic Earth, the island is constantly changing.

Waves crash along the shore, breaking down rock born of volcanic activity.

Discovery *Activity*

Sand

1. Examine some sand with a magnifying glass. What do you observe?

2. Form a pile of sand in a large waterproof container such as a dishpan. Pour water from a paper cup onto the sand. Does the speed at which you pour make a difference in what you observe?

3. Fill the bottom of a small plastic container to a depth of 2 centimeters with wet sand. Stir 25 grams of alum into the sand. Allow the mixture to dry completely (about 2 days). After the mixture has dried, gently twist the sides of the container to free its contents.

   ■ How do you think the observations you made in this activity relate to events that occur in nature?

Movement of the Earth's Crust

Guide for Reading

After you read the following sections, you will be able to

10–1 Earth's Changing Surface
■ Describe how the Earth's crust is deformed.

10–2 The Floating Crust
■ Define isostasy and explain its effect on the movement of the Earth's crust.

Have you ever had the exhilarating experience of standing at the edge of a mountain and looking down into a valley far below? Did you know that millions of years ago the mountain and valley probably looked quite different? The land may have been completely flat, without so much as a hill. Perhaps the area was once beneath an ocean. What caused the land to change? How did the mountain and the valley form?

Throughout the Earth's long history, its surface has been lifted up, pushed down, bent, and broken by forces beneath the surface. Although the resulting movements of the Earth's surface are usually too small and too slow to be directly observed, they are constantly changing the appearance of the Earth. Thus the Earth looks different today from the way it did millions of years ago. For example, what were once small hills may now be mountains that stand almost 9 kilometers above sea level!

What are the forces that cause mountains and valleys to form and grow? How do they work? Read on and find out.

Journal *Activity*

You and Your World Perhaps you have hiked to the top of a high mountain, traveled down into a valley, or imagined doing so. In your journal, discuss your experiences, real or imagined. Accompany your description with some illustrations.

 These towering mountains did not always exist. But over time, forces deep within the Earth have pushed them up far above the surrounding land.

10–1 Earth's Changing Surface

Stress! This word is probably all too familiar to most people. Think about the last time you were under a lot of stress. Perhaps you were getting ready to take a hard math test, arguing with a friend or family member, making a difficult decision, or waiting for your turn to perform in a musical or athletic competition. You may have felt as if you were being pulled in many directions at once. Or you may have felt so tense inside that you thought something might snap.

Like you, the Earth also experiences **stress**. This kind of stress, however, is not the result of emotionally difficult situations. Rather, it is caused by forces within the Earth itself. These forces push and pull on the part of the Earth known as the crust. As you learned in Chapter 9, the crust is the surface, or outermost, layer of the Earth. Because this is where stress occurs, it might be helpful to review its composition.

There are two major sections of the crust. One section is called continental crust. Continental crust makes up the Earth's landmasses, such as the North American continent. In most places, continental crust is about 32 kilometers thick. The other section, called oceanic crust, is found under the ocean floor. It is thinner than continental crust. Oceanic crust is usually about 8 kilometers thick.

Figure 10–1 *The rocks of the Earth's crust may be carved into strange and beautiful forms by the action of wind, water, and weather. The Needle's Eye is found in the Black Hills of South Dakota (left). The red-orange pinnacles are found in Bryce Canyon National Park in Utah (right).*

Figure 10–2 *These rocks on the coast of New Zealand have been deformed by stress. What does the term deformation mean?*

As you have just read, stress pushes and pulls on the Earth's crust. **As the rocks of the crust undergo stress, they slowly change shape and volume.** (Volume is the amount of space an object takes up.) **They also move up or down or sideways.** The movement causes the rocks to break, tilt, and fold. The breaking, tilting, and folding of rocks is called **deformation.** The prefix *de-* means undo; the root word *form* means shape or configuration. Can you explain why the term deformation is appropriate?

There are three basic types of stress, each of which deforms the crust in a different way. The three types of stress are **compression, tension,** and **shearing.** Refer to Figure 10–3 as you read about these different types of stress.

Compression squeezes the rocks of the crust. This often causes the particles in the crustal rocks to

Figure 10–3 *Each of the different forms of stress deforms the crust in a different way. The large arrows show the directions of the forces acting on the rocks. How are rocks affected by compression? Tension? Shearing?*

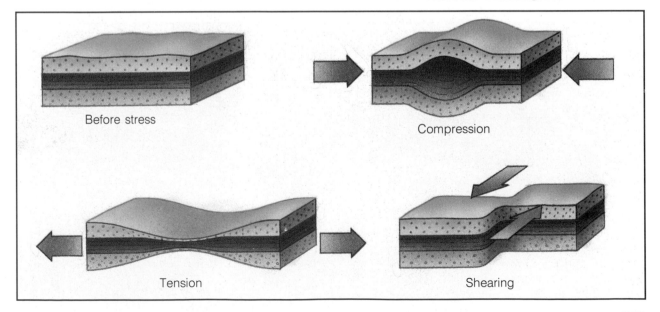

Before stress

Compression

Tension

Shearing

The Changing Earth

1. During the next two months, collect newspaper clippings dealing with earthquakes, floods, volcanoes, and other Earth-changing events.

2. On a map of the world, indicate the site of each event. Use a different-colored pencil for each category of event. Include a key with your map.

■ How did each event alter the Earth's surface?

move closer together, making the rocks denser and smaller in volume. In this case, compression is acting rather like a trash compactor, squeezing a large amount of matter into a smaller amount of space. As crustal rocks are compressed, they are pushed both higher up and deeper down. To understand this movement, imagine you are squeezing clay in your hand. As you squeeze the clay, some of it is pushed out of the opening at the top of your fist and some of it is pushed out of the opening at the bottom.

Tension pulls on the rocks of the crust, causing them to stretch out over a larger area. Like a piece of warm taffy being pulled, a rock under tension becomes thinner in the middle than at the ends. In addition, as the volume of the rock increases, its density decreases.

Shearing pushes rocks of the crust in two opposite directions. This causes the rocks to twist or tear apart. During shearing, then, rocks are not compressed or stretched. They simply bend or break apart.

Compression, tension, and shearing can change a rock's volume, its shape, or both. These stresses can also cause the rocks to **fracture,** or crack. If the rocks fracture along numerous flat surfaces which show no displacement, the cracks are called joints. Joints are generally parallel to one another. Some rocks have joints that form in more than one direction. Such rocks may break into blocks. The blocks form where the different sets of joints cross one another.

Figure 10–4 *Joints divide the face of the cliff behind the waterfall into tall, six-sided blocks. The joints formed as molten rock cooled and shrank. What shape are the blocks formed by the joints in the cliff overlooking the sea?*

Figure 10–5 *Based on the diagram and the photograph, what type of stress was acting on the sandstone? How can you tell?*

Faulting

Stress sometimes causes rocks to break. A break or crack along which rocks move is called a **fault.** The rocks on one side of the fault slide past the rocks on the other side of the fault. Movements along a fault can be up, down, or sideways. Earthquakes often occur along faults in the Earth's crust. What are some other possible results of movements along a fault?

Look at the cross sections of faulted rocks in Figure 10–5. As you can see, there are two blocks of rock, one on top of the other. The block of rock above the fault is called the **hanging wall.** The block below the fault is called the **foot wall.**

Stress can cause either the hanging wall or the foot wall to move up or down along a fault. If tension is acting on a fault, the hanging wall will move down relative to the foot wall. If this occurs, the fault between the two blocks is called a **normal fault.** If compression is acting on a fault, the hanging wall will move up relative to the foot wall. This type of fault is called a **reverse fault.**

A special type of reverse fault is a **thrust fault.** A thrust fault is formed when compression causes the hanging wall to slide over the foot wall. Thrust faults are special because they are almost horizontal, whereas regular reverse faults and normal faults are almost vertical. Thrust faults usually carry rocks many kilometers from their original position. Rocks are usually severely bent at the same time that thrust faulting occurs. In addition, thrust faults mix up the order of the layers in rock. Normally, older rock layers are found under younger rock layers. But a thrust fault pushes older rocks on top of younger rocks. The Lewis Overthrust Fault in Glacier National Park, Montana, is an example of a thrust fault. Here very old rocks have slid eastward more than 48 kilometers and now rest on top of younger rocks.

Figure 10–6 *A thrust fault is a special kind of reverse fault in which the hanging wall slides over the foot wall. How does a thrust fault affect the order of the rock layers in an area?*

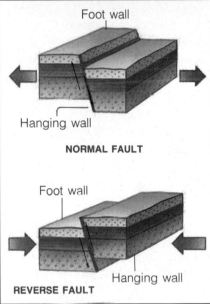

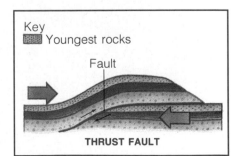

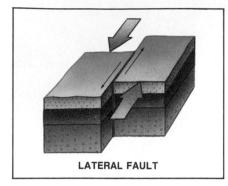

Figure 10–7 *In a lateral fault, which is also known as a strike-slip fault, the blocks of rock move horizontally past each other.*

Figure 10–8 *A fault-block mountain is formed when a block (or blocks) of rocks between two normal faults is pushed up. The rock layers in the diagram are flat, so you can clearly see the mountain-forming process. However, the rock layers in real mountains, such as the Grand Tetons in Wyoming, are usually tilted. One of the slopes of each mountain was once a horizontal surface!*

Stress does not cause blocks of crustal rock to move only up and down. Shearing will cause the blocks of rock to slide horizontally past each other. One block moves to the left or right in relation to the other block. The fault along which the blocks move horizontally past each other is called a **lateral fault.**

Faulted Mountains and Valleys

When there are many normal faults in one area, a series of mountains and valleys may form. Mountains formed by blocks of rock uplifted by normal faults are called **fault-block mountains.** A vast region in western North America called the Cordilleran Mountain region contains many fault-block mountains. The region extends from central Mexico to Oregon and Idaho and includes western Utah, all of Nevada, and eastern California.

Valleys also form when mountains form. Some valleys are formed when the block of land between two normal faults slides downward. Valleys created in this way are called **rift valleys.** One example of a rift valley is Death Valley in California. It is a long, narrow valley 87 meters below sea level. Scientists believe that the valley was formed by a series of small movements along two faults at either side of the valley. They estimate that the land along the eastern fault of Death Valley will move another 3 meters during the next 1000 years.

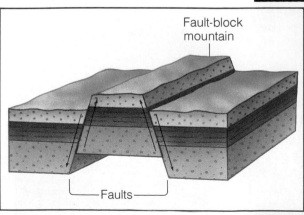

Fault-block mountain

Faults

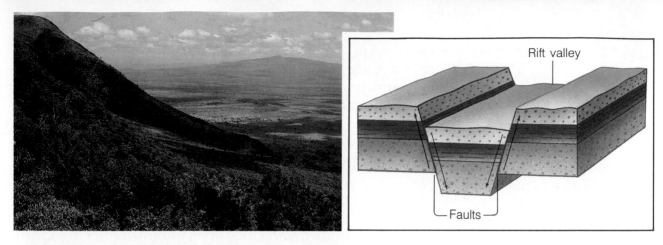

Figure 10-9 *A rift valley is formed when a block of rock between two normal faults slides down. The flat plain formed by this Kenyan rift valley is home to zebras, wildebeest, lions, and many other living things. How did the low mountains on either side of the valley form?*

Folding

Sometimes when stress is applied to the rocks of the crust, the rocks bend but do not break. The rocks bend in much the same way a rug wrinkles as it is pushed across a floor. A bend in a rock is called a **fold.** As you can see in Figure 10–10, a rock can fold either upward or downward. An upward fold in a rock is called an **anticline** (AN-tih-klighn). A downward fold in a rock is called a **syncline** (SIHN-klighn).

Folds vary in size. Some folds are so small that you need a magnifying glass to see them clearly. Others are large enough to form mountains. Layered rocks with large folds often have smaller folds within the layers. The Appalachian Mountains in the eastern United States are made up of many anticlines and synclines. This folded mountain chain extends from Canada to Alabama.

Figure 10-10 *Anticlines are upward folds in rocks. Synclines are downward folds in rocks. Some folds are quite large. The speck at the top of the English hill is a person.*

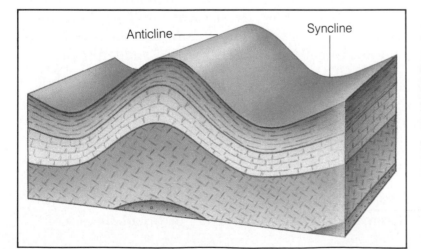

Under Pressure

1. Flatten three pieces of different-colored modeling clay into thin, rectangular layers on a piece of waxed paper. (If you do not have clay, you can substitute three equal-sized carpet scraps or pieces of foam rubber.)

2. Place the flattened layers of clay on top of one another.

3. Place your hands at opposite ends of the clay rectangle. Slowly push the two ends together. What happens to the clay?

■ How does this relate to the processes that build mountains?

Even though an anticline is an upward fold, it is not always higher than the surrounding land. An anticline can be under hills, valleys, or flat areas. An anticline may be hidden by layers of rock that build up in the low-lying areas around it after it forms. Or the stress may not have been great enough to bring the fold to the Earth's surface.

Fault or Fold?

A number of factors determine whether rocks will fault or fold. One factor is temperature. If the rocks become extremely hot during compression, they are more likely to fold than to fault. Do you know why? If you ever left a box of crayons in the sun when you were young, you may have firsthand experience with the effect of temperature on folding and faulting. At normal temperatures, crayons snap in two when stress is applied. In other words, they fault. But warm crayons can bend without breaking—they fold.

Another factor that affects whether rocks will fault or fold is pressure. The greater the pressure applied to the rocks, the more likely they are to fold rather than fault.

Rock type is yet another factor that determines whether rocks will fault or fold. Some types of rocks break easily when stress is applied. Such fragile rocks are said to be brittle. Sandstone is one example of brittle rock. Other rocks, such as rock salt, bend easily under stress. Rocks that bend easily are said to be ductile. Ductile rocks are more likely to fold, whereas brittle rocks are more likely to fault.

Another factor that determines whether rocks will fault or fold is how the stress is applied to the rocks. If the stress is applied gradually, the rocks will usually fold. But if the stress is applied suddenly, the rocks will usually fault.

Plateaus

A **plateau** (pla-TOH) is a large area of flat land that is raised high above sea level. You can get a pretty good idea of what a typical plateau looks like if you place a sandwich on a plate and look at it from the side. The flat layers of bread slices, cold cuts, cheese, lettuce, tomato, and mayonnaise (or whatever you put in your sandwich) correspond roughly to the horizontal rock layers that make up a plateau. Like a sandwich, a plateau is wider than it is tall. In addition, a plateau is often surrounded by steep cliffs that rise sharply from the surrounding land, much as a sandwich rises above the surface of the plate on which it is placed.

Although plateaus are often raised up by the same processes that form mountains, the rock layers in a plateau remain flat. (This is not the case with mountains, in which the rock layers are tilted and broken by faulting or are warped by folding.)

One way a plateau may be formed is by a slow, flat-topped fold. The Appalachian Plateau, which lies just west of the folded Appalachian Mountains, was created millions of years ago by such a fold. This plateau covers much of New York, Pennsylvania, Ohio, Kentucky, West Virginia, and Tennessee.

Another way a plateau may be formed is through vertical faulting. The Colorado Plateau, which is located west of the Rocky Mountains, was uplifted when the underlying region of the inner Earth became hotter and expanded. As this region expanded, it pushed up on the crust above it. The rocks at the edge of the forming Colorado Plateau fractured, and the plateau was slowly pushed upward. The Colorado Plateau covers parts of New Mexico, western

Figure 10–11 *A river cutting through the Colorado plateau reveals the horizontal rock layers that lie beneath its surface (left). Lake Titicaca is located on a plateau on the border of Peru and Bolivia. Rock, mud, and sand washed down from the sides of the surrounding mountains and piled up in flat layers to form the plateau (right). How else are plateaus formed?*

Colorado, eastern Utah, and northern Arizona. Most of the plateau is more than 1500 meters above sea level. The Colorado Plateau was formed hundreds of millions of years after the Appalachian Plateau.

Plateaus can also be formed by a series of molten rock flows on the surface of the Earth. Molten rock at the surface of the Earth is called lava. Molten rock deep within the Earth is called magma. Magma reaches the Earth's surface through long cracks in the ground. Great floods of hot molten rock periodically stream out of the cracks. The flowing lava spreads out over a large area and hardens into a sheet. The lava sometimes fills in valleys and covers hills. The flowing and spreading out of the lava is repeated over and over again. The hardened lava sheets pile up and form a raised plateau. The Columbia Plateau, which covers parts of Oregon, Washington, and Idaho, is a lava plateau. Here lava built up a large flat region covering almost 5 million square kilometers. The plateau is 1 to 2 kilometers thick.

Rivers often carve one large plateau into many smaller plateaus or cut deep valleys and canyons through plateaus. One of the most spectacular canyons formed by a river is the Grand Canyon in the Colorado Plateau.

Domes

You know now that lava flows out onto the Earth's surface to form plateaus. Sometimes, however, magma pushes upward but does not reach the Earth's surface. The stress caused by the magma causes the rock layers above it to fold upward, forming an uplifted area. At some point, the magma cools and forms hardened rock.

The uplifted area created by rising magma is called a **dome.** A dome is a raised area shaped roughly like the top half of a sphere. The outline of a dome is oval or circular. You can think of a dome as rather like a blister on the surface of the Earth. Like a blister, a dome is formed when fluid collects beneath the surface and pushes up on overlying layers, forming a raised spot in the immediate area but leaving the surrounding regions flat and undisturbed.

Figure 10–12 *A dome may be formed when rising magma causes the rock layers above it to fold upward (left). Over a long period of time, the uppermost rock layers may be worn away to reveal the dome's core of hardened magma (right).*

Domes that have been worn away in places form many separate peaks called dome mountains. The Black Hills of South Dakota and Wyoming are dome mountains. In this region, many layers of flat-lying rocks were arched up. Over a long period of time, the rocks on top were worn away. The hardened magma that caused the uplifting was then exposed.

10–1 Section Review

1. How does stress affect the Earth's crust?
2. Compare faulting and folding.
3. How are plateaus formed?
4. What is a dome? A dome mountain?

Connection—*Paleontology*

5. A paleontologist is a scientist who studies organisms that lived on the Earth long ago (such as dinosaurs). Most of the information about these long-gone organisms comes from fossils, or the preserved remains of ancient organisms. The majority of fossils are found in certain kinds of rock layers. Why is it important for a paleontologist to understand faulting and folding?

ACTIVITY

WRITING

A Geological Trip

Using information from the text, write a 300-word essay about an imaginary trip you are taking across the United States. Describe any important and dramatic geological formations you find along the way. In your essay, use the following vocabulary words.

plateau
dome mountain
fault
anticline
thrust fault
fault-block mountain
rift valley
fold
syncline
normal fault

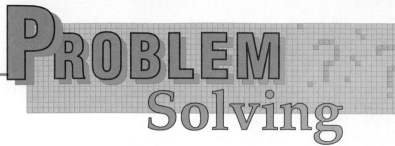

PROBLEM Solving

Studying Sidewalks

Ever since her class had started studying the movements of the Earth's crust in science, Jenny had noticed that she was paying a lot more attention to the ground at her feet. For example, she had observed that the sidewalk in her neighborhood had a number of cracks, sunken areas, raised bumps, seams, and breaks in it. In one place, one broken edge of the sidewalk stuck up two to three centimeters above the matching edge. As Jenny's brother had found out the hard way, it was easy to stub one's toe on that protruding edge.

Obviously, Jenny thought, the sidewalk was not made with cracks in it, or with low places where puddles formed, or with raised areas that tripped people. Like the Earth's crust, the sidewalk had changed. But why did it change?

Applying Concepts

1. What do you think causes the cracks and other changes in the sidewalk?

2. How are the forces that act on the sidewalk similar to the ones that act on the crust of the Earth? How are they different?

3. Suppose that Jenny hypothesizes that tree roots, acting rather like the magma in a dome, are responsible for a broken, raised ridge on the sidewalk. How might she test her hypothesis?

Guide for Reading

Focus on these questions as you read.

▶ *What is isostasy?*

▶ *How does isostasy affect the Earth's crust?*

10–2 The Floating Crust

You have learned how areas of the Earth's crust can be moved up and down through faulting, folding, and uplifting. But there is another process in which the crust moves up and down. Here is how it works.

Beneath the Earth's crust is a layer called the **mantle.** The mantle is the layer of the Earth that

Figure 10–13 *These four diagrams show the effect a heavy icecap has on an area's elevation. When an icecap forms on a flat area of crust (A), the added material increases the force with which the area pushes down on the mantle. This causes the area to sink (B). When the icecap melts, the downward force of the crust decreases, so the upward force of the mantle pushes the crust slowly upward (C). Eventually, the upward force of the mantle balances the downward force of the crust (D). What is the balancing of these two forces called?*

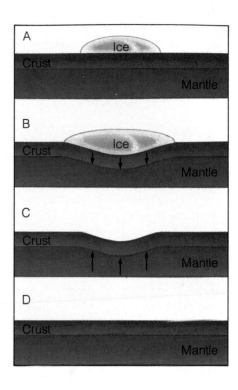

extends from the bottom of the crust downward about 2900 kilometers to the Earth's core. The mantle is made of rock that flows slowly—sort of like molasses or hot, thick tar. Because the mantle is much denser than the crust, the solid, rocky crust floats on the mantle. (A less dense object always floats on a more dense object.)

The floating crust exerts a downward force on the mantle. But the mantle also exerts a force. The mantle exerts an upward force on the crust. **A balance exists between the downward force of the crust and the upward force of the mantle.** The balancing of these two forces is called **isostasy** (igh-SAHS-tuh-see). The prefix *iso-* means equal, and the root word

Burning Up, p.762

Figure 10–14 *Material carried by rivers is deposited on the ocean floor, where it builds up in thick, heavy layers. You might think that eventually the ocean would be filled in. But this does not happen. Why?*

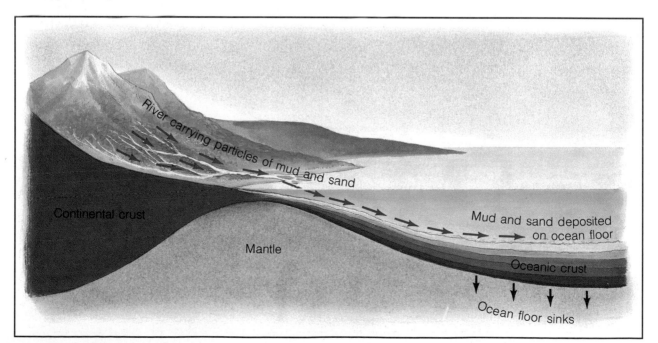

339

ACTIVITY

DISCOVERING

Exploring Density

Here's a riddle that may be familiar to you: Which is heavier—a pound of feathers or a pound of lead?

The answer, of course, is that neither is heavier. They weigh exactly the same amount. However, a pound of feathers fills a large bag and a pound of lead is a rather small chunk. Lead has more mass per unit volume than feathers do. In other words, lead has a greater density.

How do the densities of other substances compare to one another? Find out for yourself. Some materials that you might use in your experiments include a large glass jar, water, vegetable oil, glycerine, food coloring, ice, salt, a block of wood, a small plastic object, and a rock.

■ Which substances have the greatest density? The least density? How can you tell?

■ How might density account for the fact that mountains are high and oceans are deep?

stasis means standing still. Why is isostasy an appropriate term for this balancing act?

If material is added to an area of the crust, that area will float lower on the mantle. If material is removed, that area will float higher. So the crust is always balanced on the mantle.

Isostasy explains why some low-lying regions—such as Norway, Sweden, and Finland—have slowly risen. Thousands of years ago, these northern European countries were covered by tons of ice. The melting of the ice removed material from the crust. As a result, the land began to float higher on the mantle. In fact, the land is still rising today—and it is expected to rise about 200 meters in the next few thousand years! What do you think would happen to the elevation of Antarctica if the ice sheets covering most of the continent melted?

Crustal rock can also sink. For example, the Mississippi River has dropped millions of tons of mud and sand particles into the Gulf of Mexico. Will the accumulation of particles cause the Gulf to grow shallower and eventually disappear? Thanks to isostasy, the answer is no. The addition of materials—mud and sand—to the crust on the Gulf floor causes it to sink. But the depth of the water in the Gulf has not changed. A balance is maintained between the building up and the sinking of the Gulf floor.

10–2 Section Review

1. What balances the downward force of the crust? What is this balancing of forces called?
2. Which are less dense, the crustal rocks or the mantle rocks?
3. What happens when sediments are deposited on the ocean floor?

Critical Thinking—*Applying Concepts*
4. Most of Greenland is hidden beneath an enormous sheet of ice. Using what you have learned about isostasy, explain why the surface rock that makes up Greenland is saucer-shaped, with its center below sea level.

CONNECTIONS

A World of Opposites

According to traditional Chinese *philosophy*, everything that exists is made up of two opposite principles: the feminine *yin* and the masculine *yang*. These two principles interact and balance each other; when one increases, the other decreases. The harmonizing of these two opposite principles is represented by a circle divided into light and dark halves.

Consider what you have learned about the movement of the Earth's crust. You have learned about tension and compression, anticlines and synclines, and the balancing of upward and downward forces in isostasy. What other opposites can you think of?

Geology (the study of the Earth) is not the only science in which you will find opposites. In chemistry, there are positive and negative ions, acids and bases, metallic and nonmetallic elements.

In biology, there are seed plants and plants without seeds, males and females, vertebrate and invertebrate animals. In physics, there are concave and convex lenses, north and south magnetic poles, positive and negative electrodes. The world of opposites is not restricted to the world of science. There are representational and abstract works of art. Music may be fortissimo (very loud) or pianissimo (very soft). Numbers may be even or odd, real or imaginary, rational or irrational, positive or negative. Dramas may be tragedies or comedies and may receive favorable or unfavorable reviews. Religions deal with good and evil. The law deals with right and wrong. What other pairs of opposites can you think of?

Invertebrates such as moths and vertebrates such as orangutans can be thought of as opposite types of animals.

Laboratory Investigation

Examining Isostasy

Problem

How does the Earth's crust float on the Earth's mantle?

Materials *(per group)*

2 blocks of wood—
    1: 10 cm x 10 cm x 2.5 cm
    2: 10 cm x 10 cm x 1.5 cm
basin of water
metric ruler
25 metal washers

	Number of Washers	Amount Above Water
Block 1		
Block 2		

Procedure

1. Label the larger block of wood 1 and the smaller block 2.

2. Float block 1 in the basin of water. Using a metric ruler, measure the amount of wood above the water's surface. Record your measurement in a data table similar to the one shown here.

3. Carefully place ten washers on the surface of block 1. Measure the amount of wood above the water's surface. Record this information in your data table.

4. Continue adding washers two at a time. Carefully measure and record the amount of wood above the water's surface after each addition. Stop adding washers when the wood sinks or the washers spill into the basin of water.

5. Repeat steps 2 through 4 for block 2.

Observations

1. Are there any differences in the way the two blocks of wood float before the washers are added? After?

2. Which block of wood is able to hold more washers before it sinks? Explain.

Analysis and Conclusions

1. How do the two blocks of wood resemble continental and oceanic crust? How does the water represent the Earth's mantle?

2. If block 1 represents continental crust and block 2 represents oceanic crust, which crust is able to support the most weight?

3. How is the Earth's crust able to stay balanced on the mantle?

4. How does this investigation illustrate isostasy?

5. **On Your Own** Design an experiment to examine isostasy in which thick mud is used to model the mantle. What do you think would be the results of this experiment? If you receive permission, you may perform this investigation and see if your predictions were correct.

Study Guide

Summarizing Key Concepts

10–1 Earth's Changing Surface

▲ As the rocks of the crust undergo stress, they slowly change shape and volume.

▲ The breaking, tilting, and folding of rocks is called deformation.

▲ Compression squeezes the rocks of the crust together.

▲ Tension pulls the rocks of the crust apart.

▲ Shearing pushes two parts of the crust in opposite directions, causing the rocks of the crust to twist or tear apart.

▲ A break or crack along which rocks move is called a fault. A break along which rocks do not move is a joint.

▲ The block of rock above a fault is called the hanging wall, and the block of rock below a fault is called the foot wall.

▲ Mountains formed by blocks of rock uplifted by normal faults are called fault-block mountains.

▲ Valleys formed when the block of land between two normal faults slides downward are called rift valleys.

▲ A bend in a rock is a fold. An upward fold is an anticline; a downward fold is a syncline.

▲ Rocks are more likely to fold than fault if they are hot, under pressure, ductile, and stressed gradually.

▲ A plateau is a large area of flat land that is raised high above sea level.

▲ Plateaus may be formed by flat-topped folds, vertical faulting, or lava flows.

▲ An uplifted area called a dome can be formed by magma that works its way toward the Earth's surface without actually erupting onto the surface and causes the rock layers above it to fold upward.

▲ Domes that have been worn away in places form many separate peaks, or dome mountains.

10–2 The Floating Crust

▲ The mantle is the layer of the Earth that extends from the core to the crust.

▲ The balancing of the downward force of the crust and the upward force of the mantle is known as isostasy.

Reviewing Key Terms

Define each term in a complete sentence.

10–1 Earth's Changing Surface
stress
deformation
compression
tension
shearing
fracture
fault
hanging wall
foot wall

normal fault
reverse fault
thrust fault
lateral fault
fault-block mountain
rift valley
fold
anticline
syncline
plateau
dome

10–2 The Floating Crust
mantle
isostasy

Chapter Review

Content Review

Multiple Choice

Choose the letter of the answer that best completes each statement.

1. The rocky outermost layer of the Earth is the
   a. core.
   b. crust.
   c. mantle.
   d. continental plate.

2. The form of stress that pulls apart rocks of the crust is
   a. tension.
   b. compression.
   c. contraction.
   d. compaction.

3. The block of rock above a fault is called the
   a. anticline.
   b. syncline.
   c. foot wall.
   d. hanging wall.

4. Older rock layers may slide up and over younger rock layers in a
   a. normal fault.
   b. lateral fault.
   c. thrust fault.
   d. anticline.

5. Rocks are more likely to fault than fold if they are
   a. ductile.
   b. extremely hot.
   c. under much pressure.
   d. brittle.

6. A downward fold in a rock is called a(an)
   a. syncline.
   b. anticline.
   c. plateau.
   d. dome.

7. A large flat area that is uplifted high above sea level and whose underlying layers of rock are flat is called a(an)
   a. plateau.
   b. syncline.
   c. dome.
   d. anticline.

8. Magma pushing on rock layers may cause them to fold sharply upward into a blisterlike structure called a
   a. syncline.
   b. dome.
   c. fault-block mountain.
   d. plateau.

9. Which of the following is formed when the block of land between two normal faults slides downward?
   a. rift valley
   b. anticline
   c. syncline
   d. horst

True or False

If the statement is true, write "true." If it is false, change the underlined word or words to make the statement true.

1. The breaking, tilting, and folding of rock is called <u>shearing</u>.
2. The blocks of rock move horizontally past one another in a <u>normal fault</u>.
3. The balancing of the force exerted by the crust and the force exerted by the mantle is called <u>isostasy</u>.
4. <u>Brittle</u> rocks are more likely to fold than fault.
5. <u>Fault-block mountains</u> are formed by blocks of rock uplifted by normal faults.
6. A downward, U-shaped fold in the rocks is known as a(an) <u>dome</u>.
7. When <u>shearing</u> acts on a fault, the foot wall slides up relative to the hanging wall.

Concept Mapping

Complete the following concept map for Section 10–1. Then contruct a concept map for the entire chapter.

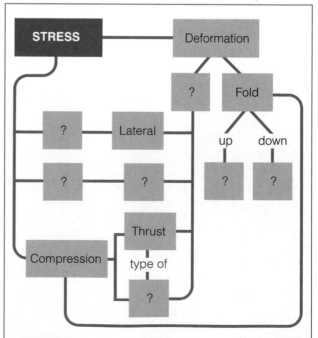

Concept Mastery

Discuss each of the following in a brief paragraph.

1. How can lava form a plateau?
2. What is the difference between a joint and a fault?
3. Compare magma and lava.
4. What is isostasy? How does isostasy affect the Earth's crust?
5. Draw a diagram that compares an anticline with a syncline.
6. How do faulting and folding result in deformation of the rocks of the crust?
7. How are compression, tension, and shearing similar? How are they different?

Critical Thinking and Problem Solving

Use the skills you have developed in this chapter to answer each of the following.

1. **Summarizing information** Prepare a table that summarizes what you have learned about the different kinds of faults. Your table should include the following information: type of fault; position of blocks; type of stress involved; sketch of fault.
2. **Making comparisons** Compare the rising and sinking of a floating ship to the floating crust.
3. **Relating concepts** Explain why a dome can be classified as an anticline. How does a dome differ from a more typical anticline?
4. **Interpreting data** Explain how the rock formation in the accompanying photograph was formed.

5. **Applying concepts** Geologists studying a rock formation have found that there are older rocks lying on top of younger rocks. How can you explain these findings in terms of faulting? In terms of folding? (*Hint:* Folds are not always symmetrical, or even on both sides.)
6. **Making inferences** Coal miners dig their tunnels along faults. The miners named the blocks above and below the faults. They called one block the hanging wall and the other block the foot wall. How do you think they came up with these names?
7. **Making generalizations** Rock salt is much less dense than surrounding rocks are. Under pressure, such as that caused by the weight of rock layers above it and around it, rock salt flows easily. Explain why and how rock salt, like magma, is able to form domes.
8. **Using the writing process** Imagine that you are an area of the Earth's crust. Write a brief autobiography describing the many changes due to stress that you have experienced over the millions of years of your existence. (*Hints:* What type of rock formation are you now? What were you in your "childhood"? Were the changes you experienced fun, scary, or exciting? How did they make you feel?)

Earthquakes and Volcanoes

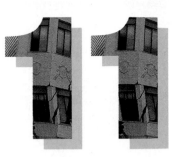

11

Guide for Reading

After you read the following sections, you will be able to

11–1 Earthquakes

- Explain what happens during an earthquake.
- Describe how earthquakes are detected.

11–2 Formation of a Volcano

- Compare the different types of lava and volcanic particles.
- Classify the three types of volcanoes.

11–3 Volcano and Earthquake Zones

- Identify the locations of major zones of earthquake and volcanic activity.

It was the World Series. People filled Candlestick Park in San Francisco to watch the Giants play the Oakland Athletics. But the game scheduled for October 17, 1989, was not to be played. The blimp, floating high above the stadium, was strategically positioned to capture the drama of the game. But instead, the blimp was dispatched to film another drama—the drama of buildings cracking and fires breaking out as underground gas mains exploded. Sportscasters became newscasters as the focus of the baseball championship changed dramatically to the streets of San Francisco. If you tuned in to watch this World Series game, you saw a major earthquake "live."

It was July 1991, and huge black clouds of smoke poured from a volcano in the Philippines. During the eruption, molten rocks, poisonous fumes, and dust-laden air poured from Mount Pinatubo. The toll in lives and property damage mounted as the volcano continued to erupt.

Volcanoes and earthquakes are dramatic examples—and not so gentle reminders—that the Earth's crust is continually moving. In this chapter, you will learn what causes some movements of the Earth's crust and how these movements are studied. You will also learn about two of the most sudden and violent movements: earthquakes and volcanic eruptions.

Journal *Activity*

You and Your World Have you ever experienced an earthquake or seen a volcano erupt? What do you think it would be like to live through an earthquake or the eruption of a volcano? Write your thoughts in your journal.

◀ *During the October 1989 earthquake, buildings in many sections of San Francisco suddenly collapsed.*

11–1 Earthquakes

The Earth seems so solid—its surface strong and stable. But the occurrence of enormous natural disturbances such as earthquakes and volcanoes indicates that perceptions about the Earth's stability often differ from reality. The surface of the Earth actually moves in ways most dramatic. One has only to see the effects of an **earthquake** to appreciate this fact.

An earthquake is the shaking and trembling that results from the sudden movement of part of the Earth's crust. A familiar example will help you to understand how an earthquake behaves. When you throw a pebble into a pond, waves move outward in all directions. In a similar manner, when rocks in the Earth's crust break, earthquake waves travel through the Earth in all directions. The ground shakes and trembles. During a severe earthquake, the ground can rise and fall like waves in an ocean. The motion of the ground causes buildings, trees, and telephone poles to sway and fall. Loud noises can sometimes be heard coming from the ground.

Scientists estimate that more than one million earthquakes occur every year. This is approximately one earthquake every thirty seconds. The vast majority of earthquakes are so small that the surface of the Earth barely moves. Several thousand earthquakes a year move the surface of the Earth, however, in ways significant enough to notice. Several hundred earthquakes make major changes in the Earth's surface features. And about twenty earthquakes a year cause severe changes in the Earth's surface. It is this last group of earthquakes that has the potential to cause serious damage to buildings and dramatic loss of life in populated areas.

The most common cause of earthquakes is faulting. As you learned in Chapter 10, a fault is a break in the Earth's crust. During faulting, parts of the Earth's crust are pushed together or pulled apart. Rocks break and slide past one another. Energy is released during this process. As the rocks move, they cause nearby rocks to move also. The rocks continue to move in this way until the energy is used up.

Figure 11–1 *The damage brought about by the 1985 earthquake in Mexico City shows the awesome power of earthquake waves.*

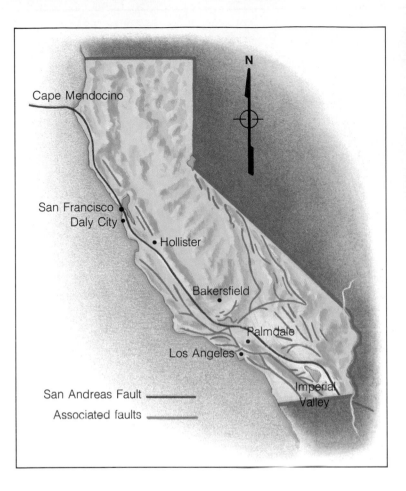

Figure 11–2 *The San Andreas Fault extends 960 kilometers along the western edge of California (left). Only a small portion of the fault is visible in the aerial photograph. However, you can see that movement along the fault has caused streams that run across the fault to become offset (top). Movement also causes rock formations to become buckled and twisted (bottom).*

The San Andreas Fault in California extends near the border with Mexico to the south through the city of San Francisco and continues on and off shore to the coast of northern California. The San Andreas Fault is about 960 kilometers long and 32 kilometers deep. The land to the west of the San Andreas Fault is slowly moving north. The land to the east of the fault is moving south. But the rocks along the fault do not all move at the same time. Earthquakes occur in one area and then in another. One of the worst of the disasters occurred in 1906, when movement along a small section of the San Andreas Fault caused the famous San Francisco earthquake.

Earthquakes also occur on the floor of the ocean. These earthquakes often produce giant sea waves called **tsunamis** (tsoo-NAH-meez). Tsunamis can travel at speeds of 700 to 800 kilometers per hour. As they approach the coast, tsunamis can reach heights of greater than 20 meters. To get a better idea of this

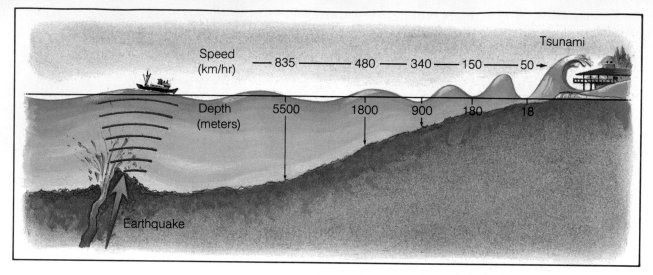

Figure 11–3 *Giant sea waves called tsunamis are caused by earthquakes on the ocean floor. When tsunamis are out at sea, they are far apart, fast moving, and low. What happens to these waves near shore?*

ACTIVITY

READING

New Madrid, Missouri

If you think that earthquakes in the United States occur only along the San Andreas Fault in California, you are incorrect. During the years 1811 and 1812, a strong series of earthquakes occurred along the New Madrid Fault in southeastern Missouri and Arkansas.

You might enjoy reading about the New Madrid Fault. Begin with an article written by Robert Hamilton called "Quakes Along the Mississippi," published in the August 1980 edition of *Natural History* magazine. Another good article is "The Rift, the River, and the Earthquake" by Arch C. Johnston, which appears in the January 1992 edition of *Earth* magazine.

height, consider the following: A 6-story building is about 20 meters tall! When a tsunami strikes the coast, it can cause great damage.

Seismic Waves

Some faults are located deep inside the Earth. Others are close to or at the Earth's surface. Most faults occur between the surface and a depth of about 70 kilometers.

The point beneath the Earth's surface where the rocks break and move is called the **focus** (FOH-cuhs) of the earthquake. The focus is the underground point of origin of an earthquake. Directly above the focus, on the Earth's surface, is the **epicenter** (EHP-uh-sehn-tuhr). Earthquake waves reach the epicenter first. During an earthquake, the most violent shaking is found at the epicenter. See Figure 11–4.

Earthquake waves are known as **seismic** (SIGHZ-mihk) **waves.** Scientists have learned much about earthquakes and the interior of the Earth by studying seismic waves. There are three main types of seismic waves. Each type of wave has a characteristic speed and manner of travel.

PRIMARY WAVES Seismic waves that travel the fastest are called **primary waves,** or **P waves.** P waves arrive at a given point before any other type of seismic wave. P waves travel through solids, liquids, and

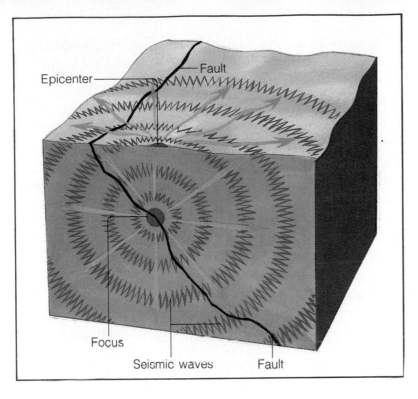

Figure 11–4 *This diagram shows the relationship between the epicenter and the focus of an earthquake. Where do the strongest seismic waves occur?*

gases. They move through the Earth at different speeds, depending on the density of the material through which they are moving. As they move deeper into the Earth, where material is more dense, they speed up.

P waves are push-pull waves. As P waves travel, they push rock particles into the particles ahead of them, thus compressing the particles. The rock particles then bounce back. They hit the particles behind them that are being pushed forward. The particles move back and forth in the direction the waves are moving. See Figure 11–5.

SECONDARY WAVES Seismic waves that do not travel through the Earth as fast as P waves do are called **secondary waves,** or **S waves.** S waves arrive at a given point after P waves do. S waves travel through solids but not through liquids and gases. Like P waves, S waves speed up when they pass through denser material.

Part of the Earth's interior is molten, or a hot liquid. Because S waves do not travel through liquids, they are not always recorded at all locations during an earthquake. What happens to S waves when they reach the liquid part of the Earth's interior?

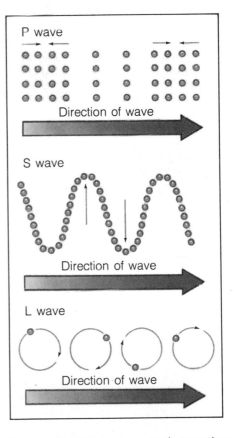

Figure 11–5 *P waves push together and pull apart rock particles in the direction the waves are moving. S waves, which are slower than P waves, move rock particles from side to side at right angles to the direction the waves are moving. How do L waves move?*

Graphing the Speed of a Tsunami

A tsunami far out to sea travels very quickly and carries a great deal of energy. Out at sea, however, tsunami waves are quite low. As a tsunami approaches shore, its speed decreases drastically, but it still carries the same amount of energy. What effect does the slowing down in speed have on the height of tsunami waves close to shore? Why are such waves so powerful?

Use the data from Figure 11–3 to make a graph plotting ocean depth against the speed of a tsunami. What general conclusions can you draw from your graph?

S waves cause rock particles to move from side to side. The rock particles move at right angles to the direction of the waves. See Figure 11–5.

SURFACE WAVES The slowest-moving seismic waves are called **surface waves,** or **L waves.** L waves arrive at a given point after primary and secondary waves do. L waves originate on the Earth's surface at the epicenter. Then they move along the Earth's surface the way waves travel in the ocean. Just as the water's surface rises and falls with each passing wave, the Earth's surface moves up and down with each L wave that passes. L waves cause most of the damage during an earthquake because they bend and twist the Earth's surface.

The Seismograph

A **seismograph** (SIGHZ-muh-grahf) is an instrument that detects and measures seismic waves. Although crude seismographs were in use hundreds of years ago, the first practical seismograph was developed by John Milne in 1893. Milne's invention has remained relatively unchanged to this day.

A seismograph consists of a weight attached to a spring or wire. See Figure 11–7. Because the weight is not attached directly to the Earth, it remains nearly still even when the Earth moves. A pen attached to the weight records any movement of the Earth on a sheet of paper wound around a constantly rotating drum.

Figure 11–6 *Earthquakes can cause blocks of land to slip along a fault. How might such slippage affect railroad tracks, roads, and streams? How has slippage affected the straight rows of orange trees in the photograph?*

Because the pen is attached to the weight, it also remains nearly still when the Earth moves. But the drum moves with the Earth. When the Earth is still, the pen records a nearly straight line. When the Earth moves, the pen records a wavy line. What kind of line would be recorded during a violent earthquake?

Seismologists (sighz-MAHL-uh-jihstz), scientists who study earthquakes, can determine the strength of an earthquake by studying the height of the wavy lines recorded on the paper. The seismograph's record of waves is called a **seismogram** (SIGHZ-muh-gram). The higher the wavy lines on the seismogram are, the stronger the earthquake is.

The height of the tallest wavy lines on a seismogram is used to calculate the strength of an earthquake on the **Richter scale,** which was created by California seismologists Charles Richter and Beno Gutenberg in 1935. The Richter scale was an important development because it gave scientists a way to determine earthquake strength based on readings from scientific instruments (namely, the seismograph). Before that, scientists were limited to estimating an earthquake's strength based on observations of the destruction the earthquake caused and eyewitness reports—sources that are not always accurate, consistent, or reliable.

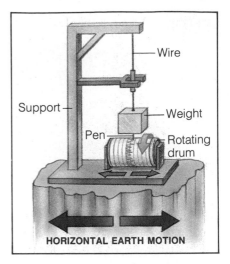

Figure 11–7 *In a seismograph, a heavy weight attached to a wire holds a pen motionless while a rotating drum moves with the Earth. What is a seismograph's record of seismic waves called?*

Figure 11–8 *In 1906, a devastating earthquake struck San Francisco. Fires that broke out after the earthquake destroyed part of the city (left). Buildings that normally stood straight and true were realigned by movements of the Earth (right).*

Shake It Up

1992 was a year for earthquakes. Large tremors shook California, Nevada, Utah, Nicaragua, and Egypt. Find out more about these earthquakes. Prepare a bar graph that shows the sizes of these earthquakes on the Richter scale. Share your graph in a presentation to your class that answers at least three of the following questions.

■ How do the 1992 quakes compare to the largest quakes on record? What number on the Richter scale corresponds to nearly total destruction? How exactly do scientists calculate the size of an earthquake on the Richter scale? What are foreshocks and aftershocks?

Figure 11–9 *By finding out how much time it takes for a laser beam from a laser field station to strike a reflector and bounce back, scientists can accurately measure the movements along a fault.*

Each number on the Richter scale represents an earthquake stronger than an earthquake represented by the preceding number. Any number above 6 indicates a very destructive earthquake. As you might imagine, an earthquake assigned the number 10 would be truly devastating!

The amount of damage caused by an earthquake depends on several different factors. The earthquake's strength, the kind of rock and soil that underlies an area, the population of the area affected, the kinds of buildings in the area, and the time at which the earthquake occurs all influence how damaging a particular earthquake is.

Predicting Earthquakes

In their study of earthquakes, scientists hope to improve the ability to accurately predict them. To be useful, earthquake prediction must be reliable and complete. The prediction must include where, when, and how strong the earthquake will be. If a strong earthquake is predicted, people can be moved from areas in danger. In 1975, Chinese scientists predicted with great accuracy that an earthquake would occur in their country. Most of the people in three areas of the country were evacuated before the earthquake struck. Many thousands of lives were saved.

If strong earthquakes could be predicted years in advance, people could better plan the growth of cities. Buildings could be reinforced to better withstand the shock waves produced by an earthquake. In some cities, attempts have already been made to construct earthquake-proof buildings. In what other ways might more accurate earthquake prediction save lives?

Seismologists have identified some warning signals that help to predict earthquakes with greater accuracy. Often changes occur in the speeds of P waves and S waves before a major earthquake strikes. Sometimes slight changes in the tilt of the Earth's surface can be detected. Land near a fault may rise or sink slightly. The water level in wells often goes up or down. And although it sounds a bit unscientific, some scientists in China believe that changes in the behavior of certain animals might help to predict earthquakes.

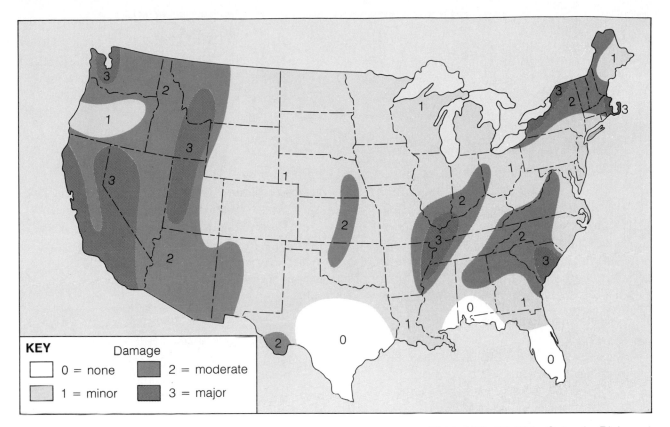

KEY Damage

- ☐ 0 = none
- ☐ 1 = minor
- ☐ 2 = moderate
- ☐ 3 = major

Figure 11–10 *This Seismic Risk Map shows areas of the United States (excluding Alaska and Hawaii) where earthquakes are likely to occur and the relative damage they are likely to cause. Where are damaging earthquakes least likely to occur? Most likely to occur?*

11–1 Section Review

1. What is an earthquake? What is the most common cause of an earthquake?
2. What is the focus of an earthquake? The epicenter?
3. Describe the three major types of seismic waves.
4. How does a seismograph work?
5. How is the strength of an earthquake measured?

Critical Thinking—*Applying Concepts*

6. Two different cities experience earthquakes of similar strength. In one city, relatively few people are injured. In the other city, there is a great loss of life. What are some possible reasons for the different effects? What kinds of plans could be developed to limit earthquake damage in the future?

PROBLEM Solving ???

Shake, Quake, and Maybe Not Break

Cities built near fault zones in the crust face a serious problem. Their existence is threatened by the land upon which they are built. Architects and engineers constantly search for ways to construct buildings that will be better able to resist the movements of the Earth's crust that occur during an earthquake.

Relating Concepts

Pretend you are an architect or engineer planning an "earthquake-proof" building. What should your building look like? How should it be built? Where should it be built? What materials should you use? These are but a few of the questions to consider. Begin your project in the library, where you can find out about ideas of others who have tried to build earthquake-proof buildings. One student faced with this problem developed a plan for a building built on giant springs. What ideas can you and your classmates come up with?

Guide for Reading

Focus on this question as you read.

▶ *How are types of volcanoes related to types of volcanic eruptions?*

Activity Bank

It's a Blast, p.763

11–2 Formation of a Volcano

Deep within the Earth, under tremendous pressure and at extreme temperatures, rock exists as a hot liquid called **magma**. This molten rock is found in pockets called magma chambers. Magma is constantly moving. In some places magma works its way toward the Earth's surface through cracks in solid rock. In other places, magma works its way toward the surface by melting the solid rock.

When magma reaches the Earth's surface, it is called **lava**. The place in the Earth's surface through which magma and other materials reach the surface (and the magma becomes lava) is called a **volcano.** You may have seen photographs of lava flowing down the sides of a volcano. A lava flow is so hot that it incinerates every burnable thing in its path. In some places, lava can build up to form a

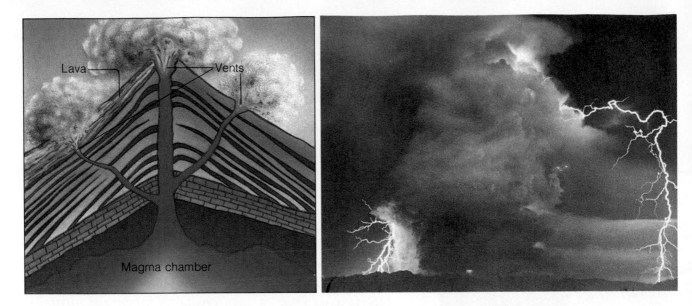

cone-shaped mountain. Such a landform, which is the result of an accumulation of volcanic material, is often referred to as a volcano as well.

The opening from which lava erupts is called a **vent.** Volcanoes often have more than one vent. If there is more than one vent, lava will sometimes pour from the sides of a volcano as well as from the top.

Volcanic Eruptions

Not all volcanic eruptions are alike. Some eruptions are quiet, with lava slowly oozing from a vent. Other eruptions are very violent, with lava and other materials being hurled hundreds of meters into the air. Gases from within the Earth's interior mix with huge quantities of volcanic dust and ash and rise into the air as great dark clouds that can be seen from many kilometers away. A violent volcanic eruption is truly an awesome sight.

Although it seems to be a dangerous endeavor, many scientists spend their working lives studying volcanoes. For volcanoes are "windows" into the interior of the Earth. By analyzing the mineral makeup of lava, geologists can determine the chemical composition of the magma from which the lava formed. Such data provide information about the composition of the part of the Earth that remains unseen. There are four main types of lava.

One type of lava is dark-colored and contains a lot of water. This lava is rich in the elements iron

Figure 11–11 *If you had been able to look inside Mount Pinatubo as it erupted in July 1991, you would have seen magma moving through the vents toward the Earth's surface.*

Figure 11–12 *Although you might not wish to touch lava with a "ten-foot pole," this potentially hazardous activity is all in a day's work for a volcanologist (scientist who studies volcanoes). The long pole contains a special probe that can measure the temperature of the lava.*

357

and magnesium. When this type of lava cools, igneous rocks such as basalt are formed. (You will learn more about rocks in Chapter 13.)

Another type of lava is light in color. This lava, which contains little water, is rich in the elements silicon and aluminum. Compounds of these elements account for its lighter color. When this type of lava cools, it forms the igneous rock rhyolite, which resembles granite.

The third type of lava has a chemical composition similar to that of both the dark-colored type and the light-colored type. Different varieties of igneous rocks in the Earth's crust, such as andesite, are formed from this type of lava.

The fourth type of lava contains large amounts of gases such as steam and carbon dioxide. When this lava hardens, it forms rocks with many holes in them. Like the holes trapped in the dough of a loaf of bread, the holes in this type of lava form as gas bubbles are trapped in the molten rock as it hardens. Pumice and scoria are igneous rocks formed from this type of lava. Do you know an unusual property of pumice?

Some dark-colored lava is thin and runny, and most tends to flow. The islands of Hawaii and Iceland were formed by many lava flows. But light-colored lava causes explosive eruptions. Because light-colored lava is rich in the element silicon, it tends to harden in the vents of a volcano. Explosive eruptions are caused when lava in the vents hardens into rocks. Steam and new lava build up under the rocks. When the pressure of the steam and new lava becomes great, a violent explosion occurs. As an example, if you place a cork in a bottle of seltzer water and shake the bottle, what do you think will happen? The cork will be pushed out of the bottle. The increased pressure exerted by the gas in the seltzer as a result of shaking the bottle causes the cork's ejection. This model illustrates what happens to a hardened lava plug in a vent as pressure builds up beneath it.

During volcanic eruptions, many rock fragments are blown into the air. The smallest particles are called **volcanic dust**. Particles of volcanic dust are very fine, less than 0.25 millimeter in diameter, or as tiny as grains of flour.

Figure 11–13 *There are two basic forms of dark-colored lava, both of which get their names from Hawaiian words. Hot, fast-flowing pahoehoe (pah-HOH-ay-hoh-ay) hardens into rounded swirls and ropy wrinkles (top). Cooler, slow-flowing aa (AH-ah) crumbles into large, jagged chunks as it oozes downhill. As a result, aa is rough and blocky (bottom). Can you explain why pahoehoe may change to aa as the lava moves away from the vent?*

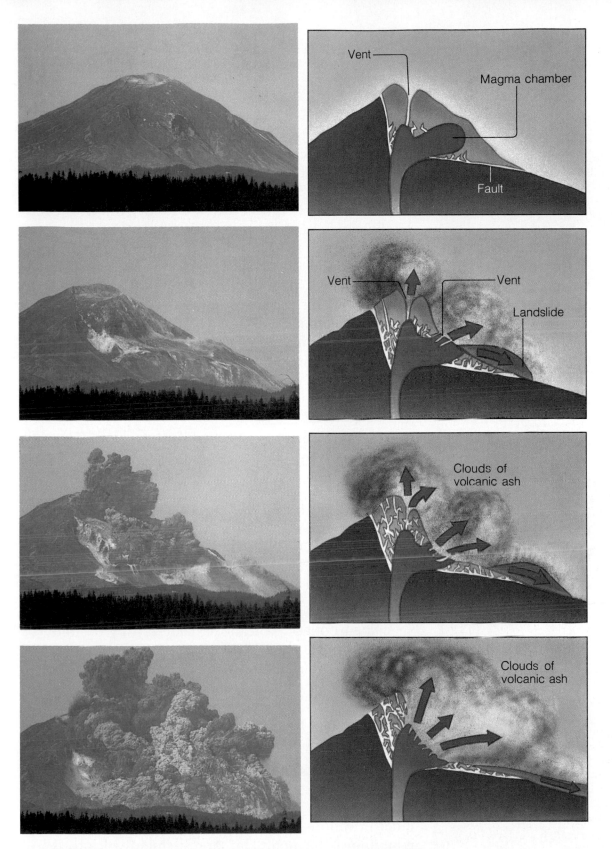

Figure 11–14 *In May 1980, Mount St. Helens in the state of Washington erupted explosively. These photographs and diagrams show the first few minutes of the eruption. What is the term for the openings from which lava erupts?*

Rock particles more than 0.25 millimeter but less than 5 millimeters in diameter are called **volcanic ash**. Particles of volcanic ash are about the size of rice grains. Volcanic ash falls to the Earth's surface and eventually forms small rocks. Both volcanic dust and volcanic ash can be carried away from a volcano by the wind. In this manner, they can fall to the Earth near the volcano, or they can be carried completely around the world.

Larger rock particles are called **volcanic bombs**. Volcanic bombs are a few centimeters to several meters in diameter. Some bombs are the size of boulders and have masses of several metric tons. Small volcanic bombs about the size of golf balls are called **cinders**. When volcanic bombs are hurled out of a volcano, they are molten. They harden as they travel through the air.

Types of Volcanoes

Different types of volcanic eruptions form different types of volcanoes. Some volcanoes are built from quiet flows of thin, runny lava that spread over a broad area. Other volcanoes are formed from violent eruptions. Some volcanoes are formed from a combination of quiet flows of lava and violent eruptions.

CINDER CONES Volcanoes made mostly of cinders and other rock particles that have been blown into the air are called **cinder cones**. Cinder cones form from explosive eruptions. Because the material in cinder cones is loosely arranged, the cones are not high. But they have a narrow base and steep sides. Paricutin in Mexico is a cinder cone.

SHIELD VOLCANOES Volcanoes composed of quiet lava flows are called **shield volcanoes**. Because it is runny, the lava flows over a large area. After several quiet eruptions, a gently sloping, dome-shaped mountain is formed. The largest shield volcano is Mauna Loa in the Hawaiian Islands. Mauna Loa rises from the bottom of the Pacific Ocean to a height of 4 kilometers above sea level.

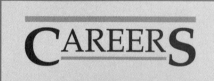

CAREERS

Volcanologist

Volcanologists are interested in the origin of volcanoes, the kinds of materials volcanoes release, the different shapes volcanoes develop, and the causes of eruptions.

After graduating from college, many volcanologists teach, do research, or work for government organizations. To learn more about this career, write to the American Geophysical Union, 2000 Florida Avenue, NW, Washington, DC 20009.

| CINDER CONE | SHIELD VOLCANO | COMPOSITE VOLCANO |

Labels: Cinders; Lava flows; Lava flows, Cinders

Figure 11–16 *Izalco in El Salvador is a cinder cone (left). Kilauea in Hawaii is a shield volcano. The crater within the caldera is clearly visible (center). Mount Egmont in New Zealand is a composite volcano (right). How does a composite volcano form?*

COMPOSITE VOLCANOES   Volcanoes built up of alternating layers of rock particles and lava are called **composite volcanoes.** During the formation of a composite volcano, a violent eruption first occurs, hurling volcanic bombs, cinders, and ash out of the vent. Then a quiet eruption occurs, producing a lava flow that covers the rock particles. After many alternating eruptions, a large cone-shaped mountain forms. The most famous composite volcanoes are Mount Vesuvius near Naples and Mount Etna in Sicily, both in Italy.

There is often a funnel-shaped pit or depression at the top of a volcanic cone. This pit is called a **crater.** If a crater becomes very large as a result of the collapse of its walls, it is called a **caldera.** A caldera may also form when the top of a volcano collapses or explodes. You may be familiar with the word caldron, a type of large cooking pot or kettle. The witches in *Macbeth*, a play written by William Shakespeare, stir their potions in a bubbling caldron. Both these words are derived from the Latin word *caldarius,* which pertains to warming. As you might guess, a volcano's caldera was at one time quite hot and contained bubbling lava.

ACTIVITY
DOING

Making a Model Volcano

1. Use the diagrams in Figure 11–16 to make a papier-mâché model of a cross section of one of the three types of volcanoes.

2. Label the structures of your volcano. You might like to team up with other students to make sure that a model of each type is constructed.

361

Figure 11–17 *Volcanic cones often have a depression known as a crater at their summit. Locate the craters of these two Indonesian volcanoes. Why is the crater of the volcano in the back considered to be quite unusual? In general, if a crater is more than three times wider than it is deep, it is called a caldera. Craters and calderas may fill with water to form lakes.*

Volcanic Activity

Volcanoes are rather unpredictable phenomena. Some volcanoes erupt fairly regularly; others have not erupted within modern history. In order to indicate the relative activity of volcanoes, scientists classify them as active, dormant, or extinct.

An active volcano is one that erupts either continually or periodically. There are several active volcanoes in the continental United States: Lassen Peak in Lassen Volcanic National Park (California), Mount St. Helens in the Cascade Range (Washington State), and Mount Katmai (Alaska).

A volcano that has been known to erupt within modern times but is now inactive is classified as a dormant, or "sleeping," volcano. Mount Rainier (Washington State), Mount Hood (Oregon), and Mount Shasta (California) are examples of dormant volcanoes in the continental United States.

A volcano not known to have erupted within modern history is classified as an extinct volcano. Volcanologists (scientists who study volcanoes) consider truly extinct volcanoes to be only those that have been worn away almost to the level of their magma chamber. But even so-called extinct volcanoes can prove unpredictable. Both Lassen Peak and Mount St. Helens suddenly erupted after long periods of inactivity.

ACTIVITY
DOING

Volcano in Motion

1. Using eight to ten unlined note cards, draw each successive step in the movement of magma up and out of a volcano. Use Figures 11–11 and 11–14 as guides and use your imagination.

2. Number each note card in sequence as you draw it.

3. Tape the cards together along the top.

Hold the cards at the taped end and flip from the first card to the last card.

11–2 Section Review

1. What is a volcano? What determines the type of volcano formed? Describe the three types of volcanoes.
2. What is the difference between magma and lava?
3. List in order of increasing size the different kinds of particles blown from a volcano.
4. How are volcanoes classified according to activity?

Connection—*Ecology*

5. How does a volcanic eruption alter the area around a volcano? What changes in plant and animal life do you think you would notice in the area around a volcano that has just erupted?

11–3 Volcano and Earthquake Zones

Have you ever wondered why California seems to have more than its share of earthquakes? Or why there are so many active volcanoes on islands in the Pacific Ocean? Volcanic eruptions and earthquakes often occur in the same areas of the world. Sometimes volcanic eruptions are accompanied by earthquakes. Although the two events need not occur together, there is a relationship between their occurrences. **Most major earthquakes and volcanic eruptions occur in three zones of the world. Scientists believe that there is a great deal of movement and activity in the Earth's crust in these zones**. You may want to look at a map of the world as you read about these zones. It is helpful to locate the places you read about on a map so that they become more "real" to you.

One major earthquake and volcano zone extends nearly all the way around the edge of the Pacific Ocean. This zone goes through New Zealand, the Philippines, Japan, Alaska, and along the western coasts of North and South America. The San Andreas Fault is part of this zone. This zone that circles the Pacific Ocean is called the **Ring of Fire**. Can you explain how it got its name?

Guide for Reading

Focus on this question as you read.

▶ *Where are volcano and earthquake zones located?*

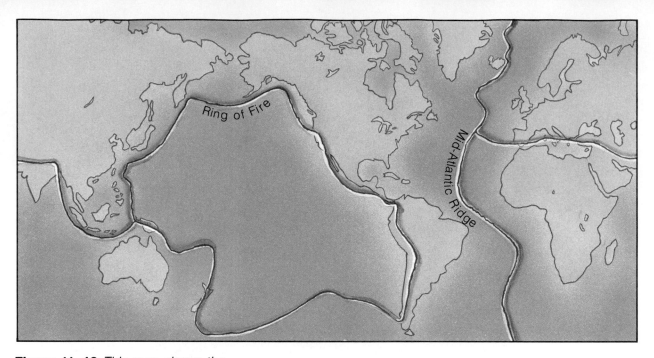

Figure 11–18 *This map shows the Ring of Fire, a zone of earthquake and volcanic activity that surrounds the Pacific Ocean. What is the name of the earthquake and volcano zone at the bottom of the Atlantic Ocean?*

A second major earthquake and volcano zone is located near the Mediterranean Sea. This zone, called the Mediterranean Zone, extends across Asia into India. Many countries in the zone, including Italy, Greece, and Turkey, have violent earthquakes. Many volcanic eruptions have also occurred in this zone.

The third major earthquake and volcano zone extends through Iceland to the middle of the Atlantic Ocean. There is under the ocean a long range of volcanic mountains called the Mid-Atlantic Ridge. Scientists believe that the volcano and earthquake activity in this area are due to the formation of new parts of the Earth's crust along the ridge. Volcanic islands in the Atlantic Ocean, such as Iceland, are part of the Mid-Atlantic Ridge.

11–3 Section Review

1. Why are earthquake and volcano activity zones located in certain areas?
2. What is the Ring of Fire?
3. What do scientists believe causes so many earthquakes in the middle of the Atlantic Ocean?

Critical Thinking—*Relating Concepts*
4. Would a volcanic eruption be likely to occur on the east coast of the United States? Explain.

The Vault of the Earth

Naples is a large sun-filled city in southern Italy. But stand in many places in the city and you are immediately aware that a dark shadow looms overhead. Across the Bay of Naples, Mount Vesuvius, an active volcano, rises to a height of 1220 meters. By world standards, Mount Vesuvius is neither very large nor very old. But it played an important role in the history of the Mediterranean region.

On August 24, AD 79, life in two ancient cities, Pompeii and Herculaneum, abruptly came to an end with the eruption of Mount Vesuvius. Pompeii was covered with a layer of fine, hot ash—a layer that trapped people and animals and preserved ancient buildings and household furnishings. Herculaneum was covered by a river of mud that contained pumice spewed forth from the volcano. Not until the eighteenth and nineteenth centuries did *archaeologists,* scientists who study the remains of past civilizations, become aware of the treasures preserved by Vesuvius's anger.

The layer of ash that covered Pompeii made casts of people frantically trying to escape the eruption. Most people died when the hot ash in the air entered their lungs, choking off a fresh supply of oxygen. The people of Herculaneum were luckier. Although their city was destroyed, they were able to flee the slow-moving mud slides.

Thus the eruption of Vesuvius, while it destroyed two lively cities of the ancient world, preserved evidence of these civilizations for almost two thousand years. Scientists are now able to study a great historical treasure preserved in a vault made from materials spewed forth during a devastating volcanic eruption.

Laboratory Investigation

Locating Patterns of Earthquake and Volcano Distribution

Problem

What is the worldwide pattern of earthquake and volcano distribution?

Materials *(per student)*

> world map showing longitude and latitude
> 4 pencils of different colors

Procedure

1. Use the information in the table to plot the location of each earthquake. Use one of the colored pencils to label on the world map each earthquake location with the letter E inside a circle.

2. Do the same thing for volcanoes. Use another colored pencil and the letter V inside a circle.

3. Use another pencil to lightly shade the areas in which earthquakes are found.

4. Use another pencil to lightly shade the areas in which volcanoes are found.

Observations

1. Are earthquakes scattered randomly over the surface of the Earth or are they concentrated in definite zones?

2. Are volcanoes scattered randomly or concentrated in definite zones?

3. Are most earthquakes and volcanoes located near the edges or near the center of continents?

4. Are there any active volcanoes near your home? Has an earthquake occurred near your home?

Analysis and Conclusions

1. Describe any patterns you observed in the distribution of earthquakes and volcanoes.

2. What relationship exists between the locations of earthquakes and of volcanoes?

3. **On Your Own** On a map of the United States, locate active volcanoes and areas of earthquake activity in the fifty states.

EARTHQUAKES		VOLCANOES	
Longitude	**Latitude**	**Longitude**	**Latitude**
120°W	40°N	150°W	60°N
110°E	5°S	70°W	35°S
77°W	4°S	120°W	45°N
88°E	23°N	61°W	15°N
121°E	14°S	105°W	20°N
34°E	7°N	75°W	0°
74°W	44°N	122°W	40°N
70°W	30°S	30°E	40°N
10°E	45°N	60°E	30°N
85°W	13°N	160°E	55°N
125°E	23°N	37°E	3°S
30°E	35°N	145°E	40°N
140°E	35°N	120°E	10°S
12°E	46°N	14°E	41°N
75°E	28°N	105°E	5°S
150°W	61°N	35°E	15°N
68°W	47°S	70°W	30°S

Study Guide

Summarizing Key Concepts

11-1 Earthquakes

▲ An earthquake is the shaking and trembling that results from the sudden movement of part of the Earth's crust.

▲ The most common cause of earthquakes is faulting.

▲ Giant sea waves called tsunamis are caused by earthquakes on the ocean floor.

▲ The underground point of origin of an earthquake is called the focus.

▲ The epicenter is located on the Earth's surface directly above the focus.

▲ Earthquake waves are called seismic waves. There are three types of seismic waves: primary (P), secondary (S), and surface (L) waves.

▲ Seismic waves are detected and measured by a seismograph.

▲ The strength of an earthquake is measured on the Richter scale.

11-2 Formation of a Volcano

▲ Magma that reaches the Earth's surface is called lava.

▲ The place where magma reaches the Earth's surface is called a volcano.

▲ The opening from which lava erupts is called a vent.

▲ The mineral makeup of lava provides a clue to the chemical composition of magma inside the Earth.

▲ Many rock fragments of varying sizes are blown into the air during volcanic eruptions. They include volcanic dust, volcanic ash, volcanic bombs, and cinders.

▲ Different types of volcanic eruptions form different types of volcanoes. These include cinder cones, shield volcanoes, and composite volcanoes.

▲ The funnel-shaped pit, or depression, at the top of a volcano cone is called a crater. A caldera forms when the walls of a crater collapse.

11-3 Volcano and Earthquake Zones

▲ There are three major earthquake and volcano zones in the world where a great deal of movement in the Earth's crust occurs.

Reviewing Key Terms

Define each term in a complete sentence.

11-1 Earthquakes
earthquake
tsunami
focus
epicenter
seismic wave
primary wave, P wave
secondary wave, S wave
surface wave, L wave
seismograph
seismologist
seismogram
Richter scale

11-2 Formation of a Volcano
magma
lava
volcano
vent
volcanic dust
volcanic ash
volcanic bomb
cinder
cinder cone
shield volcano
composite volcano
crater
caldera

11-3 Volcano and Earthquake Zones
Ring of Fire

Chapter Review

Content Review

Multiple Choice

Choose the letter of the answer that best completes each statement.

1. The most common cause of earthquakes is
   a. tsunamis.
   c. seismic waves.
   b. faulting.
   d. magma.
2. Giant sea waves caused by earthquakes on the ocean floor are called
   a. volcanoes.
   c. seismograms.
   b. faults.
   d. tsunamis.
3. The underground point of origin of an earthquake is the
   a. focus.
   c. magma.
   b. epicenter.
   d. lava.
4. During an earthquake, the most violent shaking occurs at the
   a. Ring of Fire.
   c. focus.
   b. epicenter.
   d. vent.
5. The fastest seismic waves are
   a. S waves.
   c. V waves.
   b. L waves.
   d. P waves.
6. The seismic waves that cause most of the damage during an earthquake are
   a. S waves.
   c. V waves.
   b. L waves.
   d. P waves.
7. The instrument used to detect and measure earthquake waves is called the
   a. seismograph.
   c. voltmeter.
   b. seismogram.
   d. barometer.
8. The scale used to measure the strength of an earthquake is the
   a. focus scale.
   b. Milne scale.
   c. Richter scale.
   d. San Andreas scale.
9. Hot liquid rock that is found in the interior of the Earth is called
   a. lava.
   c. ash.
   b. magma.
   d. cinders.
10. The largest rock fragments blown into the air during a volcanic eruption are
    a. volcanic ash.
    b. volcanic dust.
    c. volcanic cinders.
    d. volcanic bombs.

True or False

If the statement is true, write "true." If it is false, change the underlined word or words to make the statement true.

1. A <u>caldera</u> forms when the walls of a volcano crater collapse.
2. The <u>Ring of Fire</u> is a zone of volcano activity that surrounds the Pacific Ocean.
3. <u>Secondary</u> waves travel through solids but not through liquids.
4. The opening from which lava erupts is called a <u>fault</u>.
5. Small volcanic bombs are called <u>craters</u>.
6. Volcanoes composed of quiet lava flows are called <u>shield volcanoes</u>.
7. A funnel-shaped pit at the top of a volcanic cone is called a <u>vent</u>.

Concept Mapping

Complete the following concept map for Section 11–1. Then construct a concept map for the entire chapter.

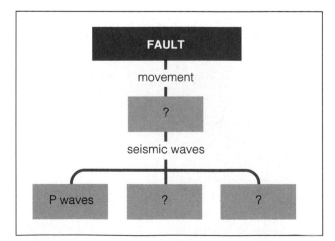

Concept Mastery

Discuss each of the following in a brief paragraph.

1. What is an earthquake? What is the most common cause of earthquakes?
2. Explain the difference between the focus of an earthquake and the epicenter of an earthquake.
3. What are seismic waves? Why are L waves more destructive than P or S waves?
4. What is the Richter scale? How is this scale used to compare earthquakes?
5. What is a volcano?
6. Describe the differences in the four kinds of lava.
7. Compare the shape and method of formation of cinder cones, shield volcanoes, and composite volcanoes.
8. Volcanoes are classified as active, dormant, or extinct. What do these classifications mean?

Critical Thinking and Problem Solving

Use the skills you have developed in this chapter to answer each of the following.

1. **Relating cause and effect** In 1883, the island of Krakatoa in the Pacific Ocean was destroyed by a tremendous volcanic explosion. Huge amounts of volcanic dust were hurled into the air. This dust remained in the air for several years before settling to the Earth. As far away as Europe scientists noted that temperatures dropped. Several years were referred to as "years without summers." Explain why this was so.

2. **Relating concepts** The Richter scale is used to rate the relative strength of earthquakes. How many times stronger than an earthquake rated 3 on the Richter scale is an earthquake rated 6? What are the advantages of using a single scale to rate the relative strengths of all earthquakes?
3. **Applying concepts** Earthquakes and volcanic eruptions occur naturally in certain zones. Does this mean that an earthquake or a volcanic eruption cannot occur outside one of these zones? What kinds of conditions would be necessary for an earthquake or volcanic eruption to occur outside these zones?
4. **Identifying relationships** In Section 11–2 you read about the formation of igneous rocks. The word igneous comes from a Latin word that means fire. What is the relationship between volcanoes and igneous rocks?
5. **Using the writing process** Pretend that you are a reporter for the *Daily Roman,* working in 79 AD. You are on assignment in Pompeii when Mount Vesuvius erupts. Write a dispatch for your newspaper describing your observations.

Plate Tectonics 12

Guide for Reading

After you read the following sections, you will be able to

12–1 Earth's Drifting Continents
- Describe the evidence for the theory of continental drift.

12–2 Earth's Spreading Ocean Floor
- Relate ocean-floor spreading to continental drift.

12–3 Earth's Moving Plates
- Discuss the theory of plate tectonics.

Have you ever looked at a globe or world map and noticed that the Earth's landmasses resemble pieces of a giant jigsaw puzzle? For example, the east coast of South America matches up with the west coast of Africa. The Arabian Peninsula and the northeast coast of Africa also seem to fit together.

Since the 1600s, people have wondered why the Earth's landmasses look like they would fit together. Were they connected at one time? If so, how were they moved apart?

In time, new discoveries caused other questions about the Earth to be asked. Why do places far from one another and with different climates have the remains of the same types of ancient organisms? Why do mountains and valleys form where they do? Why do earthquakes and volcanoes occur in the same areas over and over again?

For many years, no one came up with a theory that provided satisfactory answers. Then in 1915, a young German scientist published a radical, extremely controversial new theory. Read on, and discover more about the development of a theory that put the pieces of the puzzle together and revealed a better picture of the dynamic planet on which we live.

Journal *Activity*

You and Your World   Have you ever been in a situation in which you knew you were right, but no one would listen to you? In your journal, describe the situation and how it made you feel.

This photograph taken from space shows that the Arabian Peninsula (top) and northeastern Africa (bottom) look as if they are two pieces of a giant puzzle.

12–1 Earth's Drifting Continents

Imagine that you are browsing in the library, looking for something interesting to read. A paper on prehistoric plants and animals catches your eye, and you start to look through it. But partway through, you put the paper down and start to think. The theory presented in the paper does not sound right to you.

This is the theory: A land bridge once stretched across the Atlantic Ocean and connected South America and Africa. Evidence for this land bridge is seen in the **fossils** of plants and animals that could not possibly have crossed an ocean but are found in both South America and Africa. Fossils are the preserved remains or evidence of ancient organisms. You will learn more about them in Chapter 19.

The author of the paper states that the land bridge no longer exists because it sank to the bottom of the ocean. Knowing what you do about isostasy, you realize that continental crust cannot sink into denser oceanic crust. Why, then, are the fossils the same on both sides of the Atlantic Ocean?

Suddenly, you realize that South America and Africa must have been connected at one time—but not in the way the author of the paper envisioned. You remember noticing how well the coasts of the two continents fit together and wondering if they had once been a single landmass. At the time, you thought that idea was silly. Now it seems to be an idea worth considering.

You begin to search through the reference materials in the library, looking for evidence that will support or disprove your hypothesis. The more research you do, the more evidence you find in favor of your hypothesis: **The Earth once had a single landmass that broke up into large pieces, which have since drifted apart.** You name this giant landmass **Pangaea** (pan-JEE-ah), which means all Earth.

This story is based on real events that happened in the first half of this century to the German scientist Alfred Wegener. Wegener was not the first person to suggest that the continents had once been

ACTIVITY
DISCOVERING

Putting the Pieces Together

1. Find one or two friends who also want to do this activity.

2. Obtain one sheet of newspaper per person. (Make sure you use a paper that everyone has finished reading!)

3. Tear a sheet of newspaper into a few large pieces.

4. Trade pieces with a friend.

5. Try to fit the pieces together. How do lines of print help to confirm that you have reassembled the pieces correctly?

■ How does this activity relate to the development of the theory of continental drift?

joined together and had since moved apart. However, he was the first to build a detailed scientific case in support of the idea.

Wegener's **theory of continental drift** contradicted many of the existing, widely-accepted ideas about the evolution of the Earth. At that time, scientists thought that the crust could not move horizontally—continents were permanently fixed in the positions in which they had formed billions of years before. As you can imagine, most established scientists reacted unfavorably to being told many basic principles of geology were incorrect—especially by a young man who was not even a geologist! Wegener, you see, was a meteorologist, or weather scientist. Wegener's theory was met with great hostility and rejected by most of the world's scientists.

Despite the extremely negative response of most of the world's scientists, Wegener and his supporters continued to believe in the theory of continental drift. They kept on collecting evidence to support the theory. About thirty years after Wegener's death, enough evidence had been gathered to convince almost all scientists that continental drift was an acceptable, useful theory.

Evidence From Fossils

Evidence from fossils supports Wegener's theory of continental drift. As you read earlier, Wegener began to work seriously on the theory when he read that identical types of fossils had been found in Africa and South America. But as you can see in Figure 12–1, fossils reveal connections among other continents as well.

One organism whose fossils provide evidence for continental drift is *Glossopteris* (glahs-SAHP-teh-rihs), an extinct, or no longer living, plant.

Glossopteris fossils, which are located in rocks about 250 million years old, are found in South Africa, Australia, India, and Antarctica. *Glossopteris* seeds were too large to have been carried by wind and too fragile to have survived a trip by ocean waves. The seeds could not possibly have traveled the great distances that separate the continents today. This suggests that the places in which the plant's fossils are found must once have been closer together.

Figure 12–1 *The fossilized leaves of the extinct plant Glossopteris have been found in southern Africa, Australia, India, and Antarctica. Today, these places are widely separated and have different climates. What do the Glossopteris fossils indicate about the positions of the continents in the past?*

Figure 12–2 *Continental drift helped to explain a biological mystery: why green sea turtles living near the coast of Brazil lay their eggs on a distant island in the middle of the Atlantic Ocean. Long ago, before Africa and South America moved farther apart, this island was quite close to Brazil.*

The presence of *Glossopteris* fossils in the frozen wastelands of Antarctica indicates that Anarctica's climate millions of years ago was far different from the way it is today. Because the size and location of landmasses have a powerful effect on climate, this suggests that Antarctica and the other continents have changed position.

How did *Glossopteris* develop on such widely separated continents? Like Wegener, scientists today think that *Glossopteris* and many other organisms of the distant past lived on a single landmass—Pangaea. This landmass later split apart. The pieces of the broken landmass—today's continents—slowly drifted away from one another, carrying their fossils with them.

Evidence From Rocks

You have just read how fossils, which are located within rocks, provide support for the theory of continental drift. But fossils are not the only evidence for continental drift. The rocks themselves indicate that the continents have drifted.

One of the clearest sets of evidence is found in the rocks of Africa and South America. When the continents are "pieced" together, rock formations in Africa line up with matching ones in South America. An ancient folded mountain chain that stretches across South Africa links up with an equally ancient folded mountain chain in Argentina. Coal fields with distinctive layers in Brazil line up with coal fields with identical layers in Africa. And there are many other matches. Can you explain how these matching rock formations ended up on opposite sides of an ocean?

Rock deposits left behind by moving sheets of ice known as glaciers have also been used as evidence to support the theory of continental drift. Many glacial deposits are found in South America, Africa, India, Australia, and Antarctica. The similarity of these deposits indicates that they were left by the same ice sheets.

Many of these ancient glacial deposits have been found in areas with very warm climates. Because glaciers usually form close to the poles, scientists have concluded that these areas were once part of a giant landmass located near the South Pole.

ACTIVITY

Pangaea

1. Using a globe and paper, trace the shape of each continent and Madagascar. Also trace the shape of India and the Arabian Peninsula.

2. Cut out each piece, leaving Asia and Europe as one.

3. Disconnect India and the Arabian Peninsula from Asia.

4. Piece together the continents as they may have looked before the breakup of Pangaea. Use the directions of plate motion shown in Figure 12–8 as a guide.

5. Attach your reconstruction of Pangaea to a sheet of paper. Compare your version with those of your classmates.

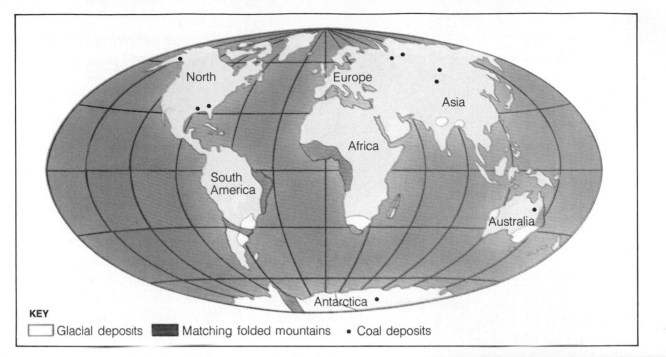

KEY
□ Glacial deposits ■ Matching folded mountains • Coal deposits

Other kinds of rock deposits—including salts, coal, and limestone derived from coral reefs—also provide evidence of changes in climate caused by continental drift. Today most salt deposits form in areas between 10° and 35° north and south of the equator. But salt deposits hundreds of millions of years old have been found as far north as Michigan. Coal forms in warm, swampy climates. Yet large coal deposits have been discovered in Antarctica. And limestone deposits from coral reefs, which form in tropical climates, have been found in western Texas, the northern central United States, and other places far from the equator.

Figure 12–3 *The map shows some of the matching rock formations, which indicate the continents were once joined together and have since moved apart. Red sandstone, which makes up this arch in Utah, is formed only in deserts near the equator. What does this imply about the location of Utah in the past?*

12–1 Section Review

1. What is continental drift? Who first developed a scientific argument for continental drift?
2. How do scientists explain the existence of fossils of the same plants and animals on continents thousands of kilometers apart?

Critical Thinking—*Evaluating Theories*

3. "Wegener's lack of formal training in geology helped him to develop the theory of continental drift, but hurt him in getting his ideas accepted." What is the reasoning behind this statement? Do you agree? Why or why not?

12–2 Earth's Spreading Ocean Floor

In spite of all the evidence from fossils and rocks, many scientists still refused to accept the theory of continental drift. They were waiting for the answer to a very important question: How could the continents plow through hard, solid ocean floor?

Until recently, there was no acceptable answer to this question. Then, during the 1950s and 1960s, new techniques and instruments enabled scientists to make better observations of the ocean floor. These observations revealed that the continents do not plow through the ocean floor like ships in an icy sea. How the continents actually move is far stranger.

New mapping techniques gave scientists a much clearer picture of the ocean floor. They discovered a large system of underwater mountains that have a deep crack, called a rift valley, running through their center. These underwater mountains are known as **midocean ridges.** What do you think is the name of the ridge in the Atlantic Ocean?

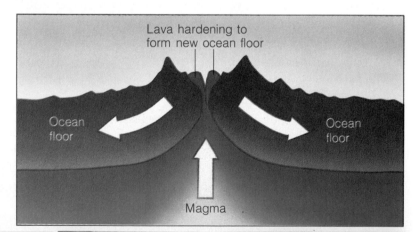

Figure 12–4 *As the ocean floor moves away from the midocean ridge, lava flows out of the rift and hardens to form new ocean floor. The island of Iceland was formed when part of the Mid-Atlantic Ridge rose above the surface of the ocean. Why does this big crack run through the center of Iceland? Why does Iceland have a lot of volcanic activity?*

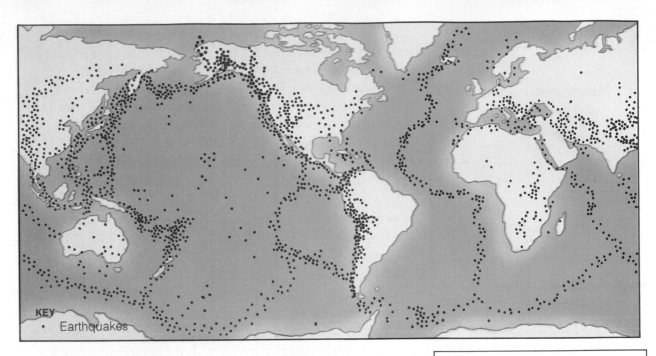

The midocean ridges form the single largest mountain chain in the world. The chain is approximately 80,000 kilometers long—roughly twenty times the distance from Los Angeles to New York City—and 3 kilometers high.

A great deal of volcanic activity occurs at the midocean ridges. Lava erupts from the rift valley that runs the length of a ridge. As the ocean floor moves away on either side of the ridge lava wells up and hardens. The hardened lava forms new ocean floor. This process is called **ocean-floor spreading.** So the ocean floor that scientists once thought was solid and immovable actually can move! **Ocean-floor spreading helps to explain how continents drift.** As a piece of the ocean floor moves, it takes its continent (if it has one) with it.

Although individual sections of midocean ridges are perfectly straight, the ridges as a whole curve. This is because the straight ridge sections are offset by thin cracks known as **transform faults.** Recall from Chapter 1 that a fault is a break or crack in the Earth's crust along which movement occurs. Look at Figure 12–5. Can you explain why a lot of earthquakes take place at the midocean ridges?

New deep-sea drilling machines also provided evidence to support the idea of ocean-floor spreading. Rock samples from the ocean floor indicate that rocks next to a midocean ridge are younger than rocks farther away. The youngest rocks are in the

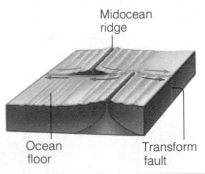

Figure 12–5 *The diagram shows how sections of ocean floor move along a transform fault. The map shows where earthquakes took place over a seven-year period. Why were scientists able to locate midocean ridges by looking for areas with lots of earthquakes?*

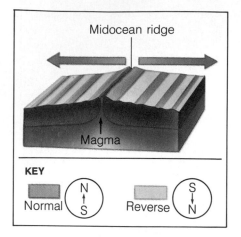

Figure 12–6 *Reversals of the Earth's magnetic poles are recorded in the rocks of the ocean floor. Because the periods of normal and reverse poles are not equal in length, the magnetic stripes in the rocks vary in width. The pattern of stripes is identical on both sides of a midocean ridge. How are these matching stripes evidence of ocean-floor spreading?*

ACTIVITY

DISCOVERING

Opposites Attract

Which way does the Earth's magnetic field lie now? Find out by securely tying one end of a piece of string about 30 cm long to the center of a bar magnet that has its north and south poles marked. Tie the other end of the string to a horizontal support, such as a shower-curtain rod, so that the magnet is suspended and can move freely. Leave the magnet alone for a few minutes. What happens?

■ What does this tell you about the Earth's magnetic field?

center of the ridge. As the ocean floor spreads, the older rocks move farther away from the ridge.

Magnetic stripes in ocean-floor rocks further convinced scientists of ocean-floor spreading. Scientists know that some minerals have magnetic properties and are affected by the Earth's magnetism. In molten rock, the magnetic mineral particles line up in the direction of the Earth's magnetic poles. When the molten rock hardens, a permanent record of the Earth's magnetism remains in the rocks. Scientists discovered that the history of the Earth's magnetism is recorded in magnetic stripes in the rocks. Although these stripes cannot be seen, they can be detected by special instruments. What, scientists wondered, caused these stripes to form?

When scientists studied the magnetic stripes, they made a surprising discovery. The Earth's magnetic poles reverse themselves from time to time. In other words, the magnetic north and south poles change places. Studies show that during the past 3.5 million years, the magnetic poles have reversed themselves nine times.

But the scientists were in for an even bigger surprise. As you can see in Figure 12–6, the pattern of magnetic stripes is identical on both sides of a midocean ridge. In other words, the pattern of magnetic stripes on one side of a ridge matches the pattern on the other side. The obvious conclusion was that as magma hardens into rock at a midocean ridge, half the rock moves in one direction and the other half moves in the other direction. The pattern of magnetic stripes provides clear evidence of ocean-floor spreading.

You might think that as a result of ocean-floor spreading, the Earth's surface is getting larger. But this is definitely not the case. Just what is going on, then? Here's some information that might help you answer this question. The oldest rocks on land are almost 4 billion years old. But the oldest rocks on the ocean floor are only 200 million years old.

Because the Earth's surface remains the same size, the ocean floor is being destroyed as fast as it is being formed by ocean-floor spreading. This would explain why the rocks on the ocean floor are so young—all the old ocean floor has been destroyed. But how does this destruction occur?

The answer involves deep, V-shaped valleys called **trenches** that lie along the bottom of the oceans. The trenches are the deepest parts of the oceans. They are found close to some continents or near strings of islands such as Alaska's Aleutian Islands. The Pacific Ocean has many trenches around its edges. Can you explain why the location of these trenches is significant? (*Hint:* Look back at Section 11–3.)

As you learned earlier, older ocean floor moves away from the midocean ridges as new ocean floor is formed. Eventually, the older ocean floor moves down deep into the Earth along the trenches. The process in which crust plunges back into the Earth is called **subduction** (suhb-DUHK-shuhn).

When the rocks are pushed deep enough, they are melted by the heat of the Earth. Some of the molten rock will rise up through the crust and produce volcanoes. But most of the molten rock will become part of the mantle. (Recall from Chapter 10 that the mantle is the layer of the Earth that extends from the bottom of the crust downward to the core.) So as new rocks are formed along the midocean ridges, older rocks are subducted into the trenches. One process balances the other. The Earth's crust remains the same size.

Activity Bank

Going Their Separate Ways, p.764

Figure 12–7 *The diagram shows how ocean floor is created and destroyed during ocean-floor spreading. What happens to the ocean floor at a midocean ridge? At a trench? The photograph shows water, cloudy with dissolved chemicals and heated by underlying magma, rising from a vent on a ridge in the eastern Pacific Ocean.*

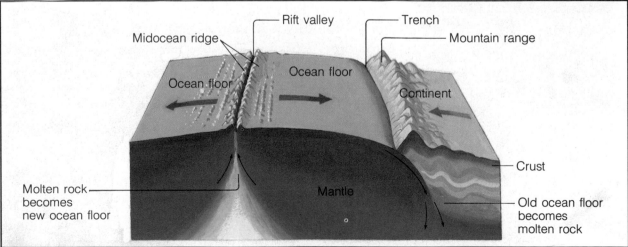

379

1. What process helps explain how continents drift?
2. Where are the youngest rocks on the ocean floor found?

Critical Thinking—*Relating Concepts*

3. How can the magnetic orientation of rocks be used to trace the way a continent moved as it drifted? (*Hint:* Special techniques exist for determining the age of rocks.)

Guide for Reading

Focus on these questions as you read.

▶ What is the theory of plate tectonics?

▶ How do plate movements relate to various features of the Earth?

ACTIVITY READING

Worlds Apart

What will the Earth look like in the future? How will the continuing evolution of Earth's surface affect the evolution of Earth's living things? For one person's vision of the Earth of the distant future, read *After Man* by Dougal Dixon.

12–3 Earth's Moving Plates

By the 1960s, it had become clear that the Earth was far more dynamic than people had once believed. The overwhelming evidence for continental drift and ocean-floor spreading caused many of the old theories about the Earth to be discarded. A new theory about the evolution of the Earth began to develop. In time, this new theory was named the **theory of plate tectonics** (tehk-TAHN-ihks). The word **plate** refers to the moving, irregularly-shaped slabs that fit together like paving stones to form the surface layer of the Earth. The plates carry the continents and are edged by trenches and ridges. The word **tectonics** refers to the branch of geology that deals with the movements that shape the Earth's crust. **The theory of plate tectonics, which links together the ideas of continental drift and ocean-floor spreading, explains how the Earth has evolved over time. It helps to explain the formation, movements, collisions, and destruction of the Earth's crust.**

The theory of plate tectonics provides a framework for understanding mountains, volcanoes, earthquakes, and other landforms and processes of the physical Earth. It also gives scientists insight into how and why life on Earth has evolved. Like all good scientific theories, the theory of plate tectonics helps people to understand the past and to predict the future.

Lithospheric Plates

According to the theory of plate tectonics, the topmost solid part of the Earth, called the **lithosphere** (LIHTH-oh-sfeer), is made of a number of plates. The plates contain a thin layer of crust above a thick layer of relatively cool, rigid mantle rock. Plates usually contain both oceanic and continental crust.

There are seven major lithospheric plates, each of which is named after its surface features. The Pacific plate, which covers one-fifth of the Earth's surface, is the largest plate. The other major plates are the North American, South American, Eurasian, African, Indo-Australian, and Antarctic plates. Can you locate the seven major plates in Figure 12–8?

There are also many smaller plates. Some of these, such as the Caribbean and Arabian plates, are fairly large. Others are so small that they are not included in maps that show the entire Earth.

Plates move at different speeds and in different directions. Some small plates that lack landmasses move as much as several centimeters per year. Large plates that are weighted down with continents move only a few millimeters per year.

In a few cases, the edges of the continents are the boundaries of plates. However, most plate

ACTIVITY
CALCULATING

Traveling Cities

Los Angeles, on the Pacific plate, is slowly moving northwest. San Francisco, on the North American plate, is slowly moving southeast. These two cities are moving toward each other at a rate of about 5 centimeters per year. About 11 million years from now, the two cities will be next to each other. How many meters does each city have to travel before they meet?

Figure 12–8 *This map shows the Earth's most important lithospheric plates. Which plate is most of the United States on? How do the boundaries of the plates relate to the earthquake zones shown in Figure 12–5 on page 377?*

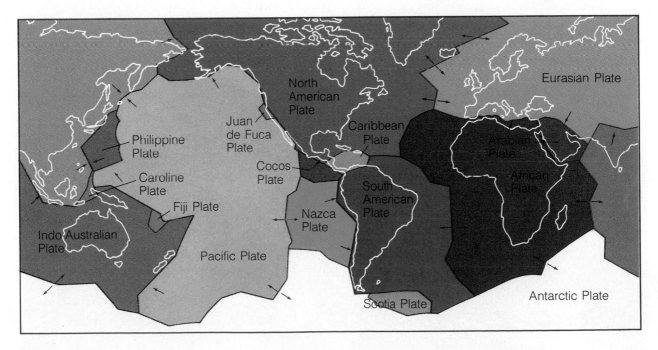

boundaries are on the ocean floor. Which two major plates have boundaries at the edges of continents? Where is the boundary between the South American and African plates? What is this boundary called?

ACTIVITY

Plate Boundaries

There are three types of plate boundaries. The first type occurs at midocean ridges. Because the plates move apart (diverge) at midocean ridges, the ridges are called **divergent** (digh-VER-jehnt) **boundaries.** These boundaries are also called constructive boundaries. Why is this an appropriate name?

The second type of plate boundary has trenches. Because the plates come together (converge) at the trenches, the trenches are called **convergent** (kuhn-VER-jehnt) **boundaries.** Why are trenches also called destructive boundaries?

The collision of plates at convergent boundaries causes tremendous pressure and friction. Severe earthquakes often result. As plate material melts in the Earth's mantle, some of it surges upward to produce volcanoes. This explains why the Ring of Fire, a line of volcanoes circling the edge of the Pacific plate, follows the major ocean trenches in that area.

The third type of plate boundary is formed by a lateral fault. Boundaries formed by lateral

Figure 12–9 *The red areas on this map indicate major volcanic and earthquake sites. These sites also outline the Earth's midocean ridges and trenches. Locate the Ring of Fire on the map.*

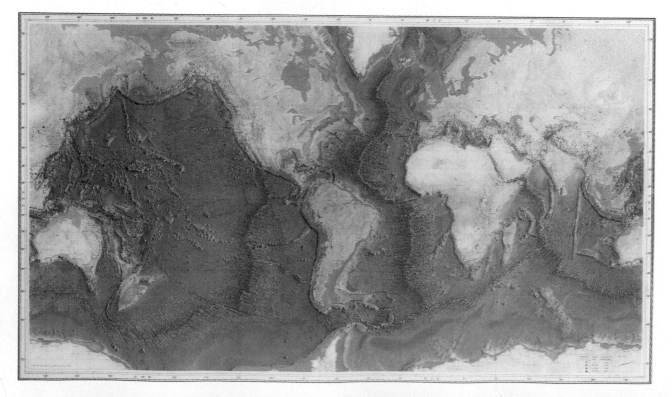

faults are called **strike-slip boundaries.** At a strike-slip boundary, two plates grind together and slip past each other horizontally. No new plate material is made, and no plate material is destroyed. Why do you think a strike-slip boundary is also known as a conservative boundary?

Earthquakes often occur along strike-slip boundaries. An example of a strike-slip boundary is the San Andreas Fault in California. The Pacific plate, on the west, is grinding slowly northwest, while the North American plate is sliding west. Today San Fransisco is farther north than Los Angeles. But someday Los Angeles, which is on the northward-moving Pacific plate, will be farther north than San Francisco, which is on the North American plate. In about 150 million years, the sliver of California containing Los Angeles will become part of Alaska!

Plate Motion

Scientists are not sure exactly what makes the plates move. They have searched a long time to find the source of the forces that can move continents. One hypothesis is that large **convection currents** within the Earth move the plates.

A convection current is the movement of material caused by differences in temperature. Convection currents move air in the atmosphere and water in the oceans. And they may move the plates of the lithosphere as well. Here's how. Mantle material close to the Earth's core is very hot. Mantle material farther from the core is cooler and denser. The cooler material sinks down toward the Earth's core. The hot material is then pushed up to replace the cooler material. As the cooler material nears the core, it becomes hot and rises once again. The rising and sinking cycle repeats over and over. This type of circular motion carries the plates of the lithosphere along with it, thus causing the continents to move.

Have you ever ridden in a bumper car at an amusement park? If so, you know that it is almost impossible to move without colliding into another bumper car. Like bumper cars, the continents collide with one another as they move. The collision between two continents, however, is far more complex than that between two bumper cars. What happens when continents collide?

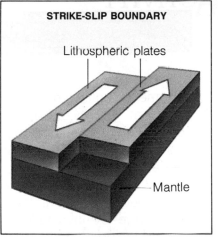

STRIKE-SLIP BOUNDARY

Lithospheric plates

Mantle

Figure 12–10 *At a strike-slip boundary, two plates move past one another horizontally. The San Andreas fault in California is an example of a strike-slip boundary.*

383

Figure 12–12 *When an oceanic and a continental plate collide, the oceanic plate is subducted. Some of the material from the melting oceanic plate rises upward and erupts as volcanoes on the continent (top). When two continental plates collide, the continental crust is pushed together and upward to form large mountain ranges (center). When two oceanic plates collide, the denser plate is subducted. Some of the material from the melting plate rises upward and erupts on the ocean floor, forming an island arc (bottom).*

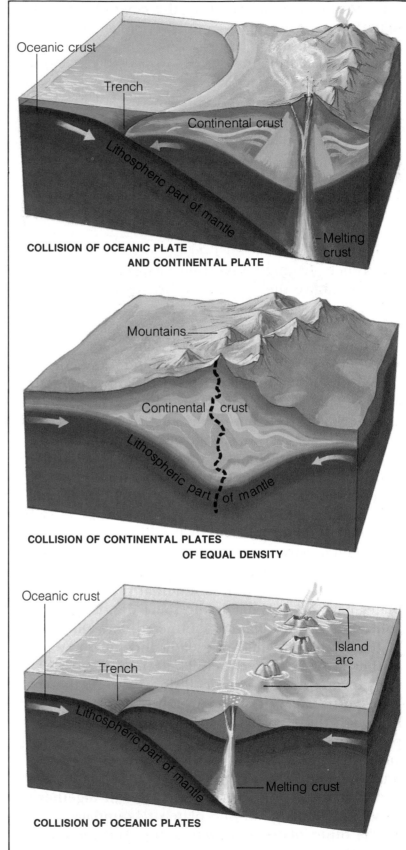

COLLISION OF OCEANIC PLATE
AND CONTINENTAL PLATE

COLLISION OF CONTINENTAL PLATES
OF EQUAL DENSITY

COLLISION OF OCEANIC PLATES

ACTIVITY

THINKING

Prefixes

Knowing the meaning of a prefix can often help you remember the meaning of a word. Using a dictionary, find the meaning of the prefixes *con-*, *di-*, *pan-*, *sub-*, and *trans-*. Relate what you have learned about the prefixes to the definition of the following vocabulary words:

convection current
constructive boundary
Pangaea
divergent boundary
subduction
transform fault

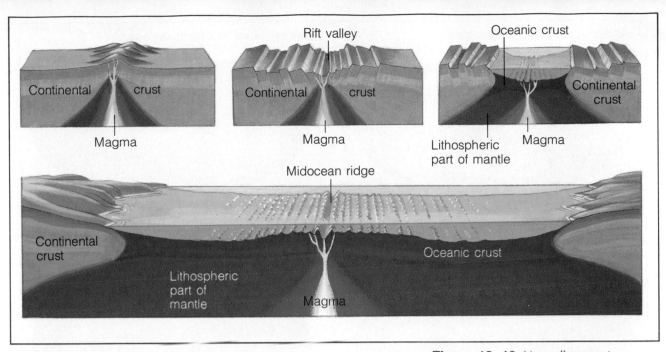

Figure 12–13 *New divergent boundaries may form in the center of continents. The formation of the new boundary begins when rising magma heats and weakens an area of a continental plate (top left). The area cracks and sections slip down to form a rift valley (top center). Eventually, ocean water fills in the widening gap between the newly formed continents. Lava erupting from the rift forms new ocean floor (top right). After millions of years, there is a mature ocean where there was once dry land (bottom).*

boundaries. Continental plates may fuse together. A trench may "switch direction" and begin to subduct a formerly overriding plate. New divergent boundaries may form in the center of continents. And plates may be completely subducted and disappear!

The theory of plate tectonics, like Wegener's theory of continental drift, explains how the Earth's surface has changed over time and predicts how it will change in the future. The diagrams in Figure 12–14 on page 388 illustrate what scientists think the Earth has looked like and what it will look like.

12–3 Section Review

1. What is the theory of plate tectonics? How does it relate to continental drift?
2. Describe the three different kinds of plate boundaries.
3. How might convection currents account for the movement of the plates?
4. Explain the origins of volcanoes, earthquakes, and mountains as they relate to plate tectonics.

Connection—*Language Arts*
5. The ocean that surrounded Pangaea is called Panthalassa. The Greek word *thalassa* means sea. Why is the term Panthalassa appropriate? (*Hint:* Look at Figure 12–14.)

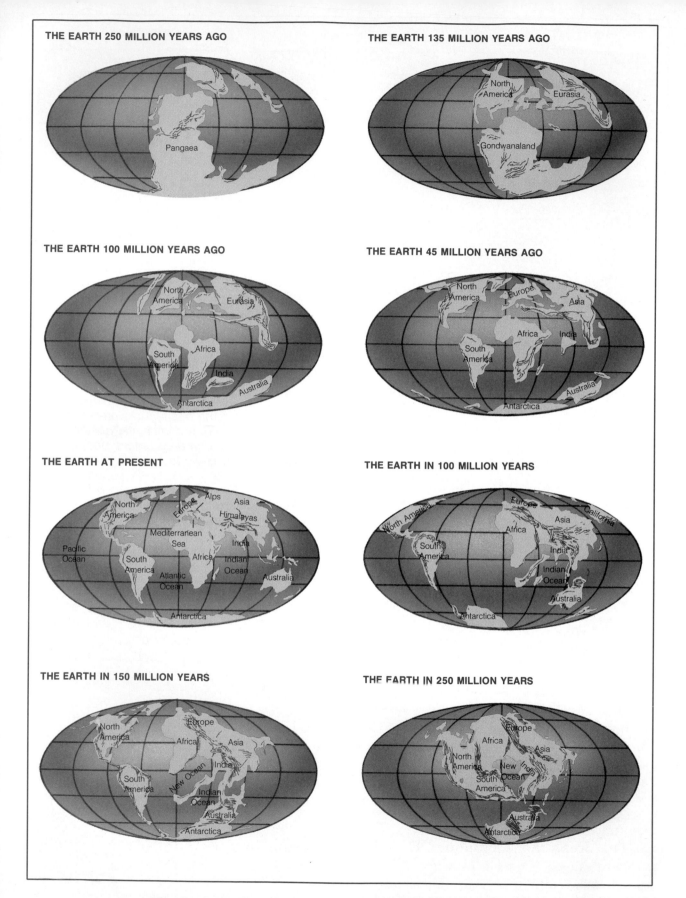

Figure 12–14 *The shapes and positions of Earth's continents have changed greatly.*

CONNECTIONS

Plate Tectonics and Life on Earth

The *evolution of Earth's living things* is strongly linked to the movements of the lithospheric plates. Why? Because living things evolve in response to changes in their environment. And the movement of the plates causes changes in climate, in geographic features such as mountains, and in the types of living things with which a species (specific type of living thing) interacts.

When the history of the Earth and its living things is studied, some basic patterns occur over and over again. One pattern is that when landmasses join together, diversity decreases. For example, fossils indicate that there were once 29 families of mammals in South America and 27 entirely different families of mammals in North America. (A family is a scientific group containing many related kinds of animals. The cat family, for example, includes lions, tigers, and house cats.) Soon after the continents joined together—about 3 million years ago—there were only 22 families left. Only the families that competed the most successfully survived; the rest died out.

Yet another pattern is that when landmasses split apart, the diversity of land animals increases. On a big landmass, animals can easily move to suitable places and avoid the more challenging environments. On a small landmass, animals are stuck where they are and thus must adapt to local conditions. At the same time, the animals are cut off from competitors and natural enemies on other landmasses. This combination of conditions results in the development of an enormous number of new species.

The world's monkeys and apes are one example of diversity caused by the breakup of a landmass. The splitting up of South America and Africa roughly 45 million years ago resulted in monkeys evolving into two distinct groups. New World monkeys are primarily tree-dwellers that have long tails used for grasping and for balance. Although Old World monkeys include tree-dwellers as well as ground-dwellers, none has a grasping tail.

Laboratory Investigation

Mapping Lithospheric Plates

Problem

How are the locations of the Earth's volcanoes, earthquakes, and mountain ranges related to the locations of the lithospheric plates?

Materials *(per student)*

colored pencils (black, red, brown, green)

paper   chapter maps

Procedure

1. With the black pencil, trace the outline of the world map onto the paper.
2. Draw with a red pencil the Ring of Fire on the world map. Also draw the other earthquake and volcano zones.
3. Shade in the general boundaries of the world's mountain ranges with a brown pencil. Be sure to include the Himalayas, Alps, Andes, and Rockies.
4. Draw in with a green pencil the boundaries of the seven lithospheric plates as well as the boundaries of the Arabian and Caribbean plates. Label each plate.

Observations

1. What is the relationship of the Ring of Fire to the Pacific plate?
2. Where are the most earthquakes, volcanoes, and mountains located in relation to the lithospheric plates?

Analysis and Conclusions

1. From the map you have made and the information in this chapter, how can you explain the apparent relationships between the lithospheric plates and the occurrence of earthquakes, volcanoes, and mountain ranges?
2. **On Your Own** Some volcanic activity is due to "hot spots." Using references from the library, find out what hot spots are and where the major hot spots are located. Using a blue pencil, mark the locations of the major hot spots on your map. Explain how hot spots provide evidence for plate movement.

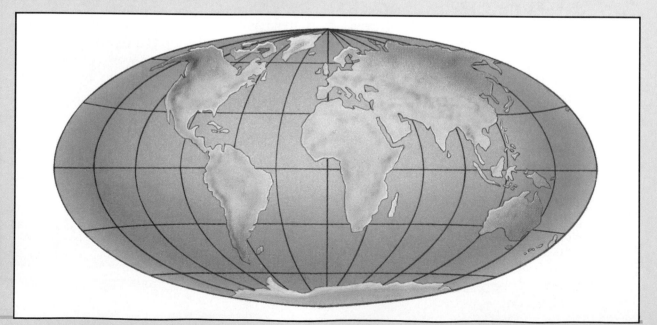

Study Guide

Summarizing Key Concepts

12–1 Earth's Drifting Continents

▲ The theory of continental drift, formulated by Alfred Wegener, states that all the continents were once part of one giant landmass, Pangaea. Pangaea split apart, and the continents slowly moved to their present positions.

▲ Wegener's theory is based on evidence from fossils and rock formations.

▲ The location of the Earth's landmasses affects their climate.

12–2 Earth's Spreading Ocean Floor

▲ Ocean-floor spreading occurs as parts of the ocean floor move away from a rift valley in the center of a midocean ridge. New ocean floor forms as molten rock rises through the rift and hardens.

▲ Ocean floor is destroyed when it is subducted into trenches and melted inside the mantle.

▲ The ocean floor is made of pieces that move from rifts to trenches. Many of these moving pieces have continents on top of them.

▲ Both the ages of the ocean-floor rocks and the magnetic stripes on the ocean floor are evidence of ocean-floor spreading.

12–3 Earth's Moving Plates

▲ The theory of plate tectonics, which links together the ideas of continental drift and ocean-floor spreading, explains how the Earth has evolved over time. It helps to explain the formation and destruction of the Earth's crust and its movements and collisions.

▲ The lithosphere, which consists of the crust and a thick layer of relatively cool, rigid mantle rock, is made of a number of plates.

▲ Plates usually contain both oceanic and continental crust.

▲ Divergent plate boundaries are formed by the midocean ridges.

▲ Convergent plate boundaries are formed by the trenches.

▲ Strike-slip boundaries are formed by lateral faults at which two plates slide horizontally past each other.

▲ Some scientists hypothesize that plate movement is caused by convection currents within the mantle.

▲ Understanding how the plates have moved in the past makes it possible to predict their future movement.

Reviewing Key Terms

Define each term in a complete sentence.

12–1 Earth's Drifting Continents
fossil
Pangaea
theory of continental drift

12–2 Earth's Spreading Ocean Floor
midocean ridge
ocean-floor spreading
transform fault
trench
subduction

12–3 Earth's Moving Plates
theory of plate tectonics
plate
tectonics
lithosphere
divergent boundary
convergent boundary
strike-slip boundary
convection current

Chapter Review

Content Review

Multiple Choice

Choose the letter of the answer that best completes each statement.

1. Alfred Wegener is most closely associated with the theory of
   a. the contracting Earth.
   b. continental drift.
   c. plate tectonics.
   d. ocean-floor spreading.
2. A deep crack that runs through the center of a midocean ridge is called a
   a. trench.   c. lithosphere.
   b. rift valley.   d. transform fault.
3. The collision of two oceanic plates creates
   a. mountain belts.   c. rift valleys.
   b. convection currents.   d. island arcs.
4. Evidence that supports the theory of continental drift has been provided by
   a. coal fields.   c. fossils.
   b. glacial deposits.   d. all of these.

5. The movement of the ocean floor on either side of a midocean ridge is best known as
   a. rifting.   c. ocean-floor spreading.
   b. glaciation.   d. subduction.
6. Plates containing crust and upper mantle form the Earth's
   a. lithosphere.   c. core.
   b. hydrosphere.   d. atmosphere.
7. The process in which the ocean floor plunges into the Earth's interior is called
   a. construction.   c. rifting.
   b. subduction.   d. convection.
8. Two plates grind past each other at a
   a. constructive boundary.
   b. divergent boundary.
   c. convergent boundary.
   d. strike-slip boundary.

True or False

If the statement is true, write "true." If it is false, change the underlined word or words to make the statement true.

1. The largest lithospheric plate is the <u>Pacific</u>.
2. Wegener proposed that all the continents were once part of one large landmass called <u>Gondwanaland</u>.
3. Ocean floor is subducted at <u>transform boundaries</u>.
4. <u>Conduction currents</u> may be the cause of plate movement.
5. <u>Midocean rifts</u> are also known as convergent, or destructive, boundaries.
6. Magnetic stripes on the ocean floor indicate that the Earth's magnetic poles <u>reverse themselves from time to time</u>.

Concept Mapping

Complete the following concept map for Section 12–1. Then construct a concept map for the entire chapter.

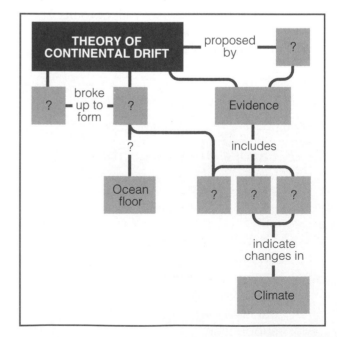

Concept Mastery

Discuss each of the following in a brief paragraph.

1. How do plate movements relate to volcanoes and earthquakes?
2. What kinds of evidence are used to support the theory of continental drift?
3. Describe what happens in the three different kinds of plate collisions.
4. What is a lithospheric plate?
5. How might convection currents account for the movement of the continents?
6. What is ocean-floor spreading? How does it relate to the theories of continental drift and plate tectonics?
7. How are the magnetic stripes on the ocean floor formed? Why are these stripes significant?
8. How does plate tectonics explain the formation of mountains?

Critical Thinking and Problem Solving

Use the skills you have developed in this chapter to answer each of the following.

1. **Making comparisons** How are the theories of continental drift and plate tectonics similar? How are they different?
2. **Developing a hypothesis** Studies have shown that continents appear to consist of small pieces that come from many different parts of the Earth. Using what you know about plate tectonics and isostasy, develop a hypothesis to explain how Earth's "crazy quilt" continents were formed.
3. **Analyzing data** The two imaginary continents in the accompanying figure each have three rock sections. The arrows show the magnetic field direction that existed when each section formed. The rocks' ages are shown in billions of years. Reptile fossils are found in sections A, B, and Z; fish fossils in sections C and X.
   On a piece of paper, trace all the information given in the figure. Cut out both continents. Then follow the instructions and answer the questions.
   a. Try to fit the two continents together. Do they fit more than one way? Choose the better fit. Explain what evidence you used to make your choice.
   b. What is your best estimate of the age of the rocks in section Z?
4. **Evaluating theories** Mountains almost always appear as long, narrow, curving ranges located at the edges of continents. Mountain ranges vary greatly in age. Most scientists once thought that mountains formed because the Earth was contracting. This caused the surface to wrinkle up like a raisin. If the contraction hypothesis were correct, what would you expect to be true about the age and distribution of mountains? Explain why the theory of continental drift better accounts for the age and distribution of mountains.
5. **Using the writing process** Write a humorous, but accurate, skit in which Alfred Wegener and one of his opponents appear on a major daytime talk show.

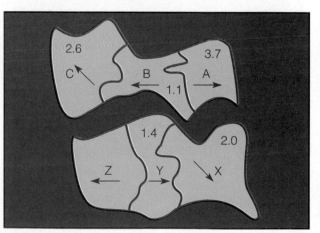

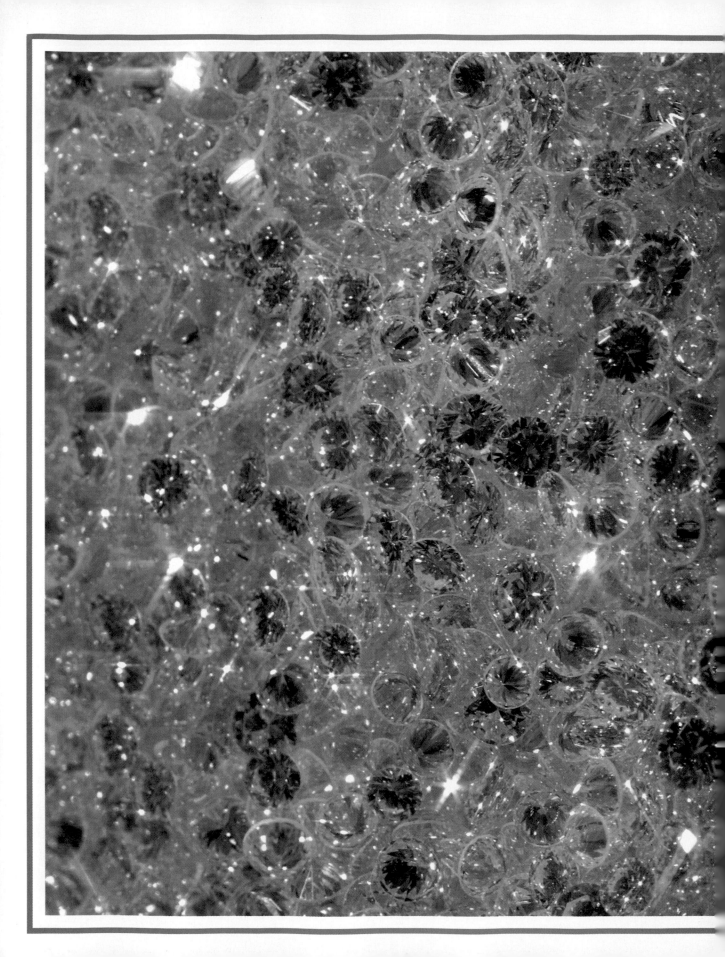

Rocks and Minerals

Guide for Reading

After you read the following sections, you will be able to

13–1 Elements, Compounds, and Mixtures

■ Describe how matter is classified.

13–2 What Is a Mineral?

■ Define the term mineral.

13–3 Uses of Minerals

■ Differentiate among metals, nonmetals, ores, and gemstones.

13–4 What Is a Rock?

■ Describe the rock cycle.

13–5 Fluid and Fire: Igneous Rocks

■ Explain how igneous rocks are classified.

13–6 Slowly Built Layers: Sedimentary Rocks

■ Identify the main types of sedimentary rocks.

13–7 Changes in Form: Metamorphic Rocks

■ Describe how metamorphic rocks are formed.

For hundreds of years, diamonds have been prized as a symbol of great wealth and power. Many of the world's largest diamonds adorn the scepters and crowns of kings and queens and decorate the jewelry of the extremely wealthy.

Some of the largest and most precious diamonds have dramatic histories. For example, the large, dark-blue gem now known as the Hope diamond is said to have once been an eye in the statue of an Indian goddess. When the diamond was stolen, the goddess is said to have cursed the stone and decreed that it would bring bad luck to all those who wore it. The diamond was owned and worn by King Louis XVI of France and his queen, both of whom were later beheaded during the French Revolution. Soon after the revolution, the diamond disappeared. When it reappeared nearly forty years later, it continued to be linked with murders, tragic accidents, and other misfortunes as it passed from owner to owner in Europe and the United States. The Hope diamond now rests in a display case at the Smithsonian Institution in Washington, DC.

Diamonds and other gemstones—rubies, emeralds, and sapphires, to name a few—are types of minerals. Minerals are the building blocks of rocks, and rocks are the building blocks of the solid Earth. Read on, and learn more about rocks and minerals.

Journal *Activity*

You and Your World You can probably think of many ways in which rocks have affected your life. In your journal, describe an incident in your life in which a rock played an important part.

◀ *Diamond is one of the most beautiful and precious of Earth's minerals.*

13–1 Elements, Compounds, and Mixtures

Look around. What do you see? Glass, wood, cloth. All the things around you are forms of matter. **Matter** is anything that takes up space and has mass. Air is matter. You are matter. All the world is made up of matter. Even the most distant stars and planets are made of matter.

Elements

All matter can be classified into three forms: elements, compounds, and mixtures. An **element** is a substance that cannot be separated into simpler substances by ordinary chemical means. Carbon and hydrogen are elements. So are iron, gold, and copper.

At present, scientists have identified 109 elements. About 90 of these elements occur naturally. The rest have been made in the laboratory. All the known elements are shown in Appendix H in a chart called the periodic table of the elements.

Each element has a name and a chemical symbol made up of one or two letters. The most recent laboratory-made elements have temporary names with three-letter symbols. Some of the symbols are the same as the first letter of the name of the element. For example, the symbol for oxygen is O, for hydrogen H, for carbon C, and for sulfur S. When the names of two elements begin with the same letter, a second letter is needed to prevent confusion. The symbol for helium is He, for chlorine Cl, and for silicon Si. The symbols for some of the elements come from the Latin names for the elements. For example, the symbol for iron, Fe, comes from the Latin word *ferrum,* and the symbol for sodium, Na, comes from the word *natrium.* The symbol for gold, Au, comes from the word *aurum.* Symbols are used as shorthand to represent the names of the elements. Figure 13–2 gives the names and symbols for some common elements.

The smallest part of an element that has all the properties of that element is an **atom.** Atoms are the

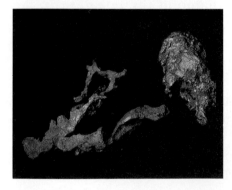

Figure 13–1 *The "lead" in a lead pencil is actually graphite, a form of carbon. A sparkling diamond is also a form of carbon. Native copper is an important mineral resource. What are some uses of copper with which you are familiar?*

basic building blocks of matter. It is possible to have a single atom of an element such as gold, aluminum, or iron. Some elements are made up of atoms that are chemically combined to form **molecules** (MAHL-uh-kyoolz). A molecule is two or more atoms held together by chemical forces. For example, a molecule of hydrogen consists of two hydrogen atoms chemically joined, or bonded together. A sulfur molecule is made up of eight sulfur atoms bonded together.

Atomic Structure

Atoms are made up of three main particles: protons, neutrons, and electrons. The center of the atom is called the nucleus. Two different kinds of particles are found in the nucleus. One of these is the proton. The proton is a positively charged particle. The other particle that makes up the nucleus is the neutron. A neutron is a neutral particle. It has no charge.

Whirling around outside the nucleus are particles called electrons. An electron has a negative charge. In a neutral atom, the number of negatively charged electrons is equal to the number of positively charged protons. What, then, is the total charge on a neutral atom?

Compounds

A **compound** is made of atoms of different elements that are bonded together. Water is a compound. As you read in Chapter 7, a water molecule is made up of two atoms of hydrogen combined with one atom of oxygen. You also learned that a water molecule is the smallest particle of water that has all the properties of water.

Common table salt, sodium chloride, is another compound. It is made up of sodium and chlorine atoms. Sodium chloride is not made up of molecules. Instead it consists of a repeating pattern of different atoms. See Figure 13–3 on page 398. As you will learn in the next section, atoms arranged in a definite pattern over and over again form solids called crystals.

Some compounds are made of several elements. Clay is made up of aluminum, magnesium, silicon, oxygen, and hydrogen.

COMMON ELEMENTS	
Name	**Symbol**
Aluminum	Al
Calcium	Ca
Carbon	C
Chlorine	Cl
Copper	Cu
Fluorine	F
Gold	Au
Helium	He
Hydrogen	H
Iron	Fe
Lead	Pb
Magnesium	Mg
Nitrogen	N
Oxygen	O
Potassium	K
Silicon	Si
Silver	Ag
Sodium	Na
Sulfur	S

Figure 13–2 *The names and symbols of some common elements are listed in this table. What is the symbol for aluminum? For calcium?*

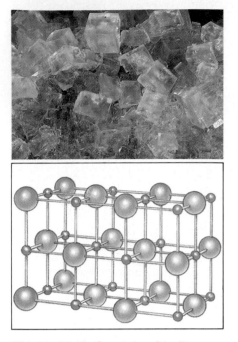

Figure 13–3 *Crystals of halite, or rock salt, are made up of repeating patterns of sodium (orange) and chlorine (green).*

Mixtures

Some forms of matter are neither elements nor compounds. Instead they are two or more substances mixed together. Such forms of matter are called mixtures. A **mixture** is two or more substances physically combined. Most rocks, soil, sea water, and air are examples of mixtures. Soil contains several substances, such as bits of clay, sand, and rocks. Air is a gaseous mixture of mostly nitrogen, oxygen, and water vapor. Air is a type of mixture called a solution because the substances that make up air are mixed on the molecular level. Sea water is another example of a solution.

Because the substances that make up a mixture are not chemically combined, the components can be separated out by physical means. For example, if you have a mixture of salt and water, you can separate the two substances by evaporating and collecting the water. The salt remains.

Chemical Formulas

You have just learned that elements can be represented by chemical symbols. Combinations of chemical symbols can also be used to represent the different atoms that make up compounds. These combinations of chemical symbols are called **chemical formulas.**

A chemical formula shows the elements that make up a compound. A chemical formula also shows the number of atoms of each element in a molecule or smallest particle of the compound. For example, the chemical formula for water is H_2O. According to this formula, every molecule of water is made up of 2 atoms of hydrogen and 1 atom of oxygen.

When writing a chemical formula, you use the symbol of each element in the compound. You also use small numbers called subscripts. Subscripts are placed to the lower right of the symbols. A subscript gives the number of atoms of the element in the compound. When there is only one atom of an element, the subscript 1 is not written. It is understood to be 1.

Figure 13–4 *Granite is a common, coarse-grained rock that is clearly a mixture of different minerals. What is the difference between a mixture and a compound?*

Figure 13–5 *The various kinds of matter can be classified into three forms: elements, compounds, and mixtures. The bars of bullion (left) are made of the element gold. The mineral formation in the Carlsbad Caverns of New Mexico (center) is made of the compound calcium carbonate. And the super burger (right) is a dazzling mixture of substances.*

Carbon dioxide is a compound of the elements carbon and oxygen. Its formula is CO_2. By looking at its formula, you can tell that every molecule of carbon dioxide is made up of 1 atom of carbon and 2 atoms of oxygen. Calcium carbonate, or limestone, makes up the beautiful cave formations shown in Figure 13–5. Its chemical formula is $CaCO_3$. What elements and how many atoms of each are there in this compound?

13–1 Section Review

1. What is the difference between an element, a compound, and a mixture?
2. How can you distinguish between an atom and a molecule?
3. What is a chemical symbol?
4. What is a chemical formula?

Critical Thinking—*Applying Concepts*
5. How could you tell if your tap water is pure water or a mixture of water and salts?

ACTIVITY

CALCULATING

Chemical Formulas

What elements and how many atoms of each are there in the following compounds?

$C_{12}H_{22}O_{11}$
Na_2SO_4
$CaCl_2$
KCl
H_2O

13–2 What Is a Mineral?

Animal, vegetable, or mineral?

If you have ever played the guessing game Twenty Questions, this phrase should be familiar to you. In the game, the word **mineral** refers to anything that is not living. In science, however, the word mineral has a more specific meaning. **A mineral is a naturally occurring, inorganic solid that has a definite chemical composition and crystal structure.** In order for a substance to be called a mineral, it must have all five of the characteristics described in this definition. Let's look at each characteristic more closely.

A mineral must occur naturally in the Earth. Silver, asbestos, and talc (the main ingredient of talcum powder), which all occur naturally, are minerals. Steel and cement, which are manufactured substances, are not minerals.

A mineral must be **inorganic,** or not formed from living things or the remains of living things. Quartz, which makes up about 11 percent of the Earth's crust, is a mineral. Coal and oil, although found in naturally occurring underground deposits, are not minerals because they are formed from the remains of living things that existed long ago.

A mineral is always a solid. Like all solids, a mineral has a definite volume and shape. Can you explain why oxygen, which occurs naturally and is inorganic, is not a mineral?

A mineral has a definite chemical composition. A mineral may be made of a single pure substance, or element, such as gold, copper, or sulfur. The minerals diamond and graphite (the main ingredient in pencil lead) are both made of the element carbon. Most minerals, however, are made of two or more elements chemically combined to form a compound.

A mineral's atoms are arranged in a definite pattern repeated over and over again. Atoms are the building blocks of matter. If not confined, the repeating pattern of a mineral's atoms forms a solid called a **crystal.** A crystal has flat sides that meet in

Figure 13–6 *The calcite crystals, fossil-bearing limestone, and pearls are all made of the compound calcium carbonate. Yet only the calcite is considered to be a mineral. Why?*

Figure 13–7 *Minerals have a definite chemical composition. Some, such as copper (left) and sulfur (bottom right), contain only one kind of element. Others are made up of compounds. Covellite (top right) is made up of a compound that contains copper and sulfur atoms.*

sharp edges and corners. All minerals have a characteristic crystal structure. In some mineral specimens, this structure is obvious from the specimen's appearance. In other specimens, this structure is apparent only on the microscopic level.

There are about 2500 different kinds of minerals. Some minerals are very common and easy to find. Others are rare and valuable. But all minerals have the five characteristics you have just read about.

Formation and Composition of Minerals

Many minerals come from magma, the molten rock beneath the Earth's surface. When magma cools, mineral crystals are formed. How and where magma cools determine the size of the mineral crystals.

When magma cools slowly beneath the Earth's crust, large crystals form. When magma cools rapidly beneath the Earth's crust, small crystals form. Sometimes the molten rock reaches the surface of the Earth and cools so quickly that no crystals at all form.

Crystals may also form from compounds dissolved in a liquid such as water. When the liquid evaporates, or changes to a gas, it leaves behind the minerals as crystals. The minerals halite, or rock salt, and calcite form in this way.

ACTIVITY

DISCOVERING

Rock-Forming Minerals

1. Collect between five and ten different kinds of rocks from your neighborhood.

2. Use a rock and mineral field guide to identify the minerals that make up each rock you found.

■ What minerals were found in your rocks?

■ What are the most common rock-forming minerals?

Figure 13–8 *These richly colored emerald crystals formed as magma slowly cooled deep inside the Earth (left). The delicate clusters of gypsum crystals known as desert roses are formed by evaporation (right).*

Activity Bank

Growing a Crystal Garden, p. 766

As you can see in Figure 13–9, the elements oxygen and silicon make up almost 75 percent of the Earth's crust. Other elements found in large amounts in the Earth's crust are aluminum, iron, calcium, sodium, potassium, and magnesium. Since these 8 elements are the most abundant elements in the Earth's crust, most common minerals are made of combinations of these elements.

There are about 100 common minerals formed from the 8 most abundant elements. Of these 100 common minerals, fewer than 20 are widely distributed in the Earth's crust. These minerals make up almost all the rocks in the crust. Scientists call these minerals rock-forming minerals. Quartz, calcite, augite, hematite, micas, and feldspars are examples of rock-forming minerals.

Identifying Minerals

Because there are so many different kinds of minerals, it is not an easy task to tell them apart. In fact, it is usually difficult to identify a mineral simply by looking at it. For example, the three minerals in Figure 13–10 all look like gold. Yet only one actually is gold.

Minerals have certain physical properties that can be used to identify them. Some of these properties can be seen just by looking at a mineral. Other properties can be observed only through special tests. By learning how to recognize the properties of minerals, you will be able to more easily identify many common minerals around you.

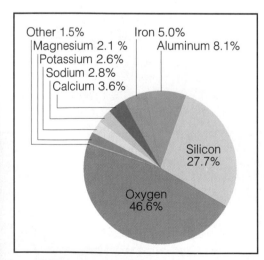

Other 1.5%
Magnesium 2.1 %
Potassium 2.6%
Sodium 2.8%
Calcium 3.6%
Iron 5.0%
Aluminum 8.1%
Silicon 27.7%
Oxygen 46.6%

Figure 13–9 *Eight elements make up more than 98 percent of the Earth's crust. Which element accounts for nearly 50 percent?*

Figure 13–10 *All that glitters is not always gold. The delicate branches among the quartz crystals are the real thing (left). The imitators are chalcopyrite (center) and pyrite (right). Can you explain why pyrite is also known as "fool's gold"?*

COLOR The color of a mineral is an easily observed physical property. But color can be used to identify only those few minerals that always have their own characteristic color. The mineral malachite is always green. The mineral azurite is always blue. No other minerals look quite the same as these.

Many minerals, however, come in a variety of colors. The mineral quartz is usually colorless. But it may be yellow, brown, black, green, pink, or purple. (The gemstone amethyst is purple quartz.) As you can see in Figure 13–11, color alone cannot be used to identify quartz and other minerals that have many different forms.

Color is not always a reliable way to identify minerals for another reason. The colors of minerals can change as a result of exposure to or treatment with heat, cold, pollution, or radiation.

Figure 13–11 *The color of lemon-yellow mimetite (right) and red-orange crocoite (center) may be their most obvious physical property. But color alone cannot be used to identify minerals. Some minerals are always the same color. Other minerals, such as quartz, come in many different colors (left).*

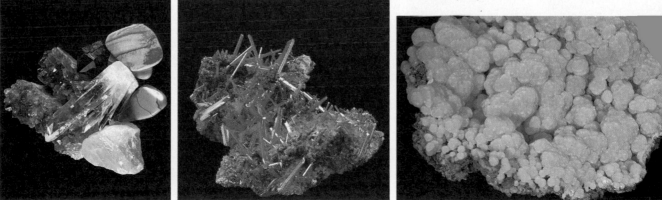

LUSTER   The **luster** of a mineral describes the way a mineral reflects light from its surface. Certain minerals reflect light the way highly polished metal does. Such minerals—including silver, copper, gold, pyrite, and graphite—have a metallic luster.

Minerals that do not reflect much light have a nonmetallic luster. Nonmetallic lusters may be described by a number of different terms: brilliant, glassy, pearly, silky, and dull, to name a few.

HARDNESS   The ability of a mineral to resist being scratched is known as its **hardness.** Hardness is one of the most useful properties for identifying minerals. Friedrich Mohs, a German mineralogist, worked out a scale of hardness for minerals. He used ten minerals and arranged them in order of increasing hardness. The number 1 is assigned to the softest mineral, talc. Diamond, the hardest of the ten minerals, is given the number 10. Each mineral will scratch any mineral with a lower number and will be scratched by any mineral with a higher number. Figure 13–13 shows the minerals of the Mohs hardness scale with their assigned numbers. What mineral is harder than talc but softer than calcite? What minerals would you expect quartz to scratch?

Quartz

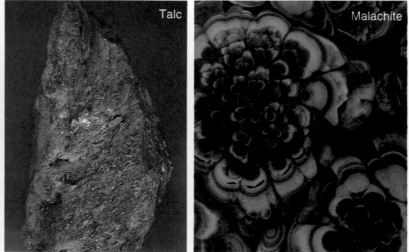
Diamond

Talc

Malachite

Figure 13–12 *Because quartz reflects light like glass, it is said to have a glassy luster. Diamond has a brilliant luster. Talc's luster ranges from pearly to greasy. And malachite's luster ranges from glassy to silky. Which end of this range is shown by the malachite in the photograph?*

To determine the hardness of an unknown mineral, the mineral is rubbed against the surface of each mineral in the hardness scale. If the unknown mineral is scratched by the known mineral, it is softer than the known mineral. If the unknown mineral scratches the known mineral, it is harder than that mineral. If two minerals do not scratch each other, they have the same hardness. What is the hardness of a mineral sample that scratches quartz and is scratched by corundum but not by topaz?

STREAK The color of the powder scraped off a mineral when it is rubbed against a hard, rough surface is called its **streak.** Streak can be an excellent clue to identifying some minerals. Even though the color of a mineral may vary, its streak is always the same. This streak, however, may be different from the color of the mineral itself. For example, hematite may be gray, green, or black, but it always has a reddish-brown streak.

Streak can be observed by rubbing the mineral sample across a piece of unglazed porcelain, which is called a streak plate. The back of a piece of bathroom tile makes an excellent streak plate. A streak

MOHS HARDNESS SCALE

Mineral	Hardness
Talc	1
Gypsum	2
Calcite	3
Fluorite	4
Apatite	5
Feldspars	6
Quartz	7
Topaz	8
Corundum	9
Diamond	10

Figure 13-13 *The Mohs hardness scale is a list of ten minerals that represent different degrees of hardness. As you might expect, quartz is about 7 times as hard as talc, and corundum (the mineral of which rubies and sapphires are made) is about 9 times as hard as talc. Diamond, however, is about 40 times (not 10 times) as hard as talc. Diamonds are extremely hard!*

FIELD HARDNESS SCALE

Hardness	Common Tests
1	Easily scratched with a fingernail (2.5)
2	Scratched by fingernail
3	Very easily scratched by a knife (5.5–6); will not scratch a copper penny (3)
4	Easily scratched by a knife
5	Difficult to scratch with a knife; will not scratch glass (5.5–6)
6	Scratched by a steel file (6.5–7); may barely scratch glass
7	May barely scratch a steel file; easily scratches glass
8–10	Scratches a steel file

Figure 13-14 *A field hardness scale can be used when the minerals from the Mohs scale are not available. What is a disadvantage of using a field scale rather than the Mohs scale?*

ACTIVITY

How Hard Could It Be?

Obtain a penny, a penknife, a piece of glass, a steel file, and at least five different mineral samples.

■ What is the approximate hardness of each of your mineral samples?

plate has a hardness slightly less than 7. Can you explain why a streak test cannot be done on a mineral whose hardness is greater than 7?

Many minerals have white or colorless streaks. Talc, gypsum, and quartz are examples. Streak is not a useful physical property in identifying minerals such as these.

DENSITY Every mineral has a property called **density.** Density is the amount of matter in a given space. Density can also be expressed as mass per unit volume. The density of a mineral is always the same, no matter what the size of the mineral sample. Because each mineral has a characteristic density, one mineral can easily be compared with any other mineral. You can compare the densities of two minerals of about the same size by picking them up and hefting them. The denser mineral feels heavier.

CRYSTAL SHAPE As you have already learned, minerals have a characteristic crystal shape that results from the way the atoms or molecules come together as the mineral is forming. As you can see in Figure 13–15, there are six basic shapes of crystals, or crystal systems.

CLEAVAGE AND FRACTURE The terms **cleavage** and **fracture** are used to describe the way a mineral breaks. Cleavage is the tendency of a mineral to split along smooth, definite surfaces. Some minerals

Figure 13–15 *The six basic crystal systems are shown here. The dashed lines on the crystal diagrams represent special lines called axes (AK-seez). The length and position of the axes relative to one another determine the system to which a crystal belongs.*

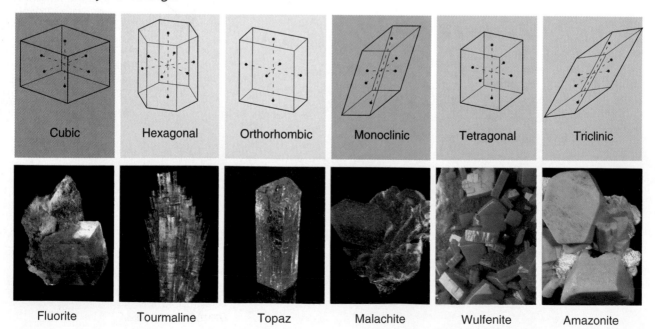

Cubic	Hexagonal	Orthorhombic	Monoclinic	Tetragonal	Triclinic
Fluorite	Tourmaline	Topaz	Malachite	Wulfenite	Amazonite

cleave quite well. Halite, for example, always cleaves in three directions, breaking into small cubes. Micas cleave along one surface, making layer after layer of very thin sheets.

Most minerals, however, do not break along smooth, definite surfaces. Instead, they break along rough or jagged surfaces. This type of break is known as fracture. Like cleavage, fracture is a property that helps to identify a mineral. For example, quartz has a shell-shaped fracture that has a number of smooth, curved surfaces and that resembles chipped glass.

SPECIAL PROPERTIES Some minerals can be identified by special properties. Magnetite is naturally magnetic. Fluorite glows when put under ultraviolet light. Halite tastes salty. Sulfur smells like rotten eggs or burning rubber. Calcite fizzes when hydrochloric acid is added to it. And uraninite (one of the sources of uranium) is radioactive.

Figure 13–16 *The way a mineral breaks is a clue to its identity. Mica cleaves into thin sheets (left). Calcite cleaves into shapes resembling slanted boxes (center). Quartz has a shell-shaped fracture. The broken surface has curved ridges like those on a clam's shell (right).*

13–2 Section Review

1. Define the term mineral. Briefly describe the five characteristics of minerals.
2. What kinds of physical properties are used to identify minerals?
3. How is a mineral's hardness tested?
4. What is the difference between cleavage and fracture?

Critical Thinking—*Applying Concepts*

5. How would you go about determining if a yellow pebble is a valuable topaz or a not-so-valuable citrine (yellow quartz)? What would you do differently if you needed to identify a cut and polished gem without damaging it? Explain.

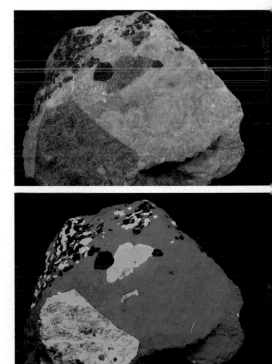

Figure 13–17 *Under ordinary light, calcite and willemite look quite plain. But under ultraviolet light, these minerals glow with unexpected colors.*

13–3 Uses of Minerals

Throughout history, people have used minerals. At first, minerals were used just as they came from the Earth. Later, people learned to combine and process the Earth's minerals. **Today many of the Earth's minerals are used to meet the everyday needs of people.** Minerals are raw materials for a wide variety of products from dyes to dishes and from table salt to televisions.

Ores

The term **ores** is used to describe minerals or combinations of minerals from which metals and nonmetals can be removed in usable amounts. **Metals** are elements that have shiny surfaces and are able to conduct electricity and heat. Metals can be hammered or pressed into thin sheets and other shapes without breaking. Metals can also be pulled into thin strands without breaking. Iron, lead, aluminum, copper, silver, and gold are examples of metals.

Most metals are found combined with other substances in ores. So after the ores are removed from the Earth by mining, the metals must be removed from the ores. During a process called smelting, an ore is heated in such a way that the metal can be

Activity Bank

One Ore in the Water, p. 768

Figure 13–18 *Chrysocolla is an ore of the metal copper. Copper is used in electrical wire. What are some other uses of copper?*

separated from it. For example, iron is obtained from ores such as limonite and hematite. Lead can be processed from the ore galena. Aluminum comes from the ore bauxite.

Metals are very useful. Iron is used in making steel. Copper is used in pipes and electrical wire. Aluminum is used in the production of cans, foil, lightweight motors, and airplanes. Silver and gold are used in dental fillings and in decorative objects such as jewelry. Pure metals may be combined to form other metallic substances. For example, lead and tin are melted together to make pewter, which is used to make bowls, platters, and decorative objects. Chromium and iron are melted together to make stainless steel. And copper and zinc are combined to make brass.

Nonmetals are elements that have dull surfaces and are poor conductors of electricity and heat. Nonmetals are not easily shaped. Sulfur and halite are examples of nonmetals.

Some nonmetals are removed from the Earth in usable form. Other nonmetals must be processed to separate them from the ores in which they are found.

Like metals, nonmetals are quite useful. Sulfur is one of the most useful nonmetals. It is used to make matches, medicines, and fertilizers. It is also used in iron and steel production.

ACTIVITY READING

Neither a Borrower Nor a Lender Be

Because of their beauty and value, gems can have a powerful effect on people. Sometimes they can even change a person's life. Read the short story *The Necklace* by Guy de Maupassant.

Figure 13–19 *Red-orange cinnabar is the main ore of mercury, a metal often used in thermometers. Purple fluorite is the main ore of the nonmetal fluorine. Fluorine compounds have many different uses—you probably use the fluorine compounds known as fluorides every time you brush your teeth!*

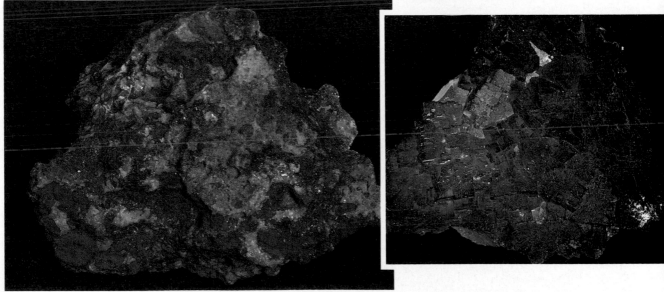

Figure 13–20 *Some minerals, such as beryl (left), topaz (center), and garnet (right), are considered gemstones. What are gemstones?*

Gemstones

Some minerals are hard, beautiful, and durable substances that can be cut and polished for jewelry and decoration. Such minerals are called **gemstones.** Once a gemstone is cut and polished, it is called a gem. The rarest and most valuable gemstones—diamonds, rubies, sapphires, and emeralds—are known as precious stones. All other gemstones are known as semiprecious stones. Amethysts, zircons, garnets, turquoises, and tourmalines are just a few examples of semiprecious stones. They are all beautiful and durable, but they are not as rare and as valuable as precious stones.

Although many gems are minerals, there are a few that are not. Pearls, which are produced by oysters and mussels, and amber, which is fossilized tree sap, are gemstones. But they are not minerals. Can you explain why?

A Gem of a Puzzle

Imagine the following situation. Hearing that you have gotten pretty good at identifying minerals, a wealthy (and rather eccentric) gem dealer has challenged you to identify three beautifully cut gems. If you can correctly identify the gems, you get to keep them.

As you can see in the accompanying figure, the gem dealer has presented you with the three gems, a table of information, and five vials containing thick, rather smelly liquids.

Applying Concepts

1. Describe the procedure you plan to use to identify the gems.

2. What results would you expect to obtain for sapphire (corundum)? For quartz?

3. Suppose that one of the gems sinks slowly in solution C, floats on the top of solution E, and stays at whatever depth you put it in solution D. What mineral is this gem made of?

4. Explain how you can tell the difference between cubic zirconia and zircon using only the materials available to you. (It can be done.)

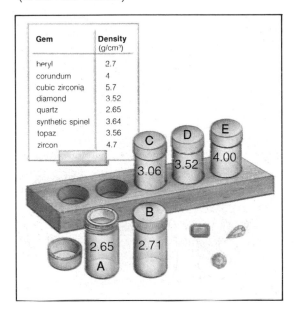

Gem	Density (g/cm³)
beryl	2.7
corundum	4
cubic zirconia	5.7
diamond	3.52
quartz	2.65
synthetic spinel	3.64
topaz	3.56
zircon	4.7

13–3 Section Review

1. Describe five different ways in which minerals are used.
2. What is an ore? Why are ores smelted?
3. How do metals differ from nonmetals?
4. List three examples each of precious and semi-precious stones.

Connection—*Economics*

5. If the demand for an object exceeds the supply, the price of the object will go up. In general, rubies and emeralds are far more expensive than diamonds. What can you infer from this?

Genuine Imitations

In the past hundred years or so, advances in *chemical technology* have made it possible to create crystals that have the same structure, composition, and appearance as natural minerals do. These synthetic (made by humans) gemstones are produced by a number of different processes and have a variety of different uses.

As you might expect, many synthetic gemstones are used for jewelry. But you might be surprised to know that most synthetic sapphires and rubies are used for more practical purposes. Fine mechanical watches have parts that are made of tiny pieces of synthetic ruby. (This is why such watches advertise that they have 17-jewel or 21-jewel movements.) The microcircuits, or chips, used in aircraft, satellites, and nuclear reactors are formed on a base of synthetic sapphire. Lasers, compasses, electric meters, quartz watches, and cloth-making machines are among the many devices that also contain parts made from synthetic rubies and sapphires. Even the glass plate in most supermarket scanners is coated with synthetic sapphire.

It is quite possible that supermarket scanners and many other objects will one day have a more scratch-resistant coating than sapphire. That coating will be made of synthetic diamond. Watch crystals, scanner windows, and stereo speakers with diamond coatings are being commercially manufactured already. Experts predict that diamond-coated razor blades, computer hard disks, drill bits, and pots and pans may be available in the not-so-distant future.

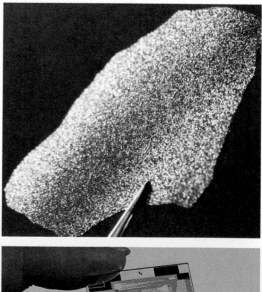

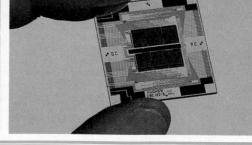

13–4 What Is a Rock?

Rocks are probably a familiar sight to you. You see them all around you in various shapes, sizes, and colors. Rocks are the building blocks of the Earth. They form beaches, mountains, the ocean floor, and all the other parts of the Earth's crust.

Humans have been using rocks for a long time. About 2 million years ago, ancestors of modern humans shaped small pieces of rocks into stone tools and weapons. Stonehenge in Great Britain, the Great Pyramid of Egypt, the Great Wall of China, the city of Machu Pichu in Peru, and the city of Great Zimbabwe in southern Africa were all built of rocks hundreds of years ago. What are some other ways in which humans used rocks in the past? How do they use rocks today?

It is easy to tell that something is made from rocks. It is also easy to recognize a rock when you see one. But what exactly is a rock?

In science, a rock is a hard substance composed of one or more minerals. Usually, a rock is made of more than one kind of mineral. Recall that the most common minerals in rocks are made of the elements that are most abundant in the Earth's crust. What are the eight most abundant elements in the crust?

A rock may also be made of or contain naturally occurring substances that do not perfectly fit the definition of a mineral. For example, rocks may be composed of volcanic glass or of opal. Both these substances lack a crystalline structure and so are not minerals in the strictest sense of the word.

Types of Rocks

To make sense of the enormous diversity of rocks in the world, it is necessary to organize them in a logical way. Geologists (people who study the structure and history of the Earth) place rocks into groups based on certain characteristics. **Rocks are placed into three groups according to how they form: igneous, sedimentary, and metamorphic.**

Igneous (IHG-nee-uhs) rocks were originally hot, fluid magma within the Earth. Igneous rocks get their name from the Latin word *ignis,* which means

Rock Around the Town

How are rocks used in your neighborhood? Make a list from memory. Then take a walk around and see how many other uses you can observe—you may be surprised!

■ How are rocks used? What are the most interesting uses of rocks you observed? How is your list similar to your classmates'? Different?

Figure 13–21 *The Aztecs, who lived long ago in what is now Mexico, created magnificent buildings and works of art out of rocks.*

Figure 13–22 *Igneous rocks are formed when molten rock cools and hardens. Red-hot lava still glows beneath a crust of basalt in this fresh lava flow in Hawaii (left). Sedimentary rocks may be formed as layer upon layer of particles build up on the bottom of a sea. These layers may be revealed as plate movements drain seas and raise the rocks that once rested on the ocean floor (center). Metamorphic rocks form when heat, pressure, and chemical reactions change existing rock into something new. The process of change may cause the minerals within the rock to separate into layers, forming distinct bands (right).*

fire. Do you think that igneous rock is an appropriate name?

Most **sedimentary** (sehd-ih-MEHN-tuh-ree) rocks are formed from particles that have been carried along and deposited by wind and water. These particles, or **sediments** (SEHD-ih-mehnts), include bits of rock in the form of mud, sand, or pebbles. Sediments also include shells, bones, leaves, stems, and other remains of living things. Over time, these particles become pressed or cemented together to form rocks.

Metamorphic (meht-ah-MOR-fihk) rocks are formed when chemical reactions, tremendous heat, and/or great pressure change existing rocks into new kinds of rocks. These new rocks (metamorphic rocks) have physical and chemical properties that are usually quite different from the original rocks. The root word *morph* means form, and the prefix *meta-* means change. Why is the term metamorphic an appropriate one?

The Rock Cycle

In the previous three chapters, you learned that the Earth's surface is not at all as permanent and unchanging as it sometimes seems to be. Mountains fault and fold upward; volcanoes build new islands in the ocean; tectonic plates move. The rocks that form the Earth's surface are also subject to change. Igneous and sedimentary rocks may be transformed by heat, pressure, or chemical reactions into metamorphic rocks. Metamorphic rocks may change into other kinds of metamorphic rocks. Metamorphic rocks may be remelted and become igneous rocks again. The continuous changing of rocks from one kind to another over long periods of time is called the **rock cycle.**

Many cycles exist in nature. Some of these cycles, such as the phases of the moon or the seasons of the year, occur in a definite sequence. For example, the sequence of the seasons is winter, spring, summer, and autumn. In contrast, the rock cycle has no definite sequence. It can follow many different pathways. Look at Figure 13–23. The outer circle shows the complete rock cycle. The arrows within the circle show alternate pathways that can be taken, and often are.

Let's follow the material in a rock on its long journey through the rock cycle. In the right-hand photograph in Figure 13–23, a huge dome of granite, an igneous rock, lies exposed to the wind and rain, the cold of winter, and the heat of summer.

Because granite is made of hard minerals such as quartz and feldspars, it is quite resistant to nature's

ACTIVITY
READING

Guides for the Perplexed

Confused by the enormous number of rocks and minerals? Don't despair—help is just a trip to the library or bookstore away! Many good field guides on rocks and minerals are available. Two of these are *Simon & Schuster's Guide to Rocks and Minerals* and *Simon & Schuster's Guide to Gems and Precious Stones.*

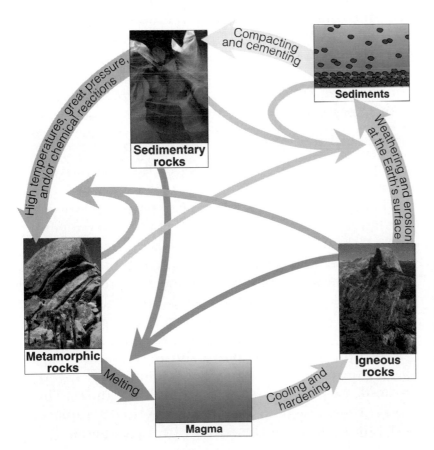

Figure 13–23 *The photographs that illustrate this diagram of the rock cycle show Half Dome, a granite formation in Yosemite National Park, California (right); sandstone in Antelope Canyon, Arizona (top); and a quartzite formation in Joshua Tree National Monument, California (left). What kind of rock does each of these photographs represent? How does rock change from one type to another?*

Figure 13–24 *The changing seasons form a cycle in nature in which events always happen in the same order. How does this cycle differ from the rock cycle?*

ACTIVITY

Famous Rock Formations

Using reference materials in the library, find out more about the following rock formations:

Giant's Causeway
Stone Mountain
Devil's Tower
Rock of Gibraltar
Garden of the Gods
Half Dome

Write a brief report about the formation that you find most interesting. In your report, you should tell where the rock formation is located, what type of rock it is composed of, how it was formed, and why it is interesting.

forces. However, under the steady force of wind, water, and temperature changes, the granite is slowly worn down. Bits of granite flake off. Dragged along in rushing streams, these bits of granite are reduced to sand.

The sand from the granite, along with other sediments, is carried by the streams to a river, which carries the sediments to the sea. As the river flows into the sea, its speed decreases and its load of sediments is deposited on the sea floor. Over the years, layers of sediment slowly pile up.

The weight of the upper layers puts pressure on the lower layers, pushing the particles closer together. Dissolved minerals—in this case, calcite—cement the particles together. What was once ground-up granite is now sandstone, a sedimentary rock.

As the layers of sandstone are buried under more and more layers of sediment, they are subjected to increasingly high temperatures and pressures. Under sufficiently high temperature and pressure, the particles in the sandstone are pressed even closer together until there are no spaces left between them. The calcite that cemented the grains together is replaced with silica (the main ingredient of the mineral quartz). The texture of the rock changes from grainy to smooth. It is now the metamorphic rock quartzite.

What happens next? One possibility is that the quartzite becomes molten deep inside the Earth. The resulting magma hardens back into granite. In time, the material in the newly formed granite may undergo the same steps of the rock cycle just described. But this is not the only possibility. What else might occur?

13–4 Section Review

1. What are the three main groups of rocks? Give one example from each group.
2. How are igneous rocks formed? Sedimentary rocks? Metamorphic rocks?
3. What is the rock cycle? What two factors in this cycle may change sandstone to quartzite?

Connection—*Architecture*

4. The sedimentary rocks limestone and sandstone are fairly good materials for building. But they do not wear as well as the metamorphic rocks— marble and quartzite—that are formed from them. Why do you think this is so? How might this affect an architect's choice of building materials?

ACTIVITY DOING

Starting a Rock Collection

1. Label each specimen by putting a dot of light-colored paint in an inconspicuous place. When the paint dries, write a number on the dot of paint with permanent ink. (Start with the number 1 for the first specimen and work your way up.)

2. Prepare an index card for each specimen. This card should provide the following information about the specimen: its number, what it is, where it was found, and the date it was collected.

13–5 Fluid and Fire: Igneous Rocks

Igneous rocks are classified according to their composition and texture. Composition refers to the minerals of which rocks are formed. Texture means the shape, size, arrangement, and distribution of the minerals that make up rocks. Both composition and texture are evident in a rock's appearance. For example, light-colored igneous rocks are typically rich in the colorless mineral quartz, whereas dark-colored igneous rocks are typically rich in the dense, greenish gray mineral augite.

Guide for Reading

Focus on this question as you read.

▶ *How are igneous rocks classified?*

417

Figure 13–25 *Igneous rocks may be classified according to their texture. Trachyte has a porphyritic texture. What kind of textures are illustrated by obsidian, basalt, and granite?*

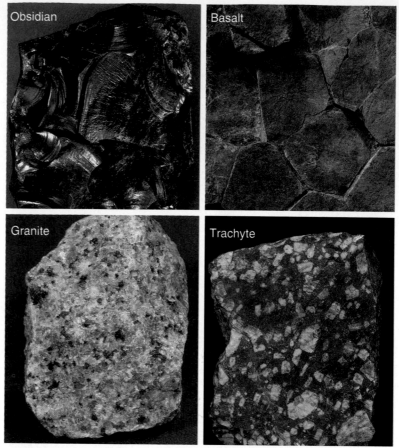

Obsidian

Basalt

Granite

Trachyte

ACTIVITY

DOING

Mineral Deposits

This activity will help you to find out where some of the major mineral deposits in the world are located.

1. In the library, find a map of the world. Draw or trace the map on a sheet of paper. Label Africa, Asia, Europe, North America, South America, Australia, and Antarctica.

2. Find out where uranium, sulfur, aluminum, iron, halite, and gold deposits are located.

3. Using a symbol to represent each mineral, show the locations of these deposits on the map.

4. Make a key by writing the name of each mineral next to its symbol. Make your map colorful and descriptive.

As you can see in Figure 13–25 igneous rocks have four basic types of textures: glassy, fine-grained, coarse-grained, and porphyritic (por-fuh-RIHT-ihk). Glassy igneous rocks are shiny and look like glass. The materials that make up a glassy igneous rock are not organized into crystals. Obsidian (uhb-SIHD-ee-uhn), which is also known as volcanic glass, has a glassy texture.

Fine-grained rocks, unlike glassy rocks, are made of interlocking mineral crystals. These crystals are too small to be seen without the help of a microscope. The dark-gray rock known as basalt (buh-SAHLT) has a fine-grained texture.

Coarse-grained rocks, such as granite, consist of interlocking mineral crystals, which are all roughly the same size. The crystals in a coarse-grained rock are visible to the unaided eye.

Porphyritic rocks consist of large crystals scattered on a background of much smaller crystals. Sometimes these small background crystals are too tiny to be seen without a microscope. This gives some porphyritic rocks a texture that resembles rocky road ice cream.

Why do igneous rocks show such a variety of textures? Recall from Section 13–2 that how magma cools and where it cools determine the size of mineral crystals. The longer it takes magma to cool, the larger are the crystals that form. Glassy and fine-grained rocks form from lava that erupts from volcanoes and hardens on the Earth's surface. Coarse-grained rocks form from molten rock that cools and hardens within the Earth instead of at the Earth's surface.

Rocks formed from lava are called **extrusive** (ehk-STROO-sihv) **rocks.** Because lava is brought to the Earth's surface by volcanoes, extrusive rocks are also known as volcanic rocks. Basalt and obsidian are two kinds of extrusive rocks. Both these rocks are quite solid. In contrast, the gray volcanic glass called pumice (PUH-mihs) is filled with bubbles. Because pumice is filled with bubbles, it can float on water.

Igneous rocks formed deep within the Earth are called **intrusive** (ihn-TROO-sihv) **rocks.** They form when magma forces its way upward into preexisting rocks and then hardens. Intrusive rocks include granite and pegmatite, an extremely coarse-grained rock that may be rich in gemstones.

Intrusive rocks are also known as plutonic rocks, after Pluto, the Roman god of the underworld. A mass of intrusive rock is known as a pluton. As you can see in Figure 13–27 on page 420, plutons are classified according to their size, shape, and position relative to surrounding rocks.

Plutons may produce landforms by pushing up the layers of rock above them. This is how the domes you had read about in Chapter 10 are formed. Plutons may also produce landforms when the softer rock around them is worn away, exposing the buried intrusive rock.

Figure 13–26 *Molten rock may cool so quickly that gases inside do not have a chance to escape. The rock hardens around the bubbles, producing rocks that have more holes than Swiss cheese. Scoria is basically bubbly basalt (left). Pumice, a volcanic glass, is so light it can float on water (right).*

ACTIVITY DOING

An Igneous Invasion

Using papier-mâché, tempera paint, markers, a hardwood base, and any other materials necessary, make a model of an igneous rock intrusion. Use Figure 13–22 to help you make your model.

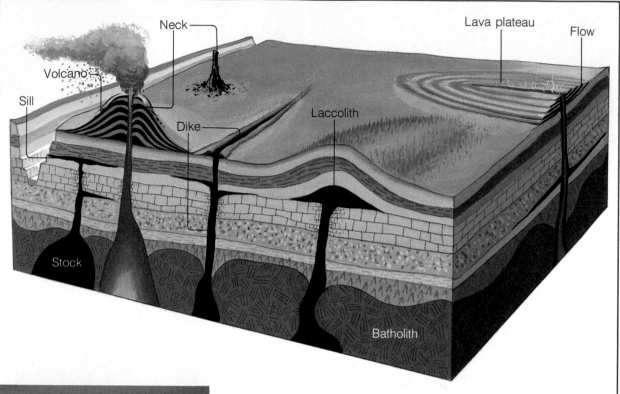

Neck

Volcano

Sill

Dike

Laccolith

Lava plateau

Flow

Stock

Batholith

Figure 13–27 *Some igneous rock formations, such as volcanoes and lava plateaus, are visible on the surface as soon as they form. Most plutons, however, are revealed only after the surrounding rocks have worn away. The photograph shows two such formations in New Mexico. Shiprock is the exposed neck, or plug, of an ancient volcano. The Devil's Backbone is the remains of a dike.*

13–5 Section Review

1. What characteristics are used to classify igneous rocks?
2. How are intrusive rocks similar to extrusive rocks? How are they different?
3. What determines the size and type of crystals in rocks?
4. What is the relationship between a rock's texture and where it was formed?

Critical Thinking—*Developing a Hypothesis*
5. Propose an explanation for how porphyritic rocks are formed.

13–6 Slowly Built Layers: Sedimentary Rocks

The most widely used classification system for sedimentary rocks places them into three main categories according to origin of the materials from which they are made. These three categories are: **clastic rocks, organic rocks,** and **chemical rocks.**

Clastic Rocks

Sedimentary rocks that are made of the fragments of previously existing rocks are known as clastic rocks. Clastic rocks are further classified according to the size and shape of the fragments in them.

Some clastic rocks are made of rounded pebbles cemented together by clay, mud, and sand. If over a third of the rock is made of pebbles, the rock is called a conglomerate (kahn-GLAHM-er-iht). The pebbles in conglomerates are smooth and rounded because they have been worn down by the action of water. Conglomerates are not as common as rocks made of smaller pieces because moving water tends to break large pieces into smaller pieces. Because they resemble an old-fashioned pudding filled with nuts and chopped fruit, conglomerates are sometimes called puddingstones.

Figure 13–28 *Clastic rocks are classified according to the size of the rock fragments they contain. Puddingstone and breccia have the largest fragments. How do the fragments in these two rocks differ? Sandstone is made up of sand-sized fragments. Shale is composed of dust-sized fragments.*

Guide for Reading

Focus on this question as you read.

▶ *What are the different categories of sedimentary rocks?*

Breccia

Shale

Sandstone

Puddingstone

Clastic rocks made of small, sand-sized grains are called sandstones. At least half the particles in a clastic rock must be sand-sized in order for it to be considered a sandstone. Sandstones are very common rocks. They are formed from the sand on beaches, in riverbeds, and in sand dunes. In sandstones, the sand grains are cemented together by minerals. The minerals harden in the small spaces, or pores, between the grains.

Many geologists use the term shale to describe all the clastic rocks that are made of particles smaller than sand. Shales form from small particles of mud and clay that settle to the bottom of quiet bodies of water such as swamps. Most shales can be split into flat pieces.

Organic Rocks

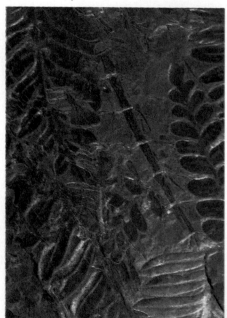

Organic rocks come from organisms; they are formed either directly or indirectly from material that was once living. Limestones, which are made primarily of the mineral calcite, are often (but not always) organic rocks. Deposits of limestone may be formed from the limestone shells of creatures such as clams and certain microorganisms. When these organisms die, their shells collect on the ocean floor. Eventually, the shells are compacted into rock.

Living organisms may create limestone directly. Sometimes many animals with limestone shells live

Figure 13–29 *Coquina is composed primarily of fossil clam shells. The white cliffs of Dover are made of chalk. Coal is formed from the remains of plants that lived millions of years ago. When chunks of coal are broken apart, the ghostly impressions of ancient leaves may be revealed. To what group of sedimentary rocks do coquina, chalk, and coal belong?*

together. They cement their shells together and over time form large structures called reefs. Corals build limestone reefs off the coast of Florida and around many of the Caribbean and Pacific islands. Oysters build limestone reefs along the Texas Gulf coast.

Have you ever written or drawn with sticks of chalk? If so, you have first-hand experience with one kind of limestone. Chalk is a type of fine-grained limestone composed of microscopic shells, small fragments of shells, and calcite crystals. Because the particles in chalk are tiny and relatively loosely packed, chalk is much softer than other limestones.

Coal is another rock that is formed from the remains of living things. It is made from plants that lived millions of years ago.

Chemical Rocks

Some sedimentary rocks are formed when a sea or a lake dries up, leaving large amounts of minerals that were dissolved in the water. As you can see in Figure 13–30, the deposited minerals may create spectacular formations. Examples of chemical rocks formed in this way include rock salt and gypsum.

Some limestone rocks are formed by inorganic processes rather than by organisms. The strange and beautiful limestone formations found in many caves are formed by mineral-rich water dripping into the

ACTIVITY

CALCULATING

Coral Conversions

The largest coral reef is the Great Barrier Reef, which parallels the northeastern coast of Australia for a distance of about 2000 kilometers. How many meters long is the Coral Reef? How many centimeters? Compare this distance to the distance across the United States, which is 4517 km from east to west.

Figure 13–30 *Chemical rocks form in many different places. As the sun beats down, evaporation forms strange towers of salt and calcium carbonate at Mono Lake, California. Spectacular formations are slowly built underground as water drips into a cave and deposits minerals.*

cave. When the water evaporates, a thin deposit of limestone is left behind. Over a long period of time, the deposits are built up into pillars, spikes, and other structures. Limestone may also be produced through chemical changes in ocean water that cause grains of calcite to form. The small grains get larger as additional thin layers are deposited from the ocean water. So these limestones are chemical rocks rather than organic rocks.

Figure 13–31 *Interesting sedimentary rock structures include geodes (top left), ripple marks (center left), concretions (bottom left), fossils (top right), and mud cracks (bottom right).*

13–6 Section Review

1. How are sedimentary rocks classified? Give an example of each major group.
2. What are clastic rocks? How are clastic rocks classified?
3. How are organic and chemical rocks similar? How are they different?

Critical Thinking—*Relating Concepts*
4. Explain how the fossil of a fish formed and ended up on the side of a mountain.

13–7 Changes in Form: Metamorphic Rocks

When already existing rocks are buried deep within the Earth, tremendous heat, great pressure, and chemical reactions may cause them to change into different rocks with different textures and structures. The changing of one type of rock into another as a result of heat, pressure, and/or chemical reactions is called **metamorphism** (meht-ah-MOR-fihz-uhm).

Guide for Reading

Focus on this question as you read.

▶ *How are existing rocks changed into metamorphic rocks?*

Figure 13–32 *Metamorphism may cause the minerals in a rock to separate into bands (right). It may also cause impurities in a rock to form minerals, such as garnets, that are not found in other types of rocks. Can you explain why schist (SHIHST), the most common metamorphic rock, may be dotted with garnets (left)?*

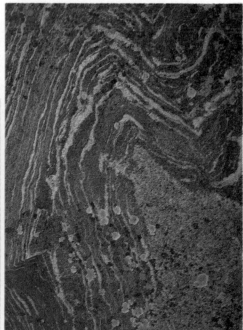

425

Shale

Slate

Granite

Gneiss

Metamorphic rocks may be formed from igneous, sedimentary, or metamorphic rocks. Although rocks remain solid during metamorphism, you can think of heat and pressure as making the rocks flexible enough to undergo change. Temperatures of about 100°C to 800°C cause some minerals to break down, allowing their atoms to form other, more heat-tolerant minerals. Under pressures hundreds or even thousands of times greater than at the Earth's surface, the atoms in rocks rearrange to form denser minerals. The combination of heat and pressure may cause the minerals in the rocks to separate into layers. Chemical reactions involving atoms from outside the original rocks may also occur. During metamorphism, a rock's texture, its mineral composition, and even its chemical composition may be changed.

The amount of heat, pressure, and chemical reactions varies during metamorphism. Thus the degree of metamorphism also varies. If the change in a rock is slight, some of the characteristics of the original rock can still be seen in the new rock. If the change in a rock is great, it may be difficult to tell what the original rock was. The characteristics of the original rock also affect the degree of metamorphism.

Figures 13–33 and 13–34 show some common metamorphic rocks. Each metamorphic rock is paired with one of the kinds of igneous or sedimentary rocks from which it is formed. Interestingly, many metamorphic rocks can be produced from more than one kind of rock. Slate, for example, can be formed from tuff, an igneous rock made of volcanic ash, as well as from shale.

Like igneous and sedimentary rocks, metamorphic rocks can be classified according to texture. The classification groups for metamorphic rocks are based on the arrangement of the grains that make up the rocks.

In the first group, the mineral crystals are arranged in parallel layers, or bands. These rocks are said to be foliated (FOH-lee-ay-tehd). The word foliated comes from the Latin word for leaf. It describes the layers in such metamorphic rocks, which

Figure 13–33 *Heat, pressure, and chemical reactions may transform one type of rock into another type of rock. How are metamorphic rocks classified?*

426

Figure 13–34 *Metamorphism may transform chalk (left) into marble (right). Marble is used to make tiles, rolling pins, and many other decorative and useful objects. Can you name some?*

are thin and flat, like leaves. Most metamorphic rocks are foliated. Foliated rocks—schist, slate, and gneiss, for example—tend to break along their bands.

In the second, smaller group of metamorphic rocks, the rocks are not banded and do not break into layers. These rocks are said to be unfoliated. Marble and quartzite are examples of unfoliated metamorphic rocks.

13–7 Section Review

1. Under what conditions do metamorphic rocks form?
2. What is metamorphism?
3. Name two metamorphic rocks. Name a rock from which each is formed.
4. How does pressure change rock?

Critical Thinking—*Relating Concepts*
5. Explain why metamorphism is often associated with intrusive igneous rocks and with tectonic plate collisions.

ACTIVITY

DISCOVERING

Between a Rock and a Hard Place

How and why do rocks become foliated? Find out by making a model with a small ball of modeling clay, sequins, 30 cm of thread, and two wood blocks.

1. Gently mix the sequins into the modeling clay.

2. Roll the clay into a ball. Using the piece of thread, cut the ball in half. How are the sequins arranged in the clay?

3. Reform the ball of clay. Put the ball on one end of one of the blocks of wood. Using the other block, slowly smear the ball across the surface of the first block.

4. Carefully lift away the top block of wood. What happened to the sequins?

■ Imagine that the sequins were mineral crystals and the clay was rock. Relate what you observed to metamorphism and foliation.

Laboratory Investigation

Creating Crystals

Problem

How do crystals form from liquids?

Materials *(per group)*

glass-marking pencil	dental floss
5 petri dishes	borax
250-mL beaker	alum
stirring rod	copper sulfate
table salt	magnifying glass

Procedure 🧪 🧰

1. With the glass-marking pencil, label the petri dishes as shown in the accompanying diagram.
2. Using a beaker and stirring rod, dissolve 25 grams of table salt in 200 milliliters of hot water.
3. Fill a petri dish with this solution.
4. Place a piece of dental floss in the solution and let it hang over the edge of the dish.
5. Repeat steps 1 through 3 for borax, alum, and copper sulfate.
6. Allow the solutions to evaporate slowly for a day or two. Note which crystals form quickly and which form slowly.
7. With a magnifying glass, observe the crystals formed in the dish and along the dental floss.

Observations

1. Write a brief statement describing the results of this investigation.
2. Describe the appearance of each of the different crystals you grew.

Analysis and Conclusions

1. Prepare a graph that shows how long it took each of your crystals to grow.
2. Why do you think some crystals took longer than others to grow? How might you test your hypothesis?
3. Relate this investigation to sedimentary rock formation.
4. The minerals halite, kalinite, and hydrocyanite are composed from salt, alum, and copper sulfate, respectively. Are the crystals you made in this investigation minerals? Explain.
5. **On Your Own** Rock candy consists of clusters of large crystals of sugar. A wooden lollipop stick is often embedded in the rock candy. How do you think rock candy is made? Design an experiment to test your hypothesis. If you receive the proper permission, perform the experiment you have designed.

Study Guide

Summarizing Key Concepts

13–1 Elements, Compounds, and Mixtures

▲ All matter can be classified into either elements, compounds, or mixtures.

13–2 What Is a Mineral?

▲ A mineral is a naturally occurring, inorganic solid that has a definite chemical composition and crystal shape.

13–3 Uses of Minerals

▲ Ores are minerals or combinations of minerals from which metals and nonmetals can be removed in usable amounts.

13–4 What Is a Rock?

▲ A rock is a hard substance composed of one or more minerals.

▲ Igneous rocks are formed when hot, fluid rock cools and hardens.

▲ Most sedimentary rocks are formed from sediments that are compacted or cemented together.

▲ Metamorphic rocks are formed when chemical reactions, heat, or pressure change existing rocks into new kinds of rocks.

▲ The continuous changing of rocks from one type to another is called the rock cycle.

13–5 Fluid and Fire: Igneous Rocks

▲ Igneous rocks are classified according to their composition and texture.

13–6 Slowly Built Layers: Sedimentary Rocks

▲ Sedimentary rocks can be classified into three categories according to origin of the materials from which they are made: clastic rocks, organic rocks, and chemical rocks.

13–7 Changes in Form: Metamorphic Rocks

▲ Rocks that have been changed from an existing type of rock into a new type of rock are called metamorphic rocks.

Reviewing Key Terms   *Define each term in a complete sentence.*

13–1 Elements, Compounds, and Mixtures
matter
atom
molecule
compound
mixture
chemical formula

13–2 What Is a Mineral?
mineral
inorganic
crystal
luster
hardness
streak
density
cleavage
fracture

13–3 Uses of Minerals
ore
metal
nonmetal
gemstone

13–4 What Is a Rock?
rock
igneous
sedimentary
sediment
metamorphic
rock cycle

13–5 Fluid and Fire
extrusive rock
intrusive rock

13–6 Slowly Built Layers
clastic rock
organic rock
chemical rock

13–7 Changes in Form
metamorphism

Chapter Review

Content Review

Multiple Choice

Choose the letter of the answer that best completes each statement.

1. All matter can be classified into elements, compounds, or
   a. molecules.   c. atoms.
   b. mixtures.   d. crystals.

2. Metamorphic rocks with mineral crystals arranged in parallel layers, or bands, are
   a. clastic.   c. porphyritic.
   b. intrusive.   d. foliated.

3. The way in which a mineral reflects light from its surface is its
   a. streak.   c. fracture.
   b. luster.   d. brilliance.

4. Which rocks can be changed into sediments by weathering and erosion?
   a. sedimentary   c. metamorphic
   b. igneous   d. all of these

5. The softest mineral in the Mohs hardness scale is
   a. fluorite.   c. diamond.
   b. talc.   d. calcite.

6. The breaking of a mineral along smooth, definite surfaces is called
   a. cleavage.   c. splintering.
   b. fracture.   d. foliation.

7. Which of these is an example of an intrusive rock?
   a. granite.   c. shale.
   b. basalt.   d. obsidian.

8. Elements that have shiny surfaces and are able to conduct electricity and heat are called
   a. metals.   c. ores.
   b. nonmetals.   d. gemstones.

True or False

If the statement is true, write "true." If it is false, change the underlined word or words to make the statement true.

1. A <u>molecule</u> is two or more atoms held together by chemical forces.
2. A solid in which the atoms are arranged in a definite and repeating pattern is called a <u>crystal</u>.
3. Substances not formed from living things or the remains of living things are <u>organic</u>.
4. The color of the powder left by a mineral after it is rubbed against a hard, rough surface is called its <u>cleavage</u>.
5. The number <u>1</u> is assigned to the hardest mineral in the Mohs hardness scale.
6. Minerals from which metals and non-metals can be removed in usable amounts are called <u>gemstones</u>.

Concept Mapping

Complete the following concept map for Section 13–2. Then construct a concept map for the entire chapter.

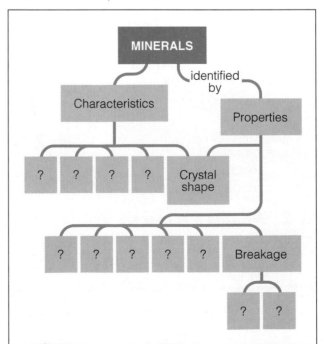

Concept Mastery

Discuss each of the following in a brief paragraph.

1. Describe eight properties used to identify minerals.
2. What are rock-forming minerals? Why are they important? List three examples of rock-forming minerals.
3. Relate the cooling rate of magma to the crystal size in igneous rocks.
4. Compare extrusive and intrusive igneous rocks. Give an example of each.
5. How can the shell of a snail become part of a sedimentary rock?
6. What is metamorphism? Describe how metamorphism affects three different kinds of rock.
7. What is a mineral? A rock?
8. What is the rock cycle? How are rocks changed into different forms in the rock cycle?

Critical Thinking and Problem Solving

Use the skills you have developed in this chapter to answer each of the following.

1. **Interpreting statements** Explain the following statement: You can determine the identity of a mineral by showing what it cannot be. Use specific properties of a mineral in your explanation.
2. **Relating concepts** Explain why scientists study sedimentary rocks to learn about prehistoric life.
3. **Developing a hypothesis** The gemstone opal is a sedimentary rock that consists of microscopic balls of silica (the main ingredient of quartz) cemented together by water and more silica. Explain how this opalized (changed to opal) fossil clam shell may have formed.

4. **Applying concepts** Obsidian and diorite are both igneous rocks. Obsidian looks like black glass. At a distance, diorite is dark gray; up close, it becomes clear that it is made of black, gray, and white grains. How do you account for the differences in these two rocks?
5. **Making inferences** Graphite and diamonds are both made of carbon. Yet they are not considered types of the same mineral. Rubies and sapphires are both made of aluminum oxide. They are considered types of the same mineral, corundum. Why do you think this is so?
6. **Identifying relationships** Suppose you have found a large mass of igneous rock between layers of sedimentary rock. Between the bottom of the igneous rock and the sedimentary rock you observe a thin layer of quartzite. The igneous rock itself is fine grained and very dark. What can you infer about the igneous formation's history?
7. **Using the writing process** Imagine that you are a particle of limestone. Write an autobiography entitled A Sedimental Journey, in which you describe your adventures as you travel through the rock cycle.

Weathering and Soil Formation

14

Guide for Reading

After you read the following sections, you will be able to

14–1 Weathering
- Distinguish between mechanical and chemical weathering.
- Recognize several factors that affect the rate of weathering.

14–2 Soil Formation
- Explain how soil is formed.

14–3 Soil Composition
- Identify the layers of mature soil.
- Recognize the importance of organic material and pore spaces to the quality of soil.

If you have ever been to the Black Hills of South Dakota, you have probably visited Mount Rushmore. Carved into a high granite cliff of this mountain are the faces of four famous presidents—George Washington, Thomas Jefferson, Abraham Lincoln, and Theodore Roosevelt. Since their completion in 1941, these carvings have attracted visitors from all over the world.

Yet several years ago, this beautiful monument was almost ruined. After a little more than forty years, the granite rock on these mammoth carvings was beginning to crumble. The presidents' faces were beginning to wear away. Trees and grass were sprouting from the head of George Washington! Worst of all, large pieces of the carved rock were falling off. Can you imagine what Lincoln would look like without his nose?

Luckily, workers for the National Park Service were able to save the monument before more serious damage occurred. Using plaster and metal spikes, they were able to keep the presidents' faces from crumbling. But what had made hard, solid granite crumble and crack? As you read this chapter, you will discover the answer.

Journal *Activity*

You and Your World   Plant a few seeds in a pot of soil. It does not make much difference what seeds you plant. Keep the soil moist, but not too wet. Watch the pot for several weeks. Record your observations, either as words or as drawings, in your journal.

This National Park Service worker is repairing damage to the Mount Rushmore National Memorial caused by weathering. Look below the worker to see where a crack in President Lincoln's nose has been filled with plaster.

Guide for Reading

Focus on these questions as you read.

▶ What is weathering?

▶ How do mechanical and chemical weathering affect the surface of the Earth?

Activity Bank

The Brass Is Always Greener, p. 769

Figure 14–1 *The effects of weathering often take only a short time to become evident—as you may know if you have ever left a bicycle or roller skates out in the rain! Rust, which results from weathering, may appear quite quickly on exposed metal objects (right). Most of the time, however, weathering takes a long time. It took thousands of years for this talus in Glacier National Park in Montana to form (left). How does a talus form?*

14–1 Weathering

The reason the rocks of Mount Rushmore—as well as many other natural features of the Earth's surface—have cracked and crumbled is that the Earth's surface is constantly undergoing a natural breaking-down process. **The breaking down of rocks and other materials on the Earth's surface is called weathering.** A slow, continuous process, **weathering** affects all substances exposed to the atmosphere.

Because weathering of rocks is such a slow process, the effects are not always easily observed. But other types of weathering are more obvious. You have probably seen the effects of weathering if you have ever noticed paint peeling on the side of a house. Or perhaps you have noticed changes that occur on a brick building. New bricks have a bright red color and sharp corners and edges. The bricks of an old building are darker in color. The corners and edges are rounded. Pieces of the bricks may have broken off.

As you have just read, rocks on the Earth's surface also undergo weathering. Large pieces often break off the rocks. Over a long period of time, the rocks crumble and decay. You can see the results of weathering at the base of a mountain or on a mountain slope. Pieces of broken rocks pile up in these areas. These piles of rock fragments are called talus (TAY-luhs).

Rocks on the Earth's surface are broken down by two types of weathering. When the forces of

weathering break rocks into smaller pieces but do not change the chemical makeup of the rocks, the process is called **mechanical weathering.** When the chemical makeup of the rocks is changed, the process is called **chemical weathering.**

Mechanical Weathering

During **mechanical weathering,** rocks are broken into different shapes and smaller pieces. At the beginning of the weathering process, typical rock fragments are sharp and angular. As weathering continues, they become smooth and rounded. Although there are several different agents, or causes, of mechanical weathering, each results in the breaking down of rocks.

TEMPERATURE Rocks can be broken apart by changes in temperature. During the day, rocks on the Earth's surface are heated by the sun's rays. The outside of the rock heats up and begins to expand. But the inside of the rock remains cool and does not expand. When the air temperature drops at night, the outside of the rock cools and contracts.

The next day, the heat from the sun causes the outside of the rock to expand again. The cycle of heating and cooling continues. The repeated changes in temperature cause particles on the surface of the rock to crack or flake off. Often the pieces break off in curved sheets or slabs parallel to the rock's surface. This type of breaking off of rock is called **exfoliation** (ehks-foh-lee-AY-shuhn). Other agents of mechanical weathering also cause exfoliation.

FROST ACTION Unlike most liquids, water expands when it freezes. The repeated freezing and melting of water is a common cause of mechanical weathering. This process of weathering is called **frost action.**

Frost action occurs when water seeps into a small opening or crack in a rock. When the temperature falls below 0°C, the freezing point of water, the water in the crack freezes and expands. The crack in the rock is made larger by the pressure of the expanding water. In time, the freezing and melting of the water cause the rock to break into pieces. The cracks and potholes you see in roads or in cement driveways are often the result of frost action.

Figure 14–2 *Pieces of this granite rock in Yosemite National Park in California are flaking off in curved sheets parallel to the rock's surface. What is this process called? What causes it?*

ACTIVITY

DISCOVERING

Expanding Water

1. Fill a clear plastic container about three-fourths full of water. Mark the water level on the outside of the container. Use a piece of tape or a marking pencil.

2. Place the water-filled container in the freezer for at least 6 hours.

3. Remove the container and observe the level of the ice that has formed. Explain your observations.

■ Develop a plan to use frozen water to break up large rocks.

435

Figure 14–3 *As this cedar tree grows, its roots pry apart the boulder on which it is growing. What is this type of mechanical weathering called?*

ORGANIC ACTIVITY Plants and animals can cause mechanical weathering. The roots of plants sometimes loosen rock material. A plant growing in a crack in a rock can make the crack larger as the plant's roots grow and spread out. This type of mechanical weathering is called **root-pry.** Root-pry is an organic activity, or an activity caused by living things.

GRAVITY Gravity is another agent of mechanical weathering. Sometimes gravity pulls loosened rocks down mountain cliffs in a **landslide.** A landslide is a large movement of loose rocks and soil. As the rocks fall, they collide with one another and break into smaller pieces. Falling rocks generally occur in areas where a road or highway has been cut through a rock formation, leaving cliffs on one or both sides of the road.

ABRASION Wind-blown sand causes mechanical weathering of rocks by **abrasion** (uh-BRAY-zhuhn). Abrasion is the wearing away of rocks by solid particles carried by wind, water, or other forces. In desert regions, the wind easily picks up and moves sand particles. The sharp edges of the sand particles scrape off small pieces of exposed rocks. Over a long period of time, the abrading sand can create unusual shapes in exposed rocks. See Figure 14–4.

Water also causes abrasion of rocks. Running water such as a river carries along loose rocks and other particles. The moving rocks and particles collide,

Figure 14–4 *Mechanical weathering can tear down the sides of mountains or wear away rocks to produce unusual formations. What agent of mechanical weathering caused this road-blocking landslide to occur (right)? How were the "Sunbonnet Rock" and "Navaho Twins" formed (left)?*

scrape against one another, and eventually break. In addition, the moving rocks scrape the rocks in the riverbed. This action makes riverbed rocks smooth and rounded.

Chemical Weathering

During **chemical weathering,** changes occur in the mineral composition, or chemical makeup, of rocks. As chemical changes take place, minerals can be added to or removed from rocks. Or the minerals in rocks can be broken down in a process called decomposition. Many substances react chemically with rocks to break them down.

WATER Most chemical weathering is caused by water and carbon dioxide. (You will learn more about the action of carbon dioxide on the next page.) Water can dissolve most of the minerals that hold rocks together. Rocks that dissolve in water are said to be soluble.

Water can also form acids when it mixes with certain gases in the atmosphere. These acids often speed up the decomposition of rocks. Water can also combine with a mineral to form a completely different mineral. For example, when the mineral feldspar reacts with water, it forms clay.

OXIDATION Chemical weathering is also caused by **oxidation** (ahk-suh-DAY-shuhn). Oxidation is the process in which oxygen chemically combines with another substance. The result of oxidation is the formation of an entirely different substance.

Figure 14–5 *Oxidation has turned the rocks red in the Valley of Fire, Nevada. Water may dissolve away solid limestone to form vast networks of underground caverns. Can you explain how chemical weathering at the surface resulted in the formation of stalactites and stalagmites within this cave?*

437

Weathering in Action

1. Place a piece of steel wool outside your school in an area where it will be exposed to the air.

2. Place another piece of steel wool in a sheltered place in your classroom.

3. Examine both pieces of steel wool daily for one month. Record your observations each day.

What changes do you observe? What are the conditions that contributed to these differences?

■ Devise a way to protect a piece of steel wool from weathering. With your teacher's help, plan an investigation to see if your method of protection works.

Figure 14–6 *Lichens, like plants, are living things that can release weak acids into their environment. How do these lichens affect the rock on which they grow?*

Iron in rocks combines with oxygen in the air to form iron oxide, or rust. This is one example of chemical weathering by oxidation. The color of some rocks is an indication that oxidation is occurring. If oxidation is taking place, the inner material of a rock will be a different color from the outer material. What color is iron rust?

CARBONATION When carbon dioxide dissolves in water, a weak acid called carbonic acid is formed. Carbonic acid is the acid used to give soft drinks their fizz. When carbonic acid reacts chemically with other substances, the process of **carbonation** occurs.

In nature carbonic acid is formed when carbon dioxide in the air dissolves in rain. This slightly acidic rain falls to the ground and sinks into the soil. The carbonic acid is able to dissolve certain rocks on or beneath the surface of the Earth. Fortunately, carbonic acid is too weak to be harmful to plants and animals. But it does slowly decompose feldspars and limestone.

SULFURIC ACID The air in certain areas is polluted with sulfur oxides. Sulfur oxides are a byproduct of the burning of coal as a source of energy. These compounds dissolve in rainwater to form sulfuric acid. Rain that contains sulfuric acid is one type of acid rain. Sulfuric acid is a much stronger acid than carbonic acid. Sulfuric acid corrodes, or wears away, rocks, metals, and other materials very quickly. What effects do you predict sulfuric acid would have on monuments and buildings?

PLANT ACIDS You have read before that plants can be agents of mechanical weathering. Plants can also cause chemical weathering. Plants produce weak acids that dissolve certain minerals in rocks.

For example, mosses produce weak acids. Mosses are low-growing plants that resemble a soft green carpet. Mosses often grow in damp areas. As they grow, the acids they produce seep into rocks and dissolve some of the minerals. Gradually, the rocks break into smaller pieces. Lichens are another type of living thing that produces weak acids capable of dissolving the minerals in rocks. The chemical weathering produced by mosses and lichens is important in the formation of soil.

Rate of Weathering

The rate of weathering, or how fast weathering takes place, depends on several factors. One factor is the composition of the rocks. Two different types of rock in the same climate can weather differently, depending on the minerals that make up each rock type. If the minerals in a rock resist chemical weathering, the rock is called a **stable rock.**

The stability of a rock can vary, depending on the climate in which that rock is found. Limestone, for example, weathers vary little in a dry, warm climate. But in a wet climate, moisture in combination with weak acids can completely dissolve limestone.

Granite is a stable rock in cool, dry climates. But in tropical climates, granite decomposes relatively quickly. The abundant rainfall hastens the breakdown of feldspars, a main ingredient of granite. The feldspars become clay minerals, which are too weak to hold the rock together. The more moisture there is in an area, the faster rocks will weather.

The amount of time that rock is exposed on the Earth's surface also affects its rate of weathering. A very old rock that has not been exposed to the various forces of weathering can remain almost unchanged. But if a newly formed rock is immediately deposited on the Earth's surface, it will begin to weather right away.

The amount of exposed surface area on a rock also affects its rate of weathering. As rocks are broken down into many small pieces, more rock surfaces are exposed and more weathering takes place. In rocks that contain many joints or cracks, various chemicals easily come in contact with the rock surfaces and break them down.

ACTIVITY
DISCOVERING

Weathering Rates

1. Place an antacid tablet inside a folded piece of paper. Put on safety goggles. Carefully tap the tablet with a hammer until the tablet has broken into small pieces.

2. Place the broken tablet in a glass. Place an unbroken tablet in another glass.

3. Add 10 mL of water to both glasses at the same time. Observe both reactions until they are finished. Record your observations.

What differences in the rate of reaction did you observe?

■ What relationship can you identify from the activity?

■ Develop a hypothesis that relates the results of this activity to the weathering process in nature.

Figure 14–7 *Granite weathers slowly in the cool, dry climate of Yosemite National Park (left). In tropical climates, granite weathers more quickly (right).*

1. What is weathering? Describe the two types.
2. In what two ways do plants contribute to the weathering of rocks?
3. Identify several factors that influence the rate at which weathering occurs.

Connection—*Ecology*
4. A limestone statue of a dog is placed in a park in Miami, Florida. What types of natural forces would affect the weathering of this statue?

Guide for Reading

Focus on this question as you read.

▶ How does soil form?

14–2 Soil Formation

The weathering of rocks on the Earth's surface results in the formation of soil. **Soil is formed when rocks are continuously broken down by weathering.** As rocks weather, they break into smaller pieces. These pieces are broken down into even smaller pieces to form soil.

The formation of soil is extremely important to most living organisms. Plants depend on soil directly as a source of food. Soil supplies plants with minerals and water needed for growth. Animals depend on soil indirectly for the materials they need to live. Some animals eat plants; other animals eat animals that eat plants. You may already know that a lion

Figure 14–8 *Almost all living things depend on soil. Plants require minerals from the soil in order to live and grow. Why is this bison, as well as other animals, dependent on soil? Many living things make their home in the soil. The mole's broad, shovel-shaped paws are just one adaptation for its life underground.*

eats other animals. But even a mighty lion depends on plants that grow in soil. The zebras and gnus that are food for a lion eat plants. In this way a lion depends on soil for its survival.

Sometimes soil remains on top of its parent rock, or the rock from which it was formed. This soil is called **residual** (rih-ZIHJ-oo-uhl) **soil.** Residual soil has a composition similar to that of the parent rock it covers. Some soil is moved away from its parent rock by water, wind, glaciers, and waves. Soil that is moved away from its place of origin is called **transported soil.** Transported soil can be very different in composition from the layer of rock it covers. In either case, the layer of rock beneath the soil is called **bedrock.**

Living organisms help to form soil. Some organisms produce acids that chemically break down rocks. Mosses and lichens are two examples that you should recall from the previous section. Certain bacteria in the soil cause the decay of dead plants and animals. Decay is the breaking down of plants and animals into the substances they are made of. This decaying material is called **humus** (HYOO-muhs). Humus is a dark-colored material that is important for the growth of plants. Some of the chemicals

Figure 14–9 *Soil formation begins when solid parent rock is broken down into smaller pieces by weathering (left). As weathering continues, the rock is broken down further into soil particles (center). Under certain conditions, a thick layer of soil will develop above the parent rock (right).*

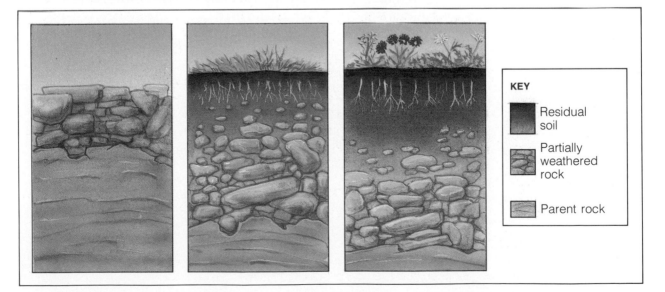

KEY

Residual soil

Partially weathered rock

Parent rock

PROBLEM Solving

Plants in Pots

José and Carol spent a day in a commercial greenhouse. Walking up and down the rows of plants, the two friends noticed that different kinds of soils were used to grow various plants. For example, the soil in pots that had cactuses growing was very sandy. The pots that held tropical plants had a dark brown soil rich in humus.

On their return home, the two friends wondered about their observations. What could explain the differences they observed in the kinds of soils used to grow different plants?

Designing an Experiment

Design an investigation to determine if the kind of soil used to grow a particular kind of plant is important. If you decide to do this investigation and have your teacher's approval, keep a picture record of your observations.

produced during the process of decay speed up the breakdown of rocks into soil.

Living things such as moles, earthworms, ants, and beetles help to break apart large pieces of soil as they burrow through the ground. The burrows allow water to move rapidly through the soil. The water speeds up weathering of the underlying rock.

14–2 Section Review

1. How is soil formed?
2. Compare residual soil and transported soil.
3. What is humus? Why is it important for plant growth?

Critical Thinking—*Applying Concepts*

4. Plants get water and minerals needed for growth from soil. What do animals get from soil?

14-3 Soil Composition

Pieces of weathered rock and organic material, or humus, are the two main ingredients of soil. Organic material is material that was once living or was formed by the activity of living organisms. Rock particles form more than 80 percent of soil. Air and water are also present in soil.

Clay and quartz are the most abundant minerals in soil. Because clay and quartz are very stable minerals, they exist in the greatest quantities. Potassium, phosphorus, and the nitrogen compounds called nitrates are important chemicals in soil. Because these chemicals are vital to plant growth, they are included in the fertilizers added to soil.

Air and water fill the spaces between soil particles. These spaces are called **pore spaces.** Plants and animals use the water and air in these spaces, as well as the minerals dissolved in the water. Pore spaces are important for healthy plant roots. Plant roots need oxygen, which they get from the air in the pore spaces.

The composition of soil varies from place to place. The type of rock broken down by weathering determines the kinds of minerals in the soil. For example, soil formed largely from a parent rock of limestone will be different from soil formed from a parent rock of sandstone.

The type of weathering also affects the composition of soil. Mechanical weathering produces soil with a composition similar to the rock being weathered. Chemical weathering produces soil with a composition different from that of the rock being weathered. Why do you think this is so?

Soil Texture

The type of weathering also affects soil texture. Texture refers to the size of individual soil particles. Soil particles vary from very small to large.

Both mechanical and chemical weathering first break rocks down into gravel. Gravel particles are between 2 and 64 millimeters in diameter. Both types of weathering then break gravel down into

Guide for Reading

Focus on these questions as you read.

▶ What are the two main ingredients of soil?

▶ What are some characteristics of each soil horizon?

Figure 14–10 *The reddish, sandy soil is low in humus. How can you tell that the silty clay soil is high in humus?*

sand. Sand particles are less than 2 millimeters in diameter.

Silt is made of very small broken crystals of rock formed in the same way as sand is. Silt particles are less than 1/16 of a millimeter in diameter. Clay is the smallest soil particle produced by chemical and mechanical weathering. Clay particles are smaller than silt particles. They are, in fact, less than 1/256 millimeter in diameter.

Soil Horizons

As soil forms, it develops separate soil layers called horizons (huh-RIGH-zuhns). Each soil **horizon** is different. Imagine making a vertical slice through these horizons. You would observe one horizon piled on top of another. Such a view is called a cross section. A cross section of the soil horizons is called a **soil profile.** A soil profile shows the different layers of soil. A soil profile is shown in Figure 14–11.

Soil that has developed three layers is called mature soil. It takes many thousands of years and the proper conditions for soil to develop three layers. Some soil contains only two layers. This soil is called immature soil. Immature soil has been formed more recently than mature soil has.

Figure 14–11 *As soil forms, it develops distinct layers called horizons (right). What horizons can you identify in the forest soil profile (left)?*

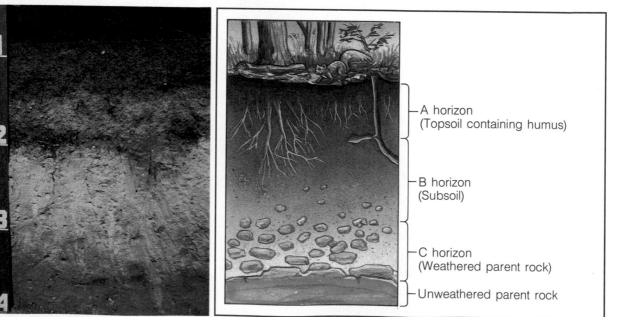

A horizon
(Topsoil containing humus)

B horizon
(Subsoil)

C horizon
(Weathered parent rock)

Unweathered parent rock

The uppermost layer of mature soil is called the A horizon. The A horizon is a dark-colored soil layer in which much activity by living organisms takes place. Bacteria, earthworms, beetles, and other organisms in this horizon constantly add to the soil through the process of decay. These organisms also break apart large pieces of soil as they move through the ground.

The soil in the A horizon is called **topsoil.** Topsoil consists mostly of humus and other organic materials. Humus supplies minerals essential for plant growth. Because humus is spongy, it stores water. It also contains many pore spaces through which air and water can reach plant roots. Topsoil is the most fertile part of the soil. Plants are able to grow well in the fertile, or nutrient-rich, soil of the A horizon.

Water that soaks into the ground washes some minerals from the A horizon into the second layer of soil, or the B horizon. This process is called **leaching** (LEECH-ihng). The B horizon is just below the A horizon. In addition to leached-out minerals, the B horizon is made of clay and some humus. The soil in the B horizon is called **subsoil.** Subsoil is formed very slowly. The B horizon may take more than 100,000 years to form!

The third layer of soil is called the C horizon. The C horizon consists of partly weathered rock. The C horizon extends down to the top of the unweathered parent rock. The composition of soil in the C horizon is similar to that of the parent rock.

Whether all three soil horizons develop depends on several factors. Time is one of the most important factors in soil formation. The longer a rock is exposed to the forces of weathering, the more it is broken down. Mature soil is formed if all three layers have had time to develop.

In some places, the upper layers of soil are removed, and the rocks below the soil are exposed. The weathering process then forms new soil from the exposed rocks. This recently formed soil is immature because there has not been enough time for all three soil layers to form. For example, soil in the northern regions, where glacial erosion has taken place, is immature soil. The glaciers that covered the area removed much of the soil from the top horizons. Since then, weathering has produced new soil.

Figure 14–12 *A backyard garden can be a source of vegetables, flowers, and fun. How does the soil in a garden affect the plants grown there? Why do many people add topsoil to their garden?*

A**CTIVITY**

Studying a Soil Profile

1. Use a shovel to dig down about 0.5 m to obtain a soil sample from your yard or from a yard in your neighborhood. Remember to ask permission before you begin to dig. Try not to disturb the soil too much, or you will not be able to observe the different soil layers.

2. Observe the soil sample. Answer the following questions:

a. How deep is the topsoil layer? What color is it?

b. How deep is the subsoil layer? What color is it?

c. How does the soil in the two layers differ?

d. Did you find the layer of parent rock? If so, describe this layer.

Is your soil sample mature soil?

Figure 14–13 *The soil that once covered this rock has been removed by large moving sheets of ice known as glaciers. The broad horizontal groove in the rock was carved by a large stone embedded in the bottom of a slowly moving glacier (right). Soil may also be removed by the action of heavy rains or floods (left).*

Climate is another important factor in the formation of soil. In areas with heavy rainfall and warm temperatures, weathering takes place more rapidly. Organisms are more plentiful in the soil in these areas. They speed up the chemical and mechanical weathering of rocks. Heavy rainfall in tropical regions of the world washes much of the topsoil away. But because many plants and animals live in this climate, soil that is washed away is replaced quickly.

The type of rock in an area also affects soil formation. Some rocks do not weather as rapidly as others do. Rocks that do not break down easily do not form soil rapidly. For example, in some climates it takes a long time for granite to break down. So soil formation from granite in these climates is relatively slow. But sandstone breaks and crumbles into sand very quickly. Soil formation from the weathering of sandstone is rapid.

The surface features of the region also determine the speed at which soil is formed. On very steep slopes, rainwater running off the land erodes the soil and exposes rock to weathering.

ACTIVITY READING

Blowing Sands

One of the great tragedies of the first half of the twentieth century was the creation of the dust bowl. John Steinbeck wrote about the lives of people who lived in the area of the dust bowl in a powerful novel called *The Grapes of Wrath.* You might like to read this moving novel that details the triumph of the human spirit over disastrous living conditions.

14–3 Section Review

1. What is a soil horizon?
2. Describe a typical soil profile.
3. What two factors affect soil composition?

Critical Thinking—*Relating Concepts*
4. Some people buy topsoil from a garden center to add to their own garden soil. Why is this added topsoil beneficial for plant growth?

A Search for Soil to Produce Food

If you could fly over a *tropical rain forest,* you would notice a thick covering of trees. In fact, the trees grow so thick that you would not see the plants that grow low to the ground. And obviously, from the air, you wouldn't even catch the tiniest glimpse of the soil.

From your observations, you might logically conclude that the soil in a tropical rain forest is rich and fertile—good soil for plants to grow in. If you were a farmer, it might seem to you that the land here could produce abundant crops.

Appearances in a tropical rain forest are deceiving, however. When the forest is cleared to make room for crops or for pastures, something strange and terrible happens.

The first year or two, crops or grasses grow well. But with each successive year, the growth of the crops or grasses is greatly diminished. The soil loses its fertility, and the loss is permanent. Why does this happen?

The answer lies in two apparent opposites: fire and rain. Tropical forests are cleared by what is called a *slash-and-burn* technique. The ashes from the burned forest act like fertilizer, adding minerals to the soil. This is why crops and grasses can be grown on newly cleared areas. In a year or two, however, heavy rains wash the minerals from the soil. The rains even wash away the soil itself. In between the rains, the soil bakes in the sun and develops a hard crust that discourages plant growth.

The rains are not a problem in an undisturbed tropical rain forest. There, the loss of minerals is balanced by the formation of humus. The thick vegetation prevents soil from washing away. The native plants also keep the soil moist and loose, so a crust does not form.

But rains eventually destroy the land that was cleared for cropland and pastures. More forest lands are slashed-and-burned, and this sad cycle continues. Meanwhile, the abandoned fields and pastures become scrubland or deserts.

Laboratory Investigation

Observing the Effect of Chemical Weathering on Rocks

Problem

What rocks are affected by carbonated water—a form of carbonic acid?

Materials (per group)

> 8 baby food jars
> carbonated water
> masking tape
> 2 fragments of each of the following rocks:
>   limestone, marble, granite, sandstone

Procedure 🧪

1. Fill four baby food jars three-fourths full of carbonated water. Fill the remaining four baby food jars three-fourths full of tap water. Carefully place the jars on your desk.

2. Use masking tape to label the jars: limestone and carbonated water, limestone and tap water, marble and carbonated water, marble and tap water, granite and carbonated water, granite and tap water, sandstone and carbonated water, sandstone and tap water.

3. Place the appropriate rock fragment into each labeled jar.

4. Observe the effects. Record your observations in a chart similar to the one shown.

5. Continue to observe the rock specimens. After 20 minutes, record your observations again.

6. Let the jars stand overnight. Observe them again the next day. Record any changes in the rock fragments.

Observations

1. Which samples show that a change has taken place?

2. For each sample, how did the effects produced by carbonated water compare with the effects produced by tap water?

Analysis and Conclusions

1. What evidence supports the idea that a chemical change has occurred?

2. What is the effect of time on the rate of weathering?

3. How does carbonic acid affect rocks?

4. **On Your Own** Obtain some other rock samples. Perform a similar investigation to determine the effect of carbonic acid on these rock samples. Then using all your rock samples, design an experiment to determine whether temperature has an effect on chemical weathering.

Rock	Carbonated Water			Tap Water		
	Initial	20 min	24 hr	Initial	20 min	24 hr
Limestone						
Marble						
Granite						
Sandstone						

Study Guide

Summarizing Key Concepts

14–1 Weathering

▲ Mechanical weathering causes rocks to be broken into smaller pieces, but the chemical makeup of the rocks is not changed.

▲ The agents of mechanical weathering are temperature, frost action, organic activity, gravity, and abrasion.

▲ Chemical weathering causes a change in the mineral composition of rocks.

▲ Chemical weathering is caused by water, oxidation, carbonation, sulfuric acid, and acids produced by plants.

▲ The rate of weathering depends on the composition of the rock, the amount of time the rock is exposed on the Earth's surface, and the amount of exposed surface area of the rock.

14–2 Soil Formation

▲ Soil is formed when rocks are continuously broken down by weathering.

▲ Soil forms above a solid layer of rock called bedrock.

▲ Residual soil remains on top of its parent rock. Transported soil is moved from its place of origin.

▲ Humus is the material formed from the decay of plants and animals.

14–3 Soil Composition

▲ The two main ingredients of soil are pieces of weathered rock and organic material.

▲ Air and water fill the pore spaces between particles of soil.

▲ The type of rocks broken down by weathering determines the kinds of minerals in the soil.

▲ As soil forms, it develops separate layers, or horizons. A cross section of the soil horizons is called a soil profile.

▲ A typical soil profile has an A horizon, or topsoil, a B horizon, or subsoil, and a C horizon.

Reviewing Key Terms

Define each term in a complete sentence.

14–1 Weathering
weathering
mechanical weathering
exfoliation
frost action
root-pry
landslide
abrasion
chemical weathering
oxidation
carbonation
stable rock

14–2 Soil Formation
residual soil
transported soil
bedrock
humus

14–3 Soil Composition
pore space
horizon
soil profile
topsoil
leaching
subsoil

Chapter Review

Content Review

Multiple Choice

Choose the letter of the answer that best completes each statement.

1. The breaking off of rock pieces in curved sheets parallel to the rock's surface is
   a. oxidation.
   b. carbonation.
   c. root-pry.
   d. exfoliation.

2. Rocks can be broken apart by
   a. organic activity.
   b. root-pry.
   c. frost action.
   d. all of these.

3. The wearing away of rocks by solid particles carried by wind, water, and other forces is called
   a. exfoliation.
   b. abrasion.
   c. oxidation.
   d. gravity.

4. Most chemical weathering is caused by
   a. air pollution.
   b. water.
   c. sulfuric acid.
   d. gravity.

5. The decayed parts of plants and animals in soil are called
   a. humus.
   b. topsoil.
   c. residual soil.
   d. mature soil.

6. If the minerals in a rock enable the rock to resist chemical weathering, the rock is described as
   a. stable.
   b. soluble.
   c. organic.
   d. residual.

7. The solid rock layer beneath the soil is called
   a. transported soil.
   b. bedrock.
   c. residual rock.
   d. mature soil.

8. The size of individual soil particles is called soil
   a. profile.
   b. horizon.
   c. texture.
   d. porosity.

9. The process in which water washes minerals from one soil horizon to another is called
   a. leaching.
   b. oxidation.
   c. exfoliation.
   d. claying.

True or False

If the statement is true, write "true." If it is false, change the underlined word or words to make the statement true.

1. When gravity pulls loosened rocks down a mountain cliff, a <u>landslide</u> occurs.
2. When the chemical makeup of rocks is changed, <u>mechanical</u> weathering occurs.
3. A rock that dissolves easily in water is said to be <u>stable</u>.
4. Rain that contains <u>humus</u> is called acid rain.
5. <u>Transported</u> soil has a composition similar to that of the bedrock it covers.
6. <u>Clay and quartz</u> are the most abundant minerals in soil.
7. The largest particles found in soil are <u>silt</u>.
8. The soil in the B horizon is called <u>topsoil</u>.

Concept Mapping

Complete the following concept map for Section 14–1. Then construct a concept map for the entire chapter.

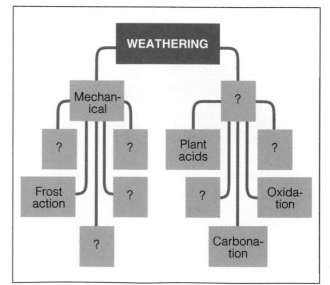

Concept Mastery

Discuss each of the following in a brief paragraph.

1. What is the difference between mechanical and chemical weathering?
2. How is the weathering of rocks helpful to life on Earth?
3. Briefly describe how soil is formed.
4. What is acid rain? How does it contribute to weathering?
5. Some scientists say the "soil is alive." What does this statement mean?
6. What is the difference between residual soil and transported soil?
7. Why are pore spaces important for good plant growth?
8. How does weathering affect the texture of soil?
9. Describe a typical soil profile.
10. Compare the following types of soil particles: gravel, sand, silt, and clay.

Critical Thinking and Problem Solving

Use the skills you have developed in this chapter to answer each of the foillowing.

1. **Relating concepts** Why would frost action not be a major cause of weathering in polar climates?
2. **Making predictions** Predict what would happen if you rubbed a piece of granite with sandpaper. If you rubbed a piece of sandstone. What type of weathering is simulated in this activity?
3. **Analyzing data** In an experiment to measure soil's ability to hold water, particle size and the amount of humus the soil contained were tested. The accompanying data table shows the results.

   Use the data to construct a graph that represents the relationship between the amount of water retained and the size of the soil particles.

   Based on your graph, describe a type of soil that would supply water for plant roots during a period of little rainfall.

4. **Making inferences** How would you determine if a soil was formed by mechanical or by chemical weathering?
5. **Relating concepts** If you overwater a potted plant for a period of time, the plant will probably die. However, in nature plants do not usually die after periods of heavy rain. Explain why this is so.
6. **Using the writing process** Many farmers and scientists are concerned that topsoil is being washed away from the land at a dangerous rate. They feel that we are in danger of losing one of our most valuable assets. Yct few people outside the scientific and farming community seem concerned. Write a letter to your representative in Congress, voicing your concern about this problem. Make sure you explain why it is important to protect our valuable soil resources.

	Small Particles		Medium Particles		Large Particles	
	With humus	Without humus	With humus	Without humus	With humus	Without humus
Water retained by soil	50.0 mL	20.8 mL	44.6 mL	13.6 mL	39.8 mL	10.2 mL

Erosion and Deposition

15

To the people of the Huaylas Valley, the glacier
(a huge mass of ice and snow perched on the steep
northwest face of Peru's highest peak) was a familiar
sight. The people hardly took notice of the glacier.
It had been there for as long as they could remember—creeping forward when fed by winter snows
and shrinking back when warmed by summer
temperatures. For this glacier, named Glacier 511
by Peruvian geologists, was only one of hundreds
that dotted the Andes Mountains.

Then at 6:13 PM on January 10, 1962, Glacier 511
stirred. A great mass of ice about 182 meters long
and nearly 1 kilometer wide broke loose. As it
hurtled down the cliff, it picked up tons of rock
material. It plowed up chunks of granite as large
as houses. It swept up everything in its path. Within
8 minutes, the wall of ice, snow, rock, and mud had
covered a distance of 16 kilometers and buried an
estimated 4000 people from 9 villages. It had
demonstrated the awesome power of moving ice.

Glaciers—along with winds, waves, running water,
and gravity—constantly reshape the Earth's surface.
In this chapter you will learn about the effects of
these powerful forces of nature.

Journal *Activity*

You and Your World Have you ever visited the Grand Canyon or seen
pictures of it? It is a remarkable place. In your journal, write a postcard to
a friend describing a visit, real or imaginary, to the Grand Canyon. Try to
capture in words the immense size of the canyon.

 *A glacier similar to Glacier 511 sits peacefully above a village
in the Huaylas Valley of Peru.*

15–1 Changing the Earth's Surface

Millions of years ago, the Colorado River flowed slowly across a broad flat area in present day Arizona. If you were to visit the area today, you would see a huge gorge called the Grand Canyon. The Grand Canyon was carved out of the Earth by **erosion** (ih-ROH-zhuhn). Erosion is the process by which weathered rock and soil particles are moved from one place to another. In Chapter 14 you learned that weathering is the breaking down of rocks and other materials on the Earth's surface. Erosion carries away the products of weathering.

Rocks and soil particles carried away by erosion are deposited in other places. Over time, these materials build up to create new landforms. The process by which sediments are laid down in new locations is called **deposition** (dehp-uh-ZIHSH-uhn). Both erosion and deposition change the shape of the Earth's surface. Erosion moves materials from place to place. Deposition builds new landforms. Weathering, erosion, and deposition form a cycle of forces that wear down and build up the Earth's surface.

Erosion can be caused by gravity, wind, running water, glaciers, and waves. These are the five agents of erosion. An agent of erosion is a material or force that moves sediments from place to place.

Figure 15–1 *For millions of years, the Colorado River carved a huge gorge out of a once broad, flat area of the Earth's surface. Today, a small raft is dwarfed by the tall cliffs of the Grand Canyon.*

15–1 Section Review

1. What are the five agents of erosion? How does erosion change the Earth's surface?
2. What is deposition? How does deposition change the surface of the Earth?

Critical Thinking—*Relating Concepts*
3. A girl using a garden hose to water a vegetable bed notices that a slight depression forms where the water hits the ground. She also notices that excess water running down a cement path is brown. Relate these observations to the formation of the Grand Canyon.

15–2 Gravity

Gravity pulls rocks and soil down slopes. The downhill movement of sediments caused by gravity is called **mass wasting.** Mass wasting can occur rapidly or slowly. In either case, sediments come to rest at the bottom of a slope in a formation called a talus. You have read about a talus in Chapter 14.

One example of rapid mass wasting is a landslide. A landslide is a tumbling of soil, rocks, and boulders down a slope. A landslide can be caused by an earthquake, a volcanic eruption, or the weakening of supporting rocks as a result of heavy rain. Once a landslide begins, it can move millions of tons of rocks down a slope and cause tremendous damage.

A mudflow is another example of rapid mass wasting. A mudflow usually occurs after a heavy rain. The rain mixes with the soil to form mud. The mud begins to slide downhill, picking up more soil and becoming thicker. A mudflow can move just about anything in its path—including boulders and houses.

Sometimes a block of rock or soil on the face of a steep slope will slip down so that its upper surface is tilted backward as it moves. This type of mass wasting is called slump. Slump, which may involve more than one block of material, is also known as slope failure. Can you see why?

Guide for Reading

Focus on this question as you read.

▶ *How does gravity cause erosion?*

Figure 15–2 *Loose rocks can be moved down a hill by the force of gravity in a form of mass wasting known as a landslide (left). A mudslide (center) and a slump (right) are two other examples of earth movement due to gravity.*

Earthflows and soil creep are two examples of slow mass wasting. An earthflow usually occurs after a heavy rain. A mass of soil and plant life slowly slides down a slope. Soil creep is the slowest kind of mass wasting. Alternating periods of freezing and thawing, animal activity, or water movement disturb the soil particles. As the particles begin to move, gravity pulls them slowly downhill.

15–2 Section Review

1. How does gravity cause erosion?
2. What is rapid mass wasting? Give two examples.
3. What is slow mass wasting? Give two examples.

Critical Thinking—*Language Arts*
4. Why is mass wasting an appropriate term?

Guide for Reading

Focus on this question as you read.

▶ *Where does wind cause the greatest amount of erosion?*

ACTIVITY
DISCOVERING

Jump Start

1. Put 15 Ping-Pong balls together on the floor. The balls represent sand grains.

2. Pick up one of the balls. Bounce it onto the others. What happens?

■ How do most sand grains move?

■ Is a camel rider in a sandstorm doomed? Explain.

15–3 Wind

Have you ever seen a person lose his or her hat to a brisk gust of wind? If so, you know that wind is a powerful force—often powerful enough to move materials from one place to another. Certain locations are more easily affected by wind erosion than others are. **Wind is the most active agent of erosion in deserts, in plowed fields, and on beaches.** In these places loose material is exposed at the Earth's surface. This loose material can easily be picked up and carried by the wind. You will learn more about winds in Chapter 16.

Types of Wind Erosion

Wind erodes the Earth's surface in two ways. Wind removes loose materials such as clay, silt, and sand from the land. This type of wind erosion is called deflation (dih-FLAY-shuhn). Fine particles are carried many meters up into the air. Larger particles rise only a few centimeters. Do you know why?

As the wind blows, the larger particles roll or bounce along the ground. These particles slowly wear away exposed rocks. The particles often act like a sandblaster, cutting and polishing rocks. This type of wind erosion is called abrasion. In nature the rock particles worn away by abrasion are carried away by the wind. What effect can these particles have on other rock surfaces?

The amount of erosion caused by wind depends on the size of the particles being carried, the speed of the wind, and the length of time the wind blows. It also depends on the resistance of the rocks exposed to the wind.

In many desert regions wind erosion forms wind caves by wearing away less-resistant material. Sometimes wind erodes desert sands down to the depth where water is present. With water available on the surface, trees, shrubs, and grasses grow. Then a green, fertile area within a desert, called an oasis (oh-AY-suhs), forms.

Deposits by Wind

The amount of rock and soil particles carried by wind depends on the speed of the wind. The faster the wind blows, the more particles it can carry. The slower the wind blows, the fewer particles it can carry. As the speed of the wind decreases, the particles it can no longer carry are deposited.

DUNES In desert areas and along shorelines, windblown sand is often deposited near rocks and

Figure 15–3 *Wind erosion carved these beautiful caves in Sandstone Canyon, Arizona. In some places in a desert, wind erodes sand away to a depth where water is present. With water, plants are able to grow and eventually an oasis forms.*

Figure 15–4 *Formed by wind-blown sand, a dune on the shore of Lake Michigan is populated by a variety of plants. A dune formed by wind-blown sand in Death Valley shows no plant life. What accounts for this difference in the two dunes?*

bushes. Wind blowing over these deposits is slowed down. More sand is deposited. The mounds of sand continue to grow and to form **sand dunes.** A sand dune is a mound of sand deposited by wind. Sand dunes are very important features of a beach area. They protect the area on the side of the dune away from the ocean from further wind erosion. Small plants often grow on a sand dune. The roots and stems of these plants hold the sand in place. In this way the plants protect the dune from erosion. On some dunes, you may have seen signs cautioning you to avoid stepping on or removing plants. Can you now explain why these signs are important?

Sand dunes vary in size and in shape. Figure 15–6 shows how a sand dune forms. Notice that the side of the dune facing the wind has a gentle slope. Sand is carried up the gentle slope, or windward side, to the crest, or top of the dune. At the crest, the sand is dropped by the wind. The sand slides down the other side. This side of the dune, the slip face, has a steep slope.

As the wind blows, sand dunes move across the areas where they form. They move in the direction the wind is blowing. A sand dune moves by being eroded on one side and built up on the other side. Sometimes moving sand dunes cover buildings, farmlands, and trees.

LOESS Some fine particles of sand and silt are not deposited in dunes. Instead, they are deposited by the wind many kilometers from where they were picked up. When many layers of fine sand and silt are deposited in the same area, **loess** (LOH-ehs) is formed. Loess deposits are very fertile.

Deposits of loess are light in color and may be many meters thick. Loess deposits are found near the northern and central parts of the Mississippi River Valley. They are also found in northeast China.

Figure 15–5 *This loess deposit is a nearly vertical cliff of sand and silt. Does a loess deposit show any visible layers?*

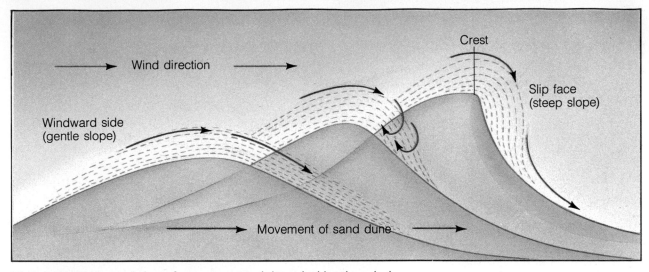

Figure 15–6 *A sand dune forms as material carried by the wind moves up the gentle slope, or windward side, of the dune and accumulates at the crest. Then this material moves down the steep slope, or slip face, of the dune and forms a series of layers. In this same way, a sand dune moves across the area where it forms. On what side of the dune does erosion take place? Deposition?*

Large dust storms in the Gobi desert in Asia have formed loess deposits hundreds of meters thick.

A windbreak is often used to decrease wind erosion and aid in wind deposition. A windbreak is a barrier that causes the wind to slow down. What happens when the wind slows down? When wind speed is decreased, the load carried by the wind is dropped. Fences are often used as windbreaks. So are plants. Consequently, many farmers surround their fields with bushes or trees to help stop wind erosion.

15–3 Section Review

1. Where is wind the most active agent of erosion?
2. How are deflation and abrasion different?
3. What are two kinds of deposits caused by wind?

Connection—*Ecology*

4. At certain beaches, you can often observe a short fence made of thin slats of vertical wood held together at the top and bottom by thin strands of wire. These fences are not tall enough or strong enough to make effective barriers to animals or people. They have an important function, however. Propose a hypothesis that explains what these fences are used for.

ctivity Bank

Down by the Old Mill Stream, p. 770

Running Water and Erosion

1. After a heavy rain, collect a sample of runoff in a clear plastic container.

2. Let the water stand for about 10 minutes.

3. Observe the bottom of the container for sediments carried by the runoff.

4. Collect and observe samples from several other areas.

Are there any differences in the samples? Was the runoff from one particular area carrying more sediments than the runoff from other areas? Explain your answer.

15–4 Running Water

From gently falling raindrops to rushing rivers, running water changes more of the Earth's surface than any other agent of erosion. **Running water is the major cause of erosion.**

Rivers, streams, and runoff are forms of running water. Runoff is water that flows over the Earth's surface, usually after a rainfall or a spring thaw. Runoff flows into streams and rivers.

Runoff and Erosion

When rain falls on the surface of the Earth, three things can happen to the water. The rain can evaporate, it can sink into the ground, or it can flow over the land surface as runoff.

When water moves across the Earth's surface as runoff, it picks up and carries particles of clay, sand, and gravel. Because of gravity, the water and sediments move downhill. As the water and sediments move downhill, they cut into the soil and form tiny grooves, called rills. As erosion continues, the rills become wider and deeper. Eventually, gullies form. Gullies act as channels for runoff. You may have seen gullies on slopes alongside highways. Where else might you see gullies caused by erosion?

The amount of runoff is affected by several factors. One factor is the amount of rainfall in an area. In areas with a high average rainfall, there is a lot of runoff. When there is a lot of runoff, there is a lot of erosion.

The amount of runoff is also affected by the amount of plant growth in an area. Plant roots hold soil particles in place. The soil absorbs some of the water. The plant roots also absorb some of the water. Areas with little plant growth have greater runoff and therefore greater erosion. Soil with little plant life can easily be washed away since there are few roots to hold the soil in place.

The shape of the land also affects the amount of runoff. Areas that have steep slopes have the greatest amount of runoff. On a steep slope the water moves too fast to soak into the ground. As the water

moves rapidly downhill, a lot of erosion takes place. If land surfaces have adequate plant life and are properly cared for, little erosion will occur. Why is it important to control runoff?

Streams and Erosion

Gullies formed by runoff are actually tiny stream valleys. When runoff from several gullies comes together, a larger stream forms.

Streams are important agents of erosion because they carry large amounts of sediments. The soil particles and rock materials carried by a stream are called the stream's **load.** Large and fast-moving streams can carry big loads.

Sediments in a stream's load are transported in different ways. Large, heavy sediments, such as pebbles and boulders, are pushed or rolled downstream. Lighter sediments, such as silt or clay, are picked up and carried along by the force of the moving water. Still other sediments, such as salts, dissolve in the stream water.

Streams cause erosion by abrasion. Sediments carried by streams constantly collide with rocks, chipping away pieces and wearing down the rocks.

Sometimes the layers of rocks beneath a stream are eroded by abrasion. If the stream flows first over hard rock layers and then over soft rock layers, a waterfall will form. This is because abrasion wears away the soft rocks faster than it does the hard rocks. In time, the level of the stream flowing over the soft rocks is lower than the level of the stream flowing over the hard rocks. A waterfall results.

ACTIVITY READING

The Good Earth

Although Pearl Buck was born in the United States, she spent a good part of her life in China. One of her novels, *The Good Earth,* describes the effects of river floods on the lives of people. You might enjoy reading this book, considered to be a classic by many people.

You might be interested to learn that Pearl Buck was also the first woman to win the Nobel prize for literature—a very great honor indeed.

Development of a River System

As you have just read, runoff forms rills. Rills deepen and widen to form gullies. Gullies then join to form streams. Finally, streams join to form rivers. Rivers usually begin in mountains or hills. The downward pull of gravity gives them energy to cut away the land and form valleys. Rivers are important agents of erosion because they affect a large area.

The network of rills, gullies, streams, and rivers in an area is called a **drainage system.** You can compare the pattern of channels in a drainage system to the pattern of branches on a tree. The small twigs of a tree that grow from small branches are like the rills and gullies that join to form streams. The small branches are connected to larger branches just as the small streams flow into larger streams. These larger streams are called **tributaries** (TRIHB-yoo-tehr-eez). The tributaries flow into the main river in much the same way as the larger branches are joined to the trunk of the tree. The main river is like the tree trunk. In time the main river empties into another river, a lake, or an ocean at a place called the mouth of the river.

The area drained by a main river and its channels is called a **drainage basin.** The land that separates one drainage basin from another is called a divide. One of the largest divides is the Continental Divide, located about 80 kilometers west of Denver, Colorado. The Continental Divide is a continuous line that runs north and south the length of North America. West of the divide, all water eventually flows into the Pacific Ocean. East of the divide, all water eventually flows into the Atlantic Ocean.

Figure 15–9 *The pattern of a drainage system can be seen in this satellite photograph. What does this branching system resemble?*

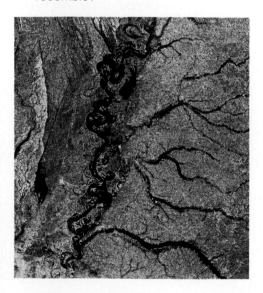

A divide starts off as a wide area. But as the drainage system of a river develops, the divide becomes narrower. Sometimes a drainage system will cut through its divide and steal runoff from another drainage basin.

A drainage system grows larger by deepening its channels, widening its valleys, and adding more rills and gullies to its system. The river grows larger and faster, and the river valley grows deeper and wider. In time the river reaches a balance between the processes of erosion and deposition.

Life Cycle of a River

An **immature river,** or young river, is a river in an early stage of development. An immature river cuts a valley with steep sides into the Earth's surface. The valley is typically V-shaped, and the river covers almost the entire valley floor. The waters of an immature river flow very quickly over rocks, producing rapids. Waterfalls are also commonly found in immature rivers. These rivers erode the surrounding areas rapidly. What size particles do you think an immature river is able to carry?

A river that has been developing for many thousands of years is called a **mature river.** Because of continuous erosion, the rapids and waterfalls have largely disappeared. The river has also eroded much of the valley floor. The valley walls are far from the river itself. The floor of the valley is broad and flat. What shape do you think such a valley is described as having? The course of the river has also become curved and winding, forming loops called **meanders** (mee-AN-derz). The river has slowed down, so erosion has slowed down. What size particles do you think a mature river is able to carry?

Figure 15–10 *The Upper Bow River, in Banff National Park, Canada, is an example of an immature river (right). The Niobrara River in Nebraska is an example of a mature river (left). How are these two rivers different?*

Deposits by Rivers

A stream or river carries a large amount of sediments. In places where the stream or river slows down, sediments are deposited. Some of the larger sediments settle on the riverbed, or the bottom of the river channel. Some sediments are deposited along the river bank, or the side of the river. These deposits constantly change surrounding land areas.

Sediments are usually deposited on a river bank where a river bends, or curves. This is because the speed of a river decreases at a bend. Rivers tend to erode material on the outside of the curve and deposit it on the inside. The outside of the curve receives the full impact of the current. The water on the inside of a river bend moves more slowly.

OXBOW LAKES Sometimes the meanders of a river form large, U-shaped bends. Erosion along such bends can cut these bends off from the river. Deposited sediments dam up the ends of the meander. A small lake called an **oxbow lake** is formed. An oxbow lake is separated from the river. Figure 15–11 shows how an oxbow lake forms.

ALLUVIAL FANS When a river leaves the mountains and runs out onto a plain, its speed decreases. Nearly all the sediments the river is carrying are dropped. They build up to form an **alluvial fan.** The sediments spread out from the river channel in a fanlike shape.

DELTAS Large amounts of sediments deposited at the mouth of a large river that flows into a lake or an ocean form a **delta.** A delta forms because the river's speed decreases as it runs into the body of

Figure 15–11 *An oxbow lake is often formed when a meander is cut off from the rest of the river. What type of river might have oxbow lakes along its course?*

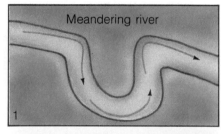

1 — Meandering river

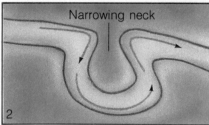

2 — Narrowing neck

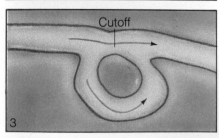

3 — Cutoff

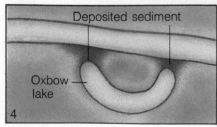

4 — Deposited sediment — Oxbow lake

standing water. The river cannot carry as much material when it is moving slowly. So it deposits much of the sediments. Sediments deposited during flood stages can gradually build up above the river's normal water level.

FLOOD PLAINS AND LEVEES On both sides of a mature river or stream, flat areas called **flood plains** form. After heavy rains or spring thaws, the river overflows its banks and covers the flood plain. Sediments are deposited on the plain. Repeated flooding causes sediments to build up. Flood plains have fertile soil. For example, the flood plains on either side of the Mississippi River are very fertile areas as a result of the periodic flooding of the river. What might be a good use for these areas?

Sediments deposited on a flood plain usually consist of fine particles. The larger particles, which settle first, are deposited along the sides of the river. These larger particles accumulate to form ridgelike deposits called **levees** (LEHV-eez).

Figure 15–12 *An alluvial fan forms when a river leaves the mountains and slows down as it runs out onto a plain (right). As a large river flows into a lake or ocean, its speed decreases and it deposits large amounts of sediments. These deposits form a delta (left).*

15–4 Section Review

1. What is the major cause of erosion?
2. What factors affect the amount of runoff?
3. What is a drainage system? A drainage basin?
4. Compare an immature river to a mature river.
5. How are deltas and flood plains formed?

Connection—*Ecology*

6. Flood plains have fertile soil and can produce good crops. However, flood plains might not be good places to build houses. Explain why.

465

15–5 Glaciers

As you learned in Chapter 7, a **glacier** (GLAY-shuhr) is a large mass of moving ice and snow. Glaciers form where there are many large snowfalls and the temperatures remain very cold. Some glaciers form in high mountains where the snow that falls in the winter does not completely melt in the summer. The snow builds up over the years and gradually turns to ice. These glaciers, called valley glaciers, move very slowly down the mountains.

Other glaciers form in the polar regions of the world. Some of these glaciers are huge sheets of ice called continental glaciers or icecaps. They often cover millions of square kilometers. See Figure 7–8. What areas of the Earth do you think are covered with continental glaciers?

Glacial Ice and Erosion

A glacier is one of the most powerful agents of erosion. **Glacial ice erodes by abrasion and by plucking away at the rock beneath it.**

As a glacier moves through a valley, rock materials of all sizes—from immense boulders to tiny particles of clay—are carried along and pushed in front of it. Rock materials carried by a glacier are called glacial debris. Some glacial debris is frozen into the ice of the glacier. The glacier gains more debris as it scrapes materials from the valley walls.

A glacier may carry along large boulders as well as smaller particles of rocks. These make up the

Figure 15–13 *This field of boulders in Hickory Run State Park, Pennsylvania, was left behind by a retreating glacier during the last Ice Age. What are rocks and boulders carried by a glacier called?*

glacier's load. The load of a glacier helps to wear down the land surface by grinding and polishing the rock it passes over. The moving glacier scrapes away soil and carves distinctive grooves into rocks as it moves over an area. Glacial erosion changes V-shaped mountain valleys into U-shaped mountain valleys.

During the Ice Age, huge icecaps covered a large part of North America. The Rocky Mountains, the mountains of New England, and many of the states in the Northeast and Midwest were at one time covered by glaciers. Glacial erosion caused many of the surface features that are present in these areas. For example, the Great Lakes were formed by glaciers.

Deposits by Glaciers

When the lower end of a glacier reaches a warm area, the ice at the front begins to melt. The glacier continues to move forward, but it may be melting so rapidly at the front that it appears to be moving backward. Such a glacier is said to be retreating. As it retreats, rocks and debris are deposited.

Rocks and soil deposited directly by a glacier are called **till.** Till is a mixture of material that varies in size from large boulders to very fine clay particles. Till is not sorted out by the action of running water. In other words, the material in till is not separated into layers according to its size.

Other glacial deposits are sorted out by running water from melting glaciers. The coarse and fine materials are separated into layers. Both sorted and unsorted materials are found in different features of the land formed by glaciers.

MORAINES When a glacier melts and retreats, it leaves behind till. The till forms a ridge called a **moraine.** There are different types of moraines. Till deposited at the front end of a glacier is called a terminal moraine. Till deposited along the sides of a glacier is called a lateral moraine.

Scientists can find out about glaciers that have melted by studying moraines. The rocks found in a moraine are evidence of where the glacier formed. Rocks can be carried great distances by glaciers. The position of a terminal moraine indicates how far the glacier advanced before retreating.

Figure 15–14 *This boulder in New York City's Central Park shows grooves etched by rocks carried along by retreating glaciers. You might be surprised to learn that much of New York City was covered by a glacier during the last Ice Age. The Great Lakes were also formed by the action of glaciers.*

Figure 15–15 *Till left behind when a glacier melts and retreats forms ridges called moraines. Where is a lateral moraine located? A terminal moraine?*

DRUMLINS A **drumlin** is an oval-shaped mound of till. Its tip points in the direction that the glacier was moving. Scientists believe that drumlins are formed as deposits of till are rounded by the glacial ice.

MELTWATER DEPOSITS When valley glaciers stop advancing, melting ice forms streams that flow out from the glacier. These streams are called **meltwater** streams. The meltwater carries away sand and gravel. The sand and gravel sediments are deposited along the meltwater stream in long trainlike deposits called valley trains. The meltwater may also form small lakes and ponds near the glacier. Many present-day rivers were originally meltwater streams.

Sediments deposited by rivers of glacial meltwater form areas called **outwash plains.** Outwash plains are fan-shaped and form in front of terminal moraines. Outwash plains are very fertile land areas. Today many farms can be found in outwash plains.

ICEBERG DEPOSITS Valley glaciers and continental glaciers sometimes reach the sea. When this happens, the glaciers form cliffs of ice and snow. Parts of the glaciers break off and drift into the sea. These glacial parts are called icebergs. The continental glaciers of Greenland and Antarctica are the major sources of icebergs.

Figure 15–16 *What appear to be gently rolling hills are actually glacial deposits called drumlins. A drumlin is an oval-shaped mound of till. What is till?*

Figure 15-17 *A kettle pond forms when a block of glacial ice, surrounded by or covered with sediments, melts and leaves a hole that fills with water. Kettle ponds can be seen in Yosemite National Park.*

Icebergs may contain rocks and debris picked up from the land. As the icebergs melt, the rocks and debris are deposited on the ocean floor. These sediments are often found thousands of kilometers from their source.

GLACIAL LAKES Glaciers created many of the lakes in the United States. The Finger Lakes in New York, the Great Lakes, and many smaller lakes were formed by glaciers. Do you know of any other lakes that were formed by glaciers?

Figure 15-18 *The various land features formed by glacial deposits are shown in this diagram. What are some of these features?*

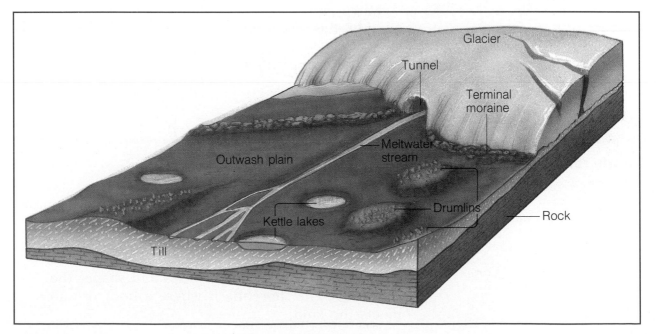

ACTIVITY DISCOVERING

Glacial Erosion

1. Cover a sheet of cardboard with a layer of clay 1 centimeter thick.

2. Rub some sand on top of the clay.

3. Slide an ice cube slowly along a path in the sand. Then hold the ice cube in one place and allow some of it to melt.

Describe the appearance of the sand after the ice cube has slid over it. What do you notice about the ice cube? What happened in the place where you held the cube?

■ How does this activity relate to the erosion processes of glaciers?

Glaciers can form lakes in two ways. Glacial till or deposits of sorted sediments from meltwater sometimes pile up in low-lying river channels and other areas. These deposits keep water from flowing away from the area. The land areas fill with water, and lakes are formed.

Sometimes huge blocks of glacial ice are left behind by a glacier. The ice blocks are surrounded by or covered with sediments deposited by the glacier. When the ice melts, it leaves a depression, or hole, in the ground. The depression fills with water and forms a lake. Lakes formed in this way are called **kettle lakes.** Kettle lakes are usually round and very deep.

15–5 Section Review

1. How does a glacier erode the Earth's surface?
2. Compare a valley glacier and a continental glacier.
3. What is till? A moraine? A drumlin?
4. What are two meltwater deposits?
5. How are glacial lakes formed?

Critical Thinking—*Applying Concepts*
6. While walking in a valley in a national park located near a snow-capped mountain range, Betty noticed large piles of rocks, boulders, sand, and fine clay particles all mixed together. The piles were unlike the small rocks she had previously noticed. Propose a theory to explain Betty's observations.

Guide for Reading

Focus on this question as you read.

▶ *How do waves affect a shoreline?*

15–6 Waves

If you have ever been to an ocean beach, you are probably familiar with waves. Waves are caused by winds, by tides, and sometimes even by earthquakes. Waves can be extremely powerful. **The powerful force of waves constantly erodes and shapes the shoreline.** The shoreline is where a body of water meets the land.

Waves and Erosion

Waves cause erosion in several ways. As ocean waves reach shallow water near the shore, they begin to break. As the breaking waves hit the shoreline, their force knocks fragments off existing rock formations. Waves also carry small rocks and sand. The force of the small rocks and sand particles hitting other rocks on the shoreline chips off fragments. What kind of weathering is taking place in these two types of wave erosion?

Another way waves cause erosion is by forcing water into cracks in the rocks at the shoreline. The water causes pressure to build up in the cracks. Over time, the cracks become larger, and the pressure breaks the rocks. Because some rocks dissolve in salt water, the chemical action of salt water also breaks down rocks.

Erosion at the shoreline can occur at different rates. Various conditions cause these different rates. The size and force of the waves hitting the shoreline have an effect on the rate of erosion. Under normal conditions, waves may erode the shoreline at a rate of 1 to 1.5 meters per year. During storms, however, wave action is increased. Larger waves hit the shoreline with greater force. The rate of shoreline erosion may increase to 25 meters in one day. The type of rock that makes up the shoreline also affects the rate of erosion. Some rocks do not erode as quickly as others. How might wave erosion differ along ocean shores and lake shores?

ACTIVITY

CALCULATING

Storm Action

If the rate of shoreline erosion during a storm is 25 meters per day, how many kilometers of shoreline would be eroded if an area had 50 days of storms a year?

Figure 15–19 *The powerful force of waves constantly erodes rocks and reshapes the shoreline. Why are people cautioned about building homes near the shoreline?*

Figure 15–20 *Sea stacks are the remains of a cliff that was eroded away by waves. A sea cave is a hollowed-out portion of a sea cliff.*

ACTIVITY

DISCOVERING

Wave Erosion

1. Fill one end of a shallow pan with sand. Shape the sand into a slope.

2. Mark on the side of the pan where the edge of the sand slope ends.

3. Add 1 cm of water.

4. Make gentle waves with a piece of cardboard.

What changes do you observe in the sand?

■ How does this activity relate to beach erosion?

■ What variables in the waves would affect beach erosion?

SEA CLIFFS AND TERRACES   Wave erosion forms a variety of features along a shoreline. Erosion by waves sometimes produces steep faces of rock called **sea cliffs.** Over a long period of time the bottom of a sea cliff may be worn away by wave action. Overhanging rocks may break off the top of the cliff and fall into the sea. Waves will then grind the rocks into sand and silt.

As the sea cliff continues to be eroded, the buildup of rocks, sand, and silt forms a flat platform at the base of the cliff. This flat platform is called a **terrace.** As waves move across the terrace, they are slowed down. They strike the cliff with less force. Terraces slow down erosion of sea cliffs.

SEA STACKS AND CAVES   As waves erode a sea cliff, columns of resistant rock may be left standing. These columns are called **sea stacks.** Sometimes part of a sea cliff is made of less-resistant rock. When wave action erodes this rock, a cave is formed. A **sea cave** is a hollowed-out portion of a sea cliff.

Deposits by Waves

Waves carry large amounts of sand, rock particles, and pieces of shells. At some point waves deposit the material they carry. Sand and other sediments carried away from one part of the shoreline by waves may be deposited elsewhere on the shoreline. The shape of the shoreline is always changing.

BEACHES   Eroded rock particles deposited on the shoreline form beaches. Beaches may consist of fine sand or of large pebbles. Some beach materials come directly from the erosion of nearby areas of the shoreline. Other beach materials can come from rivers that carry sediments from inland areas to the sea. Waves transport the sediments from the mouths of rivers to different parts of the shoreline.

The type of material found on a beach varies according to its source. The color of the sand provides a clue to its origin. Beaches along the Atlantic coast have white sand. White sand usually consists of quartz material that originated in the eastern part of the United States. For example, most of the white sand on the Atlantic coast of Florida came from the erosion of the southern Appalachian Mountains. On Hawaii and other islands in the Pacific, some sand is black. This black sand comes from broken fragments of dark, volcanic rocks. Still other beaches may have deposits of shell fragments and coral skeletons.

SAND BARS AND SPITS Waves do not usually move straight into the shore. Instead, they approach the shore at an angle. The water is then turned so it runs parallel to the shoreline. The movement of water parallel to a shoreline is called a **longshore current.**

If the shoreline bends or curves, material carried by waves in a longshore current is deposited in open water. A long, underwater ridge of sand called a **sand bar** forms. If the sand bar is connected to the curving shoreline, it is called a **spit.**

Sometimes large sand bars are formed during the winter. At this time of year waves are large and carry more material away from the beaches. This material is deposited offshore. What do you think happens during the summer?

Figure 15–21 *The sand found on a beach varies according to its source. The color of sand is a clue to its origin and composition. What is the likely origin of white sand? Black sand? Pink sand?*

473

Figure 15–22 *Longshore currents slow down and deposit sand when shorelines curve or bend. What are these deposits called?*

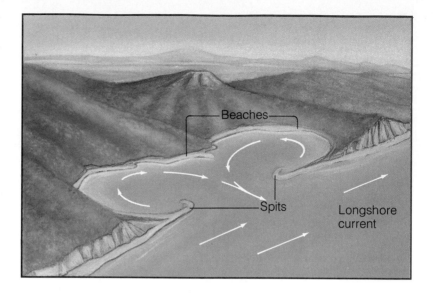

The Shape of a Shoreline

The shape of a shoreline often results from changes in the level of the sea. If the sea level drops, the resulting shoreline has many sea cliffs and terraces. The drop in sea level exposes new areas of shore to wave erosion, which forms many sea cliffs and terraces.

If the sea level rises, the resulting shoreline has many bays and harbors. The rise in sea level floods streams and small rivers, forming bays and harbors.

15–6 Section Review

1. How do waves affect a shoreline?
2. What is a sea cliff? A sea stack?
3. Why do different beaches have different colored sand?
4. How does a longshore current form sand bars and spits?

Connection—*Ecology*

5. Many people have built houses on beaches. The view of the ocean causes land along the shore to be highly valued. However, many scientists warn against building a house on the beach front. Why do you think the scientists warn against this?

Nature's Gifts From the Nile

Life on Earth often forms webs of great complexity. In this chapter, you have read about the fertility of lands that form a river's flood plains. These lands, renewed by periodic deposits of silt and minerals, are part of the river's bounty of life. The crops produced in fertile flood plains provide food and fibers for millions of people who often live many, many kilometers from the river's banks.

The Nile River performed this life-giving role in ages past. Heavy rains caused the Nile to flood every year. As the river's waters overspilled the banks, land in the flood plains was inundated. Deposits carried by the river were left behind as the water receded. These deposits enhanced the soil's fertility—Egypt could produce enough food to feed its people.

Today progress and technology have altered life along the Nile. The Aswan Dam, completed in 1971, was viewed with hope and promise. It was thought that the dam would control the annual flooding of the Nile, as well as generate enough electricity to power industrial plants that would provide jobs for millions of Egypt's inhabitants. It did all that. But it also altered the web of life that had existed almost unchanged for thousands of years along the river.

Today farmers along the Nile cannot depend on the annual flooding of the Nile to enrich their soil. They must add artificial fertilizers to provide food for their crops. Some scientists have calculated that the power produced by the dam today equals the power needed to make fertilizers for the area's crops. In this case, nature might have known best. The Nile River is controlled by modern technology, and its annual floodings are no more. However, one must wonder if the lives of those living in the area have been improved very much, if at all.

Laboratory Investigation

Observing Erosion and Deposition in a Model Stream

Problem

How is a stream's ability to erode and deposit materials affected by a change in its flow?

Materials *(per group)*

> lab table
> support, such as books
> stream pan (2 cm x 50 cm x 8–10 cm)
> sand
> 2 buckets
> 2 25-cm lengths of rubber tubing (1 cm in diameter)
> screw clamp
> food coloring or ink

Procedure

1. Set up a stream table similar to the one shown in the illustration.

2. Raise one end of the large pan slightly, so that the pan forms a very low angle with the table. To start the water flowing, siphon the water out of the bucket. Use the screw clamp to set the water flow at a low volume.

3. As the water runs to the end of the pan, observe and record the changes that occur on the land surface, on the lake, and on the stream itself. Note any deposition features that may form. A drop of food coloring or ink can help to reveal patterns of change.

4. Next, change the slope of the stream, making it steep by increasing the angle between the pan and the table. Observe and record the effects of this change.

5. Now increase the stream's volume by opening the screw clamp or by pouring water down the stream table. Observe and record the effects of this change.

Observations

1. What, if any, deposition features formed?

2. What evidence of erosion did you observe?

3. What changes in the stream occurred when you increased the steepness of the slope of your stream table? When you increased the volume of water?

Analysis and Conclusions

1. What effects does an increase in the speed at which the stream flows have on the processes of erosion and deposition? An increase in stream volume?

2. Why do you think old rivers meander?

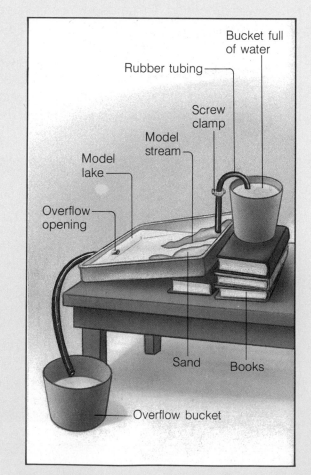

Study Guide

Summarizing Key Concepts

15–1 Changing the Earth's Surface

▲ Erosion is the process by which weathered rock and soil particles are moved from one place to another.

▲ Deposition is the process by which sediments are laid down in new locations.

▲ The five agents of erosion are gravity, wind, running water, glaciers, and waves.

15–2 Gravity

▲ The downhill movement of sediments caused by gravity is called mass wasting.

15–3 Wind

▲ Wind erodes by deflation and abrasion.

▲ Sand dunes and loess are wind deposits.

15–4 Running Water

▲ Running water in the form of rivers, streams, and runoff is the major agent of erosion.

▲ The network of rills, gullies, streams, and rivers in an area is called a drainage system.

▲ Deposits by rivers include oxbow lakes, alluvial fans, deltas, flood plains, and levees.

15–5 Glaciers

▲ A glacier is a large mass of moving ice and snow. Two types of glaciers are valley glaciers and continental glaciers.

▲ Rocks and soil deposited directly by a glacier are called till.

▲ Other glacial deposits include moraines, drumlins, meltwater streams, outwash plains, icebergs, and lakes.

15–6 Waves

▲ Waves erode and shape the shoreline.

▲ Wave erosion forms sea cliffs, terraces, sea stacks, and sea caves.

▲ Deposits by waves include beaches, sand bars, and spits.

Reviewing Key Terms

Define each term in a complete sentence.

15–1 Changing the Earth's Surface
erosion
deposition

15–2 Gravity
mass wasting

15–3 Wind
sand dune
loess

15–4 Running Water
load
drainage
  system
tributary
drainage basin
immature river
mature river
meander
oxbow lake
alluvial fan
delta
flood plain
levee

15–5 Glaciers
glacier
till
moraine
drumlin
meltwater
outwash plain
kettle lake

15–6 Waves
sea cliff
terrace
sea stack
sea cave
longshore
  current
sand bar
spit

Chapter Review

Content Review

Multiple Choice

Choose the letter of the answer that best completes each statement.

1. The process by which sediments are laid down in new locations is called
   a. erosion.
   b. deposition.
   c. abrasion.
   d. mass wasting.

2. Two examples of rapid mass wasting are
   a. slump and soil creep.
   b. landslides and earthflows.
   c. soil creep and earthflows.
   d. landslides and slump.

3. Layers of fine sand and silt deposited in the same area by wind are called
   a. loess.
   b. dunes.
   c. terraces.
   d. till.

4. The network of rills, gullies, and streams that forms a river is called a
   a. drainage basin.
   b. tributary.
   c. levee.
   d. drainage system.

5. Rich, fertile soil deposited on the sides of a river as it overflows forms flat areas called
   a. terraces.
   b. sand bars.
   c. flood plains.
   d. valley trains.

6. A ridge of till deposited as a glacier melts and retreats is called a
   a. moraine.
   b. terrace.
   c. levee.
   d. flood plain.

7. Glacial meltwater forms very fertile deposits of sediments called
   a. flood plains.
   b. outwash plains.
   c. kettle lakes.
   d. drumlins.

8. Columns of resistant rock left as waves erode sea cliffs are called
   a. spits.
   b. sea stacks.
   c. terraces.
   d. sand bars.

9. A sand bar connected to a curving shoreline is called a
   a. terrace.
   b. sea stack.
   c. spit.
   d. drumlin.

10. A shoreline that has many sea cliffs and terraces may indicate that the sea level has
    a. dropped.
    b. risen.
    c. remained constant.
    d. reversed direction.

True or False

If the statement is true, write "true." If it is false. change the underlined word or words to make the statement true.

1. The downhill movements of sediments is called <u>mass wasting</u>.
2. The most active agent of erosion in deserts and on beaches is <u>waves</u>.
3. When wind or water moves <u>slowly</u>, the amount of particles it can carry <u>increases</u>.
4. Areas with little plant growth have <u>more</u> erosion than areas with lots of plant growth.
5. A large deposit of sediment at the mouth of a river is called a <u>levee</u>.
6. Rocks and debris deposited directly by a glacier are called <u>till</u>.
7. Parts of glacial ice that break off and drift into the sea are called <u>drumlins</u>.

Concept Mapping

Complete the following concept map for Section 15–1. Then construct a concept map for the entire chapter.

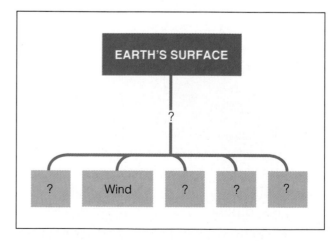

Concept Mastery

Discuss each of the following in a brief paragraph.

1. Explain why the rate of erosion along a shoreline increases during a storm.
2. Explain how both erosion and deposition occur at the same time in the formation of sand dunes.
3. What can scientists learn about glaciers by studying moraines?
4. List several agents of erosion that might affect land areas in a large city. Compare these agents with ones that might affect land areas in the country. Explain why different agents work in different areas.
5. Describe the formation of a waterfall. What role does water play?
6. Explain why farmland near rivers is often very productive.
7. Dams are usually built across rivers and streams. If the dam is large enough, a huge lake may form behind it. In what ways does a dam slow down erosion?
8. Continental glaciers may cause problems in areas that are far away from the site of the glacier. What kind of dangers can continental glaciers pose?
9. Wind erosion in a desert area is usually harmful. In one instance, however, it can be helpful. Explain how wind erosion in the desert can be helpful.

Critical Thinking and Problem Solving

Use the skills you have developed in this chapter to answer each of the following.

1. **Sequencing events** The following steps are stages in the formation of a river system from the time rain falls to the Earth to the time a steadily flowing river forms. The steps, however, are not in order. Read the steps and place them in the proper order.
   a. Runoff from several slopes collects in low places.
   b. Rain falls to the Earth's surface.
   c. Water tumbles in broad sheets.
   d. Branch gullies develop and then become tributaries.
   e. A gully is formed.
   f. A V-shaped valley with streams, waterfalls, and rapids forms.
   g. Erosion lengthens the gullies.
   h. The gully gets larger and collects more water.
2. **Relating concepts** Use glaciers as an example to explain how the erosion of a land area usually involves more than one agent of erosion.
3. **Making inferences** Why would a flood plain be characteristic of a mature river valley and not of an immature river valley?

4. **Applying concepts** What are two ways in which people cause erosion? What are two ways in which people can prevent erosion?
5. **Making diagrams** Make a diagram to show how an immature and a mature river would look in a photograph taken from a high-flying plane. How would each river look in a topographic map?
6. **Using the writing process** In order to protect shorelines, a proposal has been made to prohibit the construction of homes near beach dunes. Write a letter to your governor explaining your views.

GAZETTE

Alan Kolata & Oswaldo Rivera

THE MYSTERIOUS CANALS OF BOLIVIA

The Pampa Koani, a treeless plain in northern Bolivia, was rich in strange ridges and depressions but poor in crops. The Aymara Indians, the inhabitants of this flood plain, were forced to watch as their crops succumbed to frost and their potatoes rotted in the boggy soil. The Aymara knew that nearly one thousand years ago their ancestors had farmed the land successfully. That powerful pre-Incan civilization, called the Tiwanaku state, had flourished from 200 to 1000 AD. What farming methods did the Tiwanakus know so many years ago that the Aymara lacked today?

In 1981, two archaeologists suggested a possible answer. Alan Kolata (bottom left),

a professor of archaeology and anthropology at the University of Chicago, and Oswaldo Rivera (bottom right), an archaeologist at Bolivia's National Institute of Archaeology, had been studying the Tiwanaku culture since the late 1970s. The two scholars believed that the secret lay in the ridges and ruts that ran across the flood plain. They had observed similar topographical patterns in Mayan and Aztec farming sites in the jungles of Central America. The archaeologists suggested that the patterns were part of a sophisticated system of canals and raised planting surfaces that had allowed the Tiwanakus to grow their crops successfully.

Kolata and Rivera needed to test their hypothesis. A proven, correct theory would be more than simply a credit to the archaeologists' research abilities. It would also be

a way to rejuvenate the failing Aymara farms and produce hardy crops. In 1981, the archaeologists' first attempt to rehabilitate the Aymara fields was met with a severe drought. It was not until 1987 that Kolata and Rivera were able to convince the Aymara to try again. At first, only one man agreed to cooperate. As a result, he was scorned by his neighbors, who thought the archaeologists were meddling foreigners who would only harm Aymara agriculture. The Aymaras continued to plant their crops away from the rutted fields on nearby hillsides. But the archaeologists and the lone Aymara farmer persevered. Together, the three redug the channels, planted the potato crop, and watched excitedly as the plants grew to record heights.

Then, only a few days before the first harvest, frost struck the area. The Aymara farmers looked on helplessly as 90 percent of their hillside crops were lost. They expected the same fate for the crops Kolata and Rivera had helped to cultivate. The coldest, heaviest air, they thought, would flow downhill onto the flood plain, killing every plant.

The archaeologists hoped for a different outcome. And indeed, when they went out before dawn to investigate, they beheld a remarkable sight! Across the entire flood plain, a white mist lay like a blanket over the potato crops. With the first rays of sunlight, the mist disappeared, revealing undamaged potato plants. Almost the entire crop had survived the killing frost! It was then that Kolata and Rivera, along with the Aymara farmers, recognized the ingenuity of the early Tiwanakus. These ancient people knew how to use the system of canals and ridges to protect their harvest. Can you guess how they did it?

During the day, the soil absorbs heat from the sun. But the soil quickly loses its warmth during the cold night, putting the crops at risk. Water, however, retains heat for a much longer time than soil does. A temperature difference between the water in the canals and the air causes the water to evaporate. This causes a protective, blanketlike mist to form over the crops. In addition, warm water is drawn by capillary action into the

▲ **These Bolivian farmers are harvesting potatoes produced in raised fields bordered by canals.**

raised platforms, conducting warmth into the soil and into the plants' root systems.

Kolata and Rivera were pleased with their discovery—and particularly with the fact that the Aymara began to trust them and treat them like friends. But nobody was more pleased than the Aymara people themselves. With the "new" farming system, their crops began to prosper, yielding bountiful harvests of potatoes, barley, oats, lettuce, and onions. As a bonus, algae and nitrogen-fixing bacteria began to thrive in the canals, providing a useful source of fertilizer after the crops were harvested and the canals were drained. And the Aymara had done all this by returning to the ways of their ancestors!

Meanwhile, Kolata and Rivera continue to research the Tiwanaku culture, which reached its peak in 600 AD. They are especially interested in the daily life of the Tiwanaku people—what they ate, what they wore, and how their society was structured. With a team that includes hydrologists and computer scientists, they study the sophisticated Tiwanaku temples and pyramids as well as their canal system. But Kolata and Rivera are just as interested in the present as in the past. The raised-field technology they helped the Aymara to implement can be used in other areas of Bolivia to help feed a hungry population.

U N I T F O U R

Exploring Earth's Weather

Seen from space, the Earth is a "big blue marble" floating in the infinite blackness of the universe. The first astronauts to travel into space looked back at the Earth and were struck by the delicate beauty of their home planet—a tiny oasis of life in a hostile universe. As one astronaut said: "I was terrified by its fragile appearance."

For the first time, the astronauts saw the Earth's atmosphere—the "ocean of air"—as a thin blue ribbon surrounding the planet. They found that bands of white storm clouds swirling above dark blue oceans were the most visible features on the Earth's surface. The state of the atmosphere, as shown by the presence of these clouds, represents the Earth's weather. In this book you will learn about weather and how it affects your life. You will find out what causes weather and what people can do to predict (and perhaps control) it. You will also learn about long-term weather conditions, or climate.

▲ *Weather forecasters make use of computers to coordinate data from weather satellites and ground-based observers.*

The destructive power of a hurricane can clearly be seen in the damage caused to Galveston, Texas, by Hurricane Alicia. ▶

Although climate seems to remain about the same from year to year, it is actually changing slowly over a period of thousands or even millions of years. What causes changes in climate? Are humans speeding up these climate changes? You will learn the answers to these and other questions you may have as you read the chapters that follow. And you will also learn how climate influences life—plants, animals, and people—on Planet Earth.

▼ *A winter snowstorm and a scorching day at the beach illustrate contrasting climates in different parts of the United States.*

Discovery *Activity*

Weather Watch

Look out your classroom window. Is the sun shining? Are there clouds in the sky? Is it raining or snowing? Every day that you use this textbook, describe the weather where you live. Record the temperature, precipitation, and any other weather factors that are important to you.

■ Based on your observations, what can you predict about the weather the week after you finish this textbook? How about the following year?

What Is Weather?

16

Guide for Reading

After you read the following sections, you will be able to

16–1 Heating the Earth
- Identify the factors that interact to cause weather.

16–2 Air Pressure
- Describe the three factors that affect air pressure.

16–3 Winds
- Explain the difference between local and global wind patterns.

16–4 Moisture in the Air
- Identify the three basic types of clouds.

16–5 Weather Patterns
- Describe how fronts affect weather patterns.

16–6 Predicting the Weather
- Explain how weather forecasts are made.

The animal in the photograph is a groundhog. You might be wondering what a groundhog has to do with the weather. Well, many people believe that a groundhog can forecast the weather! In fact, in some countries of the Northern Hemisphere, February 2 is called Groundhog Day. Early on Groundhog Day, people anxiously wait for a groundhog to come out of its burrow. They believe that if the groundhog sees its shadow, six more weeks of winter are to come.

The belief that groundhogs can forecast the weather is just one example of weather folklore. You may have heard the weather proverb: "Red sky at night, sailors delight. Red sky at morning, sailors take warning." Perhaps you can think of other examples of weather folklore. Such folklore is common because weather influences every aspect of our lives.

People have been trying to make accurate weather predictions for centuries. Today, scientists know a great deal about the conditions that influence weather. Modern instruments help them predict the weather more accurately than ever before. In this chapter you will learn about weather and how scientists use weather satellites and computers—not groundhogs—to make their forecasts.

Journal *Activity*

You and Your World Have you ever experienced a violent storm, such as a hurricane or tornado? What was the storm like? How did you feel during the storm? Did the storm cause any damage? What questions came to mind as you observed the storm? In your journal, describe your favorite storm story.

◀ *If a groundhog sees its shadow when it emerges from its burrow on February 2, weather folklore says there will be six more weeks of winter.*

16–1 Heating the Earth

When you woke up this morning, did you stop to think about the weather? Was the sun shining? Was it warm enough for a picnic? Did you take your umbrella with you?

Weather affects your daily life and influences you and the world around you. The type of homes people build, the clothes they wear, the crops they grow, the jobs they perform, and the ways in which they spend their leisure time are all determined by the weather.

Today, people have a good understanding of the weather. Weather satellites, computers, and other kinds of weather instruments provide accurate information about weather conditions. Meteorologists (meet-ee-uh-RAHL-uh-jihsts), people who study the weather, use this information to predict the weather. Their forecasts help you plan your daily activities. But what exactly is weather and what causes it?

You can think of weather as the daily condition of the Earth's **atmosphere** (AT-muhs-feer). The atmosphere is a mixture of gases that surround the Earth. Weather is caused by the interaction of several factors in the atmosphere. **The atmospheric factors that interact to cause weather are heat energy, air pressure, winds, and moisture.**

Figure 16–1 *Weather plays an important role in our daily lives–from the clothes we wear to the crops we grow.*

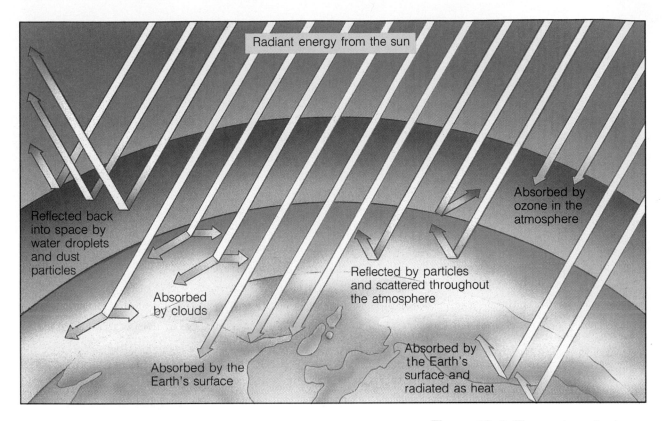

Figure 16–2 *The sun's radiant energy helps warm the atmosphere. According to the diagram, what happens to the sun's radiant energy?*

Labels in figure:
Radiant energy from the sun

Reflected back into space by water droplets and dust particles

Absorbed by clouds

Absorbed by the Earth's surface

Reflected by particles and scattered throughout the atmosphere

Absorbed by ozone in the atmosphere

Absorbed by the Earth's surface and radiated as heat

Heat Energy and the Atmosphere

Almost all of the Earth's energy comes from the sun. This energy is called radiant energy. The sun's radiant energy warms the Earth. The atmosphere also helps warm the Earth by absorbing, storing, and recycling the sun's radiant energy. Let's see how this happens.

As the sun's energy reaches the atmosphere, part of it is reflected (bounced back) into space and part is scattered throughout the atmosphere. This happens when incoming rays of sunlight strike water droplets and dust particles in the atmosphere.

Much of the sun's energy that is scattered throughout the atmosphere is absorbed by the atmosphere. In the upper atmosphere, a layer of ozone gas (O_3) absorbs one form of radiant energy called ultraviolet radiation. You have probably heard that ultraviolet radiation, which causes sunburn, can be dangerous to people. Too much ultraviolet radiation can cause skin cancer. That is why the ozone layer, which absorbs much of the ultraviolet radiation from the sun, is so important to life on Earth. Ultraviolet radiation does, however, have some

How Can You Prevent Food From Spoiling?, p. 772

ACTIVITY

Convection Currents

1. Pour water into a small beaker until it is almost full.

2. Add two or three drops of food coloring to the surface of the water.

3. Put on safety goggles and light a candle. **CAUTION:** *Be careful when working near an open flame.*

4. Put on heat-resistant gloves. Using laboratory tongs, hold the beaker about 10 centimeters above the candle flame.

What happens to the food coloring? Why? How are your observations related to the heating of the air? At what location on the Earth would air constantly be rising because of convection currents?

Figure 16–3 *Conduction is the direct transfer of heat energy from one substance to another. Convection is the transfer of heat in a fluid. Radiation is the transfer of energy through space in the form of waves. How is most of the heat energy in the atmosphere transferred?*

beneficial uses. Ultraviolet lamps are used to kill bacteria in hospitals and in food-processing plants, where bacteria could cause packaged foods to spoil.

Radiant energy that is neither reflected nor absorbed by the atmosphere reaches the Earth's surface. Here it is absorbed by the Earth and changed into heat. **The sun's energy that is absorbed by the Earth is spread throughout the atmosphere in three basic ways: conduction, convection, and radiation.**

Heat Transfer in the Atmosphere

Conduction is the direct transfer of heat energy from one substance to another. As air above the Earth's surface comes into contact with the warm ground, the air is warmed. So temperatures close to the ground are usually higher than temperatures a few meters above the ground. However, soil, water, and air are poor conductors of heat. So conduction plays only a minor role in heating the land, ocean, and atmosphere.

Convection is the transfer of heat energy in a fluid (gas or liquid). Air is a fluid. When air near the Earth's surface is heated, it becomes less dense and rises. Cooler, denser air from above sinks. As the cool air sinks, it is heated by the ground and begins to rise. This process of warm air rising and cool air sinking forms convection currents. Convection currents are caused by the unequal heating of the

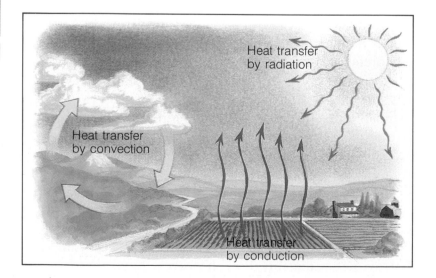

atmosphere. Most of the heat energy in the atmosphere is transferred by convection currents.

Radiation is the transfer of energy by waves such as light. Energy that is transferred by radiation does not need the presence of a solid, liquid, or gas. It can travel through a vacuum, or empty space. Energy from the sun reaches the Earth by radiation. When radiant energy from the sun is absorbed by the Earth, it is changed into heat.

The Greenhouse Effect

As you have just read, some of the sun's radiant energy (in the form of sunlight) is absorbed by the Earth and changed into heat. Sunlight passes easily through the atmosphere and reaches the Earth. Later, this energy is radiated back from the Earth to the atmosphere in the form of infrared rays. You cannot see infrared rays, but you can feel them as heat. (Although humans cannot see infrared rays, rattlesnakes and some other snakes have heat-sensitive pits on their head that "see" the heat given off by small animals.)

You may actually be more familiar with infrared rays than you realize. The heat lamps often used in

Figure 16–4 *In a greenhouse, the glass windows prevent heat from escaping (left). Carbon dioxide and other gases in the atmosphere act like the glass windows in a greenhouse (right). In what form is energy radiated from the Earth to the atmosphere?*

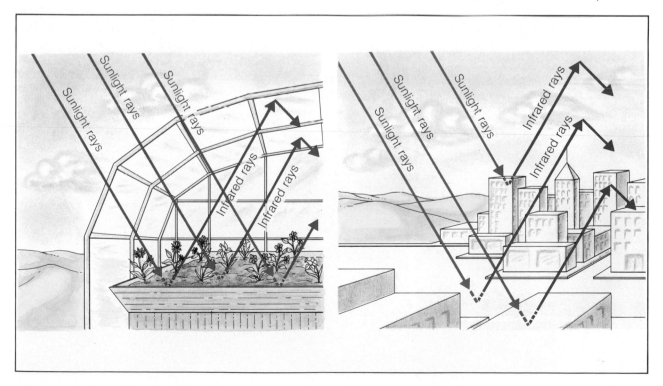

489

Figure 16–5 *Rattlesnakes have special heat-detecting organs. These pit organs are so sensitive they can detect differences in temperature of only 0.003°C!*

Figure 16–6 *The extremely high surface temperatures on Venus are the result of a runaway greenhouse effect. Carbon dioxide released by burning fossil fuels may already be causing higher temperatures on Earth.*

restaurants to keep food warm make use of infrared radiation. If you hold your hand near a light bulb or stove, you can feel the heat given off as infrared rays.

Infrared rays are not like visible light, however. Infrared rays cannot pass through the atmosphere and out into space. Carbon dioxide (CO_2), water vapor, and other gases in the atmosphere absorb the infrared rays, forming a kind of "heat blanket" around the Earth. This process is called the **greenhouse effect** because the gases act like the glass in a greenhouse to trap heat. The greenhouse effect makes the Earth a comfortable place to live. What do you think would happen to the temperature at the Earth's surface if there were no greenhouse effect?

Because most of the infrared rays are absorbed by carbon dioxide, the amount of this gas in the atmosphere is very important. Carbon dioxide is produced by burning fossil fuels, such as coal, oil, and natural gas. As the amount of carbon dioxide in the atmosphere increases, more infrared rays will be absorbed. The greenhouse effect will increase and temperatures at the Earth's surface will go up.

Higher temperatures might result in altered weather patterns, including warmer winters and changes in rainfall. You will learn more about the results of the greenhouse effect in Chapter 17.

Temperature Variations

If the Earth's atmosphere is warmed by heat rising from the surface, how can the air temperature vary so much from place to place? To help you answer this question, look at Figure 16–7.

The angle at which the sun's rays strike the surface is not the same everywhere on Earth. At the equator (the imaginary line that separates the Earth into two halves), the sun is nearly overhead. The sun's rays strike the Earth at a 90° angle all year long. The greatest heating occurs where the sun's rays are most direct; that is, at or near an angle of 90°. So areas at or near the equator receive the most radiant energy and have the highest temperatures.

The farther away from the equator an area is, the less radiant energy it receives. Why is this so? In these areas, the angle at which the sun's rays strike the Earth is less than 90°. As the angle of the sun's

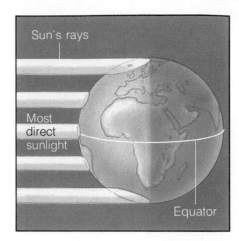

Figure 16–7 *Radiant energy from the sun strikes the Earth at different angles, causing uneven heating of the Earth's surface. Which area receives the most direct sunlight? In which areas is the same amount of radiant energy spread over a wider area?*

Figure 16–8 *What is responsible for the wide variations in air temperature in different regions of the Earth?*

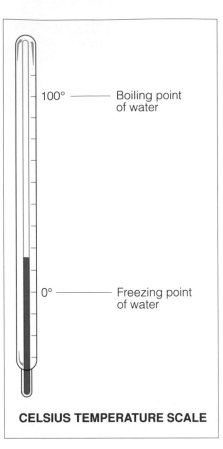

CELSIUS TEMPERATURE SCALE

Figure 16–9 *The temperature of the air is measured with a thermometer in units called degrees. What is the freezing point of water on the Celsius scale? The boiling point?*

rays becomes smaller, the rays become less direct. The same amount of radiant energy is spread over a wider area. The result is less heat and lower temperatures.

Measuring Temperature

Air temperature is measured with a **thermometer.** Most thermometers consist of a thin glass tube with a bulb at one end. The bulb is filled with a liquid, usually either mercury or alcohol that is colored with dye.

Thermometers make use of the ability of a liquid to expand and contract. When a liquid is heated, it expands, or takes up more space. When a liquid is cooled, it contracts, or takes up less space. What happens to the liquid in a thermometer when the air temperature rises? What happens to the liquid when the air temperature falls?

Temperature is measured in units called degrees (°). The temperature scale used by scientists is the Celsius (SEHL-see-uhs) scale. On the Celsius scale, the freezing point of water is 0°. The boiling point of water is 100°C. Normal human body temperature is 37°C.

16–1 Section Review

1. What are the factors that interact to cause weather?
2. What are three ways by which heat energy is spread throughout the atmosphere?
3. How does the angle at which the sun's rays strike the Earth affect the temperature at the Earth's surface?
4. How is carbon dioxide gas in the atmosphere similar to the glass in a greenhouse?

Connection—*Environmental Science*
5. Why do you think some scientists are concerned about increased levels of carbon dioxide in the atmosphere as a result of burning fossil fuels? What effect might an increase in carbon dioxide have on the environment?

16–2 Air Pressure

Hold the eraser of a pencil against the palm of your hand. Now press down. What you feel is the force of the pencil pressing against your hand. You feel pressure. Atmospheric pressure, or **air pressure,** is a measure of the force of the air pressing down on the Earth's surface. The air pressure at any point on the Earth is equal to the weight of the air directly above that point. We are walking on the bottom of an "ocean" of air about 800 kilometers deep!

Air pressure can vary from one point to another on the Earth's surface. **The air pressure at any particular point on the Earth depends on the density of the air.** (Density is equal to mass divided by volume.) Denser air has more mass per unit volume than less dense air. So denser air exerts more air pressure against the Earth's surface than less dense air does.

Factors That Affect Air Pressure

The density of the Earth's atmosphere, and thus air pressure, is affected by three factors: temperature, water vapor, and elevation. As you learned in Section 16–1, the density of a fluid (gas or liquid) decreases when the fluid is heated. Less dense air exerts less air pressure. So places with high

Guide for Reading

Focus on this question as you read.

▶ *What is the relationship between the density of air and air pressure?*

Figure 16–10 *Elevation, or altitude, is one of the factors that affect air pressure. Is the air pressure at the top of Mt. McKinley, Alaska, higher or lower than the air pressure at sea level?*

ACTIVITY
CALCULATING

A Water Barometer

Mercury has a density of 13.5 g/cm³. If standard air pressure supports a column of mercury 76 cm high, how high could the column of water rise when supported at this pressure? (The density of water is 1 g/cm³.)

Figure 16–11 *When air pressure increases, the column of mercury rises in the barometer tube (right). What happens to the column of mercury when air pressure decreases (left)?*

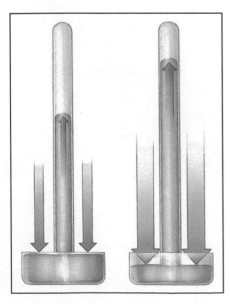

temperatures usually have lower air pressure than places with low temperatures.

At a given pressure, moist air is less dense than dry air. This is because a water molecule has less mass than either a nitrogen or an oxygen molecule. Thus air with a large amount of water vapor in it exerts less air pressure than dryer air.

Elevation, or altitude, also affects air pressure. As the elevation (height above sea level) increases, the air becomes thinner, or less dense. So the air pressure decreases with increasing elevation.

Measuring Air Pressure

Because air pressure changes with changes in temperature and elevation, standard air pressure is measured at a temperature of 0°C at sea level. Air pressure is measured with an instrument called a **barometer** (buh-RAHM-uh-ter). There are two types of barometers. One type, called a mercury barometer, is shown in Figure 16–11.

The mercury barometer was invented in 1643 by an Italian scientist named Evangelista Torricelli. A mercury barometer consists of a glass tube closed at one end and filled with mercury. The open end of the glass tube is placed in a container of mercury. At sea level, air pressure pushing down on the surface of the mercury in the container supports the column of mercury at a certain height in the tube. As the air pressure decreases, the column of mercury drops. What will happen to the column of mercury if the air pressure increases?

A more common type of barometer, called an aneroid (AN-uh-roid) barometer, is shown in Figure 16–12. An aneroid barometer consists of an airtight metal box from which most of the air has been removed. (The word aneroid comes from a Greek word and means without liquid.) A change in air pressure causes a needle to move along a dial, which indicates the new air pressure.

Air Pressure and Weather

Barometers can be used to help forecast the weather. Air pressure may become relatively high when large masses of air come together in the upper

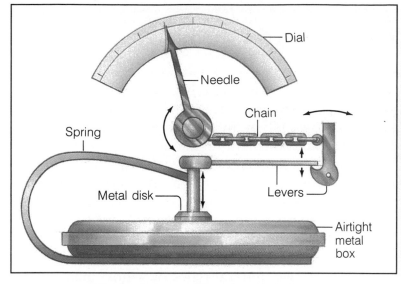

Figure 16–12 *An aneroid barometer is often used in homes, offices, and classrooms to detect changes in air pressure.*

atmosphere. These air masses press down on the layers of air below. This pressure usually prevents warm, moist air from rising into the upper atmosphere. As a result, clouds do not form. So high pressure usually means fair weather. But there are exceptions.

Air pressure may become relatively low when large air masses move apart in the upper atmosphere. This reduces pressure on the layers of warm air below. As a result, the warm air rises. If the warm air is moist, clouds will form in the upper atmosphere. So low pressure can lead to cloudy, rainy weather. But, again, there are exceptions.

16–2 Section Review

1. What is air pressure? What is the relationship between the density of air and air pressure?
2. List and describe three factors that affect air pressure.
3. How is air pressure measured?

Critical Thinking—*Relating Concepts*
4. Which of the following cities has the highest air pressure? Which has the lowest? Explain.
   Atlanta, Georgia   elevation: 320 meters
   Boise, Idaho   elevation: 825 meters
   Denver, Colorado   elevation: 1600 meters
   Salt Lake City, Utah   elevation: 1300 meters

ACTIVITY

Using a Barometer to Forecast the Weather

1. For five days, use a barometer to measure air pressure. Make your measurements before school, during science class, and after school. Record your measurements.

2. At the same time, observe and record the weather conditions.

3. Make a graph of your air pressure measurements.

■ Did you see any relationship between your air pressure measurements and the weather conditions? Can a barometer help you to predict the weather? Explain.

The Density of Water

Is cold water denser than hot water? Try this activity to find out.

1. Fill a deep pan three-fourths full of cold water.

2. Fill a small bottle with hot (not boiling) water. Add a few drops of food coloring to the hot water.

3. Hold your finger over the opening of the bottle. Carefully place the bottle on its side in the pan of cold water. Make sure the bottle is completely under water.

4. Take your finger away from the opening of the bottle. Observe what happens.

What happened when you removed your finger? What does this tell you about the density of hot water and cold water?

■ What do you think would happen if you put hot water in the pan and cold water in the bottle? Try it and find out.

Figure 16–13 *Wind is air in motion. The force of the wind enables the crew of this racing yacht to enjoy an exciting ride.*

16–3 Winds

Have you ever flown a kite at the beach? A beach is a good place to fly a kite because of the winds that usually blow near the shore. What causes these winds to blow? When air is heated, its density decreases. The warm air rises and produces an area of low pressure. Cooler, denser air, which produces an area of high pressure, moves in underneath the rising warm air. So air moves from an area of high pressure to an area of lower pressure. **Winds** are formed by this movement of air from one place to another.

There are two general types of winds: local winds and global winds. Local winds are the type you are most familiar with. They blow from any direction and usually cover short distances. Global winds blow from a specific direction and almost always cover longer distances than local winds. **Both local winds and global winds are caused by differences in air pressure due to unequal heating of the atmosphere.**

Local Winds

During the day, the air over a land area is often warmer than the air over a nearby lake or sea. The air is warmer because the land heats up faster than the water. As the warm air over the land rises, the cooler air over the sea moves inland to take its place.

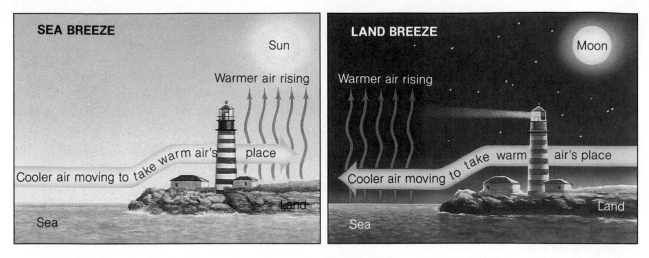

Figure 16–14 *Land and water absorb and lose heat at different rates, causing a sea breeze during the day and a land breeze during the night. Which heats up faster: land or water?*

This flow of air from the sea to the land is called a **sea breeze.** If you have ever spent a summer's day at the beach, you have probably felt a sea breeze.

During the night, the land cools off faster than the water. The air over the sea is now warmer than the air over the land. This warm air over the sea rises. The cooler air over the land moves to replace the rising warm air over the sea. A flow of air from the land to the sea, called a **land breeze,** is formed. If you have stayed at the beach after sunset, then you are probably familiar with a land breeze, too. A land breeze is also called an off-shore breeze.

The name of a wind tells you from which direction the wind is blowing. A land breeze blows from the land to the sea. A sea breeze blows from the sea to the land. Most local winds that you are familiar with are named according to the direction from which they are blowing. For example, a northwest wind blows from northwest to southeast. From what direction does a southwest wind come? In what direction is it blowing?

A major land and sea breeze is called a monsoon (mahn-SOON). A monsoon is a seasonal wind. (The word monsoon is derived from an Arabic word that means season.) During part of the year, a monsoon blows from the land to the ocean. During the rest of the year, it blows from the ocean to the land. When a monsoon blows from the ocean to the land, it brings in warm, moist air. This results in a rainy season with warm temperatures and huge amounts of rain. The rainy season is important to many countries because it supplies the water needed for farming. Monsoon winds are very common in Asia.

ACTIVITY

DISCOVERING

Heating Land and Water

Obtain the following materials: two beakers, sand, water, a thermometer, a watch or clock, and a bright light bulb (or a sunny window). Using these materials, design an experiment to answer these questions.

1. Which heats up faster: land or water?

2. Which one cools down faster?

3. Which one holds heat longer?

■ Based on the results of your experiment, explain why land and sea breezes occur.

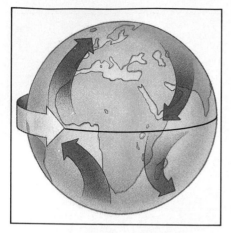

Figure 16–15 *Because of the Earth's rotation, winds appear to curve to the right in the Northern Hemisphere and to the left in the Southern Hemisphere. What is the name for this shift in wind direction?*

Global Winds

Unequal heating of the Earth's surface also forms large global wind systems. In areas near the equator, the sun is almost directly overhead for most of the year. The direct rays of the sun heat the Earth's surface rapidly. The polar regions receive slanting rays from the sun. The slanting rays do not heat the Earth's surface as rapidly as the direct rays do. So temperatures near the poles are lower than those near the equator. At the equator, the warm air rises and moves toward the poles. At the poles, the cooler air sinks and moves toward the equator. This movement produces a global pattern of air circulation.

Global winds do not move directly from north to south or from south to north as you might expect. Because the Earth rotates, or spins on its axis, from west to east, the paths of the winds shift in relation to the Earth's surface. All winds in the Northern Hemisphere curve to the right as they move. In the Southern Hemisphere, winds curve to the left. This shift in wind direction is called the **Coriolis effect.**

The Coriolis effect is the apparent shift in the path of any fluid or object moving above the surface of the Earth due to the rotation of the Earth. For example, suppose you are in an airplane flying south from Seattle, Washington, to San Jose, California. If the pilot does not adjust for the Coriolis effect, the airplane will land west of the point for which it is headed. In other words, an invisible force seems to be pushing the airplane west. You might wind up in the Pacific Ocean!

The diagram in Figure 16–16 shows the Earth's global wind systems. Refer to it often as you read the description of each global wind system. Remember, wind systems describe an overall pattern of air movement. At any particular time or place, local conditions may influence and change the pattern.

DOLDRUMS At the equator (0° latitude), surface winds are quite calm. These regions are called the doldrums (DOHL-druhmz). A belt of air around the equator receives much of the sun's radiant energy. The warm, rising air produces a low-pressure area that extends many kilometers north and south of the equator. Cooler, high-pressure air would normally flow into such an area, creating winds. But the

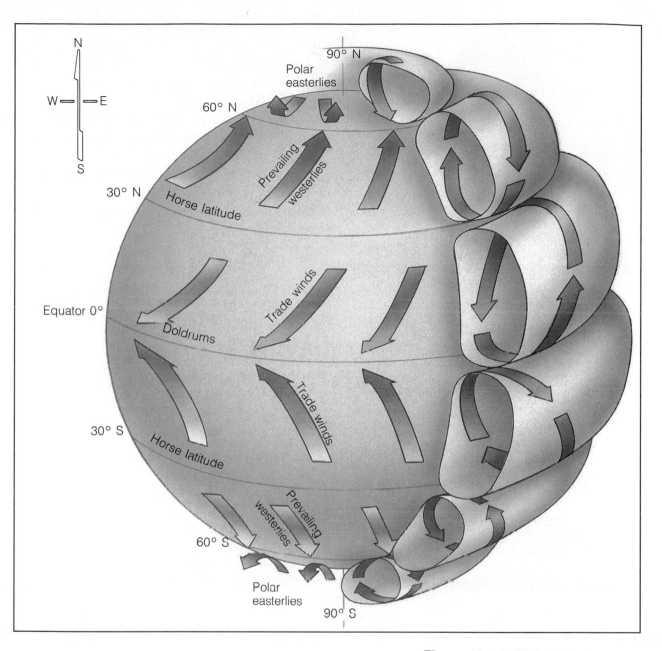

N
W——**E**
S

90° N
Polar
easterlies
60° N
Prevailing
westerlies
30° N
Horse latitude
Equator 0°
Trade winds
Doldrums
Trade winds
30° S
Horse latitude
Prevailing
westerlies
60° S
Polar
easterlies
90° S

Figure 16–16 *Global wind patterns are caused by the unequal heating of the Earth's surface and by the rotation of the Earth. Warm air rises, cold air sinks, and the Coriolis effect causes the winds to curve. What are the three major global winds?*

cooler air is warmed so rapidly near the equator that the winds which form cannot move into the low-pressure area. As a result, any winds that do form are weak. The doldrums can be a problem for sailing ships. Because there may be no winds, or weak winds at best, sailing ships can be stuck in the doldrums for many days. Have you ever heard people refer to themselves as being "in the doldrums"? What did they mean?

TRADE WINDS About 30° north and south of the equator, the warm air rising from the equator cools and begins to sink. Here, the sky is usually clear.

499

Figure 16–17 *The overall movement of global wind systems can be seen in the pattern of the Earth's cloud cover.*

Figure 16–18 *Unlike the trade winds, the prevailing westerlies are strong winds. Where are the prevailing westerlies located?*

There are few clouds and little rainfall. Winds are calm. Hundreds of years ago, sailing ships traveling to the New World were sometimes unable to move for days or weeks because there was too little wind. Sailors sometimes had to throw horses overboard when the horses' food supply ran out. For this reason the latitudes 30° north and south of the equator are called the horse latitudes.

At the horse latitudes, some of the sinking air travels back toward the equator. The rest of the sinking air continues to move toward the poles. The air moving back toward the equator forms a belt of warm, steady winds. These winds are called trade winds.

In the Northern Hemisphere, the Coriolis effect deflects the trade winds to the right. These winds, called the northeast trades, blow from northeast to southwest. In the Southern Hemisphere, the trade winds are deflected to the left. They become the southeast trades. In what direction do the southeast trades blow?

Early sailors used the trade winds when they traveled to the New World. The trade winds provided a busy sailing route between Europe and America. Today, airplane pilots use the trade winds to increase speed and save fuel when they fly this route from east to west.

PREVAILING WESTERLIES The cool, sinking air that continues to move toward the North and South poles is also influenced by the Coriolis effect. In the Northern Hemisphere, the air is deflected to the right. In the Southern Hemisphere, it is deflected to the left. So in both hemispheres, the winds appear to travel from west to east. These winds are called the prevailing westerlies. (Remember, winds are named according to the direction from which they blow.) As you can see from Figure 16–16, the prevailing westerlies are located in a belt from 40° to 60° latitude in both hemispheres. Unlike the trade winds, the prevailing westerlies are often particularly strong winds.

POLAR EASTERLIES In both hemispheres, the westerlies start rising and cooling between 50° and 60° latitude as they approach the poles (90° latitude). Here they meet extremely cold air flowing toward the equator from the poles. This band of cold air is deflected west by the Coriolis effect. As a result, the winds appear to travel from east to west and are called the polar easterlies. The polar easterlies are cold but weak winds. In the United States, many changes in the weather are caused by the polar easterlies.

Jet Streams

For centuries, people have been aware of the global winds you have just read about. But it was not until the 1940s that another global wind was discovered. This wind is a narrow belt of strong, high-speed, high-pressure air called a jet stream. Jet streams flow from west to east at altitudes above 12 kilometers. Wind speeds in the jet streams can reach 180 kilometers per hour in the summer and 220 to 350 kilometers per hour in the winter. Airplane pilots flying from west to east can use a jet stream to increase speed and save fuel.

Figure 16–19 *A high-altitude jet stream moves over the Nile River Valley and the Red Sea. In which direction do jet streams flow?*

PROBLEM Solving

North Pole Smog Alert

No place on the surface of the Earth is farther away from industry and human development than the land above the Arctic Circle near the North Pole. Yet scientists have discovered sulfur particles in the arctic air that are identical to those found in the polluted air of some European cities. These particles are so thick that they form a blue-gray haze similar to that seen over many large cities. Using your knowledge of global wind systems, explain how air pollution has reached the Arctic. Draw a map to illustrate your explanation.

Figure 16–20 *Wind speed is related to the rate at which the cups of the anemometer revolve. What other weather instrument can you see in the photograph?*

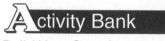
ctivity Bank

Build Your Own Anemometer, p. 773

Build a Wind-Speed Meter

1. Obtain a square piece of cardboard.

2. Stick a push pin into the upper left corner.

3. Hang a 3-cm strip of metal from the push pin.

4. Calibrate your wind-speed meter by holding it out the window of a moving car. The metal strip will move higher as the wind speed increases. Mark the position of the strip at different speeds.

Jet streams do not flow around the Earth in regular bands. They wander up and down as they circle the Earth. At times, they take great detours north and south. The wind speed and depth of a jet stream can change from season to season, or even from day to day.

The wandering jet streams affect the atmosphere below them. The rush of a jet stream creates waves and eddy currents, or swirling motions opposite to the flow of the main stream, in the lower atmosphere. These disturbances cause air masses in the lower atmosphere to spread out. This produces areas of low pressure. The low-pressure areas serve as the centers of local storms.

Measuring Wind

As you have been reading about local and global winds, you have probably noticed that two measurements are needed to describe wind: wind direction and wind speed. Meteorologists and weather observers use a wind vane to determine the direction of the wind on the Earth's surface. A wind vane points into the wind. An **anemometer** (an-uh-MAHM-uh-ter) is used to measure wind speed. Wind speed is usually expressed in meters per second, miles per hour, or knots. One knot is equal to 1850 meters per hour.

16–3 Section Review

1. What are the differences between local winds and global winds? How are they alike?
2. What causes winds in the Northern Hemisphere to curve to the right as they move?
3. Name the Earth's four major wind belts.
4. Describe the movements of the three major global winds in terms of unequal heating and the Coriolis effect.

Connection—*You and Your World*
5. An airplane trip from New York City to Los Angeles takes longer than the return trip from Los Angeles to New York. Explain why.

16–4 Moisture in the Air

As you walk to the supermarket on a summer afternoon, you can feel your shirt sticking to your back. Beads of salty perspiration cling to your forehead and upper lip. The air around you feels damp. You can't wait to get into the air-conditioned store!

Why does the air sometimes feel damp? Moisture enters the air through the **evaporation** of water. Evaporation is the process by which water molecules escape into the air. Through evaporation, the sun's radiant energy turns liquid water into a gas, or water vapor. (The liquid water comes from oceans, rivers, lakes, soil—even from plants and animals.) Winds transport the moisture all over the Earth. At any given time, the atmosphere holds about 14 million tons of moisture! **Water vapor, or moisture, in the air is called humidity.**

The amount of moisture in the air can vary greatly from place to place and from time to time. You will often hear the amount of moisture in the air referred to in terms of **relative humidity** (hyoo-MIHD-uh-tee). Relative humidity is the percentage of moisture the air holds relative to the amount it could hold at a particular temperature.

Suppose that at a certain temperature, 1 kilogram of air can hold 12 grams of water vapor. However, it is actually holding 9 grams. The relative humidity of the air at that temperature would be 9/12 × 100, or 75 percent. If the same kilogram of air held 12

Guide for Reading

Focus on these questions as you read.

▶ *How are the terms humidity and relative humidity related?*

▶ *What are the forms of water vapor in the air?*

Figure 16–21 *Fog, seen here enveloping the skyscrapers of Chicago, is formed when water vapor in the air condenses at a temperature called the dew point. Dew that forms overnight can often be seen on leaves or blades of grass or pine needles in the early morning.*

RELATIVE HUMIDITY

Dry-Bulb Thermometer Readings (°C)	Difference Between Wet- and Dry-Bulb Thermometer Readings (°C)				
	1	2	3	4	5
10	88	77	66	55	44
11	89	78	67	56	46
12	89	78	68	58	48
13	89	79	69	59	50
14	90	79	70	60	51
15	90	80	71	61	53
16	90	81	71	63	54
17	90	81	72	64	55
18	91	82	73	65	57
19	91	82	74	65	58
20	91	83	74	66	59
21	91	83	75	67	60
22	92	83	76	68	61
23	92	84	76	69	62
24	92	84	77	69	62
25	92	84	77	70	63
26	92	85	78	71	64
27	92	85	78	71	65
28	93	85	78	72	65
29	93	86	79	72	66
30	93	86	79	73	67

Figure 16–22 *If the difference between the readings on the wet-bulb and dry-bulb thermometers is 2°C and the air temperature is 19°C, what is the relative humidity?*

grams of water vapor, it would be holding all the moisture it could hold at that temperature. The relative humidity would then be 100 percent ($12/12 \times 100$). When the relative humidity is 100 percent, the air is said to be saturated. That is, it is holding all the water vapor it can hold at that particular temperature.

Measuring Relative Humidity

Meteorologists measure relative humidity with a **psychrometer** (sigh-KRAHM-uh-ter). A psychrometer consists of two thermometers. The bulb of one thermometer is covered with a moist cloth. This thermometer is the wet-bulb thermometer. The other thermometer is the dry-bulb thermometer.

When air passes over the wet bulb, the water in the cloth evaporates. Evaporation requires heat energy. So evaporation of the water from the cloth cools the thermometer bulb. If the humidity is low, evaporation will take place quickly and the temperature of the wet-bulb thermometer will drop. If the humidity is high, evaporation will take place slowly and the temperature of the wet-bulb thermometer will not change much. In other words, the temperature of the wet-bulb thermometer will be close to the temperature of the dry-bulb thermometer, which is measuring air temperature.

To determine the relative humidity, meteorologists first find the difference between the dry-bulb temperature and the wet-bulb temperature. Then they use a chart similar to the one in Figure 16–22 to find the relative humidity expressed as a percentage. Suppose the dry-bulb thermometer reads 28°C. The difference between the two thermometer readings is 4°C. What is the relative humidity?

Clouds

Warm air can hold more moisture than cold air. As warm, moist air rises in the atmosphere, its temperature begins to drop. Because cold air cannot hold as much water vapor as warm air, the rising air soon becomes saturated. At this point, the water vapor in the air begins to condense, or change into a liquid. The temperature at which water vapor

Figure 16–23 *The three basic cloud types are fluffy cumulus (left), layered stratus (center), and wispy cirrus (right). What type of weather is usually associated with each cloud type?*

condenses is called the dew point. Have you ever seen drops of water, or dew, on blades of grass early in the morning? What do you think caused dew to form on the grass?

Clouds form when moisture in the air condenses on small particles of dust or other solids in the air. The tiny droplets of water that form make up the clouds. A cloud is really a mixture in which particles of a liquid (water) are suspended in a gas (air).

As you can see for yourself just by looking at the sky, clouds come in all sorts of shapes and sizes. Scientists use the basic shape and the altitude of clouds to classify them. The three main types of clouds are cumulus (KYOO-myoo-luhs) clouds, stratus (STRAT-uhs) clouds, and cirrus (SEER-uhs) clouds. Each type of cloud is generally associated with a certain type of weather.

Cumulus clouds look like piles of cotton balls in the sky. These clouds are fluffy and white with flat bottoms. They form at altitudes of 2.4 to 13.5 kilometers. Cumulus clouds usually indicate fair weather. However, when cumulus clouds get larger and darker on the bottom, they produce thunderstorms. These large thunderclouds are called cumulonimbus clouds.

Figure 16–24 *Clouds are classified according to their shape and altitude. Cumulus and stratus clouds that develop at altitudes between 2 and 7 kilometers have the prefix* alto- *in their names. What prefix is used for these clouds if they are at an altitude above 7 kilometers?*

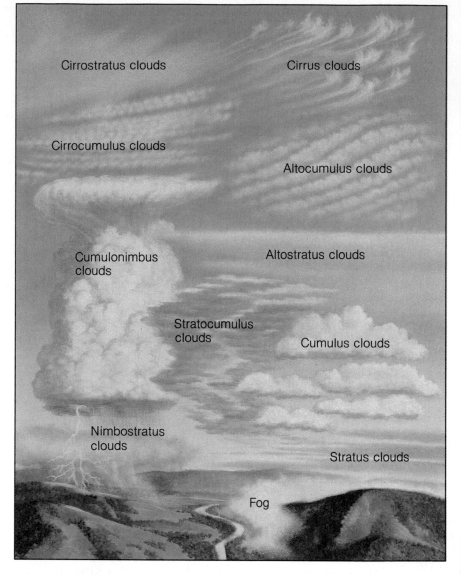

Cirrostratus clouds

Cirrus clouds

Cirrocumulus clouds

Altocumulus clouds

Cumulonimbus clouds

Altostratus clouds

Stratocumulus clouds

Cumulus clouds

Nimbostratus clouds

Stratus clouds

Fog

ACTIVITY

DOING

Fog in a Bottle

1. Fill a narrow-necked bottle with hot water. **CAUTION:** *Do not use water hot enough to cause burns.*

2. Pour out most of the water, leaving about 3 centimeters at the bottom of the bottle.

3. Place an ice cube on the mouth of the bottle.

4. Repeat steps 1 through 3 using cold water instead of hot water.

In which bottle does fog form? Why? Why is it helpful to repeat the activity with cold water?

Smooth, gray clouds that cover the whole sky and block out the sun are called stratus clouds. They form at an altitude of about 2.5 kilometers. Light rain and drizzle are usually associated with stratus clouds. Nimbostratus clouds bring rain and snow. When stratus clouds form close to the ground, the result is fog. Ground fog is formed when air above the ground is cooled rapidly at night. Warmer temperatures during the day cause the fog to disappear.

Feathery or fibrous clouds are called cirrus clouds. Sometimes these clouds are called mares' tails. Can you tell from looking at the picture of cirrus clouds in Figure 16–23 why they are called mares' tails? Cirrus clouds form at very high altitudes,

Figure 16–25 *Dark storm clouds gather over a field. What is the name for the type of cloud that usually brings thunderstorms?*

usually between 6 and 12 kilometers. Cirrus clouds are made of ice crystals. You can see cirrus clouds in fair weather, but they often indicate that rain or snow will fall within several hours.

Precipitation

Water vapor that condenses and forms clouds can fall to the Earth as rain, sleet, snow, or hail. Water that falls from the atmosphere to the Earth is called **precipitation** (pree-sihp-uh-TAY-shuhn).

Before water falls to the Earth as precipitation, cloud droplets must increase in size. Cloud droplets increase in size by colliding and combining with other droplets. At some point, the droplets become too large to remain suspended in the cloud. Gravity then pulls these larger drops of water to the Earth as rain. An average raindrop contains about one million times as much water as a cloud droplet!

When falling raindrops pass through an extremely cold layer of air, they sometimes freeze into small ice pellets called sleet. Sleet reaches the Earth only in the winter. Why? What do you think happens to sleet in the summer?

Snow forms when water vapor changes directly into a solid. Snowflakes are flat six-sided ice crystals that have beautiful shapes. Because snowflakes sometimes clump together, it is often hard to see the

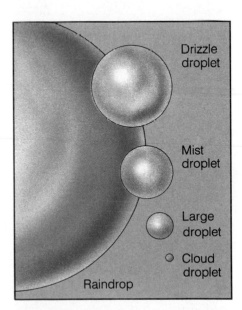

Figure 16–26 *Notice the relative sizes of water droplets in a cloud. Which droplet is the smallest? The largest? When water droplets get large enough, they fall to Earth.*

507

separate crystals. If you could look at many individual snowflakes, you would find that they all have different shapes. In fact, no two snowflakes are exactly alike!

Hail is one of the most damaging forms of precipitation. It is usually formed in cumulonimbus clouds. Hailstones are small balls or chunks of ice ranging from 5 to 75 millimeters in diameter. Hailstones are formed when water droplets hit ice pellets in a cloud and freeze. If the updraft (upward movement of the wind) is strong enough, the hailstones remain in the cloud for a long time. As more water droplets strike them, new layers of ice are added. Finally, the hailstones get so big and heavy that they fall to the ground. One of the largest hailstones ever found fell on Coffeywill, Kansas, in September 1970. This hailstone measured 140 millimeters in diameter!

Measuring Rainfall

Precipitation in the form of rain is measured with a **rain gauge.** A rain gauge is a straight-sided container with a flat bottom that collects rain as it falls. The amount of rain collected in a rain gauge over a given period of time is usually expressed in millimeters or centimeters. Weather observers in the United States, however, usually express the amount of rainfall in inches.

Figure 16–27 *When huge numbers of individual snowflakes (top) accumulate, they form a lovely winter scene (center). These hailstones became large and heavy enough to fall to the ground (bottom).*

16–4 Section Review

1. What is the difference between humidity and relative humidity?
2. How does moisture enter the air?
3. What are the three main types of clouds? What are the four main types of precipitation?
4. How is relative humidity measured? How is rainfall measured?

Critical Thinking—*Making Calculations*
5. Suppose 1 kilogram of air can hold 16 grams of water vapor but actually holds 8 grams. What is the relative humidity?

16–5 Weather Patterns

As you have already learned in the first part of this chapter, there are many factors that interact in the Earth's atmosphere to cause weather. You know from experience that weather is constantly changing. Clouds and rain may move quickly into an area and move away just as quickly. Days of blue, sunny skies and warm temperatures may change overnight to gray, stormy skies and freezing rain. What atmospheric conditions and patterns cause these changes in the weather?

Air Masses

Changes in the weather are caused by movements of large bodies of air called **air masses.** Air masses usually cover thousands of square kilometers. The properties of the air in an air mass are nearly the same, or uniform, throughout the air mass. Like clouds, air masses are classified according to some basic characteristic. For clouds, the characteristic is shape; for air masses, it is where they form. Where air masses form determines two of their most important properties: temperature and humidity, or moisture content. Air masses that form over tropical regions are warm. Those that form over polar regions are cold. Continental air masses, which form over continents, are relatively dry. Maritime air masses form over oceans, and they are relatively humid. **The four major types of air masses that affect the weather in the United States are maritime tropical, maritime polar, continental tropical, and continental polar.** Figure 16–28 on page 510 shows where these air masses form and the areas of the United States they most influence.

The maritime tropical air mass forms over the ocean near the equator. It holds warm, moist air. In the summer, the maritime tropical air mass brings hot, humid weather. But if the warm, moist air comes in contact with a cold air mass in the winter, rain or snow will fall.

The maritime polar air mass forms over the Pacific Ocean in both winter and summer. It forms over the cold North Atlantic waters in the summer.

Guide for Reading

Focus on these questions as you read.

▶ *What are the four major air masses that affect the weather in the United States?*

▶ *How do different types of fronts and storms affect weather in the United States?*

ACTIVITY

DISCOVERING

Does Air Have Mass?

1. Using a balance, find the mass of a fully deflated ball.

2. Use an air pump to completely inflate the ball. What do you think the mass of the inflated ball will be?

3. Place the inflated ball on the balance and find its mass. What is the mass of the inflated ball? Was your prediction correct?

■ Does air have mass? How do you know?

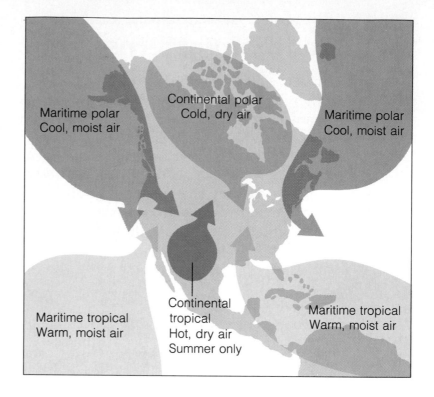

During the summer, the maritime polar air mass brings cooler temperatures to the eastern states and fog to California and other western states. Heavy snow and cold temperatures are produced by the maritime polar air mass in the winter.

During the summer, the continental tropical air mass forms over land in Mexico. This air mass brings dry, hot air to the southwestern states. The continental polar air mass forms over land in northern Canada. In winter, this cold, dry air mass causes extremely cold temperatures in the United States.

Fronts

When two air masses that have different properties meet, they do not mix readily. Instead, a boundary forms between the two air masses. This boundary is called a **front.** (The term front was first applied to weather during World War I, when opposing armies faced one another across a battlefront.) The weather at a front is usually unsettled and stormy. **There are four different types of fronts: cold fronts, warm fronts, occluded fronts, and stationary fronts.**

A cold front forms when a mass of cold air meets and pushes under a mass of warm air, as shown in Figure

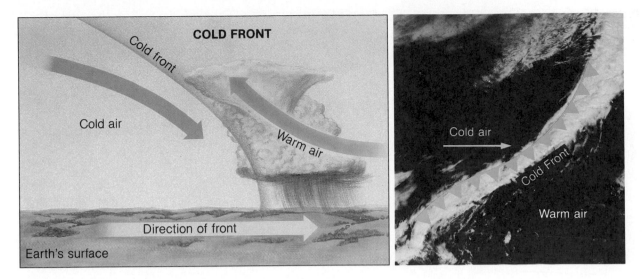

16-29. The cold air mass forces its way underneath the warm air mass and pushes it upward. What do you know about cold air and warm air that explains why this happens? Violent storms are associated with a cold front. Fair, cool weather usually follows.

A warm front forms when a mass of warm air overtakes a cold air mass and moves over it. This process is shown in Figure 16-30. Rain and showers usually accompany a warm front. Hot, humid weather usually follows.

A cold front travels faster than a warm front. When a cold front overtakes a warm front, an occluded front forms. An occluded front is shown in Figure 16-31 on page 512. As the warm air is pushed upward, the cold air meets cool air. An occluded

Figure 16-29 *A cold front forms when a mass of cold air meets and pushes under a mass of warm air, as shown in the illustration (left). Notice the weather symbols showing the edge of the cold front on the satellite weather photograph (right).*

Figure 16-30 *A warm front forms when a mass of warm air overtakes a cold air mass and moves over it, as shown in the illustration (left). Notice the weather symbols showing the edge of the warm front on the satellite weather photograph (right).*

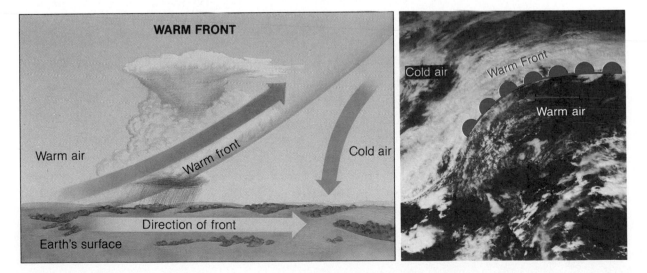

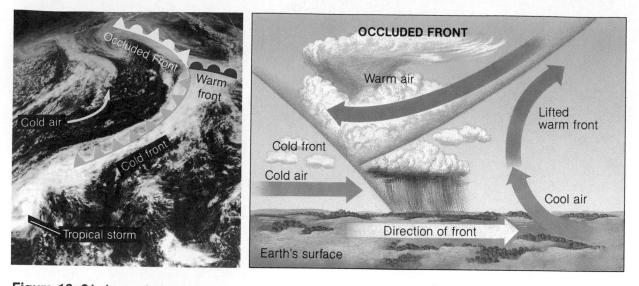

Figure 16–31 *An occluded front forms when a cold front overtakes a warm front, as shown in the illustration (right). Notice the weather symbols showing the occluded front on the satellite weather photograph (left).*

front may also occur when cool air overtakes a cold front and warm air is pushed upward. An occluded front produces less extreme weather than a cold front or a warm front.

When a warm air mass meets a cold air mass and no movement occurs, a stationary front forms. Rain may fall in an area for many days when a stationary front is in place.

Storms

A storm is a violent disturbance in the atmosphere. It is marked by sudden changes in air pressure and rapid air movements. Some storms may cover a huge area, whereas others cover only a small area. You are probably familiar with one or more of the storms described here. As you read about these storms, compare the descriptions with your own experiences.

RAINSTORMS AND SNOWSTORMS When two different fronts collide, rainstorms or snowstorms form. When a warm front moves in and meets a cold front, heavy nimbostratus clouds develop. In the summer, the result is a steady rainfall that lasts for several hours. In the winter, a heavy snowfall occurs. If the wind speed is more than 56 kilometers per hour and the temperature is below −7°C, a blizzard results.

Sometimes, heavy rain falling over a wide area freezes instantly on trees, power lines, and other surfaces. The result is an ice storm. Although the layer

of glittering ice may look beautiful, ice storms can cause great damage by knocking down trees and power lines. Some interesting effects of an ice storm are shown in Figure 16–32.

THUNDERSTORMS When a cold front moves in and meets a warm front, cumulonimbus clouds produce thunderstorms. Thunderstorms are heavy rainstorms accompanied by thunder and lightning. These storms can be quite dangerous. Violent downdrafts and strong wind shear (a great change in wind velocity over a short distance) are often associated with thunderstorms. These conditions are of great concern to airplane pilots and air-traffic controllers during take-offs and landings.

The other factor that makes thunderstorms dangerous is lightning. What is lightning? You may have heard the story about Benjamin Franklin flying a kite into a thunderstorm to prove that lightning is a form of electricity. During a thunderstorm, areas of positive and negative electric charges build up in the storm clouds. Lightning is a sudden discharge, or spark, of electricity between two clouds or between a cloud and the ground.

Lightning striking the ground is the leading cause of forest fires in the western states. Lightning may also strike people, animals, or buildings. In fact, more people are killed every year by lightning than as a result of any other violent storm! There are some important safety rules you should remember when you see a lightning storm coming. Avoid open

Figure 16–32 *An ice storm covers everything in its path like frosting on a cake or glaze on a doughnut. Although it may look beautiful, an ice storm can cause much damage.*

Activity Bank

What Causes Lightning?, p. 774

ACTIVITY

CALCULATING

Storms and Lightning

Every day, an average of 45,000 storms occur across the Earth's surface. How many storms occur in a year?

Lightning can occur with or without a thunderstorm. Lightning strikes somewhere in the United States about 50 million times a year. On the average, how many times each day does lightning strike the United States?

Figure 16–33 *Why should you never stand under a tree during a thunderstorm?*

Speed of Sound

1. Working with a partner, measure a distance of 100 meters in an open outdoor area.

2. Stand at one end of this 100-meter distance with a stopwatch. Have your partner stand at the opposite end and make a loud, sharp noise—for example, by striking an old aluminum pot with a metal spoon.

3. Start the stopwatch exactly when you see your partner strike the pot. Stop the watch exactly when you hear the noise. How long did it take for you to hear the noise?

4. Repeat the procedure two more times and calculate the average for the three trials. Divide the distance by the average time to find the speed of sound in meters per second.

spaces, but do not take shelter under a tree. The best shelter is inside a building. Remember, however, to stay away from sinks, bathtubs, and televisions. (Some people have even been injured by lightning when talking on the telephone.) And never try to repeat Benjamin Franklin's experiment with a kite!

Loud thunder claps usually accompany the lightning in a thunderstorm. The electrical discharge of lightning heats the air. When the air is heated, it expands rapidly. This sudden expansion of the air results in sound waves, which we hear as thunder. Do you know why you see lightning before you hear thunder? Although lightning and thunder occur at the same time, you see the lightning almost instantly. The sound waves of thunder, however, travel much more slowly than light (340 meters per second compared with 300,000 kilometers per second). If you hear thunder about 3 seconds after you see a flash of lightning, the lightning is about 1 kilometer away. How can you tell if a thunderstorm is moving toward or away from you?

CYCLONES AND ANTICYCLONES Air pressure has a great effect on the weather. An area of low pressure that contains rising warm air is called a cyclone. In a cyclone, cooler air moves in to take the place of the rising warm air. The air currents begin to spin. Winds spiral around and into the center of the cyclone. The winds move in a counterclockwise direction in the Northern Hemisphere. Cyclones usually cause rainy, stormy weather. What do you think causes the air currents in a cyclone to spin?

A high-pressure area that contains cold, dry air is called an anticyclone. Winds spiral around and out from the center of an anticyclone. In the Northern Hemisphere, the winds move in a clockwise direction. The weather caused by anticyclones is usually clear, dry, and fair.

HURRICANES A hurricane is a powerful cyclone (a low-pressure area containing rising warm air) that forms over tropical oceans. Hurricanes that form over the western Pacific Ocean are called typhoons. During late summer and early autumn, low-pressure areas often form over the Caribbean or the Gulf of Mexico. Warm, moist air begins to rise rapidly. Cooler air moves in, and the air begins to spin. As

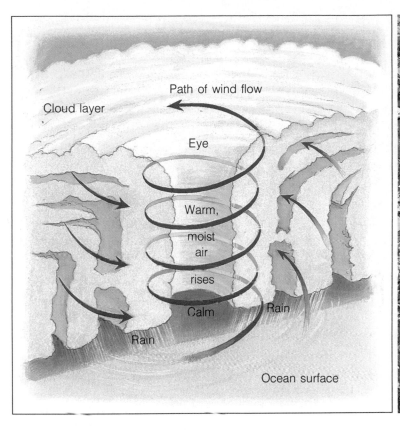

the air pressure in the center drops, more air is drawn into the spinning system. The system begins to spin faster. The rapidly spinning, rising air forms a doughnut-shaped wall of strong winds, clouds, and rainfall. Inside the wall, the air is calm. This calm center is called the eye of the hurricane. Outside the eye, winds may reach rotational speeds close to 480 kilometers per hour.

The high waves and strong winds of a hurricane often cause great damage, especially in coastal areas. Heavy rain may also cause serious flooding. Meteorologists can track the path of a hurricane and issue watches or warnings to people living near the coast as the storm approaches. A typical hurricane lasts for about 9 days. In extreme cases, hurricanes can last as long as 3 to 4 weeks. In terms of the total energy involved, hurricanes are the most powerful storms on Earth. As a hurricane moves inland, it loses its force and power. Can you explain why?

TORNADOES Tornadoes are also incredibly destructive. A tornado is a whirling, funnel-shaped cloud. It develops in low, heavy cumulonimbus clouds. The air pressure at the bottom of the funnel

Figure 16–34 *This photo shows some of the destruction caused by Hurricane Andrew when it hit south Florida in August 1992. A hurricane has a large counterclockwise movement of air surrounding a low-pressure center. What is the name for the calm center of a hurricane?*

of swirling air is extremely low. When this low-pressure area touches the ground, it acts like a giant vacuum cleaner. Some tornadoes occur over water. A tornado over a lake or ocean is called a waterspout.

Meteorologists are not sure how tornadoes form. Tornadoes occur most often in spring during the late afternoon or early evening. In the United States, they are most common on the Great Plains. In fact, tornadoes are so common that this part of the United States is often called Tornado Alley. Here, cool, dry air from the west collides with warm, moist air from the Gulf of Mexico.

The diameter of an average tornado is only about 0.4 kilometer. The length of a tornado's path varies, but it averages 6 kilometers. Tornadoes generally last only a few minutes. But because they are so concentrated, they are intensely violent and dangerous storms. Tornadoes have strong winds that can reach speeds of more than 95 kilometers per hour. Roofs and walls of buildings may be blown out by the winds. Houses, railroad cars, automobiles, and even people may be picked up and thrown hundreds of meters. A tornado in Nebraska tossed a 225-kilogram baby grand piano almost 400 meters across a corn field!

16–5 Section Review

1. What are two important properties of an air mass? What are the four major types of air masses that affect the weather in the United States?
2. What is a front? Name four different types of fronts.
3. What is the difference between a cyclone and an anticyclone?
4. Describe the differences between a hurricane and a tornado.

Connection—*Geography*
5. Saskatchewan, Canada, has hot summers, cold winters, and stormy weather in spring and autumn. Explain this weather in terms of major air masses.

16–6 Predicting the Weather

As Lisa was about to leave for school, her mother called after her, "Don't forget to take your umbrella." Lisa looked out the window. The sun was shining brightly, and there were only a few fluffy white clouds in the sky. How could Lisa's mother know that she would need her umbrella later in the day?

Accurate weather predictions are important for planning many human activities. Farmers need to know the best times to plant and harvest their crops. Airplane takeoffs, landings, and flight paths are scheduled according to local weather conditions. Weather forecasts alert people to severe storms that could endanger life or property. And most people want to know what the weather will be like as they go to and from work and school or plan outdoor activities.

Meteorologists rely on up-to-date observations of current weather conditions to make their forecasts. Most weather forecasts are made for periods of a few hours up to five days. **Meteorologists interpret weather information from local weather observers, balloons, satellites, and weather stations around the world.** Weather stations are located on land and on ships at sea. Meteorologists also use computers to help them interpret weather data.

Weather Maps

Accurate weather forecasts are made possible by studying information about atmospheric conditions at several places. In the United States, weather data are gathered from more than 300 local weather stations. These data include temperature, air pressure, precipitation, and wind speed and direction. Weather data are used to prepare a daily weather map. Information about cloud cover, air masses, and fronts may also be included on a weather map. So a weather map is a "picture" of local weather conditions.

The information on weather maps is often recorded in the form of numbers and symbols. Symbols are used to show wind speed and direction,

Figure 16–36 *Here you see two meteorologists releasing a weather balloon. A computer monitor displays weather data transmitted from a weather satellite.*

517

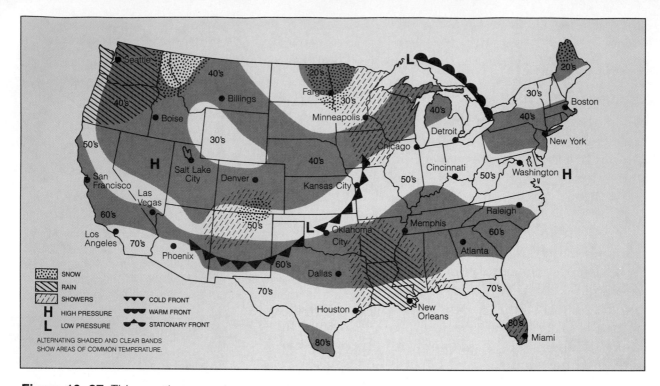

Figure 16-37 *This weather map is similar to those often printed in newspapers. The legend at the bottom left tells you how to read the symbols on this map. These symbols are not exactly the same as those on an official National Weather Service map. What was the weather in Minneapolis on this particular day?*

cloud cover, precipitation, position and direction of fronts, and areas of high and low pressure. The symbols on official National Weather Service weather maps are used by all nations. As with other branches of science, it is important that meteorologists from different countries be able to understand universal weather symbols. In chemistry, universal symbols are used to identify the different chemical elements. For example, chemists in the United States, Russia, Japan, and China all recognize H as the symbol for hydrogen and C as the symbol for carbon. In the same way, meteorologists all over the world recognize the universal weather symbols. You might notice, however, that the official National Weather Service symbols differ from those used on the simplified weather map in your local newspaper. A typical newspaper weather map is shown in Figure 16-37.

Recording Weather Data

Look closely at Figure 16-38, which shows how weather data from a particular location are presented. The circle represents an observation station. Weather data are placed in specific positions inside and outside the station circle. Think of the station circle as the point of an arrow. Attached to the station circle is a line, which is like the shaft of an arrow. The wind direction is represented as moving along the shaft of the arrow toward the station circle. The wind direction is the direction from which the wind is blowing. According to this station circle, how is the wind blowing? You are correct if you said from southwest to northeast.

Small lines at the end of the shaft are symbols for the wind speed. Each full line represents a wind speed of 9–14 miles per hour. (Notice that in the United States, English units are commonly used instead of metric units.) In this station circle, the wind speed is about 18 miles per hour. Average daily temperature is given in degrees Fahrenheit next to the station circle. Other data shown include percentage of cloud cover and atmospheric pressure in millibars and inches of mercury. One millibar equals about 0.03 inch of mercury. (Inches of mercury are usually given to the nearest hundredth and range from 28.00 to 31.00 inches.) What were the temperature and percentage of cloud cover when the data at this weather station were recorded?

The data from weather stations all around the country are assembled into weather maps at the National Weather Service. Figure 16–39 on page 520 shows such a weather map. Notice that this map includes most of the weather station data shown in Figure 16–38. How does this weather map compare with weather maps in your local newspaper?

A warm front is shown on a weather map as a line with half circles pointing in the direction of its movement. A cold front is shown as a line with triangles pointing in the direction of its movement. To show a stationary front, the symbols for a warm front and a cold front are combined. Why is this appropriate? The symbols are shown as pushing against each other, to illustrate that a stationary front does not move in either direction. The symbols for a warm front and a cold front are also combined to show an occluded front. But the symbols are on the same side to illustrate that both fronts are moving in the same direction.

Isotherms and Isobars

On some weather maps, you may see curved lines called **isotherms** (IGH-soh-thermz). The word

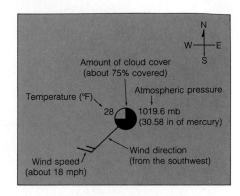

Figure 16–38 *These weather data indicate readings taken at a weather observation station.*

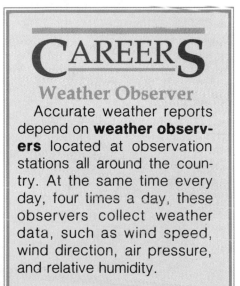

CAREERS

Weather Observer

Accurate weather reports depend on **weather observers** located at observation stations all around the country. At the same time every day, four times a day, these observers collect weather data, such as wind speed, wind direction, air pressure, and relative humidity.

If you would like to learn more about weather observers, write to the United States Department of Commerce, NOAA, National Weather Service, Silver Spring, MD 20910.

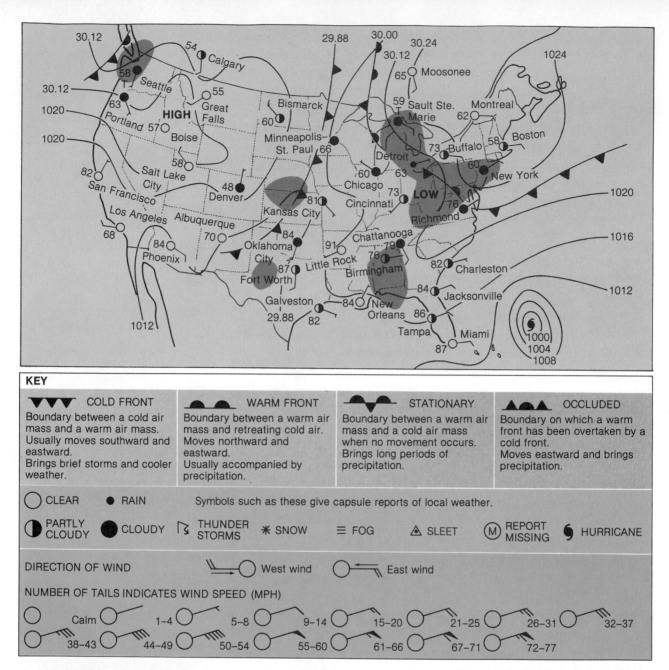

Figure 16–39 *This illustration shows a typical weather map with data from observation stations all over the country. Use the key below the map to determine the weather conditions in your state on this particular day.*

isotherm is made up of the prefix *iso-*, meaning equal, and the root word *-therm*, meaning heat. Isotherms are lines that connect locations with the same temperature. The number on the end of an isotherm indicates the temperature at all points along the isotherm.

Notice the curved lines running through the weather map in Figure 16–39. These lines are called **isobars** (IGH-soh-barz). From the prefix and root word, what do you think isobars are? Isobars are lines that join places on a weather map that have the same air pressure. The number at the end of an isobar represents the air pressure recorded at each observation station along the isobar. The air pressure can be given in millibars, inches of mercury, or both. On this weather map, the isobars are marked at one end with air pressure in inches and at the other end with air pressure in millibars.

Controlling the Weather

An American writer and humorist once said, "Everybody talks about the weather, but nobody does anything about it." Actually, people have always tried to do something about the weather. Because rain is so important for the growth of crops, many efforts to control the weather have centered around rainmaking. Native Americans tried to encourage rainfall by performing elaborate rain dances. In 1901, French farmers fired an "antihail" cannon into the air. They were hoping to break up large hailstones that could destroy their crops and to produce a gentle rain instead. But all they got was a loud bang!

If something could be done about the weather, the results would be important to many people. By controlling the weather, damage from hailstorms, tornadoes, lightning, and hurricanes could be avoided. Droughts and floods could be prevented by controlling rainfall.

At the present time, weather control is limited to the seeding of clouds. Cloud seeding involves the sprinkling of dry ice (solid carbon dioxide) or silver iodide crystals into supercooled layers of stratus clouds. (Supercooling occurs when water remains a liquid below its freezing point.) Seeding causes water droplets to evaporate, or change into a gas. As they evaporate, the water droplets absorb heat from nearby supercooled droplets. The supercooled droplets then freeze and form ice crystals. The crystals grow rapidly. At some point, the crystals become large enough to fall to the Earth as rain or snow.

Experiments have shown that seeding hailstorms and hurricanes decreases their force. However, the most successful use of cloud seeding has been in the partial removal of cool fog at airports. Dry ice is sprinkled onto the fog, causing ice crystals to form. As a result, the fog loses some of its moisture. In

Figure 16–40 *A Sioux member of the Big Thunder Dance Company is shown performing a rain dance.*

ACTIVITY

DOING

Observing and Predicting the Weather

1. Cut out the weather map from your local newspaper every day for a week. Each day note what type of weather is predicted for your area for the following day.

2. Each day write a brief description of the actual weather conditions.

3. Obtain a copy of the *Farmer's Almanac* and read the weather predictions for those days.

How do the long-range predictions in the *Farmer's Almanac* compare with the daily weather map predictions and your observations?

Figure 16–41 *Notice how this airplane is releasing silver iodide crystals from the back of the wing as it flies through the clouds. Cloud seeding was first used in the 1940s as a method of producing rain during dry periods. Earlier in the century, some people were willing to try more creative methods to cause rainfall!*

this way, a clear area, or "hole," is made in the fog so airplanes can take off and land. Unfortunately, most fog is warm and is not affected by seeding. But warm fog can be removed by mixing the fog with warmer, drier air from above or by heating the air from the ground. The fog evaporates when it is heated.

In the future, we may be able to improve living conditions on the Earth by controlling the weather. Do you think weather control could damage the environment? If so, in what way?

16–6 Section Review

1. What are some sources of weather information used by meteorologists?
2. What are the lines on a weather map that connect areas of equal pressure? Equal temperature?
3. Using the weather map in Figure 16–39, describe the weather conditions in Fort Worth. What is the wind speed in Denver? What is the temperature in San Francisco?
4. Why is controlling the weather important?

Critical Thinking—*Making Predictions*
5. Predict how your life might change if the weather could be carefully controlled.

CONNECTIONS

Desalting California's Water Supply

Schoolchildren, hoping for sunny weather, chant, "Rain, rain go away. Come again another day." But what happens if the rain goes away and does *not* come again? Too little precipitation in an area can result in a drought—a prolonged period of dry weather. The United States experienced the worst drought in its history during the 1930s.

In 1991, California was in the fifth year of a drought that was the worst since the great drought of the 1930s. Animals, plants, and people suffered from the lack of water. With reservoirs down to half their normal levels, many cities had to look elsewhere for their water supplies. So they turned to the Pacific Ocean. Cities such as Santa Barbara made plans to build desalting plants to turn seawater into fresh water.

Desalting plants have been used for more than 30 years in very dry parts of the world such as the Middle East. These desalting plants remove the salts and other impurities from seawater and produce fresh water. The largest desalting plant in the world, in Saudi Arabia, produces more than 1 billion liters of fresh water a day from the salty water of the Persian Gulf.

There are two basic kinds of desalting technology. Most desalting plants use a distillation process in which the seawater is boiled to produce steam. The salt-free steam is then condensed (changed to a liquid), and the resulting fresh water is collected and stored. Another kind of desalting process is called reverse osmosis. In this process, seawater is filtered to remove suspended and dissolved solids.

Unfortunately, it is expensive to make fresh water from seawater— as much as four times as expensive as obtaining fresh water from natural sources. However, as natural sources of fresh water in California become less available and more costly, desalting may become a more practical alternative.

Dried-up reservoir in California (top)

Desalting plant in Saudi Arabia (bottom)

Laboratory Investigation

Using a Sling Psychrometer to Determine Relative Humidity

Problem

How can you determine relative humidity using a handmade sling psychrometer?

Materials *(per group)*

sling psychrometer
medicine dropper

Procedure 🧪

1. Using a medicine dropper, add a few drops of water to the gauze on one thermometer. This is the wet-bulb thermometer.

2. Hold the dowel in your hand and slowly spin the thermometers around the nail. This spinning motion will speed up the evaporation process. **Note:** *Be sure to stand away from other students and to spin the thermometers slowly.*

3. From time to time, check the temperature of the wet-bulb thermometer. Keep spinning the thermometers until the temperature stops dropping.

4. When the temperature of the wet-bulb thermometer has stopped dropping, read the temperatures on both the wet-bulb and dry-bulb thermometers. Calculate the difference between the two readings.

5. Using the dry-bulb temperature and the difference between the dry-bulb and the wet-bulb temperatures, determine the relative humidity. (Refer to Figure 16–22.) Express your answer as a percentage.

Observations

1. Which of the two thermometers measures the air temperature?

2. What is the relative humidity in your classroom?

Analysis and Conclusions

1. What is the relationship between evaporation and the wet-bulb temperature?

2. What is the relationship between evaporation and relative humidity?

3. What would the relative humidity be if both the wet-bulb thermometer and the dry-bulb thermometer measured the same temperature? Explain.

4. **On Your Own**   How do you think the relative humidity inside your classroom compares with the relative humidity outdoors? How could you find out whether you are right or wrong?

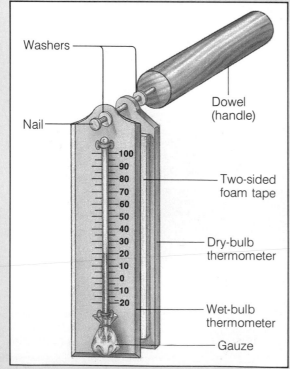

Washers

Nail

Dowel (handle)

Two-sided foam tape

Dry-bulb thermometer

Wet-bulb thermometer

Gauze

100
90
80
70
60
50
40
30
20
10
0
-10
-20

Study Guide

Summarizing Key Concepts

16–1 Heating the Earth

▲ Factors that interact to cause weather are heat energy, air pressure, winds, and moisture in the air.

▲ Heat energy is transferred by conduction, convection, or radiation.

▲ Air temperature varies depending on the angle at which the sun's rays strike the Earth.

16–2 Air Pressure

▲ Air pressure depends on the density of the air.

▲ Factors affecting air pressure are temperature, water vapor in the air, and elevation.

16–3 Winds

▲ Local and global winds are caused by differences in air pressure due to unequal heating of the air.

▲ Local winds blow from any direction and cover short distances; global winds blow from a specific direction and cover long distances.

16–4 Moisture in the Air

▲ Water vapor, or moisture, in the air is called humidity.

▲ There are three main types of clouds: cumulus, stratus, and cirrus.

▲ Water vapor that condenses and forms clouds can fall to the Earth as precipitation in the form of rain, sleet, snow, or hail.

16–5 Weather Patterns

▲ The four major air masses that affect weather in the United States are maritime tropical, maritime polar, continental tropical, and continental polar.

▲ When two air masses meet, a cold front, a warm front, an occluded front, or a stationary front may form.

16–6 Predicting the Weather

▲ Meteorologists use data from local weather observers, balloons, satellites, and weather stations to predict the weather.

Reviewing Key Terms

Define each term in a complete sentence.

16–1 Heating the Earth
atmosphere
conduction
convection
radiation
greenhouse effect
thermometer

16–2 Air Pressure
air pressure
barometer

16–3 Winds
wind
sea breeze
land breeze
Coriolis effect
anemometer

16–4 Moisture in the Air
evaporation
relative humidity
psychrometer
precipitation
rain gauge

16–5 Weather Patterns
air mass
front

16–6 Predicting the Weather
isotherm
isobar

Chapter Review

Content Review

Multiple Choice

Choose the letter of the answer that best completes each statement.

1. The factors that cause weather include heat, air pressure, wind, and
   a. temperature.   c. moisture.
   b. elevation.   d. storms.

2. Most of the heat energy in the Earth's atmosphere is transferred by
   a. conduction.   c. radiation.
   b. convection.   d. ultraviolet rays.

3. Isobars on a weather map connect places with the same
   a. temperature.   c. precipitation.
   b. wind speed.   d. air pressure.

4. A wind that blows from the sea to the land is called a
   a. land breeze.   c. jet stream.
   b. trade wind.   d. sea breeze.

5. A powerful storm that forms over tropical oceans is called a
   a. thunderstorm.   c. hurricane.
   b. tornado.   d. blizzard.

6. Air pressure is measured with a
   a. thermometer.   c. anemometer.
   b. barometer.   d. psychrometer.

7. The type of front formed when a mass of warm air moves over a mass of cold air is a(an)
   a. cold front.   c. occluded front.
   b. warm front.   d. stationary front.

8. Fair weather clouds that may develop into thunderstorms are called
   a. cumulus clouds. c. cirrus clouds.
   b. stratus clouds. d. nimbostratus clouds.

True or False

If the statement is true, write "true." If it is false, change the underlined word or words to make the statement true.

1. Winds that blow from a specific direction are called <u>local</u> winds.
2. Ozone gas in the Earth's atmosphere absorbs <u>infrared</u> rays from the sun.
3. Isotherms on a weather map connect places with the same <u>temperature</u>.
4. Air pressure <u>increases</u> at higher elevations.
5. A front that forms when a warm air mass meets a cold air mass and no movement occurs is <u>an occluded</u> front.
6. When <u>cirrus</u> clouds form close to the ground, the result is ground fog.
7. The Coriolis effect causes all winds in the Northern Hemisphere to curve to the <u>left</u>.
8. Water vapor, or moisture, enters the air through the process of <u>evaporation</u>.

Concept Mapping

Complete the following concept map for Section 16–1. Then construct a concept map for the entire chapter.

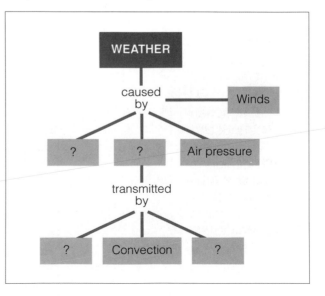

Concept Mastery

Discuss each of the following in a brief paragraph.

1. How are rain, sleet, snow, and hail formed?
2. How is weather information from a particular observation station shown on a weather map? What kinds of weather data are recorded on a weather map?
3. Describe the three main types of clouds.
4. What is the difference between a cyclone and an anticyclone?
5. Describe the greenhouse effect. What is its importance?
6. Compare how heat energy is transferred by conduction, by convection, and by radiation.
7. Describe the formation of a hurricane.
8. Explain how the Coriolis effect determines the direction of global winds.

Critical Thinking and Problem Solving

Use the skills you have developed in this chapter to answer each of the following.

1. **Making calculations** Suppose that 1 kilogram of air can hold 15 grams of water vapor but actually holds only 10 grams. What is the relative humidity? How much water vapor is in the air if the relative humidity is 100 percent? What if the relative humidity is 30 percent?
2. **Interpreting a map** Use the weather map in Figure 16–39 on page 520 to answer the following questions. Find the isobar passing through New York. What is the air pressure in New York? What other locations have the same air pressure as New York? What type of front is approaching Kansas City? Predict the probable weather conditions in Kansas City the day after this map was issued.
3. **Applying concepts** Another instrument that can be used to measure relative humidity is called a hair hygrometer. A hair hygrometer can be read directly without using a chart. It works on the principle that human hair changes length in proportion to changes in relative humidity. Hair gets longer as relative humidity increases. How is this related to the fact that people with curly hair find that their hair gets "frizzy" in humid weather?
4. **Making inferences** Is it possible for both the temperature and the amount of water vapor in the air to change while the relative humidity remains the same? Why or why not?
5. **Relating concepts** The diagram shows how the air pressure changes toward the center of a hurricane. Does the air pressure increase or decrease toward the center of the hurricane? How is your answer related to what you know about hurricanes and how they form?
6. **Making inferences** Explain why an aneroid barometer can be used to measure elevation as well as air pressure.
7. **Using the writing process** Pretend that you are the captain of a nineteenth-century sailing ship. You are preparing to make a voyage from the east coast of the United States to England and back again. Write a letter to a friend or relative describing the route you will take in order to make the best use of global wind patterns. (You may wish to refer to the diagram in Figure 16–16.)

What Is Climate? 17

Just imagine that you can travel into the distant past or the far-off future by means of a time machine. You enter your time machine in the midwestern United States at the end of the twentieth century. What will you find as you step out into the world of 6000 years ago?

The air is warm. But it is also much more humid than you are used to. Tall grasses grow everywhere. Many different types of flowers add splashes of brilliant color. The world you have reached is a tropical grassland. Obviously, the climate 6000 years ago was markedly different from the climate today. What type of climate might you find farther back in time?

Returning to the time machine, you set the controls for 16,000 years ago. When you step out of the machine again, a blast of bitter-cold air hits you. Stretching away to the north is a vast sheet of ice. In the distance, a herd of woolly mammoths grazes in a bleak, snow-covered landscape. You quickly retreat to the warmth of the time machine! As you set the controls for 30,000 years in the future, you think about how drastically the climate has changed over thousands of years. What might await you in the future?

Journal *Activity*

You and Your World What does the word climate mean to you? Hot? Cold? Wet? Dry? In your journal, briefly describe the climate in the area where you live. Then describe how you think the climate in your area might be different in the future. How might it have been different in the past?

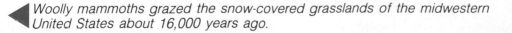

Woolly mammoths grazed the snow-covered grasslands of the midwestern United States about 16,000 years ago.

17–1 What Causes Climate?

On your way to school today, you may have made some observations about the weather. Even before you left your house, you were probably aware of two important weather factors: temperature and precipitation. You may have looked at an outdoor thermometer to check the morning temperature. Was the air cold, cool, warm, or hot? You also may have checked the precipitation. Was it raining or snowing?

If you were to keep a record of the weather in your area for an extended period of time, you would discover some general conditions of temperature and precipitation (rain, snow, sleet, hail). Such general conditions are described as the average weather for your area. **Climate** is the name for the general conditions of temperature and precipitation for an area over a long period of time. Every place on Earth has its own climate. For example, the climate of the southwestern United States tends to be hot and dry all year. The climate of Florida is also hot, but it is much wetter than the climate of the Southwest. What is the climate like where you live?

The climate of any region on the Earth is determined by two basic factors: temperature and precipitation. Different combinations of temperature and precipitation are used to classify the Earth's major climates. Temperature and precipitation are in turn influenced by several other factors.

Factors That Affect Temperature

Latitude, elevation, and the presence of ocean currents are three natural factors that affect the temperature at a particular location. The extent to which these factors influence climate varies from place to place.

Figure 17–1 *Climate is all the characteristics of the weather in an area over a long period of time. Some parts of the world are dominated by bleak, snow-capped mountain ranges. White sandy beaches and palm trees are the rule in tropical regions.*

LATITUDE   Latitude is a measure of the distance north and south of the equator, as you have learned. Latitude is measured in degrees (°). Areas close to the equator, or 0° latitude, receive the direct rays of the sun. (See Figure 16–7.) These direct rays provide the most radiant energy. So areas near the equator have a warm climate. Polar regions have a cold climate.

Farther from the equator, the sun's rays are not as direct. As a result, areas farther from the equator receive less radiant energy. So climates are cooler in latitudes farther north and south of the equator. In general, the lowest average temperatures occur near the poles (90° north and south latitude), where the sun's rays are least direct.

ELEVATION Elevation, or altitude, is distance above sea level. As elevation increases, the air becomes less dense. This means that there are fewer gas molecules in the air and they are spread farther apart. Less-dense air cannot hold as much heat as denser air. So as elevation increases, the temperature decreases. The temperature at the top of a mountain is lower than the temperature at sea level.

OCEAN CURRENTS As you learned in Chapter 6, an ocean current is a "river" of water that flows in a definite path in the ocean. Some ocean currents are warm water currents. Other ocean currents are cold water currents. The major warm currents and cold currents are shown in Figure 6–33.

The surface temperature of water affects the temperature of the air above it. Warm water warms the air and cold water cools the air. So land areas near warm water currents have warm temperatures.

Figure 17–2 Although Mt. Kilimanjaro in Tanzania, Africa, is located near the equator, snow is visible on top of the mountain. What factors other than elevation affect temperature?

Activity Bank

What Are Density Currents?, p. 775

Figure 17–3 Ireland (right) is at the same latitude as many parts of central Canada. Why do you think Ireland has a warmer climate?

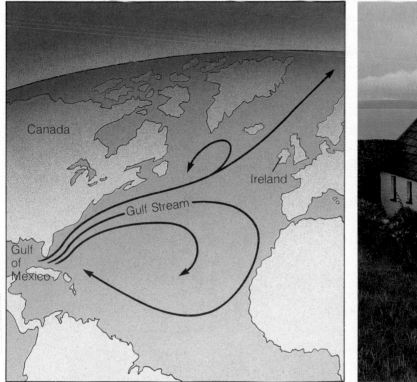

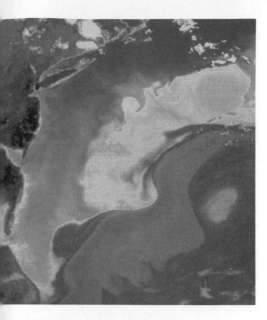

Figure 17–4 *The Gulf Stream appears purple in this satellite photograph. You can see the eastern coast of the United States on the left side of the photo.*

Land areas near cold water currents have cool temperatures.

Ocean currents traveling away from the equator are warm water currents. Land areas located near these currents have warm temperatures. The Gulf Stream is an ocean current that carries warm water from the southern tip of Florida along the eastern coast of the United States. How do you think the warm waters of the Gulf Stream affect the climate of the eastern United States?

Ocean currents traveling toward the equator are cold water currents. Areas located near these currents have cool temperatures. Off the western coast of the United States, the California Current flows toward the equator. What kind of temperatures would you expect along the coast in this area?

Factors That Affect Precipitation

The two natural factors that affect the amount of precipitation at a particular location are prevailing winds and mountain ranges. As with temperature factors, the effects of precipitation factors vary from place to place.

PREVAILING WINDS A wind that blows more often from one direction than from any other direction is called a **prevailing wind.** (Recall the global winds called prevailing westerlies that you read about in Chapter 16. From what direction do these winds blow?) Prevailing winds have a great influence on the climate of regions in their path. Different prevailing winds carry different amounts of moisture. The amount of moisture carried by a prevailing wind affects the amount of precipitation a region receives.

Warm air can hold more moisture than cold air. As warm air rises, it cools and cannot hold as much moisture. The moisture the air can no longer hold falls to the Earth as some form of precipitation. Thus winds formed by rising warm air tend to bring precipitation. As cold air sinks, it becomes warmer and can hold more moisture. So winds formed by sinking cold air tend to bring little precipitation.

The direction from which a prevailing wind blows also affects the amount of moisture it carries. Some prevailing winds blow from the land to the water (a land breeze). Others blow from the water to the land (a sea breeze). Which kind of prevailing wind do you think carries more moisture? Remember that moisture gets into the air as a result of the evaporation of water from the Earth's surface. Where is there more water? The prevailing winds that blow from the water carry more moisture than those that blow from the land. So areas in the path of a prevailing wind that originates over water usually receive a lot of precipitation. How much precipitation do you think areas receive in the path of a prevailing wind blowing from inland?

A region that receives a very small amount of precipitation (less than 25 centimeters of rainfall a year) is called a desert. The combined effect of a prevailing wind's moisture content and its direction can make it possible for a desert to exist near a large body of water.

Let's see how this happens. The Sahara in northern Africa is the largest desert on Earth. (In fact, the name sahara is the Arabic word for desert.) It is also one of the driest places on Earth. Yet the Sahara is bordered on the west by the Atlantic Ocean! However, the prevailing winds that blow across the Sahara (and carry little moisture) originate far inland, where they are caused by sinking cold air (which brings little precipitation). These two factors combine to make the prevailing winds over the Sahara very dry. As a result, little precipitation reaches the Sahara, even though a large body of water is nearby.

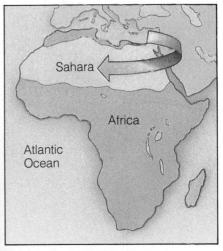

Figure 17–5 *Although the Sahara in Africa is bordered on the west by the Atlantic Ocean, it is one of the driest places on Earth! The prevailing winds, which originate far inland, carry little moisture as they sweep south and then west across the region.*

To get a better idea of how dry the Sahara really is, pour water into a graduated cylinder up to the 25-centimeter mark. This is the total amount of water that falls on the Sahara in one year. In some parts of the Sahara, no rain at all has fallen for more than 20 years!

MOUNTAIN RANGES   The amount of precipitation at a particular location is also affected by mountain ranges. A mountain range acts as a barrier to prevailing winds. As you can see from Figure 17–6, mountains cause air to rise. As the air rises, it cools. Remember that cold air cannot hold as much moisture as warm air. So the moisture in the rising air falls to the Earth as precipitation. As a result, the **windward side** of a mountain, or the side facing toward the wind, receives a great deal of precipitation. The region on the windward side of a mountain has a wet climate.

Conditions are far different on the **leeward side** of a mountain, or the side facing away from the wind. By the time the prevailing winds reach the top of the mountain, they have lost most of their moisture in the form of precipitation. So relatively dry air moves down the leeward side of the mountain. As

Figure 17–6 *There is a rainy climate on the windward slopes of a mountain range because moist air rises, cools, and forms rain clouds. Dry air moving down the leeward slopes results in a desert climate.*

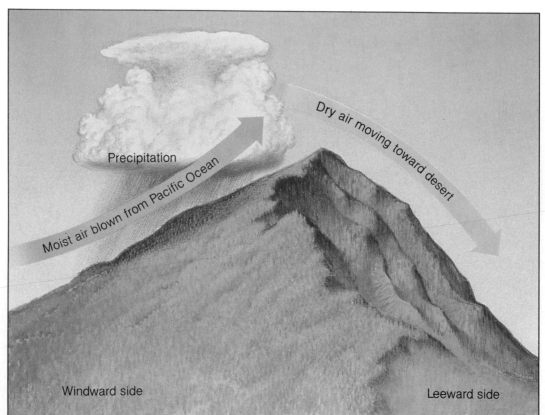

Precipitation

Moist air blown from Pacific Ocean

Dry air moving toward desert

Windward side

Leeward side

a result, there is little precipitation on the leeward side of a mountain. The area on the leeward side of a mountain is called a rain shadow. What kind of climate does this area have? You are correct if you said this area has a dry climate. In fact, there are usually dry areas called rain-shadow deserts on the leeward side of a mountain range.

On the west coast of the United States is a mountain range called the Sierra Nevadas. Areas to the west of the Sierra Nevadas (the windward side) receive a large amount of precipitation from the prevailing winds, which blow in from the Pacific Ocean. Land areas east of the Sierra Nevadas (the leeward side) receive little precipitation because the prevailing winds have lost most of their moisture by the time they cross the mountain range. The result is a rain-shadow desert called the Great Basin on the eastern side of the Sierra Nevada mountain range. The Great Basin extends south from Washington State into Nevada and Utah.

Figure 17–7 *The western side of the Sierra Nevada mountain range has a moist climate (top). The Great Basin in Utah, on the eastern side of the Sierra Nevadas, has a desert climate (bottom). Which is the windward side? The leeward side?*

17–1 Section Review

1. What two factors determine climate? What conditions influence these factors?
2. Describe how cold water currents and warm water currents affect the climate in locations near these currents.
3. Explain the following conditions:
   a. The peak of a mountain near the equator is covered with snow throughout the year.
   b. Deserts are located on the eastern side of the Rocky Mountains.

Critical Thinking—*Applying Concepts*
4. Suppose that you live in a coastal region on the windward side of a mountain range. A warm water current flows along the coast. Describe the climate in your region.

Guide for Reading

Focus on this question as you read.

▶ *How are the Earth's climates classified into major climate zones?*

17–2 Climate Zones

An Alaskan Inuit trudges on snowshoes through the frozen wasteland above the Arctic Circle. Nearby, a polar bear hunts seals in the icy-cold Arctic Ocean. Thousands of kilometers farther south, tourists wander through the steamy rain forests of Hawaii. Exotic tropical birds call to each other from the dense treetops. Why do Alaska and Hawaii have such different climates?

The Earth's climates can be divided into general climate zones according to average temperatures. These climate zones can be broken down into subzones. Even the subzones have further subdivisions. In fact, scientists even classify very localized climates as **microclimates.** A microclimate can be as small as your own backyard!

The three major climate zones on the Earth are the polar, temperate, and tropical zones. Temperatures in these three climate zones are determined mainly by the location, or latitude, of the zone. Figure 17–8 shows the locations of the three major climate zones. In what climate zone is Alaska located? Hawaii? In what climate zone do you live?

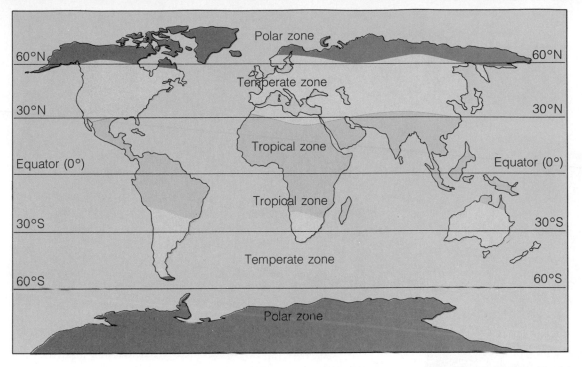

Figure 17–8 The Earth's three major climate zones are shown in this diagram. In which zone is most of the United States located?

Polar Zones

In each hemisphere, the **polar zone** extends from the pole (90°) to about 60° latitude. Polar climates have the coldest average temperatures. Within the polar zones, the average yearly temperature remains below freezing (below 0°C). Polar climates have no summer. Even during the warmest months of the year, the average temperature does not rise above 10°C. There is little precipitation in the polar zones.

Polar zones are also known as high-latitude or arctic climates. The polar zones include the icecaps of Greenland in the Northern Hemisphere and Antarctica in the Southern Hemisphere. These icecaps remain frozen throughout the year. However, there are some places in the polar zones where the snow melts during the warmest part of the year. The northern coasts of Canada and Alaska and the southern tip of South America are examples of these places.

Temperate Zones

In each hemisphere, the **temperate zone** is found between 60° and 30° latitude. In the areas of the temperate zones farther from the equator, snow is common in the winter. In the areas of the temperate

Activity Bank

What Is Your Latitude?, p. 776

Figure 17–9 Adelie penguins enjoy a brisk swim in the cold waters off Antarctica, which is in the polar climate zone.

537

Figure 17–10 *The yellow-bellied racer is one of several snakes that make their home in Arizona's Sonoran Desert.*

ACTIVITY

DISCOVERING

Examining a Microclimate

1. Locate two separate areas in your neighborhood that appear to have different microclimates.

2. Carefully observe each area for several days.

■ Describe the similarities and differences in your two microclimates. What factors cause these differences? How is a microclimate related to the Earth's major climate zones?

zones closer to the equator, rain normally falls all year round. But the average amount of precipitation is about the same throughout the temperate zones. Average temperatures in the temperate zones vary greatly. They range from about 5°C to more than 20°C. These temperatures fall between those of the polar and the tropical zones.

Temperate zones, or middle-latitude climates, cover a huge portion of the Earth. So the temperate zones can include the cool rain forests of Washington State as well as the hot rain forests of southern China, with many different climates in between. Most of the United States is in the temperate zone.

Deserts in the temperate zones are usually located inland, far away from the oceans. The winds that blow across these inland deserts carry little moisture. Inland deserts are found in Australia (the Great Sandy Desert) and Central Asia (the Gobi Desert).

Many people mistakenly believe that temperate deserts are always hot. Certainly this is true of most deserts during the day. But at night, the temperature in the desert can drop to below freezing! How is this possible? The low humidity and cloudless skies allow a tremendous amount of radiant energy to reach the ground and heat it during the day. But these same conditions also allow the heat to escape rapidly at night, causing the temperature to drop dramatically. As a result, temperatures in the desert can range from 20°C at 2 o'clock in the afternoon to 0°C at 2 o'clock in the morning.

Another common misunderstanding people have about deserts is that they are barren and lifeless. However, several kinds of plants and animals are able to live in the desert. For example, in the Sonoran Desert of the southwestern United States and Mexico, plants such as sagebrush and giant saguaro cacti grow. Animals such as lizards, snakes, and cougars also live in this desert.

Tropical Zones

The **tropical zones,** which extend from 30° north and south latitude to the equator (0°), have high temperatures and high humidity. Precipitation in the tropical zones is usually very heavy during part of the year. Tropical zones are also known as low-latitude climates.

Tropical climates have the warmest average yearly temperatures. There is no winter in tropical climates. In a tropical climate, the average temperature during the coldest month of the year does not fall below 18°C.

In the tropical zones, many deserts are located on the western coasts of continents. This is because the prevailing winds in the tropical zones (the northeast and southeast trades) blow from east to west. High mountains along the western coast of a continent block these prevailing winds from reaching the coast. Rain falls on the eastern (windward) side of

ACTIVITY
DISCOVERING

Radiant Energy and Climate

Radiant energy from the sun strikes different areas of the Earth at different angles. Using a flashlight and a piece of paper taped to the wall, design an experiment to show how the angle of sunlight affects the intensity of the light.

■ Relate your observations to the three major climate zones of the Earth.

Figure 17–11 *When you think of the tropical climate zone, images such as the lush Hawaiian rain forest probably come to mind. But the barren Atacama Desert, a cold desert in Peru, is also in the tropical zone.*

the mountains. Areas on the western (leeward) side of the mountains do not receive much rainfall and thus become deserts. These deserts are often cold deserts due to the presence of cold ocean currents along the western coasts of the continents. For example, the Atacama Desert in parts of Chile and Peru is a cold desert located on the western coast of South America.

Marine and Continental Climates

Within each of the three major climate zones there are **marine climates** and **continental climates.** Areas near an ocean or other large body of water have a marine climate. Areas located within a large landmass have a continental climate.

Areas with a marine climate receive more precipitation than areas with a continental climate. Can you explain why? Temperatures in areas with a marine climate do not vary greatly. Areas with a marine climate have warm (not hot) summers and mild winters. This is because their nearness to a large body of water has a moderating effect on the air temperature.

A continental climate is drier than a marine climate. Why? There is usually a great range in average temperatures during the year. Areas with a continental climate have hot summers and cold winters. Most of the world's deserts that are located just north and south of the equator have a continental climate.

17–2 Section Review

1. What are the Earth's three major climate zones?
2. Describe the location of each major climate zone. What conditions of temperature and precipitation are typical of each zone?
3. What is the difference between a marine climate and a continental climate?

Critical Thinking—*Relating Concepts*
4. Explain in terms of radiant energy why polar zones have the coldest average temperature and tropical zones have the warmest.

17–3 Changes in Climate

You know from experience that weather changes from day to day. Sometimes weather seems to change from hour to hour! Climate, however, seems to remain relatively unchanged. But climates do change slowly over time. In fact, the climate of a region can change from a temperate rain forest to a tropical desert within a relatively short time in the Earth's history. (Remember, however, that the Earth is about 4.6 billion years old. So a "short time" in the Earth's history could be thousands or even millions of years!)

What causes climates to change? Major climate changes may be caused by one or more of three natural factors. **The three natural factors responsible for climate changes are the slow drifting of the continents, changes in the sun's energy output, and variations in the position of the Earth relative to the sun.** These "natural" factors are not related to human activities. However, the results of human activities, which include increased atmospheric levels of carbon dioxide caused by burning fossil fuels, may also lead to changes in climate.

As you might guess, major climate changes have a tremendous impact on the Earth and on the organisms that inhabit it. Just think of the changes in climate you saw during your imaginary trip into the

Guide for Reading

Focus on this question as you read.

▶ *What causes the changes in the Earth's climate?*

Figure 17–12 *Climate changes may have caused the extinction of the dinosaurs 65 million years ago. But were those changes brought about by the slow drifting apart of the continents or by a sudden, catastrophic asteroid impact?*

past. Major climate changes that occurred in the past have had dramatic effects on the Earth, including a series of ice ages and perhaps the extinction (dying out) of the dinosaurs. Scientists have not yet determined the causes of past climate changes. Once they do, they will be better able to predict future climate changes and their effects on the Earth and its living things, including humans.

Ice Ages

From time to time throughout the Earth's history, much of the Earth's surface has been covered with enormous sheets of ice. Such periods are called ice ages. Scientists have found evidence of at least four major ice ages during the last 2 million years. Earth scientists call these ice ages **major glaciations.**

During an ice age, or major glaciation, the average temperature on the Earth was about 10° to 15°C below the average temperature today. Each glaciation probably lasted about 100,000 years or more. The most recent glaciation began about 1.75 million years ago and ended only about 10,000 years ago. (Remember, 10,000 years is like the blink of an eye compared with the age of the Earth!) During the last glaciation,

Figure 17–13 Geological evidence indicates that the white areas on this map were covered with huge masses of ice during the last ice age. What is another name for an ice age?

a great sheet of ice covered the United States as far south as Iowa and Nebraska. So much water was locked in the ice that the average sea level rose about 90 meters when the ice melted. That is enough water to cover a 20-story building!

The time periods between major glaciations are called **interglacials.** Interglacials are warm periods. During an interglacial, the average temperature was about 4° to 6°C higher than the average temperature during a major glaciation. A cold period, often called the Little Ice Age, lasted from 1500 to 1900. The Earth is now in an interglacial.

Although there are many theories about the cause of ice ages, the exact causes are not known. However, major glaciations are probably associated with gradual changes in the tilt of the Earth's axis and in variations in the shape of the Earth's path, or orbit, around the sun. Based on what you know about the sun's radiant energy, how could these changes influence the Earth's climate?

Drifting Continents

About 230 million years ago, all the Earth's landmasses were joined in one supercontinent. About 160 million years later, this supercontinent had broken apart and the individual continents had drifted close to their present locations.

The slow drifting apart of the continents caused dramatic climate changes. As the continents moved toward their present-day locations, the sea level dropped, volcanoes erupted, and much of the

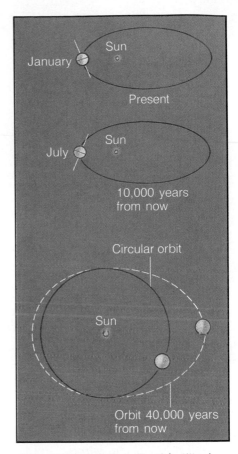

Figure 17–14 *The Earth's tilted axis changes direction like a spinning top. As a result, the time at which the Earth is closest to the sun gradually changes over a period of 10,000 years (top). The shape of the Earth's orbit is also changing—from nearly circular to slightly elliptical and back again (bottom). How might these changes affect the Earth's climate?*

Earth's Elliptical Orbit, p. 777

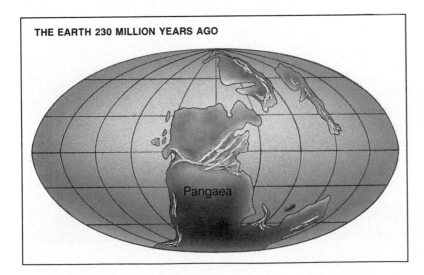

THE EARTH 230 MILLION YEARS AGO

Pangaea

Figure 17–15 *Over millions of years, the shapes and positions of the Earth's continents have changed. What was the name of the supercontinent that existed 230 million years ago?*

Earth's surface was pushed upward. The combined effect of all these changes was a drop in temperature and precipitation all over the Earth. Because the continents move only a few centimeters per year, the climate changes caused by continental drift are very gradual and happen only over millions of years.

Extinction of the Dinosaurs

The climate changes caused by the drifting apart of the continents may have resulted in the extinction, or dying out, of the dinosaurs. About 65 million years ago, dinosaurs—and most other kinds of animals and plants—became extinct. Scientists do not know exactly what caused this mass extinction. Some biologists think it was caused by the slow process of climate change as a result of continental drift. Dinosaurs could not adapt fast enough to these drastic climate changes and died out. Also, many types of plants became extinct as a result of the climate changes. Without plants to eat, the plant-eating dinosaurs died out. And without the plant-eating dinosaurs as a food source, the meat-eating dinosaurs died out as well.

The theory of gradual climate change caused by drifting continents is only one explanation for dinosaur extinction. Many scientists think that the climate changes which caused the mass extinction

Figure 17–16 *Evidence found in different parts of the world indicates that a gigantic asteroid collided with the Earth 65 million years ago. Many scientists think that the extinction of the dinosaurs was the direct result of this catastrophe.*

happened suddenly, rather than slowly. In 1978, the geologist Walter Alvarez and his father, the Nobel prize-winning physicist Luis Alvarez, found evidence suggesting that a giant asteroid probably struck the Earth 65 million years ago. This collision resulted in a huge explosion. The explosion raised enormous clouds of dust and set off planetwide forest fires. As dust and smoke rose into the atmosphere, they may have blocked the sun's rays and caused the Earth's temperature to drop. The dinosaurs could not survive in the suddenly colder climate and died out.

Variations in Radiant Energy

Some scientists have tried to relate changes in the Earth's climate to changes in the sun's energy output. If the sun's energy output changes over time, these changes could have an effect on the Earth's temperature. During periods of high energy output, the Earth's temperature would rise. When the sun's energy output dropped, the Earth's temperature would fall. Although this seems logical, a relationship between variations in the sun's energy and climate changes on the Earth has not yet been demonstrated. In fact, scientists have found no evidence for any variations in the sun's energy output.

Global Warming

Humans have probably been altering the Earth's climate in some way ever since the discovery of fire. Only recently, however, have humans had a measurable effect on climate. In the mid-nineteenth century, industrialization led to the increased burning of fossil fuels. Fossil fuels include coal, oil, and natural gas. When these fuels are burned, they release carbon dioxide (CO_2) into the atmosphere. Recall from Chapter 16 that a buildup of CO_2 in the atmosphere results in a greenhouse effect. Like the glass in a greenhouse, CO_2 absorbs heat reflected from the Earth's surface and prevents the heat from escaping into space. As a result, the atmosphere becomes warmer.

Over the past 25 years, the amount of CO_2 in the atmosphere has increased by about 8 percent. By the middle of the next century, the percentage of CO_2 in

Figure 17–17 *Carbon dioxide is released into the atmosphere by burning gasoline in automobile engines. What effect might a buildup of carbon dioxide have on the Earth's climate?*

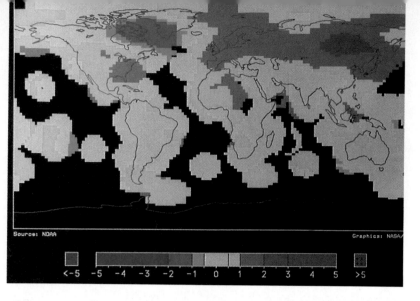

Figure 17–18 *This computerized chart shows average global temperatures for 1990. Blue represents the coldest temperatures and red represents the hottest.*

Source: NOAA   Graphics: NASA

<-5 -5 -4 -3 -2 -1 0 1 2 3 4 5 >5

Figure 17–19 *The arrival of El Niño is unpredictable. But it usually results in surprising weather for some parts of the world. Unexpected weather may include floods in Louisiana and severe droughts in Africa.*

the atmosphere could be twice as much as it is today. How will this affect the Earth's climate? Climatologists have developed computer models to predict what will happen to the Earth's climate as a result of increased CO_2 levels. Most of these models predict an increase in temperatures of 1.5° to 5°C. These higher temperatures could lead to significant changes in the Earth's climate. Can you suggest what some of these changes might be?

Are we already beginning to feel the effects of global warming? Measurements made at weather stations around the world showed that the average surface temperature during 1990 was the highest in more than 100 years. However, scientists are not sure whether this warming trend resulted from an increase in CO_2 in the atmosphere. Yet many scientists and environmentalists recommend that people reduce their use of fossil fuels and thus limit the amount of CO_2 that escapes into the atmosphere. How can you and your classmates help in this effort?

El Niño

Some short-term climate changes may be the result of changes in ocean currents and global winds. Ocean currents help transfer heat to the atmosphere. This process generates global winds. The global winds, in turn, help move the ocean currents. Any major change in an ocean current can cause a change in climate. El Niño is an example of such a change. Let's see why.

A cold current that flows from west to east across the southern part of the Pacific Ocean turns toward

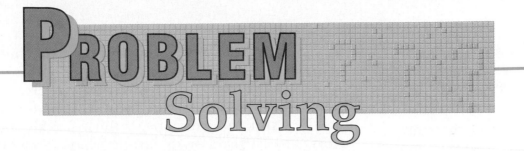

PROBLEM Solving

Analyzing a Feedback Mechanism

At an international conference on global warming, British scientists presented the following theory: If the temperature of the Earth rises significantly as a result of global warming, the speed of global winds will increase. Increased wind speed will cause a greater disturbance of ocean water, which in turn will cause larger clouds to form. The clouds might either increase or decrease global warming. This theory is an example of a feedback mechanism. In a feedback mechanism, one event causes a series of other events, which in turn influence the first event.

Imagine that you are a scientist at the conference. You have been given a copy of the diagram shown here, which illustrates the feedback mechanism described by the British scientists. It is your job to interpret the diagram and to analyze how this particular feedback mechanism might influence global warming.

Relating Cause and Effect

1. According to the diagram, what changes will occur in the atmosphere as a result of global warming? What do you think will cause these changes to occur?

2. How will the changes in the atmosphere affect the ocean? Explain.

3. How will the changes in the ocean affect cloud formation?

4. Based on your knowledge of weather and climate, how might larger clouds make the Earth warmer? How might larger clouds make the Earth cooler?

5. Do you think that this feedback mechanism will increase or decrease the effects of global warming? Why?

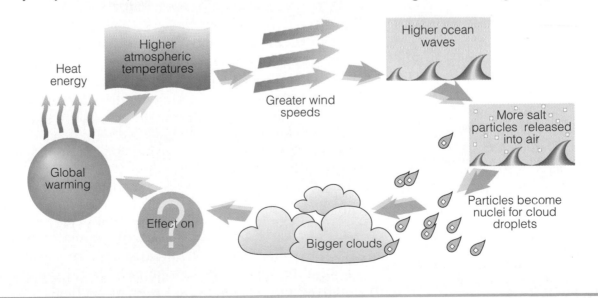

El Niño

Use reference materials in the library to find out more about El Niño. Write a brief essay, including answers to the following questions:

■ What do scientists think may be the causes of El Niño?

■ What are some of the worldwide weather changes that result from El Niño?

■ Do scientists have any methods for predicting El Niño?

■ What is upwelling? What effect does it have on ocean life in areas where it occurs?

■ What effect does El Niño have on upwelling?

the equator along the coast of South America. As the current flows north along the coast of Chile and Peru, it is known as the Peru Current. Occasionally, the cold water of the Peru Current is covered by a thin "sheet" of warm water from the equator. Usually the warm water disappears fairly quickly. But every 2 to 10 years or so, strong winds spread the warm water over a large area. This unusual behavior of the Peru Current is known as El Niño.

El Niño, then, is a temporary current that arrives with little warning, usually around Christmas. (*El Niño* means the child in Spanish.) The warming caused by El Niño in the tropical zone results in dramatic changes in world climates. In 1982 and 1983, the strongest El Niño in history caused severe droughts in some regions. Other regions were subjected to unusually heavy rains and flooding. The extreme changes in climate resulted in more than 1000 deaths and much economic damage throughout the world.

Scientists have not yet discovered just what causes El Niño to appear. However, important progress has been made in understanding the interaction of the ocean and the atmosphere. Accurate predictions of future El Niños may be possible within a few years.

17–3 Section Review

1. What natural factors do scientists think may cause climate changes?
2. How might the slow drifting of the continents have caused the extinction of the dinosaurs? How might a collision with a large asteroid have caused the extinction of the dinosaurs?
3. What is another name for an ice age? What is the period between ice ages called?
4. What is El Niño? What effect does it have on climate?

Connection—*Geology*

5. Some scientists think that volcanic eruptions may cause changes in the Earth's climate. How might volcanic dust in the atmosphere cause global temperatures to change? Would the resulting temperatures be lower or higher?

The Birth of Agriculture

According to *archaeologists* Dr. Frank Hole and Joy McCorriston from Yale University, wild cereals were first domesticated about 10,000 years ago. (The word domesticate means to tame plants or animals to be able to use them for the benefit of humans.) This revolutionary event in human history took place in a region near the Dead Sea called the southern Levant. This region includes parts of the modern countries of Israel, Lebanon, and Jordan. The people of this region—who were called Natufians—were forced to learn how to grow cereals for food as a result of a change in climate.

About 12,000 years ago, the climate in the region became much hotter and dryer. As freshwater lakes dried up, the Natufians crowded into smaller and smaller areas where water was still available. The growing population led to food shortages. To reduce the food shortages, the Natufians began saving seeds from wild wheat, planting the seeds, and harvesting them for food.

The Natufians had previously relied only on the wild wheat for their food supply. But the wild wheat plants tended to scatter their seeds when they were cut, making them difficult to harvest. Then a genetic mutation, or change, in the wheat resulted in a few wheat plants with tougher stems that did not shed their seeds.

The Natufians found that the mutant wheat plants were easier to harvest than the wild plants. Gradually, more and more of the mutant wheat was selected and harvested. After about 20 years, only mutant plants were growing in the Natufians' wheat fields. The Natufians had domesticated wheat and thereby invented agriculture. So when you dig into a bowl of delicious, nutritious cereal, remember to thank the Natufians, who made it all possible!

Laboratory Investigation

Graphing Climate Information

Problem

How can you use temperature and precipitation data to classify the climates of cities in different parts of the world?

Materials *(per student)*

2 sheets of graph paper
3 different-colored pencils

Procedure

1. On a sheet of graph paper, plot the data for average monthly precipitation in Winnipeg, Canada.
2. On another sheet of graph paper, plot the data for average monthly temperature for Winnipeg.
3. Repeat steps 1 through 4 using the data for Izmir, Turkey, and for Ulan Bator, Mongolia.

Observations

1. Which city has the highest winter temperatures? The lowest?
2. Which city has the greatest temperature range from winter to summer? Which city has the smallest range?
3. Which city has the driest summers? The wettest?
4. Which city has the driest winters? The wettest?

Analysis and Conclusions

1. In which climate zone is each city located?
2. Which of the three cities has a marine climate? Which has a continental climate?
3. **On Your Own** How could you gather similar climate information about familiar locations? Choose three nearby cities and repeat this laboratory investigation using the climate information you gathered for those cities.

WINNIPEG, CANADA

Month	J	F	M	A	M	J	J	A	S	O	N	D	Year
Temperature (°C)	−18	−16	−8	3	11	17	20	19	13	6	−5	−13	3
Precipitation (cm)	2.6	2.1	2.7	3	5	8.1	6.9	7	5.5	3.7	2.9	2.2	51.7

IZMIR, TURKEY

Month	J	F	M	A	M	J	J	A	S	O	N	D	Year
Temperature (°C)	9	9	11	15	20	25	28	27	23	19	14	10	18
Precipitation (cm)	14.1	10	7.2	4.3	3.9	0.8	0.3	0.3	1.1	4.1	9.3	14.1	69.5

ULAN BATOR, MONGOLIA

Month	J	F	M	A	M	J	J	A	S	O	N	D	Year
Temperature (°C)	−26	−21	−13	−1	6	14	16	14	9	−1	−13	−22	−3
Precipitation (cm)	0.1	0.2	0.3	0.5	1	2.8	7.6	5.1	2.3	0.7	0.4	0.3	21.3

Study Guide

Summarizing Key Concepts

17–1 What Causes Climate?

▲ The basic factors that determine climate are temperature and precipitation.

▲ Factors that affect temperature are latitude, elevation, and the presence of ocean currents.

▲ Factors that affect precipitation are prevailing winds and the presence of mountain ranges.

17–2 Climate Zones

▲ The Earth's three major climate zones are the polar, temperate, and tropical zones.

▲ Marine climates and continental climates occur within each of the three major climate zones.

17–3 Changes in Climate

▲ Natural factors that may cause changes in climate are continental drift, changes in the sun's energy output, and variations in the tilt of the Earth's axis and the shape of the Earth's orbit.

▲ The effects of human activities may lead to global warming.

Reviewing Key Terms

Define each term in a complete sentence.

17–1 What Causes Climate?
climate
prevailing wind
windward side
leeward side

17–2 Climate Zones
microclimate
polar zone
temperate zone
tropical zone
marine climate
continental climate

17–3 Changes in Climate
major glaciation
interglacial

Chapter Review

Content Review

Multiple Choice

Choose the letter of the answer that best completes each statement.

1. The climate in any region of the Earth is determined by temperature and
   a. latitude.
   b. humidity.
   c. precipitation.
   d. elevation.

2. A low-latitude climate is a climate that is
   a. polar.
   b. temperate.
   c. arctic.
   d. tropical.

3. The measure of distance north and south of the equator is called
   a. altitude.
   b. elevation.
   c. latitude.
   d. climate.

4. The climate zone with the coldest average temperatures is
   a. tropical.
   b. polar.
   c. temperate.
   d. marine.

5. The climate zone with the greatest temperature range is
   a. tropical.
   b. polar.
   c. temperate.
   d. marine.

6. Three factors that affect the temperature in an area are latitude, elevation, and
   a. prevailing winds.
   b. ocean currents.
   c. mountain ranges.
   d. deserts.

7. Most of the land area in the United States has a
   a. polar climate.
   b. tropical climate.
   c. marine climate.
   d. temperate climate.

8. Ice ages are thought to be associated with changes in
   a. the Earth's axis and orbit.
   b. ocean currents.
   c. prevailing winds.
   d. the sun's energy output.

True or False

If the statement is true, write "true." If it is false, change the underlined word or words to make the statement true.

1. The <u>temperate</u> zone is also called a high-latitude climate.
2. The <u>leeward</u> side of a mountain usually receives a lot of precipitation.
3. Increased CO_2 levels may cause the Earth's climate to <u>cool</u>.
4. As the amount of <u>carbon dioxide</u> in the atmosphere increases, the Earth's temperature will probably <u>increase</u>.
5. A land area near a large lake would probably have a <u>continental</u> climate.
6. The Gulf Stream, which flows away from the equator, is a <u>cold</u> water current.
7. A region that receives <u>less</u> than 25 centimeters of rainfall a year is a desert.
8. The warm periods between ice ages are called <u>major glaciations</u>.

Concept Mapping

Complete the following concept map for Section 17–1. Then construct a concept map for the entire chapter.

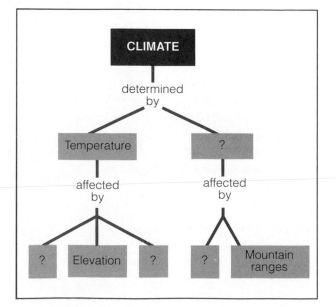

Concept Mastery

Discuss each of the following in a brief paragraph.

1. Describe how latitude, elevation, ocean currents, prevailing winds, and mountain ranges affect climate.
2. Explain how a large body of water such as an ocean can keep a nearby land area cool in the summer and warm in the winter.
3. Why do deserts have such a large daily temperature range? What are two mistaken beliefs that many people have about conditions in a desert?
4. How might changes in climate have resulted in the extinction of the dinosaurs?
5. Explain why the Sahara is one of the driest places on Earth even though it is near the Atlantic Ocean.
6. How was the climate during a major glaciation different from the climate during an interglacial? How was a major glaciation different from the climate today? What was the Little Ice Age?
7. Would a desert in the tropical zone be more likely to be found on the eastern or western coast of a continent? Why?

Critical Thinking and Problem Solving

Use the skills you have developed in this chapter to answer each of the following.

1. **Making predictions** Suppose a warm ocean current flowing along a coast suddenly becomes a cold ocean current. Predict what would happen to the climate along the coast. Explain why.
2. **Relating cause and effect** Explain how two areas at the same latitude and elevation on the Earth's surface could have different climates.
3. **Interpreting a diagram** Study the diagram shown here. Which side of the mountain is the windward side? Which side is the leeward side? On which side would you be more likely to find a desert? Explain.

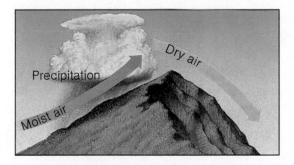

4. **Making inferences** Why do you think meteorologists record both the maximum and the minimum temperatures rather than the average temperature in order to determine the climate of a desert?
5. **Making inferences** Why do you think polar, temperate, and tropical climate zones are also called high-, middle-, and low-latitude climates, respectively?
6. **Relating concepts** The specific heat of a substance is the amount of heat needed to raise the temperature of 1 gram of the substance 1°C. Water has a relatively high specific heat. Use this information to explain why the presence of a large body of water has a moderating effect on temperatures in marine climate regions.
7. **Using the writing process** Write a science fiction story describing a trip by time machine into the future or the past. Be sure to include a detailed description of the climate in your story.

Climate in the United States

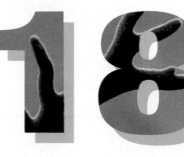

18

Guide for Reading

After you read the following sections, you will be able to

18–1 Climate Regions of the United States

■ Describe the kinds of climates that occur in the United States.

18–2 Land Biomes of the United States

■ Explain what a biome is and how land biomes are classified.

■ Describe the kinds of land biomes located in the United States.

Herds of caribou were once common in Maine. Then hunting and other human activities drove the caribou farther north. Many people hope that Maine may once again be home to the caribou.

As part of the Maine Caribou Reintroduction Project, game wardens captured 30 caribou in Canada and brought them to the University of Maine at Orono. These 30 caribou became a "nursery herd" for breeding more caribou that were slowly introduced to their new homes in Maine. Members of the Reintroduction Project hoped that as many as 100 caribou would be roaming through Maine by 1996. Unfortunately, all of the caribou that were released mysteriously vanished. However, other programs to reintroduce deer herds in Pennsylvania and red wolves in New York were more successful. Perhaps the caribou will return to Maine in the future.

Today, caribou spend the summer in an area called the tundra. In the winter, the caribou often travel south to coniferous forests. In this chapter you will learn the difference between tundras and coniferous forests. You will also learn about the climate in these and other areas of the United States, and about the plants and animals that live there.

Journal *Activity*

You and Your World What kinds of plants and animals live in your part of the United States? In your journal, sketch two kinds of plants and two kinds of animals that are common where you live. Did you ever wonder why these plants and animals are characteristic of your area?

 A solitary caribou bull will join with thousands of other caribou in vast herds to migrate in search of food.

Guide for Reading

*Focus on this question as
you read.*

▶ *What are the six major
climate regions of the
United States?*

18–1 Climate Regions of the United States

Where in the United States do you live? Do you live among the corn and wheat fields of the Midwest plains? Do you live out on the West Coast? Do you live in the hot, dry deserts of the Southwest? Or are you one of the millions of people living along the Eastern Seaboard? Wherever you live, you know that your section of the United States has its own climate (the average weather conditions there over a long period of time).

The three climate zones that you learned about in Chapter 17—polar, temperate, and tropical—are all represented in various sections of the United States. Alaska is located in the polar zone. Hawaii and southern Florida are located in the tropical zone. But most of the United States is located in the temperate zone.

Within the temperate zone, there are many different climates. To describe each climate precisely, scientists have divided the mainland United States into six major climate regions. **The six climate regions of the United States are Mediterranean, marine west coast, moist continental, moist subtropical, desert, and steppe.** The division of the mainland United States into six major climate

Figure 18–1 *From the busy streets of New York City to an Iowa corn field to a tranquil rice paddy in Arkansas, each region of the United States has its own climate.*

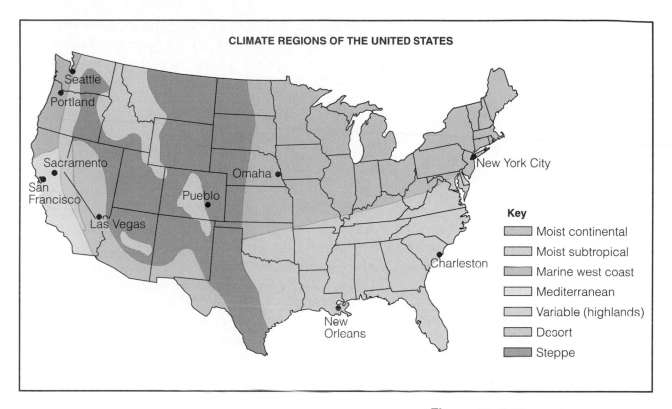

CLIMATE REGIONS OF THE UNITED STATES

Key
- Moist continental
- Moist subtropical
- Marine west coast
- Mediterranean
- Variable (highlands)
- Desert
- Steppe

regions is based on the average precipitation and temperature in each region. But it is important to remember that even within a particular climate region, variations in precipitation and temperature exist. The map in Figure 18–2 shows the six major climate regions of the United States. According to Figure 18–2, in which climate region do you live?

In the pages that follow, you will read about the six major climate regions of the United States. You will learn about the average weather conditions for each region, and also about some of the living things that are characteristic of the region. As you read this information, keep in mind the ways in which the climate of a particular region affects the plants and animals (including humans) that live in the region. Look for connections among the region's climate, ecology (relationship of living things to the environment), and economy (what people do for a living).

Figure 18–2 *The major climate regions of the United States are shown on this map, along with representative cities in each region. Remember that the climate does not change suddenly as you cross an invisible line from one climate region to another! The climate regions actually blend gradually into one another.*

Mediterranean Climate Region

The narrow coastal area of California has a **Mediterranean climate.** The name of this climate region comes from the area around the Mediterranean Sea. In winter, cyclones and moist maritime

MEDITERRANEAN CLIMATE	Summer	Winter
Average Temperature (°C)		
San Francisco	17.3	10.0
Sacramento	24.0	9.0
Average Precipitation (cm/month)		
San Francisco	0.2	9.8
Sacramento	0.2	8.0

Figure 18–3 *Variations in temperature and precipitation occur within each climate region. San Francisco, California, and Sacramento, California, both have a Mediterranean climate. How did this climate region get its name?*

Figure 18–4 *Mixed shrubs and stunted trees are characteristic of California's Mediterranean climate. The Napa Valley in California is ideal for vineyards.*

polar air masses bring heavy precipitation to the Mediterranean climate region. In summer, however, there is almost no rain. (This type of climate is also known as a dry-summer subtropical climate.) Winters throughout the Mediterranean climate region are cool. Summer temperatures are only slightly higher than winter temperatures. The chart in Figure 18–3 shows the average temperature and precipitation in summer and winter for the Mediterranean climate region.

The Mediterranean climate of wet winters and dry summers results in two basic types of plant life in this region. One type of plant life is a dense growth of shrubs and stunted (shorter than normal) trees. The other type consists of scattered oak and olive trees with a ground cover of grasses. You will learn more about the types of plants characteristic of each region of the United States in the next section.

With the help of extensive irrigation, agriculture is a major occupation in the Mediterranean climate region. Most crops produced in California are grown in the Central Valley. There are still some citrus groves near Los Angeles despite the city's expansion. Grapes are grown in many places, including the Napa Valley (the wine-making center) and Fresno (the raisin center). Other important crops include peaches, a variety of vegetables, rice, cotton, and alfalfa.

Marine West Coast Climate Region

The northwestern coast of the United States has a **marine west coast climate.** This is a rainy climate because moist air from the Pacific Ocean rises, cools, and releases precipitation onto the western slopes of the Cascade Mountains. Mild winters and cool summers are characteristic of the marine west coast climate. The temperature range from one season to another is small due to the moderating effect of the nearby Pacific Ocean.

The type of plant life most common to the marine west coast climate region is the forests of needle-leaved trees. These thick forests consist of mixed cedar, spruce, redwood, and fir trees. In fact, the most valuable needle-leaved forests in the world are located in the Pacific Northwest. These forests contribute greatly to the economy of this region. Processing wood for lumber, paper, and furniture is the major industry.

Moist Continental Climate Region

The northern portion of the United States extending from the Midwest (central Nebraska and Kansas) to the Atlantic coast has a **moist continental climate.** Continental polar air masses flowing south across this region produce very cold winters. In

MARINE WEST COAST CLIMATE		
	Summer	Winter
Average Temperature (°C)		
Seattle	17.0	5.3
Portland	18.5	5.0
Average Precipitation (cm/month)		
Seattle	2.3	11.9
Portland	2.3	15.5

Figure 18–5 *Seattle, Washington, and Portland, Oregon, both have a marine west coast climate. What variations in temperature occur from summer to winter in this climate region?*

Figure 18–6 *Mt. Hood in Oregon provides a dramatic background for the thick forests of needle-leaved trees characteristic of a marine west coast climate. These forests have made the lumber industry an important part of the economy.*

MOIST CONTINENTAL CLIMATE

	Summer	Winter
Average Temperature (°C)		
New York City	22.0	–0.3
Omaha	23.7	–4.3
Average Precipitation (cm/month)		
New York City	10.0	8.4
Omaha	8.7	2.2

Figure 18–7 *New York City, New York, and Omaha, Nebraska, share a moist continental climate. What characteristics does this climate have?*

Figure 18–8 *The moist continental climate region includes both pine trees in Maine and the endless wheat fields of Nebraska.*

summer, tropical air masses flowing north across the region produce high temperatures throughout the region.

The moist continental climate region receives a moderate amount of precipitation throughout the year. During the summer, however, there is a marked increase in precipitation for all locations within the region. During the winter, the decrease in precipitation varies from place to place. Look at Figure 18–7. What is the difference in average monthly precipitation for Omaha, Nebraska, from summer to winter?

In some sections of the moist continental climate region, forests of broad-leaved and needle-leaved trees are dominant. In other sections, much of the land was once covered with tall grasses. Farms now have largely replaced both the forests and the tall grasses.

Commercial agriculture is the principle occupation in this region. The moist continental climate region includes all of the Corn Belt as well as the eastern half of the Winter Wheat Belt. After corn and wheat, soybeans are the next most important crop in the region. Hogs, poultry, and beef cattle are also a major part of the economy.

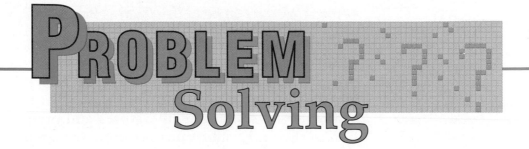

PROBLEM Solving

What Causes a Drought?

In 1988, the midwestern United States experienced a severe drought—a prolonged period of extremely dry weather. Little rain fell to help irrigate the corn and wheat fields. Many farmers lost their entire crops, leading to great economic hardships in this region. What were the causes of this harmful drought?

The map shown here illustrates the events that led to the drought in the Midwest. The numbers show the order in which the events occurred. Study the map and then answer the questions that follow.

Relating Cause and Effect

1. What event began the process that led to the drought?

2. What was the final event that caused the drought to occur? What was the immediate cause of this event?

3. What unusual storm activity contributed to the drought? What was the direct result of this storm activity?

4. Summarize the ways in which changes in global winds and changes in the temperature of ocean water contributed to the drought.

5. How are the changes you described in question 4 related?

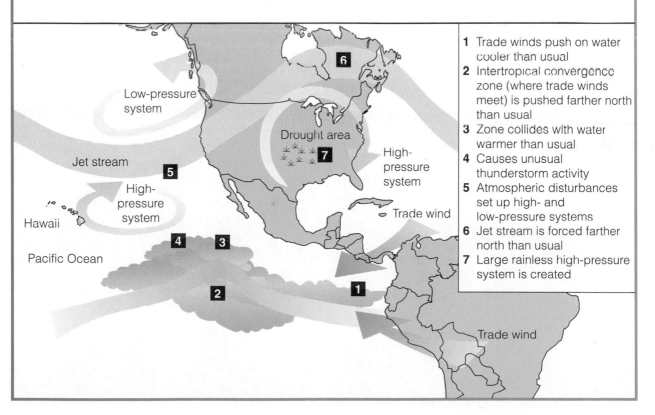

1 Trade winds push on water cooler than usual
2 Intertropical convergence zone (where trade winds meet) is pushed farther north than usual
3 Zone collides with water warmer than usual
4 Causes unusual thunderstorm activity
5 Atmospheric disturbances set up high- and low-pressure systems
6 Jet stream is forced farther north than usual
7 Large rainless high-pressure system is created

MOIST SUBTROPICAL CLIMATE		
	Summer	Winter
Average Temperature (°C)		
New Orleans	26.3	12.7
Charleston	27.2	11.3
Average Precipitation (cm/month)		
New Orleans	14.0	10.1
Charleston	15.0	7.6

Figure 18–9 *A moist subtropical climate is typical of New Orleans, Louisiana, and Charleston, South Carolina. Are the variations in temperature and precipitation from summer to winter extreme in this climate region?*

Figure 18–10 *Live oak trees flourish in Florida, which has a moist subtropical climate. Cotton, which was once the major crop in the South, is still grown today in many southern states.*

Moist Subtropical Climate Region

The southeastern United States has a **moist subtropical climate.** Summers are hot in the moist subtropical climate region. The average precipitation in summer is greater than it is in winter. In fact, the characteristic summer temperatures and precipitation in the moist subtropical region are similar to those of the tropical climate zone. Maritime tropical air masses moving inland from the tropical zones greatly influence the summer climate in this region. So in summer, the climate of the moist subtropical region of the United States is similar to the climate of the Earth's tropical zones. (As you may recall from Chapter 17, the tropical zones extend from 30° north and south latitude to the equator.)

The similarity between the moist subtropical climate and the tropical climate ends in winter. Although winters in the moist subtropical climate region are generally cool and mild, the mixing of polar air masses with maritime tropical air masses causes the temperature to drop below freezing occasionally. Severe frosts sometimes occur in the northern areas of the region. In late summer and early autumn, hurricanes are common along the coast. In spring and summer, tornadoes are common in the western parts of the region.

Figure 18–11 *The American alligator and the green heron are two inhabitants of the Florida Everglades.*

The plant life of the moist subtropical climate region consists of forests of broad-leaved and needle-leaved trees. Oak, chestnut, and pine trees grow in this region. The "River of Grass" of the Florida Everglades is also located in this region. The Everglades is home to a large variety of animals, including herons, egrets, alligators, crocodiles, and manatees.

At one time, cotton was the major crop in the South. Cotton is still grown in the region today, but other crops have become an important part of the economy. For example, citrus fruits are grown in central Florida, peaches and peanuts in Georgia, sugar cane in Mississippi, and rice in Louisiana.

Desert and Steppe Climate Regions

Located within the western interior of the United States are two regions that have similar climates.

DESERT AND STEPPE CLIMATES

	Summer	Winter
Average Temperature (°C)		
Las Vegas	28.3	8.2
Pueblo	22.5	–0.3
Average Precipitation (cm/month)		
Las Vegas	10.3	1.4
Pueblo	4.2	1.2

Figure 18–12 *The desert and steppe climates of Las Vegas, Nevada, and Pueblo, Colorado, receive the lowest amounts of precipitation of any region in the United States.*

Figure 18–13 *Several types of cacti and other hardy plants are able to survive the harsh conditions of the southwestern deserts. Sheep herding is important to the economy of the steppe climate region.*

These climates are the **desert climate** and the **steppe climate.** The desert climate region and the steppe climate region begin just east of the mountain ranges along the west coast and end in the central midwestern part of the United States (the Great Plains).

The desert and steppe climate regions receive the lowest amount of precipitation of any climate region in the United States. However, the steppe climate region receives slightly more precipitation than the desert climate region does.

One reason precipitation is so low in these climate regions is that they are located far inland, away from the oceans that are the sources of moist maritime air masses. (The desert and steppe climate regions are also called dry continental climates.) In addition, high mountain ranges along the western borders of these regions block most of the maritime air masses. In winter, dry continental polar air masses further reduce the amount of precipitation these regions receive.

In spite of the harsh conditions found in the desert climate region, many plants—including cactus, yucca, and sagebrush—grow well in this region. The slightly higher precipitation of the steppe climate encourages the growth of short grasses and scattered forests of needle-leaved trees.

Grazing for livestock—beef cattle and sheep—is an important part of the economy of the Great Plains. Goats are also raised in this region, especially in Texas. Because this region is so dry, overgrazing can be a serious problem. Overgrazing exposes the dry soil so that it can be blown away by the wind. These conditions led to the dust bowl of the 1930s.

Highlands (Variable) Climate Region

You probably noticed a climate region identified as highlands, or variable, in Figure 18–2 on page 557. These regions are located in mountain areas. The climate varies with latitude and elevation. Generally, the temperature in highlands regions is low—the higher the elevation, the lower the temperature. Average precipitation increases with elevation and is higher than in the surrounding lowlands.

ACTIVITY WRITING

What's in a Name?

Grasslands in different parts of the world are known by many names. Using library references, find out where each of the different types of grasslands listed here is found. Write a brief report describing the location and characteristics of each of the following grassland biomes: steppes, savannas, pampas, plains, prairies, llanos, veldts.

Figure 18–14 *This diagram illustrates the effects of latitude and elevation on climate. Climbing 1000 meters higher in elevation has about the same effect as traveling 1700 kilometers north. How are conditions at the highest elevations on a mountain similar to those at the North Pole?*

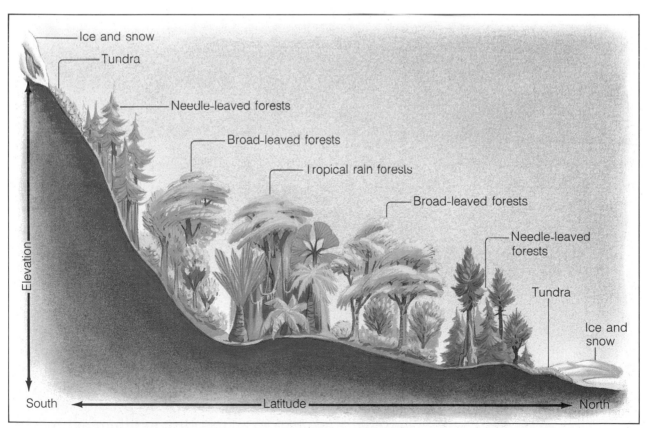

Forestry is the major industry in the mountain regions of the western United States. Fir and pine are the most important commercial trees. Mountain areas are also used as summer grazing grounds for livestock (especially sheep), which are transported from the Great Plains.

18–1 Section Review

1. What are the major climate regions of the United States? What factors determine this classification?
2. Why are summer temperatures in San Francisco, California, cooler than summer temperatures in Sacramento, California?
3. What are three reasons for the low precipitation in desert and steppe climate regions?
4. Why does the east coast of the United States receive more precipitation in the summer, whereas the west coast receives more precipitation in the winter?

Critical Thinking—*Making Comparisons*
5. What changes in climate would you expect if you were to travel from New York City to New Orleans, Louisiana, during the summer? What if you were to make the same trip during the winter?

Guide for Reading

Focus on this question as you read.

▶ *What are the major land biomes of the United States?*

18–2 Land Biomes of the United States

Imagine that you are taking a trip across the United States. As you travel from one part of the country to another, you quickly discover that different plants and animals live in different areas. So you would probably be really surprised to see an alligator in the middle of the Mojave Desert or a cactus in the Everglades!

Why do some kinds of plants and animals survive in one area but not in another? Why do different groups of plants and animals live in different areas?

You can probably answer these questions easily once you think about them. The kinds of animals that live in an area depend largely on the kinds of plants that grow there. For example, the midwestern United States was once home to millions of grazing bison. Today, however, most of the grasses that once grew in the Midwest have been replaced by corn and wheat fields. What effect do you think this has had on the bison population? You are right if you said that the herds of bison have greatly decreased and have almost disappeared. (Today, small herds of bison have been established on private land.)

If the plant life in an area determines the animal life in that area, what determines the plant life? The plant life in an area is determined mainly by climate. Recall that climate refers to the general conditions of temperature and precipitation for an area over a long period of time. As you learned in Section 18–1, the United States has six major climate regions. Scientists classify areas with similar climates, plants, and animals into divisions called **biomes** (BIGH-ohmz).

Biomes are divisions that help scientists better understand the natural world. But as is often the case in science, not all scientists agree on the kinds and number of biomes. However, most scientists accept at least six land biomes. Each of these biomes is located in some area of the United States. **The major land biomes of the United States are tundras, coniferous forests, deciduous forests, tropical rain forests, grasslands, and deserts.** There are also several types of aquatic, or water, biomes. Because aquatic biomes do not depend on climate, they will not be considered here.

Figure 18–15 *At one time, millions of bison could be seen grazing on the Great Plains. Today, only a few scattered herds remain.*

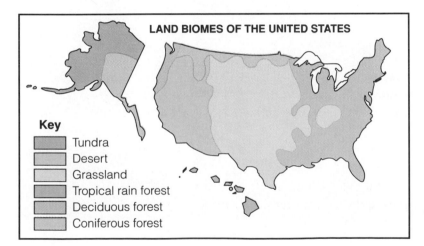

LAND BIOMES OF THE UNITED STATES

Key

	Tundra
	Desert
	Grassland
	Tropical rain forest
	Deciduous forest
	Coniferous forest

Figure 18–16 *This map shows the distribution of major land biomes in the United States. In which biome do you live?*

Tundras

Tundra biomes cover about 10 percent of the Earth's surface. In the United States, tundra biomes are found only in parts of Alaska. (Recall from Chapter 2 that Alaska is in the polar climate zone.) The climate of a tundra is extremely cold and dry. In fact, you could think of a tundra as a cold desert. Less than 25 centimeters of rain and snow fall on a tundra during most years. (On the average, a snowfall 10 centimeters deep is the equivalent of 1 centimeter of rainfall.) The little water that is found on a tundra is permanently frozen in the soil. This frozen layer of soil is called **permafrost.** Almost 85 percent of the ground in Alaska is permafrost.

Plant life on a tundra consists mostly of mosses and grasses. Carpetlike lichens, which are actually fungi and algae growing together, cover the rocks and bare ground. Because of the permafrost, large trees cannot root on a tundra. The few trees that do grow here are mainly knee-high willows and birches.

Figure 18–17 *British soldier lichen (top) are common on the tundra as are tundra willow, dwarf birch, and sedge (bottom).*

Lichens are the favorite food of the caribou herds you read about at the beginning of this chapter. The caribou roam the tundras in the summer before moving farther south for the winter. Wolves often follow close behind the caribou, preying on the old and weak animals. Birds such as ptarmigan and small animals such as lemmings also inhabit the tundras. Some animals are only seasonal residents of the tundras. Arctic terns, for example, make round-trip migrations of 34,000 kilometers to mate and raise their young during the short tundra ''summer.''

Figure 18–18 *The Alaska tundra is home to the white-tailed ptarmigan, the arctic tern, and the shaggy musk ox.*

Coniferous Forests

South of the tundra biomes are the coniferous forest biomes. Unlike the permafrost of the tundras, the soil in a coniferous forest thaws every spring, making the forest floor wet and swampy. For this reason, a coniferous forest biome is also called a **taiga** (TIGH-guh), a Russian name that means swamp forest. A coniferous forest biome, or taiga, is found in parts of Alaska as well as at the higher elevations of the Rocky Mountains. Temperatures in coniferous forest biomes are cold. The yearly rainfall is between 50 and 125 centimeters.

Few types of trees can survive the cold climate of the coniferous forests. The trees that do live in these biomes are needle-leaved trees, or **conifers.** Conifers produce their seeds in cones. They include firs, spruces, and pines. Giant redwoods grow along the coasts of Washington State, Oregon, and northern California. These conifers, which may grow as tall as 60 meters, are among the tallest trees in the world. (The tallest redwood ever found was 110 meters tall—almost 20 meters taller than the Statue of Liberty!) The Mediterranean climate of southern California supports a coniferous forestlike biome called a chaparral. A chaparral consists mainly of short, shrublike plants.

Large animals in the coniferous forests include wolves, deer, black bears and grizzly bears, and moose. (Parts of the coniferous forests are even called "spruce-moose" belts.) Many smaller animals, such as beaver, hares, and red squirrels, also live in

Figure 18–19 *Soaring redwoods and other conifers can be seen in Sequoia National Park, California.*

Activity Bank

Soil Permeability, p. 778

Figure 18–20 *The brown bear shares its home in the coniferous forest with the moose and the great horned owl. What is another name for a coniferous forest?*

Figure 18–21 *In autumn, a deciduous forest becomes a blaze of vivid colors. When the leaves decay, nutrients that help new trees grow are returned to the soil.*

the coniferous forests. Crows and great horned owls are some of the birds that build their nests among the conifers. Grouse roost in the branches.

Deciduous Forests

South of the coniferous forest biomes are the deciduous forests. Deciduous forests begin at the northeastern border, between the United States and Canada, and cover the eastern United States. Deciduous trees shed their leaves in the autumn. New leaves grow back in the spring. The summers in the deciduous forests are warm and the winters are cold, but they are not as cold as in the coniferous forests. Rainfall in the deciduous forests is between 75 and 150 centimeters a year.

There are more than 800 kinds of deciduous trees in North America. Oak, birch, maple, beech, and hickory are the most common varieties found in the deciduous forests of the United States. Autumn in the deciduous forests is one of the most beautiful seasons of the year because of the bright colors the leaves display before they fall to the ground. In the spring, wildflowers and ferns cover the forest floor.

Many different kinds of animals make their homes in the deciduous forests. Thrushes, woodpeckers, cardinals, and blue jays are some of the many birds you might see in a deciduous forest. Snails, worms, snakes, and salamanders slither along the forest floor. Small mammals, such as gray squirrels and raccoons, live among the branches of the trees.

Figure 18–22 *The hollow trunk of a deciduous tree makes a cozy home for the pileated woodpecker and its young, as well as for these baby raccoons. The black bear cub is just visiting, however! Black bears live in dens on the ground.*

Tropical Rain Forests

In the United States, tropical rain forests are found only in Hawaii. (Recall that Hawaii is in the tropical climate zone.) As you might expect, rain forests get a great deal of rain—at least 200 centimeters a year. Kauai, Hawaii, may be the wettest place on Earth. It receives an average rainfall of 1215 centimeters every year! Temperatures in the tropical rain forests remain warm all year, so plants grow well here throughout the year.

Rain forests have more varieties of plant life than any other biome. Trees grow to a height of 35 meters or more. High above the forest floor, the tops of the trees meet to form a green roof, or layer, called a **canopy** (KAN-uh-pee). The canopy is so dense that rainfall may not reach the forest floor for 10 minutes after hitting the canopy! Most of the other plants in a rain forest grow in the canopy, where sunlight can reach them. Woody vines up to 90 meters long hang from the trees. Orchids and ferns grow on the branches of trees instead of on the ground.

Like the plant life, animal life in a rain forest is rich and varied. Some rain forest animals spend their entire lives high in the trees and never touch the ground. Parrots, toucans, and hundreds of other birds live in the canopy. At night, huge colonies of bats come out to hunt among the trees. Insects, tree frogs, and snakes crawl on the trunks and branches of the trees.

ACTIVITY
CALCULATING

Daily Rainfall

The island of Kauai, Hawaii, receives an average of 1215 centimeters of rain every year. What is the average rainfall each day?

Figure 18–23 *Exotic orchids (left) are among the many different plants you can expect to see growing in the tropical rain forest on Maui, Hawaii (center). Compare the tropical rain forest with the temperate rain forest of Olympic National Park, Washington (right).*

Figure 18–24 *The iiwi and the nene goose are birds that are native to Hawaii. The ti plant grows on the slopes of Hawaiian volcanoes.*

Grasslands

The first European explorers found an endless sea of grass in the midwestern plains of the United States. French explorers from Canada called these grasslands a prairie, a French word that means meadow. Some of the grasses on the prairie were over 2 meters tall! The grassland biomes in the United States receive between 25 and 75 centimeters of rain every year. The grasslands of the midwestern plains are characterized by hot summers and cold winters.

Grasses make up the main group of plants in a grassland biome. There are few trees because of the low rainfall. Fires, which often sweep over the grasslands, also prevent widespread tree growth. Today, most of the original grasslands in the United States have been replaced by farms and pastures. Wheat, corn, and other grains are now widely farmed in the midwestern plains of the United States.

Gophers, prairie dogs, and other small animals live on the grasslands. Blackbirds, prairie chickens, and meadow larks are among the birds that feed on the grasshoppers, locusts, and other insects. Large plant eaters, such as elk and bison, were once common on the plains. They were hunted by wolves and cougars. Now that farms have replaced most of the original grasslands, however, most of the large animals live only in national parks and other protected areas.

Figure 18–25 *Although most of the midwestern plains have been converted to corn or wheat fields, native grasslands have been restored in the Flint Hills Preserve in Kansas.*

Figure 18–26 *The greater prairie chicken is a common resident of the grasslands. The round structure in its throat is its vocal sac, not an orange! Two other inhabitants are the grasshopper and the tiny harvest mouse.*

Deserts

Unlike the other biomes, deserts can be classified by what they do not have: water. Deserts receive less than 25 centimeters of rain a year. Desert biomes are located in the southwestern part of the United States. Although deserts can be hot or cold, the deserts of the American Southwest are hot.

Plants in a desert are adapted to the lack of rainfall. For example, the thick, fleshy stems of cacti help them to store water. A giant saguaro cactus in the Sonoran Desert of Arizona can store up to a ton of water! The Joshua tree, in spite of its name, is really a giant yucca—a member of the lily family. Most flowering plants in the southwestern deserts flower, produce seeds, and die within a few weeks of a rare desert rainfall.

Like the plants, desert animals must be able to survive on little water. Plant-eating animals, such as kangaroo rats and jack rabbits, obtain most of their water from the plants they eat. Meat-eating animals, such as cougars, obtain most of their water by eating

Figure 18–27 *Tall saguaro cacti may take hundreds of years to reach full height. Flowering hedgehog cacti and organ pipe cacti must bloom and produce seeds in a brief growing season. The Joshua tree thrives in the desert.*

Figure 18–28 *The jack rabbit, the mountain lion, and the white-winged dove all have adaptations that allow them to survive in the desert. What adaptations for survival does the cactus have?*

the plant eaters. Most desert animals hide from the hot sun during the day and come out to eat only at night, when temperatures are cooler.

18–2 Section Review

1. Identify and describe the main characteristics of the major land biomes of the United States.
2. Compare the climates of the three forest biomes.
3. What is another name for a coniferous forest?
4. How are plants and animals adapted for life in a desert?

Connection—*Social Studies*

5. About 10 percent of all workers in the seven states that make up the midwestern plains are employed on farms, whereas only about 1 percent are employed in forestry. Based on your knowledge of the midwestern plains biome, explain why this is so.

A Pharmacy on the Prairie

Growing among the tall and short grasses of the prairie are many colorful wildflowers and weeds. The Native Americans who lived on the Great Plains before the coming of settlers from the East learned to use some of these plants as remedies, or cures, for common illnesses. This type of traditional *medicine* using plants is called folk medicine. Scientists have found that some traditional folk remedies have real medicinal value.

A common grasslands weed called fleabane was used by the people living on the prairie as an insect repellant. (The word bane means poison or killer. So fleabane is a ''flea killer.'') Fleabane was also used to cure sore throats and to help heal minor cuts and bruises. Laboratory tests have confirmed that substances in fleabane promote healing and help protect against infection.

An herb called blue cohosh was used by Native American women as an aid in childbirth. Before giving birth, pregnant women drank a tea made from the plant's roots. Modern research has shown that a substance derived from blue cohosh stimulates contractions of the uterus, or birth canal, which could lead to a faster and easier birth.

There are many other examples of folk remedies that have only recently been found to have a scientific basis. These examples should remind us to use caution when we change the *environment* to suit our own needs. By destroying wilderness areas, we may unknowingly be destroying many beneficial organisms at the same time.

Common fleabane

Blue cohosh

Laboratory Investigation

Comparing Climate Regions and Biomes

Problem

How can you use climate information to determine the biomes of the United States?

Materials (per student)

tracing paper
5 different-colored pencils

Procedure

1. Study the map of North America shown here. The lines on the map are isotherms (connecting places with the same temperature). The key shows the average yearly precipitation in different areas.

2. On a sheet of tracing paper, trace the outline of the United States from the map of North America. **Note:** *Be sure to trace Alaska. (Hawaii, which is a tropical rain forest biome, is not shown on this map.)*

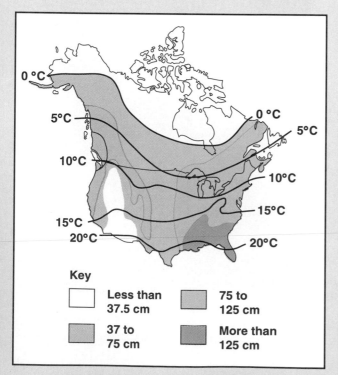

Key

☐ **Less than 37.5 cm**

☐ **37 to 75 cm**

☐ **75 to 125 cm**

☐ **More than 125 cm**

3. Study the data table, which shows the average yearly precipitation and temperature in five land biomes of the United States.

4. Using the information in the data table, draw the approximate boundaries of each biome on your map of the United States. **Note:** *Be sure to use a different-colored pencil for each biome.*

Observations

1. What is the average yearly temperature in each of the biomes listed in the data table?

2. What is the average yearly precipitation in each of the biomes listed in the data table?

Analysis and Conclusions

1. What happens to the average yearly precipitation as you travel across the United States from the west coast to the east coast?

2. Which biome covers the largest land area in the United States?

3. What is the average yearly temperature and precipitation where you live? In which biome do you live?

4. **On Your Own**   Add a key to your map showing the main crops grown in each biome.

Biome	Average Yearly Precipitation	Average Yearly Temperature
Tundras	0 to 25 cm	below 0°C
Coniferous forests	50 to 125 cm	0° to 12°C
Deciduous forests	75 to 150 cm	5° to 25°C
Grasslands	25 to 75 cm	5° to 25°C
Deserts	0 to 25 cm	10° to 25°C

Summarizing Key Concepts

18–1 Climate Regions of the United States

▲ Most of the United States is located in the temperate climate zone.

▲ The six major climate regions of the United States are Mediterranean, marine west coast, moist continental, moist subtropical, desert, and steppe.

▲ The classification of climate regions is based on the average temperature and precipitation in each region.

▲ In the highlands, or variable, climate region, climate varies with latitude and elevation.

▲ The climate, ecology, and economy of a particular region are all interrelated.

18–2 Land Biomes of the United States

▲ The kinds of animals that live in an area depend on the kinds of plants that grow in the area, which are determined mainly by the climate of the area.

▲ Areas with similar climates, plants, and animals are classified into biomes.

▲ The major land biomes of the United States are tundras, coniferous forests, deciduous forests, tropical rain forests, grasslands, and deserts.

▲ Aquatic, or water, biomes are not determined by climate.

Reviewing Key Terms

Define each term in a complete sentence.

18–1 Climate Regions of the United States

Mediterranean climate
marine west coast climate
moist continental climate
moist subtropical climate
desert climate
steppe climate

18–2 Land Biomes of the United States

biome
permafrost
taiga
conifer
canopy

Chapter Review

Content Review

Multiple Choice

Choose the letter of the answer that best completes each statement.

1. The climate zone that includes most of the mainland United States is the
   a. polar zone.
   b. temperate zone.
   c. tropical zone.
   d. subtropical zone.
2. The type of climate found along the coast of California is called a
   a. marine west coast climate.
   b. moist continental climate.
   c. Mediterranean climate.
   d. moist subtropical climate.
3. Which of the following trees is a conifer?
   a. pine   c. beech
   b. oak   d. hickory
4. In the United States, the type of biome found only in Alaska is a
   a. desert.   c. coniferous forest.
   b. grassland.   d. tundra.

5. Redwoods, which are among the tallest trees in the world, grow in
   a. tropical rain forests.
   b. coniferous forests.
   c. deciduous forests.
   d. tundras.
6. The most important crops grown in the moist continental climate region of the United States are
   a. trees for lumber.
   b. fruits and vegetables.
   c. wheat and corn.
   d. cotton and citrus fruits.
7. The type of biome that has a greater variety of plant life than any other biome is the
   a. coniferous forest biome.
   b. deciduous forest biome.
   c. grassland biome.
   d. tropical rain forest biome.

True or False

If the statement is true, write "true." If it is false, change the underlined word or words to make the statement true.

1. Dry-summer subtropical climate is another name for the <u>marine west coast</u> climate region.
2. The Russian name for a <u>deciduous</u> forest is taiga.
3. The climate in a variable, or <u>lowlands</u>, climate region varies with latitude and elevation.
4. Climate is not a factor in determining <u>water</u> biomes.
5. Like other <u>coniferous</u> trees, oak and maple trees shed their leaves in autumn.
6. The Florida Everglades is located in the <u>moist continental</u> climate region.

Concept Mapping

Complete the following concept map for Section 18–1. Then construct a concept map for the entire chapter.

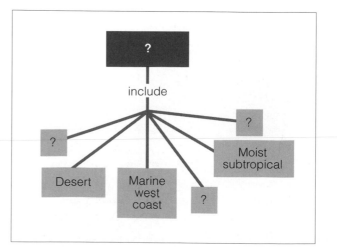

Concept Mastery

Discuss each of the following in a brief paragraph.

1. Briefly describe the kinds of plants and animals that live in each of the six major land biomes of the United States.
2. Why are tundra biomes sometimes referred to as cold deserts?
3. What crops are grown in the Mediterranean climate region? Why is extensive irrigation needed to grow crops in this region?
4. Why is climate an important factor in determining land biomes?
5. Why do you think it is difficult for scientists to agree on the number and kinds of biomes?
6. How are the desert and steppe climate regions similar? How are they different?
7. Why is wood processing a major industry in the Pacific Northwest?
8. How is the climate of the moist subtropical climate region in the United States similar to the climate of the Earth's tropical climate zones? How is it different?

Critical Thinking and Problem Solving

Use the skills you have developed in this chapter to answer each of the following.

1. **Making charts** Make a chart in which you list each of the six major land biomes in the United States, the average yearly temperature and precipitation in each biome, and the kinds of plants and animals that live in each biome.
2. **Classifying** In which climate region or regions of the United States would you expect to find each of the following plants?
   a. olive trees   d. sagebrush
   b. tall grasses   e. pine trees
   c. redwood trees   f. short grasses
3. **Classifying** In which biome or biomes would you expect to find each of the following animals?
   a. caribou   d. moose
   b. parrots   e. kangaroo rats
   c. raccoons   f. prairie dogs
4. **Applying concepts** As you climb a mountain, you may pass through several biomes. Explain how this is possible.
5. **Making predictions** The Arctic National Wildlife Refuge is part of the tundra biome in northeastern Alaska. The refuge is home to caribou, musk oxen, polar bears, and other animals. Now some oil companies want to explore the refuge for oil and natural gas. How might large-scale development of the refuge affect the animals (and plants) living in this biome?
6. **Interpreting photographs** Which biome is shown in this photograph? How do you know? What kinds of animals would you expect to find in this biome?

7. **Using the writing process** Pretend that you and your family are pioneers who have just settled on the Great Plains. Write a letter to a friend back home on the east coast describing life on the prairie during the 1800s.

SCIENCE

JOANNE SIMPSON'S STORMY STRUGGLE

 oanne Simpson spent the year 1943 contributing to the American effort in World War II by teaching weather forecasting to air force personnel. At the same time, she was fighting a more personal battle. Simpson, who had graduated from the University of Chicago, wanted to return there to earn additional degrees in meteorology. Her efforts, however, were met with much opposition from professors at the university. They told Simpson that the idea of a woman meteorologist was a "lost cause." The concept of a female scientist, they claimed, was a "contradiction in terms," and "there was no point" in her trying to get an advanced degree. Yet, in 1949, the determined Simpson became the first American woman to receive a PhD in meteorology.

Simpson's interest in meteorology began when she was a young girl. Her father was

▶ From information gathered by weather satellites, meteorologists such as Joanne Simpson hope to learn more about various weather conditions and to be able to forecast severe storms.

a journalist who wrote about aviation, and she sometimes went flying with him. During her teen years, Simpson spent summers as an assistant to the director of aviation for the state of Massachusetts. She also began to take flying lessons.

In 1940, Simpson enrolled at the University of Chicago. She was introduced to meteorology while training for her pilot's license. The ability to read and understand a weather map, as well as knowledge of weather patterns and the atmosphere, are important to flying. Simpson was so fascinated by the subject that she signed up for a course at the university.

After receiving her undergraduate degree and teaching military personnel for a year, Simpson decided to continue her studies in meteorology. At first none of the faculty at the University of Chicago would support her venture. But Simpson, a very determined young scientist, eventually won the support of Herbert Riehl. He agreed to supervise her research project, which involved the study of cumulus clouds—their interaction with the environment and their relationship to tropical waves.

Woods Hole, Massachusetts, a small town at the southwest tip of Cape Cod, provided an ideal natural environment for Simpson's research on cumulus clouds. Simpson studied at both Woods Hole and the University of Chicago before receiving her PhD in meteorology in 1949.

Simpson's interesting and dynamic career has included teaching at several universities—among them, the University of California at Los Angeles and the University of Virginia. In 1979, she was invited to head the Severe Storms Branch of the Goddard Space Flight Center Laboratory for Atmospheric Sciences. This laboratory is part of the National Aeronautics and Space Administration (NASA).

Dr. Simpson enjoys a challenge, so for her NASA is a perfect place to be. She contin-

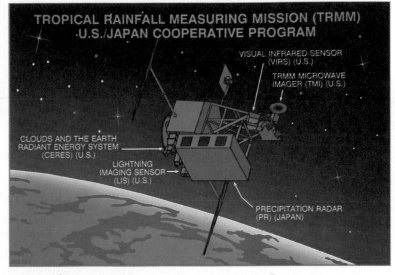

▲ This diagram shows what the Tropical Rainfall Measuring Mission satellite will look like when it is placed in orbit around the Earth.

ues to study the formation and development of cumulus clouds. And she is currently working on a new weather satellite that will provide accurate measurements of the rainfall in tropical ocean areas. The satellite, called TRMM (Tropical Rainfall Measuring Mission), which is scheduled to be launched in 1996 or 1997, should give meteorologists a better understanding of various changes in climate. These discoveries could enable scientists to make more accurate and longer range weather forecasts.

In the last 40 years, Simpson has published 115 scientific research papers, won numerous awards and honors, traveled across the globe, and served on many scientific councils and committees. The honors that have given her the greatest personal satisfaction are the Meisinger Award, given to her in 1962 for her work on cumulus clouds; NASA's Exceptional Scientific Achievement Medal; and the Carl-Gustav Rossby Research Medal, the American Meteorological Society's highest award. Simpson's courage and determination have earned her the respect of her colleagues and the public. She has truly paved the way for a generation of women meteorologists.

UNIT FIVE
History of the Earth

A gentle breeze sent ripples across the shimmering surface of the shallow pond. The ground shook slightly as a giant ground sloth walked clumsily out of the nearby woods. Dipping its head toward the water, the sloth drank deeply. Suddenly, the sloth raised its head and stood very still, trying to detect a whisper of danger from the trees.

Hearing nothing, the sloth bent its head toward the water again. At that moment, a saber-toothed cat leaped from the woods. With

▼ *Although neither the saber-toothed cat nor the ground sloth will survive its sticky encounter with the La Brea tar pits, their remains may become fossils found by scientists thousands of years in the future.*

claws bared and teeth flashing, the cat flew through the air toward its startled prey. With the giant cat on its back, the sloth plunged into the pond. Its feet splashed through the water but did not find solid ground. Instead, a sticky, gooey tar trapped the animal, pulling it further and further down into the pond.

In a matter of minutes, both animals were stuck in the tar. They remained there for thousands of years. In the early 1900s, scientists discovered their remains and pieced together a picture of the area in which the sloth and the cat had made their home. Today, this place is known as the La Brea tar pits in Los Angeles, California.

The types of fossils that were found in the La Brea pits are not the only kinds of fossils that have been found. As you read this book, you will discover some other types of evidence that help scientists gain an understanding of the Earth's past.

▲ *A model of an elephantlike creature trapped in tar can be seen at the La Brea tar pits in Los Angeles, California.*

Discovery Activity

Looking Into the Earth's Past

Take a walk through a nearby park or through your neighborhood and look for fossils embedded in the surfaces of sidewalks, building walls, rocks, and roads.

■ What do the fossils look like?

■ What do the fossils tell you about the kinds of living things that formed them?

■ How do you think the fossils formed?

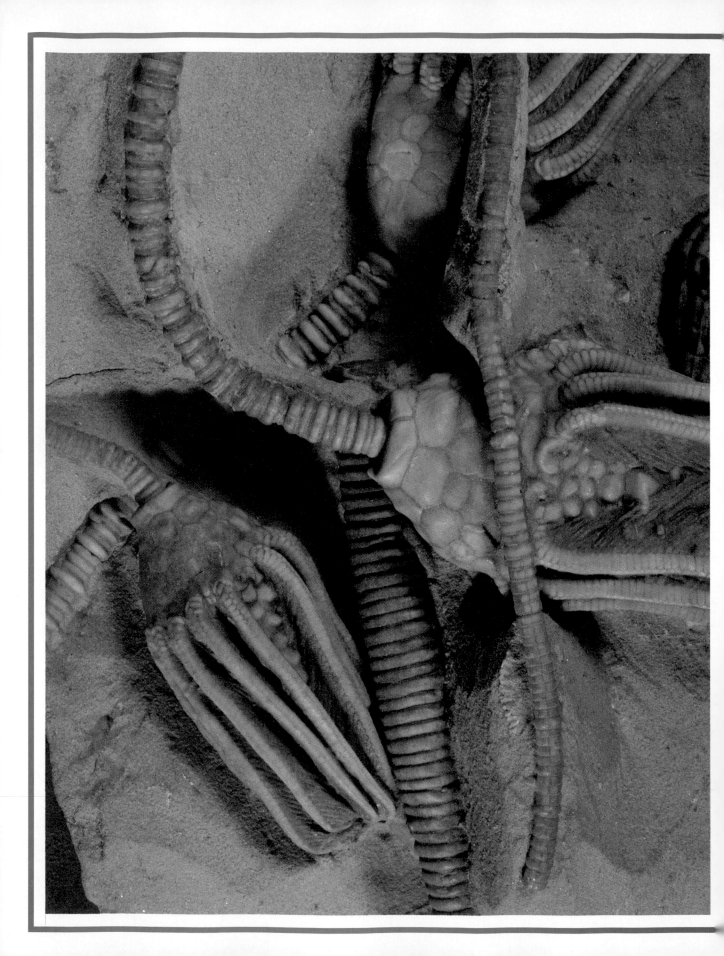

Earth's History in Fossils 19

Guide for Reading

After you read the following sections, you will be able to

19–1 Fossils—Clues to the Past

■ Describe how scientists use fossils as clues to events in Earth's past.

■ List some different types of fossils and explain how each forms.

19–2 A History in Rocks and Fossils

■ Define the law of superposition and describe how it is used to find the relative age of rocks and fossils.

■ Describe how the half-life of radioactive elements is used to find the absolute age of rocks and fossils.

What do you think these remains of living things are? You might guess that they are plant remains. In fact, they are called sea lilies because they look so much like flowers. But they are really the remains of animals called crinoids. Crinoids are relatives of starfish and sea urchins.

People have known for hundreds of years about sea lilies like these preserved in rocks and thought they were extinct. Imagine their surprise when a dredge brought up some living specimens from the ocean bottom! The animals live attached to the bottom by stalks that can be very long. When undisturbed, the branched arms are widely spread. Grooves on their upper surfaces sweep food into the central mouth.

In this chapter, you will learn how remains like these sea lilies can provide clues to the Earth's past history. You will also discover how scientists determine the age of the rocks in which they are found and, ultimately, the age of the Earth itself.

Journal *Activity*

You and Your World The Chinese were among the first to record past events. But their records only go back 2500 years. How do you think scientists find out how long ago these sea lilies lived on the ancient sea bottom? In your journal describe one way you know of measuring time indirectly, without a clock.

These fossil crinoids, or sea lilies, once grew at the bottom of the sea more than 500 million years ago. Today, crinoids like these still live in deep ocean water.

 Activity Bank

Turned to Stone, p.779

19–1 Fossils—Clues to the Past

The remains of living things like the sea lilies you have just read about were a great mystery for a long time. People wondered how they came to be preserved in rocks. To scientists, such remains provide clues that help create a picture—a picture of Earth's past. How exactly can they do this?

If you see a fish, you can conclude that somewhere on Earth there must be water, for that is where fishes live. If you see a polar bear, you can conclude that somewhere on Earth there is ice and cold temperatures—the environment in which polar bears live. In much the same way, scientists who study prehistoric forms of life use **fossils** to form a picture of Earth's past.

As you learned in Chapter 12, **a fossil is the remains or evidence of a living thing.** A fossil can be the bone of an organism or the print of a shell in a rock. A fossil can even be a burrow or tunnel left by an ancient worm. The most common fossils are bones, shells, pollen grains, and seeds.

Most fossils are not complete organisms. Fossils are generally incomplete because only the hard parts of dead plants or animals become fossils. The soft tissues either decay or are eaten before fossils can form. Decay is the breakdown of dead organisms into the substances from which they were made.

Figure 19–1 *Scientists carefully reassemble fossil bones to better understand the living things that existed long ago. What are fossils?*

Most ancient forms of life have left behind few, if any, fossils as evidence that they once lived on Earth. In fact, the chances of any plant or animal leaving a fossil are slight at best. For most fossils to form, the remains of organisms usually have to be buried in **sediments** soon after the organisms die. Sediments are small pieces of rocks, shells, and other materials that were broken down over time. Quick burial in sediments prevents the dead organisms from being eaten by animals. It also slows down or stops the decay process.

Plants and animals that lived in or near water were preserved more often than other organisms were. Sediments in the form of mud and sand could easily bury plants and animals that died in the water or along the sides of a body of water. When the sediments slowly hardened and changed to sedimentary rocks, the organisms were trapped in the rocks. Sedimentary rocks are formed from layers of sediments. Most fossils are found in sedimentary rocks.

Rocks known as igneous rocks are formed by the cooling and hardening of hot molten rock, or magma. Most magma is found deep within the Earth, where no living things exist. Sometimes the magma flows onto the Earth's surface as hot, fiery lava. Can you explain why fossils are almost never found in igneous rocks?

A third type of rock is called metamorphic rock. Metamorphic rocks are formed when sedimentary or igneous rocks are changed by heat, pressure, and chemical reactions. If there are fossils in a rock that undergoes such changes, the fossils are usually destroyed or damaged. So fossils are rarely found in metamorphic rocks as well.

There are many different kinds of fossils. Each kind is identified according to the process by which it was formed.

Petrification

When the dinosaurs died, the soft parts of their bodies quickly decayed. Only the hard parts—the bones—were left. Many of these bones were buried under layers of sediments of mud and wet sand. As water seeped through the layers of sediments, it dissolved minerals in the mud and sand. The water and

Figure 19–2 *These coiled shells once housed octopuslike animals that lived millions of years ago. How did the shells end up trapped in solid rock?*

Animal Footprints

1. Spread some mud in a low, flat-bottomed pan. Make sure the mud is not too wet and runny. Smooth the surface of the mud.

2. Have your pet or a neighbor's pet walk across the mud. Let the mud dry so that it hardens and the footprints are permanent.

3. Bring the footprints to science class. Exchange your set of footprints for the set of another student.

Examine the footprints and predict what type of animal made them. Explain how you arrived at your answer.

How is this activity similar to the way scientists determine what organism left the fossils that have been found?

Figure 19–3 *The Petrified Forest in Arizona has stone copies of trees that once grew there. The stone trees are the result of a process called petrification. How does petrification occur?*

ACTIVITY

DISCOVERING

Preservation in Ice

1. Place fresh fruit—such as apple slices, strawberries, and blueberries—in an open plastic container. Completely cover the fruit with water. Put the container in a freezer.

2. Put the same amount of fresh fruit in another open container. Place it somewhere where it will not be disturbed.

3. After three days, observe the fruit.

■ How do the samples in the two containers compare? How can you account for these differences?

minerals flowed through pores, or tiny holes, in the buried bones. When the water evaporated, the minerals were left behind in the bones, turning the bones to stone. This process is called **petrification,** which means turning into stone.

Petrification can occur in another way as well. Water may dissolve away animal or plant material. That material is replaced by the minerals in the water. This type of petrification is called replacement. Replacement produces an exact stone copy of the original animal or plant.

In the Petrified Forest of Arizona are some fossil trees that were created by replacement. Great stone logs up to 3 meters in diameter and more than 36 meters long lie in the Petrified Forest. Scientists suspect that the trees were knocked down by floods that swept over the land more than 200 million years ago. The remains of the trees—the fossil logs—show almost every detail of the once-living forest. For example, the patterns of growth rings in the trunks of many trees show up so clearly that scientists can count the growth rings and determine how long the trees lived.

Molds and Casts

Two types of fossils are formed when an animal or a plant is buried in sediments that harden into rock. If the soft parts of the organism decay and the hard parts are dissolved by chemicals, an empty space will be left in the rock. The empty space, called a **mold**, has the same shape as the organism.

Sometimes the mold is filled in by minerals in the sediment. The minerals harden to form a **cast,** or filled-in mold. The cast is in the same shape as the original organism.

Imprints

Sometimes a fossil is formed before the sediments harden into rock. Thin objects—such as leaves and feathers—leave **imprints,** or impressions, in soft sediments such as mud. When the sediments harden into rock, the imprints are preserved as fossils.

One particular imprint fossil has provided scientists with a clue to the development of the first

birds. The imprint shows that the bird's skeleton was like that of a reptile with a toothed beak. Why do scientists believe the imprint was made by an ancient bird? The imprint also shows feathers around the skeleton, and only birds have feathers.

Figure 19–4 *Molds, casts, and imprints are types of fossils. Which part of the fossil shell is the mold? Which is the cast? The wing and tail feathers of this ancient bird are imprinted around its fossilized bones.*

Preservation of Entire Organisms

Perhaps the most spectacular kinds of fossils are those in which the whole body, or complete sections of it, is preserved. Although it is quite rare for both the soft and the hard parts of an organism to be preserved, some entire-organism fossils exist. How was the decay of these organisms stopped completely so that they could be preserved?

FREEZING You probably know that freezing substances helps to preserve them. Freezing prevents substances from decaying. On occasion, scientists have found animals that have been preserved through freezing. Several extinct (no longer living on Earth) elephantlike animals called woolly mammoths have been discovered frozen in large blocks of ice. Woolly mammoths lived some 10,000 years ago. Another extinct animal, the furry rhinoceros, has been found preserved in the loose frozen soil in the arctic. So well preserved are the woolly mammoths and the furry rhinoceroses that wolves had sometimes eaten parts of the flesh when the ice had thawed.

ACTIVITY
WRITING

Terrible Lizards

Using reference materials in the library, look up information about these reptiles:

    Brachiosaurus
    Ankylosaurus
    Plesiosaurus

Write a report that includes a description of each reptile and its habitat. Accompany your descriptions with drawings of the reptiles.

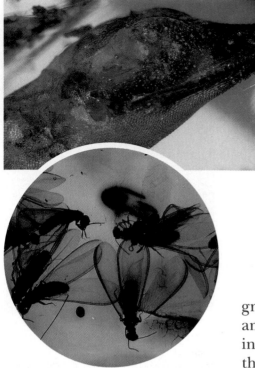

Figure 19–5 *Fossils may form when living things are trapped in tree resin that later hardens into amber. The tiny scales of the lizard, the hairlike bristles on the cricket's hind legs, and the delicate wings of the termites are perfectly preserved.*

AMBER When the resin (sap) from certain evergreen trees hardens, it forms a hard substance called amber. Flies and other insects are sometimes trapped in the sticky resin that flows from these trees. When the resin hardens, the insects are preserved in the amber. Insects found trapped in amber are usually perfectly preserved.

TAR PITS Tar pits are large pools of tar. Tar pits contain the fossil remains of many different animals. The animals were trapped in the sticky tar when they went to drink the water that often covered the pits. Other animals came to feed on the trapped animals and were also trapped in the tar. Eventually, the trapped animals sank to the bottom of the tar pits. Bison, camels, giant ground sloths, wolves, vultures, and saber-toothed cats are some of the animals found as fossils in the tar pits. In the La Brea tar pits in present-day Los Angeles, California, the complete skeletons of animals that lived more than a million years ago are perfectly preserved.

Most of the fossils recovered from tar pits are bones. The flesh of the trapped animals had either decayed or been eaten before the animals could be preserved. But whole furry rhinoceroses have been found in tar pits in Poland.

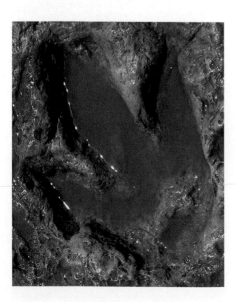

Figure 19–6 *Dinosaur footprints are an example of trace fossils. What are some other types of trace fossils? Why are such fossils important to scientists?*

Trace Fossils

Trace fossils are fossils that reveal much about an animal's appearance without showing any part of the animal. Trace fossils are the marks or evidence of animal activities. Tracks, trails, footprints, and burrows are trace fossils. Trace fossils can be left behind by animals such as worms, which are too soft to be otherwise preserved.

Interpreting Fossils

Scientists can learn a great deal about Earth's past from fossils. **Fossils indicate that many different life forms have existed at different times throughout Earth's history.** In fact, some scientists believe that for every type of organism living today, there are at least 100 types of organisms that have become extinct.

When fossils are arranged according to age, they show that living things have **evolved,** or changed over time. By examining the changes in fossils of a particular type of living thing, scientists can determine how that living thing has evolved over many millions of years. You will learn more about evolution at the end of Chapter 20.

Fossils also indicate how the Earth's surface has evolved. For example, if scientists find fossils of sea organisms in rocks high above sea level, they can assume that the land was once covered by an ocean.

Fossils also give scientists clues to Earth's past climate. For example, fossils of coral have been found in arctic regions. Coral is an animal that lives only in warm ocean areas. So evidence of the presence of coral in arctic regions indicates that the climate in the Arctic was once much warmer than it is today. Fossils of alligators similar to those found in Florida today have been located as far north as Canada. What kind of climate might once have existed when these fossils were living?

Fossils also tell scientists about the appearance and activities of extinct animals. From fossils of footprints, bones, and teeth, scientists construct models of extinct animals. They can even tell how big or heavy the animals were. Fossil footprints provide a clue as to how fast a particular animal could move.

Figure 19–7 *Scientists can learn much about the Earth's past from fossils. Although today's alligators live only in warm climates, alligatorlike fossils have been found as far north as Canada. What does this suggest about the past climate of Canada? What do the fossil shark teeth from a desert of Morocco indicate about that area's past? What characteristics of the shark's teeth indicate that it was a meat-eater?*

Although we may think of dinosaurs as being slow and plodding creatures, fossil footprints indicate that some dinosaurs could run as fast as 50 kilometers per hour. Fossils of teeth provide clues about the kind of food the animals ate. How might the shape of a tooth help scientists determine if an animal ate plants or other animals?

19–1 Section Review

1. What is a fossil? List five different types and describe how each forms.
2. Do molds and casts represent the remains of organisms or evidence of those organisms? Explain.
3. How can fossils provide evidence of climate changes on Earth?

Critical Thinking—*Applying Concepts*
4. The Hawaiian Islands are volcanic in origin. Would you expect to find many fossils of ancient Hawaiian organisms on the islands?

Guide for Reading

Focus on these questions as you read.

▶ *How do scientists use the law of superposition to determine the relative ages of rocks and fossils?*

▶ *How does the half-life of a radioactive element enable scientists to determine the absolute age of rocks and fossils?*

19–2 A History in Rocks and Fossils

Using evidence from rocks and fossils, scientists can determine the order of events that occurred in the past: what happened first, second, third, and so on. And scientists can often approximate the time at which the events happened. In other words, scientists can "write" a history of Earth.

One way to think of Earth's history is to picture a very large book filled with many pages. Each page tells the story of an event in the past. The stories of the earliest events are in the beginning pages; the stories of later events are in the pages near the end.

Although you could tell from such a book which events occurred before others, you could not know when the events occurred. In other words, you could tell the order of the events, but not their dates. To know when an event occurred, you would need numbers on the pages. If each number stood for a certain period of time—one million years perhaps—then you would have a fairly accurate calendar of Earth's history. As it turns out, scientists have both kinds of "history books" of Earth—one without page numbers but with a known order of pages, and one with page numbers as well.

The Law of Superposition

How, you might wonder, can scientists determine what events in Earth's history occurred before or after other events? That is, how do scientists develop their "book without dates"?

As you have read, most fossils are found in sedimentary rocks. Sedimentary rocks are made of layers of sediments that have piled up one atop the other. If the sediments have been left untouched, then clearly the layers of rocks at the bottom are older than those at the top. Put another way, the sedimentary layers are stacked in order of their age.

The **law of superposition** states that in a series of sedimentary rock layers, younger rocks normally lie on top of older rocks. The word superposition means one thing placed on top of another.

The law of superposition is based on the idea that sediments have been deposited in the same way throughout Earth's history. This idea was first proposed by the Scottish scientist James Hutton in the late eighteenth century. Hutton theorized that the processes acting on Earth's surface today are the same processes that have acted on Earth's surface in the past. These processes include weathering, erosion, and deposition. Weathering is the breaking down of rocks into sediments. Erosion is the carrying away of sediments. Deposition is the laying down of sediments.

Scientists use the law of superposition to determine whether a fossil or a layer of rock is older or younger than another fossil or layer of rock. Think of the layers of sedimentary rocks as the unnumbered pages of the "history book" that you have just read about. Remember, the beginning pages hold stories of long ago, while the end pages hold more recent stories. Now think of the words on each page as being a fossil. The words (fossil) on an earlier page (layer of rock) are older than the words (fossil) on a later page (layer of rock).

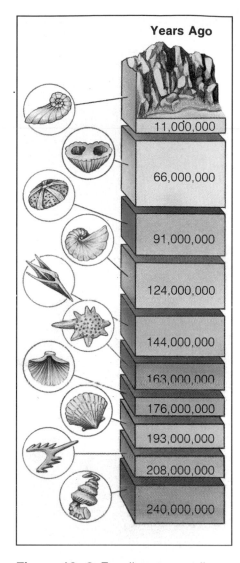

Years Ago

11,000,000
66,000,000
91,000,000
124,000,000
144,000,000
163,000,000
176,000,000
193,000,000
208,000,000
240,000,000

Figure 19–8 *Fossils are usually found in sedimentary rocks. If the sedimentary rock layers are in the same positions in which they formed, lower layers are older than upper ones. This principle is known as the law of superposition. How old are the fossils in the bottom layer of the diagram? The top layer?*

Figure 19–9 *The law of superposition helps scientists to determine the sequence of changes in life forms on the Earth. Is the spiral shell fossil older or younger than the cone-shaped shell fossil? How can you tell?*

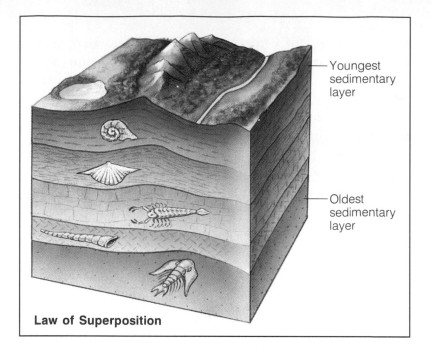

Youngest sedimentary layer

Oldest sedimentary layer

Law of Superposition

The process of sedimentation still occurs today. As you read these words, the fossils of tomorrow are being trapped in the sediments at the bottoms of rivers, lakes, and seas. For example, the Mississippi River deposits sediments at a rate of 80,000 tons an hour—day after day, year after year—at the point where the river flows into the Gulf of Mexico.

Index Fossils

The law of superposition helps scientists put in order the record of Earth's past for one particular location. But how can scientists get a worldwide picture of Earth's past? Is there a way of using the knowledge about the ages of rock layers in one location to find the relative ages of rock layers in other parts of the world? The relative age of an object is its age compared to the age of another object. Relative age does not provide dates for events, but it does provide a sequence of events.

In the early 1800s, scientists working on opposite sides of the English Channel came up with a way to determine relative ages of rock layers in different parts of the world. The scientists were digging through layers of sedimentary rocks near the southern coast of England and the northern coast of France. In both locations, the scientists discovered fossils of sea-dwelling shellfish. Clearly, both coasts had been under water at some time in the past.

ACTIVITY

WRITING

Index Fossils

Index fossils are used to identify the age of sedimentary rock layers. Using reference materials from the library, find out the names of several index fossils. Identify the period during which the fossilized organisms lived. Present your findings in a written report.

As you can see from Figure 19–10, four distinct kinds of shellfish fossils were found on both sides of the channel. Fossil 1 was found only in the upper layers. Fossil 2 was found in various layers. Fossil 3 was found only in middle layers. And fossil 4 was found only in the lower layers. Because the same fossils were found in similar rock layers on both sides of the channel, the scientists concluded that layers with the same fossils were the same age. Thus fossils 1, 3, and 4 were clues to the relative ages of the rock layers. Fossil 2 was not. Explain why.

Fossils such as fossils 1, 3, and 4 in Figure 19–10 are called **index fossils.** Index fossils are fossils of organisms that lived during only one short period of time. Scientists assume that index fossils of the same type of organism are all nearly the same age. So a layer of rock with one type of index fossil in it is close in age to another layer of rock with the same type of index fossil in it. Even though the rock layers may be in different regions of the world, the index fossils indicate that the layers are close in age. Why would the fossil of an organism that lived for a long period of time not be a good index fossil?

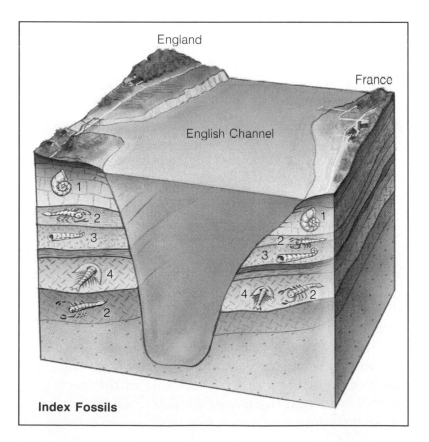

Index Fossils

Figure 19–10 *Index fossils are fossils of organisms that lived during only one short period of time. This illustration shows the rock layers on both sides of the English Channel. Even though the rock layers are separated by about 30 kilometers, there are three kinds of index fossils that are found on both sides. So scientists concluded that the English rock layers were the same age as the French rock layers that contain the same index fossils. Which three fossils helped scientists to reach this conclusion? Which fossil cannot be used to determine the relative age of the English and French rock layers?*

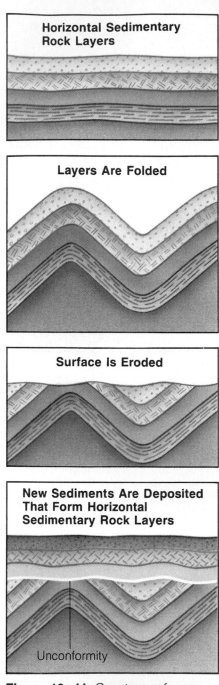

Horizontal Sedimentary Rock Layers

Layers Are Folded

Surface Is Eroded

New Sediments Are Deposited That Form Horizontal Sedimentary Rock Layers

Unconformity

Figure 19–11 *One type of unconformity forms when forces within the Earth fold and tilt previously horizontal sedimentary rock layers (top and top center). In time, the layers are worn down to almost a flat surface (bottom center). After a long period of time, new rock layers form, covering the old surface and producing an unconformity (bottom).*

Unconformities

Sedimentary rock layers and the fossils found within them may be disturbed by powerful forces within the Earth. The rock layers may be folded, bent, and twisted. Sometimes older, deeply buried layers of rocks are uplifted to the Earth's surface. At the surface, the exposed rocks are weathered and eroded. Sediments are then deposited on top of the eroded surface of the older rocks. The deposited sediments harden to form new horizontal sedimentary rock layers. The old eroded surface beneath the newer rock layers is called an **unconformity.** Tilted sedimentary rock layers covered by younger horizontal sedimentary layers is an example of an unconformity. See Figure 19–11.

There is a wide gap in the ages of the rock layers above and below an unconformity. There is also a wide gap in the ages of the fossils in these rock layers. By studying unconformities, scientists can tell where and when the Earth's crust has undergone changes such as tilting, uplifting, and erosion. In addition, scientists can learn about the effects of these changes on the organisms living at that time.

Faults, Intrusions, and Extrusions

There are other clues to the relative ages of rocks and the history of events on Earth. During movements of the Earth's crust, rocks may break or crack. A break or crack along which rocks move is called a **fault.** The rock layers on one side of a fault may shift up or down relative to the rock layers on the other side of the fault.

Because faults can occur only after rock layers are formed, rock layers are always older than the faults they contain. The relative age of a fault can be determined from the relative age of the sedimentary layer that the fault cuts across. Scientists can determine the forces that have changed the Earth's surface by examining the faults in rock layers.

The relative ages of igneous rock formations can also be determined. Magma often forces its way into layers of rocks. The magma hardens in the rock layers and forms an **intrusion.** An intrusion is younger than the sedimentary rock layers it passes through.

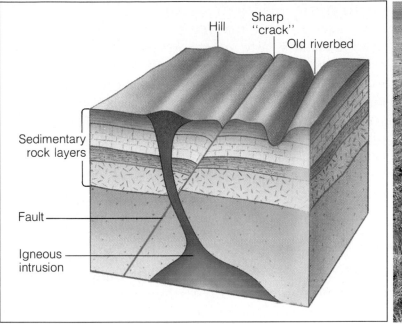

Figure 19–12 *Intrusions of igneous rock may be exposed when the overlying rock has been worn away. The diagram shows how intrusions and faults affect the arrangement of the rocks in an area.*

Sometimes magma reaches the surface of the Earth as lava and hardens. Igneous rock that forms on the Earth's surface is called an **extrusion.** Extrusions are younger than the rock layers beneath them. What do extrusions tell scientists about the Earth's past?

A History With Dates

By the end of the nineteenth century, scientists had developed a clear picture of Earth's past as recorded by fossils and rocks. The picture showed great and varied changes. The continents had changed shape many times. High mountains had risen and had been worn away to hills. Life had begun in the sea and had later moved onto land. Living things had evolved through many stages to the forms that exist today. Climates around the world had also changed many times.

Scientists knew that these changes had taken place. They knew the order in which the changes had happened. But what they did not know was how many years the changes had taken. How many years ago had each event happened? It seemed clear that all the changes had taken a lot of time—certainly millions of years. But could a clock made of rock layers measure such lengths of time?

Figure 19–13 *The formation and wearing away of sedimentary rock layers do not occur at steady rates throughout geologic history. These rocks on the coast of New Zealand may have been built faster and worn away slower—or vice versa— than they were elsewhere. And the rates at which the rocks were built and destroyed may have varied greatly over time.*

To create a clock to measure time, you need to have a series of events that take place at a steady rate, like the steady movement of the second hand on a watch. The first clock developed by scientists to measure Earth's age was the rate at which sedimentary rock is deposited.

The scientists decided to assume that sediment was deposited at a steady rate throughout Earth's past. That rate, they reasoned, should be the same as it is in the present. Let's say the rate is 30 millimeters per century (100 years). If the total depth of sedimentary rocks deposited since the depositing began was measured and then divided by the yearly rate, the age of the oldest sedimentary rock could be calculated. In fact, this method could be used to determine the age of any sedimentary rock layer— and the fossils it contained.

In 1899, a British scientist used this method and came up with a maximum age for sedimentary rocks of about 75 million years. Although in some parts of the world this dating system seemed to work fairly well, it was not actually an accurate method of measuring time. Its greatest drawback was that there is not, and never has been, such a thing as a steady rate of deposition. A flood of the Mississippi River can lay down two meters of muddy sediment in a single day. But hundreds of years may pass before one meter of mud piles up at the bottom of a lake or pond.

So using the deposition of sediments to determine the age of Earth is like trying to use a clock that runs at widely different rates. Nevertheless, the invention of this "sedimentary clock" marked the beginning of efforts to measure the absolute age of events on Earth. Absolute age gives the precise time an event occurred, not just the order of events that relative age provides.

By the beginning of the twentieth century scientists who study the history and structure of the Earth agreed that Earth was at least several hundred million years old. Today, scientists know Earth's age to be about 4.6 billion years. What kind of clock do scientists use to measure the Earth's age so accurately? Strange as it may seem, the clock they use is a radioactive clock!

Radioactive Dating

The discovery of radioactive elements in 1896 led to the development of an accurate method of determining the absolute age of rocks and fossils. An atom of a radioactive element has an unstable nucleus, or center, that breaks down, or decays. During radioactive decay, particles and energy called radiation are released by the radioactive element.

As some radioactive elements decay, they form decay elements. A decay element is the stable element into which a radioactive element breaks down. **The breakdown of a radioactive element into a decay element occurs at a constant rate.** Some radioactive elements decay in a few seconds. Some take thousands, millions, or even billions of years to decay. But no matter how long it takes for an element to decay, the rate of decay for that element is absolutely steady. No force known can either speed it up or slow it down.

Scientists measure the decay rate of a radioactive element by a unit called **half-life.** The half-life of an element is the time it takes for half of the radioactive element to decay.

For example, if you begin with 1 kilogram of a radioactive element, half of that kilogram will decay during one half-life. So at the end of one half-life, you will have 0.50 kilograms of the radioactive element and 0.50 kilograms of the decay element. Half of the remaining element (half of a half) will decay during another half-life. At this point one quarter of the radioactive element remains. How much of the decay element is there? This process continues until all the radioactive element has decayed. Figure 19–15 on page 602 illustrates the decay of a radioactive element with a half-life of 1 billion years.

If certain radioactive elements are present in a rock or fossil, scientists can find the absolute age of the rock or fossil. For example, suppose a rock contains a radioactive element that has a half-life of 1 million years. If tests show that the rock contains

on page 602

ACTIVITY
CALCULATING

Half-Life

1. Suppose a radioactive element has a half-life of 30 days. Of an 8-gram sample, how much will be unchanged after 90 days?

2. Suppose a radioactive element has a half-life of 20,000 years. How much of the original sample will be left after 40,000 years?

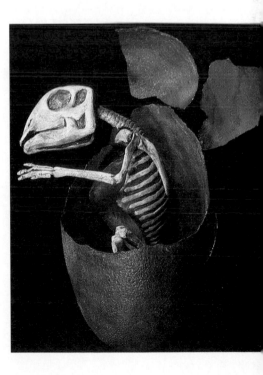

Figure 19–14 *A knowledge of life science was needed to correctly reassemble the tiny bones in the skeleton of a hatching dinosaur. How does a knowledge of physical science help a scientist to determine the absolute age of the fossil?*

601

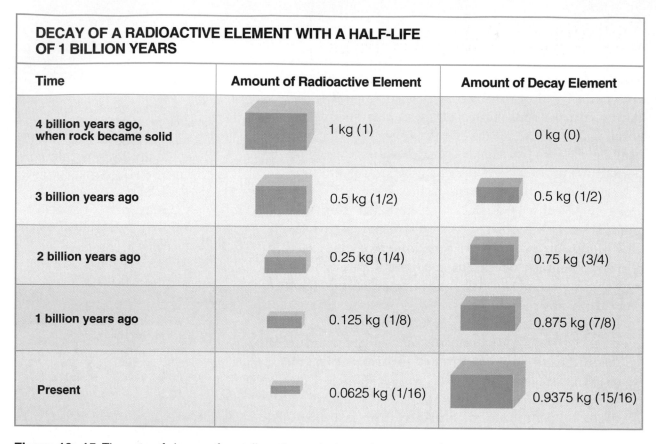

DECAY OF A RADIOACTIVE ELEMENT WITH A HALF-LIFE OF 1 BILLION YEARS

Time	Amount of Radioactive Element	Amount of Decay Element
4 billion years ago, when rock became solid	1 kg (1)	0 kg (0)
3 billion years ago	0.5 kg (1/2)	0.5 kg (1/2)
2 billion years ago	0.25 kg (1/4)	0.75 kg (3/4)
1 billion years ago	0.125 kg (1/8)	0.875 kg (7/8)
Present	0.0625 kg (1/16)	0.9375 kg (15/16)

Figure 19–15 *The rate of decay of a radioactive substance is measured by its half-life. How much of the radioactive element remains after 2 billion years?*

equal amounts of the radioactive element and its decay element, the rock is about 1 million years old. Since the proportion of radioactive element to decay element is equal, the element has gone through only one half-life. Scientists use the proportion of radioactive element to decay element to determine how many half-lives have occurred. If the rock contains three times as much decay element as it does radioactive element, how many half-lives have occurred? How old is the rock?

Many different radioactive elements are used to date rocks and fossils. Figure 19–16 lists some radioactive elements and their half-lives. One radioactive element used to date the remains of living things is carbon-14. Carbon-14 is present in all living things. It can be used to date fossils such as wood, bones, and shells that were formed within the last 50,000 years. It is difficult to measure the amount of

HALF-LIVES OF ELEMENTS USED TO FIND THE AGE OF ROCKS AND FOSSILS

Element	Half-life	Used to Find Age of
Rubidium-87	50.00 billion years	Very old rocks
Thorium-232	13.90 billion years	Very old rocks
Uranium-238	4.51 billion years	Old rocks and fossils in them
Potassium-40	1.30 billion years	Old rocks and fossils in them
Uranium-235	713 million years	Old rocks and fossils in them
Carbon-14	5730 years	Fossils (usually no older than about 50,000 years)

Figure 19–16 *Each radioactive substance has a different half-life. These substances are used to measure the age of different rocks and fossils. What is the half-life of potassium-40? Can you explain why carbon-14 is not used to determine the age of dinosaur fossils?*

carbon-14 in a rock or fossil more than 50,000 years old because almost all of the carbon-14 will have decayed into nitrogen. Nitrogen is the decay element of carbon-14. Using the information in Figure 19–16, which radioactive elements would you choose to date a fossil or rock found in the oldest rocks on Earth?

Other Methods of Absolute Dating

Did you know you can find out how old a tree is by counting rings in the trunk? Each ring is different and usually represents a single year. The width of a ring depends on the temperature and rainfall that year. Thus tree rings provide both dates and a record of weather in the past.

A similar method of absolute dating is by using varves. A **varve** is sediment that shows a yearly cycle. These sediments are often deposited in glacial lakes. Each year a light-colored sandy layer is deposited in the summer and a dark-colored clay layer is deposited in the winter. By counting the pairs of layers, it is possible to tell how many years a glacier was in a particular place before it disappeared.

Figure 19–17 *The rings in the trunk of a tree are a permanent record of the tree's yearly growth. Can you count the number of rings shown here? If each ring represents a year's growth, how old was the tree when it was cut down?*

Figure 19–18 *In a varve, a light-colored and a dark-colored layer together represent one year's worth of glacial deposition. The word "varve" comes from the Swedish word* varv, *meaning layer.*

Another method of radioactive dating is based on the splitting, or fission, of the nuclei of radioactive atoms. The high-energy particles that are split off leave microscopic tracks that can be counted. The older the rock, the greater the number of tracks. This method can be used to date moon rock samples and meteorite samples as well as samples of Earth rocks.

The Age of the Earth

Scientists use radioactive dating to help determine the age of rocks. By finding the age of rocks, they can estimate the age of the Earth. Scientists have found some rocks in South Africa that are more than 4 billion years old—the oldest rocks found on the Earth so far.

Radioactive dating of moon rocks brought back by the Apollo missions shows them to be 4 to 4.6 billion years old. The oldest moon rocks, then, are more than a half billion years older than the oldest known Earth rocks. However, because scientists have evidence that the Earth and the moon formed at the same time, they believe that the Earth is about 4.6 billion years old.

19–2 Section Review

1. How is the law of superposition used to date fossils?
2. Do index fossils provide evidence for relative age or absolute age? Explain.
3. Compare an intrusion and an extrusion.
4. How do scientists use the half-life of a radioactive element to date rocks and fossils?

Connection—*You and Your World*
5. While digging in her backyard, Carmela finds the bones of a fish. Carmela immediately decides that the bones provide evidence that the area she lives in was once under water. Is Carmela correct in her analysis or could there be some other explanation for her findings?

PROBLEM Solving

People-Eating Dinosaurs?

As the world's leading expert on fossils, you have been called upon to resolve a growing controversy. Recently, a collection of human bones have been found at the mouth of an ancient river. Grooves on the bones show that they were chewed by a large animal. Near the bones were discovered the tracks of a meat-eating dinosaur. Newspapers throughout the world have declared the find as evidence that people and dinosaurs once lived together and that the dinosaurs hunted and ate people. However, as a scientist, you know that the dinosaurs were extinct for over 60 million years before the first humans evolved on Earth

Interpreting Evidence

1. What tests would you perform to demonstrate that the humans were not eaten by dinosaurs?

2. What other hypothesis can you provide to explain the find?

Laboratory Investigation

Interpreting Fossil Molds and Casts

Problem

What fossil evidence can be obtained from molds and casts?

Materials *(per group)*

small, empty milk carton
petroleum jelly
plaster of Paris
stirring rod or spoon
3 small objects

Procedure

1. Open completely the top of the empty milk container. Grease the inside of the container with petroleum jelly.

2. Mix the plaster of Paris, following the directions on the package. Pour the mixture into the milk container so that the container is half full.

3. Rub a coat of petroleum jelly over the objects you are going to use.

4. When the plaster of Paris begins to harden, gently press the objects into the plaster so that they are not entirely covered. After the mixture has hardened, carefully remove the objects. You should be able to see the imprints of your objects.

5. Coat the entire surface of the hardened plaster of Paris with petroleum jelly.

6. Mix more plaster of Paris. Pour it on top of the hardened plaster of Paris so that it fills the container. After the plaster hardens, tear the milk carton away from the plaster block. Gently pull the two layers of plaster apart. You now have a cast and a mold of the objects.

7. Exchange your molds and casts for those of another group. Number each cast and mold set from 1 to 3. In a chart, record the number of each set. Record your prediction of what object made each cast and mold.

8. Get the original objects from the other group and see if your predictions were correct. Record in your chart what the actual object is.

Observations

1. What are the similarities and differences between the casts and molds?

2. What are the similarities and differences between the casts and the original objects they were made from?

Number	Predicted Object	Actual Object

Analysis and Conclusions

1. Compare the formation of a plaster mold with the formation of a fossil mold.

2. Compare the way you predicted what the unknown object was with the way a scientist predicts what object left a fossil cast or mold.

3. **On Your Own** Find a set of prints or tracks left by an animal in concrete (such as a concrete sidewalk). Determine what the animal looked like, based on its "fossil" prints.

Summarizing Key Concepts

19–1 Fossils—Clues to the Past

▲ Fossils are the remains or evidence of once-living things.

▲ Fossils can form by the process of petrification, in which plant and animal parts are changed into stone.

▲ Fossils—in the form of molds, casts, and imprints—record the shapes of living things that have been buried in sediments.

▲ Fossils of entire animals are formed as the animals are buried in tar, amber, or ice.

▲ Trace fossils are any marks formed by an animal and preserved as fossils.

▲ Fossils indicate that many different life forms have existed throughout Earth's history.

19–2 A History in Rocks and Fossils

▲ The law of superposition states that in a series of sedimentary rock layers, younger rocks normally lie on top of older rocks.

▲ Scientists can tell the order in which past events occurred and the relative times of occurrence by studying sedimentary rock layers, index fossils, and unconformities.

▲ Index fossils are used to identify the age of the sedimentary rock layers containing them.

▲ The half-life of a radioactive element is the amount of time it takes for half the atoms in a sample of that element to decay.

▲ Scientists can determine the absolute age of rocks and fossils by using radioactive-dating techniques.

Reviewing Key Terms

Define each term in a complete sentence.

19–1 Fossils—Clues to the Past
    fossil
    sediment
    petrification
    mold
    cast
    imprint
    trace fossil
    evolve

19–2 A History in Rocks and Fossils
    law of superposition
    index fossil
    unconformity
    fault
    intrusion
    extrusion
    half-life
    varve

Chapter Review

Content Review

Multiple Choice

Choose the letter of the answer that best completes each statement.

1. The shape of an organism preserved in rock is called a(an)
   a. mold and cast. c. imprint.
   b. footprint. d. petrification.
2. Bodies of whole animals have been preserved in
   a. ice. c. amber.
   b. tar. d. all of these
3. Rocks formed from the piling up of layers of dust, dirt, and sand are called
   a. igneous. c. magma.
   b. metamorphic. d. sedimentary.
4. A crack in a rock structure that moves the rocks on either side out of line is a(an)
   a. fault. c. intrusion.
   b. cast. d. extrusion.
5. The decay rate of a radioactive element is measured by a unit called
   a. period. c. half-life.
   b. era. d. unconformity.
6. Sediment that shows a yearly cycle is known as
   a. varve. c. imprint.
   b. clay. d. deposition.
7. Insects are often found preserved in
   a. ice. c. tar.
   b. amber. d. magma.
8. A measure of how many years ago an event occurred or an organism lives is
   a. absolute age. c. decay time.
   b. relative age. d. sedimentary age.

True or False

If the statement is true, write "true." If it is false, change the underlined word or words to make the statement true.

1. The <u>soft</u> parts of plants or animals usually become fossils.
2. An empty space called a <u>cast</u> is left in a rock when a buried organism dissolves.
3. Footprints of extinct dinosaurs are examples of <u>trace fossils</u>.
4. Sediments are usually deposited in <u>vertical</u> layers.
5. The measure of how many years ago an event occurred or an animal lived is called <u>relative age</u>.
6. <u>Faults</u> are always younger than the rock layers they cut through.
7. The time it takes for half the atoms in a sample of a radioactive element to decay is called its <u>half-life</u>.

Concept Mapping

Complete the following concept map for Section 19–1. Then construct a concept map for the entire chapter.

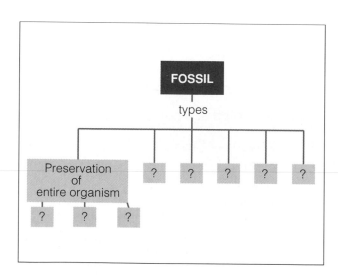

Concept Mastery

Discuss each of the following in a brief paragraph.

1. How are radioactive elements used to determine the age of rocks and fossils?
2. How does the law of superposition help determine the age of rocks?
3. Why is sedimentation rate an inaccurate way of measuring geologic time?
4. Why are few fossils found in igneous or metamorphic rock?
5. Discuss five ways fossils can form.
6. Why isn't the fossil of an organism that lived for a long period of time a good index fossil?

Critical Thinking and Problem Solving

Use the skills you have developed in this chapter to answer each of the following.

1. **Making calculations** A radioactive element has a half-life of 500 million years. After 2 billion years, how many half-lives have passed? How many kilograms of a 10-kilogram sample would be left at this time? If the half-life were 4 billion years?
2. **Analyzing diagrams** Use the diagram to answer the following questions.
   a. According to the way in which layers C, D, E, and F lie, what might have happened in the past?
   b. Which letter shows an unconformity? Explain your answer.
   c. List the events that occurred from oldest to youngest. Include the order in which each layer was deposited and when the fault, intrusion, and unconformity were formed. Explain why you chose this order.

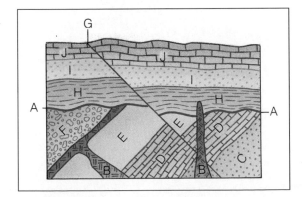

3. **Interpreting evidence** Suppose you are a scientist who finds some fossils while looking at a cross section of rock in an area. One layer of rock has fossils of the extinct woolly mammoth. In a layer of rock below this, you discover the fossils of an extinct alligator. What can you determine about changes over time in the climate of this area?
4. **Developing a theory** Explain why an animal species that reproduces every year would have a better chance of surviving a change in its environment than an animal species that reproduces only once or twice in ten years does.
5. **Sequencing events** List five events in your life in the order they happened. Have a friend or classmate list five events in his or her life in the order they happened. Now try to list all ten events in the order they happened.

   What difficulties did you have in deciding whether a certain event occurred before or after other events? How has this activity helped you understand the difficulty scientists had in developing a time scale without radioactive dating?
6. **Using the writing process** Choose one of the animals that lived near the La Brea Tar Pits and write a short story depicting a day in its life.

A Trip Through Geologic Time 20

Guide for Reading

A cloud of volcanic ash rises toward the sky above a strange landscape. Beneath the cloud, firs, pines, and tall palmlike trees sway in a warm, gentle breeze. Furry mammals, most no larger than a rat, scurry about on the forest floor. One day, descendants of these mammals will become the dominant animals on Earth. But that day is a long way off: The time is 140 million years ago, and the world belongs to the dinosaurs.

The world is changing, however. A great mountain chain is rising—a mountain chain that will eventually stretch from Alaska to Central America. Soon the landscape will be quite different. The Age of Dinosaurs will come to an end. All that will be left of these magnificent reptiles will be their bones.

One day in the distant future, a shepherd will build a cabin of dinosaur bones—the only such building in the world. Quite naturally, the place will be called Bone Cabin Quarry. And the vast area around it will be known as Wyoming!

In this chapter, you will learn about the Earth's past. You will also take a trip through time and discover many of the changes that have taken place in the Earth's 4.6-billion-year existence.

Journal *Activity*

You and Your World   Although people and dinosaurs often do battle in Hollywood movies, all the dinosaurs were actually gone long before people evolved on Earth. But for now, imagine that you are alive during the Age of Dinosaurs. In your journal, write a brief story about a day in your life.

Slashing with their terrible sickle-shaped claws, a pack of fierce meat-eating dinosaurs attack an Iguanodon *in this scene from 140 million years ago.*

20–1 The Geologic Time Scale

The Earth's clock began ticking long ago. So long ago that the major units of time of this clock could not be seconds, hours, days, weeks, months, or even years. There would be just too many of these units for them to be useful in setting up a calendar of Earth's history. For example, more than 1.5 trillion days have passed since Earth formed. If each of these days took up one page of an ordinary office calendar, the calendar would be about 140,000 kilometers thick. Not very practical—and a bit difficult to carry around.

In order to divide geologic time into workable units, scientists have established the geologic time scale. **Earth's history on the geologic time scale is divided into four geologic eras: Precambrian Era, Paleozoic Era, Mesozoic Era, and Cenozoic Era.** An era is the largest division of the geologic time scale. Eras are broken into smaller subdivisions called periods.

The eras of Earth's geologic time scale are of different lengths. Geologic time is the length of time Earth has existed. The **Precambrian** (pree-KAM-bree-uhn) **Era** is the longest era. It lasted about 4 billion years and accounts for about 87 percent of Earth's history. The **Paleozoic** (pay-lee-oh-ZOH-ihk) **Era**

Figure 20–1 *Many unusual animals lived long ago, such as the meat-eating saber-toothed cat (top) and the plant-eating dinosaur (bottom).*

lasted about 345 million years, and the **Mesozoic** (mehs-oh-ZOH-ihk) **Era** about 160 million years. The **Cenozoic** (see-nuh-ZOH-ihk) **Era,** the era in which we now live, has lasted for only 65 million years.

Figure 20–3 on pages 614 and 615 is a chart that shows the geologic history of the Earth. The chart gives you a preview of the major life forms and events during the geologic eras. To get a better understanding of these eras and the events that occurred during each one, you will now take a short imaginary trip through Earth's history.

As you learned in Chapter 3, Earth's history began with a spinning cloud of gas and dust called a nebula. According to the nebular theory, shock waves from a supernova caused the nebula to collapse and condense into the sun and planets. One of those planets is Earth.

You begin your trip in space, gazing upon planet Earth from a safe distance. The time is 4.6 billion years ago, and Earth is a planet of molten rock much too hot to set foot upon. The atmosphere, unlike today's atmosphere, contains mainly poisonous gases. Because of widespread volcanic eruptions and cooling and hardening of lava, there is no record in the rocks from this distant time.

Skip ahead in your mind about 1.5 billion years later. The Earth is cooler now. Continents and oceans have formed. Although the air is warm and quite humid, little oxygen exists in the atmosphere. In fact, much of the atmosphere contains sulfur dioxide gas that has been released by volcanic eruptions. It is a dynamic and restless time in Earth's history. As you will see, this is the time when life began.

Figure 20–2 *Many volcanic eruptions occurred during the early geologic history of the Earth.*

20–1 Section Review

1. What are the four eras of geologic time?
2. How is a geologic period different from an era?
3. What occurred on Earth 4.6 billion years ago?

Critical Thinking—*Analyzing Charts*
4. Look at Figure 20–3. What seems to be the major trend in the development of life forms during geologic history?

GEOLOGIC HISTORY OF THE EARTH

Era	Precambrian	Paleozoic			
Began (millions of years ago)	4600	570			
Ended (millions of years ago)	570	225			
Length (millions of years)	4030	345			
Period	None	**Cambrian**	**Ordovician**	**Silurian**	**Devonian**
Began (millions of years ago)	4600	570	500	430	395
Ended (millions of years ago)	570	500	430	395	345
Length (millions of years)	4030	70	70	35	50

Earth's history begins; seas form; mountains begin to grow; oxygen builds up in atmosphere; first life forms in sea; as time passes, bacteria, algae, jellyfish, corals, and clams develop

Shallow seas cover parts of continents; many trilobites, brachiopods, sponges, and other sea-living invertebrates are present

Many volcanoes and mountains form; North America is flooded; first fish (jawless) appear; invertebrates flourish in the sea

Caledonian Mountains of Scandinavia rise; coral reefs form; first land plants, air-breathing animals, and jawed fish develop

Acadian Mountains of New York rise; erosion of mountains deposits much sediment in seas; first forests grow in swampy areas; first amphibians, sharks, and insects develop

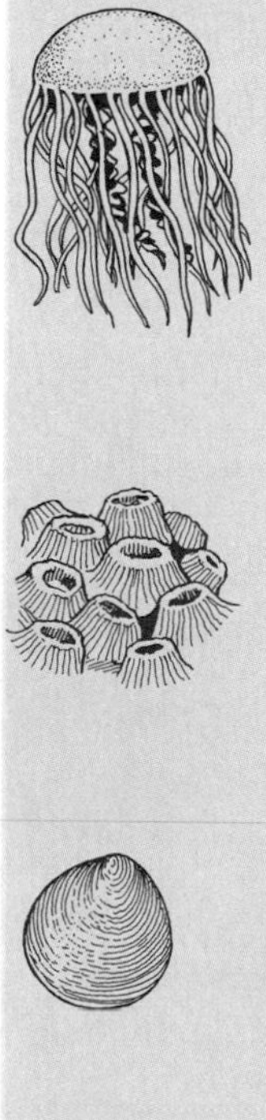

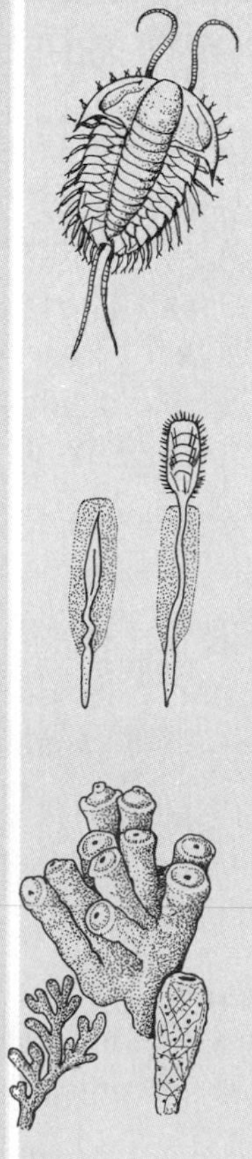

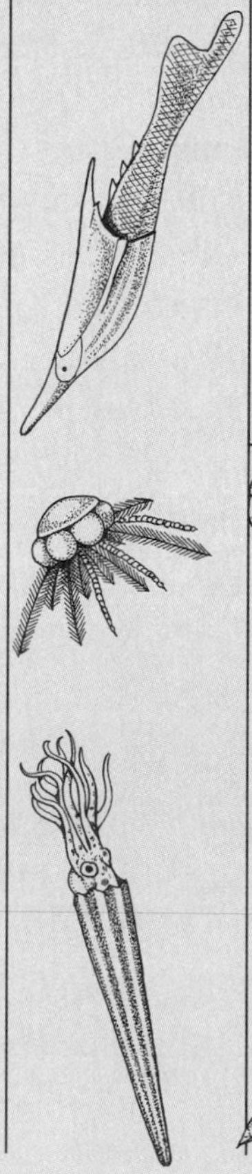

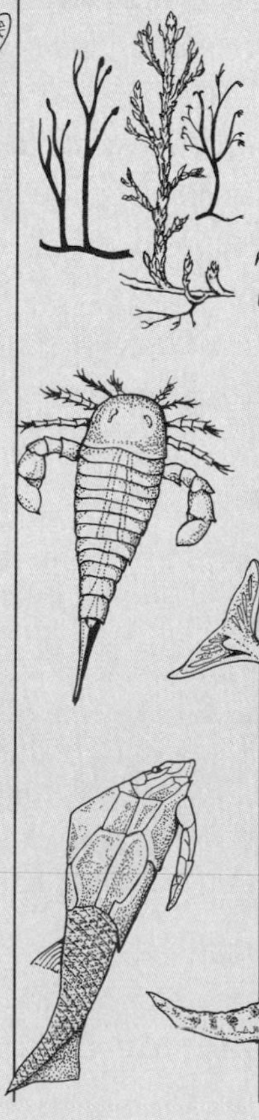

Figure 20–3 This chart illustrates the geologic history of the Earth. What events occurred during the Permian Period? When did modern humans appear?

Carboniferous*	Permian	Triassic	Jurassic	Cretaceous	Tertiary	Quaternary

*In North America, the Carboniferous Period is often subdivided into the Mississippian Period (345–310 million years ago) and the Pennsylvanian Period (310–280 million years ago).

Mesozoic	Cenozoic
225	65
65	The present
160	65

Carboniferous*	Permian	Triassic	Jurassic	Cretaceous	Tertiary	Quaternary
345	280	225	190	136	65	1.8
280	225	190	136	65	1.8	The present
65	55	35	54	71	63.2	1.8
Appalachian Mountains of North America form; ice covers large areas of the Earth; swamps cover lowlands; first mosses, reptiles, and winged insects appear; great coal-forming forests form; seed-bearing ferns grow	Ural Mountains of Russia rise; first cone-bearing plants appear; ferns, fish, amphibians, and reptiles flourish; many sea-living invertebrates, including trilobites, die out	Palisades of New Jersey and Caucasus Mountains of Russia form; first dinosaurs and first mammals appear; modern corals, modern fish, and modern insect types develop	The Rocky Mountains rise; volcanoes of North American West are active; first birds appear; palms and cone-bearing trees flourish; largest dinosaurs thrive; primitive mammals develop	First flowering plants appear; placental mammals develop; dinosaurs die out, as do many sea-living reptiles	Andes, Alps, and Himalayan Mountains rise; first horses, primates, and humanlike creatures develop; flowering plants thrive; mammals take on present-day features	Ice covers large parts of North America and Europe; Great Lakes form as ice melts; first modern human beings appear; woolly mammoths die out; civilization begins

20–2 Early Earth History

As you continue your trip through geologic history, you enter the middle and later part of a time when ancient rocks were formed that can now be seen on every continent. In North America they are found in Eastern and Central Canada, in the Lake Superior area, and in the Adirondacks, among other places. Let's imagine what you might have seen in and around the oceans in Precambrian times.

The Precambrian Era: The Dawn of Life

Gazing down on the shores of a Precambrian sea, you notice a rocky shoreline with no signs of life. The scene is the same all over Earth. Rain falls and thunder rolls. But on land there are no plants to receive the rain and no animals to hear the thunder. Nor will there be for the next 2.6 billion years!

Figure 20–4 *The oldest fossils that can be seen with the unaided eye are these fossil stromatolites (top), the remains of bacterial colonies from the Precambrian Era. Living stromatolites can be seen today in Hamlin Pool, Western Australia (bottom).*

But there is life in the seas. If you look closely you will see faint signs of it. Lying on rocks just beneath the sea surface are patches of what looks like mold. The patches are several centimeters across. They are made of millions of bacteria clumped together in a tangled mat of threadlike fibers. Billions of years later scientists will find fossils of these bacteria—the oldest fossils ever found.

Plants related to modern seaweed are in the seas as well. They use simple chemicals in the water plus energy from sunlight to make their own food, just as green plants have done ever since. In the process, they produce oxygen. Over the next billion years, more and more oxygen will dissolve in the sea water and enter the atmosphere. Animal life will become possible.

By the end of the Precambrian Era, animals such as jellyfish and worms have appeared in the seas, along with sponges and corals. Although sponges and corals look like plants, they are actually colonies of animal cells.

Figure 20–5 *Modern sponges are quite similar to their earliest ancestors, which appeared at the end of the Precambrian Era.*

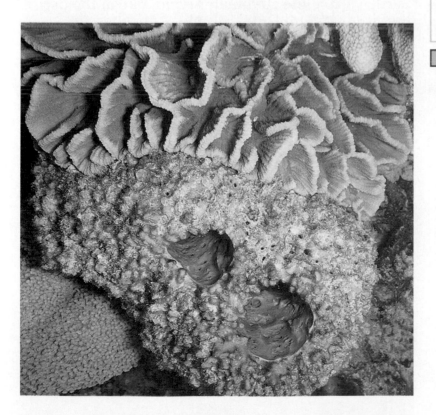

ACTIVITY DOING

The Time of Your Life

1. On white index cards, write several important events that have happened to you in your life. *Place one event on each card.*

2. Arrange the cards in the order in which the events happened.

3. Using colored index cards, write one of the following on each: Preschool Years, Early Elementary School Years, Middle Elementary School Years, Late Elementary School Years, Junior High School/Middle School Years (if applicable). Insert each colored index card in front of the group of events that occurred during those years.

How does the arrangement of the cards resemble a geologic time line?

The Paleozoic Era: Life Comes Ashore

Your imaginary trip has brought you to the Paleozoic Era. The time is 570 million years ago, and even a quick glance alerts you to the fact that the land is still lifeless. But life is abundant in the seas. Worms of many kinds crawl across the sandy bottom. Strange "plants," which seem to grow from the sea floor, resemble animal horns, vases, and bells. These formations are actually sponges.

Other sea animals have large heads, long thorny spines, and many body divisions. They have jointed legs like those of a modern insect or lobster. These animals are **trilobites.** They will become an important index fossil for the Paleozoic Era. They evolved rapidly during that era, leaving different forms in each of the era's periods, and then became extinct by the era's end.

Parts of the sea floor contain lampshade-shaped shells. The shells have two parts that close to cover and protect the soft animal within. These animals are brachiopods. See Figure 20–7.

The seas are truly teeming with life. Fishes can be found almost everywhere. Fishes are the first vertebrates, or animals with backbones, to appear on Earth. In fact, the Devonian period, one of the periods of the Paleozoic Era, is often called the Age of Fishes. See Figure 20–8.

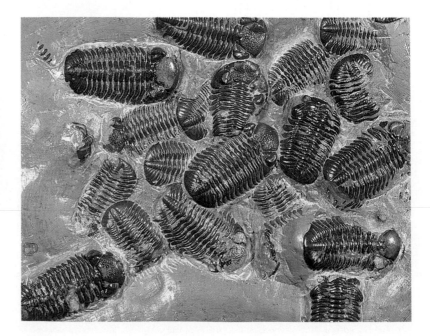

Figure 20–6 *Creatures of the Paleozoic seas included starfish (top) and trilobites (right and bottom). This starfish is unusual because it has six arms, whereas most modern starfish have five. Why are trilobites important index fossils?*

By the end of the Paleozoic Era, the land is no longer lifeless. Huge forests of ferns have developed. There are also cycads, which are trees with a crown of fernlike leaves. Cycads are among the first seed plants. In the future, the sago palm, one of the few modern cycads, will be called a living fossil. Scientists believe that the remains of these forests of ferns and other plants formed the huge coal deposits in the United States and other parts of the world.

Amphibians, such as *Eryops,* now appear as well. Amphibians are the first land vertebrates. The name amphibian, which means "living a double life," is quite appropriate, since amphibians typically spend their early lives in water and then move to land. *Eryops* is a far larger amphibian than its twentieth-century relatives, such as frogs and toads. It is almost 2 meters long, with a large head and a thick, clumsy body. *Eryops* waddles through the forest in search of king-sized roaches and other tasty meals. But because *Eryops* must keep its skin moist in order to survive, it does not move far from water. See Figure 20-9 on page 620.

By the end of the Paleozoic Era, the amphibians have run up against hard times. There is drought, and the climate has cooled. Mountains are rising in what will become Norway, Scotland, Greenland, and parts of North America. These areas, as well as all the other landmasses on Earth, are joined together as one single continent. Scientists will one day call this

Figure 20-7 *Brachiopods were quite common during the Paleozoic Era—about 30,000 species are known from their fossil shells. Although brachiopods look somewhat like clams, they are as distantly related to clams as you are.*

Figure 20-8 *Strange armored fishes swam in the waters during the Devonian Period. What is this period's nickname?*

Figure 20–9 *Amphibians evolved from fish ancestors during the Paleozoic Era. Like typical amphibians,* Eryops *lived in water when it was young. As an adult, this ancient amphibian lived in moist places on land.*

continent Pangaea, but that is still about 225 million years in the future.

New kinds of animals that live on land all the time are appearing. Their tough skin is protected by scales or hard plates. Unlike amphibians, these animals do not lose water through their skins. Their eggs have thick shells, so the eggs do not dry out. The animals are reptiles, and for the next 160 million years they will dominate Earth.

20–2 Section Review

1. What life forms developed during the Precambrian Era?
2. What is an important index fossil for the Paleozoic Era?
3. Why were amphibians like *Eryops* unable to move very far onto land areas?

Connections—*Ecology*

4. Some people are concerned that frogs and toads, the relatives of ancient amphibians, are declining in numbers. What might be causing such a decline?

20–3 Middle and Recent Earth History

Guide for Reading

Focus on these questions as you read

▶ *What life forms developed during the Mesozoic and Cenozoic Eras?*

▶ *What geologic events occurred during the Mesozoic and Cenozoic Eras?*

You've come a long way now on your journey through geologic time. This would be a good place to take stock of where you've been and where you will be going. Look back at the chart of Earth history in Figure 20–3. What is the next era after the Paleozoic? What is the era in which you live? As you move on, watch for some familiar forms of life to appear.

The Mesozoic Era: Mammals Develop

Your trip continues as you enter the Mesozoic Era, which began about 225 million years ago. The Mesozoic Era is a period of many changes—both in the land and in the living things that inhabit Earth. Scientists believe that Pangaea began to break apart during the Mesozoic Era. The expansion of the ocean floor along midocean ridges caused the continents gradually to spread apart. Midocean ridges are chains of underwater volcanic mountains. Today the continents are still moving apart at the midocean ridges.

As Pangaea broke apart, there were numerous earthquakes and volcanic eruptions. Many mountains were formed at this time. The Appalachian Mountains were leveled by erosion during the early part of the Mesozoic Era. Then they were uplifted again late in the era. The Sierra Nevada and Rocky Mountains were formed during the late stages of the Mesozoic Era.

Scientists divide the Mesozoic Era into three periods. The oldest period is called the **Triassic** (trigh-AS-ihk) **Period.** The middle period is called the **Jurassic** (joo-RAS-ihk) **Period.** The youngest period is called the **Cretaceous** (krih-TAY-shuhs) **Period.** Now let's see how life changed in these three periods.

ACTIVITY DOING

Animals in Pangaea

Fossils of the same land animals have been found on separate continents. Scientists say such findings are evidence that at one time Earth had one supercontinent called Pangaea.

Using materials in the library, find out which fossil animals support the idea of Pangaea. Write down the names of the fossil animals and where they were discovered on the continents.

Mark off these discovery sites on a world map. At which points do you think the continents came together?

Figure 20–10 *Reptiles dominated the land, sky, and seas during the Mesozoic Era. Porpoiselike ichthyosaurs and long-necked plesiosaurs swam swiftly through the oceans in search of food.*

ACTIVITY
READING

Good Mother Lizard

If you think that dinosaurs were slow-witted, slow moving creatures, you will be in for a surprise if you read *Maia—A Dinosaur Grows Up* by Jack Horner. In this book you will discover what it might have been like to be an infant dinosaur in a world with so many ferocious creatures.

THE TRIASSIC PERIOD As you enter the Triassic Period you notice that the drought that began in the Paleozoic Era has not ended. The climate, in fact, is even hotter than before. Slowly, very slowly, you see North and South America begin to separate from Africa. A narrow sea opens between North America and what is now Iceland and England. This sea will become the North Atlantic Ocean. The southern lands of Africa, South America, Antarctica, and India are still joined.

In the seas, you spot creatures that are shaped like fish. But they are not fish. The bones in their fins have five fingerlike projections, like the limbs of land animals. They have lungs and breathe air. These creatures are reptiles—land-living animals— that have returned to the sea.

Mammals appear in the Triassic Period. Mammals are animals with hair or fur, whose offspring, for the most part, do not hatch from eggs. The young grow and mature in their mother's body before birth.

Ferns and seed ferns are still common. Cycads are growing bigger. During this time, the trees that will become the Petrified Forest of Arizona are uprooted by floods. The first dinosaurs are appearing. Many are small, no bigger than chickens. They have small heads, long tails, and walk on their hind legs.

THE JURASSIC PERIOD   As you move forward into the Jurassic Period, you notice that the dinosaurs that will be found at Bone Cabin Quarry have now appeared. The Age of Dinosaurs has begun. Volcanoes are active in the American West. The mountains of the Sierra Nevada and Rocky Mountain ranges are rising. The North Atlantic is still quite narrow. The southern continents, still closely linked, are just beginning to separate. Animals and plants are similar throughout this "supercontinent."

Huge cycads and modern-looking evergreens called conifers make up the forests. There are no flowers yet. Toward the end of the Jurassic Period, one of the first birds, Archaeopteryx (ahr-kee-AHP-ter-iks), appears. Its name means "ancient wing."

THE CRETACEOUS PERIOD   The Cretaceous Period is a time of widespread flooding of continents by seas. The continents continue moving apart. By the end of the period, they are pretty much as they are now, although North America and Europe are still joined.

Dinosaurs still dominate the world. *Tyrannosaurus,* the greatest meat eater of all times, stalks the land. Among the plant eaters are the armored *Triceratops* and the strange-looking duck-billed dinosaurs. By the end of the Cretacious Period, however, all the dinosaurs will have died out. So will the sea-living reptiles. Of all the different reptiles of the Mesozoic Era, only crocodiles, turtles, lizards, and snakes will have survived. The mysterious mass extinctions of so many forms of life will puzzle scientists of the future. The scientists will debate whether the extinctions were due to a change in climate, a worldwide disease, or even the result of a gigantic asteroid crashing into the Earth.

The Cretaceous Period was a time of rapid change—rapid, that is, in terms of Earth's long past. During this period, sea levels dropped. Rivers and flood plains, where many dinosaurs thrived, dried up. Flowering plants appeared—among them such familiar trees as magnolia, oak, fig, poplar, elm,

Figure 20–11 *Dinosaurs were still masters of the land during the Cretaceous Period. But their reign was soon to come to an end.*

birch, and willow. As the new plant life spread and flourished, most of the great tree ferns and cycads died out. The world was beginning to take on a look that is much more familiar to you.

The Cenozoic Era: A World With People

You are about to enter the era that began approximately 65 million years ago—the era in which you live. The Cenozoic Era will be divided into two great periods known for the evolution of the first horses and the evolution of the first animals to walk on two feet. Great sheets of ice will sweep across the land. And finally, almost at the end of your trip through geologic time, a new kind of living thing will make its home on Earth and attempt to make sense of all that has passed.

THE TERTIARY PERIOD You find yourself near what will one day be the town of Green River, in southwest Wyoming, not too many kilometers from the site of Bone Cabin Quarry. It is about 50 million years ago. Although in many ways the land is familiar, there is something odd about it.

In a grassy meadow, you hear birds singing. There are groups of redwoods, oaks, and cedars. But there are groves of palm trees, too! Worldwide, the

climate is mild. And it will stay that way through most of this period.

Trotting through the meadow you see a beast that makes you wonder whether you are in Africa. It is about the size of an elephant, with elephantlike legs. Its skin is gray and wrinkled. Its tail, with a tuft of hair at the end, looks much like a lion's tail. But its head and ears are those of a rhinoceros. Instead

Figure 20–12 Uintatherium, *which lived during the beginning of the Tertiary Period, was one of the largest and strangest-looking mammals ever to walk the Earth.*

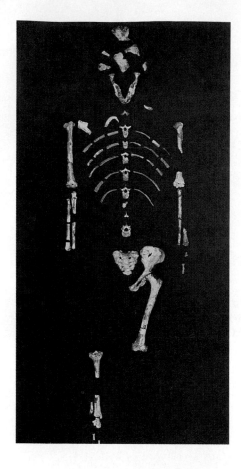

Figure 20–13 *This skeleton of* Australopithecus afarensis *was nicknamed Lucy by its discoverers. Lucy is one of the oldest and most complete of the early hominids yet to be found.*

of one or two horns, however, the animal has six horns.

The animal is *Uintatherium* (yoo-wihn-tuh-THEER-ee-uhm). The name means "Uinta beast," after the Uinta Mountains of Utah and Wyoming. Wandering the meadows with *Uintatherium* is a direct ancestor of the rhinoceros. It is no larger than a large dog.

Somewhere around 3.4 million years ago, toward the end of the Tertiary Period, humanlike creatures begin walking upright on the African plains. One is a small adult female about 1 meter tall. Scientists will find her skeleton in 1977. They will call her "Lucy."

THE QUATERNARY PERIOD The climate turns sharply colder during the Quaternary Period. On four different occasions, great sheets of ice advance from the Arctic and Antarctic regions, only to retreat as the climate becomes milder. (You read about these ice ages in Chapter 17.) At their worst, the ice ages are like winters that last thousands of years. Large parts of Europe and North and South America are ice-covered. The last ice age ends about 11,000 years ago. As the world warms, farming becomes widespread and modern civilization begins. What will happen in the Quaternary Period from this point on is modern history.

Figure 20–14 *The weather became much cooler during the Quaternary Period. Sheets of ice repeatedly advanced and retreated over the Earth.*

20–3 Section Review

1. How do mammals differ from reptiles?
2. When did the first flowering plants appear?
3. During what period did the first birds evolve?
4. Identify and describe one animal associated with the Cenozoic Era.
5. What major geologic event occurred during the Mesozoic Era?

Critical Thinking—*Making Inferences*
6. How might the collision of a huge asteroid with Earth result in the extinction of the dinosaurs? *Hint:* Assume the dinosaurs were not killed by the impact alone.

20–4 Evolution: Change Over Time

Earlier in this chapter you read about Earth's history. You learned that by studying rocks and fossils, scientists have developed a fairly accurate picture of how Earth and its inhabitants have changed over long peroids of time. Although the picture is far from complete, there is no doubt that changes have occurred and that many of the living things on Earth today are very different from the living things that existed in the past. In other words, there is no doubt that living things have changed over time.

How and why have living things changed? And which living things are more closely related to one another? Today scientists know that the answers to these questions lie in the process of **evolution.** The word evolution comes from Latin and means an unfolding or opening out. A scientific translation of this meaning is descent with modification. Descent means to come from something that lived before. And modification means change. Thus evolution means that all inhabitants of Earth are changed forms of living things that came before.

Evolution can be defined as a change in species over time. A species is a group of organisms that share similar characteristics and that can interbreed with one another to produce fertile offspring. Lions,

Figure 20–15 *The members of the species* Alces alces, *better known as moose, often wade into lakes and ponds to graze on water plants. What is a species?*

A Packy-Poem

Ever wonder how poets view those "terrible lizards" we call dinosaurs? For a humorous point of view, read the poem *Pachycephalosaurus* by Richard Armour.

Figure 20–16 *What evidence do you see that this saguaro cactus is well-adapted to the desert environment near Tucson, Arizona?*

for example, are a species. So are tigers. Lions and tigers share many similar characteristics and can even be bred together to produce offspring called ligers and tiglons. The offspring, however, are not fertile. That is, ligers and tiglons cannot mate and produce more of their own kind. So lions and tigers are not the same species. They are two separate species. Quite the opposite is true of a German shepherd and a French poodle. Although they appear quite different, they can interbreed and produce fertile offspring. So dogs, even though they may appear quite different, are all members of the same species.

Why have some species evolved into the plants and animals living on Earth today while other species became extinct? During the history of life on Earth, chance changes in the genes of organisms have produced new or slightly modified living things. A gene is a unit of heredity that is passed on from parent to offspring. A change in a gene will produce a change in the offspring of an organism. Changes in genes are called mutations. And mutations are one of the driving forces behind evolution.

Mutations: Agents of Change

Most of the time, a mutation in a gene produces an organism that cannot compete with other organisms. This new organism usually dies off quickly. Sometimes, however, the change in the organism is a positive one. The change makes the organism better suited to its environment. A change that increases an organism's chances of survival is called an **adaptation.**

Organisms that are better adapted to their environment do more than just survive. They are able to produce offspring, which produce more offspring, and so on. Over a long period of time, so many small adaptations may occur that a new species may evolve. The new species may no longer resemble its ancient ancestors. In addition, the new species may be so successful in its environment that the species from which it evolved can no longer compete. The original species dies off. Thus the development of a new species can result in the extinction of another species.

The Fossil Record

In Chapter 19 you read about the many types of fossils that have been found. The record of Earth's history in fossils and in fossil-containing rocks clearly demonstrates that living things have evolved, or changed over time. You can see some of these changes for yourself in Figure 20–18 on page 630, which shows the fossil record of the camel. Scientists have cataloged the evolution of many such organisms.

The fossil record provides evidence about the changes that have occurred in living things and their way of life. In 1983, for example, scientists found a buried skull belonging to an animal that had lived more than 50 million years ago. The skull was very similar to that of a whale. But the bony structure that allowed the animal to hear could not have worked underwater. So scientists concluded that the whalelike skull belonged to an ancestor of modern whales that spent some of its life on land. Scientists also concluded that at some point the ancestors of whales left the land completely and became water-dwelling creatures.

Although the fossil record is not complete—and never will be because many organisms have come and gone without leaving any fossils—it does provide ample evidence that evolution has indeed occurred.

Figure 20–17 *A hummingbird's beak, a giraffe's neck, and a vampire bat's sharp teeth are all examples of adaptations for feeding. What are adaptations? How do these particular adaptations affect the animals that have them?*

Figure 20–18 *Living things have evolved, or changed over time. The diagram shows the fossil record of the past 65 million years in the evolution of the camel. How are modern camels similar to their ancestors? How are they different?*

Pleistocene

Pliocene

Miocene

Oligocene

Eocene

Paleocene

20–4 Section Review

1. Define evolution, using the term species.
2. Give an example of how fossils show change in living things over time.

Critical Thinking—*Ecology*

3. There is evidence that Earth's climate is getting warmer. How might such global warming affect the evolution of living things?

CONNECTIONS

Another Mass Extinction?

Some of the most significant events in the history of life on Earth have been the periods of mass extinction. The geological record reveals at least five times when a major portion of the living species died out. The most dramatic of these events took place at the end of the Paleozoic Era, when 96 percent of all marine species disappeared. Of course, the best known mass extinction occurred at the end of the Mesozoic Era, when the dinosaurs became extinct.

Scientists have proposed many theories to account for these extinctions. Changes in climate, periods of high volcanic activity, and collisions with asteroids are some of the possible explanations.

Today, many people are concerned that Earth may be entering a new period of mass extinction. Unlike the others, the cause of this biological catastrophe is known—it is the activity of humans.

As the number of humans has increased, hunting and fishing have reduced the populations of many species. Entire habitats, such as the tropical rain forests, are in danger of destruction. The wildlife on islands such as the Hawaiian Islands is also at great risk. At the current rate, conservationists estimate that one fifth of the 5 million plants, animals, and microorganisms now living in the rain forests will be extinct within 50 years.

It is far too late to save the dinosaurs. But it is not too late to prevent a modern-day mass extinction. Because we humans can think, we can also devise ways to maintain the diversity of life. For example, we can stop hunting endangered species, limit the use of pesticides, set up wildlife preserves, and replant forests. How do you think you can help?

Laboratory Investigation

Analyzing a Geologic Time Line

Problem

How can the relationships between evolutionary events be plotted on a time line?

Materials *(per student)*

meterstick
pencil
5 meters of adding-machine tape

Procedure

1. For your time line, use a scale in which 1 mm = 1 million years, or 1 m = 1 billion years.

2. Using the meterstick, draw a continuous straight line down the middle of the tape. Draw a straight line across one end. Label this line *The Present*. Assuming each meter represents 1 billion years, place a label at the spot representing 4.6 billion years ago. Add the label *Earth's Beginning?* to this line.

3. Using the table provided, plot each event on the time-line tape. Label both the number of years ago and the event.

Observations

1. Which time period is the longest? The shortest?

2. In which era did dinosaurs exist or begin to exist? In which era did mammals exist or begin to exist?

3. Which lived on Earth the longer time, dinosaurs or mammals?

Analysis and Conclusions

1. How many years does 1 cm represent on your time scale?

2. Why is there a question mark in the label Earth's Beginning?

3. If you had any difficulty plotting some of the events on the list, explain why.

4. What general conclusions con you draw from your time line regarding the rate of evolution?

5. **On Your Own** Add any events to your time line that you feel are significant. Use the information you have read in both Chapters 19 and 20.

INFERRED AGES OF EVENTS IN YEARS BEFORE PRESENT	
Event Label	**Number of Years Ago**
First mammals and dinosaurs	200 million
Beginning of Carboniferous Period	345 million
Oldest fungi	1.7 billion
Beginning of Jurassic Period	190 million
Beginning of Devonian Period	395 million
Last ice age	10,000
Beginning of Cretaceous Period	136 million
Beginning of Paleozoic Era (first abundant fossils)	570 million
Oldest rocks known	3.5 billion
Beginning of Quaternary Period	1.8 million
Oldest carbon from plants	3.6 billion
Beginning of Ordovician Period	500 million
First birds	160 million
Beginning of Cenozoic Era	65 million
First humanlike creatures	2–4 million
Beginning of Silurian Period	430 million
First reptiles	290 million
Beginning of Mesozoic Era	225 million
Modern humans make tools	500,000
Beginning of Permian Period	280 million

Summarizing Key Concepts

20–1 The Geologic Time Scale

▲ Scientists have set up a geologic calendar divided into four eras: the Precambrian, the Paleozoic, the Mesozoic, and the Cenozoic.

▲ The eras of Earth's geologic time scale are of different lengths. The longest era, the Precambrian, accounts for 87 percent of Earth's history.

▲ There were widespread volcanic eruptions during the earliest part of geologic history. Earth's atmosphere contained mainly poisonous gases.

20–2 Early Earth History

▲ The Precambrian Era began 4.6 billion years ago. During this era, the first plant and animal life formed in the seas.

▲ The Paleozoic Era began 570 million years ago. Sea animals, including fish, were abundant.

▲ The first land plants and animals appeared during the Paleozoic Era. Reptiles were the first land animals able to survive out of water.

20–3 Middle and Recent Earth History

▲ The Mesozoic Era—containing the Triassic, Jurassic, and Cretaceous periods—began about 225 million years ago. During this time, dinosaurs, birds, mammals, and the first flowering plants evolved.

▲ The supercontinent Pangaea broke apart during the Mesozoic Era and the continents began to form. Many mountains were also formed.

▲ The Cenozoic Era, which includes the Tertiary and Quaternary periods, began 65 million years ago. During that time, the first humans evolved and great ice ages occurred.

20–4 Evolution: Change Over Time

▲ Evolution can be defined as a change in species over time. A species is a group of organisms that share similar characteristics and can interbreed to produce fertile offspring.

▲ Changes in genes called mutations are one of the driving forces behind evolution. Such changes can make an organism better adapted to its environment.

▲ Scientists use fossil evidence to demonstrate that evolution has occurred during Earth's history.

Reviewing Key Terms

Define each term in a complete sentence.

20–1 The Geologic Time Scale
Precambrian Era
Paleozoic Era
Mesozoic Era
Cenozoic Era

20–2 Early Earth History
trilobite

20–3 Middle and Recent Earth History
Triassic Period
Jurassic Period
Cretaceous Period

20–4 Evolution: Change Over Time
evolution
adaptation

Chapter Review

Content Review

Multiple Choice

Choose the letter of the answer that best completes each statement.

1. The longest geologic era is the
   a. Precambrian.
   b. Cenozoic.
   c. Quaternary.
   d. Mesozoic.
2. The first mammals appeared in the
   a. Precambrian Era.
   b. Jurassic Period.
   c. Triassic Period.
   d. Cretaceous Period.
3. Pangaea began to break up into continents during the
   a. Tertiary Period.
   b. Precambrian Era.
   c. Mesozoic Era.
   d. Cenozoic Era.
4. Mountains that formed during the Jurassic Period are the
   a. Rocky Mountains.   c. Alps.
   b. Appalachians.   d. Urals.

5. Ice covered large areas of North America and Europe during the
   a. Tertiary Period.
   b. Quaternary Period.
   c. Triassic Period.
   d. Jurassic Period.
6. Dinosaurs found at Bone Cabin Quarry lived during the
   a. Paleozoic Era.
   b. Jurassic Period.
   c. Cretaceous Period.
   d. Tertiary Period.
7. The animal used as an index fossil for the Paleozoic Era is the
   a. sago palm.   c. trilobite.
   b. dinosaur.   d. *Eryops.*
8. A change that increases an organism's chances for survival is called a(n)
   a. mutation.   c. evolution.
   b. adaptation.   d. gene.

True or False

If the statement is true, write "true." If it is false, change the underlined word or words to make the statement true.

1. Brachiopods were common during the <u>Paleozoic</u> Era.
2. <u>Ferns</u> were among the first seed plants.
3. *Eryops* was a <u>reptile</u>.
4. *Tyrannosaurus* was a <u>reptile</u>.
5. During the Tertiary Period, the climate was <u>mild</u>.
6. Most members of a species show <u>variation</u>.
7. Evolution can be defined as a change in <u>an organism</u> over time.

Concept Mapping

Complete the following concept map for Section 20–1. Then construct a concept map for the entire chapter.

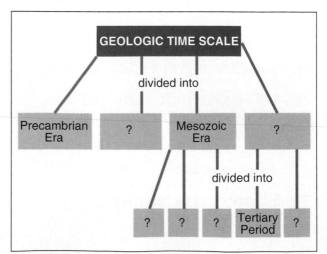

Concept Mastery

Discuss each of the following in a brief paragraph.

1. Trilobites are important index fossils for the Paleozoic Era. Explain what is meant by this statement.
2. Describe some of the geologic changes that occurred during the Paleozoic Era.
3. Why might the dinosaurs have become extinct at the end of the Cretaceous Period?
4. *Uintatherium,* an ancestor of the rhinoceros, lived during the Tertiary Period. Describe two other mammals that also lived in this period.
5. Evolution is an ongoing process. It continues as it has for millions of years. Why are scientists usually unable to see evolution in action?

Critical Thinking and Problem Solving

Use the skills you have developed in this chapter to answer each of the following.

1. **Applying Concepts** Many Precambrian rocks are metamorphic. How might this help explain why there are so few fossils in them?
2. **Interpreting Evidence** This fossil was found deep in a Pennsylvania coal mine. What does the fossil suggest about the conditions that existed when the coal was formed?

3. **Making Comparisons** Many scientists think that present-day birds evolved from dinosaurs. What are some similarities between birds and dinosaurs that might have led them to this conclusion? What are some differences?
4. **Sequencing** Arrange these organisms in the order in which they first appeared on Earth: insects, sponges, humans, birds, dinosaurs, bacteria, ferns, fish, cycads, horses, amphibians, flowering plants.
5. **Relating Cause and Effect** Certain snails that live in grasses and in woods are eaten by birds. The snails that live in grasses are yellow; the snails that live on the woodland floor are dark colored. Explain how the snails have become adapted to their environment.
6. **Using the Writing Process** Choose one of the four geologic eras and write a short story depicting a day in the life of an organism living during that era.

SARA BISEL UNCOVERS THE PAST WITH

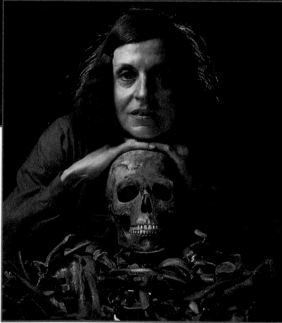

ANCIENT BONES

You probably know a bone when you see one. And you might even be able to tell the difference between a chicken bone and a steak bone. But if you saw a pile of bones, you probably couldn't tell much more about them. Dr. Sara Bisel is different. She studies bones to reveal a story within the bones—a story of ancient times. Dr. Bisel is an anthropologist, a person who studies the physical characteristics and cultures of people who lived in the past. She has studied chemistry, nutrition, and art. All of these fields help her in her work with bones.

Today, Sara Bisel works in Italy. There she studies the remains of a great disaster that occurred almost two thousand years ago. On August 24, AD 79, Mount Vesuvius, a volcano in southern Italy, erupted. For many people living near the volcano, this day was their last.

Herculaneum, a busy port city on the Bay of Naples, was located at the base of the volcano. The people of Herculaneum fished in the surrounding waters. They stored their fishing boats in stone huts on the beach. In one of the stone huts Sara Bisel made her most important discovery—not boats, but the remains of people who perished during the eruption of Mount Vesuvius. Although these remains are now only silent witnesses to a dreadful event, they tell a story to Sara Bisel.

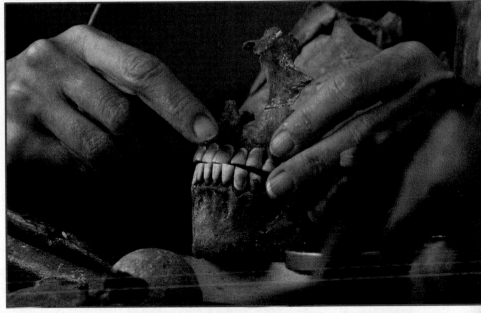

▲ "Who says dead men don't talk?" From bones such as these, Dr. Bisel is reconstructing the lives of people buried during the eruption of Mount Vesuvius in AD 79.

"Who says dead men don't talk?" Dr. Bisel asks. "These bones will have a lot to say about who these people were and how they lived." For Dr. Bisel uncovers more than bones in her work. She tries to bring the lives of ancient people into focus.

In 1982 Dr. Bisel began to reconstruct the lives of people who hid in the boat shed during the eruption of Mount Vesuvius. That eruption was followed by an avalanche that buried the dead under thirty meters of lava and mud. This volcanic covering sealed the bones from the air. The mud hardened and preserved the skeletons.

Near the boat shed, Dr. Bisel found the remains of a woman she calls Portia. In examining Portia's badly crushed skull, Dr. Bisel concluded that Portia fell from a great height during the eruption. By measuring one of Portia's leg bones, Dr. Bisel was able to determine Portia's height. The condition of the bones also told Dr. Bisel about the kind of life Portia lived. For example, Dr. Bisel analyzed Portia's bones with special chemical tests. These tests could tell if Portia was well nourished and if she had any diseases. The shape and texture of the bones could tell what Portia did for a living. Ridges and rough spots on the arm bones indicated to Dr. Bisel the way in which Portia used her arm muscles. "I think she was a weaver."

Sara Bisel works carefully, loosening the fragile bones from their stony resting place. If the bones are treated roughly, they can break as easily as eggshells. She washes each bone and dips it into a liquid plastic solution to preserve it. Next she stores the bones in special yellow plastic boxes. To date, Dr. Bisel has collected the bones of 48 men, 38 women, and 25 children.

Putting the pieces of a skull together requires artistic skills as well as scientific knowledge. Sara Bisel is an expert at solving these complex, three-dimensional puzzles. "Just look at her profile and that delicate nose," Dr. Bisel exclaimed excitedly about Portia's reconstructed skull. "In your mind's eye, spread a little flesh over these bones. She was lovely!"

In one family, Dr. Bisel found four men, three women, and five children. One of the children was very young, only about seven months old the day of the eruption. Because the baby wore jewelry, Dr. Bisel thinks this family was wealthy.

Dr. Bisel, who works six days a week, truly enjoys her interesting job. She takes great delight in reconstructing the skeletons and discovering the stories they silently tell.

UNIT SIX
Ecology
Earth's Natural Resources

▲ *Is there a solar-powered telephone in your future? As nonrenewable energy resources are used up, solar energy and other alternative sources of energy will become increasingly important.*

Like the United States, most countries rely on coal and oil, mined or drilled from the Earth, to produce the energy they need. But Iceland, a small island nation in the North Atlantic, mines "volcanic fires." Iceland sits atop a chain of volcanoes covering one third of its territory. Heat generated within the Earth, or geothermal energy, provides Iceland with energy for home heating, electricity, and manufacturing.

Iceland's use of geothermal energy demonstrates how clean, inexpensive alternative energy sources can be used to meet people's energy needs. As you read the chapters that follow, you will learn about various energy resources and their importance for present and future use. You will also learn about Earth's other nonliving resources: land, water, and air. You will read about the damage that people have done to these resources and find out what can be done to protect them.

An off-shore oil-drilling platform lights up the ocean at dusk. But obtaining and using energy resources such as oil can be harmful to the environment. ▶

▲ *How can we save the Earth from polluted air and water? The use of wind generators and widespread recycling can help.*

Discovery *Activity*

Reusable Paper

1. Soak some shredded newspaper in warm water overnight.

2. Mash the soaked newspaper into a pulpy mixture.

3. Cover your work area with a sheet of waxed paper. Spread a thin layer of the pulpy mixture on the waxed paper.

4. Cover the mixture with plastic wrap. Let the mixture dry overnight. What does the dried mixture look and feel like?

■ What could you use your reusable paper mixture for?

■ Why is reusing paper a good idea?

Energy
Resources

Guide for Reading

*After you read the following
sections, you will be able to*

21–1 What Are Fossil Fuels?

■ Describe three main
types of fossil fuels and
their uses.

21–2 Energy From the Sun

■ Compare active and
passive solar heating.

21–3 Wind and Water

■ Discuss the use of wind
generators and
hydroelectric power.

21–4 Nuclear Energy

■ Compare nuclear fission
and nuclear fusion.

■ Describe the parts of a
nuclear reactor.

**21–5 Alternative Energy
Sources**

■ Discuss the nature and
importance of alternative
energy sources.

What is 221 meters high, 379 meters long,
14 meters thick at the top, 201 meters thick at the
bottom, and contains 2.5 million cubic meters of
concrete? Give up? The answer is the Hoover Dam,
the highest concrete dam in the Western Hemisphere. This huge dam is located in a canyon on the
Colorado River between Nevada and Arizona.

You may wonder why enormous amounts of time
and money were spent to build this mammoth structure. One reason for the effort was to control the
flow of the Colorado River and provide irrigation
for surrounding farmlands. The other equally
important reason was to generate hydroelectric
power. Hoover Dam's 17 electric generators provide
electricity for 500,000 homes in Nevada, Arizona,
and California.

Hydroelectric power—electricity generated by
water—currently provides 9.5 percent of all the
electricity produced in the United States. Where
does the rest of our electricity come from? What are
some other sources of energy for today and tomorrow? You will find the answers to these questions in
the pages that follow.

Journal *Activity*

You and Your World What do you think your life might have been like 100
years ago, before the widespread use of electricity? How would it have
been different from your life today? In your journal, describe what a typical
day without electricity might be like.

◀ *This aerial view of Hoover Dam in Nevada shows the dam and
the power plant in the foreground and Lake Mead in the background.*

21–1 What Are Fossil Fuels?

Stop for a minute and think about the many ways in which you use energy every day. Pretty impressive list, isn't it? Where does all this energy come from? About 90 percent of the energy used in the United States—energy to light and heat your home and to run the family car—comes from **fossil fuels**. Fossil fuels formed hundreds of millions of years ago from the remains of dead plants and animals. The dead plants and animals were buried under layers of sediments such as mud, sand, silt, and clay. Over millions of years, heat and pressure changed the sediments into rocks and the plant and animal remains into fossil fuels. **The three main fossil fuels are coal, oil, and natural gas.**

Why are fossil fuels so useful as energy sources? The answer has to do with their chemical makeup. Fossil fuels are rich in **hydrocarbons**. Hydrocarbons are substances that contain the elements hydrogen and carbon (thus their name). The chart in Figure 21–1 lists some simple hydrocarbons.

Figure 21–1 *This chart lists some simple hydrocarbons and their chemical formulas. What is the name of the hydrocarbon used for bottled gas? What is its formula?*

SOME SIMPLE HYDROCARBONS

Name	Chemical Formula	Use
Methane	CH_4	Major part of natural gas; raw material for many synthetic products
Ethane	C_2H_6	Used to make ethyl alcohol, acetic acid, and other chemicals; refrigerant
Propane	C_3H_8	"Bottled gas" for home heating, portable stoves and heaters; refrigerant
Butane	C_4H_{10}	Used in portable lighters, home heating fuel, portable stoves and heaters
Pentane	C_5H_{12}	Solvent; measuring column in low-temperature thermometers
Hexane	C_6H_{14}	Major component of materials used in certain motor fuels and dry-cleaning solvents
Heptane	C_7H_{16}	Main part of turpentine from Jeffrey pine
Octane	C_8H_{18}	Important part of gasoline fuel for cars, trucks, buses, and the like

When the hydrocarbons in fossil fuels are combined with oxygen at high temperatures, heat energy and light energy are released. This process, commonly called burning, is known as **combustion.**

Other types of fuels also give off heat and light during the process of combustion. For example, people have been burning wood as a fuel ever since early cave dwellers learned how to start a fire. But wood does not produce as much energy per kilogram as fossil fuels do. One kilogram of coal, for example, provides twice as much heat as one kilogram of wood. The amount of heat energy provided by oil and natural gas is more than three times that provided by wood. In addition, fossil fuels are easier to transport, store, and use than wood is.

Despite these advantages, the use of fossil fuels presents several problems. Some deposits of coal and oil contain large amounts of sulfur. When these high-sulfur fuels are burned, they release dangerous pollutants such as sulfur dioxide into the atmosphere. You will learn more about the problem of pollution caused by the burning of fossil fuels in Chapter 23.

Coal

Coal is a solid fossil fuel. Historical records show that coal has been used in Europe for at least 4000 years. And Native Americans were using coal 400 years before Christopher Columbus was born! There are four types of coal, each of which represents a different stage of development. Each type of coal can be used as a fuel.

The first type of coal is **peat.** (Actually, peat is not really coal but only the first stage in the development of coal.) Peat is a soft substance made of decayed plant fibers. When burned, it gives off a great deal of smoke but little heat energy.

Pressure from the layers of rock above it changes peat into **lignite** (LIHG-night), the second type of coal. Lignite, or brown coal, is soft and has a woody texture. It is also low in heat energy.

Added pressure turns lignite into **bituminous** (bigh-TOO-muh-nuhs) **coal,** the third type of coal. Bituminous coal, which is dark brown or black, is also called soft coal. It is found deep within the

Figure 21–2 *The four types of coal are shown in this photograph. Going counterclockwise from the top left, they are peat, lignite, bituminous, and anthracite. Which is the hardest type of coal?*

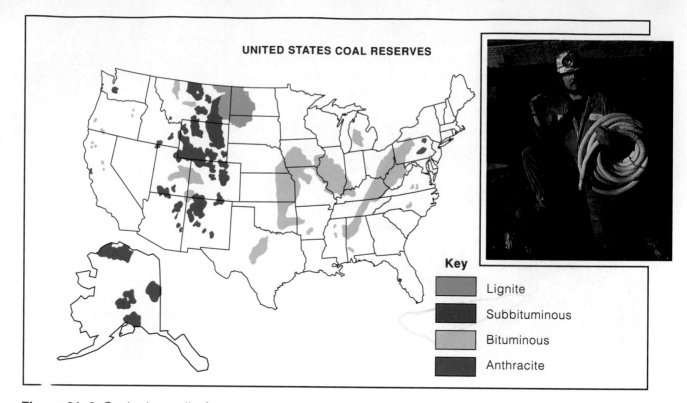

UNITED STATES COAL RESERVES

Key

Lignite

Subbituminous

Bituminous

Anthracite

Figure 21–3 *Coal miners dig for coal in deep underground mine shafts. Major coal reserves are located throughout the United States. Where is the coal deposit nearest your home located?*

Earth. Bituminous coal is the most abundant type of coal.

Tremendous pressure causes bituminous coal to change into **anthracite** (AN-thruh-sight), the fourth type of coal. Anthracite, or hard coal, is extremely hard and brittle. It is almost pure carbon. The map in Figure 21–3 shows the major coal reserves in the United States. Reserves are known deposits that can be developed economically using current technology. According to the map in Figure 21–3, where are the only reserves of anthracite located in the United States?

Oil and Natural Gas

Liquid fossil fuel is called oil, or petroleum. Oil is found in areas that were once covered by oceans. When plants and animals in the oceans died, they sank to the ocean floor and were covered by sediments. In time, the layers of sediments changed into rocks such as limestone, sandstone, and shale. Pressure from these rock layers, as well as great heat and the action of certain bacteria, changed the plant and animal remains into oil.

Limestone and sandstone contain tiny pores, or openings. Oil droplets probably seeped through

these pores and through cracks in the rock layers, forming underground pools of oil. Oil that is removed from these underground deposits is called crude oil.

Almost all the crude oil used in the world today is obtained by drilling wells into underground deposits. Some oil, however, is located near the surface of the Earth. Two sources of oil located near the Earth's surface are tar sands and oil shale. Tar sands are layers of sand soaked with thick, gooey petroleum. Oil shale is a gray rock containing a tarlike material. When oil shale is heated to a high temperature (about 600°C), it releases a hydrocarbon vapor that can be condensed (changed from the gas phase to the liquid phase) into crude oil. Unfortunately, obtaining oil from tar sands and oil shale is difficult and, therefore, not economical.

The third type of fossil fuel is natural gas. Natural gas is usually found associated with oil deposits. Because natural gas is less dense than oil, it rises above the oil. As a result, natural gas deposits are usually located above oil deposits. See Figure 21–5. The most common natural gas is methane.

Figure 21–4 *To obtain crude oil, wells may be drilled beneath the ocean floor. Oil from deposits in Alaska is transported through the Alaska pipeline. Oil shale may contain enough oil to be ignited.*

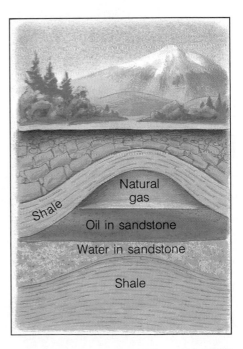

Figure 21–5 *Oil and natural gas are often found in the same deposit. Why is the natural gas usually found above the oil?*

Uses of Fossil Fuels

Making Plastic

Plastics are a part of modern life. Most of the plastics we use are made from petroleum products, or petrochemicals. However, plastics can also be made from other materials. In this activity you will make plastic from milk!

1. Pour 300 mL of milk into a large beaker. Add some food coloring to the milk.

2. Gently warm the milk over a Bunsen burner. Do not boil the milk. **CAUTION:** *Be careful when using a Bunsen burner.*

3. Slowly stir 15 mL of vinegar into the milk.

4. Pour the mixture through a sieve. Rinse the solid that remains in the sieve with water.

5. Remove the solid from the sieve and form it into an interesting shape using a cookie cutter as a mold.

6. Allow the plastic to dry. After the plastic has set, remove it from the mold. Compare your plastic with other plastic objects. What similarities or differences do you observe?

Fossil fuels—coal, oil, and natural gas—are the main sources of energy for industry, transportation, and homes. Industry is the major consumer of fossil fuels, closely followed by transportation. The charts in Figure 21–6 illustrate the major uses of oil and coal in the United States. Most of the coal produced in the United States is used to generate electricity. Transportation relies on liquid fuels, such as gasoline, that are produced from crude oil.

Crude oil is used to make many of the products you use every day. The crude oil brought up from beneath the Earth's surface is a mixture of many hydrocarbons in addition to certain impurities. Before the crude oil can be used, it must be refined. That is, the impurities must be removed. Then the oil is used to make heating oil for homes, gasoline for automobiles, kerosene for lamps, waxes for candles, asphalt for roads, and **petrochemicals.** Petrochemicals are useful substances that are derived from oil or natural gas. Some petrochemicals are used to make plastics, fabrics, medicines, and building materials. Can you name some other petrochemical products?

Natural gas is a popular source of energy for home heating because it is less expensive and cleaner to use than oil or coal. Limited reserves, however, may cut down on the use of natural gas in the future.

Figure 21–6 *These charts show the various uses of oil and coal in the United States. What percentage of the oil is used for transportation? What is most of the coal used for?*

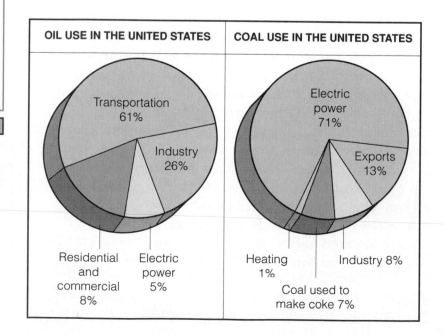

OIL USE IN THE UNITED STATES | COAL USE IN THE UNITED STATES

Transportation 61%
Industry 26%
Residential and commercial 8%
Electric power 5%

Electric power 71%
Exports 13%
Heating 1%
Coal used to make coke 7%
Industry 8%

Figure 21–7 *A wide variety of products, such as plastics, can be derived from crude oil after it is refined. What are useful products derived from oil or natural gas called?*

Fossil Fuel Shortages

Since 1900, the population of the United States has increased from 76 million people to more than 250 million at the time of the most recent census in 1990. During the same period, energy use in the United States has increased 10 times. In fact, the United States, with only 5 percent of the world's population, now uses more than 30 percent of all the energy produced in the world today!

The reserves of fossil fuels in the Earth are limited. In fact, scientists estimate that in a relatively brief period in the Earth's history (less than 500 years), we will have used up almost all the coal, oil, and natural gas formed over a period of 500 million years! In only one day, humans use an amount of oil that took about 1000 years to form. At the present rate of use, the United States may run out of fossil fuels by the year 2060. By the year 2080, the entire world may run out of fossil fuels. How do you think the absence of fossil fuels will affect living conditions in the United States? Worldwide?

In the United States, coal is more abundant than oil and natural gas. Today, coal supplies about 20 percent of the energy used in this country. At the present rate of use, coal reserves may last another

Figure 21–8 *Coal is the most abundant fossil fuel present in the United States. What will eventually happen to these coal reserves?*

300 years. But more coal is used for energy production—chiefly electricity—every year. Coal may become the main fossil fuel resource by the year 2000. In that case, reserves of coal will run out much sooner than originally estimated. It is important to remember, however, that mining and burning coal is harmful to the environment. You will learn more about the problems associated with the production and use of coal in Chapter 23.

Geologists are hard at work trying to find new sources of fossil fuels. Alternative energy sources are also being developed. Some of these alternative sources are discussed in the sections that follow. But conservation of current fossil fuel resources is still the best way to provide energy for the future. A thorough discussion of the need for conservation of energy resources is included in Chapter 24. Think about ways of conserving energy as you read the sections that follow and as you go about your daily routine. For example, what ways can you think of to conserve fossil fuels?

CAREERS

Geophysical Prospector

Oil deposits exist beneath every ocean and continent. But before oil can be recovered, it must be located. Scientists who locate oil reserves are **geophysical prospectors.** They study rock formations from which they prepare maps. The maps are then used to determine drilling spots.

To learn more about a career as a geophysical prospector, write to the Society of Exploration Geo-Physicists, PO Box 702740, Tulsa, OK 74101.

21–1 Section Review

1. Identify the three main types of fossil fuels.
2. What are the major uses of fossil fuels in the United States?
3. What are the four types of coal? Which represents the first stage in the development of coal? The last?
4. What are petrochemicals? List three products that are derived from petrochemicals.

Critical Thinking—*Making Inferences*
5. Oil and natural gas deposits were formed from the remains of plants and animals that lived in the oceans millions of years ago. Today, however, many oil and natural gas wells are located on dry land. Suggest an explanation for this fact.

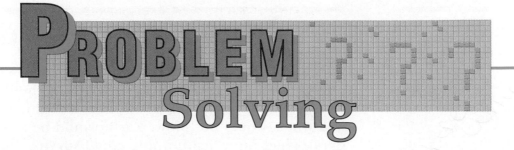

PROBLEM Solving

Examining World Oil Production

The graph below illustrates the world's crude oil production for the years 1900 to 1990. The dotted lines represent a prediction of crude oil production from 1990 to 2100. Use the graph to answer the questions that follow. (OPEC stands for the Organization of Petroleum Exporting Countries. The OPEC countries are Algeria, Ecuador, Gabon, Indonesia, Iran, Iraq, Kuwait, Libya, Nigeria, Qatar, Saudi Arabia, United Arab Emirates, and Venezuela.)

1. When was the production of crude oil in the United States at its peak?

2. According to the prediction, when will the United States stop producing crude oil?

3. What was the largest amount of crude oil produced in the world in a single year?

4. According to the prediction, what is the total amount of crude oil that will be produced by all countries in the year 2100?

5. Making Predictions According to the prediction, most of the crude oil reserves in the United States will be exhausted early in the next century. What sources of energy do you think we may be using for heating, cooling, transportation, and electricity in 2050?

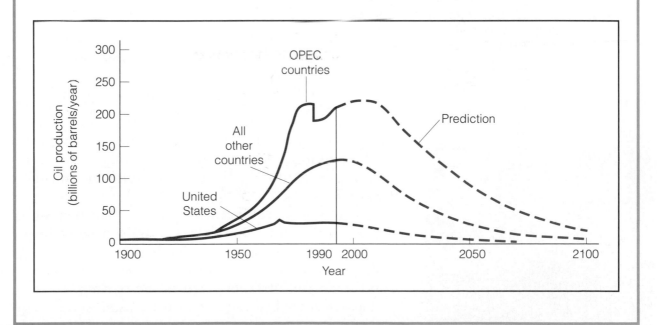

Guide for Reading

Focus on this question as you read.

▶ *What are some uses of solar energy?*

ACTIVITY

DOING

A Solar Oven

Solar energy has many practical uses. Before reading this section, design and build a simple solar oven to cook a hot dog or boil an egg. After reading this section, what changes would you make in your oven based on what you have learned?

Figure 21–9 *Without energy from the sun, life on Earth would not be possible. What is another name for energy from the sun?*

21–2 Energy From the Sun

Life on Earth would not be possible without energy from the sun, or **solar energy.** Without solar energy, plants would not grow, rain would not fall, and winds would not blow. Earth would be a cold, dark planet on which nothing could survive.

Scientists estimate that the solar energy received by the Earth in one day is enough to meet the world's energy needs for 30 years at the present rate of energy use. **Solar energy can be used to heat buildings and to produce electricity.** To be useful, however, solar energy must first be collected, converted, and stored.\Why are collection, conversion, and storage necessary?

Solar energy is spread out over a wide area, not concentrated in one place. So solar energy must be collected before it can be used. In addition, most of the sun's energy is received in the form of light. Thus, sunlight must be converted into other forms of energy, such as heat and electricity, before it can be used. And finally, solar energy must be stored for use when the sun is not shining (at night or during cloudy weather). There are several ways to solve the problems of collection, conversion, and storage of solar energy. Solar-heating systems for homes, schools, and commercial buildings may be one answer.

Passive Solar Heating

Solar-heating systems can be either passive or active. In a passive solar-heating system, the windows of a building are positioned so that sunlight enters directly and heats the building. Shades covering the windows hold in the heat during the night. An overhang prevents too much heat from entering during the summer.

The obvious problem with passive solar heating is that when the sun is not shining, the source of heat is removed. To solve this problem, a backup heating system is needed. In a passive solar home, a small wood stove can often be used as the backup system.

Passive solar heating can also be used to heat water for home use, such as for bathing, showering,

Figure 21–10 *Some modern homes are designed to make use of passive solar-heating systems. Why is the position of the windows important in a passive solar home?*

and washing dishes. Although you may not realize it, between 30 and 50 percent of the energy used in most homes is used to heat water. Solar hot-water systems, which can be used all year round, could save up to 50 percent of the energy cost of heating water. Today, about 800,000 solar hot-water systems are being used in the United States.

Active Solar Heating

An active solar-heating system involves collecting the sun's energy in a device called a **solar collector.** In a typical solar collector, a black surface absorbs energy from the sun and converts it to heat. The surface is covered with glass or plastic panels to trap the heat. Water is heated by pumping it through pipes on the surface. The heated water in the pipes then flows through a storage tank filled with water. Heat is transferred from the water in the pipes to the water in the storage tank. The heated water in the storage tank is pumped throughout the building to provide heat and hot water. At the same time, the water in the pipes returns to the solar collector to be reheated by the sun. You can get a better idea of how an active solar-heating system works by studying Figure 21–11.

Figure 21–11 *Water in a solar collector on the roof of a home is heated by the sun (top). The heat is then transferred in a heat exchanger and used to provide hot water and heat for the home.*

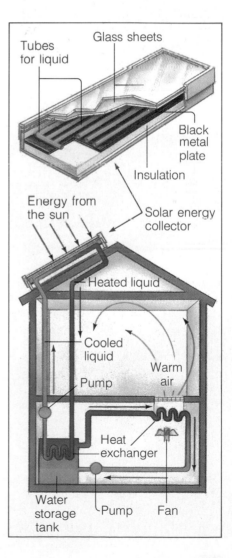

651

Solar Cells

At the present time, solar-heating systems represent the most common use of solar energy. In the future, however, solar cells may become much more common as sources of usable energy. Solar cells, or **photovoltaic cells,** convert sunlight directly into electricity. (The prefix *photo-* means light, and the suffix *-voltaic* means electrical.) You may be familiar with the use of solar cells in pocket calculators.

A solar cell is a "sandwich" made of extremely thin layers of the element silicon. When sunlight strikes the surface of this sandwich, electrons (negatively charged particles) flow across the layers. This flow of electrons is an electric current, which can be put to work in electric motors or other electrical devices.

Unfortunately, each solar cell produces only a small amount of electricity. A single solar cell can now provide only about 1 watt of electricity—while the sun shines. (The watt is the unit of electric power.) This is about the same amount of power produced by a standard flashlight battery. So large numbers of solar cells are needed to produce useful amounts of electricity. Roof panels consisting of about 5000 solar cells would be needed to provide electricity for an average American home!

Solar cells were first used on a large scale in 1958 to generate electricity aboard the United States satellite *Vanguard I.* Since then, they have been used to generate electricity on many other satellites and spacecraft. Why do you think solar cells would be especially effective in space?

When it comes to providing solar energy for the widest possible use, cost and storage are important considerations. The major disadvantage of solar cells in terms of meeting the everyday electricity needs of homes, schools, and factories has been their cost. In 1959, electricity from solar cells cost about $500 per watt. The cost is now down to about $6 per watt. But it will probably be many years before solar cells

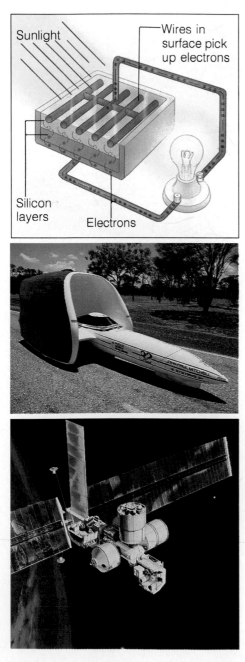

Figure 21–12 *A solar cell, or photovoltaic cell, converts sunlight directly into electricity. A solar-powered car gets all its energy from solar cells. In future space stations, energy will be provided by huge panels of solar cells.*

can compete with the cost of electricity from fossil fuels (about $1 per watt).

Looking further into the future, the National Aeronautics and Space Administration (NASA) has proposed using solar satellites in Earth orbit to provide electricity for people on Earth. These huge panels of solar cells, several kilometers on a side, would be assembled in space. Sunlight falling on the solar panels would produce electricity. The electricity would then be converted to microwaves, a form of radio waves now used in microwave ovens. The microwaves would be beamed to receiving stations on Earth and changed back into electricity for general distribution.

Power Towers

Have you ever used a magnifying glass to focus sunlight onto a spot on a piece of paper or on a leaf? If so, you were probably able to burn a hole through the paper or the leaf. This simple activity illustrates another way of using solar energy. An array of mirrors can be used to focus sunlight onto a boiler mounted on a tower. The sun's heat converts water in the boiler into steam, which drives a turbine to generate electricity. The first such solar plant, called Solar One, is shown in Figure 21–13. Several other similar plants are now being tested. As research continues and new technology is developed, solar energy will probably play an increasingly important role in your life.

Figure 21–13 In a solar-energy plant, curved mirrors reflect the sun's rays toward a tower of water. Here the heat turns the water into steam, which is used to turn turbines and generate electricity.

21–2 Section Review

1. What are two uses of solar energy?
2. Briefly describe two types of solar-heating systems.
3. What is a photovoltaic cell? How does it work?

Connection—*You and Your World*
4. In what ways is solar energy now used in your home? Considering the area of the country in which you live, what other uses of solar energy might be appropriate in your home?

Blowing in the Wind, p. 781

21–3 Wind and Water

Throughout history, people have made use of the energy of wind and water. Wind energy has been used to propel sailing ships, turn mill wheels, and pump water from wells. Water mills were once common along thousands of small rivers and streams in the United States, where they were used to grind corn and grain. **Today, the energy of wind and water is used to generate electricity.**

Wind Energy

Winds are caused by the uneven heating of the Earth's atmosphere by the sun. So wind energy can be thought of as an indirect form of solar energy. People have been taking advantage of this readily available source of energy for thousands of years.

Around 1860, small windmills started appearing on farms across the United States. Lightweight, efficient, relatively inexpensive, and easy to install, the early windmills were used to pump water out of the ground. These wind-powered pumps were essential in providing water for crops and farm animals in the farming regions of the Midwest and Southwest.

In 1890, a Danish inventor developed a windmill that could produce small amounts of electricity. American farmers could now enjoy the benefits of electricity provided by their own windmills. Windmill generators were common until the 1930s and 1940s, when transmission lines brought electricity from central power plants to even the most isolated farms.

Figure 21–14 *Windmills on farms are used mainly to pump water. At Altamont Pass in California, thousands of wind generators are used to produce electricity. Why is wind energy considered an indirect form of solar energy?*

As a source of electricity, wind generators were not always reliable. Can you think of some reasons why? They did not work on calm days. And they were easily knocked down or blown apart by strong winds. So when hydroelectric power plants started supplying electricity to rural areas, farmers welcomed the change. The electricity provided by power plants was more dependable than that produced by the wind. By 1950, most wind generators had been abandoned.

But wind energy was not ignored for long! The oil shortages of the early 1970s caused concern about an energy crisis and sparked renewed interest in wind generators. The designs of modern wind generators range from airplane-type propellers to giant "eggbeaters." Designers of large wind generators must select a location where the wind is strong (13 kilometers per hour or more) and blows steadily most of the time. Then they design and build a wind generator to suit that location.

Instead of giant individual wind generators, some developers have built "wind farms" that contain up to several hundred smaller windmills. Today, more than 100 of these wind farms are in operation, and the use of wind energy is growing rapidly. Unfortunately, wind energy will not meet all our energy needs. But some energy planners predict that by the year 2000, almost 10 percent of the electricity generated in the United States will be produced by wind energy. In addition, the increased use of wind energy will save fossil fuels and reduce pollution.

Water Energy

Like wind energy, water energy is an indirect form of solar energy. Energy from the sun causes water to evaporate from lakes and oceans. This water vapor enters the atmosphere and condenses to form clouds. From the clouds, water falls back to the Earth as rain, snow, sleet, or hail. Runoff from rain and melting snow forms rushing streams and rivers, which eventually empty into the oceans—and the cycle continues.

In the late 1700s, water mills in the United States provided energy for machine looms to make cloth or for turning millstones to grind grain. By the 1800s,

Figure 21–15 *For centuries, the mechanical energy of moving water has been used in water mills. Today, falling water at Glen Canyon Dam is used to generate electricity. Is water energy a direct or an indirect form of solar energy?*

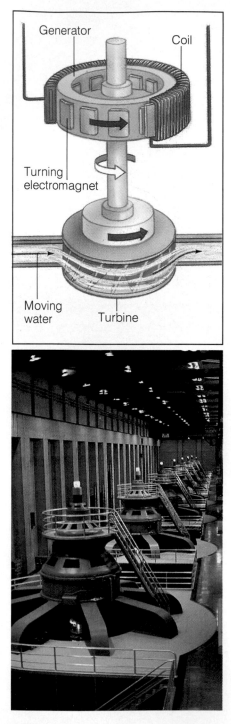

Generator

Coil

Turning electromagnet

Moving water

Turbine

most water mills had been replaced by steam engines. But with the invention of the electic light bulb by Thomas Edison in 1879, the demand for electricity increased tremendously. Water energy became important once again as a means of generating electricity.

The use of the mechanical energy of falling or running water to generate usable electricity is called **hydroelectric power.** (The prefix *hydro-* means water.) In a hydroelectric power plant, dams—such as Hoover Dam, which was described at the beginning of this chapter—hold back millions of tons of water in reservoirs. Some of this water is drawn through pipes into the power plant, where it flows through turbines within the plant. The rushing water spins the blades of the turbines, producing electricity in generators. You can see the basic plan and operation of a hydroelectric power plant in Figure 21–16.

Although new hydroelectric power plants are being built, the number of locations in which large dams can be constructed is limited. In this sense, the use of hydroelectric power as a source of energy is limited. In addition, hydroelectric power plants can be somewhat harmful to the environment. For example, patterns of fish migration in rivers may be altered by dams on those rivers. The reservoirs formed behind dams may flood land that might have been used for farming or that might have had great cultural value. For these and other reasons, energy planners do not expect the use of hydroelectric power to increase significantly in the future.

Figure 21–16 *Inside a generator at Hoover Dam, the mechanical energy of moving water spins a turbine. The spinning turbine causes large electromagnets to turn. The turning electromagnets generate electricity.*

21–3 Section Review

1. Describe how the energy of wind and the energy of water are being used today.
2. Why can both wind energy and water energy be considered indirect forms of solar energy?
3. Why were early wind generators not reliable energy sources?

Critical Thinking—*Making Comparisons*

4. Compare the use of wind generators and hydroelectric power plants in terms of the benefits and problems associated with each.

21–4 Nuclear Energy

As you have read in Section 21–2, life on Earth would not be possible without the energy we receive from the sun. Where does the sun get its energy? The heat and light of the sun (and of all other stars) are produced as a result of reactions taking place deep within the nuclei (NOO-klee-igh; singular, nucleus: NOO-klee-uhs) of atoms. Atoms are the basic building blocks of matter. All objects in the universe are made of matter—and thus of atoms. The **nucleus** is the tiny center of an atom. It is made up of positively charged particles called protons and electrically neutral particles called neutrons. In 1905, Albert Einstein, one of the greatest scientists who ever lived, predicted that if the nucleus of an atom could be split, a new and powerful energy source would be available. This energy, called **nuclear energy,** is the energy locked within the atomic nucleus.

Nuclear Fission

In 1939, **nuclear fission** was discovered. In 1942, the first sustained nuclear fission reaction was carried out by scientists at the University of Chicago. **Nuclear fission is the splitting of an atomic nucleus into two smaller nuclei, during which nuclear energy is released.** Figure 21–18 on page 658 illustrates how a nuclear fission reaction can be made to happen. The diagram shows the most common type of fission reaction, which involves the splitting of a uranium-235 nucleus. (Uranium-235 is a form of the element uranium, containing 92 protons and 143 neutrons in its nucleus.)

To split a uranium-235 nucleus, scientists must shoot a nuclear "bullet" into the nucleus. The nuclear bullet in a fission reaction is a neutron. When a neutron strikes a uranium-235 nucleus, the nucleus is split into two smaller nuclei. During this process, two or more neutrons are released from the uranium-235 nucleus. Energy is released as well.

Each neutron released during a fission reaction is capable of causing another fission reaction by splitting another uranium-235 nucleus. The neutrons released by each of these reactions can then split

Guide for Reading

Focus on this question as you read.

▶ *How is energy released by means of nuclear fission and nuclear fusion?*

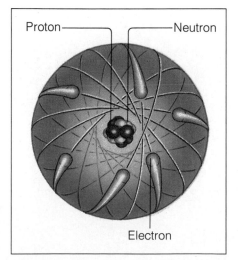

Figure 21–17 *An atom consists of a central core, or nucleus, made up of protons and neutrons. A cloud of whirling electrons surrounds the nucleus.*

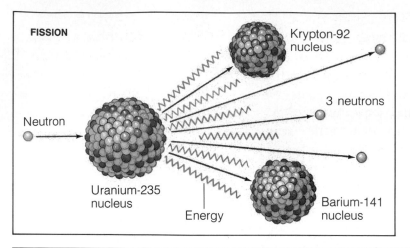

FISSION

Krypton-92 nucleus

Neutron

Uranium-235 nucleus

Energy

3 neutrons

Barium-141 nucleus

Figure 21–18 *In a fission reaction, a uranium-235 nucleus is split by a neutron "bullet." The additional neutrons produced by the fission reaction may cause a nuclear chain reaction. What are the products of a fission reaction?*

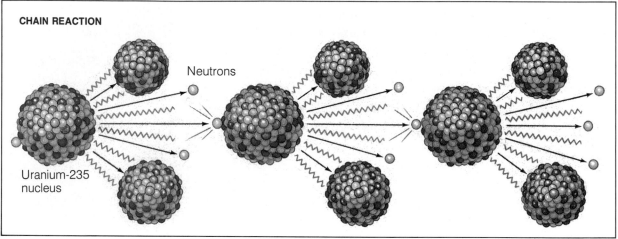

CHAIN REACTION

Neutrons

Uranium-235 nucleus

several more nuclei. In other words, one neutron striking one uranium-235 nucleus starts a chain of nuclear fission reactions. The process in which the splitting of one nucleus causes the splitting of additional nuclei is called a nuclear **chain reaction.**

If a nuclear chain reaction is uncontrolled, the nuclear energy that is released will create a huge explosion. That is just what happens in an atomic bomb in which the energy is released all at once. If the chain reaction is carefully controlled, however, the energy that is released can be a valuable energy resource. Controlled nuclear chain reactions take place in nuclear power plants.

Nuclear Power Plants

The energy released during nuclear fission is mostly in the form of heat energy. In a nuclear power plant, this heat energy is used to convert water into steam. The steam then passes through a turbine in an electric generator. The steam spins the blades of the turbine, which produces electricity. So nuclear power plants produce electricity from the energy locked within the nuclei of atoms.

Fission reactions in a nuclear power plant are produced and controlled in a nuclear reactor. The main parts of a nuclear reactor are the containment building and the reactor vessel, which contains the fuel rods and the control rods. Figure 21–19 shows a typical nuclear reactor. Refer to the diagram as you read the description that follows.

The reactor vessel is the central part of a nuclear reactor. It is within the reactor vessel that nuclear fission takes place. To begin a fission reaction, nuclear fuel rods are placed in the reactor vessel. The most common nuclear fuel is uranium-235. When neutrons strike the fuel rods containing pellets of uranium-235, nuclear fission begins. It is important to note that a single nuclear fuel rod does not contain enough uranium-235 to support a chain reaction. Only when many fuel rods are placed close together does a chain reaction occur.

In order for a fission reaction to produce useful energy, the overall speed of the reaction must be

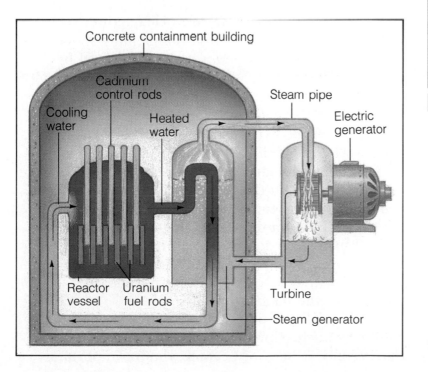

Figure 21–19 *The first nuclear reactor was built under the football stadium at the University of Chicago. This illustration shows the design of a typical modern nuclear reactor. How is the heat produced by a chain reaction converted into electricity?*

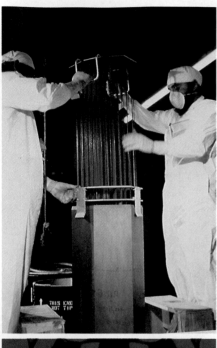

carefully controlled. To control the rate of the reaction, neutron-absorbing control rods are placed between the fuel rods. In many reactors, the control rods are made of the element cadmium. When the cadmium control rods are inserted into the reactor, they "soak up" neutrons and slow down the reaction. When the control rods are removed, the fission reaction is speeded up. Thus, the rate of the reaction is controlled by moving the cadmium control rods into or out of the reactor.

Even if a nuclear reactor should get out of control, a nuclear explosion similar to an atomic bomb is impossible. However, it is possible for the reactor to overheat. To prevent the reactor from overheating, water is circulated through the reactor vessel. The hot water from the reactor vessel then passes through a steam generator, where it produces steam to spin a turbine and generate electricity.

Problems With Nuclear Power

At one time, energy planners predicted that nuclear power would become the world's leading source of energy. Just 0.5 kilogram of uranium-235 can produce as much energy as 900 metric tons of coal! And nuclear power does not produce the kinds of pollution caused by burning fossil fuels. Yet predictions of widespread use of nuclear power have not come true. In the United States, only 14 percent of the total electricity generated is produced by nuclear power plants. What went wrong?

Safety is the most obvious concern of many people when they discuss nuclear power. The problem of safety can be divided into four major areas. First, there is the possibility of harmful radiation leaking into the environment. Second, there is the question of what to do with the dangerous radioactive wastes produced by nuclear power plants. Third, there is the possibility of a disastrous meltdown resulting from overheating due to a loss of cooling water in the reactor vessel. And fourth, there is the problem of security; that is, of preventing nuclear fuel from falling into the hands of terrorists.

Aside from the potential safety problems associated with nuclear power plants, the main reason nuclear power has not become a more important energy resource is an economic one. Nuclear power

Figure 21–20 *Before being placed in a reactor, nuclear fuel rods are carefully inspected. When the fuel rods are placed at just the right distance from one another, a controlled chain reaction will occur. What is the most common fuel used in nuclear fuel rods?*

plants are expensive to build. And the electricity produced by nuclear power plants costs more than electricity produced by other energy sources, such as coal.

The problems associated with the use of nuclear power will be discussed more fully in Chapter 23. Scientists are now trying to solve these problems. Will they be able to make nuclear power safer and more cost effective? If they succeed, nuclear power may become a greater source of energy in the future.

Nuclear Fusion

Just as splitting an atomic nucleus releases energy, so does combining two atomic nuclei. **Nuclear fusion is the combining of two atomic nuclei to produce one larger nucleus, with the release of nuclear energy.** In fact, **nuclear fusion** produces far more energy per atom than nuclear fission. Nuclear fusion is the reaction that produces the energy given off by stars such as our sun.

Like other stars, the sun is composed mainly of hydrogen. Within the sun, enormous heat and pressure cause the nuclei of hydrogen atoms to combine, or fuse, into helium nuclei. During this fusion process, some of the mass of the hydrogen is converted into energy. This is the same process that results in the uncontrolled release of nuclear energy in a hydrogen bomb.

To be able to generate useful energy from nuclear fusion, scientists must be able to produce

Figure 21–21 *Three Mile Island nuclear power plant in Pennsylvania was the site of a serious accident in 1979. Radiation escaped into the atmosphere when the reactor's cooling system failed and the reactor overheated.*

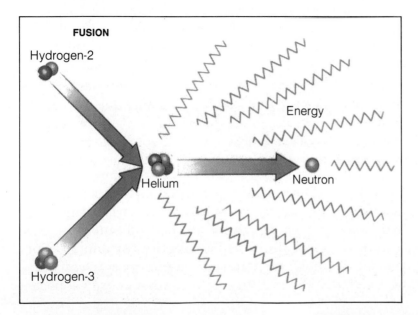

Figure 21–22 *Tremendous amounts of energy are released when two hydrogen nuclei collide to form a helium nucleus. What is this type of nuclear reaction called?*

controlled fusion reactions. If controlled nuclear fusion were practical, it would solve all our energy needs. Because a nuclear fusion reactor would use hydrogen from water, an inexpensive and unlimited supply of fuel would be available. In addition, nuclear fusion would be safer and less polluting than nuclear fission. Unfortunately, scientists have not yet been able to solve the problems involved in producing and sustaining the extremely high temperatures and pressures needed for fusion. Research is continuing, but it will probably be many years before nuclear fusion becomes a practical source of energy.

Figure 21–23 *Scientists at Princeton University are trying to produce a controlled nuclear fusion reaction in this test reactor. If nuclear fusion could be controlled, why would it provide a source of energy that could meet all our future needs?*

21–4 Section Review

1. How is energy released in a nuclear fission reaction? In a nuclear fusion reaction?
2. What is the "bullet" used to start a nuclear fission reaction? Why is the fission reaction that takes place in a nuclear reactor called a chain reaction?
3. What fuel is used in a nuclear fission reaction? In a nuclear fusion reaction?
4. What are the main parts of a nuclear fission reactor? How is the rate of the fission reaction in a nuclear reactor controlled?

Critical Thinking—*Relating Concepts*
5. Why would safe, economical nuclear power provide a good alternative to the use of fossil fuels?

21–5 Alternative Energy Sources

Most of our energy—90 percent—comes from fossil fuels. The remaining 10 percent comes from other energy sources—nuclear, solar, wind, and hydroelectric. Today, there are enough energy sources to meet the world's appetite for energy. For the future, however, alternative energy sources will be needed. Why are these alternative energy sources needed? The answer is twofold. One reason people must look for new, clean sources of energy is pollution. Pollution problems are associated with many energy resources, not just fossil fuels. You will read about some of these pollution problems in Chapter 23.

The other reason people must develop new energy resources is to meet the future energy needs of a growing population. The global population is now more than 5 billion people, and it is expected to reach 6 billion by the year 2000. The present available energy resources cannot be used up today without preparing for tomorrow. Today's generation must use energy wisely to ensure its availability for future generations. **Throughout the world, scientists are working to develop alternative energy sources, such as geothermal energy, tidal energy, biomass, and hydrogen power.**

Geothermal Energy

You may not have realized it, but there is a lot of energy right beneath your feet! **Geothermal energy** is energy produced from the heat energy within the Earth itself. (The word geothermal is made up of the prefix *geo-* meaning Earth and the suffix *-thermal* meaning heat.) The interior of the Earth is extremely hot. Molten (melted) rock deep within the Earth has an average temperature of 1800°C. In some places, the molten rock comes close to the Earth's surface. These places are called hot spots. When water near the Earth's surface comes into contact with these hot spots, the water is heated and bursts forth from the Earth in fountains of steam and boiling water known as geysers. Old Faithful, in Yellowstone National Park, is an example of such a geyser.

In some parts of the world, steam from geysers is used to generate electricity. Steam from geysers can also be used to heat homes, greenhouses, and other buildings directly. In some places, steam is obtained from geothermal wells drilled into reservoirs of hot water.

Hot spots can be used to obtain geothermal energy in another way. Wells can be drilled into hot, dry rock. When water is pumped into these dry wells, the heat in the hot rock turns the water into steam. The steam is then pumped to the surface and

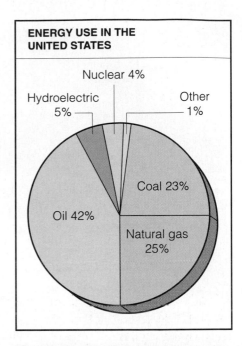

ENERGY USE IN THE UNITED STATES

- Nuclear 4%
- Hydroelectric 5%
- Other 1%
- Coal 23%
- Oil 42%
- Natural gas 25%

Figure 21–24 *This chart shows the sources of energy used in the United States. How much energy is presently obtained from fossil fuels?*

ACTIVITY
WRITING

Dinosaur Power

A dinosaur called *Stegosaurus* roamed the Earth about 150 million years ago. Some scientists believe *Stegosaurus* used solar energy in an unusual way. Find a picture of *Stegosaurus* in a library. Based on the picture, write a hypothesis describing how you think *Stegosaurus* might have used part of its body to absorb solar energy.

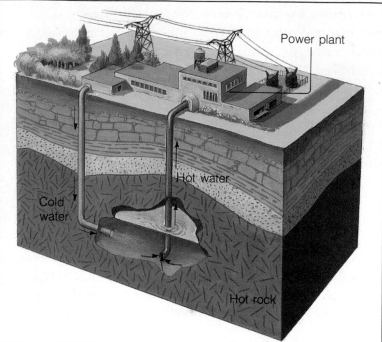

Figure 21–25 *Old Faithful geyser erupts, carrying geothermal energy from deep within the Earth. In a geothermal power plant, cold water is pumped into the Earth, where it is heated, returned to the power plant, and used to generate electricity.*

used to generate electricity or, if the geothermal wells are near a city, to heat homes and other buildings directly.

Geothermal energy is currently being used in Iceland, New Zealand, and parts of the United States, including California and Hawaii. Because the number of hot spots on the Earth is limited, however, geothermal energy is unlikely to keep pace with the world's growing energy needs.

Tidal Energy

Twice a day, the waters of the oceans rise and fall. These high tides and low tides are caused by the gravitational interactions of the sun, the moon, and the Earth. In areas where the difference between high tides and low tides is great, the movement of water can be used as a source of **tidal energy.**

In a tidal power plant, a low dam is built across the entrance to a shallow bay. As the rising and falling tides cause water to flow into and out of the bay, the dam holds back the flow of tidal water. The water then flows past turbines to generate electricity. (This is similar to the way in which electricity is generated in hydroelectric power plants.) Tidal power plants are now in use in France, Canada, and other countries. The use of tidal power as an energy

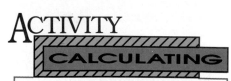

ACTIVITY

CALCULATING

Time and Tide . . .

At Cape May, New Jersey, along the shore of the Atlantic Ocean, there are two high tides every 24 hours and 50 minutes. If the first high tide occurs at 6:00 AM on Tuesday, at what time will it occur on Wednesday? On Thursday?

resource is quite limited, however, since there are relatively few areas in the world where tidal power plants can be built.

Biomass

Any materials that can be burned are said to be combustible. Combustible materials can be used in a variety of ways to produce energy. They can be burned to produce steam, which can then be passed through a turbine to generate electricity. Combustible materials can also be burned to provide heat for homes and factories. The oldest and still most widely used combustible material is wood. Wood is an example of a group of materials known as **biomass.** The term biomass refers to any materials that come from living things. (Remember that wood was once part of a living tree.) Biomass can be burned directly as a fuel or converted into other types of fuels.

DIRECT BURNING Biomass has been burned for cooking and heating purposes for thousands of years. In addition to wood, other forms of biomass are plants and animal wastes. Plants used as biomass fuels include corn husks, sugar cane, sunflowers, and seaweed. In many parts of the world, animal wastes are dried in the sun and used as heating fuel.

Some cities in the United States have recently built power plants that produce steam by burning garbage and other trash. The steam produced in these plants is used directly as a source of heat and hot water or indirectly to generate electricity.

ALCOHOL PRODUCTION Another use of biomass is to produce an alternative fuel to gasoline. Almost all cars in the United States are powered by gasoline. During the gasoline shortages of the 1970s, scientists began looking for alternatives to gasoline. One alternative that was developed is **gasohol.** Gasohol is a mixture of gasoline and alcohol. Ethanol, or ethyl alcohol, is the alcohol that is commonly used in gasohol.

Ethanol is produced by the action of yeast cells on various grains such as corn, wheat, and barley. The yeast cells convert the sugar in the grain into ethanol and carbon dioxide in a process called fermentation (fer-muhn-TAY-shuhn). The use of gasohol was begun in Brazil, which now has large-scale

Figure 21–26 Sunflowers are combustible materials that can be burned to provide energy. A power plant in California uses discarded automobile tires to generate electricity.

Figure 21–27 Gasohol is a fuel that is a mixture of gasoline and alcohol. Where does the alcohol used in gasohol come from?

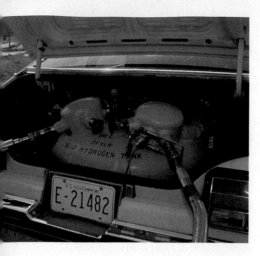

Figure 21–28 *Hydrogen gas may someday provide a clean source of energy for automobiles, buses, and other motor vehicles.*

fermentation plants that use sugar cane. Gasohol is widely used in cars in Brazil. Scientists are now experimenting with cars that run entirely on ethanol.

Hydrogen Power

Hydrogen has often been called the "fuel of the future." With the exception of sunlight, hydrogen is the only truly unlimited energy source on Earth. Oceans, rivers, and lakes all contain hydrogen as part of water. Hydrogen gas can be burned in place of fossil fuels such as natural gas. Experimental cars and buses that run on hydrogen gas have been built. And unlike gasoline, the only exhaust from burning hydrogen gas is water!

The problem with using the hydrogen in water is that it is bound to oxygen atoms. A water molecule (H_2O) contains 2 hydrogen atoms bonded to 1 oxygen atom. To obtain hydrogen gas for combustion (burning), a water molecule must be broken down. This is usually done by passing an electric current through water. The process of using electricity to break down water into hydrogen and oxygen is called electrolysis. Electrolysis, however, uses more energy in the form of electricity to produce hydrogen gas than can be obtained by burning hydrogen gas. So at this time, hydrogen power does not appear to be a major alternative energy source.

ACTIVITY

WRITING

Other Energy Sources

Prepare a report on one of the following energy sources:

Liquid Metal Fast Breeder Reactor
Magnetohydrodynamic Generators
Ocean Thermal Energy Conversion
Fuel Cells
Synfuels
Methane Gas

21–5 Section Review

1. What are four possible alternative energy sources?
2. What is gasohol? How is it produced?
3. What is biomass? Describe two ways of using biomass to produce energy.
4. What is tidal energy? How are tidal power plants similar to hydroelectric power plants?

Connection—*Chemistry*

5. When water is broken down into hydrogen gas and oxygen gas during the process of electrolysis, twice as much hydrogen gas as oxygen gas is produced. Explain this fact using the formula for a water molecule given in this section.

CONNECTIONS

Cold Fusion or ConFusion?

Fusion—the energy that powers the stars—could supply an unlimited source of inexpensive, clean energy. But fusion requires tremendously high temperatures and pressures. *Physicists* have been experimenting with different ways to produce a controlled fusion reaction for nearly 20 years. So far, however, they have not been able to sustain a reaction that produces more energy than is needed to start the reaction.

In 1989, two *chemists* startled the scientific world with a surprising announcement. They claimed to have produced fusion reactions in a simple table-top experiment at room temperature! ''Fusion in a bottle''—or cold fusion, as it came to be called—could solve all the world's future energy needs.

Researchers worldwide immediately tried to repeat the original experiment. A National Cold Fusion Research Institute was set up. Hundreds of research papers were published in scientific journals. Although some interesting observations were reported, the results were generally disappointing. More than five years after the first announcement, the existence of cold fusion still had not been confirmed. What was going on?

Some researchers think that the normal procedures of science were ignored because the potential benefits of cold fusion are so great. After all, the first description of cold fusion was given at a press conference, not in a scientific journal. In addition, the two chemists did not share the details of their experimental procedure with researchers trying to duplicate their results.

SCIENCE NEWS TODAY
Fusion Claim Stuns Scie

The stakes couldn't be much higher. On March 23, two highly respected chemists parachuted onto the center stage of physics in a public announcement...

fusion unleashes energy when the nuclei of lighter elements fuse into heavier ones. To achieve these unions, the enormous repulsive forces between positively charged nuclei must be overcome or ...vented. To date, most fusion re-

SCIENCE NEWS WEEKLY
New Find Heats Up the Cold Fus

An unpublished finding that cold fusion experiments apparently created helium has rekindled debate about the still thus far confounded researchers' efforts to show that cold fusion experiments...

Cold ConFusio
Despite the doubts of their colleagues, a few scientists ...tly contested reaction.

Today, although a few researchers are still trying to produce a cold fusion reaction, most have given up. Almost all scientists are convinced that it has been disproved on the basis of theory and experiments. It is unlikely that energy from cold fusion will ever be widely available.

Laboratory Investigation

Solar Heating

Problem

How does the color of an object affect the amount of solar energy it absorbs?

Materials   *(per group)*

black and white construction paper
tape
scissors
2 metal or plastic containers with plastic lids
2 Celsius thermometers
clock or watch

Procedure

1. Tape two layers of black paper around one container. Tape two layers of white paper around the other container.

2. Using the scissors, carefully punch a small hole through the center of each lid. Each hole should be large enough to hold a thermometer. **CAUTION:** *Be careful when using scissors.*

3. Fill each container with water at room temperature and cover with a plastic lid.

4. Carefully insert a thermometer through the hole in each lid. Make sure the bulb of the thermometer is below the surface of the water in the container.

5. Place the containers on a sunny window-sill. Be sure each is in direct sunlight.

6. Record the temperature of the water in each container every 3 minutes for 36 minutes. Record your data in a data table.

Observations

1. During which time interval did the temperature in the black container begin to rise? During which time interval did the temperature in the white container begin to rise?

2. What was the final temperature of the water in the black container? In the white container?

3. Make a graph of your data, plotting temperature on the vertical axis and time on the horizontal axis.

Analysis and Conclusions

1. How effectively did the sun's energy heat the water in the containers?

2. Did the color of the containers affect the amount of solar energy they absorbed? Explain your answer.

3. What hidden variable might have affected your results?

4. Based on the results of this experiment, what color clothing would you be likely to wear in the winter? In the summer?

5. **On Your Own**   Design an experiment to test the effects of different colors, such as red, orange, and yellow, on the absorption of solar energy.

Summarizing Key Concepts

21–1 What Are Fossil Fuels?

▲ The three main fossil fuels are coal, oil, and natural gas.

▲ Fossil fuels were formed millions of years ago from the remains of dead plants and animals.

▲ Fossil fuels are used to produce energy for industry, transportation, and home use.

21–2 Energy From the Sun

▲ Life on Earth would not be possible without energy from the sun, or solar energy.

▲ Solar energy is used to heat buildings and to produce electricity.

▲ Solar-heating systems may be either active or passive.

▲ Solar energy is converted directly into electricity by photovoltaic cells.

21–3 Wind and Water

▲ Energy from wind and water can be used to generate electricity.

▲ The use of the energy in moving water to generate electricity is hydroelectric power.

21–4 Nuclear Energy

▲ Nuclear energy is the energy trapped within the nuclei of atoms.

▲ In nuclear fission, energy is released by splitting an atomic nucleus into two smaller nuclei.

▲ In nuclear fusion, energy is released by combining two atomic nuclei into one larger nucleus.

21–5 Alternative Energy Sources

▲ Geothermal energy is produced from heat energy within the Earth.

▲ Tidal energy is produced by the movement of the tides.

▲ Biomass materials, which come from living things, can be used to produce energy.

▲ Hydrogen gas can be burned in place of fossil fuels to produce energy.

Reviewing Key Terms

Define each term in a complete sentence.

21–1 What Are Fossil Fuels?
fossil fuel
hydrocarbon
combustion
peat
lignite
bituminous coal
anthracite
petrochemical

21–2 Energy From the Sun
solar energy
solar collector
photovoltaic cell

21–3 Wind and Water
hydroelectric power

21–4 Nuclear Energy
nucleus
nuclear energy
nuclear fission
chain reaction
nuclear fusion

21–5 Alternative Energy Sources
geothermal energy
tidal energy
biomass
gasohol

Chapter Review

Content Review

Multiple Choice

Choose the letter of the answer that best completes each statement.

1. Wind energy and water energy are both indirect forms of
   a. electric energy.   c. nuclear energy.
   b. solar energy.   d. heat energy.

2. Which of the following is *not* a product made from crude oil?
   a. kerosene   c. gasoline
   b. heating oil   d. oil shale

3. The fuel rods in a nuclear reactor contain pellets of the element
   a. carbon.   c. silicon.
   b. cadmium.   d. uranium.

4. Before being used, solar energy must be converted to other forms of energy because it is
   a. spread out over a wide area.
   b. not available at night.
   c. received mostly in the form of light.
   d. not concentrated in one place.

5. The three main fossil fuels are coal, oil, and
   a. tar sands.   c. hydrogen gas.
   b. natural gas.   d. petroleum.

6. The process by which yeast cells produce alcohol from biomass materials is called
   a. combustion.   c. fermentation.
   b. electrolysis.   d. fusion.

7. Solar cells, or photovoltaic cells, are made of thin layers of the element
   a. carbon.   c. silicon.
   b. uranium.   d. hydrogen.

8. Which of the following is a problem associated with the use of nuclear power?
   a. possible radiation leaks
   b. storing radioactive wastes
   c. meltdown due to overheating
   d. all of these

True or False

If the statement is true, write "true." If it is false, change the underlined word or words to make the statement true.

1. In a nuclear <u>fission</u> reaction, two hydrogen nuclei combine to form a helium nucleus.

2. Large windmills <u>cannot</u> be used to generate electricity.

3. The "bullet" used to start a nuclear chain reaction is a <u>proton</u>.

4. The form of coal that is almost pure carbon is <u>lignite</u>.

5. The alcohol that is mixed with gasoline to produce gasohol is <u>ethanol</u>.

6. Most of the energy used in this country comes from <u>alternative energy sources</u>.

7. A backup heating system usually <u>is not</u> needed in a passive solar home.

Concept Mapping

Complete the following concept map for Section 21–1. Then construct a concept map for the entire chapter.

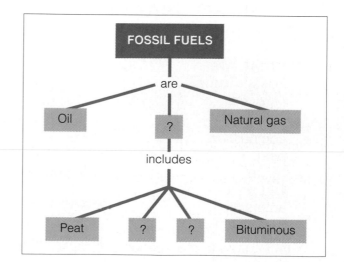

690

Concept Mastery

Discuss each of the following in a brief paragraph.

1. Discuss the advantages and disadvantages of solar cells.
2. Describe the four stages in the development of coal.
3. Describe how a nuclear fission reaction is controlled in a nuclear reactor.
4. Explain what is meant by a nuclear chain reaction.
5. Compare the benefits and risks of nuclear fission and nuclear fusion as a source of energy.

6. Trace the use of wind energy in the United States from 1860 to the present.
7. Describe two uses of biomass as a source of energy.
8. Explain why the use of geothermal energy, hydroelectric power, and tidal power is limited.

Critical Thinking and Problem Solving

Use the skills you have developed in this chapter to answer each of the following.

1. **Making calculations** The population of the United States is approximately 250 million people. For each person, approximately 35 kilograms of fossil fuels are consumed every day. How much fossil fuel is used in the United States every day? Every month? Every year?
2. **Making observations** Keep a list of the ways in which you use energy every day for a period of several days. Be sure to identify the source of each type of energy used. Are there any ways in which you could have reduced your use of energy?
3. **Making maps** Choose either geothermal energy or tidal power. Find out where in the world these energy resources are located. Identify these locations on a world map.
4. **Making predictions** Some states, such as Texas, Louisiana, and Alabama, depend on oil and natural gas reserves for much of their income. What do you think might happen to the economy of these states if the oil and natural gas reserves were used up? How do you think this could be prevented from happening?
5. **Interpreting diagrams** Describe what is happening in this diagram. What is this process called?

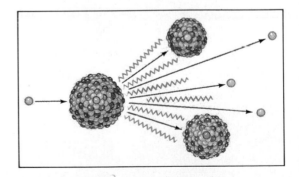

6. **Using the writing process** Write an essay explaining why you agree or disagree with the following statement: The United States should abandon the use of nuclear reactors as a source of energy and concentrate on developing alternative energy sources.

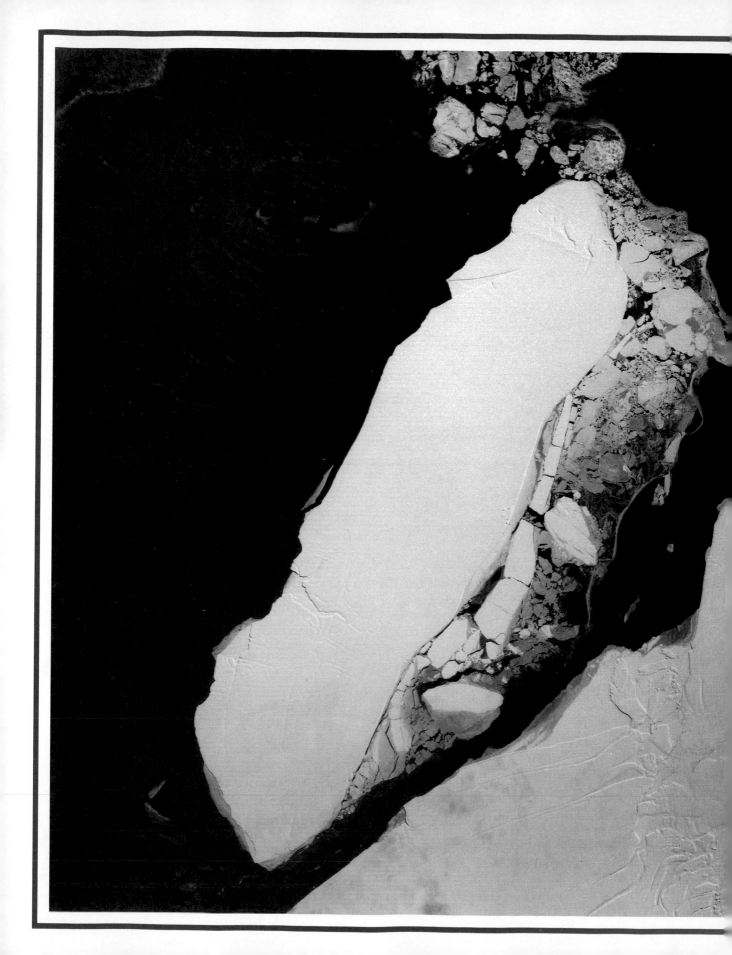

Earth's Nonliving Resources

Guide for Reading

After you read the following sections, you will be able to

22–1 Land and Soil Resources
- Identify ways in which people use land and soil resources.
- Define erosion and describe some methods of preventing erosion.

22–2 Water Resources
- Relate freshwater supplies to people's needs.

22–3 Mineral Resources
- Identify common metallic and nonmetallic minerals.

Like a ghostly floating island, a huge iceberg drifts through the polar ocean past the frozen coast of Antarctica. The floating island of ice—154 kilometers long, 35 kilometers wide, and 225 meters deep—broke away from Antarctica's Ross Ice Shelf in 1987. Before splitting up into three smaller pieces in 1990, the mountainous iceberg floated a distance of 2000 kilometers. Scientists tracking the iceberg estimated that it contained enough fresh water to provide everyone on Earth with two glasses of water a day for the next 1977 years!

A good deal of the Earth's freshwater supply is locked up in the ice at the North and South poles. Antarctica alone contains a huge amount of the world's ice. Might we someday be using this ice as a source of fresh water? Where does most of our drinking water come from today? You will find the answers to these questions as you read this chapter about the Earth's nonliving resources. You will also learn about some of the Earth's other nonliving resources—land, soil, and minerals.

Journal *Activity*

You and Your World Are you a "water waster"? In your journal, keep a record of all the ways in which you use water every day. Identify the ways in which you may be wasting water. Then make a list of ways in which you might be able to use less water every day. (No, skipping a shower or not brushing your teeth doesn't count!)

◀ *Icebergs are large chunks of ice that break off glaciers and drift into the oceans. Do you think icebergs may someday provide a source of fresh water?*

22–1 Land and Soil Resources

More than 5 billion people now inhabit the Earth. Everything people need to survive must come from the Earth itself. In fact, the Earth is like a giant storehouse of useful materials. Materials removed from the Earth and used by people are called **natural resources**. The fossil fuels—coal, oil, and natural gas—you read about in Chapter 1 are examples of the Earth's natural resources. Natural resources are the riches of the Earth. They provide a treasure chest of materials that improve our lives. And they are the inheritance we will leave to our children and grandchildren.

Scientists divide the Earth's natural resources into two groups. One group is the **nonrenewable resources**. These resources cannot be replaced by nature. Fossil fuels are nonrenewable resources. Once they are gone, they cannot be replaced. Minerals, such as copper and iron, are also nonrenewable resources. They are not replaced by nature. Mineral resources are discussed in Section 22–3.

The other group of natural resources is the **renewable resources**. Renewable resources can be replaced by nature. Wood is a renewable resource because forests can be replanted. Water is a renewable resource because it is constantly replaced by rain, snow, sleet, and hail. You will learn more about the Earth's water resources in the following section.

Figure 22–1 *All the natural resources humans need to survive—land, water, and minerals—come from the Earth. Is land a renewable or a nonrenewable resource?*

Soil, too, is a renewable resource because new soil is formed on the Earth every day. Soil formation, however, is an extremely slow process. Although land and soil resources are renewable, nature may take anywhere from 500 years to 1000 years to replace every 2.5 centimeters of topsoil that have been lost.

Land Use

One third of the Earth's surface—about 13 billion hectares—is covered by land. But only a portion of this land can be used for farming or for living space. All land is not suitable for all uses. **Land is used for cities, highways, forests, farms, and pastures.** And even though a growing population needs more and more land, it is a limited resource. As the American writer and humorist Mark Twain said about land, "They don't make it anymore."

Land is needed for building cities and towns to house the increasing human population. Land is also needed for industry and for farming. These needs must be carefully weighed and balanced. If too much land is used for cities, there may not be enough left for farms. But both uses are important.

An increasing population requires an increase in food production. The Earth's farmland must be used to its fullest potential. New and improved crop varieties must be developed. Better growing methods must be used to make existing farms more productive.

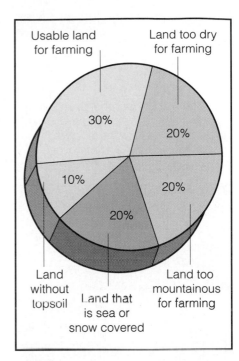

Figure 22–2 *Land is a valuable resource that is used for many purposes. What percentage of the Earth's land is used for farming?*

Figure 22–3 *Land that is too dry for farming may be irrigated or it may be used as grazing land for cattle. These pigs are enjoying a hearty barnyard meal. Where does the food used to feed pigs and other farm animals come from?*

Figure 22–4 *Nodules, or lumps, of nitrogen-fixing bacteria grow on the roots of soybean plants. How do farmers use crops such as clover to prevent depletion of nutrients from the soil?*

And land that is now unusable for farming must be made fertile. One way to do this is by **irrigation** (ihr-uh-GAY-shuhn). Irrigation is the process of supplying water to dry regions. As a result of irrigation, regions that do not have enough water for crops can be made suitable for farming.

Land is also needed for raising animals. Pigs, sheep, chickens, and cattle are renewable resources. But they must be fed. An enormous amount of farmland is used to grow food for animals. For example, more than 10 kilograms of grain are required to produce only 1 kilogram of beef from a steer! In fact, about 60 percent of all the grain grown in the world is used to feed livestock (farm animals). And land that is used as pasture or open range for grazing animals cannot be used to grow crops at all.

Land Management

If limited land resources are to be preserved, land use must be carefully planned and managed. Different land areas are best suited for different purposes. For example, some land areas are best for growing trees. Other land areas are best used as pastures for cattle and sheep. Areas that can produce the best crops should become farmland. Recreational areas should be carefully developed so as not to damage nearby farmlands and forests. Cities, towns, and factories should be built in areas where the least harm will be done to the environment. What do you think happens when cities are built without careful planning?

Even farming must be a planned activity. Crops use up nutrients (NOO-tree-uhnts) in the soil. Nutrients are chemical substances necessary for plant growth. When one type of crop is grown on the same land for too long, **depletion** may result. Depletion occurs when nutrients are removed from the soil. Corn, for example, removes nitrogen from the soil. Certain crops naturally put back nutrients that others remove. Crops such as clover and peanuts put nitrogen back into the soil. So farmers alternate crops on the same land each year. They may plant a nitrogen-using crop, such as corn, one year and a nitrogen-producing crop, such as clover, the next. This method of farming is called **crop rotation**.

Figure 22–5 *Two methods of preventing erosion are contour plowing (left) and strip cropping (right). What are two cover crops often used in strip cropping?*

Crop rotation keeps nutrients in the soil from being depleted. Why is this important?

Two other good land-management practices are **contour plowing** and **strip cropping**. Contour plowing involves planting crops across the face of a slope of land instead of up and down the slope. See Figure 22–5. In strip cropping, farmers plant strips of low cover crops between strips of other crops. Cover crops are crops that completely cover the soil. They help to hold down the soil between other crops. Hay and wheat are two common cover crops that are often planted between rows of corn.

Erosion

Growing crops is one of the most important uses of soil. Crops are grown in topsoil, which is the rich upper layer of soil. It can take anywhere from 200 to 400 years to form 1 centimeter of topsoil. In many areas, topsoil is being lost because of **erosion**. Erosion is the carrying off of soil by water or wind. Although erosion is a natural process, poor land-management practices can speed up its rate. Worldwide, topsoil is being lost up to ten times faster than new soil is being formed.

Both contour plowing and strip cropping can prevent erosion. Another method for preventing erosion is called **terracing**. Terracing is plowing a

Growing Plants With Nutrients

1. Obtain two plants that have recently sprouted in potting soil. Make sure the plants belong to the same species and have grown to about the same height.

2. Add some fertilizer to one plant. Do not add fertilizer to the other plant.

3. Observe the height of each plant every three days for at least two weeks. Record your observations.

Did the fertilizer affect plant growth? If so, in what ways? What was the reason for not adding fertilizer to one of the plants?

■ Were there any hidden factors that affected your results? If so, what were they? Design an experiment to eliminate those factors.

Figure 22–6 *To prevent soil erosion due to water running down the sides of a hill in Bali, the hill has been plowed into a series of level steps. What is this method of plowing called?*

slope into a series of level steps, or terraces, for planting. The use of terracing and contour plowing on slopes slows down the runoff of water after heavy rains or from melting snow. Both methods help prevent the water from rushing downhill and carrying away valuable topsoil.

To prevent erosion due to wind, farmers often plant windbreaks. Windbreaks are rows of trees planted between fields of crops. The trees act as a barrier to help prevent topsoil from being blown away by the wind.

Some regions are too dry for crops to be grown, but they can support grasslands. These grasslands have traditionally been used for grazing animals, such as cattle and sheep. If there are too many animals on the land, however, they may eat all the available grasses. This results in overgrazing the land. Overgrazing leaves the topsoil exposed to wind erosion. As a result of erosion caused by overgrazing, dry grasslands become deserts. This process is called **desertification** (dih-zert-ih-fih-KAY-shuhn). Desertification is taking place all over the world, even in parts of the United States. The United States Bureau of Land Management has warned that vast areas of land are currently in danger of desertification because of overgrazing.

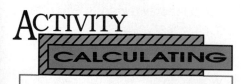

ACTIVITY

CALCULATING

Erosion Losses

It has been estimated that the Earth loses 1.8 billion kilograms of soil to erosion every year. How many kilograms of soil are lost in 5 years? In 10 years?

Figure 22–7 *A woman in Zimbabwe, Africa, carries a load of firewood. Cutting down trees for firewood speeds up soil erosion and may lead to desertification.*

Land and Soil Reclamation

Sometimes valuable land resources must be disturbed to get at resources of fossil fuels or minerals below the surface. Coal just beneath the surface of the land often can be removed only by strip mining. In strip mining, huge power shovels dig up the land above the coal and remove the coal. But this does not necessarily mean that the land must be destroyed forever. It may be possible for the land to be reclaimed, or restored to its original condition.

Land reclamation involves several steps. First, the valuable topsoil is carefully removed and stored. Then the less valuable layers of soil beneath the topsoil are stripped away. The coal, which is now exposed, is removed and shipped to coal-processing plants. During this procedure, the disturbed soil must be protected from erosion, and water in the area must be monitored to make sure it does not become chemically polluted. After all the coal has been mined, the layers of soil and the topsoil are put back in place. The final step in land reclamation is seeding and planting the land. Although strip mining is not as destructive as it once was, it still has harmful effects on the land. What do you think some of these effects are?

The Ethics of Land Use

Often, making decisions about land use is not easy. In his book *The Sand County Almanac,* published in the 1940s, Aldo Leopold pointed out the need for a land ethic. An ethic is a system of values by which decisions are made and on which actions are based. Leopold called for an ethic by which decisions about land use are based on the ecological value of land resources. What do you think about this idea?

Figure 22-8 *Mining coal just beneath the surface of the land causes ugly scars on the land. But the land can be reclaimed and returned to its natural beauty. What is this kind of coal mining called?*

22-1 Section Review

1. What are some ways in which people use land and soil resources?
2. What is the difference between renewable and nonrenewable resources? Name at least two nonrenewable and two renewable resources.
3. Describe two farming methods that help prevent soil erosion due to water runoff.
4. Why is it important to prevent overgrazing of grasslands?

Critical Thinking—*Making Predictions*
5. Predict how an increase in population will affect land use in the future.

Guide for Reading

Focus on this question as you read.

▶ *Why is it important to preserve supplies of fresh water?*

22-2 Water Resources

"Water, water everywhere" is probably the first thought that comes to mind when you look at a photograph of the Earth from space. As the science fiction writer Arthur C. Clarke has pointed out, although our planet is called Earth, it might just as well be called Water. In fact, there are billions of liters of water above, on, and in the Earth! The problem is that only a small percentage of this vast water resource is available for use by people. **Even though water is a renewable resource, there is a limited supply of fresh water.** Most of the Earth's water—97 percent—is in the oceans. But ocean water cannot be used for drinking, irrigation, or industrial processes. Do you know why? You are correct if you said because it is too salty.

Uses of Water

In the United States, billions of liters of water are used every day. The chart in Figure 22–10 shows the estimated daily use of water for an average American family of four. Each person drinks about 1.5 liters of water per day. People also need water for other uses, such as bathing, cooking, and cleaning. It has been estimated that each person in the United States uses more than 260 liters of water daily! Based on this estimate, what would be the total amount of water used by your class in one year?

In the United States, industry uses more than 60 billion liters of water every day. And it takes more than 375 billion liters of water per day to irrigate farmlands in the southern and western United States. Where do you think this water comes from?

Figure 22–9 *Without water, life on Earth would be impossible. But most of the Earth's water is in the oceans. And ocean water is too salty to be used for drinking or for irrigation.*

Activity Bank

Too Much, Too Little, or Just Right?, p. 784

Figure 22–10 *According to the graph, about how much water does a family of four use for bathing every day?*

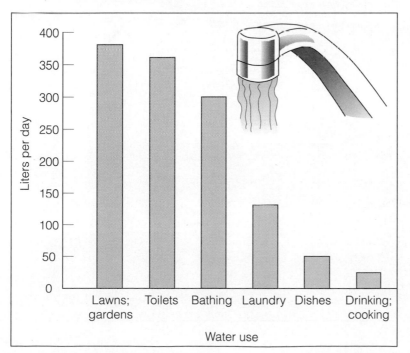
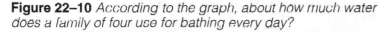

The Water Cycle

The Earth's supply of fresh water is constantly being renewed by means of the **water cycle**. A cycle is a continuous, repeating chain of events. The water cycle is the movement of water from the Earth's surface to the atmosphere (the envelope of air surrounding the Earth) and back to the surface. Three basic steps make up the water cycle. Refer to the diagram in Figure 22–11 as you read the description that follows.

In the first step of the water cycle, water on the Earth's surface is heated by the sun and evaporates (changes from a liquid to a gas). This gas, or water vapor, then rises into the atmosphere. As water vapor rises into the upper atmosphere, the vapor cools, condenses (changes from a gas to a liquid), and forms clouds. This is the second step of the water cycle. During the third step of the water cycle, the water falls back to the surface of the Earth as precipitation—rain, snow, sleet, or hail. Most precipitation falls directly into oceans, lakes, rivers,

Figure 22–11 *The water cycle constantly renews Earth's supply of fresh water. What happens to the water that falls to Earth as precipitation?*

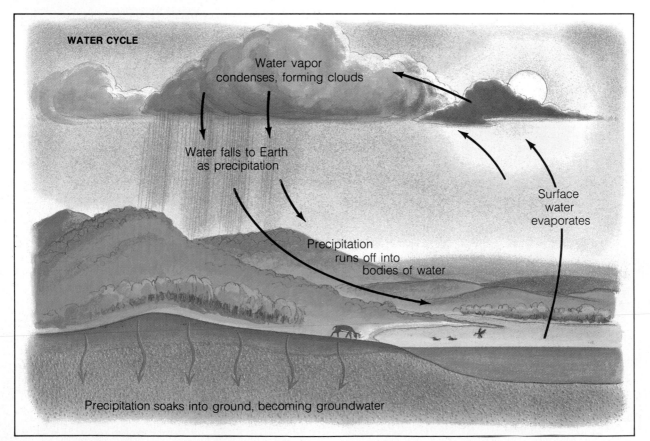

WATER CYCLE

Water vapor condenses, forming clouds

Water falls to Earth as precipitation

Precipitation runs off into bodies of water

Surface water evaporates

Precipitation soaks into ground, becoming groundwater

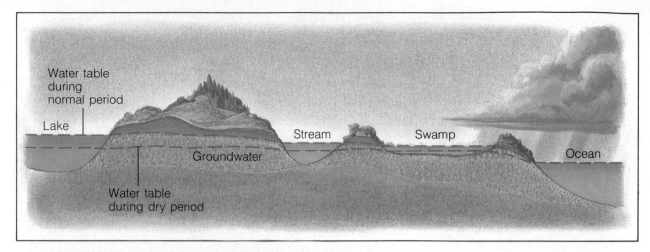

Figure 22–12 *Water that is stored in the soil is called groundwater. The level below which the soil is soaked with water is called the water table. As you can see in the diagram, the water table follows the shape of the land.*

and streams. Some precipitation falls onto the land and runs off into these bodies of water. Eventually, the water returns to the atmosphere through evaporation, and the cycle continues.

Sources of Fresh Water

Most of the Earth's water resources are in oceans, lakes, rivers, and streams. Water is also found in the soil as **groundwater** and frozen as ice in glaciers and polar icecaps. As you know, water in the oceans is too salty to be used. And the ice in glaciers is not directly available. So the main sources of fresh water for human use are groundwater, freshwater lakes, and rivers.

More than 300 billion liters of groundwater are taken out of the ground daily in this country, mostly for use on farms and in factories. Half of the drinking water in the United States comes from groundwater. Although the United States has a plentiful supply of groundwater, it takes hundreds of years for large amounts of groundwater to accumulate. In many parts of the country, groundwater is being used up faster than it is being replaced. As a result, the level of groundwater is dropping and lakes and rivers may eventually dry up. Wells must be drilled deeper and deeper as the groundwater level drops. Where can we turn for new sources of fresh water?

Figure 22–13 *A severe drought, or dry period, may cause reservoirs and other sources of fresh water to dry up.*

Using reference materials in the library, find out what each term means.

New Sources of Fresh Water

An abundant supply of fresh water can be made available by **desalination** (dee-sal-uh-NAY-shuhn) of ocean water. Desalination is the process by which salt is removed from ocean water. (The word salt comes from the Latin word *sal*.) Some cities in the United States, such as Key West, Florida, and Freeport, Texas, have already built desalination plants. The desalination plants supply these cities with more than 20 million liters of fresh water daily. Other plants are planned for California, which has a serious shortage of fresh water.

What about the fresh water locked in the ice of glaciers? Is there any way to obtain this water for human use? In fact, some scientists have suggested that it might be possible to tow icebergs from around the poles to large coastal cities in the United States. Once there, the icebergs could be mined for fresh water. Scientists are not sure, however, what effects such a project might have on the environment.

In order to have enough usable fresh water in the future, harmful substances and dangerous organisms must be removed from our water supplies. The problem of water pollution is discussed in detail in Chapter 23. In addition, everyone must learn to use our limited sources of fresh water wisely. You will learn more about the importance of safeguarding our water resources in Chapter 24.

Some Words About Water

The following terms can be used to describe water:
- water quality
- fresh water
- salt water
- brackish water
- hard water
- soft water
- polluted water
- purified water

Figure 22–14 *Yuma, Arizona, in the middle of a desert, gets some of its fresh water from a desalination plant. Most of the Earth's fresh water is frozen in glaciers.*

PROBLEM Solving

Oil in the Soil

What do you think of when you hear the words oil spill? You probably have an image of a large black oil slick floating on the surface of the ocean or of beaches covered with gooey tar. Most oil spills do fit these descriptions. But there is another kind of oil spill that can be just as damaging although it usually receives little or no publicity. This type of oil spill occurs underground.

Unlike dramatic above-ground oil spills, underground oil spills are usually slow leaks that may take years to be noticed. Most underground spills come from leaks in underground petroleum storage tanks, gas station tanks, or home-heating-oil tanks. Some underground oil spills have been known to exist for years, even decades. But it is only recently that the danger of these spills has been recognized.

Making Inferences

1. What do you think is the danger of underground oil spills? (*Hint:* Where does most of our drinking water come from?)

2. Do you think underground oil spills are more difficult to clean up than above-ground oil spills?

22–2 Section Review

1. Why might it be necessary to find new sources of fresh water?
2. About how much water does each person in the United States use daily?
3. What is a cycle? Trace the sequence of steps in the water cycle.
4. What are the main sources of fresh water now used by people? What are some possible new sources of fresh water?

Connection—*You and Your World*

5. Using Figure 22–10, estimate the amount of water you use daily. Suppose a water shortage existed in your region and people were asked to decrease their use of water by 25 percent. How would you cut back on your water use?

22–3 Mineral Resources

Since the dawn of human civilization, people have used materials from the Earth to make tools. Archaeologists have uncovered primitive tools from the Stone Age, the Iron Age, and the Bronze Age. Even the names given to these periods in human history reflect the importance of toolmaking and of the materials used to make the tools. Many of these materials are even more important in today's modern technological society.

In this textbook, a **mineral** is defined as a naturally occurring chemical substance found in soil or rocks. Today, minerals are used to make a variety of products, from aluminum cans to silver jewelry. Minerals are nonrenewable resources. Why do you think minerals are considered nonrenewable resources?

Minerals are either metallic or nonmetallic. **Metallic minerals include copper, iron, and aluminum. Nonmetallic minerals include quartz, limestone, and sulfur.** The chart in Figure 22–15 lists some common metallic and nonmetallic minerals. Both metallic and nonmetallic minerals are important natural resources.

Ores

To obtain a useful mineral, the mineral must be mined, or removed from the Earth. Deposits of

Figure 22–15 *The chart lists some important metallic and nonmetallic minerals. What is the mineral potash used for?*

SOME IMPORTANT MINERAL RESOURCES			
Nonmetallic		**Metallic**	
Mineral	**Use**	**Mineral**	**Use**
Calcite	Cement	Hematite	Cast iron
Quartz	Watches	Bauxite	Aluminum cans
Sulfur	Chemicals	Argentite	Silver jewelry
Halite	Salt	Cuprite	Copper wire
Potash	Fertilizer	Rutile	Titanium aircraft parts
Clay	Brick	Wolframite	Tungsten steel

minerals that can be mined at a profit are called **ores**. If the percentage of a mineral in an ore is high, the ore is called a high-grade ore. If the percentage of the mineral is low, the ore is called a low-grade ore. Ores are found all over the Earth. Do you know of any ores that are mined in your state?

The Earth's crust is a storehouse of mineral riches. Iron is the most widely used metal extracted from metallic ores. Other elements, including chromium, nickel, and carbon, can be added to iron to produce steel. Steel is an **alloy**, or a substance made of two or more metals. By combining various amounts of chromium, nickel, and carbon with iron, different alloys of steel with different properties can be made. Chromium is added in the steelmaking process to provide resistance to rusting. A low percentage of carbon results in very soft steel, such as that used in paper clips.

Other metals removed from metallic ores include copper, which is used in electric wires, and aluminum, which is used in cans. Gold and silver, used in jewelry, are also found in metallic ores. What other metals do you use in your daily life?

Figure 22–16 *Simple tools made of copper were used by the people of Peru thousands of years ago. Where did they obtain the copper to make the tools?*

Mining and Processing Ores

Once mineral deposits have been located, they must be mined. Unfortunately, the only practical way to obtain most minerals—especially from low-grade ores—is through open-pit mining. And open-pit mining can have disastrous effects on land and groundwater resources. You will learn more about

Figure 22–17 *Copper, which is obtained from open-pit mines, is today used to make wire, pipes, and nails. One common source of copper is the mineral bornite.*

Figure 22–18 *Potato-sized nodules of the mineral manganese are found on the ocean floor.*

the problems associated with open-pit mining, or strip mining, in Chapter 23.

Mining the ore is only the first step in obtaining a useful mineral. To extract the mineral from the ore, impurities in the ore are removed. A purified mineral remains. Then the mineral is processed so that it can be sent to manufacturing plants in a usable form. At the manufacturing plant, the mineral is used to make the final product.

Mining the Oceans

The minerals in the Earth's crust have been formed over millions, or even billions, of years. The Earth contains only a limited amount of the minerals used today. The mining of minerals cannot continue at its present rate or we will run out of minerals. What is the answer to this dilemma? One answer is to recycle, or reuse, minerals. Another is to find other materials to take their place in the products we use. You will learn more about these options in Chapter 24.

Another possibility is to search for minerals in the last unexplored place on Earth—the ocean floor. Deposits of manganese, nickel, cobalt, and perhaps copper have already been located on the ocean floor. If these deposits can be mined economically, they may provide a valuable new source of mineral resources.

ACTIVITY

DOING

From the Earth

Many of the items you use every day are made from mineral resources. All mineral resources come from the Earth's crust or oceans.

1. List all the items in your classroom that are made from metallic or nonmetallic mineral resources.

2. Draw a floor plan of the classroom showing where each item you identified is located. Use different symbols to identify the metallic and nonmetallic items.

3. Identify the metallic and nonmetallic mineral resources that were used to make each item.

22–3 Section Review

1. Name three metallic and three nonmetallic minerals.
2. What is the difference between an ore and an alloy?
3. Trace the sequence of steps involved in mining and processing an ore.
4. What are some minerals that might someday be mined from the ocean floor?

Connection—*Life Science*

5. What are some ways in which fishes and other living things in the ocean might be affected by large-scale mining of the ocean floor?

Washing Away History

Not all erosion takes place on farmland or grazing land. Today, the United States is in danger of losing 90 percent of its coastline to erosion caused by ocean waves. One of the most visible victims of this threatened erosion is the historic 110-year-old Cape Hatteras Lighthouse located on the Outer Banks of North Carolina. The lighthouse, which was built in 1870, once stood at a safe distance of 450 meters from the pounding surf. Today the distance has shrunk to 90 meters. One big Atlantic storm could wash the lighthouse into the sea!

What can be done to save the Cape Hatteras Lighthouse? Geologists, engineers, and environmentalists disagree on the answer. The National Park Service has approved a suggestion to move the lighthouse back to a safe distance from the ocean. The U.S. Army Corps of Engineers has come up with a plan to build a series of protective structures around the lighthouse. Some environmental groups, however, are in favor of letting nature takes its course and sacrificing the lighthouse to the sea. But it may not be just the lighthouse that is sacrificed. In addition to the lighthouse, the fate of a nearby wildlife refuge as well as North Carolina's profitable tourist industry are at stake. What course of action would you choose?

Groin

Groin

Sand

Vegetation

Laboratory Investigation

Erosion by Raindrops

Problem

How can raindrops splashing against bare soil cause erosion?

Materials *(per group)*

2 petri dishes	meterstick
silt	medicine dropper
2 sheets of paper	sod

Procedure 🧪 👁

1. Fill one petri dish with silt to a depth of about 1 cm. Make sure the surface of the silt is smooth and level.

2. Place the petri dish in the center of a large sheet of paper.

3. Hold the meterstick next to the petri dish. Using the medicine dropper, allow a drop of water to fall from a height of 1 meter onto the surface of the silt. Observe what happens to the silt. **CAUTION:** *Wear your safety goggles.*

4. Measure the greatest distance in centimeters that the silt splashed from the dish. Record the distance in a data table.

5. Repeat steps 3 and 4 two more times. Calculate the average distance the silt splashed from the dish. Record the average distance in the data table.

6. Place a small piece of sod in the second petri dish. Repeat steps 2 through 5.

Observations

1. What happened to the silt in the petri dish when it was hit by a water drop? What happened to the sod?

2. What was the average splash distance from the dish with the silt? From the dish with the sod?

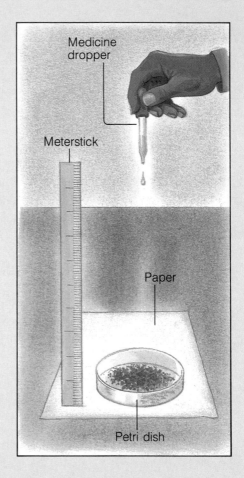

Medicine dropper

Meterstick

Paper

Petri dish

Analysis and Conclusions

1. How did using sod instead of silt affect the splash distance? Explain.

2. Erosion caused by raindrops striking bare soil is called splash erosion. Why is this an appropriate name for this type of erosion?

3. Would overgrazing of grasslands increase or decrease the likelihood of splash erosion? Explain.

4. **On Your Own** How are different types of soil affected by splash erosion? Repeat this investigation using different types of soil, such as coarse sand, clay, fine gravel, and potting soil. Compare your results with the results of this investigation.

Study Guide

Summarizing Key Concepts

22–1 Land and Soil Resources

▲ Materials removed from the Earth and used by people are called natural resources.

▲ Scientists divide natural resources into two groups: renewable resources and nonrenewable resources.

▲ Renewable resources can be replaced by nature, whereas nonrenewable resources cannot.

▲ Although land and soil are renewable resources, anywhere from decades to millions of years are required to replace land and soil that have been lost.

▲ Land use must be carefully planned and managed.

▲ Strip cropping, contour plowing, terracing, and windbreaks can help prevent soil erosion.

▲ Depletion of nutrients in the soil can be prevented by crop rotation.

▲ Land that has been damaged by strip mining may be reclaimed, or restored to its original condition.

22–2 Water Resources

▲ Although water is a renewable resource, there is a limited supply of fresh water.

▲ The Earth's supply of fresh water is constantly being renewed by means of the water cycle.

▲ The main sources of fresh water are groundwater, freshwater lakes, and rivers.

▲ Half the drinking water in the United States comes from groundwater.

▲ Fresh water can be produced from ocean water by the process of desalination.

22–3 Mineral Resources

▲ A mineral is a natural substance found in soil or rocks.

▲ Deposits of minerals that can be profitably mined are called ores.

▲ An alloy is a substance that combines two or more metals.

▲ It may be possible to obtain certain minerals from deposits located on the ocean floor.

Reviewing Key Terms

Define each term in a complete sentence.

22–1 Land and Soil Resources
natural resource
nonrenewable resource
renewable resource
irrigation
depletion
crop rotation
contour plowing
strip cropping

erosion
terracing
desertification

22–2 Water Resources
water cycle
groundwater
desalination

22–3 Mineral Resources
mineral
ore
alloy

691

Chapter Review

Content Review

Multiple Choice

Choose the letter of the answer that best completes each statement.

1. Which of the following is a nonrenewable resource?
   - a. copper
   - b. water
   - c. soil
   - d. wood
2. Plowing the land across the face of a slope is called
   - a. terracing.
   - b. contour plowing.
   - c. crop rotation.
   - d. strip cropping.
3. A natural substance found in soil or rocks is called a(an)
   - a. crop.
   - b. mineral.
   - c. alloy.
   - d. strip mine.
4. Which of the following is a metallic mineral?
   - a. sulfur
   - b. copper
   - c. quartz
   - d. limestone
5. In the United States, the percentage of drinking water supplied by groundwater is
   - a. 25 percent.
   - b. 50 percent.
   - c. 75 percent.
   - d. 100 percent.
6. The process by which nutrients are removed from the soil is called
   - a. erosion.
   - b. crop rotation.
   - c. depletion.
   - d. desertification.
7. Most of the Earth's water is found in
   - a. rivers.
   - b. groundwater.
   - c. lakes.
   - d. oceans.
8. Erosion due to wind can be prevented by
   - a. irrigation.
   - b. windbreaks.
   - c. terracing.
   - d. overgrazing.
9. The process by which salt is removed from ocean water is called
   - a. desalination.
   - b. cloud seeding.
   - c. purification.
   - d. irrigation.

True or False

If the statement is true, write "true." If it is false, change the underlined word or words to make the statement true.

1. <u>Renewable</u> resources cannot be replaced once they are used up.
2. Rock deposits that contain minerals mined at a profit are called <u>ores</u>.
3. Wood, soil, and water are examples of <u>nonrenewable</u> resources.
4. Restoring the land to its original condition after resources have been mined is called land <u>management</u>.
5. The first step of the water cycle involves <u>evaporation</u>.
6. The process by which grasslands are turned into deserts as a result of wind erosion is called <u>terracing</u>.

Concept Mapping

Complete the following concept map for Section 22–1. Then construct a concept map for the entire chapter.

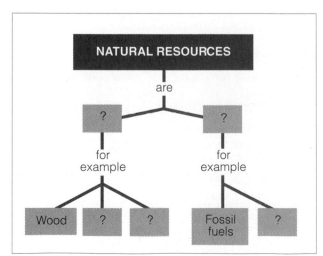

Concept Mastery

Discuss each of the following in a brief paragraph.

1. In what ways does an increase in population affect land and water resources?
2. Compare renewable and nonrenewable natural resources. Give at least two examples of each.
3. Identify and describe three methods of good land management used by farmers to protect soil resources.
4. Describe the basic steps that make up the water cycle.
5. What is strip mining? Describe the process of land reclamation involved in strip mining.
6. Explain the relationship among overgrazing, erosion, and desertification.

Critical Thinking and Problem Solving

Use the skills you have developed in this chapter to answer each of the following.

1. **Interpreting a chart** The pie chart shows how land that is available to grow crops in the United States is currently being used. What is the total land area available to grow crops? Of that total, how much land is currently being used as farmland? What percentage is that of the total? What other uses are shown on the chart? What percentage of the total available land area do these uses together represent?

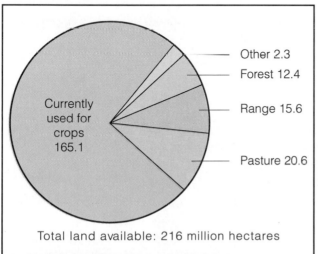

Total land available: 216 million hectares

Other 2.3
Forest 12.4
Range 15.6
Pasture 20.6
Currently used for crops 165.1

2. **Applying concepts** Why is it an advantage for a farmer to use good land-management methods?

3. **Making a graph** From AD 650 to AD 1650 the Earth's population doubled from 250 million to 500 million people. This doubling of the Earth's population took 1000 years. But now the Earth's population doubles about every 33 years. The population of the Earth in 1990 was 5 billion people. Assuming that the growth rate does not change, determine the Earth's population for the years 2023, 2056, and 2089. Graph your results. How much greater will the Earth's population be 100 years from now? Relate this population increase to our use of natural resources.

4. **Developing a model** Plan a "new town" to replace the town you live in. Consider the placement of factories, shopping malls, parks and recreational facilities, housing developments, farms, and roads. Draw a map of your new town and explain why you located each facility where you did.

5. **Using the writing process** A land developer has recently bought a large area of productive farmland near your town. The developer plans to convert the land into a low-rent housing development. Write an article for your local newspaper explaining why you think this use of the land will or will not be good for the town.

Pollution

Guide for Reading

After you read the following sections, you will be able to

23–1 What Is Pollution?
- ■ Define pollution and give some examples of it.

23–2 Land Pollution
- ■ Describe how obtaining and using energy resources can cause land pollution.

23–3 Air Pollution
- ■ Describe how using fossil fuel resources can cause air pollution.

23–4 Water Pollution
- ■ Describe how obtaining and using certain energy resources can cause water pollution.
- ■ Discuss other sources of water pollution.

23–5 What Can Be Done About Pollution?
- ■ Discuss some ways to reduce pollution.

The first sign of danger came with the southeast wind. Instruments at a Swedish nuclear power plant detected twice as much radioactivity in the atmosphere as usual on April 28, 1986. At first the Swedes feared a malfunction in their own power plant. But it soon became apparent that the excess radioactivity was being carried by winds from the Soviet Union.

An explosion and fire at the Chernobyl nuclear power plant in the Ukraine had released a huge cloud of radioactive dust. The cloud was blown by winds across Poland and into Scandinavia. Later the winds shifted and blew the deadly cloud over Switzerland and Italy. Everywhere the cloud was blown, people were warned to avoid contaminated water, vegetables, and milk.

The accident at Chernobyl undoubtedly will have an effect on the further development of nuclear power. Once thought to be the energy source of the future, nuclear power is now viewed with skepticism by many people. Our society could not exist without sources of energy. But, as we must keep in mind, using energy presents certain problems. In this chapter you will learn about some of these problems—their causes and solutions.

Journal *Activity*

You and Your World Have you seen any examples of pollution in your neighborhood? If so, was it litter, smog, polluted water, or some other type of pollution? In your journal, draw a picture of the kind of pollution you observed. Describe the pollution and what you think could be done to prevent it.

 The damage caused by the explosion and fire at the Chernobyl nuclear power plant can be seen in the center of this photograph.

23–1 What Is Pollution?

Of all the planets in our solar system, only Earth (as far as we know) is home to humans and other living things. Earth provides everything—air, water, food, energy—we need to survive. The environment seems to contain such an abundance of the natural resources needed by humans and other living things that it is hard to imagine ever being without them. Yet that is just what might happen if we are not careful. Despite the richness of Earth's natural resources, a delicate balance between plenty and scarcity exists in our environment.

The balance of the environment can be upset by the way in which humans obtain and use natural resources. If we use renewable resources faster than they can be replaced, the balance will be upset. If we quickly consume nonrenewable resources, which cannot be replaced, the balance will be upset. And if we damage one resource in the process of obtaining or using another resource, the balance will be upset. It is this last problem—the problem of **pollution**—that is the focus of attention in this chapter.

Figure 23–1 *Keeping our environment beautiful is something everyone favors (right). Yet litter discarded by careless people can quickly upset the balance of the environment (left). How can littering be prevented?*

Pollution has become a household word. But what exactly is pollution? Pollution is the release into the environment of substances that change the environment for the worse. Most pollution is the result of human activities. In obtaining and using the natural resources we depend on, we produce pollutants. As one ecologist (a person who studies the relationships among living things and their environment) has written, pollutants are the "normal byproducts of people."

The Trail of Pollution

To better understand the process of pollution, consider a can of soda. To obtain the aluminum to make the can, ore containing aluminum is dug out of the ground. This digging scars the land. Later, in various factory processes, chemicals are used to remove the aluminum from the ore. Any remaining chemicals and impurities are often washed away with water. The waste water is then discarded—and may end up in a river or a stream. The chemicals, so useful in the factory, become pollutants in the water.

Next, the purified aluminum is sent to a manufacturing plant to be turned into a can. Energy is needed to make the can. So a fuel such as coal or oil is burned to provide the energy. As a result of burning fuel, smoke, soot, and gases are released as pollutants into the air. Making the soda that goes into the can also produces land, air, and water pollutants.

Finally, the can of soda may be transported to a supermarket by a truck that burns gasoline and releases air pollutants. But the trail of pollution does not end at the market. Eventually, the can of soda ends up in the hands of a consumer. That person drinks the soda and may then carelessly toss the empty can into the gutter at the side of a road. There it becomes part of an unsightly collection of cans, bottles, plastic bags, old newspapers, and all sorts of other trash. In other words, it becomes litter! This litter is more than an eyesore. It is a danger to wildlife, and it can contribute to the poisoning of our soil and water resources.

ACTIVITY DISCOVERING

A Pollution Survey

Conduct a survey of the area in which you live to determine the extent of land, air, and water pollution.

1. Draw a map of the area. Identify major landmarks, streets, roads, rivers, streams, lakes, and factories.

2. Label the directions north, south, east, and west on the map.

3. Mark any polluted areas and include a key using a different symbol for each type of pollution. Which sections of the area were most polluted? With which types of pollution?

■ What was the cause of pollution in each area you identified?

Figure 23–2 *The trail of pollution leads from waste water discharged into a stream to an overflowing garbage can on a city street.*

Sources and Solutions

As the example of the soda can illustrates, pollution can be thought of as the damage done to one resource by our use of other resources. Although pollution cannot be blamed entirely on our use of energy resources, a great amount of pollution is tied directly to energy use. Our heavy dependence on fossil fuels (coal, oil, and natural gas) has made pollution a major concern in the last several decades. The activities involved in obtaining and using fossil fuels have led to serious land, air, and water pollution.

There is no easy answer to the problem of pollution. Fortunately, there are ways to avoid polluting the environment. Maintaining the balance of the environment does not necessarily mean we must abandon all activities that threaten the balance. Rather, the solution may involve new ways to regulate and reuse materials so that they become new resources. Let's now examine more closely the three main types of pollution—land, air, and water pollution—and the ways in which people are fighting them.

23–2 Land Pollution

In Chapter 21, you learned about many different types of energy resources: fossil fuels, solar energy, wind and water energy, and nuclear energy, as well as various alternative energy resources. Solar, wind, water, and alternative resources together account for only 5 percent of the energy used by people. Most of our energy (about 90 percent) comes from fossil fuels. The remaining 5 percent of the energy we use comes from nuclear power plants. **Obtaining and using certain energy resources—fossil fuels and nuclear energy—can pollute the land.**

The use of coal as a fuel was an important step in the industrialization of the United States. Unfortunately, the environment has often paid heavily for our use of coal. Coal near the surface of the ground is obtained by the process of strip mining. As you learned in Chapter 22, strip mines are gouged out of the surface of the land. This process badly damages the land. In addition to scarring the landscape, strip mining also causes land and soil pollution.

During the strip-mining process, fertile topsoil is buried under tons of rock. When the rock is exposed to precipitation (rain, snow, sleet, and hail), acids

Guide for Reading

Focus on these questions as you read.

▶ *How is our use of energy resources related to the problem of land pollution?*

▶ *What are solid wastes, and where do they come from?*

and other dangerous chemicals may be washed out of the rock by rainwater. The acids and chemicals then seep into the ground, polluting the land and soil.

Hazardous Wastes

Strip mining is just one example of how using energy resources can pollute the land. Another example involves the wastes produced by factories. Wastes from factories may pollute the land with toxic, or poisonous, chemicals. These toxic chemicals are called **hazardous wastes.** Hazardous wastes are any wastes that can cause death or serious damage to human health.

Factories that produce fuels and petrochemicals from petroleum are the major sources of hazardous wastes. When improperly stored in barrels buried in waste dumps, hazardous wastes can seep into the soil and cause land pollution. Cleaning up wastes that were improperly disposed of in the past is a serious problem today.

There are several possible solutions to the management of hazardous wastes. The best way to solve the problem of hazardous wastes, of course, is to produce less of them. In some cases, it might be possible for industry to reuse certain hazardous wastes. Other wastes might be chemically treated to change the toxic substances they contain into nontoxic

Figure 23–3 *When hazardous wastes are not properly disposed of, toxic chemicals may leak into the environment. Cleaning up these wastes is difficult, dangerous, and expensive.*

substances before disposing of them. But chemical treatment of hazardous wastes is usually expensive. Most hazardous wastes wind up buried deep underground, where they are a potential source of land pollution.

Radioactive Wastes

Perhaps the most threatening form of land pollution today involves the disposal of **radioactive wastes.** Radioactive wastes are the wastes produced as a result of the production of energy in nuclear power plants. Radioactive wastes are classified as either high-level or low-level wastes.

High-level wastes are primarily the used fuel rods from a nuclear reactor. Low-level wastes are, by definition, any radioactive wastes that are not high-level wastes. Low-level wastes may include contaminated clothing worn by the power-plant workers or contaminated equipment used in the power plant.

Low-level wastes have relatively short half-lives. The half-life of a radioactive substance is the time it takes for half the substance to decay, or change into a nonradioactive substance. Low-level wastes decay quickly. The disposal of these wastes usually does not cause major land-pollution problems. When properly stored, the wastes can be isolated from the environment until they are no longer radioactive.

High-level wastes, however, may have half-lives of 10,000 years or more. Isolating these wastes from the environment for that length of time is practically impossible. In the past, a common practice was to seal high-level wastes in concrete or glass containers and then bury the containers deep underground. The problem with this procedure is that the containers may eventually corrode or leak, allowing the radioactive wastes to escape and pollute the land.

Recently, several alternative solutions for the disposal of high-level wastes have been suggested. These include geologic disposal, or disposal deep in the Earth. For example, wastes can be buried in rock formations that are not subject to movement or in salt mines. Disposal in deep ocean beds is another alternative. Some scientists have even suggested that it might be possible to shoot rockets carrying high-level wastes into the sun. Finding a way to dispose of

Figure 23–4 High-level radioactive wastes from nuclear reactors are buried in special containers (top). Some low-level wastes are the result of beneficial nuclear medicine. In Brazil, part of a radiotherapy machine from a clinic was illegally dumped in a junk yard. Several people died after handling the exposed radioactive material. Here you see their lead coffins (bottom). A technician monitors the area for excess radiation.

high-level radioactive wastes safely is one of the most important environmental issues facing us at this time.

Solid Wastes

Americans produce about 11 billion tons of solid wastes every year. **Solid wastes are useless, unwanted, or discarded materials. They include agricultural wastes, commercial and industrial wastes, and household wastes.** Another word for solid wastes is garbage. The solid wastes found in a garbage dump may include old newspapers and other paper products, glass bottles, aluminum cans, rubber and plastics, discarded food, and yard wastes.

Mountains of garbage in solid-waste dumps once surrounded many cities. Solid-waste dumps are offensive to the eyes as well as to the nose! One way to deal with solid-waste dumps is to cover open dumps with thick layers of soil. In 1976, the United States Congress prohibited open dumps. They ruled that all existing open dumps were to be converted to **sanitary landfills.** In a sanitary landfill, all garbage is compacted, or packed into the smallest possible space. And the garbage is covered at least once a day with a layer of soil. No hazardous wastes are allowed to be dumped in a sanitary landfill. One of the advantages of sanitary landfills is that once they are filled to capacity, they can be landscaped and used as parks, golf courses, and other recreational facilities.

Sanitary landfills can still pose problems, however. Wastes can ooze out of landfills and pollute the surrounding soil. And although sanitary landfills are not supposed to be used for hazardous wastes, household wastes often include pesticides, cleaning materials, paint and paint thinners, and other toxic chemicals.

Another problem with sanitary landfills is that when compacted garbage begins to decompose, or break down, methane gas is produced. Methane gas burns easily and is therefore a fire hazard. A number of landfill fires have smoldered underground for years, and a few landfills have exploded. This problem can be solved by installing a "gas well" in a landfill. In this way, the methane gas can be removed and used as a fuel.

ACTIVITY
DISCOVERING

Reducing Packaging Waste

Many of the foods you eat come in packages that you throw away every day. Packaging accounts for one third of all the solid wastes in landfills. Suppose that you could make your own lunch. How could you reduce the amount of packaging waste?

1. Pack an imaginary brown-bag lunch using only disposable, single-serving containers. You might include a container of milk, a sandwich, a bag of potato chips, and a cup of yogurt. Also include a straw, a plastic spoon, and a paper napkin.

2. Pack the same brown-bag lunch, but this time use only reusable containers. Include a metal spoon and a cloth napkin.

3. Compare the amount of packaging waste you would throw away for each lunch. Which lunch would be easier to prepare? To clean up? Which do you think would cost more per serving?

■ Considering all the factors involved, which lunch would you be more likely to pack? Why?

Figure 23–5 *Solid wastes are disposed of in a sanitary landfill (left). Shea Stadium in New York City is one of many recreational facilities around the country built on the site of a sanitary landfill (right).*

But the most serious problem with sanitary landfills may be finding a place to put them. At present, sanitary landfills cannot handle more than a fraction of the solid wastes produced in this country. A city of a million people can produce enough garbage to fill a football stadium in just a year! Most residents probably would not be happy with a landfill nearby. So finding sites to build new sanitary landfills is difficult.

Alternatives to sanitary landfills include ocean dumping, burning, and recycling. At one time, solid wastes were commonly towed offshore and dumped into the ocean. Even today, about 50 million tons of wastes are dumped into the oceans every year. Ocean dumping often results in washed-up debris on beaches, causing more land pollution. But because of the low cost of ocean dumping, many coastal cities consider it an alternative to landfills.

Figure 23–6 *Why is ocean dumping of garbage not a good alternative to sanitary landfills?*

Figure 23–7 *Recycling reduces the volume of solid wastes and helps preserve natural resources. How can you make recycling a part of your life?*

Burning garbage in open dumps and in the incinerators of apartment buildings, hospitals, and factories was at one time a popular alternative to landfills. Because burning releases harmful gases, however, this practice is being halted. Sometimes the old incinerators are replaced with highly efficient incinerators fitted with emission controls. But there is another way to burn garbage that is increasingly being used. Since the 1960s, several European countries have used special waste-to-energy incinerators to burn their garbage. The heat produced is used to convert water into steam, which is then used to generate electricity or to heat the buildings. Some of these waste-to-energy incinerators are in use in the United States, and more are planned for the future.

Recycling, which not only gets rid of solid wastes but also creates useful materials, is considered the solid-waste solution of the future by most environmentalists. You will learn more about recycling in Chapter 24. Recycling often involves high technology. Technology alone, however, can do little. People must also be involved. Recycling begins at home. An aluminum can or a glass bottle carelessly tossed to the side of the road can take thousands of years to decompose. Everybody, to a certain degree, causes land pollution. And everybody can help to stop it.

23–2 Section Review

1. Describe two ways in which obtaining and using fossil-fuel resources results in land pollution.
2. What are radioactive wastes? What is the difference between high-level and low-level wastes?
3. What are solid wastes? What are three sources of solid wastes?
4. Describe four methods of solid-waste disposal.

Connection—*You and Your World*
5. For one week, keep a list of all the solid wastes you throw away. What percentage of your solid wastes consists of renewable resources (paper, wood, and so on)? What percentage consists of nonrenewable resources (metals, plastics, and so on)?

PROBLEM ???
Solving

The Diaper Dilemma

Disposable paper diapers make up 2 percent of all the garbage produced in this country, adding to the mountains of solid wastes in sanitary landfills. As a result, many parents have chosen reusable cloth diapers instead. But are these reusable diapers really less harmful to the environment than disposable diapers? You decide. The following chart compares resources used and pollutants produced per week by both kinds of diapers.

Based on the risks and benefits associated with their use, which kind of diaper would you choose? Why? What other factors might you consider in making your decision?

	Reusable Diapers	Disposable Diapers
Resources Used		
Renewable	0.18 kilogram	9.72 kilograms
Nonrenewable	1.44 kilogram	1.67 kilograms
Water Used	547 liters	90 liters
Energy Used		
Renewable Sources	14,890 BTU*	3,720 BTU
Nonrenewable Sources	64,000 BTU	19,570 BTU
Pollutants Produced		
Air	0.39 kilogram	0.04 kilogram
Water	0.05 kilograms	0.005 kilogram

*BTU stands for British thermal unit. One BTU is the amount of heat needed to raise the temperature of one pound of water one degree Fahrenheit.

Guide for Reading

Focus on this question as you read.

▶ *What are the major sources of air pollution?*

23–3 Air Pollution

When you think of the Earth's natural resources—land, water, minerals, fossil fuels—the one resource that may not come to mind immediately is air. Yet air is probably the most important resource of all. Where would we be without fresh, clean air to breathe? We usually do not think of air as a resource because, although it is all around us, air is normally invisible—odorless, colorless, and tasteless.

But now imagine a place where the sky is always gray, the buildings are blackened by soot, and the air smells like rotten eggs. Do you think people would choose to live in such a place? Would you? The people of Donora, Pennsylvania, did live in such a place in the 1940s.

The city of Donora boasted one of the largest steel mills in the world. The economy of the city was thriving as mills and factories operated 24 hours a day. Millions of tons of coal were burned every hour to provide energy for this growing industrial center. And the people of Donora reasoned that the gray sky, the soot, and the smell were the price they had to pay for progress.

But in October 1948 the price became too high. The air became almost unbreathable. Noontime looked like late evening. People could barely see. They suffered from eye irritations and chest pains. Even the animals became sick. What had happened to this Pennsylvania city in which the autumn air was usually cool and damp? The answer is that on that October day in Donora, a phenomenon known as a **temperature inversion** had settled over the city.

A temperature inversion occurs when cool air near the Earth's surface becomes trapped under a layer of warm air. Normally, cool air is heated by the Earth's surface and rises, taking pollutants with it. But during a temperature inversion, the layer of warmer air acts as a lid, and the pollutants are trapped in the cooler air near the surface. The temperature inversion in Donora, in which 20 people died and thousands more were hospitalized, lasted for four days.

Figure 23–8 *During a temperature inversion, cool air containing pollutants becomes trapped under a layer of warm air. Why is a temperature inversion dangerous to human health?*

Cold, clean air

Warm air

Trapped cool air with pollutants

Since the Donora disaster, cities and states have passed laws to control emissions of pollutants from factories and power plants. Yet the problems associated with burning coal and other fossil fuels still remain. **Although much air pollution comes from the industrial burning of coal and other fossil fuels, the most significant source of air pollution is motor vehicles.** Now let's find out how motor vehicles contribute to air pollution.

Smog

The air that makes up the Earth's atmosphere is a mixture of several gases. These gases include oxygen, nitrogen, carbon dioxide, and water vapor. When fossil fuels are burned, a brew of pollutants enters the air. The gasoline burned in the engines of automobiles and other motor vehicles contains hydrocarbons, or compounds of hydrogen and carbon. Pollution occurs when the gasoline is not completely burned in the engine. Some hydrocarbons escape into the air. At the same time, the poisonous gas carbon monoxide is produced and also enters the air.

Hydrocarbons, carbon monoxide, and several other gases often react in sunlight to form a thick brownish haze called **smog.** (The word smog is a combination of the words smoke and fog.) Smog contains chemicals that irritate the eyes and make

Figure 23–9 *In this photograph, much of Los Angeles is hidden by the smog caused by a temperature inversion. How does automobile exhaust add to the smog problem in Los Angeles?*

ACTIVITY
DISCOVERING

How Acid Is Your Rain?

Find out if there is an acid rain problem in your area.

1. The next time it rains, collect a sample of rainwater in a clean glass jar. Label it Sample A.

2. Place some distilled water in another jar and label it Sample B.

3. Obtain some pH paper (used to measure acidity) from your teacher. Your teacher will show you how to use the pH paper to test the acidity of each of your samples. Record your results.

■ Was there a difference in acidity between the two water samples?

■ If so, what might have caused the difference?

breathing difficult. Smog is expecially damaging—even deadly—for people with lung diseases or other respiratory disorders, such as asthma. The pollutants in smog can also damage or kill plants.

Smog can build up over a city because of the flip-flop in layers of air that takes place during a temperature inversion. This is what happened in Donora for four days in 1948. But it happens in Los Angeles all the time. Los Angeles has frequent temperature inversions. As a result, the air in the city is unhealthy for more than 200 days out of the year. Other cities in the United States also have smog problems.

Acid Rain

Factory smokestacks and automobile exhausts release various pollutants into the air. Some of these pollutants include sulfur and nitrogen compounds called oxides. In the atmosphere, sulfur oxides and nitrogen oxides combine with water vapor through a series of complex chemical reactions. These reactions result in the formation of two of the strongest acids known: sulfuric acid and nitric acid. These acids can fall to the Earth as precipitation in the form of rain, snow, sleet, and even fog. The general term used for precipitation that is more acidic than normal is **acid rain.**

Figure 23–10 *The damage to trees caused by acid rain can be clearly seen in this photograph. What is the source of acid rain?*

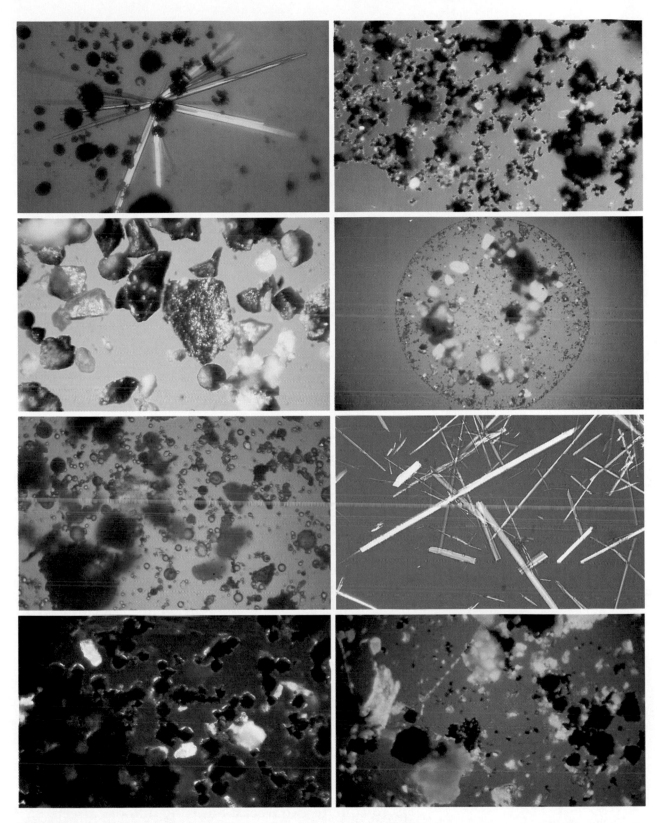

Figure 23–11 *These photographs show some pollutants found in the air. Reading from left to right are sulfate crystals, automobile exhaust, steel mill emissions, a drop of acid rain, coal ash, asbestos particles, oil ash, and emissions from a power plant.*

A Homemade Indicator

1. Shred several leaves of red cabbage and boil them in some water until the liquid turns dark purple. **CAUTION:** *Be careful when boiling a liquid. Wear safety goggles.*

2. When the cabbage and liquid have cooled, pour the liquid through a sieve into a container.

3. Pour 4 mL of lemon juice into a separate container. Add 2 mL of the red cabbage juice. Stir and observe any color change. Based on the fact that lemon juice is an acid (citric acid), what color does red cabbage juice turn in the presence of an acid?

Figure 23–12 *Smoking is a leading cause of indoor air pollution. Why is smoking not allowed on public transportation?*

Very often, acid rain falls many kilometers away from the original source of the pollution. Acid rain from factories in Germany, France, and Great Britain is being blamed for killing fishes and trees in Sweden. Acid rain blown by winds from industrial areas in the midwestern United States is being blamed for damage to lakes and forests in the northeastern United States and in Canada.

The damage caused by acid rain is a serious problem. Naturally, the best way to control acid rain is to stop releasing sulfur and nitrogen oxides into the air. For example, factories could burn coal with a low sulfur content. But low-sulfur coal is expensive and hard to find. So scientists continue to search for additional ways to prevent acid rain and other forms of air pollution.

Indoor Air Pollution

After reading about all the problems caused by air pollution, you may think that the safest place to be is indoors. But think again! Indoor air pollution is an issue that has often been overlooked. Recently, however, scientists have realized that some homes and offices may have serious air-pollution problems.

Several factors combine to make indoor air pollution a serious problem. Some appliances used in homes and offices give off potentially dangerous gases. In addition, many homes and office buildings are well insulated for increased energy efficiency. This means that pollutants that might otherwise escape through cracks and leaks are trapped inside. Also, most people spend more time indoors than they do outdoors.

There are many sources of indoor air pollution. These include the gases given off by wood, coal, and kerosene stoves, as well as the chemicals in air fresheners, disinfectants, and oven and drain cleaners. One of the leading causes of indoor air pollution is smoking. In fact, smoking only one cigarette is the equivalent of breathing the smoggy air of Los Angeles for one to two weeks! Smoking indoors affects nonsmokers as well as smokers. Many communities have recognized the harmful effects of smoking indoors by banning smoking in restaurants, offices, and other public spaces.

CONNECTIONS

Plants Versus Pollution

Can houseplants reduce indoor air pollution? Dr. W. C. Wolverton thinks they can. Dr. Wolverton has designed a filter system using plants, such as English ivy and peace lilies, that absorb harmful gases and chemicals from the air in homes and offices. But Dr. Wolverton is neither a *florist* nor a *gardener*. He is a former researcher with the National Aeronautics and Space Administration (NASA). In fact, Dr. Wolverton began his research with plants while searching for ways to reduce air pollution on space stations such as *Skylab*. Now he has brought the results of his research down to Earth.

Some scientists are skeptical of Dr. Wolverton's system. They say that the process by which plants absorb air pollutants has still not been determined. Others think that the best way to reduce indoor air pollution is to use materials that do not release pollutants and to improve ventilation. Wolverton, however, is so sure of his results that he has installed a "self-contained bioregeneration system" in his home in Mississippi. In addition, a community college in Mississippi is planning to construct a new math-and-science building using Dr. Wolverton's plant filtration system. This will be the first large-scale test of the system.

If Dr. Wolverton is correct, it may be possible to control indoor air pollution while at the same time adding beauty to our homes and offices. As another researcher has said, even if the system does not work, "having a lot of plants around is nice."

23–3 Section Review

1. What are the major sources of air pollution?
2. What is a temperature inversion? How is it related to air pollution?
3. What is acid rain? How can acid rain cause damage in lakes and forests far from the source of air pollution?
4. What are some sources of indoor air pollution?

Critical Thinking—*Making Inferences*
5. What might be the effect on the economy of an industrial city if strict limitations were placed on the emissions from factories?

ACTIVITY
DISCOVERING

Acidity of Pond Water

1. With adult supervision, collect a sample of fresh water from a pond or lake in your area.

2. Using either pH paper or red cabbage juice indicator, test the acidity of your water sample.

■ Do your results indicate an acidity problem with the water in your area? If so, what might have caused the problem?

23–4 Water Pollution

Water! No living thing—plant, animal, or human—can long survive without this precious liquid. As you have learned in Chapter 22, people use water for drinking, bathing, cooking, and growing crops. Water is also essential for industry and manufacturing. Water is a popular source of recreation, too. As the human population increases, however, agriculture and industry demand more and more water—often more water than is readily available. While some parts of the world have adequate water supplies, other parts of the world are dry.

More and more of the water on the Earth is becoming unusable. One reason for a shortage of usable water is water pollution. **Obtaining and using energy resources are the major causes of water pollution.**

Pollution From Fossil Fuels

In the last section, you read how the emissions from motor vehicles and factories that burn fossil fuels can cause droplets of sulfuric acid and nitric acid to form in the atmosphere. When these droplets fall to the Earth as acid rain, they increase the acidity of lakes, rivers, and streams. Most fishes and

Figure 23–13 *Clean water is one of our most precious natural resources.*

other organisms that live in water can survive in only a narrow range of acidity. By increasing the water's acidity, acid rain kills many of the organisms living in the water. In some parts of the world, entire lakes are now lifeless as a result of acid rain.

Unfortunately, there are other ways in which our energy needs contribute to water pollution. Strip mining for coal releases pollutants that may run off into lakes and streams or may seep into the soil to contaminate groundwater. (Recall from Chapter 22 that half of our drinking-water supply comes from groundwater.)

Our dependence on oil and petroleum products is another source of water pollution. Petroleum is often found under the ocean floor. To obtain this petroleum, offshore oil wells are constructed. Although great precautions are taken during the construction of such wells, drilling accidents do occur. As a result of such accidents, huge amounts of oil spill into the oceans.

Oil spills also occur when tankers carrying oil are damaged, causing their oil to leak into the surrounding water. The first major accident involving an oil tanker took place in 1967, when the tanker *Torrey Canyon* spilled more than 700,000 barrels of oil onto the beaches of England and France. Sadly, there have been many such disasters in the years since— from the *Amoco Cadiz* in 1978 to the *Exxon Valdez* in

Figure 23–14 *During the war in the Persian Gulf, oil was deliberately leaked into the Gulf, creating a huge oil spill (left). Cleaning up a California beach after an oil spill is not an easy task (right).*

1989. It might surprise you to know, however, that more water pollution is caused by the day-to-day operation of oil tankers than by major oil spills. This happens because oil tankers often deliberately flush waste oil directly into the ocean.

Whatever the cause, an oil spill is an environmental disaster. Plants and animals, especially sea birds and aquatic mammals, that come in contact with the oil may be killed. If the oil reaches the shore, it contaminates beaches and may contribute to the death of shore-dwelling organisms. Despite improved cleanup technology, oil spills remain one of the more difficult types of water pollution to remedy.

Pollution From Nuclear Power

Water is needed to cool the reactors in nuclear power plants. Cold water from lakes and rivers is usually used for this purpose. As a result of the cooling process, a large amount of hot water is generated. This heated water is then discharged back into the lakes and rivers. The addition of the heated water causes the temperature of the lakes and rivers to rise. This temperature increase is called **thermal pollution.** Most fishes and other water-dwelling organisms can survive in only a narrow temperature range. When the water temperature rises, many organisms die as a result. In what ways is thermal pollution similar to acid rain?

You read in the last section how radioactive wastes from nuclear power plants can pollute the land. In much the same way, radioactive wastes can become a source of long-term water pollution. Radioactive wastes stored in underground containers may leak out of the containers and pollute groundwater supplies. Pollution of the oceans may result if the containers are dumped at sea.

Hazardous Wastes

Although using and obtaining energy are the major sources of water pollution, they are by no means the only sources. Prior to the 1970s, many industries dumped chemicals and other hazardous wastes directly into streams and other nearby bodies of water. The Cuyahoga River in Cleveland, Ohio,

Figure 23–15 *The cooling towers of a nuclear power plant discharge heated water into a nearby body of water, resulting in thermal pollution. How does thermal pollution affect fishes living in the water?*

was once so polluted with flammable chemical wastes that it caught fire!

Today, chemicals and hazardous wastes are no longer discharged directly into bodies of water. Instead, they are often buried in special landfills. However, even when these wastes are properly contained and buried, it is possible for leaks to occur. Leaks from hazardous-waste landfills may result in groundwater pollution.

Illegal dumping of hazardous wastes is another serious source of groundwater contamination. Containers of hazardous wastes have been dumped illegally in abandoned factories, sanitary landfills, and even vacant lots. This method of illegally disposing of hazardous wastes is called "midnight dumping." Why do you think this name is appropriate for this practice?

Figure 23–16 *Leaking drums of hazardous wastes add to the problem of groundwater pollution.*

Sewage and Agricultural Runoff

Probably the greatest water-pollution threat to human health comes from sewage. Sewage is the waste material that is carried away by sewers and drains. Sewage is sometimes dumped directly into rivers and streams. This sewage often contains disease-causing bacteria and viruses. Drinking water and water used for swimming may become contaminated with these disease-causing organisms. The result is a serious threat to the health of the people who use the contaminated water. Contamination with sewage also makes fishes and other organisms living in the polluted water unfit for human consumption.

Untreated sewage dumped into lakes and rivers is harmful to the fishes and other organisms that live in these bodies of water. Bacteria in the water break down the sewage. In the process, the bacteria use up oxygen. If too much sewage is dumped, too much oxygen is used up. Fishes and other organisms may then die from lack of oxygen.

The runoff of animal wastes and chemicals from farmlands also contributes to water pollution. Chemicals such as phosphates and nitrates are used in fertilizers to improve the growth of crops. When fertilizers run off the land into a lake, they stimulate the growth of algae. The algae then use up the oxygen supply in the lake. Pesticides, which are

ACTIVITY

DOING

Pond Scum

What kinds of organisms are normally found in lakes and ponds? Let's find out.

1. With adult supervision, collect a sample of water from a lake or pond in your area.

2. Place a drop of your water sample on a microscope slide. Cover the drop with a coverslip.

3. Use a microscope to observe the drop of water. What do you see? Draw any organisms you see. Using reference books, try to identify the organisms you observed.

Figure 23-17 *Waste water must be treated at a sewage-treatment plant to prevent contamination of lakes and rivers (left). Runoff of fertilizers into a pond causes an explosion in the growth of algae (right).*

Pond Water + Fertilizer = Algae Explosion, p. 786

poisonous chemicals used to kill harmful insects and other pests, can also cause water pollution when they enter lakes and rivers in the runoff from farmlands.

There are a number of ways in which water pollution can be prevented. And scientists are always searching for methods to clean up polluted water. You will learn what can be done to prevent water pollution, as well as land pollution and air pollution, in the section that follows.

ACTIVITY READING

Silent Spring

In 1962, Rachel Carson published her classic book *Silent Spring,* in which she warned of the dangers of pesticides and other chemicals released into the environment. Read *Silent Spring* and decide if her conclusions still apply today.

23-4 Section Review

1. What are the major sources of water pollution?
2. Describe two ways in which our use of fossil fuels contributes to water pollution.
3. What is thermal pollution? What is the cause of thermal pollution?
4. Describe what happens when fertilizers build up in a lake.

Critical Thinking—*Making Predictions*

5. Predict at least one problem that could result from dumping hazardous wastes into the ocean.

23–5 What Can Be Done About Pollution?

Guide for Reading

Focus on this question as you read.

▶ *What are some ways in which pollution can be reduced?*

Because pollutants are the normal byproducts of human activities, environmental pollution is a problem that will not go away. On the contrary, pollution will get worse as the human population increases. But there are some things that can be done to reduce pollution. **Pollution can be reduced by conserving energy, by finding cleaner ways to use energy, and by making sure that wastes are disposed of in the safest possible ways.** Let's examine some of the ways in which people can help fight pollution.

Conservation

Today, many people are concerned about saving and protecting our natural resources. **Conservation** is the wise use of natural resources so that they will not be used up too quickly or used in a way that will damage the environment. When natural resources are conserved, the environment is benefited in two ways. First, nonrenewable resources last longer. Second, pollution is reduced. Conservation of natural resources will be discussed more fully in Chapter 24.

There are many ways in which energy can be conserved at home. Washing one large load of clothing or dishes instead of several small loads will save energy. Turning down the thermostat on the home heating system a few degrees in the winter and turning up the thermostat on the air conditioner a few degrees in the summer will save energy. And making sure that a house or apartment is well insulated will also save energy.

Because a lot of energy is used by motor vehicles, changing driving habits can make a real difference in the quality of the environment. The use of car pools and public transportation saves fuel and reduces air pollution. So does keeping an automobile well tuned and in good operating condition. Riding a bicycle instead of driving a car for short trips also helps. And don't forget the most ancient (and nonpolluting) form of transportation: walking!

Figure 23–18 *Everyone can learn to use energy wisely. How does home insulation help to conserve energy?*

Figure 23-19 *Reducing pollution does not have to depend on the development of new technologies. If more people rode bicycles or used public transportation, what effect would this have on air pollution?*

A form of conservation that has received considerable public attention is recycling. You probably have a recycling center in your neighborhood or town. Resources that are reclaimed from recycled materials can be sent to factories and used again. Recycling has been successful in reclaiming paper, glass bottles and jars, and aluminum cans.

New Technologies

New technologies can reduce pollution by creating cleaner and more efficient ways of obtaining and using energy resources. Technology can also help develop alternatives to fossil fuels. You have learned about some of these alternative energy sources in Chapter 21. If a clean, renewable source of energy such as solar energy or nuclear fusion could be used on a large scale, many of our current pollution problems would be solved.

The burning of coal has been made less damaging to the environment by the use of scrubber systems. A scrubber system works like a shower. As sulfur oxides are released from burning coal, a high-pressure spray of water dissolves the oxides before they can react with water vapor in the atmosphere. Scrubber systems and other air-pollution-control devices can be used on smokestacks to prevent the release of pollutants into the atmosphere.

Pollution from automobile exhaust has been reduced by equipping cars with pollution-control devices. This type of pollution could be further reduced by the development of engines that burn fuel more completely.

Scientists are exploring new methods of drilling for oil under the ocean floor in order to reduce the possibility of underwater leaks. In addition, several new methods have been developed for cleaning up oil spills. These include vacuum systems that can pump oil out of the water, certain types of absorbent materials that can soak up oil near the shore, and "oil-eating" bacteria that have been developed through genetic-engineering techniques.

ACTIVITY

DISCOVERING

Car Pooling

Select a safe spot where you can observe cars as they go by. (Do not choose a busy highway because you will not be able to keep track of every car.) Try to observe the cars at different times each day for several days. For 10 minutes each day, record the number of people in each car that goes by. Make a chart to display your observations.

How many cars have only the driver? At what times of day? How many have one or more passengers?

■ How might the environment benefit from car pooling?

Waste Disposal

Much pollution is caused by industry. Industrial hazardous wastes and other solid wastes are often buried underground in landfills. But if not buried properly, these wastes can leak out of their containers and severely damage the environment.

Of course, the best way to reduce the problem of pollution from hazardous wastes is to reduce the production of these wastes. But there are also several ways to dispose of hazardous wastes safely. First, the hazardous wastes should be separated from other industrial wastes. Second, as much of the wastes as possible should be reused or recycled. Third, the wastes should be chemically treated to destroy the toxic materials they contain. Finally, the wastes should be buried in secure landfills with many safeguards to prevent leaks into the environment.

Figure 23–20 *The message in this environmental demonstration is "Recycle the trash monster!"*

Everyone's Responsibility

At the beginning of this chapter, you read that pollution is caused mainly by the activities of people. It is important to realize that the activities of people can also reduce pollution. And everyone—young and old, scientist and nonscientist—can help. Remember that in the future you will be responsible for making decisions about ways to reduce pollution. Now is the time to begin. What can you do to help reduce pollution?

23–5 Section Review

1. How can pollution be reduced?
2. What is conservation? How does conservation reduce pollution and protect resources?
3. How can new technologies reduce pollution?
4. List four steps involved in the safe disposal of hazardous wastes.

Connection—*You and Your World*
5. What pollution problems do you think you will face in the next five to ten years? What will you do to solve these problems?

ACTIVITY
THINKING

Pro or Con?

Write a brief essay that either supports or refutes the following statement: ''I think this whole environmental thing has gone too far. If industrial profits go down because of all these government regulations, the country will be worse off than ever.''

Laboratory Investigation

Observing Air Pollutants

Problem

How can you observe solid particles in the air that cause air pollution?

Materials

6 petri dishes
petri dish cover
petroleum jelly
glass-marking pencil
graph paper
magnifying glass

Procedure 🧪

1. Coat the flat surface of each petri dish with a thin layer of petroleum jelly.

2. Immediately place the cover on one of the petri dishes. Put the covered dish aside.

3. Place the other five petri dishes in different locations outdoors where they will not be disturbed.

4. Use the glass-marking pencil to write the name of the location on the side of each dish.

5. Leave the dishes undisturbed for 3 days.

6. After 3 days, collect the dishes. Place each dish, one at a time, on the graph paper. Use the magnifying glass to count the number of particles in each square of the graph-paper grid. Calculate the total number of particles in each dish. Record your observations in a data table similar to the one shown here.

Observations

1. Compare the data from each location.

2. Compare the covered dish with the five dishes you placed outdoors.

3. Compare your data with data from other groups. Record the locations of the dishes from the other groups and the number of particles counted in each dish.

Dish	Location	Number of Particles
1		
2		

Analysis and Conclusions

1. Which dish was the control in this investigation? Explain your answer.

2. The solid particles you counted are evidence of air pollution. How can you account for the difference in the number of particles at the various locations?

3. How can you account for the difference in the number of particles found in other locations by your classmates?

4. **On Your Own** Make a bar graph of your data, plotting location on the horizontal axis and number of particles counted on the vertical axis. What conclusions can you draw from your graph?

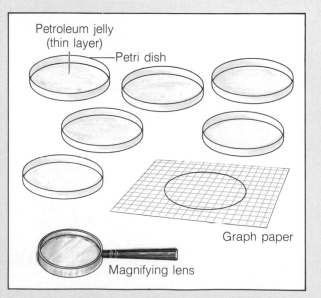

Petroleum jelly (thin layer)
Petri dish
Graph paper
Magnifying lens

Study Guide

Summarizing Key Concepts

23–1 What Is Pollution?

▲ The balance of the environment can be upset by the way in which humans obtain and use natural resources.

▲ Pollution is the release into the environment of substances that change the environment for the worse.

▲ The three main types of pollution are land pollution, air pollution, and water pollution.

23–2 Land Pollution

▲ Obtaining and using fossil fuels and nuclear energy can cause land pollution.

▲ Other sources of land pollution are hazardous wastes, radioactive wastes, and solid wastes.

▲ Solid wastes include agricultural wastes, commercial and industrial wastes, and household wastes.

23–3 Air Pollution

▲ The major sources of air pollution are motor vehicles and the burning of coal and other fossil fuels by industry.

▲ Acid rain is caused when sulfur and nitrogen oxides released by burning fossil fuels combine with water vapor in the air to form sulfuric acid and nitric acid.

▲ Indoor air pollution is a serious problem that is often overlooked.

23–4 Water Pollution

▲ Obtaining and using energy resources, especially fossil fuels and nuclear energy, are the major causes of water pollution.

▲ Other sources of water pollution are industrial hazardous wastes, sewage, and agricultural runoff.

23–5 What Can Be Done About Pollution?

▲ Pollution can be reduced by conserving energy, by finding cleaner ways to use energy, and by disposing of wastes in the safest possible ways.

Reviewing Key Terms

Define each term in a complete sentence.

23–1 What Is Pollution?
pollution

23–2 Land Pollution
hazardous waste
radioactive waste
sanitary landfill

23–3 Air Pollution
temperature inversion
smog
acid rain

23–4 Water Pollution
thermal pollution

23–5 What Can Be Done About Pollution?
conservation

Chapter Review

Content Review

Multiple Choice

Choose the letter of the answer that best completes each statement.

1. The major source of air pollution is
   a. hazardous wastes.
   b. radioactive wastes.
   c. burning coal.
   d. motor vehicles.
2. The damage done to one natural resource in the process of using another resource is called
   a. ecology.   c. conservation.
   b. pollution.   d. recycling.
3. Which of the following is an example of hazardous wastes?
   a. toxic chemicals
   b. plastics
   c. yard wastes
   d. old newspapers
4. High-level radioactive wastes are difficult to dispose of because they
   a. take up too much space.
   b. have long half-lives.
   c. are poisonous.
   d. have short half-lives.

5. Pollution can be reduced by
   a. conserving energy.
   b. finding clean ways to use energy.
   c. disposing of wastes safely.
   d. all of these
6. The release of excess heat into nearby bodies of water results in
   a. thermal pollution.
   b. acid rain.
   c. hazardous waste pollution.
   d. groundwater pollution.
7. The term midnight dumping refers to the illegal disposal of
   a. yard wastes.
   b. solid wastes.
   c. hazardous wastes.
   d. untreated sewage.
8. A temperature inversion occurs when
   a. winds are calm.
   b. warm air is trapped under cool air.
   c. cool air is trapped under warm air.
   d. warm air rises.

True or False

If the statement is true, write "true." If it is false, change the underlined word or words to make the statement true.

1. Acid rain is formed when oxides of sulfur and nitrogen combine with <u>oxygen</u> in the air.
2. The wise and careful use of natural resources is called <u>recycling</u>.
3. The wastes produced by nuclear power plants are <u>agricultural</u> wastes.
4. Sanitary landfills are used to dispose of <u>solid</u> wastes.
5. Indoor air pollution <u>is not</u> a serious problem.
6. Growth of algae results from the runoff of <u>fertilizers</u> into a lake.

Concept Mapping

Complete the following concept map for Section 23–1. Then construct a concept map for the entire chapter.

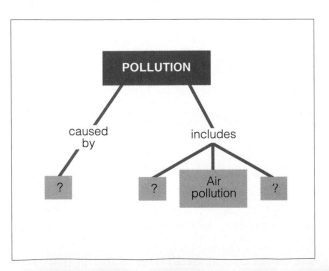

Concept Mastery

Discuss each of the following in a brief paragraph.

1. Explain how the balance of the environment is related to obtaining and using energy resources.
2. What is the relationship between conservation and pollution?
3. Explain why land, air, and water pollution cannot really be separated from one another.
4. Describe the trail of pollution involved in manufacturing a can of soda.
5. What is the most serious problem involved with the use of sanitary landfills? What are three alternatives to the use of sanitary landfills?
6. Describe the chain of events that led to the air-pollution disaster in Donora, Pennsylvania, in October 1948.
7. Why is smog a serious problem in Los Angeles?
8. What is the difference between high-level and low-level radioactive wastes?
9. One serious form of land pollution is solid waste: garbage and litter. Instead of being buried in sanitary landfills, garbage and litter can be burned. Why is burning garbage and litter not an environmentally sound idea? How could it become an environmentally sound idea?

Critical Thinking and Problem Solving

Use the skills you have developed in this chapter to answer each of the following.

1. **Making predictions** Imagine that the year is now 2010. Air pollution has become so bad that Congress has passed a law forbidding the use of private automobiles. How do you think your life might be changed by this law?
2. **Interpreting photographs** Describe the situation shown in this photograph and explain its probable cause.

3. **Applying concepts** Pollutants can be thought of as resources in the wrong place. Make a list of some of the pollutants discussed in this chapter. How could they be useful if they were in the right place?
4. **Relating concepts** Discuss how each of the following groups might react to the problem of acid rain in a certain area.
   a. tourists
   b. factory owners
   c. wildlife conservationists
   d. campers on a fishing trip
5. **Using the writing process** Write a short science fiction story describing what you think life will be like in the year 2061. The focus of your story should be the kinds of energy resources used and the environmental problems that may exist.

Conserving Earth's Resources

24

Guide for Reading

After you read the following sections, you will be able to

24–1 Fossil Fuels and Minerals
- Discuss various methods of conserving fossil fuel and mineral resources.

24–2 Protecting the Environment
- Identify ways to prevent land, air, and water pollution.

It was a typically peaceful early morning near the remote town of Valdez on Alaska's southern coast. Then suddenly, at 12:27 AM, came the emergency call from the huge oil tanker *Exxon Valdez:* ''I've run aground and we've lost 150,000 barrels.'' And so began the worst oil-spill disaster on record in the United States.

On March 24, 1989, the *Exxon Valdez* struck Bligh Reef in Prince William Sound. The reef ruptured the hull of the ship, eventually releasing more than 240,000 barrels of crude oil into the water. As the oil slick began to grow, environmentalists, state officials, and experts from Exxon and the federal government tried to develop a plan to clean up the oil as quickly as possible. Their response, however, was too slow to stop the oil from spreading onto the beaches. Despite massive cleanup efforts, it will be many years before the damage to the environment can be corrected.

The Earth's natural resources, such as oil, can cause great harm to the Earth and its inhabitants when used carelessly. They can also be of great value to people when used wisely. In the following pages, you will learn how people can help to protect the environment by the wise use of natural resources.

Journal *Activity*

You and Your World What do you think is meant by the wise use of natural resources? In your journal, draw a picture showing ways in which you, your family, and your community can use resources wisely.

◀ *The oil spill caused by the* Exxon Valdez *(the larger of the two ships in the photograph) resulted in great harm to wildlife in and around Prince William Sound.*

24–1 Fossil Fuels and Minerals

You use natural resources every day of your life. Some of these resources are fossil fuels: coal, oil, and natural gas. Others are minerals, such as aluminum, copper, and iron. Recall from Chapter 22 that fossil fuels and minerals are classified as nonrenewable resources. This means that once they are used up, they cannot be replaced. Because society relies so heavily on nonrenewable resources, conservation of these resources is extremely important. As you learned in Chapter 23, conservation is the wise use of natural resources so that they will not be used up too quickly or used in a way that will damage the environment. **Fossil fuels and minerals can be conserved by saving energy and by recycling.** Let's examine these methods of conservation more closely.

Energy Conservation

The year is 1973. A sea of automobiles stretches for several kilometers. As the sun peeks over the horizon, some motorists read the morning newspapers or try to sleep. The more sociable drivers use the opportunity to chat with their neighbors. The rest just sit in their cars and scowl.

Figure 24–1 *During the gas shortage of 1973, motorists in Connecticut—and elsewhere—had to wait in long lines to buy gasoline. Do you think such shortages could happen again?*

Is this the scene of an early-morning traffic jam? No, it represents the first experience Americans had with an oil shortage. At that time, shipments of oil to the United States were drastically reduced. Motorists had to wait in long lines at gas stations for what had become a most precious resource: gasoline.

Fortunately, the oil crisis of 1973 did not last long. The discovery of new oil fields combined with serious conservation efforts produced a relative abundance of oil by 1986. But the oil shortages of the 1970s remain dramatic illustrations of how dependent people are on fossil fuels and how dangerously close we are to running out of them.

Could the events of 1973 be repeated in the future? Unfortunately, the answer is yes. Modern society relies on fossil fuels for transportation, for industry, for heating and cooling buildings, and for generating electricity. But supplies of fossil fuels are dwindling. Sooner or later, we will run out of them. The goal of energy conservation is to make existing supplies last as long as possible.

How can you help to conserve energy? Here is a list of ways in which you can conserve energy in the home:

- Replace burned-out light bulbs with new energy-efficient bulbs.
- Turn off lights when they are not needed.
- Turn off the television when you are not watching it.

ACTIVITY
DISCOVERING

Current Events

Start a scrapbook of current news items concerning environmental problems. Bring your scrapbook to class and organize a class discussion around one or more of the news items. Are the problems worldwide or are they limited to certain parts of the world? How might these events affect you and your classmates? How might they affect living things in the environment?

■ What solutions can you suggest for some of these problems?

Figure 24–2 *By saving energy and using energy efficiently, we may be able to make our natural resources last longer. Why does thawing frozen food before cooking help save energy?*

- Take a quick shower instead of filling the tub for a bath.
- Fix leaking water faucets and pipes.
- Use the clothes washer and dryer only for full loads.
- Use the dishwasher only for full loads or do dishes by hand.
- Allow dishes to air dry instead of using the dry cycle on the dishwasher.
- Thaw frozen foods before putting them in the oven.
- Cook the entire meal in the oven instead of using several burners on the stove.
- Make sure refrigerators and freezers are properly sealed.
- Defrost refrigerators before the ice becomes too thick.
- Set the thermostat on the home heating system as low as possible.

What other ways can you think of to conserve energy in the home?

Energy Efficiency

Another way to conserve fossil fuels is to use them more efficiently. More efficient car engines use less gasoline. Smaller, less massive cars also use less gasoline than larger, more massive cars do. Adding 100 kilograms to the mass of a car increases its consumption of gasoline by 6 percent. Driving slowly also saves gasoline, as well as lives. But the best way to save energy is to leave the car at home and use public transportation: buses, passenger trains, and subways. Most forms of public transportation are much more energy efficient than cars. Riding a bicycle or walking are also energy-saving alternatives.

Recycling

The problem with minerals is similar to the problem with fossil fuels. Once minerals are used up, they are gone forever. One solution to this problem is to find other materials to take the place of minerals. For example, large amounts of steel are used in car engines. Steel is an alloy of iron and several

Figure 24–3 *In Portland, Oregon, many commuters use a new light rail service instead of driving their cars to work. How does such public transportation save energy and also cut down on pollution?*

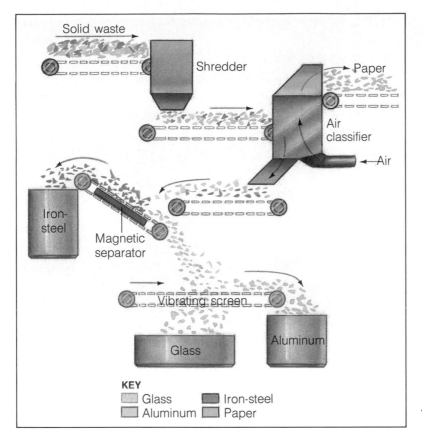

Solid waste

Shredder

Paper

Air classifier

Air

Iron-steel

Magnetic separator

Vibrating screen

Glass

Aluminum

KEY
Glass — Iron-steel
Aluminum — Paper

Figure 24–4 *This diagram shows how solid wastes can be separated for recycling. Separating wastes in this way is expensive. Does the value of recycling justify the cost of separation?*

other metals, including chromium and nickel. (Recall that an alloy is a substance made of two or more metals.) Today, scientists are working to replace some parts of these metal engines with plastic parts. If plastics and other materials can replace some minerals, supplies of these minerals will last longer.

Another solution is to keep minerals in usable form by **recycling** them. If recycling became an accepted part of everyday life, existing mineral resources would last longer, less land would be dug up and destroyed in the search for new mineral resources, and the solid-waste problem would be reduced. Recycling also contributes to energy conservation. Making aluminum from recycled cans, for example, uses much less energy than making aluminum from ore.

Although community recycling of solid wastes has become increasingly common, most industries still do not recycle on a large scale. The reason for this is primarily an economic one. Separating solid wastes for recycling is expensive. And even if the separation is done, there is little consumer demand for recycled

ACTIVITY
DOING

Magnetic Separation

In this activity you will make a model to illustrate how metals are separated from solid wastes for recycling.

1. Make a mixture of approximately equal amounts of iron filings, shredded paper, and sawdust.

2. Using a bar magnet, try to separate the iron filings from the paper and sawdust. Why can you use a magnet to separate the iron filings from the mixture?

How could separating solid wastes—newspapers, glass bottles, aluminum cans—into individual containers before they are collected help to reduce the cost of recycling?

Figure 24–5 *Many tons of paper are being recycled at this recycling center. Recycling helps save trees, from which paper is made. Writing paper and envelopes made from maps are some of the products made from recycled paper that are now available to consumers. What other recycled products are you familiar with?*

products. This situation may be changing, however. For example, cellulose insulation made from recycled paper fibers is now competitive with other types of home insulation, such as fiberglass. Finally, when the cost of solid-waste disposal and of the pollution involved is compared with the cost of recycling, recycling can be seen as an economical alternative to disposal.

24–1 Section Review

1. What are two ways to conserve fossil fuels and minerals?
2. What is the goal of energy conservation? List at least four ways to conserve energy in the home.
3. How can automobiles be made to use gasoline more efficiently?
4. Why is recycling not practiced on a large scale by most industries? What can be done to change this?

Critical Thinking—*Relating Concepts*
5. Using plastics instead of steel in car engines is one way to conserve minerals. However, the use of plastics presents other problems. What are some of these problems?

Helping the Victims of an Oil Spill

You have been reading about Earth's nonliving resources and what can be done to protect them. Earth has living resources as well. Among these living resources are the thousands of sea birds and other *wildlife* that may be injured or killed as the result of an oil spill. What can be done to protect these living resources?

In 1988, a relatively "small" oil spill off the coast of Washington State resulted in the deaths of tens of thousands of sea birds. Fortunately, about 4000 birds survived long enough to struggle onto the beaches. When the oil-soaked birds reached shore, volunteers were waiting to transport them to emergency treatment centers. Here the volunteers slowly and carefully washed and dried the birds, trying to remove all traces of oil from their feathers. The volunteers had to treat the birds gently to avoid damaging the feathers. Each bird required at least an hour to bathe and rinse thoroughly.

In spite of all the care they received, fewer than 1000 birds survived to be released back into the environment. And there was no way to know for sure if these birds were able to survive on their own after being released. Even with modern technology and good intentions, humans cannot duplicate an animal's natural survival equipment. Yet they can easily destroy it with just one careless act.

24–2 Protecting the Environment

If nothing is done to prevent pollution, the problem will only get worse as the human population increases. As you learned in Chapter 23, pollution is the release into the environment of substances that change the environment for the worse. Although pollution can be classified as land, air, and water pollution, it is important to remember that all parts of the environment are interrelated. Anything that damages one part of the environment can also damage other parts. Acid rain, for example, begins as air

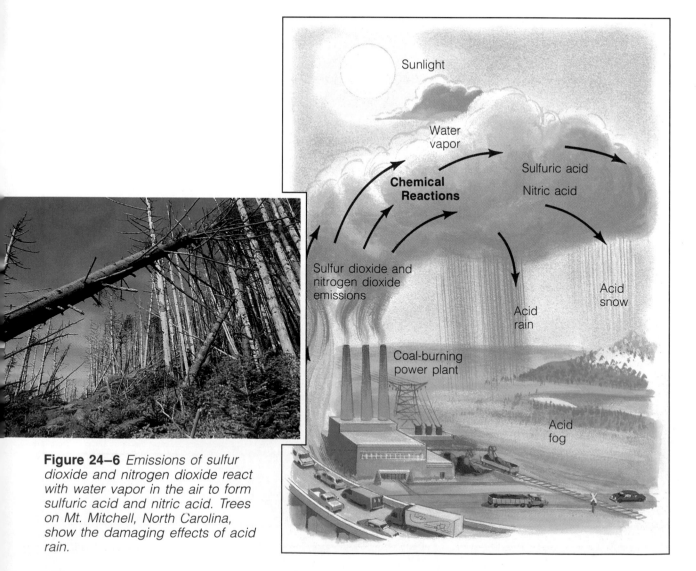

Figure 24–6 *Emissions of sulfur dioxide and nitrogen dioxide react with water vapor in the air to form sulfuric acid and nitric acid. Trees on Mt. Mitchell, North Carolina, show the damaging effects of acid rain.*

pollution. As acid rain falls into lakes and rivers, the problem becomes water pollution. Then as acid rain seeps into the soil, land pollution results. In this example of a "pollution chain," all aspects of the environment are damaged.

What can be done to prevent pollution? There is no easy answer to this question; no single solution to the problem. But there are some actions that can be taken now—before it is too late. **People can help prevent pollution by using energy wisely and by discarding wastes safely.** In the previous section you learned about ways to use energy wisely and efficiently. In the following pages you will read about some specific examples of what can be done to prevent pollution of the environment.

Safeguarding the Air

Gases and particles given off when fossil fuels are burned are called **emissions** (ee-MIHSH-uhnz). In theory, if the burning of fossil fuels such as coal, oil, and natural gas is complete—that is, with enough oxygen present—the only waste products should be carbon dioxide and water vapor. In practice, however, some pollution-causing emissions are always given off as well. These emissions include the poisonous gas carbon monoxide as well as nitrogen oxides

ACTIVITY
WRITING

The Greenhouse Effect

The carbon dioxide released into the air by motor vehicles and the burning of fossil fuels by industry contributes to the greenhouse effect. Using reference books in the library, write a report on the greenhouse effect. In your report, explain how carbon dioxide increases the greenhouse effect. Also include a discussion of how scientists think the greenhouse effect may change the Earth's climate, as well as the results of such changes.

Figure 24–7 *Emissions released into the air from factory smokestacks cause acid rain and other forms of air pollution. Scrubbers are pollution-control devices that reduce emissions from factory smokestacks.*

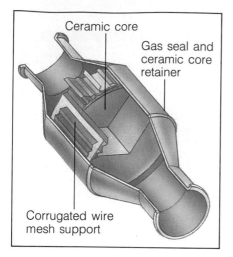

Ceramic core

Gas seal and ceramic core retainer

Corrugated wire mesh support

Figure 24–8 *Automobiles manufactured today are required to have catalytic converters. How does a catalytic converter work?*

ACTIVITY

DOING

Natural Pollution

Pollution is caused by people. But sometimes nature may cause pollution too. Using reference books in the library, look up information about the eruption of the volcano on the island of Krakatoa, which took place in 1883. Write a short report about the effect of this eruption on the Earth's weather in the years that followed. Then compare the Krakatoa eruption with the eruption of Mt. Pinatubo in the Philippines in 1991. Prepare a poster or diorama to illustrate your report.

and sulfur oxides, which cause acid rain when they react with water vapor in the air. But the pollution-causing emissions can be reduced in various ways.

Devices called scrubbers frequently are used to wash suspended particles and sulfur oxides out of smokestack fumes. In some scrubbers, the fumes are passed through a blanket of steam. In the process, most of the pollution-causing emissions are dissolved in the steam. Then as the steam cools, the dissolved waste products rain down into a special collector and are removed. Another kind of scrubber uses a spray of liquid chemicals instead of steam. In this kind of scrubber, sulfur oxides react with the chemical spray to form a solid "sludge" that is then removed.

Emissions from motor vehicles, which are the main sources of air pollution, can be reduced by the use of **catalytic converters.** A catalytic converter is an emission-control device that changes the hydrocarbons and carbon monoxide in automobile exhaust into carbon dioxide and water vapor.

Scrubbers and catalytic converters are only two of the ways scientific technology is helping to clean up the air. In many ways, the air today is much cleaner than it was 10 or 20 years ago. But in some ways, it is more polluted. Environmentalists say that some pollution laws, such as the Clean Air Act of 1970, must be tightened if we are to ensure clean air in the future. The Clean Air Act set up emission standards, which limit the amount of pollutants that can be released into the air from a particular source. And emission-control technology must be improved. In addition, alternative sources of cleaner energy, such as gasohol and hydrogen, must be further developed.

Alternative sources of energy will never eliminate all possible sources of air pollution. And devices to clean emissions will be of little value if they are not used. So it is vital that industry and other sources of air pollution make every effort to meet air-pollution standards set by the government. Furthermore, much air pollution can be traced directly to people. People, for example, drive the cars that add to air pollution. So people should make sure that their cars are well tuned and that the engines and exhaust systems are in good working order.

Figure 24–9 *To eliminate the huge number of cars entering Yosemite National Park every year, the National Park Service hopes to build a solar train to carry visitors through the park. Nonpolluting solar-powered trucks are already being used in Natural Bridges National Monument in Utah.*

Safeguarding Our Water Supplies

In 1972 and 1974, the United States Congress passed two strict laws to fight water pollution. They were the Clean Water Act of 1972 and the Safe Drinking Water Act of 1974. Both these laws were intended to stop the flow of untreated wastes into waterways from **point sources.** Point sources include sewers, pipes, and channels through which wastes are discharged.

These laws set up rules to greatly reduce water pollution from point sources. Towns and cities were required to build sewage-treatment plants or to improve existing plants. Such plants clean wastewater before it is discharged into waterways. Similar treatment plants purify water for drinking. Industries also were required to clean their wastewater before releasing it into lakes, streams, and rivers. Most of these actions were successful. Water quality improved.

The 1972 and 1974 laws greatly reduced water pollution from point sources. Similar laws now exist

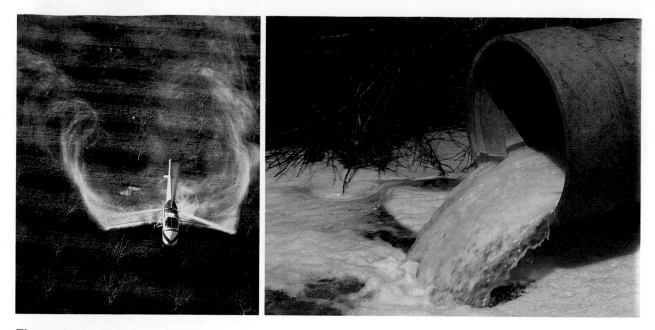

Figure 24–10 *Raw sewage is treated at a sewage-treatment plant before being discharged. Nonpoint sources of pollution include pesticides sprayed on crops.*

Waste Not, Want Not, p. 787

ACTIVITY

READING

Save the Earth

For an interesting perspective on protecting the environment, read *This Bright Land: A Personal View* by the American journalist and drama critic Brooks Atkinson (1894–1984). Then, to find out what you can do to help, read *Save the Earth: An Ecology Handbook for Kids* by Laurence Pringle.

to reduce pollution from **nonpoint sources**. Nonpoint sources of water pollution include sanitary landfills that ooze poisonous liquids and industrial waste ponds that leak into the surrounding ground. Nonpoint sources also include illegally dumped hazardous wastes and runoff of pesticides and fertilizers from various sources.

Unfortunately, the wastes from nonpoint sources are usually the most harmful to the environment. And they are often difficult to find and clean up. For example, drums of hazardous wastes may lie in solid-waste dumps for many years. Often, the drums are not identified as containing hazardous wastes. The drums may even be buried with ordinary garbage in sanitary landfills. When the drums decay, hazardous wastes may leak into the soil and groundwater. The drums may be uncovered years later, causing a nightmare for the people who must clean up the damage—if it can indeed be cleaned up.

What is the solution? Obviously, hazardous waste dumps must be checked carefully for leakage. Whenever possible, hazardous wastes should be disposed of properly at the factory or manufacturing plant where they are produced. Such disposal can be difficult and expensive. But proper disposal is far less difficult and costly than removing these hazardous wastes from the environment years later.

PROBLEM Solving

People Are Part of the Environment Too

Environmental problems cannot be viewed only as scientific problems. Because they involve people and the way people live, they must be viewed as economic, social, and political problems as well. Consider, for example, the following situation:

The city of Pleasant Grove centers around a large factory that makes machine parts. About half the families in Pleasant Grove have at least one family member working at the factory. The factory contributes significantly to air and water pollution through smokestack emissions and large amounts of chemical wastes. The factory manager recently announced that the factory will increase operations by 35 percent during the next year. The expansion will include the addition of a night shift and the purchase of a wooded area next to the factory. This land will be used for additional manufacturing facilities and for a second parking lot.

Imagine that you are a magazine reporter who has been sent to Pleasant Grove. Your assignment is to find out how the following people feel about the planned expansion of the factory: a scientist; a conservationist; an economist; an average citizen; a local politician. Write a magazine article describing the reactions of each person.

24–2 Section Review

1. How can people help prevent pollution of the environment?
2. Use the example of acid rain to describe how pollution affects all parts of the environment.
3. How do scrubbers and catalytic converters reduce harmful emissions from smokestacks and automobiles?
4. What is the difference between point sources and nonpoint sources of pollution?

Connection—*You and Your World*
5. In what ways can you personally help reduce pollution?

Laboratory Investigation

Comparing the Decomposition of Different Types of Litter in a Landfill

Problem

Large amounts of litter and garbage are buried in sanitary landfills every day. How fast do different materials decompose in a model landfill?

Materials *(per group)*

4-L glass jar with lid
topsoil
litter (orange peels, paper, scrap metal, and so forth)
glass-marking pencil

Procedure 🧪

1. Cover the bottom of the glass jar with a layer of soil.

2. Place one third of the litter in the jar. Make sure the litter is near the sides of the jar so you can see it.

3. With the glass-marking pencil, circle the location of each item of litter on the outside of the jar.

4. Add another layer of soil on top of the litter.

5. Place another one third of the litter in the jar. Mark the location of each item of litter with the glass-marking pencil.

6. Add another layer of soil on top of the litter.

7. Place the last of the litter in the jar. Mark the location of each item of litter.

8. Cover the litter with a final layer of soil. Add water to the jar until all the soil is slightly moist. Put the lid on the jar.

9. Observe your model landfill once a week for a month. Predict whether or not each item of litter will decompose.

Observations

1. Describe the appearance of each item of litter in the jar after one day, one week, two weeks, and one month. Record your observations in a data table.

2. Which items of litter decomposed fastest? Which items decomposed more slowly? Which items did not decompose at all?

Analysis and Conclusions

1. Compare the kinds of litter and their decomposition rates. Were your predictions correct? Is there any pattern to the litter that decomposed as compared with the litter that did not decompose?

2. Based on your observations, what recommendations would you make to a town that was planning to build a sanitary landfill?

3. **On Your Own** Suppose the soil, jar, water, and litter had been sterilized before the investigation. Would the results have been the same? Explain. Design an experiment to test your conclusion.

Summarizing Key Concepts

24–1 Fossil Fuels and Minerals

▲ Fossil fuels and minerals are classified as nonrenewable resources.

▲ Conservation is the wise use of natural resources so that they will not be used up too quickly or used in a way that will damage the environment.

▲ Fossil fuels and minerals can be conserved by saving energy and by recycling.

▲ The goal of energy conservation is to make existing supplies of fossil fuels last as long as possible.

▲ There are many ways in which you can conserve energy in your home—from turning off lights to lowering the thermostat.

▲ Two ways to make mineral resources last longer are to use other materials in place of minerals and to keep minerals in usable form by recycling.

24–2 Protecting the Environment

▲ Although pollution can be classified as land, air, and water pollution, all parts of the environment are interrelated, and thus pollution of one part often affects the others.

▲ Pollution can be prevented by using energy wisely and by discarding wastes safely.

▲ Emissions are gases and particles given off when fossil fuels are burned.

▲ Emissions from smokestacks can be removed by scrubbers.

▲ Emissions from motor vehicles can be removed by catalytic converters.

▲ Laws have been passed to reduce water pollution from point sources, such as sewers.

▲ Pollution from nonpoint sources, such as hazardous wastes and agricultural runoff, is especially harmful to the environment.

Reviewing Key Terms

Define each term in a complete sentence.

24–1 Fossil Fuels and Minerals
recycling

24–2 Protecting the Environment
emission
catalytic converter
point source
nonpoint source

Chapter Review

Content Review

Multiple Choice

Choose the letter of the answer that best completes each statement.

1. Using resources wisely is called
   a. ecology.
   c. pollution.
   b. conservation.
   d. waste disposal.
2. A catalytic converter changes pollution-causing emissions in automobile exhaust into carbon dioxide and
   a. carbon monoxide.
   b. water vapor.
   c. hydrocarbons.
   d. sulfur dioxide.
3. Automobiles can be made to burn fuel more efficiently by
   a. making them larger.
   b. driving faster.
   c. driving slower.
   d. increasing their mass.
4. Recycling is not done by most industries because it
   a. is too expensive.
   b. requires too much energy.
   c. is cheaper to use plastics.
   d. is too time consuming.

5. Emissions from factory smokestacks can be reduced through the use of
   a. catalytic converters.
   b. high-sulfur coal.
   c. scrubbers.
   d. all of these
6. Acid rain is a serious form of
   a. air pollution.
   c. land pollution.
   b. water pollution.
   d. all of these
7. Energy can be conserved by
   a. fixing leaky faucets.
   b. taking showers instead of baths.
   c. lowering the thermostat.
   d. all of these
8. Aluminum and copper are examples of
   a. fossil fuels.
   c. minerals.
   b. pollutants.
   d. emissions.
9. Point sources of pollution include
   a. sewers.
   b. hazardous wastes.
   c. agricultural runoff.
   d. sanitary landfills.

True or False

If the statement is true, write "true." If it is false, change the underlined word or words to make the statement true.

1. Fossil fuels and minerals are <u>renewable</u> resources.
2. Automobiles are <u>more</u> energy efficient than most forms of public transportation.
3. Making aluminum from ore requires <u>less</u> energy than making aluminum from recycled cans.
4. As the human population increases, the problem of pollution will <u>decrease</u>.
5. Two kinds of emission-control devices are scrubbers and <u>catalytic converters</u>.
6. Sewers are examples of <u>nonpoint</u> sources of water pollution.
7. Pollution of one part of the environment <u>cannot</u> affect other parts.

Concept Mapping

Complete the following concept map for Section 24–1. Then construct a concept map for the entire chapter.

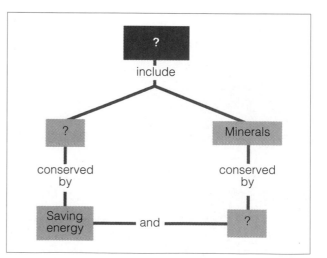

Concept Mastery

Discuss each of the following in a brief paragraph.

1. What are some ways to conserve energy in the home?
2. Why is the conservation of fossil fuels important?
3. What was the purpose of the Clean Water Act and the Safe Drinking Water Act?
4. What are some benefits of recycling?

5. What are emissions? How can pollution-causing emissions be reduced?
6. What are two ways to conserve mineral resources?
7. Why is pollution from nonpoint sources a more serious threat to the environment than pollution from point sources?

Critical Thinking and Problem Solving

Use the skills you have developed in this chapter to answer each of the following.

1. **Relating concepts** How does recycling contribute to energy conservation?
2. **Interpreting a photograph** Does the photograph show a point source or a nonpoint source of pollution? How can you tell?

3. **Applying concepts** Explain how each of the following helps to conserve energy:
   a. Turning off the TV when no one is watching it
   b. Defrosting the refrigerator
   c. Driving an energy-efficient car
   d. Taking a shower instead of a bath
4. **Making diagrams** Draw a chart or diagram that shows a pollution chain in which emissions from burning fossil fuels or fumes from toxic chemicals begin as air pollutants and then become water pollutants and land pollutants.
5. **Relating cause and effect** Identify a possible cause for each of the following:
   a. Most farmers stop using pesticides.
   b. The United States runs out of oil.
   c. Industries routinely recycle materials.
   d. More and more people use public transportation.
6. **Using the writing process** Write a brief essay in which you express your opinion about the following statement: "These gloomy predictions about running out of oil are greatly exaggerated. And even if we do run out, I feel confident that humans, with all their resourcefulness, will find another way to produce the energy they need."

GAZETTE

DR. MBAYMA ATALIA

PHOTOS: RAYMOND BONNER/NEW YORK TIMES PICTURES

Keeping the White Rhino Alive

Taking care not to let the animal catch his scent, the researcher crouches down in the tall grass and begins to take notes. The object of his attention is a white rhinoceros—a bulky grayish mammal with a pointed horn and a large square mouth. Quickly, the researcher notes the time of day, what the rhino is eating, its geographical location, and how far it has moved since last seen. Meanwhile, the rhino continues to graze like a vacuum cleaner, eating everything in sight. After about 20 minutes of intense eating, the temporarily satisfied rhino moves off at a half trot in search of its next meal.

Constant eating is a well-established habit of the white rhino, the world's second largest land mammal. Few people know the habits of this great creature better than Dr. Mbayma Atalia, a researcher and protection officer at Garamba National Park in Zaire, Africa. Dr. Mbayma has spent years studying the sleeping and grazing patterns of the white rhino. He knows his subjects so well that he can recognize every rhinoceros in the park simply by the shape of its horn and the contours of the wrinkles around its snout.

On this particular day, Dr. Mbayma is observing an adult male rhino named M–5. The time is late afternoon, and M–5 is grazing after his midday sleep. Dr. Mbayma has found that white rhinos sleep mostly between 10 AM and 2 PM, when the temperature rises above 32°C. During the rest of the daylight hours, the rhinos eat—and eat!

M–5 may not know it, but he is lucky to be alive. Fifty years ago, Garamba National Park was set aside as a preserve for animals such as M–5, who is one of a rare subspecies of white rhinoceroses that are native to this part of Africa. At that time, more than 1000 of these animals were in existence. But by 1983, only 15 of M–5's relatives were left. What had happened? That question can be answered in one word: poaching.

▲ Poachers beware! Members of Dr. Mbayma Atalia's anti-poaching unit are setting off to patrol the 7800 square kilometers of Garamba National Park.

Poaching is illegal hunting. When Garamba National Park was set aside as a wildlife preserve, guards were hired to make sure that the rhinos in the park would be free to live and reproduce. Many hunters, however, managed to outwit the guards and slaughtered the rhinos. To make matters worse, some corrupt guards joined the poachers, using their jobs as an easy way to get rich on bribes or as a source of free rhino meat.

The rewards for poaching run high. Today, a single horn from a white rhinoceros is valued at about $24,000. The value of the horn is based on the fact that it can be ground up for medicinal purposes or used to make decorative objects, just as elephant tusks are illegally sold for ivory. In addition to the valuable horn, rhinoceros meat is a tempting source of food for poor African villagers who have little nutritious food to eat.

With the white rhinoceros on the brink of extinction, conservation groups joined with the government of Zaire to clean up the corruption at Garamba. The first step was to hire a new park warden to replace the one who had been compromised by the poachers. The next step was to make the job of park guard attractive in terms of salary and other incentives. The final step was to engage highly motivated researchers, such as Dr. Mbayma, whose knowledge of the white rhino makes them ideally suited to serve as protection officers. An additional step has since been taken. The new park warden, Dr. Muhindo Mesi, has begun a program to help local villagers improve their sheep and goat herds so that they will not be tempted to poach rhinos for meat.

Today, Garamba National Park is a model for wildlife conservation in Africa. Not one white rhinoceros has been poached since 1984, and the birth of new animals has brought the total number of white rhinos at Garamba up to 28. In some African countries, the rhinos have totally disappeared. In others, their numbers have dropped alarmingly. Only in Zaire is the white rhinoceros population growing rather than shrinking. Thanks to people like Dr. Mbayma Atalia and Dr. Muhindo Mesi, Garamba National Park has succeeded where many other conservation efforts have failed.

For Further Reading

If you have been intrigued by the concepts examined in this textbook, you may also be interested in the ways fellow thinkers—novelists, poets, essayists, as well as scientists—have imaginatively explored the same ideas.

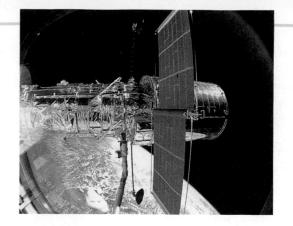

Chapter 1: Exploring Earth Science

Ames, Mildred. *Anna to the Infinite Power.* New York: Scribner.

Freeman, Ira, and Mae Freeman. *Your Wonderful World of Science.* New York: Random House.

Walsh, Jill Paton. *Toolmaker.* New York: Seabury.

Chapter 2: Stars and Galaxies

Anker, Charlotte. *Last Night I Saw Andromeda.* New York: Henry Z. Walck.

Clarke, Arthur C. *2001: A Space Odyssey.* New York: New American Library.

Ride, Sally, with Susan Okie. *To Space and Back.* New York: Lothrop, Lee & Shepard.

Chapter 3: The Solar System

Cameron, Eleanor. *The Wonderful Flight to the Mushroom Planet.* Boston: Little Brown and Co.

Gallant, Roy A. *The Constellations: How They Came to Be.* New York: Four Winds.

Harris, Alan, and Paul Weissman. *The Great Voyager Adventure: A Guided Tour Through the Solar System.* Englewood Cliffs, NJ: Julian Messner.

Chapter 4: Earth and Its Moon

Del Rey, Lester. *Prisoners of Space.* Philadelphia, PA: Westminster Press.

Heinlein, Robert A. *Rocket Ship Galileo.* New York: Charles Scribner's Sons.

Lawrence, Louise. *Moonwind.* New York: Harper & Row.

Chapter 5: Earth's Atmosphere

Carson, Rachel. *Silent Spring.* Boston, MA: Houghton Mifflin.

Verne, Jules. *Around the World in Eighty Days.* New York: Bantam Books.

Young, Louise B. *Sowing the Wind: Reflections on the Earth's Atmosphere.* New York: Prentice Hall Press.

Chapter 6: Earth's Oceans

Berill, N.J., and Jacquelyn Berill. *1001 Questions Answered About the Seashore.* New York: Dover.

Heyerdahl, Thor. *Kon-Tiki: Across the Pacific by Raft.* New York: Washington Square Press.

Verne, Jules. *Twenty Thousand Leagues Under the Sea.* New York: New American Library.

Chapter 7: Earth's Fresh Water

Pringle, Laurence. *Water: The Next Great Resource Battle.* New York: Macmillan.

Thomas, Charles B. *Water Gardens for Plants and Fish.* Neptune, NJ: TFH Publications.

Twain, Mark. *Life on the Mississippi.* New York: Harper & Row.

Chapter 8: Earth's Landmasses

Adams, Ansel. *Photographs of the Southwest.* New York: New York Graphic Society.

Riffel, Paul. *Reading Maps.* Northbrook, IL: Hubbard Science.

Rugoff, Milton. *Marco Polo's Adventures in China.* New York: Harper & Row.

Chapter 9: Earth's Interior

Jackson, Julia. *Treasures From the Earth's Crust.* Hillside, NJ: Enslow.

Rossbocker, Lisa A. *Recent Revolutions in Geology.* New York: Watts.

Verne, Jules. *Journey to the Center of the Earth.* New York: New American Library.

Chapter 10: Movement of the Earth's Crust

Hintz, Martin. *Norway.* Chicago, IL: Children's Press.

Lye, Keith. *Mountains.* Englewood Cliffs, NJ: Silver Burdett.

McPhee, John. *Rising from the Plains.* New York: Farrar, Straus & Giroux.

Chapter 11: Earthquakes and Volcanoes

Gilbreath, Alice. *Ring of Fire: And the Hawaiian Islands and Iceland.* Minneapolis, MN: Dillon.

Hills, C.A.R. *A Day that Made History: The Destruction of Pompeii and Herculaneum.* London, England: Dryad Press.

House, James. *The San Francisco Earthquake.* San Diego, CA: Lucent Books.

Chapter 12: Plate Tectonics

Corbalis, Judy. *The Ice-Cream Heroes.* Boston, MA: Little, Brown.

Miller, Russell. *Continents in Collision.* Alexandria, VA: Time-Life.

Ullman, James Ramsey. *Banner in the Sky.* Philadelphia, PA: Lippincott.

Chapter 13: Rocks and Minerals

Martin, John H. *A Day in the Life of a High-Iron Worker.* Mahwah, NJ: Troll.

Pope, Elizabeth Marie. *The Sherwood Ring.* Boston, MA: Houghton Mifflin.

Pullman, Philip. *The Ruby in the Smoke.* New York: Knopf.

Chapter 14: Weathering and Soil Formation

Cleaver, Vera, and Bill Cleaver. *Dust of the Earth.* New York: Harper & Row Junior Books.

St. George, Judith. *The Mount Rushmore Story.* New York: Putnam.

Steinbeck, John. *The Grapes of Wrath.* New York: Viking.

Chapter 15: Erosion and Deposition

Bramwell, Martyn. *Glaciers and Ice Caps.* New York: Watts.

Smith, Don. *The Grand Canyon: Journey Through Time.* Mahwah, NJ: Troll.

Steele, David H. *The Pebble Searcher.* London, England: A.H. Stockwell.

Chapter 16: What Is Weather?

Aaron, Chester. *An American Ghost.* New York: Harcourt, Brace, Jovanovich.

Babbitt, Natalie. *The Eyes of the Amaryllis.* New York: Farrar, Straus & Giroux.

Mayo, Gretchen. *Earthmaker's Tales: North American Indian Stories About Earth Happenings.* New York: Walker.

Chapter 17: What Is Climate?

O'Dell, Scott. *Island of the Blue Dolphins.* Boston, MA: Houghton Mifflin.

Skurzynski, Gloria. *Trapped in the Slickrock Canyon.* New York: Lothrop, Lee & Shepard.

Strieber, Whitley. *Wolf of Shadows.* New York: Alfred A. Knopf.

Chapter 18: Climate in the United States

Dyer, T.A. *A Way of His Own.* Boston: Houghton Mifflin.

George, Jean Craighead. *Julie of the Wolves.* New York: Harper & Row.

Turner, Ann. *Grasshopper Summer.* New York: Macmillan.

Chapter 19: Earth's History in Fossils

Katz, Welwyn Wilton. *False Face.* New York: Margaret K. McElderry Books.

Kelleher, Victor. *Baily's Bones.* New York: Dial Press.

Lammers, George E. *Time and Life: Fossils Tell the Earth's Story.* New York: Hyperion Press.

Chapter 20: A Trip Through Geologic Time

Denzel, Justin. *Boy of the Painted Cave.* New York: Philomel Books.

Lampton, Christopher. *Mass Extinctions: One Theory of Why the Dinosaurs Vanished.* New York: Watts.

Niven, Larry, and Jerry Pournelle. *The Mote in God's Eye.* New York: Pocket Books.

(continued)

Chapter 21: Energy Resources

Beatty, Patricia. *Jonathan Down Under.* New York: Morrow.

Perez, Norah H. *Breaker.* Boston, MA: Houghton Mifflin.

Sharpe, Susan. *Waterman's Boy.* New York: Bradbury.

Chapter 22: Earth's Nonliving Resources

Collier, James Lincoln. *When the Stars Begin to Fall.* New York: Delacorte Press.

Rubinstein, Robert E. *When Sirens Scream.* New York: Dodd, Mead.

Sargent, Sarah. *Seeds of Change.* New York: Bradbury.

Chapter 23: Pollution

Chester, Aaron. *Spill.* New York: Atheneum.

George, Jean. *Who Really Killed Cock Robin?* New York: Dutton.

Thackeray, Sue. *Looking at Pollution.* London, England: Trafalgar Square.

Chapter 24: Conserving Earth's Resources

Bond, Nancy. *The Voyage Begun.* New York: Atheneum.

St. George, Judith. *Do You See What I See?* New York: Putnam.

Shute, Nevil. *On the Beach.* New York: Morrow.

Activity Bank

Welcome to the Activity Bank! This is an exciting and enjoyable part of your science textbook. By using the Activity Bank you will have the chance to make a variety of interesting and different observations about science. The best thing about the Activity Bank is that you and your classmates will become the detectives, and as with any investigation you will have to sort through information to find the truth. There will be many twists and turns along the way, some surprises and disappointments too. So always remember to keep an open mind, ask lots of questions, and have fun learning about science.

747

ALL THE COLORS OF THE RAINBOW

Stars come in many different colors—from blue stars, to yellow stars such as the sun, all the way to red stars at the opposite end of the spectrum. The visible light emitted by stars is also made up of different colors. To study starlight, astronomers use a spectroscope. A spectroscope breaks up light into its characteristic colors. In this activity you will build a simple spectroscope.

Materials

shoe box
scissors
cardboard
tape
diffraction grating
black construction paper
uncoated light bulb

Procedure

1. Carefully cut two small, square holes in opposite ends of a shoe box.

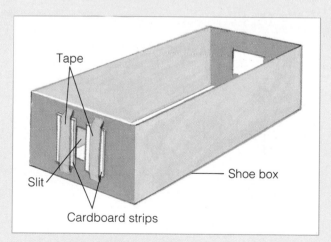

2. Tape two small pieces of cardboard on either side of one hole to make a narrow slit.

3. Tape a piece of diffraction grating over the other hole. **Note:** *Before you tape the diffraction grating in place, hold it up in front of a light. Turn the diffraction grating so that the light spreads out into a horizontal spectrum.*

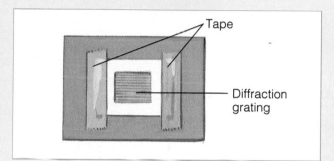

4. Cover the inside of the shoe box, except for the two holes, with black construction paper. Then tape the shoe box closed.

5. Hold your spectroscope so that the slit is parallel to the bright filament of an uncoated light bulb. Look at the light and describe what you see. **CAUTION:** *Do not point your spectroscope at the sun. Never look directly at the sun.*

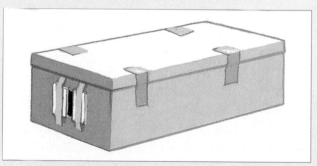

Going Further

If a fluorescent light bulb or a neon light is available, look at it through your spectroscope and describe its spectrum.

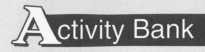
SWING YOUR PARTNER

Gravity is the force of attraction between all objects in the universe. The more mass an object has, the stronger its gravitational attraction. The Earth has the largest mass of any nearby object, so we are always aware of the Earth's gravity. On Earth, gravity keeps our feet firmly on the ground! Gravity also causes falling bodies to accelerate, or change their velocity, as they fall toward the Earth's surface. The acceleration caused by the Earth's gravity is equal to 1 g. In this activity you will measure the value of g in meters per second per second (m/sec^2).

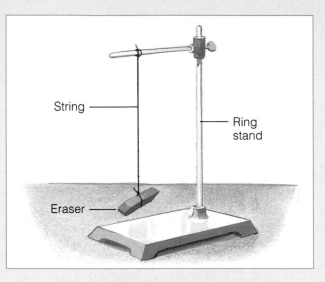

String

Ring stand

Eraser

Materials

string
metric ruler
eraser
ring stand
clock or watch with second hand

Procedure

1. Tie an eraser to a piece of string about 50 cm long.

2. Make a pendulum by tying the free end of the string to the arm of a ring stand. Record the length of the string, in meters, in a data table similar to the one shown.

3. Pull the eraser to one side and release it. Count the number of complete swings the eraser makes in 60 sec. Record this number in your data table.

4. Use the following equation to find the period (T) of the pendulum: $T = 60$ sec/number of swings. Record the period, in seconds, in your data table.

5. Repeat steps 3 and 4 three more times. Find the average period of the pendulum.

6. Calculate the gravitational acceleration g using the following formula:

$$g = 4\pi^2 L/T^2$$

In this formula, $\pi = 3.14$, L is the length of the pendulum in meters, and T is the average period of the pendulum in seconds. What value did you find for g?

DATA TABLE

Trial	Length (m)	Time (sec)	Number of Swings	Period (sec)
1		60		
2		60		
3		60		
4		60		

Think for Yourself

You may have heard astronauts refer to the "gee forces" they experienced during lift-off. What do you think they were referring to?

Activity Bank

HOW CAN YOU OBSERVE THE SUN SAFELY?

As you know, it is extremely dangerous to look directly at the sun. Viewing the sun directly can result in permanent damage to your eyes. Is there a safe way to observe the sun? The answer is yes. The best way of looking at the sun is to project an image of the sun onto a piece of white paper. You can demonstrate this by making a simple pinhole viewer. You will need a shoe box, a white index card, tape, and a pin.

1. Tape the index card to the inside of one end of the shoe box. Use a pin to make a small hole in the opposite end of the shoe box. In a darkened room, hold the shoe box so that sunlight enters the pinhole. You should see an image of the sun projected onto the index card. Describe what you see.

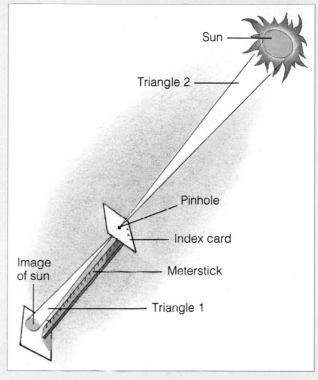

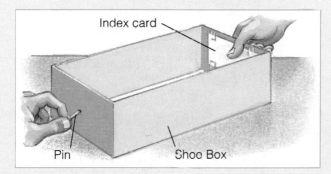

With a little simple mathematics, you can use a similar setup to measure the diameter of the sun. You will need a meterstick, two index cards, tape, and a pin.

2. Tape an index card to one end of the meterstick to make a screen. Make a pinhole in the other index card and hold it at the opposite end of the meterstick. Sunlight passing through the pinhole will form an image of the sun on the screen. Measure the diameter, in centimeters, of the sun's image on the screen. What is the diameter of the image?

As you can see in the diagram, light rays passing through the pinhole to form the image make two similar triangles. This means that the ratio of the sun's diameter to its distance from the pinhole is the same as the ratio of the diameter of the image to the length of the meterstick. Use the following equation to calculate the sun's diameter:

Sun's diameter/150,000,000 km
  = Image diameter/100 cm

What value did you find for the diameter of the sun?

Think for Yourself

The Latin name for the pinhole viewer you made in this activity is *camera obscura,* which means dark chamber or room. Do you think this is an appropriate name for this device? Why or why not?

RUSTY NAILS

Mars is often called the Red Planet. The surface of Mars appears red because the soil contains iron oxide—more commonly known as rust. You are probably familiar with rust closer to home. Anything made of iron that is exposed to air and moisture will become rusted. Junked cars, iron fences, and old bicycles are all subject to rusting. Is there any way to prevent objects from rusting? In this activity you will explore some ways to prevent rusting.

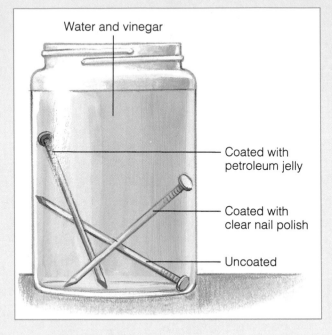

Water and vinegar

Coated with petroleum jelly

Coated with clear nail polish

Uncoated

Materials

3 iron nails
clear nail polish
petroleum jelly
glass jar
vinegar

Procedure

1. Coat one of the nails with clear nail polish. Coat the second nail with petroleum jelly. Do not put anything on the third nail.

2. Place the nails into a jar of water. Add some vinegar to the water to speed up the rusting process.

3. Allow the nails to stand in the glass jar overnight. Then examine the nails. Which nail shows signs of rusting? How do you think the nail polish and petroleum jelly prevented the nails from rusting?

Going Further

What are some other substances that would prevent the nails from rusting? Repeat this experiment to test your ideas.

Do It Yourself

Rusting can cause a great deal of damage to bridges and other objects made of iron by wearing away the metal. Rusty objects can also be dangerous to your health. If you accidentally cut yourself on a rusty nail or other sharp object, you should see a doctor immediately. Using first-aid books or other reference materials, find out why cuts caused by rusty objects are so dangerous.

ACTION, REACTION

According to Newton's third law of motion, every action causes an equal and opposite reaction. This is the principle of reaction engines, such as rockets. It is also the principle that may cause you to get soaked if you try jumping from a small boat onto the dock! Here's a simple experiment you can perform to demonstrate Newton's third law of motion for yourself.

Materials

skateboard
cardboard strip, 15 cm x 75 cm
windup toy car

Procedure

1. Place the skateboard upside down on the floor.

2. Place the strip of cardboard on top of the wheels of the skateboard. The cardboard will be the "road" for the toy car.

3. Place the toy car on the cardboard, wind it up, and let it go. Observe what happens. Does the car or the road move?

Think for Yourself

1. Are you aware of the road moving away from you when you are driving in a real car? Why or why not?

2. Would you be able to drive a car forward if you were not "attached" to the Earth?

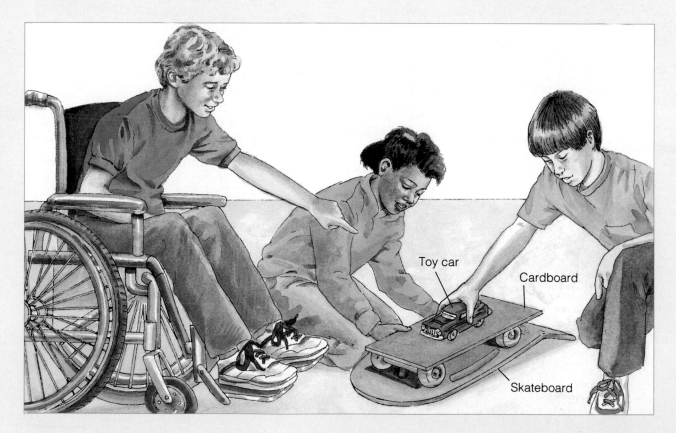

Toy car

Cardboard

Skateboard

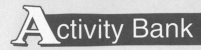

WHAT CAUSES HIGH TIDES?

The rise and fall of Earth's oceans—the tides—are caused by the pull of the moon's gravity on the Earth. Because the moon exerts different gravitational forces on different parts of the Earth, there are two high tides and two low tides every day at any given place. You can demonstrate the forces that cause the tides in this activity.

Materials

construction paper
tape
drawing compass
3 equal masses
3 springs

Procedure

1. Tape a piece of construction paper onto a smooth, flat surface. Using the compass, draw a circle 30 cm in diameter on the construction paper.

2. Label the three masses A, B, and C.

3. Attach the springs to the three masses as shown in the diagram. Place mass B in the center of the circle. The circle represents the Earth.

4. Apply a force to mass A by pulling on the spring. This force represents the gravitational pull of the moon on the Earth.

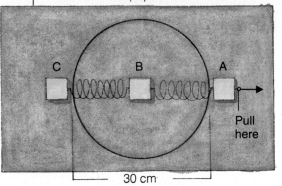

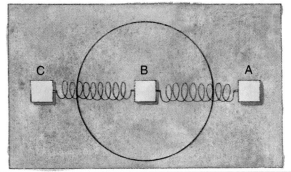

Analysis and Conclusions

1. What happens to the other two masses when you exert a force on mass A?

2. How does this demonstration illustrate the two high tides on opposite sides of the Earth caused by the pull of the moon?

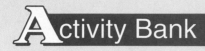

A MODEL OF ACID RAIN

In many parts of the country, rain contains chemical pollutants that produce harmful effects. You may have read about acid rain. Acid rain can kill fishes in lakes and damage the leaves of trees. In cities, acid rain can damage statues and buildings. You can make a model of acid rain and observe some of the harmful effects acid rain produces.

Materials

3 saucers
3 pennies
vinegar
teaspoon

Procedure

1. Place one penny in each of the three saucers.

2. Place two teaspoons of water on the penny in the first saucer.

3. Place two teaspoons of vinegar on the penny in the second saucer. Leave the third penny alone.

4. Set the three saucers aside and observe the three pennies the next day. (You may want to cover the saucers with a piece of plastic wrap to keep the liquids from evaporating.)

Observations

Describe the appearance of the three pennies. You may want to draw a picture of each penny.

Analysis and Conclusions

1. Explain the changes that occurred in the appearance of the three pennies.

2. What do you think happens to rocks and other objects that are exposed to acid rain over a period of time?

Going Further

With your classmates, see if you can devise a plan to protect the pennies from acid rain. Assume that you cannot stop acid rain from occurring. Present your ideas to your teacher before you test them out.

Activity Bank

SINK OR SWIM—IS IT EASIER TO FLOAT IN COLD WATER OR HOT?

Can you float? You may already know that it is easier to float in salt water than in fresh water. Salt water is denser than fresh water. Is it easier to float in warm water or cold? Try this investigation to find out.

Materials

large, deep pan
cold tap water
hot tap water
food coloring
dropper bottle

Procedure

1. Fill a large pan three-quarters full of cold water.

2. Put a few drops of food coloring in a dropper bottle and fill the bottle with hot tap water. **CAUTION:** *Be careful not to scald yourself. The hot water from some taps is very hot indeed!*

3. Place your finger over the opening of the dropper bottle. Carefully place the bottle on its side in the pan of cold water. The dropper bottle should be submerged completely.

4. Slowly take your finger off the opening of the bottle. Observe what happens.

Observations

1. Describe what happened to the hot water.

2. Why did you add food coloring to the hot water?

Analysis and Conclusions

1. Which water, cold or hot, was more dense? Why?

2. Which water, cold or hot, would be easier to float in? Why?

Going Further

Suppose you had placed cold water and food coloring in the dropper bottle and hot water in the pan. What do you think would have happened when you removed your finger from the dropper bottle? With your teacher's permission, test your hypothesis.

Food coloring

HOW DOES A FISH MOVE?

Fishes are well adapted for life in water. In this activity you will observe a fish and discover for yourself how fishes are suited to live in water.

Materials

small goldfish
aquarium
fish food
thermometer

watch or clock
several sheets of unlined paper

Procedure

1. On a sheet of unlined paper, draw an outline of the fish from the side. On the same sheet of paper, draw an outline of the fish as seen head-on. On the same sheet of paper, draw an outline of the fish as seen from the top.

2. As you observe your fish, draw its fins on your outlines. Use arrows to show how each fin moves. If a fin doesn't appear to move, indicate this on your drawing.

3. Feed the fish. Record its reaction to food.

4. Take the temperature of the water. Enter the temperature reading in a data table similar to the one shown here. Now count the number of times the fish opens and closes its gills in 1 minute. (The gills are located at the front end

of the fish just behind its eyes. In order to live, fish take oxygen from the water. They swallow water through their mouth and pass it out through their gills.)

5. Add a little warm water to the aquarium. You want to raise the temperature of the water only a few degrees, so be careful. Do not make too drastic a change in the water temperature. Count the number of times the gills open and close in the warmer water in 1 minute.

Observations

1. What fin or fins move the fish forward in the water?

2. What fins help the fish turn from side to side?

3. How does the movement of the gills relate to the temperature of the water?

DATA TABLE

	Gills open and close
Temperature 1	
Temperature 2	

Analysis and Conclusions

What special structures and behaviors enable fishes to survive in a water world?

Going Further

You might like to set up an aquarium that reflects a fish's natural environment more accurately. For example, add a gravel layer to the bottom of the aquarium. Place some rocks and plants in the aquarium. You should then examine your fish's behavior after you have completed this task. What changes, if any, do you note?

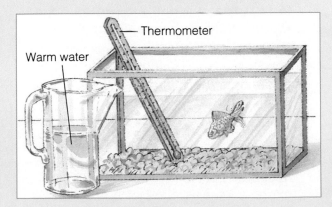

Thermometer

Warm water

WHAT IS THE EFFECT OF PHOSPHATES ON PLANT GROWTH?

Sometimes seemingly harmless chemicals have effects that are not easily predictable. For example, detergents are often added to water to clean clothes and dishes. When the clothes and dishes are rinsed, the detergents in waste water enter home septic systems or town sewage systems. Detergents in water may eventually be carried to streams, lakes, and sources of groundwater. So far this story seems unremarkable.

However, some detergents contain phosphates. Because of their effects on plant growth, detergents that contain phosphates have been banned by some communities. In this investigation you will measure the effects of phosphates on plant growth. You will uncover reasons why communities try to keep phosphates out of water supplies, and thus ban the use of certain detergents used to clean clothes and dishes.

Materials

2 large test tubes
  with corks or
  stoppers to fit
test-tube rack, or
  large plastic jar
  or beaker

2 sprigs of *Elodea*
detergent that
  contains
  phosphates
sunlight or a lamp
small scissors

Before You Begin

Make sure that the detergent you will be using contains phosphates; many do not. *Elodea* is a common water plant used in home aquariums. A local pet store is a good source of supply.

Procedure 🧪 🔲

1. Take two sprigs of *Elodea* and use your scissors to cut them to the same length. Measure the length of the sprigs and record the length in a data table similar to the one shown on the next page. Place a sprig of *Elodea* into each test tube.

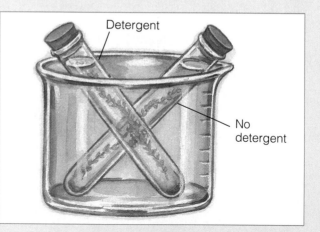

Detergent

No detergent

2. Add enough water to each test tube to fill it nearly to the top. Be sure the *Elodea* sprig is covered with water.

3. Place a small pinch of detergent into one test tube. Gently swirl the test tube to mix the water and detergent. Leave plain water in the other test tube.

4. Stopper each test tube.

5. Place the test tubes in a test-tube rack or plastic jar or beaker. Place the rack (or jar or beaker) in a sunny window or under another source of light.

6. Every three days for a month, carefully remove each *Elodea* sprig and measure it. Record your measurements in your data table. Place the sprigs back into the test tubes they were removed from each time. Do not mix up the sprigs!

Observations

1. What was the control in this experiment? Why?
2. Describe the *Elodea* that was placed in plain water.
3. Describe the *Elodea* that was placed in water that contained the detergent drops.
4. Why was it important to return each sprig to the correct tube?

Analysis and Conclusions

1. Did the detergent affect the *Elodea's* growth?
2. How do you explain the results of this investigation?
3. How might the effect of phosphates on water plants affect a community's water supply?

Going Further

Design an Investigatation that compares the effects of detergents and fertilizers on plant growth. Have your teacher check the design of your investigation before you begin.

DATA TABLE

	Day	Detergent	No Detergent
	1		
	4		
	7		
	10		
	13		
	16		
	19		
	22		
	25		
	28		
	31		

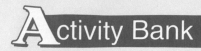

MAKING SOIL

Soil is a substance that is certainly taken for granted by most people. This common substance, often underfoot and easy to see, contributes greatly to human survival. Plants need soil to grow well—it is good, fertile soil that makes our croplands so productive. In this activity you will "make" some soil. Keep in mind, however, that what you can accomplish in an afternoon takes nature's forces many years to produce.

Materials

rocks
sand
magnifying glass
dried leaves

plastic pan or bucket
soil sample

Procedure

1. Use the magnifying glass to examine the rocks and the sand. Draw what you observe on a separate sheet of paper.

2. Place a thick layer of sand in the bottom of the plastic pan or bucket.

3. Break up the dried leaves into tiny pieces. You might even grind the dried leaves between two flat rocks.

4. Add a layer of the ground-up plant material to the sand. Use your hands to gently mix the sand and dried leaves together.

5. Use the magnifying glass to compare the soil mixture you made with the soil sample provided by your teacher. Draw what you observe.

Observations

1. How does the sand compare with the rock samples?

2. Did you observe leaves or other pieces of plant material in the soil sample provided by your teacher?

3. In what ways did the soil you made resemble the soil sample? In what ways was it different?

4. How could you make your soil more like the soil in the sample?

Analysis and Conclusions

1. Where does sand come from in natural soil?

2. Where does the plant material come from in natural soil?

3. Why is plant material an important part of soil?

4. Why are sand and other rock material important parts of soil?

Going Further

Design an experiment to compare the growth of plants in the soil you made with the growth of plants in natural soil. Discuss your plan with your teacher, and get his or her permission before you begin.

HOW HARD IS THAT ROCK?

Rocks in the Earth's crust are made up of minerals, and hardness is one of the properties used to identify them. In this activity you will determine the hardness of several mineral samples relative to each other and to some common substances.

The Mohs hardness scale shown on page 405 is used by geologists to determine hardness. But if you are collecting minerals in the field, it is often easier to use commonly available substances to perform a hardness test. For example, a fingernail has a hardness of about 2.5 and a copper penny has a hardness of 3.0. A steel knife blade has a hardness of about 5.5 and a piece of glass has a hardness of 5.5 to 6.0.

Materials
selection of mineral samples
square glass plate
steel kitchen knife
copper penny

Procedure

1. Select two mineral specimens. Try to scratch one with the other. Keep the harder of the two specimens. Put the softer one aside.

2. Select another mineral and use the same scratch test. Keep the harder of these two and set the other aside.

3. Keep repeating the procedure until you have identified the hardest mineral specimen you have.

4. Compare the minerals to find the second hardest one. Continue this procedure until all the mineral specimens have been put in order from the hardest to the softest.

5. Now compare the mineral specimens to the other materials of known hardness to determine the actual hardness of as many of your specimens as possible. **CAUTION:** *Use care when handling sharp materials. Your teacher will show you the proper way to proceed.* Share your results with your classmates. Use their findings to confirm yours.

Observations

1. Did you find any minerals that were softer than your fingernail?

2. Did any minerals scratch the penny?

3. Were any minerals unscratched by the steel blade?

4. Did any minerals scratch the glass plate?

Analysis and Conclusions

1. Calcite has a rating of 3 on the Mohs scale. Would calcite be scratched by a penny?

2. Many people think that diamond (10 on the Mohs scale) is the only mineral that can scratch glass. Is this correct? Why?

BURNING UP

The Earth's crust can be moved up and down through faulting and folding. It can also move vertically as the result of the interaction of the downward force of the crust and the upward force of the mantle. The balance between these forces constantly changes as surface processes add material to areas of the crust or take materials away. You can get an idea of how a downward force is balanced by an upward force by doing this activity and observing how a change in the amount of matter in an object affects the way it floats.

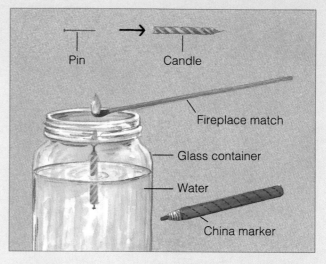

Materials

birthday-cake candle

straight pin

tall glass container (such as a jar, a
    beaker, or a water glass)

china marker

clock or watch with a second hand

long fireplace matches (If you do not have
    fireplace matches, you may use regular
    matches and a spring clothespin or a
    spring test-tube holder.)

Procedure 🔨 🔥

1. Carefully and slowly push the pin into the bottom of the candle. **CAUTION:** *Be careful when handling sharp objects.* Continue pushing the pin into the center of the candle until the head of the pin is about 2 mm from the bottom of the candle.

2. Fill the container about three-fourths full with water.

3. Hold the candle by its wick and lower it into the water. **Note:** *Do not let the wick get wet.* The candle should float upright in the water.

4. With the china marker, make a line on the side of the glass to indicate the position of the bottom of the candle.

5. Carefully light the candle. **CAUTION:** *Be careful when working with matches and open flames.* (If you are using regular matches, securely grip the base of the lit match with the clothespin or test-tube holder.) Extinguish the match by dipping it into the water.

6. Every 2 minutes, mark the position of the bottom of the candle on the side of the container.

Analysis and Conclusions

1. What happened to the position of the bottom of the candle?

2. What do you think happened to the weight of the candle?

3. What relationship do you perceive between an object's weight and how high it floats?

4. What does this activity have to do with isostasy?

IT'S A BLAST

Impress your family and friends! Create a model volcano that "erupts." All you need is a few everyday ingredients you probably have around your home.

What You Need

bottle (the 296–355 mL glass or plastic ones that contain soda or juice work well)

baking soda

funnel

vinegar

cup

red food coloring

spoon

large, shallow container (such as a plastic dishpan or a disposable aluminum baking pan)

dirt, sand, or clay

What You Do

1. Put the funnel in the mouth of the bottle. Pour baking soda into the funnel until the bottle is about half full. Then remove the funnel and rinse it clean.

Baking soda

Funnel

Bottle

2. Pour vinegar into the cup. The amount of vinegar in the cup should be about the same as the amount of baking soda in the bottle.

3. Add a few drops of red food coloring to the vinegar and stir with the spoon. Add a few more drops, if needed, to make the vinegar bright red in color.

4. Put the bottle in the pan. Mound moist dirt, sand, or clay around the bottle to form a mountain-shaped structure.

Bottle containing baking soda

Dirt

5. Gather your audience. Put the funnel in the mouth of the bottle. Pour in the vinegar, then immediately remove the funnel and step back. What happens?

Share What You Learned

1. How is what you observed similar to what actually happens in certain volcanic eruptions?

2. How might you apply what you observed to unclogging a stopped-up drain?

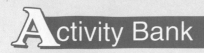
GOING THEIR SEPARATE WAYS

It is not easy to see how some processes work, especially if you cannot observe them directly. Thus it is often helpful to create a model. In this activity you will make a model that helps to show how ocean-floor spreading works.

Procedure

1. Obtain two sheets of unlined notebook paper, scissors, a colored pencil or pen, and a metric ruler.

2. Using the colored pen or pencil, draw stripes across one sheet of paper, parallel to the short sides of the paper. The stripes should vary in spacing and thickness. Fold the paper in half lengthwise. Write the word Start at the top of both halves of the paper. Then, using the scissors, cut the paper in half along the fold line to form two strips.

3. Take the second sheet of paper and lightly fold it into eighths, as shown in the accompanying diagram. Unfold the paper. Then fold it in half lengthwise.

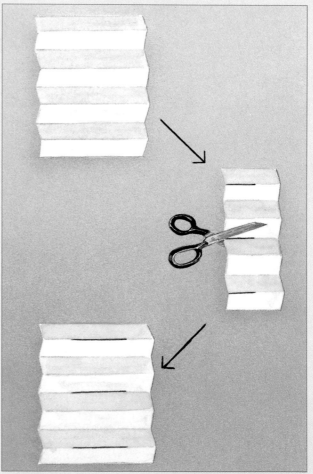

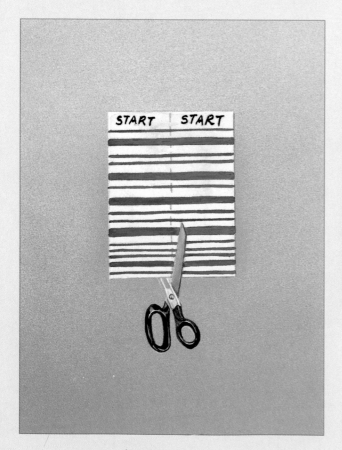

4. Draw lines 5.5 cm long, starting at the fold, on the middle crease and the two creases closest to the ends of the paper. Then use the scissors to cut along the lines you drew. Unfold the paper. You should have three slits in the center of the paper.

5. Put the two striped strips of paper together so that the Start labels touch one another. Insert the strips up through the center slit, then pull them toward the side slits.

6. Insert the ends of the strips into the side slits. Pull the ends of the strips and watch what happens at the center slit.

7. Practice pulling the strips through the slits until you can make the stripes come up and go down at the same time.

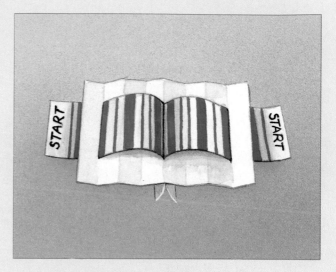

Analysis and Conclusions

1. What does the center slit represent?

2. What do the side slits represent?

3. What kind of plate boundaries are demonstrated in the model?

4. What do the striped strips represent?

5. What do the stripes on the strips represent?

6. Describe the process of ocean-floor spreading in your own words.

7. Why are models useful in studying scientific concepts?

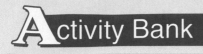

GROWING A CRYSTAL GARDEN

All minerals are made up of crystals. Crystals are solids made up of atoms or molecules that are arranged in a definite, orderly, repeating pattern. If crystals are given enough room to grow, they will develop forms whose flat sides and sharp edges reflect the orderly internal structure of the crystals. In this activity you will observe the development of crystals that have plenty of room to grow.

Materials

old newspapers

clean clear plastic jar (such as the ones used for peanut butter)

liquid laundry bluing

table salt

ammonia

measuring spoons

spoon

large, clean plastic container (such as those that contain margarine or frozen dessert-topping)

charcoal briquette

crumpled paper towel

piece of sponge

porous rocks—such as sandstones, pumice, or lava rocks (optional)

pieces of brick or clay flowerpots (optional)

Procedure 🧰

1. Assign roles to each member of the group. Possible roles include: Recorder (the person who records observations and coordinates the group's presentation of results), Materials Manager (the person who makes sure that the group has all the materials it needs), Maintenance Director (the person who coordinates cleanup), Principal Investigator (the person who reads instructions to the group, makes sure that the proper procedure is being followed, and asks questions of the teacher on behalf of the group), and Specialists (people who perform specific tasks such as arranging the collected objects in the plastic container or preparing the chemical mixture). Your group may divide up the tasks differently, and individuals may have more than one role, depending on the size of your group.

2. Soak the rocks and pieces of brick or clay in water overnight.

3. Spread old newspapers over your work area.

4. Put the charcoal, paper towel, sponge, rock, and pieces of brick or clay flowerpots into the plastic container.

5. Sprinkle 1 tablespoon of salt over the objects in the container.

6. Measure 3 tablespoons of water, 3 tablespoons of bluing, and 3 tablespoons of salt into the jar. With the spoon, stir the ingredients together slowly until they are well mixed. Then add 1 tablespoon of ammonia and stir it in well. **CAUTION:** *Ammonia has irritating fumes. Keep ammonia away from your face and avoid inhaling the fumes. Follow the safety instructions on the bottle.*

7. Spoon the mixture over the materials in the container. **Note:** *Try to leave as little of the mixture as possible on the bottom of the container. The more mixture at the bottom of the container, the slower the crystals will grow. If you have only a few objects, you may have some of the mixture left over.* Clean up any spills immediately.

8. Place your container on old newspapers in a place where it is out of drafts and will not be disturbed. Observe your container once or twice a day for about three days. Record your observations. Make drawings of what you see.

Observations and Conclusions

1. How do the contents of your container change over time?

2. What do the crystals look like?

3. Where do the materials in the crystals come from?

4. Compare your results to those obtained by your classmates. Are your results similar? Are they different? Why do you think this might be the case?

5. Many factors affect the results of this experiment. Name the three factors that you think are the most important. Explain why you selected these factors.

ONE ORE IN THE WATER

Many of the metals we use are pure elements—they contain only one kind of atom. But in nature, most substances exist as combinations of different kinds of atoms. How are the desirable metal atoms separated from the other, less desirable atoms? Discover one method by doing the following activity.

What You'll Need

black copper oxide
powdered charcoal
test tube
test-tube holder
Bunsen burner
jar

What You'll Do 🧪 🔥 👁

1. Put some copper oxide and powdered charcoal into a test tube.

2. Holding the test tube with a test tube holder, carefully heat the copper oxide and charcoal over a Bunsen burner. **CAUTION:** *Make sure you know the proper way to light and use a Bunsen burner. Be very careful when working with an open flame. Always point the mouth of the test tube away from you and others.*

3. Pour the heated mixture into a jar of water.

What You'll Discover

1. What happened when you poured the heated mixture into the water?

2. Why do you think this occurred?

3. How can metals such as copper be removed from ores such as copper oxide?

4. Thin deposits of nearly pure metal are sometimes found in places where solid rock has come into contact with hot magma rising from deep within the Earth. Using what you have learned about removing metal from ores in this activity, explain why these deposits form.

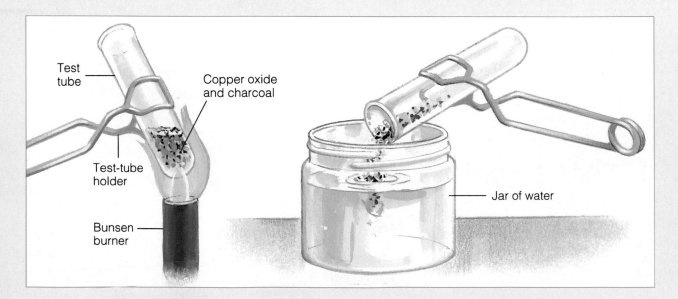

Test tube

Copper oxide and charcoal

Test-tube holder

Bunsen burner

Jar of water

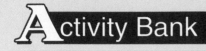
THE BRASS IS ALWAYS GREENER

Many decorative and useful objects are made of metal. But metals, like all other materials on the Earth's surface, are subject to weathering. In this activity you will see one form of weathering for yourself and make inferences from your observations. As you continue reading Section 14–1, you will find out the details about how this breaking down of metals occurs.

You Will Need

a copper penny (The date to the right of Lincoln's head must be 1981 or earlier. If you can't find an appropriate penny, you may use a piece of copper foil.)

a flat waterproof dish, such as a plate or an aluminum pie pan

vinegar

salt

Now you are ready to begin.

Vinegar — Salt

Penny

You Will Do

1. Put the penny on the plate. What color is the penny? Record your observations.

2. Sprinkle a little salt on the penny. Then pour a little vinegar over the penny. What do you observe? What do you think will happen to the penny after it has been standing for a few days? Record your prediction and explain the thinking behind it.

3. Let the penny stand for a few days. Record your observations.

You Will Discover

1. What happened to the penny after it had been standing for a few days? Why do you think this occurred?

2. Was your prediction accurate? Why do you think you were "on target" or "missed your mark"?

3. Using what you have learned from your reading of Section 14–1, what kind of weathering is the tarnishing of metal? How can you tell?

4. Compare your results with those obtained by your classmates. Explain why they are similar or different.

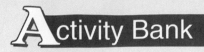
DOWN BY THE OLD MILL STREAM

Running water is a major force of erosion and deposition. It picks up and wears away materials as it flows over the land. It carries dissolved minerals and particles of mud. On rare occasions, running water can even sweep away large objects such as boulders, train engines, and houses. Obviously, running water has a lot of energy. In this activity you will find out how this energy can be harnessed and put to work for humans.

Procedure

1. Obtain a drawing compass, ruler, small disposable aluminum pan (such as a pie plate), scissors, pencil, piece of string 45 cm long, and small weight (such as a metal nut or an eraser).

2. With the compass, draw a circle about 10 cm in diameter on the bottom of the aluminum pan. Then, using the same center hole, draw a circle 3 cm in diameter.

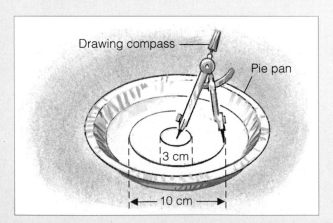

3. Using the scissors, cut out a 10 cm aluminum disk along the line you drew in step 2. **Note:** *Do not cut along the line you drew for the 3 cm circle.* **CAUTION:** *The cut edges of the pan may be sharp. Handle with care.*

4. With the scissors, make eight cuts in the disk as shown in the accompanying diagram. Notice that the cuts start at the edge of the disk, stop at the 3 cm circle, and are evenly spaced.

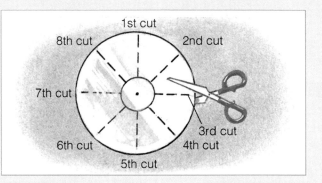

5. Twist each section of the disk a quarter-turn clockwise, as shown in the accompanying diagram. **CAUTION:** *Be careful—the edges may be sharp.*

6. Punch a hole in the center of the disk with the compass point. Enlarge the hole with the tip of the scissors. Then push the pencil through the hole. Slide the pencil through the hole until the disk is in the middle of the pencil.

7. Tightly tie one end of the string to the pencil about 3 cm from the disk. The string around the pencil should not be able to slip. (If it can, try securing it with tape.)

8. Tie the other end of the string to the weight.

9. Hold the disk under a stream of water from a faucet, as shown in the accom-panying diagram. **Note:** *The pencil should rest lightly on the tips of your thumbs and first fingers, so that it is able to move freely.* What happens?

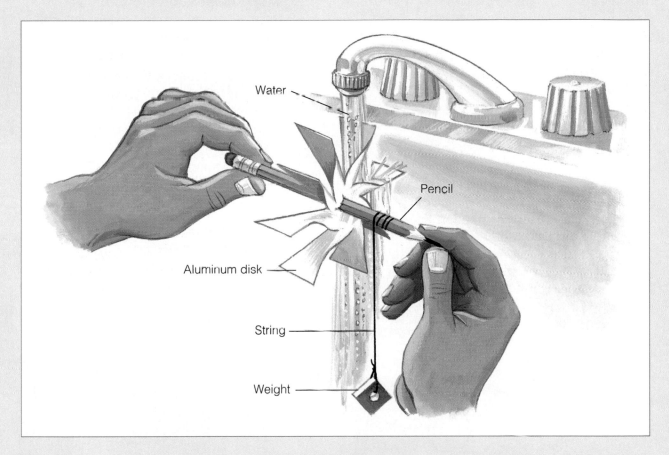

■ The disk you made in this activity is an example of a wheel that is turned by water. Such wheels played an important role in the technology of the past, and continue to play an important role today. How? A little sleuthing in the library will help you to solve this mystery! Prepare a report or poster and share your findings.

HOW CAN YOU PREVENT FOOD FROM SPOILING?

The growth of bacteria, which can cause packaged foods to spoil, can be prevented by the use of ultraviolet light. What are some other ways in which food manufacturers can slow down or stop the growth of bacteria in their food products? To stop the growth of bacteria, it is necessary to take away one or more of the conditions bacteria need in order to grow. In this activity you will investigate some of these conditions and find out how they are changed to prevent bacterial growth. All you will need are packages and labels from different food products.

1. Carefully examine each food product. Identify each food product and describe the way in which it is pack-aged. For example, is the food in a glass jar, an aluminum can, a card-board box, or some other type of package? Is the food frozen? Include as much information as you can about each food.

2. Read the package label for each food product. According to the label, what has been done to prevent bacteria from growing in each food? For example, has salt been added to the food? Bacteria cannot grow if too much salt is present. So adding salt is one way to prevent food from spoiling.

3. Share your results with the entire class. Based on your observations of the food packages and labels, what are some conditions necessary for bacterial growth? How are these conditions changed to slow down or prevent bacterial growth in packaged food?

Think for Yourself

If you have ever canned fruits or vegetables at home, you know that the food must first be heated and then sealed in airtight jars. How does this process prevent bacterial growth?

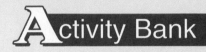
BUILD YOUR OWN ANEMOMETER

Meteorologists use an anemometer to measure wind speed. An anemometer usually has three or four cups at the ends of horizontal arms that are attached to a vertical shaft. When the wind blows into the cups, the arms turn and a meter records the wind speed in miles per hour. In this activity you will build your own simple anemometer.

Materials

2 strips of cardboard, 10 cm x 30 cm	2 washers
	screw
scissors	screwdriver
metric ruler	wooden shaft, 30 cm long
4 Styrofoam cups	
marking pen	clock or watch with second hand
stapler	

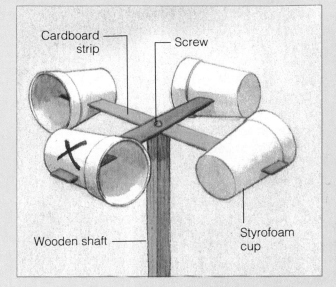

Cardboard strip — Screw

Wooden shaft — Styrofoam cup

Procedure

1. With a marking pen, draw a large X on one of the Styrofoam cups.

2. Carefully cut vertical slits in the front and back of each cup. Make the slits wide enough so that you can push a cardboard strip through them.

3. Make an X by placing one cardboard strip on top of the other. Staple the strips together.

4. Attach the four cups to the four arms of the X by sliding the cardboard strips through the slits in the cups. The openings of the cups should face counterclockwise.

5. To mount the X on the wooden shaft, make a hole in the center of the X.

Place a washer on the screw and push the screw through the hole in the X. Place the second washer on the screw below the X and screw the X to the top of the shaft. Be sure that your anemometer can turn freely.

6. Position your anemometer in a spot where the wind can hit it from all directions. To measure the wind speed, count the number of times the anemometer turns in 30 seconds and divide by 5. The result is the wind speed in miles per hour. (*Hint:* Use the cup marked with an X as a guide.)

Do It Yourself

As a class project, you might want to set up your own weather observation station. What other instruments, in addition to an anemometer, could you add to your weather station to help you make weather observations and forecasts?

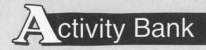
WHAT CAUSES LIGHTNING?

As Benjamin Franklin discovered, lightning is a form of electricity. Lightning is caused when electric charges build up in storm clouds, resulting in a discharge, or flash of lightning. There are two kinds of electric charges: positive and negative. In this activity you will investigate what happens when electrically charged objects are brought together.

1. To begin your investigation, obtain two balloons, two pieces of string, a glass rod, and a silk scarf.

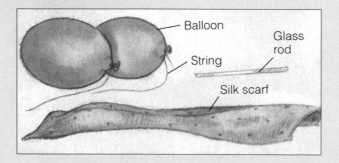

2. Blow up the balloons and tie a piece of string to each balloon.

3. Rub each balloon with the silk scarf. Hold the balloons by the string and bring them near one another. What happens to the balloons? Rubbing the balloons with silk gave each balloon a positive electric charge. Based on your observations, what happens when two objects with like charges are brought together?

4. Rub one balloon again with the silk scarf. Hold the scarf near the balloon. What happens? Rubbing the balloon with silk gave the balloon a positive charge and the silk a negative charge. Based on your observations, what happens when two objects with unlike charges are brought together?

5. Rub the glass rod with the silk scarf. What kind of electric charge does the glass rod have after being rubbed with silk?

6. Turn on a stream of water from a faucet. The water is neutral—that is, it has no electric charge. What do you predict will happen if you bring the charged glass rod near the stream of water? Try it and find out. Was your prediction correct? Based on your observations, what happens when a charged object is brought near an uncharged (neutral) object?

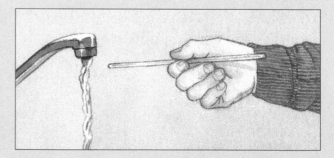

Think for Yourself

Has this ever happened to you? You walk across a room with a thick wool carpet on the floor and reach out to touch a metal doorknob. As you touch the doorknob, you feel a tingle in your fingertips. Based on what you now know about electric charges, what do you think causes the tingle you feel?

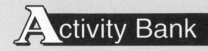

WHAT ARE DENSITY CURRENTS?

An ocean current is a river of water in the ocean. Ocean currents caused by wind patterns are called surface currents. Surface currents are either cold-water currents or warm-water currents. Other ocean currents, called deep currents, are caused mainly by differences in the density of ocean water. In this activity you will investigate how adding salt to water affects the density of water.

Materials

200-mL beaker
clear plastic container
salt
plastic spoon
food coloring, blue and red
sheet of paper

Procedure

1. Fill a 200-mL beaker with water. Add some blue food coloring to the water. Add a spoonful of salt and stir to dissolve.

2. Fill the plastic container with water. Add some red food coloring and stir.

3. Tear a sheet of paper into small pieces. Sprinkle several pieces of paper onto the surface of the water in the container.

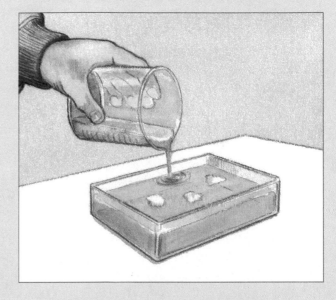

4. Gently pour the salt water down one side of the container. What happens? Do the pieces of paper move?

5. Leave the container undisturbed and continue to make observations every 5 minutes for the next 20 to 30 minutes. What happened when you poured salt water into fresh water? What effect does adding salt have on the density of water? What caused the paper to move?

Going Further

Repeat steps 1 to 3. To a second beaker, add water, a spoonful of salt, a few ice cubes, and some yellow food coloring. Pour the blue salt water into the container as you did in step 4. Then add the yellow salt water in the same way. How many layers do you see in the container?

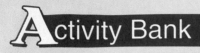
WHAT IS YOUR LATITUDE?

Early sailors used an instrument called an astrolabe to help them navigate across open waters on long ocean voyages. An astrolabe measures the altitude, or angular distance, of Polaris, the North Star, above the horizon. This angular distance, in degrees, is equal to the latitude at the observer's location. In this activity you will make a simple astrolabe and use it to determine the altitude of Polaris at your location. This will give you a good approximation of your latitude.

Materials

protractor
piece of cardboard
small weight
drinking straw
tape
string, 30 cm
thumbtack

Procedure ▄▄▄

1. Tape a protractor to a small piece of cardboard.

2. Tape a drinking straw to the straight edge of the protractor.

3. Use a thumbtack to attach a piece of string to the center hole of the protractor. Tie a small weight to the free end of the string.

4. On a clear night, go outside and locate Polaris. (*Hint*: You might want to use a star chart to help you find Polaris.) Sight Polaris through the straw as shown.

5. When you have sighted Polaris, press the string against the protractor and read the number of degrees on the protractor. The number of degrees is equal to the altitude of Polaris and also to your approximate latitude. What is your latitude?

6. Compare your observed latitude with the actual latitude listed in an atlas for your location. How accurate was your astrolabe measurement? What might have caused any difference between your observed latitude and the actual latitude? How could you improve the accuracy of your measurement?

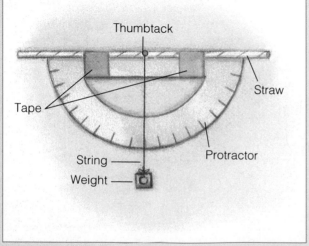

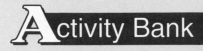
EARTH'S ELLIPTICAL ORBIT

The shape of the Earth's orbit, like the orbits of all the other planets in the solar system, is an ellipse. An ellipse is a geometrical figure drawn around two fixed points, or foci (singular: focus). For an elliptical planetary orbit, one focus is the sun. The other focus is a point in space. In this activity you will explore how the shape of the Earth's orbit affects its distance from the sun. You will need a piece of cardboard, two thumbtacks, a piece of string, and a pencil.

1. Stick two thumbtacks into a piece of cardboard. Place the thumbtacks about 10 cm apart. The thumbtacks will represent the foci of your ellipse. Label one focus "Sun."

2. Use a piece of string 30 cm long. Tie the ends of the string together and wind the string around the thumbtacks as shown.

3. With a sharp pencil, trace an ellipse on the cardboard. Be sure to keep the string taut as you draw the ellipse.

4. Repeat steps 1 to 3, but this time place the thumbtacks 5 cm apart. Compare the shapes of the two ellipses you have drawn. How does the distance between the foci affect the shape of an ellipse? Which elliptical orbit would bring the Earth closer to the sun? How would this affect the amount of radiant energy the Earth received? How would changing the amount of radiant energy affect the Earth's climate?

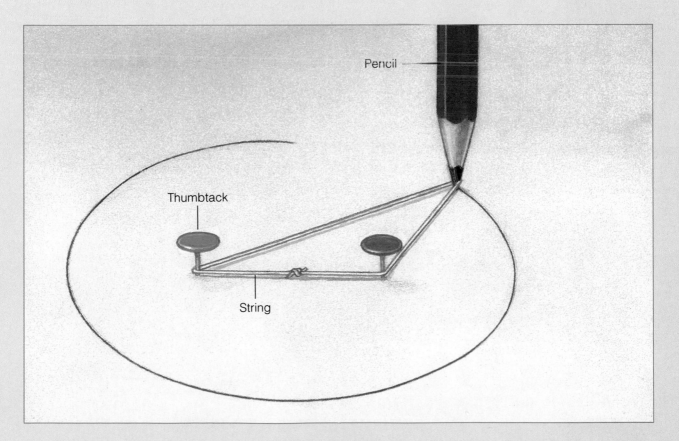

Pencil

Thumbtack

String

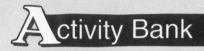
SOIL PERMEABILITY

The types of plants that can grow in different biomes depend to some extent on the type of soil present in those biomes. For example, because of the permanently frozen layer of soil called permafrost, plant growth in a tundra biome is limited to low-growing shrubs, mosses, and grasses. There are many different types of soil. Some soils soak up water better than others. The ability of soil to soak up water is called permeability. In this activity you will compare the permeability of different soils.

Materials

3 aluminum cans
can opener
100-mL graduated cylinder
clock or watch with second hand

Procedure

1. With your teacher's permission, choose three different locations on the school grounds where you can test the soil.

2. Remove the tops and bottoms from three empty aluminum soft drink cans.

3. In each location, press a can into the soil up to about 3 cm from the top of the can. **CAUTION:** *Use your foot to press the cans into the soil. Do not use your hands.*

4. Fill a 100-mL graduated cylinder with water. Pour the water into one of the cans.

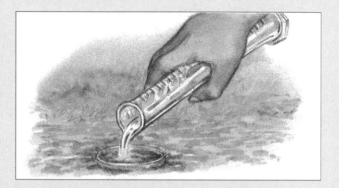

5. Measure how much time it takes for the water in the can to soak into the soil. Record your observations.

6. Repeat steps 4 and 5 for the other two cans. Compare your results. Which location had the most permeable soil? The least? How can you tell? How might the permeability of the soil in a particular biome affect plant growth in that biome?

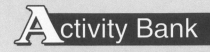
TURNED TO STONE

Fossils, some of the most interesting formations associated with sedimentary rock, are the preserved remains or traces of organisms that lived long ago. Fossils give us a glimpse into the past and reveal how organisms have evolved, or changed over time. In this activity you will discover how fossils are formed by making models of several different kinds of fossils.

Part A: Casting Call

1. Obtain a shell with a distinct texture and shape, petroleum jelly, plaster of Paris, two plastic spoons, food coloring, and two paper cups.

2. Fill a paper cup about two-thirds full with water. Add dry plaster of Paris to the water a little at a time, stirring with a spoon. Stop adding plaster when the mixture is about the consistency of honey.

3. Coat the shell with a thin layer of petroleum jelly. Press the shell into the surface of the plaster. Allow the plaster of Paris to dry overnight. What does the dry plaster look like?

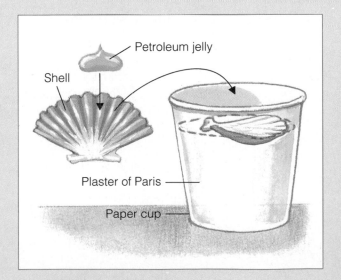

Petroleum jelly

Shell

Plaster of Paris

Paper cup

4. Under certain conditions, the shell, bone, or other fossil-forming structure dissolves after the sediments surrounding it have been cemented and compacted into rock. Represent this process by removing the shell. What do you observe? Imagine that a shell was completely buried in sediments and dissolved after the sediments had turned to rock. What kind of impression would it leave in the rock?

5. Coat the surface of the plaster of Paris with a thin layer of petroleum jelly.

6. Fill a paper cup about halfway with water. Mix another batch of plaster of Paris, as you did in step 1. Stir a few drops of food coloring into the fresh plaster. Slowly pour the fresh, colored plaster into the cup containing the hardened, white plaster. What does the colored plaster represent?

7. Allow the plaster to dry overnight. Carefully tear away the paper cup. Gently pry apart the colored and un-colored blocks of plaster. Describe the two blocks of plaster.

■ Fossils such as the one simulated in the white plaster are known as molds. Why is this name appropriate?

■ Fossils such as the one simulated by the colored plaster are known as casts. Why is this name appropriate? (*Hint:* Look up the word cast in the dictionary.)

(continued)

Part B: A Sticky Situation

Amber is a beautiful orange-gold semi-precious stone. Because it formed from the sticky sap of evergreen trees that lived long ago, amber is a fossil. But amber may also contain fossils.

1. Obtain a dead, unsquashed, hard-bodied insect such as a beetle or an ant, a piece of waxed paper about 10 cm square, and white glue.

2. Put a drop of white glue on the waxed paper. Imagine that the waxed paper is the bark of a tree and that the glue is sap oozing from a damaged spot in the bark. Now put your insect on the spot of glue. Why do you think amber often contains insect fossils?

3. Cover the insect with more white glue. Allow the glue to dry. Describe your "fossil."

■ Explain why insects in amber are often extremely well preserved.

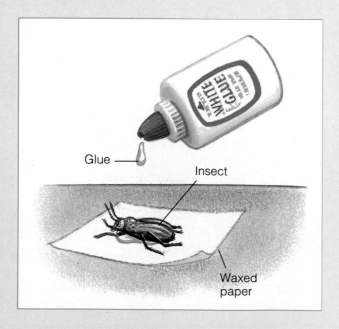

Glue

Insect

Waxed paper

Part C: Chill Out

Imagine eating steaks from a woolly mammoth (a shaggy relative of the elephant) that had been dead for thousands of years! Although this may seem disgusting, a few daring adventurers have actually done this. But how is it possible that the remains of organisms can be fossilized so that they are still edible thousands of years later?

1. Obtain two grapes, two paper cups, and permission to use the freezer.

2. Put one grape into each of two paper cups. Put one cup in the freezer. Put the other cup in a warm place where it will not be disturbed.

3. After a week, examine the two grapes. How do they differ in appearance? If you like, you may eat the frozen grape. **CAUTION:** *Do not eat the grape that was not frozen.*

■ Based on your results, explain how and why low temperatures affect preservation. Why are mammoth fossils found in frozen mud often well-preserved?

Sharing What You Learned

1. Write a brief, illustrated report that describes your observations and conclusions.

2. Prepare a display on fossils that includes the models you made in parts A and B, drawings of your results for part C, and one or more of the following: drawings of fossils and prehistoric animals, plastic models of dinosaurs, shoe-box dioramas, and/or real fossils. Be prepared to answer questions from your classmates and teacher about the items in your group's display.

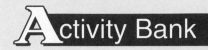

BLOWING IN THE WIND

In many parts of the world, wind is an important source of energy. In places where the wind blows steadily at 13 km/h or more, modern windmills can be used to generate electricity. Could such wind generators be used where you live? In this activity you will build a simple device to measure wind speed.

Materials

Ping-Pong ball
sewing needle
carpet thread
protractor
glue

Procedure

1. Use a sewing needle to thread 30 cm of heavy-duty carpet thread through a Ping-Pong ball. Tie a knot at the end of the thread so that the ball will not slip off.

2. Glue the free end of the thread to the center guide of the protractor.

3. Hold the protractor so that it is level. The thread holding the Ping-Pong ball should cover the 90° mark on the protractor.

4. Choose a windy spot on your school grounds. With your back to the wind, hold the protractor level so that the wind can move the Ping-Pong ball. Measure the angle on the protractor and record this angle in a data table similar to the one shown on page 782. Use the conversion table to convert the angle in degrees to the approximate wind speed in kilometers per hour.

5. Repeat your measurement twice a day every day for a week.

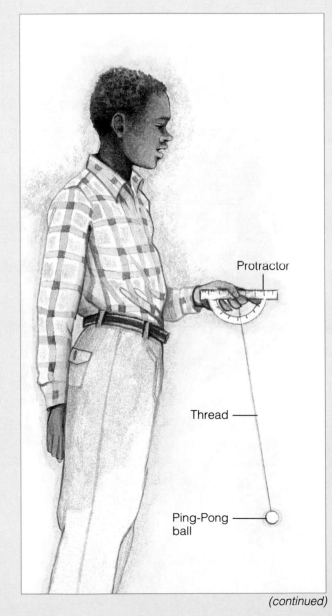

Protractor

Thread

Ping-Pong ball

(continued)

CONVERSION TABLE

Angle (°)	Wind Speed (Approximate) (km/h)
90	0
85	6
80	8
75	10
70	12
65	13
60	15
55	16
50	18
45	20
40	21
35	23
30	26
25	29
20	33

Observations

DATA TABLE

Day	Trial	Angle (°)	Wind Speed (km/h)
1	1		
	2		
2	1		
	2		
3	1		
	2		
4	1		
	2		
5	1		
	2		

Analysis and Conclusions

Share your data with the entire class and prepare a class data table. Was the wind speed constant during the week? What was the average wind speed for the week? Based on your observations, do you think wind energy could be used to generate electricity in your area? Why or why not?

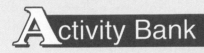
HOW DOES YOUR GARDEN GROW?

Although crop rotation is a good way to prevent depletion of nutrients from soil, many farmers also use fertilizers to help their crops grow. Imagine that you have your own vegetable garden. To get a good crop of fresh vegetables from your garden, you must add fertilizer to the soil. But you know that chemical fertilizers can cause pollution. Then a friend suggests that you make a compost pile. What is compost? Is compost a good fertilizer? How easy is it to make compost for your garden? Is it good for the environment? What will making a compost pile cost? Keep these questions in mind as you do this activity.

Materials

2-L plastic bottle with cap
soil
funnel
graduated cylinder
vegetable and fruit scraps
leaves
grass clippings
paper
glass-marking pencil

Procedure

1. Using a funnel, add some soil to a clear plastic bottle.

2. Add 20 mL of water to the soil. The soil should be moist but not soaking wet. If the soil is still dry, add some more water.

3. Add the vegetable and fruit scraps, shredded leaves and paper, and grass clippings to the soil until the bottle is about half full.

4. Screw the cap on tightly. Then turn the bottle upside down and shake it to mix the contents well.

5. Turn the bottle right-side up. Make a mark on the outside of the bottle to indicate the height of the contents.

6. Loosen the cap, but do not remove it. Place the bottle in a warm, dark place.

7. Observe the bottle at least once a week. Mix the contents and mark the height on the bottle each time. When your compost is fully decomposed, it will have a rich, brown color. Try using it as fertilizer or potting soil.

Think for Yourself

1. How difficult was it to make your compost? How would you go about making enough compost to fertilize your whole garden?

2. What are some pros and cons of composting? Do the pros outweigh the cons? Explain.

3. Do you think composting is a better idea than disposing of food wastes, leaves, and grass clippings in the trash? Why or why not?

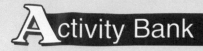
TOO MUCH, TOO LITTLE, OR JUST RIGHT?

You know that fresh water is an extremely important natural resource. One of the most important uses of water is for irrigation of farmlands. All plants need enough water to grow strong and healthy. But just how much is enough? Try this activity to find out. You will need two small flowering plants in pots, a marking pen, a metric ruler, and, of course, water.

1. Choose two small flowering plants, such as marigolds. With a marking pen, label the pots A and B.

2. Place both pots in a location where they will receive indirect sunlight.

3. Water pot A often enough so that the soil stays moist but not soaking wet.

4. Water pot B about once a week. Make sure the soil is completely dry before watering.

5. Observe the appearance of the plants every day for three weeks. Measure the height of the plants at the end of each week. Record your observations. How do the plants compare after three weeks? Which plant appeared healthier? Why?

Do It Yourself

Is it possible for a plant to receive too much water? Design and perform an experiment to find out.

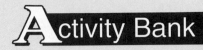
HOLD THE SALT!

Desalination is the process by which fresh water is produced from salt water. On a large scale, desalination requires a series of complex steps to remove the salt from ocean water and produce fresh water for drinking or irrigation. In this activity, however, you can turn salt water into fresh water using only the energy of the sun and a few easy-to-find materials.

Materials

salt
pencil
2-L plastic soda bottle
plastic container
3 drinking straws
plastic wrap
tape
scissors

Procedure

1. Dissolve 2 tablespoons of salt in 1 L of water.

2. Carefully cut the top off a 2-L plastic soda bottle and discard the top. Punch two holes near the open end of the bottle. Be sure the holes are directly opposite each other.

3. Punch two holes near the top of a plastic container large enough to hold the soda bottle. Again, be sure the holes are opposite each other.

4. Suspend the bottle inside the container by inserting a pencil through all four holes as shown.

5. Add the salt water to the suspended bottle.

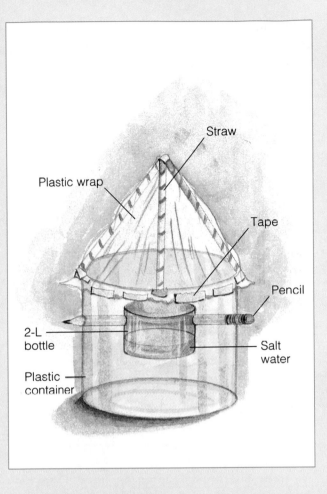

6. Tape three drinking straws together as shown and wrap a piece of clear plastic around the straws to make a tent. Tape the edges of the plastic to the outside of the container to hold the tent in place.

7. Place the apparatus in a sunny spot and observe it every day for several days. What do you see happening inside the tent? What happened to the salt water when you placed the apparatus in direct sunlight?

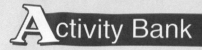

POND WATER + FERTILIZER = ALGAE EXPLOSION

Water pollution can come from many sources, including sewage, chemical wastes, pesticides, and fertilizers. In this activity you will observe how fertilizers affect the growth of algae in pond water.

Materials

glass-marking pencil
2 glass jars with lids
aged tap water
aquarium water
graduated cylinder
liquid fertilizer

Procedure

1. Label two jars A and B. Fill each jar half full with tap water that has been allowed to stand for three days. Then add aquarium water to each jar until the jar is three-fourths full.

2. Add 5 mL of liquid fertilizer to jar A. Do not add anything to jar B. Screw the lid on each jar.

3. Place both jars on a windowsill where they will receive direct sunlight. Observe the jars every day for two weeks. Compare the color of the water in the two jars. In which jar—A or B—did more algae grow? How can you tell?

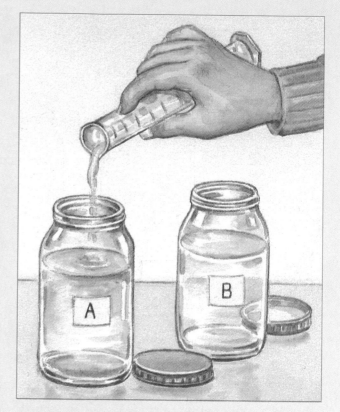

Think for Yourself

1. What was the purpose of jar B in this experiment?

2. What do you think would happen to fishes and other animals living in a lake if large amounts of fertilizer were to run off into the lake?

WASTE NOT, WANT NOT

Many of our most important mineral resources can be obtained only by mining. Each year miners dig about 24 billion metric tons of minerals from the Earth's crust. Unfortunately, mines often leave behind huge amounts of wastes, called tailings. Most of the waste contains a high concentration of sulfur. In this activity you will see how pure copper can be reclaimed from copper sulfate, such as that found in mine waste. How do you think the reclamation of copper from mine wastes might affect the environment?

Materials

copper sulfate
triple-beam balance
beaker
graduated cylinder
iron nails
litmus paper

Procedure ⚗ 📷 👁

1. Place 3 g of copper sulfate into the beaker. **CAUTION:** *Copper sulfate is poisonous. Handle it with extreme care.*

2. Add 50 mL of water to the beaker to dissolve the copper sulfate. What is the color of the solution formed?

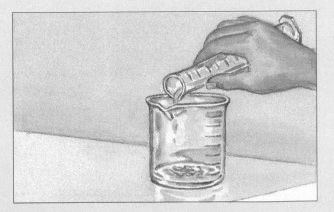

3. Test the solution with red and blue litmus paper. Does the litmus paper change color? Is the solution acidic, basic, or neutral?

4. Add several iron nails to the beaker. What is the color of the solution now? What happened to the nails after you placed them into the solution?

5. Again test the solution with red and blue litmus paper. Does the litmus paper change color? Is the solution acidic, basic, or neutral?

Think for Yourself

In this activity you have seen how a chemical reaction can be used to reclaim copper from copper sulfate. What might happen as a result of the large-scale reclamation of copper from mine waste if the water used in this process were to be flushed into a stream or river? What might happen to water supplies if this water seeped into the groundwater?

Do It Yourself

How might the water used in the reclamation process affect plants growing in the area? With your teacher's permission, design and perform an experiment to find out.

THE METRIC SYSTEM

The metric system of measurement is used by scientists throughout the world. It is based on units of ten. Each unit is ten times larger or ten times smaller than the next unit. The most commonly used units of the metric system are given below. After you have finished reading about the metric system, try to put it to use. How tall are you in metrics? What is your mass? What is your normal body temperature in degrees Celsius?

Commonly Used Metric Units

Length The distance from one point to another

meter (m) A meter is slightly longer than a yard.
1 meter = 1000 millimeters (mm)
1 meter = 100 centimeters (cm)
1000 meters = 1 kilometer (km)

Volume The amount of space an object takes up

liter (L) A liter is slightly more than a quart.
1 liter = 1000 milliliters (mL)

Mass The amount of matter in an object

gram (g) A gram has a mass equal to about one paper clip.

1000 grams = 1 kilogram (kg)

Temperature The measure of hotness or coldness

degrees Celsius (°C) 0°C = freezing point of water
100°C = boiling point of water

Metric–English Equivalents

2.54 centimeters (cm) = 1 inch (in.)
1 meter (m) = 39.37 inches (in.)
1 kilometer (km) = 0.62 miles (mi)
1 liter (L) = 1.06 quarts (qt)
250 milliliters (mL) = 1 cup (c)
1 kilogram (kg) = 2.2 pounds (lb)
28.3 grams (g) = 1 ounce (oz)
$°C = 5/9 \times (°F - 32)$

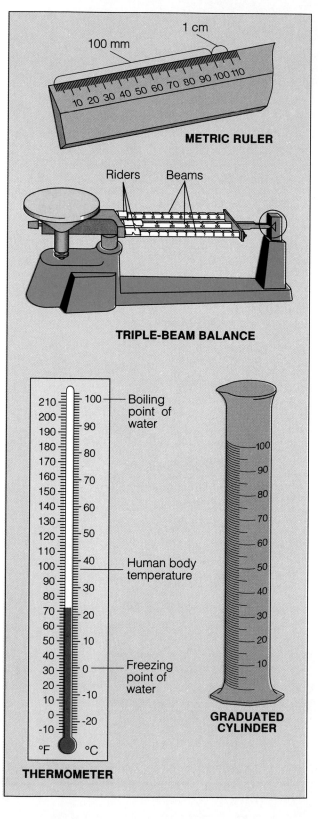

METRIC RULER

TRIPLE-BEAM BALANCE

THERMOMETER

GRADUATED CYLINDER

Appendix B

The laboratory balance is an important tool in scientific investigations. You can use the balance to determine the mass of materials that you study or experiment with in the laboratory.

Different kinds of balances are used in the laboratory. One kind of balance is the double-pan balance. Another kind of balance is the triple-beam balance. The balance that you may use in your science class is probably similar to one of the balances illustrated in this Appendix. To use the balance properly, you should learn the name, function, and location of each part of the balance you are using. What kind of balance do you have in your science class?

The Double-Pan Balance

The double-pan balance shown in this Appendix has two beams. Some double-pan balances have only one beam. The beams are calibrated, or marked, in grams. The upper beam is divided into ten major units of 1 gram each. Each of these units is further divided into units of 1/10 of a gram. The lower beam is divided into twenty units, and each unit is equal to 10 grams. The lower beam can be used to find the masses of objects up to 200 grams. Each beam has a rider that is moved to the right along the beam. The rider indicates the number of grams needed to balance the object in the left pan. What is the total mass the balance can measure?

Before using the balance, you should be sure that the pans are empty and both riders are pointing to zero. The balance should be on a flat, level surface. The pointer should be at the zero point. If your pointer does not read zero, slowly turn the adjustment knob so that the pointer does read zero.

The following procedure can be used to find the mass of an object with a double-pan balance:

1. Place the object whose mass is to be determined on the left pan.

2. Move the rider on the lower beam to the 10-gram notch.

3. If the pointer moves to the right of the zero point on the scale, the object has a mass less than

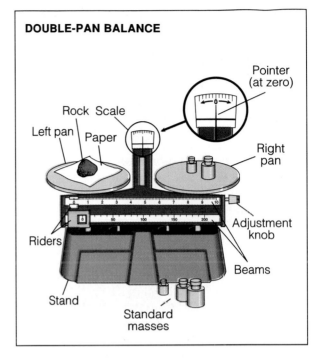

DOUBLE-PAN BALANCE

Parts of a Double-Pan Balance and Their Functions

Pointer Indicator used to determine when the mass being measured is balanced by the riders or masses of the balance

Scale Series of marks along which the pointer moves

Zero Point Center line of the scale to which the pointer moves when the mass being measured is balanced by the riders or masses of the balance

Adjustment Knob Knob used to set the balance at the zero point when the riders are all on zero and no masses are on either pan

Left Pan Platform on which an object whose mass is to be determined is placed

Right Pan Platform on which standard masses are placed

Beams Horizontal strips of metal on which marks, or graduations, appear that indicate grams or parts of grams

Riders Devices that are moved along the beams and used to balance the object being measured and to determine its mass

Stand Support for the balance

10 grams. Return the rider on the lower beam to zero. Slowly move the rider on the upper beam until the pointer is at zero. The reading on the beam is the mass of the object.

4. If the pointer did not move to the right of the zero, move the rider on the lower beam notch by notch until the pointer does move to the right. Move the rider back one notch. Then move the rider on the upper beam until the pointer is at zero. The sum of the readings on both beams is the mass of the object.

5. If the two riders are moved completely to the right side of the beams and the pointer remains to the left of the zero point, the object has a mass greater than the total mass that the balance can measure.

The total mass that most double-pan balances can measure is 210 grams. If an object has a mass greater than 210 grams, return the riders to the zero point.

The following procedure can be used to find the mass of an object greater than 210 grams:

1. Place the standard masses on the right pan one at a time, starting with the largest, until the pointer remains to the right of the zero point.

2. Remove one of the large standard masses and replace it with a smaller one. Continue replacing the standard masses with smaller ones until the pointer remains to the left of the zero point. When the pointer remains to the left of the zero point, the mass of the object on the left pan is greater than the total mass of the standard masses on the right pan.

3. Move the rider on the lower beam and then the rider on the upper beam until the pointer stops at the zero point on the scale. The mass of the object is equal to the sum of the readings on the beams plus the mass of the standard masses.

The Triple-Beam Balance

The triple-beam balance is a single-pan balance with three beams calibrated in grams. The back, or 100-gram, beam is divided into ten units of 10 grams each. The middle, or 500-gram, beam is divided into five units of 100 grams each. The front, or 10-gram, is divided into ten major units of 1 gram each. Each of these units is further divided into units of 1/10 of a gram. What is the largest mass you could find with a triple-beam balance?

The following procedure can be used to find the mass of an object with a triple-beam balance:

1. Place the object on the pan.

2. Move the rider on the middle beam notch by notch until the horizontal pointer drops below zero. Move the rider back one notch.

3. Move the rider on the back beam notch by notch until the pointer again drops below zero. Move the rider back one notch.

4. Slowly slide the rider along the front beam until the pointer stops at the zero point.

5. The mass of the object is equal to the sum of the readings on the three beams.

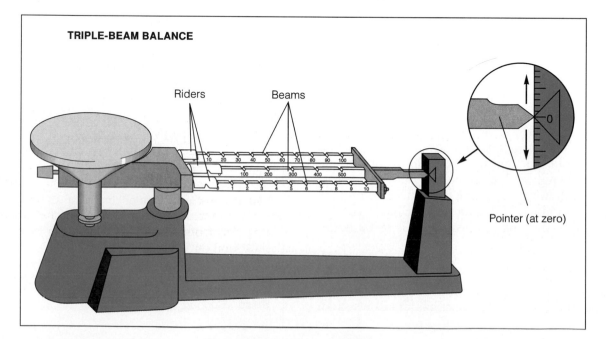

TRIPLE-BEAM BALANCE

Riders   Beams

Pointer (at zero)

Appendix **C**

One of the first things a scientist learns is that working in the laboratory can be an exciting experience. But the laboratory can also be quite dangerous if proper safety rules are not followed at all times. To prepare yourself for a safe year in the laboratory, read over the following safety rules. Then read them a second time. Make sure you understand each rule. If you do not, ask your teacher to explain any rules you are unsure of.

Dress Code

1. Many materials in the laboratory can cause eye injury. To protect yourself from possible injury, wear safety goggles whenever you are working with chemicals, burners, or any substance that might get into your eyes. Never wear contact lenses in the laboratory.

2. Wear a laboratory apron or coat whenever you are working with chemicals or heated substances.

3. Tie back long hair to keep it away from any chemicals, burners and candles, or other laboratory equipment.

4. Remove or tie back any article of clothing or jewelry that can hang down and touch chemicals and flames.

General Safety Rules

5. Read all directions for an experiment several times. Follow the directions exactly as they are written. If you are in doubt about any part of the experiment, ask your teacher for assistance.

6. Never perform activities that are not authorized by your teacher. Obtain permission before "experimenting" on your own.

7. Never handle any equipment unless you have specific permission.

8. Take extreme care not to spill any material in the laboratory. If a spill occurs, immediately ask your teacher about the proper cleanup procedure. Never simply pour chemicals or other substances into the sink or trash container.

9. Never eat in the laboratory.

10. Wash your hands before and after each experiment.

First Aid

11. Immediately report all accidents, no matter how minor, to your teacher.

12. Learn what to do in case of specific accidents, such as getting acid in your eyes or on your skin. (Rinse acids from your body with lots of water.)

13. Become aware of the location of the first-aid kit. But your teacher should administer any required first aid due to injury. Or your teacher may send you to the school nurse or call a physician.

14. Know where and how to report an accident or fire. Find out the location of the fire extinguisher, phone, and fire alarm. Keep a list of important phone numbers—such as the fire department and the school nurse—near the phone. Immediately report any fires to your teacher.

Heating and Fire Safety

15. Again, never use a heat source, such as a candle or burner, without wearing safety goggles.

16. Never heat a chemical you are not instructed to heat. A chemical that is harmless when cool may be dangerous when heated.

17. Maintain a clean work area and keep all materials away from flames.

18. Never reach across a flame.

19. Make sure you know how to light a Bunsen burner. (Your teacher will demonstrate the proper procedure for lighting a burner.) If the flame leaps out of a burner toward you, immediately turn off the gas. Do not touch the burner. It may be hot. And never leave a lighted burner unattended!

20. When heating a test tube or bottle, always point it away from you and others. Chemicals can splash or boil out of a heated test tube.

21. Never heat a liquid in a closed container. The expanding gases produced may blow the container apart, injuring you or others.

22. Before picking up a container that has been heated, first hold the back of your hand near it. If you can feel the heat on the back of your hand, the container may be too hot to handle. Use a clamp or tongs when handling hot containers.

Using Chemicals Safely

23. Never mix chemicals for the "fun of it." You might produce a dangerous, possibly explosive substance.

24. Never touch, taste, or smell a chemical unless you are instructed by your teacher to do so. Many chemicals are poisonous. If you are instructed to note the fumes in an experiment, gently wave your hand over the opening of a container and direct the fumes toward your nose. Do not inhale the fumes directly from the container.

25. Use only those chemicals needed in the activity. Keep all lids closed when a chemical is not being used. Notify your teacher whenever chemicals are spilled.

26. Dispose of all chemicals as instructed by your teacher. To avoid contamination, never return chemicals to their original containers.

27. Be extra careful when working with acids or bases. Pour such chemicals over the sink, not over your workbench.

28. When diluting an acid, pour the acid into water. Never pour water into an acid.

29. Immediately rinse with water any acids that get on your skin or clothing. Then notify your teacher of any acid spill.

Using Glassware Safely

30. Never force glass tubing into a rubber stopper. A turning motion and lubricant will be helpful when inserting glass tubing into rubber stoppers or rubber tubing. Your teacher will demonstrate the proper way to insert glass tubing.

31. Never heat glassware that is not thoroughly dry. Use a wire screen to protect glassware from any flame.

32. Keep in mind that hot glassware will not appear hot. Never pick up glassware without first checking to see if it is hot. See #22.

33. If you are instructed to cut glass tubing, fire-polish the ends immediately to remove sharp edges.

34. Never use broken or chipped glassware. If glassware breaks, notify your teacher and dispose of the glassware in the proper trash container.

35. Never eat or drink from laboratory glassware. Thoroughly clean glassware before putting it away.

Using Sharp Instruments

36. Handle scalpels or razor blades with extreme care. Never cut material toward you; cut away from you.

37. Immediately notify your teacher if you cut your skin when working in the laboratory.

Animal Safety

38. No experiments that will cause pain, discomfort, or harm to mammals, birds, reptiles, fishes, and amphibians should be done in the classroom or at home.

39. Animals should be handled only if necessary. If an animal is excited or frightened, pregnant, feeding, or with its young, special handling is required.

40. Your teacher will instruct you as to how to handle each animal species that may be brought into the classroom.

41. Clean your hands thoroughly after handling animals or the cage containing animals.

End-of-Experiment Rules

42. After an experiment has been completed, clean up your work area and return all equipment to its proper place.

43. Wash your hands after every experiment.

44. Turn off all burners before leaving the laboratory. Check that the gas line leading to the burner is off as well.

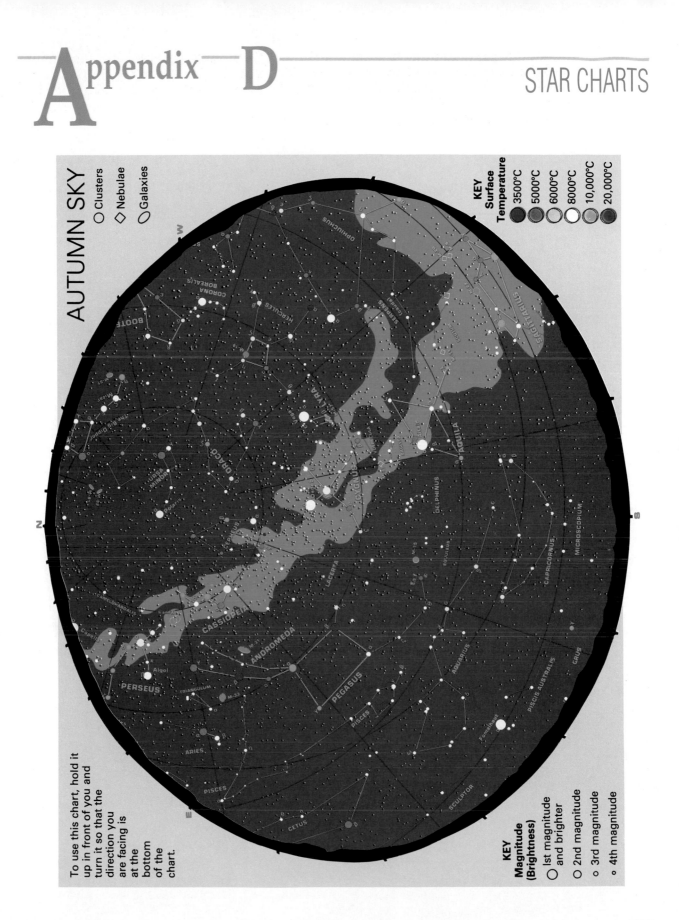

AUTUMN SKY

○ Clusters
◇ Nebulae
○ Galaxies

To use this chart, hold it up in front of you and turn it so that the direction you are facing is at the bottom of the chart.

KEY
Surface
Temperature

3500°C
5000°C
6000°C
8000°C
10,000°C
20,000°C

KEY
Magnitude
(Brightness)

○ 1st magnitude and brighter
○ 2nd magnitude
○ 3rd magnitude
○ 4th magnitude

Appendix D

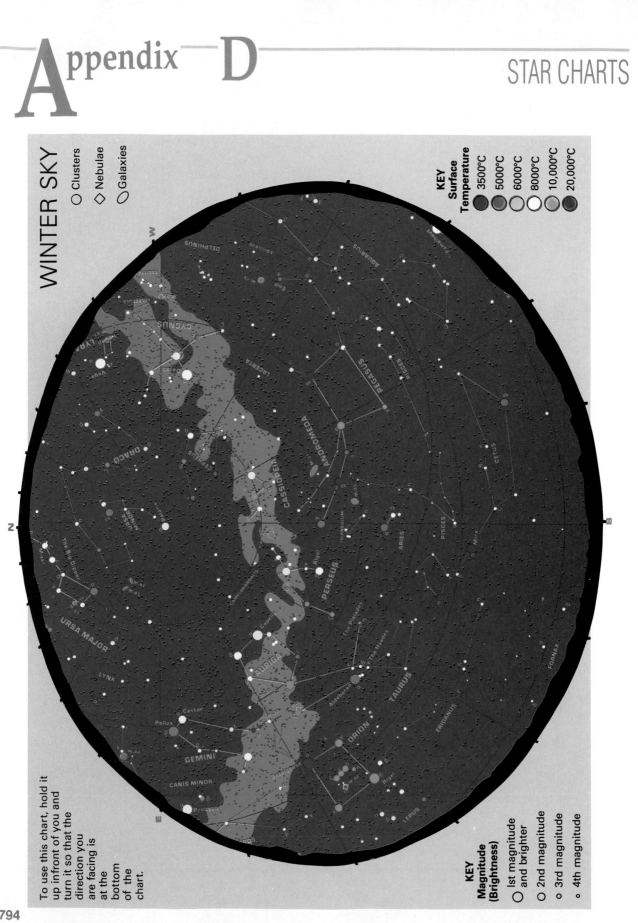

WINTER SKY

○ Clusters
◇ Nebulae
○ Galaxies

KEY
Surface
Temperature

3500°C
5000°C
6000°C
8000°C
10,000°C
20,000°C

To use this chart, hold it up infront of you and turn it so that the direction you are facing is at the bottom of the chart.

KEY
Magnitude
(Brightness)

○ lst magnitude and brighter
○ 2nd magnitude
○ 3rd magnitude
○ 4th magnitude

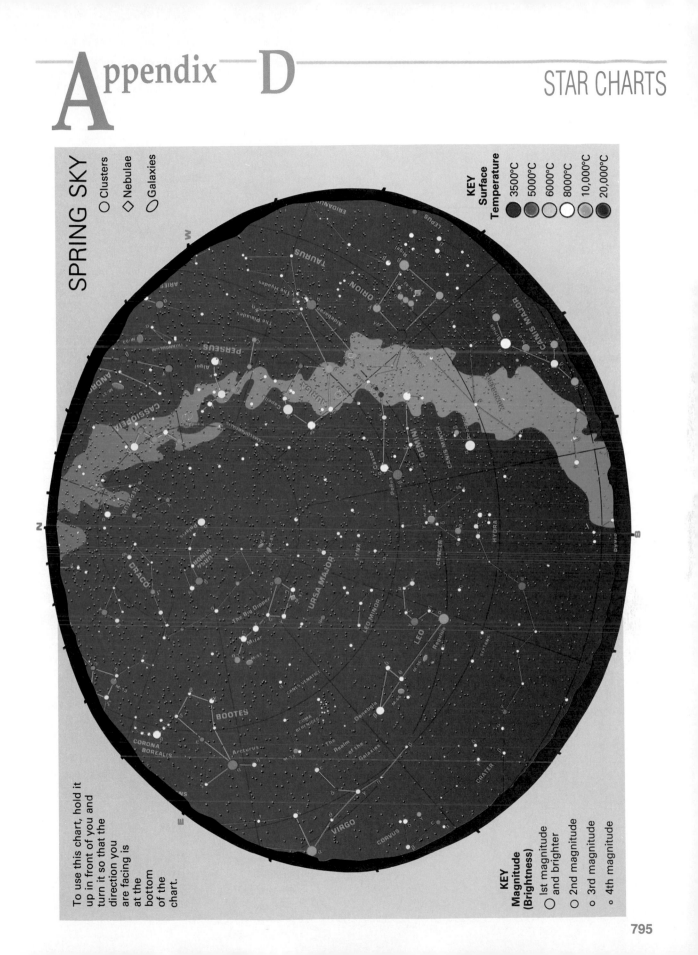

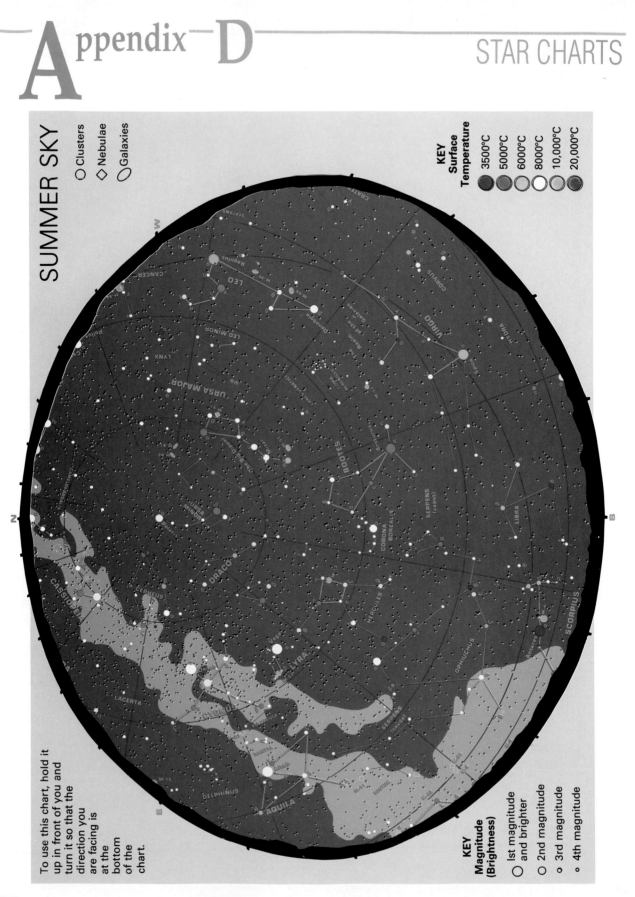

SUMMER SKY

Clusters
Nebulae
Galaxies

**KEY
Surface
Temperature**

3500°C
5000°C
6000°C
8000°C
10,000°C
20,000°C

To use this chart, hold it up in front of you and turn it so that the direction you are facing is at the bottom of the chart.

**KEY
Magnitude
(Brightness)**

1st magnitude and brighter
2nd magnitude
3rd magnitude
4th magnitude

GROUP 1
Metallic Luster, Mostly Dark Colored

Hardness	Specific Gravity	Luster/ Color	Streak	Cleavage	Other Properties/ Remarks	Chemical Formula	Mineral
6–6.5	5.02	Metallic; brass yellow	Greenish, brownish black	Uneven	Harder than chalcopyrite and pyrrhotite; called "fool's gold" but harder than gold	FeS_2	**Pyrite**
5–6	5.18	Metallic; iron black	Black	Partly octahedral	Very magnetic; important iron ore; known as "lodestone"	Fe_3O_4	**Magnetite**
5.5–6.5	5.26	Metallic; reddish brown to black	Light to dark red	Uneven	Most important ore of iron; known as "red ocher"	Fe_2O_3	**Hematite**
4	4.6	Metallic; brownish bronze	Black	Uneven	Less hard than pyrite; slight magnetism	FeS	**Pyrrhotite**
3.5–4	3.9–4.1	Resinous; brown to black	White, yellow, or brown	Dodecahedral	Important zinc ore; known as "ruby zinc"	ZnS	**Sphalerite**
3.5–4	4.1–4.3	Metallic; brass yellow	Greenish black	Uneven	Ore of copper; softer than pyrite; also known as "fool's gold"	$CuFeS_2$	**Chalcopyrite**
3	5.06–5.08	Metallic; bronze but turns to purple and black	Gray black	Uneven	Important ore of copper; known as "peacock ore" because of purple color when exposed to air for a time	Cu_5FeS_4	**Bornite**
2.5–3	8.5–9	Metallic; copper red to black	Copper red	Fracture	Can be pounded into various shapes and drawn into wires; used in making electrical wires, coins, pipes	Cu	**Copper**
2.5–3	19.3	Metallic; gold	Yellow	Fracture	Does not tarnish; used in jewelry, coins, dental fillings	Au	**Gold**
2.5	10–12	Metallic; silver white tarnishes to black	Silver to light gray	Fracture	Can be pounded into various shapes and drawn into wires; used in jewelry, coins, electrical wire	Ag	**Silver**
2.5	7.4–7.6	Metallic; lead gray	Lead gray	Cubic	Main ore of lead; used in shields against radiation, plumbing	PbS	**Galena**
1–2	2.3	Metallic; black to gray	Black	Basal cleavage (scales)	Feels greasy; very soft; used as pencil "lead" and as a lubricant	C	**Graphite**

GROUP 2
Nonmetallic Luster, Mostly Dark Colored

Hardness	Specific Gravity	Luster/ Color	Streak	Cleavage	Other Properties/ Remarks	Chemical Formula	Mineral
9	4.02	Brilliant to glassy; usually brown	White	Hexagonal	Very hard; used as an abrasive; as gems, called "ruby" (red), "sapphire" (blue)	Al_2O_3	**Corundum**
6.5–7.5	3.5–4.3	Glassy to resinous; red-brown	White, light brown	Dodecahedral	Mainly used in jewelry and as an abrasive	$Mg_3Al_2Si_3O_{12}$	**Garnet**
6.5–7	3.27–3.37	Glassy; olive green	White	Imperfect	Found in volcanic rocks; sometimes used as a gem	Mg_2SiO_4	**Olivine**
5–6	3.2–3.4	Glassy; dark green to black	Greenish gray	Perfect prism	Found in volcanic rocks	$Ca\,(Mg,\,Fe)(SiO_3)_2(Al,\,Fe)_2O_3$	**Augite**
5–6	3.2	Glassy, silky; dark green, brown, black	Gray to white	Long prism	Found in igneous and metamorphic rocks	Complex substance containing Fe, Mg, Si, O, and other elements	**Hornblende**
5	3.15–3.2	Glassy; green, brown, red	White	Hexagonal	Sometimes used as a gem	$Ca_5(PO_4)_3F$	**Apatite**
3.5–4	3.77	Glassy to dull; intense blue	Pale blue	Fibrous	Ore of copper; used as a gem	$Cu_3(CO_3)_2(OH)_2$	**Azurite**
2.5–3	2.8–3.2	Pearly, glassy; black, brown, dark green	White to light brown	Thin sheets	One of the micas; sometimes used as a lubricant	Complex substance containing Fe, Mg, Si, O, and other elements	**Biotite**
2.5	2.2–2.65	Greasy, waxy, silky; green	White	Parallel fibers	Once used in insulation but found to be cancer causing; used in fireproofing; is a form of "asbestos"	$Mg_3Si_2O_5(OH)_4$	**Serpentine**
1–5.5	3.6–4	Glassy; dark brown to black	Yellow-brown	Varies	Ore of iron; also known as "yellow ocher," a pigment; a mixture, which is not strictly a mineral	Mixture of hydrous iron oxides	**Limonite**
1–3	2–3	Dull to earthy; brown, yellow, gray, white	Colorless to gray	Uneven fracture	Ore of aluminum; smells like clay when wet; a mixture, which is not strictly a mineral	Mixture of hydrous aluminum oxides	**Bauxite**

GROUP 3
Nonmetallic Luster, Mostly Light Colored

Hardness	Specific Gravity	Luster/ Color	Streak	Cleavage	Other Properties/ Remarks	Chemical Formula	Mineral
10	3.5	Brilliant, greasy; colorless, pale yellow, red, orange, green, blue, black	Colorless	Octahedral	Hardest known substance; used in jewelry, as an abrasive, in cutting instruments	C	**Diamond**
8	3.4–3.6	Glassy; straw yellow, pink, bluish, greenish	Colorless or white	Prismatic	Valuable gem	$Al_2SiO_4(F,OH)_2$	**Topaz**
7.5–8	2.65	Glassy; greasy; colorless, white, any color when not pure	Colorless, white	Hexagonal	Many varieties are gems (amethyst, cat's-eye, bloodstone, agate, jasper, onyx); used in making glass	SiO_2	**Quartz**
6	2.55–2.75	Glassy; colorless, white, various colors	Colorless, white	In two planes at or near 90°	Most common mineral found in igneous rocks	$(K,Na,Ca)(AlSi_3O_8)$	**Feldspar**
4	3.18	Glassy; light green, yellow, bluish green, other colors	Colorless	Octahedral	Some types fluoresce (glow when exposed to ultraviolet light); used in making steel	CaF_2	**Fluorite**
3.5–4	2.85	Glassy or pearly; pink, white, gray, green, brown, black	Colorless	Conchoidal fracture	Used in making concrete and cement; type of limestone	$CaMg(CO_3)_2$	**Dolomite**
1.5–2.5	2.07	Resinous; yellow	White	Conchoidal fracture	Used in making many medicines, in producing of sulfuric acid, and in vulcanizing rubber	S	**Sulfur**
1	2.7–2.8	Pearly to greasy; gray, white, greenish	White	Uneven fracture	Very soft; used in talcum powder; found mostly in metamorphic rocks; also called "soapstone"	$Mg_3(OH)_2Si_4O_{10}$	**Talc**

TOPOGRAPHIC MAP SYMBOLS

Boundaries

National . . . .

State or territorial . . . .

County or equivalent . . . .

Civil township or equivalent . . . .

Incorporated city or equivalent . . . . .

Park, reservation, or monument . . . . .

Small park . . . .

Roads and related features

Primary highway . . . .

Secondary highway . . . .

Light-duty road . . . .

Unimproved road . . . .

Trail . . . .

Dual highway . . . .

Dual highway with median strip . . . . . .

Bridge . . . .

Tunnel . . . .

Buildings and related features

Dwelling or place of employment: small;

　large . . . .

School; house of worship . . . .

Barn, warehouse, etc.: small; large . . . .

Airport . . . .

Campground; picnic area . . . .

Cemetery: small; large . . . .

Railroads and related features

Standard-gauge single track; station . . .

Standard-gauge multiple track . . . .

Contours

Intermediate . . . .

Index . . . .

Supplementary . . . .

Depression . . . .

Cut; fill . . . .

Surface features

Levee . . . .

Sand or mud areas, dunes, or shifting

　sand . . . .

Gravel beach or glacial moraine . . . . . .

Vegetation

Woods . . . .

Scrub . . . .

Orchard . . . .

Vineyard . . . .

Marine shoreline

Approximate mean high water . . . .

Indefinite or unsurveyed . . . .

Coastal features

Foreshore flat . . . .

Rock or coral reef . . . .

Rock, bare or awash . . . .

Breakwater, pier, jetty, or wharf . . . .

Seawall . . . .

Rivers, lakes, and canals

Perennial stream . . . .

Perennial river . . . .

Small falls; small rapids . . . .

Large falls; large rapids . . . .

Dry lake . . . .

Narrow wash . . . .

Wide wash . . . .

Water well; spring or seep . . . .

Submerged areas and bogs

Marsh or swamp . . . .

Submerged marsh or swamp . . . .

Wooded marsh or swamp . . . .

Land subject to inundation . . . .

Elevations

Spot and elevation . . . .　X_{212}

Appendix G

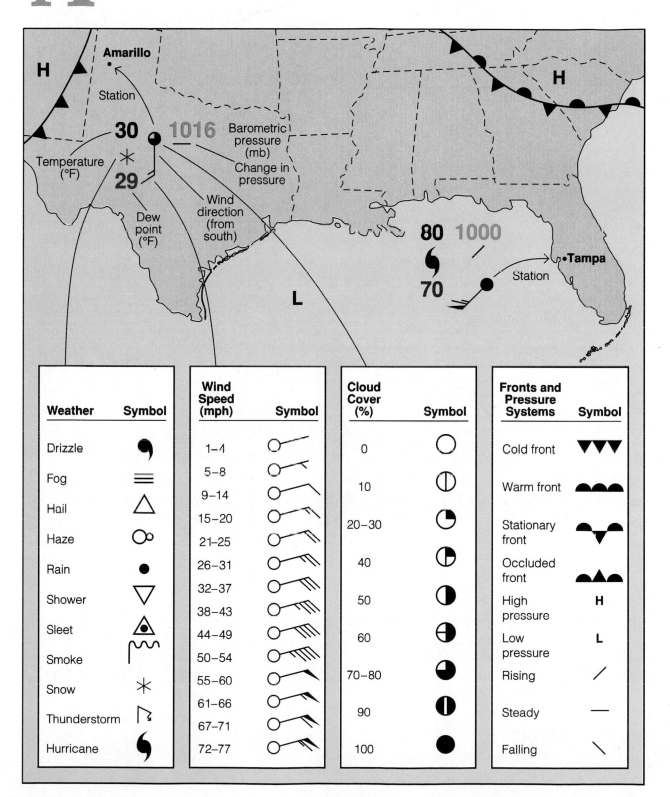

H

Amarillo

Station

30   1016   Barometric pressure (mb)

Change in pressure

Temperature (°F)

29

Wind direction (from south)

Dew point (°F)

L

H

80   1000

70

Tampa

Station

Weather	Symbol
Drizzle	
Fog	
Hail	
Haze	
Rain	
Shower	
Sleet	
Smoke	
Snow	
Thunderstorm	
Hurricane	

Wind Speed (mph)	Symbol
1–4	
5–8	
9–14	
15–20	
21–25	
26–31	
32–37	
38–43	
44–49	
50–54	
55–60	
61–66	
67–71	
72–77	

Cloud Cover (%)	Symbol
0	
10	
20–30	
40	
50	
60	
70–80	
90	
100	

Fronts and Pressure Systems	Symbol
Cold front	
Warm front	
Stationary front	
Occluded front	
High pressure	H
Low pressure	L
Rising	
Steady	
Falling	

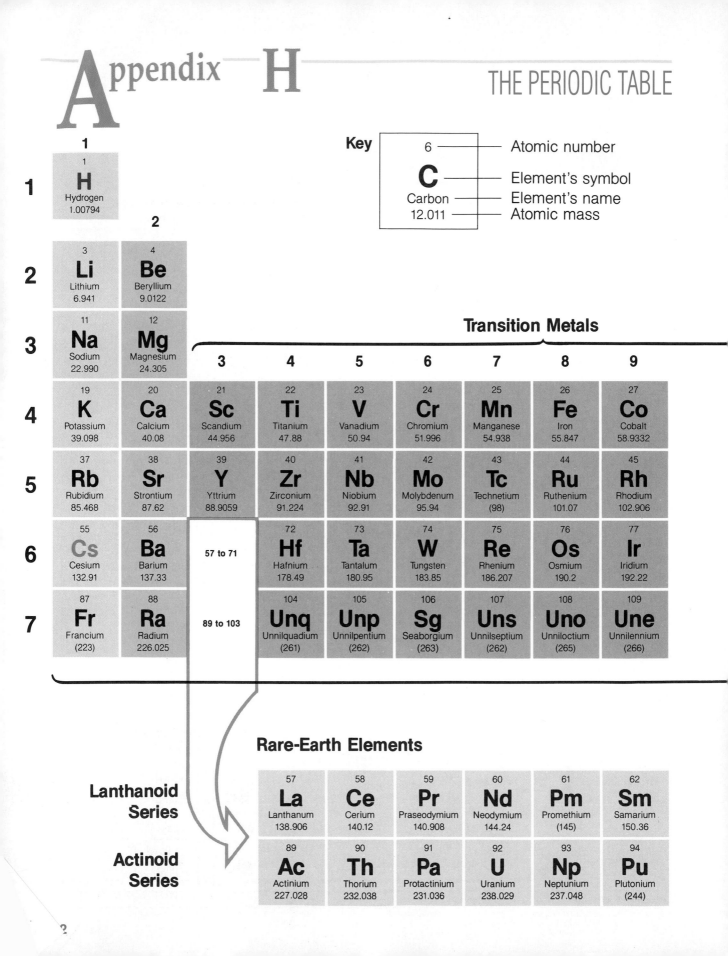

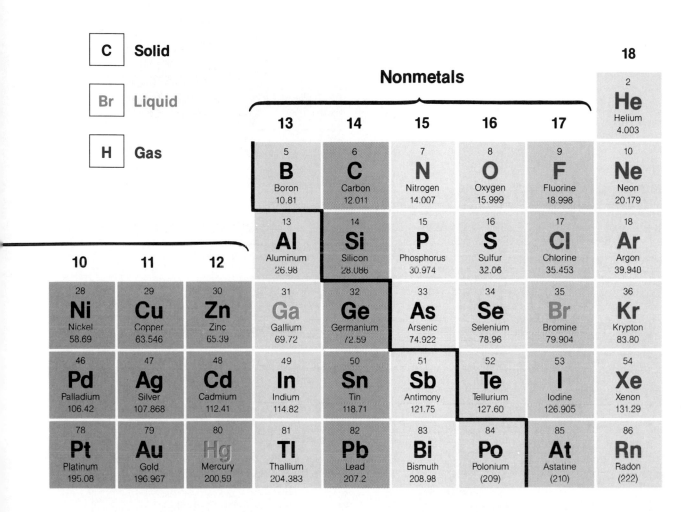

			Nonmetals				**18**
							2 **He** Helium 4.003
		13	**14**	**15**	**16**	**17**	
		5 **B** Boron 10.81	6 **C** Carbon 12.011	7 **N** Nitrogen 14.007	8 **O** Oxygen 15.999	9 **F** Fluorine 18.998	10 **Ne** Neon 20.179

C	Solid
Br	Liquid
H	Gas

10	**11**	**12**	13 **Al** Aluminum 26.98	14 **Si** Silicon 28.086	15 **P** Phosphorus 30.974	16 **S** Sulfur 32.06	17 **Cl** Chlorine 35.453	18 **Ar** Argon 39.940
28 **Ni** Nickel 58.69	29 **Cu** Copper 63.546	30 **Zn** Zinc 65.39	31 **Ga** Gallium 69.72	32 **Ge** Germanium 72.59	33 **As** Arsenic 74.922	34 **Se** Selenium 78.96	35 **Br** Bromine 79.904	36 **Kr** Krypton 83.80
46 **Pd** Palladium 106.42	47 **Ag** Silver 107.868	48 **Cd** Cadmium 112.41	49 **In** Indium 114.82	50 **Sn** Tin 118.71	51 **Sb** Antimony 121.75	52 **Te** Tellurium 127.60	53 **I** Iodine 126.905	54 **Xe** Xenon 131.29
78 **Pt** Platinum 195.08	79 **Au** Gold 196.967	80 **Hg** Mercury 200.59	81 **Tl** Thallium 204.383	82 **Pb** Lead 207.2	83 **Bi** Bismuth 208.98	84 **Po** Polonium (209)	85 **At** Astatine (210)	86 **Rn** Radon (222)

The symbols shown here for elements 104-109 are being used temporarily until names for these elements can be agreed upon.

Metals

Mass numbers in parentheses are those of the most stable or common isotope.

63 **Eu** Europium 151.96	64 **Gd** Gadolinium 157.25	65 **Tb** Terbium 158.925	66 **Dy** Dysprosium 162.50	67 **Ho** Holmium 164.93	68 **Er** Erbium 167.26	69 **Tm** Thulium 168.934	70 **Yb** Ytterbium 173.04	71 **Lu** Lutetium 174.967
95 **Am** Americium (243)	96 **Cm** Curium (247)	97 **Bk** Berkelium (247)	98 **Cf** Californium (251)	99 **Es** Einsteinium (254)	100 **Fm** Fermium (257)	101 **Md** Mendelevium (258)	102 **No** Nobelium (259)	103 **Lr** Lawrencium (260)

Glossary

Pronunciation Key

When difficult names or terms first appear in the text, they are respelled to aid pronunciation. A syllable in SMALL CAPITAL LETTERS receives the most stress. The key below lists the letters used for respelling. It includes examples of words using each sound and shows how the words would be respelled.

Symbol	Example	Respelling
a	hat	(hat)
ay	pay, late	(pay), (layt)
ah	star, hot	(stahr), (haht)
ai	air, dare	(air), (dair)
aw	law, all	(law), (awl)
eh	met	(meht)
ee	bee, eat	(bee), (eet)
er	learn, sir, fur	(lern), (ser), (fer)
ih	fit	(fiht)
igh	mile, sigh	(mighl), (sigh)
oh	no	(noh)
oi	soil, boy	(soil), (boi)
oo	root, rule	(root), (rool)
or	born, door	(born), (dor)
ow	plow, out	(plow), (owt)

Symbol	Example	Respelling
u	put, book	(put), (buk)
uh	fun	(fuhn)
yoo	few, use	(fyoo), (yooz)
ch	chill, reach	(chihl), (reech)
g	go, dig	(goh), (dihg)
j	jet, gently, bridge	(jeht), (JEHNT-lee), (brihj)
k	kite, cup	(kight), (kuhp)
ks	mix	(mihks)
kw	quick	(kwihk)
ng	bring	(brihng)
s	say, cent	(say), (sehnt)
sh	she, crash	(shee), (krash)
th	three	(three)
y	yet, onion	(yeht), (UHN-yuhn)
z	zip, always	(zihp), (AWL-wayz)
zh	treasure	(TREH-zher)

A

abrasion (uh-BRAY-zhuhn): wearing away of a substance by solid particles carried by wind, water, or other forces

absolute magnitude: amount of light a star actually gives off

abyssal (uh-BIHS-uhl) **plain:** large flat area on the ocean floor

abyssal zone: open-ocean zone that begins at a depth of about 2000 meters and extends to an average depth of 6000 meters

acid rain: general term used for precipitation (rain, snow, sleet, hail, or fog) that is more acidic than normal

adaptation: change that increases an organism's chances of survival

air mass: large body of air with uniform properties throughout

air pressure: measure of the force of air pressing down on the Earth's surface

alloy: substance made of two or more metals

alluvial fan: fan-shaped deposit of sediments formed at the point where a river leaves the mountains and runs out onto a plain

anemometer (an-uh-MAHM-uh-ter): instrument used to measure wind speed

anthracite (AN-thruh-sight): hard coal; fourth and last stage in the development of coal

anticline (AN-tih-klighn): upward fold in rock

apogee (AP-uh-jee): point of a satellite's orbit farthest from the Earth

apparent magnitude: brightness of a star as it appears on the Earth

aquifer (AK-wuh-fuhr): layer of rock or sediment that allows groundwater to pass freely

asteroid belt: region of space between Mars and Jupiter in which asteroids are found

asthenosphere (az-THEEN-oh-sfeer): layer of the Earth directly beneath the lithosphere

astronomy: study of the planets, stars, and other objects in space

atmosphere (AT-muhs-feer): mixture of gases that surrounds the Earth

atoll: ring of coral reefs surrounding an island that has been worn away and has sunk beneath the surface of the ocean

atom: smallest part of an element that has all the properties of that element; basic building block of matter

aurora (aw-ROR-uh): bands or curtains of colored lights produced when particles trapped by the Van Allen radiation belts collide with particles in the upper atmosphere

autumnal equinox (EE-kwuh-naks): time of year in the fall when day and night are of equal length; beginning of autumn in the Northern Hemisphere

axis: imaginary vertical line through the center of a body around which the body rotates, or spins

B

barometer (buh-RAHM-uh-ter): instrument used to measure air pressure

barrier reef: coral reef separated from the shore of an island by an area of shallow water called a lagoon

bathyal (BATH-ee-uhl) **zone:** open-ocean zone that begins at a continental slope and extends down about 2000 meters

bedrock: layer of rock beneath the soil

benthos (BEHN-thahs): organisms that live on the ocean floor

big-bang theory: theory that states that the universe began to expand with an explosion of concentrated matter and energy and has been expanding ever since

binary star: member of a double star system

biomass: any material, such as wood, that comes from living things and can be used as a fuel

biome (BIGH-ohm): division used to classify areas with similar climates, plants, and animals

bituminous (bigh-TOO-muh-nuhs) **coal:** soft coal; third stage in the development of coal

black hole: core of a supermassive star that remains after a supernova; the gravity of the core is so strong that not even light can escape

C

caldera: large crater formed when the sides of a volcanic cone collapse

canopy: (KAN-uh-pee): top layer of a tropical rain forest

carbonation: process in which carbonic acid reacts chemically with other substances

cast: fossil in which the space left behind in a rock by an organism has filled in, showing the same shape as the organism

catalytic converter: emission-control device that changes hydrocarbons and carbon monoxide in automobile exhaust into carbon dioxide and water vapor

cavern (KAV-uhrn): underground passage formed when limestone is dissolved by carbonic acid in groundwater

Cenozoic Era: division of geologic time that has lasted about 65 million years after the end of the Mesozoic Era

centimeter: one hundredth of a meter

chain reaction: process in which the splitting, or fission, of one atomic nucleus causes the splitting of additional nuclei

chemical formula: combination of chemical symbols used to represent compounds

chemical rock: non-clastic sedimentary rock formed by inorganic processes such as evaporation

chemical weathering: weathering that involves changes in the chemical makeup of rocks

chromosphere (KROH-muh-sfir): middle layer of the sun's atmosphere

cinder: small, rough volcanic bomb no more than several centimeters across

cinder cone: volcano made mostly of cinders and other rock particles that have been blown into the air

clastic rock: sedimentary rock formed from fragments of previously existing rocks

cleavage: tendency of a mineral to break along smooth, definite surfaces

climate: general conditions of temperature and precipitation for an area over a long period of time

coastal plain: low, flat area along a coast

comet: object made of ice, gas, and dust that travels through space

composite volcano: volcano built of alternating layers of rock particles and lava

compound: chemical substance made of atoms of different elements bonded together

compression: type of stress that squeezes rocks together

condensation (kahn-duhn-say-shuhn): process by which water vapor changes back into a liquid; second step of the water cycle

conduction: direct transfer of heat energy from one substance to another

conifer: needle-leaved tree that produces its seeds in cones

conservation: wise use of natural resources so they will not be used up too quickly

constellation: group of stars that form a pattern

continent: major landmass that measures millions of square kilometers and rises a considerable distance above sea level

continental climate: climate found in areas within a large landmass

continental glacier: thick sheet of snow and ice that builds up in polar regions of the Earth; also called polar ice sheet

continental margin: area where the underwater edge of a continent meets the ocean floor

continental rise: part of a continental margin that separates a continental slope from the ocean floor

continental shelf: relatively flat part of a continental margin that is covered by shallow ocean water

continental slope: part of the continental margin at the edge of a continental shelf where the ocean floor plunges steeply 4 to 5 kilometers

contour line: line that passes through all points on a map that have the same elevation

contour plowing: planting crops along the face, or side, of a slope instead of up and down the slope to prevent erosion

control: experiment run without a variable in order to show that any data from the experimental setup were due to the variable being tested

convection (kuhn-VEHK-shuhn): transfer of heat energy in a fluid (gas or liquid)

convection current: movement of air (or water) caused by cool, dense air (or water) sinking and warm, less dense air (or water) rising; movement of material caused by differences in temperature

convergent (kuhn-VER-jehnt) **boundary:** plate bound- ary at which plates come together

conversion factor: fraction that always equals one that is used for dimensional analysis

coral reef: large mass of limestone rocks surrounding a volcanic island in tropical waters near a continental shelf

core: center of the sun, Earth, or other object

Coriolis effect: shifts in wind direction caused by the rotation of the Earth on its axis

corona (kuh-ROH-nuh): outermost layer of the sun's atmosphere

crater: funnel-shaped pit or depression at the top of a volcanic cone

crest: highest point of a wave

Cretaceous Period: subdivision of geologic time at the end of the Mesozoic Era

crop rotation: process of alternating crops on the same land to prevent depletion of nutrients from the soil

crust: thin, outermost layer of the Earth

crystal: solid in which the atoms or molecules are arranged in a definite pattern that is repeated over and over again

cubic centimeter: metric unit used to measure the volume of solids; equal to a milliliter

D

data: recorded observations and measurements

deep current: ocean current caused mainly by differences in the density of water deep in the ocean

deep zone: area of extremely cold ocean water below the thermocline

deformation: in geology, any change in the original shape or volume of rocks

delta: triangular formation of sediments deposited at the mouth of a large river that flows into a lake or ocean

density: mass per unit volume of a substance

depletion: removal of nutrients from the soil

deposition (dehp-uh-zihsh-uhn): process by which sediments are laid down in new locations

desalination (dee-sal-uh-nay-shuhn): process by which salt is removed from ocean water

desert climate: climate found in the western interior of the United States, characterized by very low precipitation and high temperatures in summer and winter

desertification (dih-zert-uh-fih-kay-shuhn): process by which grasslands become deserts as a result of erosion caused by overgrazing

dimensional analysis: method of converting one unit to another

divergent (digh-ver-jehnt) **boundary:** plate boundary at which plates move apart

dome: raised area shaped roughly like the top half of a sphere, often formed by magma pushing upward on the rock layers above it

Doppler effect: apparent change in the wavelength of light that occurs when an object is moving toward or away from the Earth

drainage basin: area drained by a major river

drainage system: network of streams and other bodies of running water that ultimately drain into an area's main river

drumlin: oval-shaped mound of glacial till

E

earthquake: shaking and trembling that results from the sudden movement of part of the Earth's crust

electromagnetic spectrum: arrangement of electromagnetic waves that includes visible light, ultraviolet light, infrared light, X-rays, and radio waves

element: substance that cannot be separated into simpler substances by ordinary chemical means

elevation: height above sea level

elliptical galaxy: galaxy that may vary in shape from nearly spherical to flat; one of three types of galaxies

emissions (ee-MIHSH-uhnz): gases or particles given off when fossil fuels are burned

epicenter (EHP-uh-sehn-tuhr): point on the Earth's surface directly above the focus of an earthquake

equal-area projection: projection in which area is shown correctly, but shapes are distorted

equator: imaginary line around the Earth that divides the Earth into two hemispheres; parallel located halfway between the North and South poles

erosion (ee-ROH-zhuhn): process by which the products of weathering are moved from one place to another

escape velocity: velocity needed to escape the Earth's gravitational pull

evaporation (ih-vap-uh-RAY-shuhn): process by which radiant energy from the sun turns liquid water into a gas (water vapor)

evolution: change in species over time

evolve: to change over time

exfoliation (ehks-foh-lee-AY-shuhn): breaking off of curved sheets or slabs parallel to a rock's surface due to weathering

exosphere (EHK-suh-sfeer): upper part of the thermosphere that extends from about 550 kilometers above the Earth's surface for thousands of kilometers

extrusion: igneous rock that forms on the Earth's surface

extrusive (ehk-STROO-sihv) **rock:** igneous rock formed from lava that cools on the Earth's surface

F

fault: break or crack along which rocks move

fault-block mountain: mountain formed by blocks of rock uplifted along normal faults

flood plain: flat area that is found on both sides of a river or stream that is formed by sediments deposited during floods

focus (foh-kuhs): underground point of origin of an earthquake

fold: bend in rock

foot wall: block of rock below a fault

fossil: preserved remains or evidence of a living thing

fossil fuel: fuel formed hundreds of millions of years ago from the remains of dead plants and animals; coal, oil, or natural gas

fracture: break or crack in rock; in minerals, the way a mineral that does not cleave breaks along a rough or jagged surface

fringing reef: coral reef that touches the shoreline of a volcanic island

front: boundary that forms when two air masses with different properties meet

frost action: breaking apart of a rock caused by water freezing and expanding within cracks

G

galaxy: huge collection of stars

gasohol: mixture of gasoline and alcohol that can be used as a fuel

gemstone: hard, beautiful, durable substance that can be cut and polished for jewelry and decoration

geosynchronous (jee-oh-sihng-kruh-nuhs) **orbit:** orbit in which a satellite's rate of revolution exactly matches the Earth's rate of rotation

geothermal energy: energy produced from the heat energy within the Earth

giant star: star with a diameter about 10 to 100 times as large as the sun

glacier (glay-shuhr): large mass of moving ice and snow

globe: spherical, or round, model of the Earth

gram: one thousandth of a kilogram

gravity: force of attraction between objects

greenhouse effect: process in which carbon dioxide and other gases in the atmosphere absorb infrared radiation from the sun, forming a "heat blanket" around the Earth

groundwater: water that soaks into the ground and remains in the ground

guyot (gee-oh): flat-topped seamount

H

half-life: amount of time it takes for one half of the atoms of a sample of a radioactive element to decay

hanging wall: block of rock above a fault

hard water: water that contains large amounts of dissolved minerals, especially calcium and magnesium

hardness: ability of a mineral to resist being scratched

hazardous waste: any waste that can cause death or serious damage to human health; toxic chemical waste

hemisphere: northern or southern half of the Earth

Hertzsprung-Russell diagram: chart that shows the relationship between the absolute magnitude and the surface temperature of stars

highlands: mountain ranges on the moon

horizon (huh-RIGH-zuhn): soil layer

humus (HYOO-muhs): part of the soil formed by decaying organic material

hydrocarbon: substance containing the elements hydrogen and carbon

hydroelectric power: use of mechanical energy of falling or running water to generate electricity

hydrosphere: part of the Earth's surface consisting of water

hypothesis (high-PAHTH-uh-sihs): proposed solution to a scientific problem

I

iceberg: large chunk of ice that has broken off a continental glacier and drifted into the sea

igneous (IHG-nee-uhs) **rock:** rock formed from molten lava or magma

immature river: river in an early stage of development

impermeable: term used to describe material through which water cannot move quickly; opposite of permeable

imprint: fossil formed when a thin object leaves an impression in soft mud that hardens

index fossil: fossil of an organism that existed on Earth for only a short period of time and that can be used by scientists to determine the relative age of a rock

infrared telescope: telescope that gathers infrared light from distant objects in order to produce images of those objects

inner core: solid, innermost center of the Earth

inorganic: not formed from living things or the remains of living things

interglacial: time period between major glaciations, or ice ages

interior plain: low, flat area found inland on a continent; somewhat higher above sea level than a coastal plain

international date line: line located along the 180th meridian; when the line is crossed going west, one day is added; when it is crossed going east, one day is subtracted

intertidal zone: coastal region that lies between the low- and high-tide lines

intrusion: irregular formation of igneous rock formed by magma that cools beneath the Earth's crust

intrusive (ihn-TROO-sihv) **rock:** igneous rock formed from magma that cools beneath the Earth's surface

ion: electrically charged particle

ionosphere (igh-AHN-uh-sfeer): lower part of the thermosphere that extends from 80 kilometers to 550 kilometers above the Earth's surface

irrigation (eer-uh-GAY-shuhn): process of supplying water to dry regions to make them suitable for growing crops

island: small landmass completely surrounded by water

isobar (IGH-soh-bahr): line on a weather map that connects locations with the same air pressure

isostasy (igh-SAHS-tuh-see): balancing of the downward force of the crust and the upward force of the mantle

isotherm (IGH-so-therm): line on a weather map that connects locations with the same temperature

J

jet stream: strong, eastward wind that blows horizontally around the Earth

Jurassic Period: middle subdivision of geologic time in the Mesozoic Era

K

kettle lake: round, deep lake formed by a huge block of ice left behind by a glacier

kilogram: basic unit of mass in the metric system

kilometer: 1000 meters

L

land breeze: flow of air from the land to the sea

landscape: physical features of the Earth's surface found in an area

landslide: large downhill movement of loose rocks and soil caused by the pull of gravity

lateral fault: fault along which the blocks move horizontally past each other

latitude: measure of distance north and south of the equator

lava: molten rock at the Earth's surface

law: summarizing statement of observed experimental facts that has been tested many times and is generally accepted as true

law of superposition: law that states that in undisturbed sedimentary rocks each layer is older than the one above it and younger than the one below it

leaching (LEECH-ihng): process in which water washes minerals from the topsoil to the subsoil

leeward side: side of a mountain facing away from the wind

levee (LEHV-ee): in nature, a ridgelike deposit along the sides of a river

light-year: distance light travels in a year

lignite (LIHG-night): brown coal; second stage in the development of coal

liter: basic unit of volume in the metric system

lithosphere (LIHTH-uh-sfeer): topmost solid part of the Earth, which is composed of the crust and some of the mantle

load: amount of sediment carried by a stream

loess (LOH-ehs): accumulations of fine particles of sand and silt deposited by the wind

longitude: measure of distance east and west of the prime meridian

longshore current: movement of water parallel to a shoreline

lunar eclipse: blocking of the moon that takes place when the Earth comes directly between the sun and the full moon

luster: way in which a mineral reflects light from its surface

M

magma: molten rock beneath the Earth's surface

magnetosphere (mag-NEET-uh-sfeer): area around the Earth that extends beyond the atmosphere, in which the Earth's magnetic force operates

main sequence star: in the H-R diagram, a star that lies in an area from the upper left corner to the lower right corner

major glaciation: period in the Earth's history when large parts of the Earth's surface were covered with sheets of ice; ice age

mantle: layer of the Earth that extends from the bottom of the crust to the outer core

map: drawing of the Earth, or a part of the Earth, on a flat surface

maria (mahr-ee-uh; singular: mare): smooth lowland plains on the moon

marine climate: climate found in areas near an ocean or other large body of water

marine west coast climate: climate found along the northwestern coast of the United States; characterized by heavy precipitation, mild winters, and cool summers

mass wasting: downhill movement of sediments due to gravity

matter: anything that takes up space and has mass

mature river: river that has been developing for many thousands of years

meander (mee-an-der): loop in a river

mechanical weathering: weathering that does not involve changes in the chemical makeup of rocks

Mediterranean climate: climate found in the coastal area of California; characterized by heavy precipitation in winter but dry summers, with summer temperatures only slightly higher than winter temperatures

meltwater: water from melting ice or snow

Mercator projection: projection used for navigation in which the correct shape of coastlines is shown, but the sizes of land and water areas far from the equator become distorted

meridian (muh-rihd-ee-uhn): line that runs between the points on a globe or map that represent the geographic North and South poles of the Earth

mesosphere (mehs-uh-sfeer): layer of the Earth's atmosphere that extends from about 50 kilometers to about 80 kilometers above the Earth's surface

Mesozoic Era: division of geologic time, lasting about 160 million years, after the Paleozoic Era and before the Cenozoic Era

metal: element that is shiny, conducts electricity and heat, and is easily shaped

metamorphic (meht-uh-mor-fihk) **rock:** rock changed in form as a result of chemical reactions, heat, and/or pressure

metamorphism (meht-uh-mor-fihz-uhm): process in which metamorphic rock is formed

meteor: streak of light produced by a meteoroid as it burns up in the Earth's atmosphere

meteorite: meteor that strikes the Earth's surface

meteoroid (mee-tee-uh-roid): chunk of metal or stone that orbits the sun

meteorology: study of the Earth's atmosphere, weather, and climate

microclimate: localized climate in a small area

midocean ridge: undersea mountain chain where new ocean floor is produced; a constructive (divergent) plate boundary

milligram: one thousandth of a gram

milliliter: one thousandth of a liter

millimeter: one thousandth of a meter

mineral: naturally occurring, inorganic solid that has a definite chemical composition and crystal shape

mixture: two or more substances physically combined

Moho: boundary between the Earth's outermost layer (crust) and the mantle

moist continental climate: climate found from the northern Midwest to the Atlantic coast of the United States; characterized by a moderate amount of precipitation all year, with very cold winters and hot summers

moist subtropical climate: climate found in the southeastern part of the United States; characterized by more precipitation in summer than in winter, with hot summers and mild winters

mold: fossil that shows the outward shape of an organism

molecule: two or more atoms held together by chemical forces

moraine: ridge of till left behind by a retreating glacier

mountain: natural landform that reaches high elevations, with a narrow summit, or top, and steep slopes, or sides

mountain belt: large group of mountains including mountain ranges and mountain systems

mountain range: roughly parallel series of mountains that have the same general shape and structure

mountain system: group of mountain ranges in one area

N

natural resource: any material removed from the Earth and used by people

neap tide: lower than usual high tide that occurs during the first and last quarter phases of the moon

nebula: massive cloud of dust and gas between the stars

nebular theory: theory that the solar system began as a huge cloud of dust and gas called a nebula, which later condensed to form the sun and its nine planets

nekton (NEHK-ton): forms of ocean life that swim

neritic (nuh-RIHT-ihk) **zone:** area of the ocean that extends from the low-tide line to the edge of a continental shelf

neutron star: smallest of all stars

newton: basic unit of weight in the metric system

nonmetal: element that has a dull surface, is a poor conductor of electricity and heat, and is not easily shaped

nonpoint source: source of water pollution that may include sanitary landfills, hazardous wastes, and agricultural runoff

nonrenewable resource: any resource that cannot be replaced by nature, such as fossil fuels and minerals

normal fault: fault in which the hanging wall moves down relative to the foot wall

nova: star that suddenly increases in brightness in just a few hours or days

nuclear energy: energy locked within the atomic nucleus

nuclear fission: splitting of an atomic nucleus into two smaller nuclei, during which nuclear energy is released

nuclear fusion: combining of two atomic nuclei to produce one larger nucleus, with the release of nuclear energy

nucleus: center, or core, of an atom; plural, nuclei

O

ocean-floor spreading: process in which old ocean floor is pushed away from a mid-ocean ridge by the formation of new ocean floor

oceanographer (oh-shuh-NAHG-ruh-fer): scientist who studies the ocean

oceanography: study of the Earth's oceans, including their physical features, life forms, and natural resources

orbit: path an object takes when moving around another object in space

ore: mineral or rock from which useful metals or nonmetals can be profitably removed

organic rock: sedimentary rock that is formed either directly or indirectly from material that was once alive

outer core: layer of the Earth surrounding the inner core

outwash plain: flat, fan-shaped area in front of terminal moraines formed by sediments deposited by rivers of glacial meltwater

oxbow lake: U-shaped lake formed when erosion and deposition cut off a meander of a river

oxidation (ahk-suh-DAY-shuhn): process in which oxygen chemically combines with another substance

ozone: gas in the Earth's atmosphere formed when three atoms of oxygen combine

P

Paleozoic Era: division of geologic time, lasting about 345 million years, after the Precambrian Era and before the Mesozoic Era

Pangaea (pan-JEE-ah): single giant landmass that existed more than 200 million years ago and that gave rise to the present-day continents

parallax (PAR-uh-laks): apparent change in the position of a star in the sky due to the change in the Earth's position as the Earth moves around the sun

parallel: line going from east to west across a map or globe that crosses a meridian at right angles

peat: soft substance made of decayed plant fibers; first stage in the development of coal

penumbra (pih-NUHM-bruh): outer part of a shadow

perigee (PEHR-uh-jee): point of a satellite's orbit closest to the Earth

period of revolution: time it takes a planet to make one revolution around the sun

period of rotation: time it takes a planet to make one rotation on its axis

permafrost: permanently frozen layer of soil on a tundra

permeable (PER-mee-uh-buhl): term used to describe material through which water can move quickly

petrification: process by which once-living material is replaced by minerals, turning it into stone

petrochemical: any useful substance derived from oil or natural gas

photosphere: innermost layer of the sun's atmosphere

photovoltaic cell: device that converts sunlight directly into electricity; solar cell

plain: flat land area that does not rise far above sea level

plankton (PLANGK-tuhn): animals and plants that float at or near the surface of the ocean

plasticity (plas-TIHS-uh-tee): ability of a solid to flow, or change shape

plate: in plate tectonics, one of the moving, irregularly shaped slabs that make up the Earth's lithosphere

plateau (pla-TOH): large area of relatively flat land high above sea level

point source: source of water pollution that may include sewers, pipes, and channels through which wastes are discharged

polar zone: climate zone extending from the pole (90°) to about 60° latitude in each hemisphere

polarity (poh-LAR-uh-tee): property of a molecule with oppositely charged ends

pollution: release into the environment of substances that change the environment for the worse

pore space: space between particles of soil

Precambrian Era: earliest and longest division of geologic time, lasting about 4 billion years

precipitation (prih-sihp-uh-TAY-shuhn): process by which water returns to the Earth in the form of rain, snow, sleet, or hail; third step of the water cycle

prevailing wind: wind that blows more often from one direction than from any other direction

primary (P) wave: push-pull seismic wave that can travel through solids, liquids, and gases; P waves are the fastest type of seismic wave

prime meridian: meridian that runs through Greenwich, England

projection: representation of a three-dimensional object on a flat surface

prominence (PRAHM-un-nuhns): violent storm on the sun that can be seen from the Earth as a huge bright arch or loop of hot gas

protostar: new star

psychrometer (sigh-KRAHM-uh-ter): instrument used to measure relative humidity

pulsar: neutron star that gives off pulses of radio waves

Q

quasar (KWAY-zahr): quasi-stellar radio source; distant object that gives off mainly radio waves and X-rays

R

radiation: transfer of heat energy through empty space

radio telescope: telescope that gathers radio waves from distant objects in order to produce images of those objects

radioactive waste: waste produced by the generation of energy in nuclear power plants

rain gauge: instrument used to measure rainfall

reaction engine: engine, such as a rocket, in which the rearward blast of exploding gases causes the rocket to shoot forward

recycling: form of conservation in which discarded materials that can be used again are separated and sent to factories where they are reclaimed

red shift: shift toward the red end of the spectrum of a star that is moving away from the Earth

reflecting telescope: telescope that uses a series of mirrors to gather and focus visible light from distant objects

refracting telescope: telescope that uses a series of lenses to gather and focus visible light from distant objects

relative humidity: percentage of moisture the air holds relative to the amount it could hold at a particular temperature

relief: difference in a region's elevations

renewable resource: any resource that can be replaced by nature, such as water, soil, and living resources

reservoir (REHZ-uhr-vwahr): artificial lake used as a source of fresh water

residual (rih-ZIHJ-oo-wuhl) **soil:** soil that remains on top of the rock from which it was formed

retrograde rotation: reverse motion in which a planet rotates from east to west, instead of from west to east

reverse fault: fault in which the hanging wall moves up relative to the foot wall

Richter scale: scale used to measure the strength of earthquakes

rift valley: valley formed when the block of land between two normal faults slides downward

rille: valley on the moon

Ring of Fire: earthquake and volcano zone that encircles the Pacific Ocean

rock: hard substance composed of one or more minerals

rock cycle: interrelated processes that cause the continuous changing of rocks from one kind to another

root-pry: breaking apart of rocks caused by the growth of plant roots

S

salinity (suh-LIHN-uh-tee): term used to describe the amount of dissolved salts in ocean water

sand bar: long, underwater ridge of sand

sand dune: mound of sand deposited by the wind

sanitary landfill: solid-waste dump in which garbage is compacted and covered with soil

scale: used to compare distances on the Earth's surface

sea breeze: flow of air from the sea to the land

sea cave: hollowed out portion of a sea cliff

sea cliff: steep face of rock produced by wave action

sea stack: column of resistant rock left behind after a sea cliff has eroded

seamount: underwater volcanic mountain on the ocean floor

secondary (S) wave: side-to-side earthquake wave, which can travel through solids but not through liquids and gases; S waves are slower than P waves but faster than L waves

sediment (SEHD-ih-mehnt): particles of rock or organic materials that have been carried along and deposited by water, wind, or glaciers; small pieces of rock, shell, and other material that are broken down over time

sedimentary (sehd-uh-MEHN-tuh-ree) **rock:** rock formed by the compacting and cementing of sediments or by other non-igneous processes at the Earth's surface

seismic (SIGHZ-mihk) **wave:** shock wave produced by earthquakes that travels through the Earth

seismogram (SIGHZ-muh-gram): record of seismic waves recorded by a seismograph

seismograph (SIGHZ-muh-grahf): instrument used to detect and record seismic waves produced by earthquakes

seismologist (sighz-MAHL-uh-jihst): scientist who studies earthquakes

shearing: type of stress that pushes rocks of the crust in two opposite, horizontal directions

shield volcano: gently sloping volcano formed when runny lava flows over a large area

shoreline: boundary where the land and the ocean meet

smog: thick brownish haze formed when hydrocarbons, carbon monoxide, and other gases react in sunlight; combination of the words *smoke* and *fog*

soft water: water that does not contain minerals

soil profile: cross section of soil horizons

solar collector: device that absorbs energy from the sun and converts it to heat; part of an active solar-heating system

solar eclipse: blocking of the sun that occurs when the new moon comes directly between the sun and the Earth

solar energy: energy from the sun

solar flare: storm on the sun that shows up as a bright burst of light on the sun's surface

solar system: sun, planets, and all the other objects that revolve around the sun

solar wind: continuous stream of high-energy particles released into space in all directions from the sun's corona

solution: substance that contains two or more substances mixed on the molecular level

solvent (sahl-vuhnt): substance in which another substance dissolves

spectroscope: instrument that breaks up light into its characteristic colors

spectrum: band of colors formed when light passes through a prism

spiral galaxy: galaxy that is shaped like a pinwheel; one of three types of galaxies

spit: sandbar connected to the shoreline

spring tide: higher than usual high tide that occurs during the full moon and new moon phases

stable rock: rock composed of minerals that resist chemical weathering

steppe climate: climate found in the western interior of the United States; similar to a desert climate but with slightly more precipitation

stratosphere (strat-uh-sfeer): layer of the Earth's atmosphere that extends from the tropopause to an altitude of about 50 kilometers

streak: color of the powder left by a mineral when it is rubbed against a hard, rough surface

stress: in geology, the forces that push and pull on the Earth's crust, causing its deformation

strike-slip boundary: plate boundary at which two plates slip past each other horizontally

strip cropping: planting strips of cover crops, such as clover, between rows of other crops, such as corn, to prevent erosion

subduction (suhb-DUHK-shuhn): process in which crust plunges back into the interior of the Earth

submarine canyon: deep, V-shaped valley cut in the rock through a continental shelf and slope

subsoil: soil in the B horizon, or middle layer of soil

summer solstice (SAHL-stihs): time of year when the Northern Hemisphere has its longest day and the Southern Hemisphere has its shortest day; beginning of summer in the Northern Hemisphere

sunspot: dark area on the sun's surface

supergiant star: star with a diameter up to 1000 times the diameter of the sun; largest of all stars

supernova: tremendous explosion in which a star breaks apart, releasing energy and newly formed elements

surface current: ocean current caused mainly by wind patterns

surface runoff: water that enters a river or stream after a heavy rain or during a spring thaw of snow or ice

surface (L) wave: up-and-down earthquake wave; L waves are the slowest-moving seismic waves

surface zone: zone where ocean water is mixed by waves and currents

syncline (SIHN-klighn): downward fold in rock

T

taiga (TIGH-guh): another name for a coniferous forest biome; Russian word that means swamp forest

tectonics (tehk-TAHN-ihks): branch of geology that deals with the movements that shape the Earth's crust

temperate zone: climate zone located between 60° and 30° latitude in each hemisphere

temperature inversion: phenomenon that occurs when cool air containing pollutants becomes trapped near the Earth's surface under a layer of warm air

tension: in geology, the type of stress that pulls rocks apart

terrace: flat platform of rocks, sand, and silt at the base of a sea cliff

terracing: planting a slope in a series of level steps, or terraces, to prevent erosion

theory: logical explanation for events that occur in nature

theory of continental drift: theory proposed by Alfred Wegener that the continents were once joined together and have since drifted apart

theory of plate tectonics: theory that links together the ideas of continental drift and ocean-floor spreading and explains how the Earth has changed over time

thermal pollution: increase in temperature caused when cold water used to cool the reactors in nuclear power plants is heated and discharged back into lakes and rivers

thermocline (THER-muh-klighn): zone in which the temperature of ocean water drops rapidly

thermometer: instrument used to measure temperature

thermosphere (THER-muh-sfeer): layer of the Earth's atmosphere that begins at a height of about 80 kilometers and has no well-defined upper limit

thrust fault: reverse fault in which the hanging wall slides over the foot wall

tidal energy: energy produced by the rise and fall of the tides

tide: rise and fall of the oceans caused by the moon's gravitational pull on the Earth

till: rocks and debris deposited directly by a glacier

time zone: longitudinal belt of the Earth in which all areas have the same local time

topographic map: map that shows the different shapes and sizes of a land surface using contour lines

topography (tuh-PAHG-ruh-fee): shape of the Earth's surface

topsoil: soil in the A horizon, or uppermost layer of mature soil

trace fossil: mark or evidence of the activities of an organism

transform fault: fault that runs across a mid-ocean ridge

transported soil: soil that is moved away from its place of origin

trench: V-shaped valley on the ocean floor where old ocean floor is subducted; a destructive (convergent) plate boundary

Triassic Period: subdivision of geologic time at the beginning of the Mesozoic Era

tributary (TRIHB-yoo-tehr-ee): large stream or small river that flows into an area's main river

trilobite: animal that is an important index fossil for the Paleozoic Era

tropical zone: climate zone located between 30° latitude and the equator (0°) in each hemisphere

troposphere (TROH-puh-sfeer): layer of the atmosphere closest to the Earth

trough (TRAWF): lowest point of a wave

tsunami (tsoo-NAH-mee): giant sea wave produced by an earthquake

turbidity (ter-BIHD-uh-tee) **current:** flow of ocean water that carries large amounts of sediments

U

ultraviolet telescope: telescope that gathers ultraviolet light from distant objects in order to produce images of those objects

umbra (UHM-bruh): inner part of a shadow

unconformity: eroded rock surface that is much older than the younger rock layers above it

upwelling: rising of deep, cold currents to the ocean surface

V

valley glacier: long, narrow glacier that moves downhill between the steep sides of a mountain valley

Van Allen radiation belts: two doughnut-shaped regions of charged particles formed when the Earth's magnetosphere traps some of the particles in the solar wind

variable: factor being tested in an experimental setup

varve: sediment that shows a yearly cycle

vent: opening through which lava erupts

vernal equinox (EE-kwuh-naks): time of year when day and night are of equal length; beginning of spring in the Northern Hemisphere

volcanic ash: rock particles more than 0.25 mm but less than 5 mm across that are blown into the air by a volcanic eruption

volcanic bomb: rock particles larger than 5 mm in diameter that are blown into the air by a volcanic eruption

volcanic dust: smallest rock particles blown into the air by a volcanic eruption

volcano: place in the Earth's surface through which molten rock and other materials reach the surface

W

water cycle: continuous movement of water from the oceans and freshwater sources to the air and land and finally back to the oceans; also called the hydrologic cycle

water table: surface between the zone of saturation and the zone of aeration that marks the level below which the ground is saturated, or soaked, with water

watershed: land area in which surface runoff drains into a river or system of rivers and streams

wavelength: horizontal distance between two con-secutive crests or two consecutive troughs

weathering: breaking down of rocks and other materials at the Earth's surface

weight: measure of the gravitational attraction between objects

white dwarf: small dense star

wind: movement of air from an area of higher pressure to an area of lower pressure

windward side: side of a mountain facing toward the wind

winter solstice (SAHL-stihs): time of the year when the Northern Hemisphere has its shortest day and the Southern Hemisphere has its longest day; beginning of winter in the Northern Hemisphere

X

X-ray telescope: telescope that gathers X-rays from distant objects in order to produce images of those objects

Z

zone of aeration (ehr-AY-shuhn): relatively dry underground region in which pores in the soil and rocks are mostly filled with air

zone of saturation (sach-uh-RAY-shuhn): underground region in which all pores in the soil and rocks are filled with water

Index